Super Cheap USA Travel Guide

"America is a tune. It must be sung together." - Gerald Stanley Lee

Titles also by Phil Tang	11
Discover The United States of America	13
The Magical Power of Bargains	16
Who this book is for and why anyone can enjoy luxury travel on a budget	17
Weird and wonderful facts about the USA that might surprise you	18
Know Before you Go	19
Some of America's Best Bargains	21
Free Tours	21
Extremely Cheap Tours	23
Free Drink Tours	25
Free Ranger Tours	26
Fine Dining at Michelin-Starred Restaurants	28
Auctions	30
Island Hopping	32
Coupons	34
Discount Passes	35
Get Around for FREE	38
Super Cheap Buses	41
Renting a Car Cheaply	42
Ride Share	44
Flying	45
Fly for free	46
Luxury Hotels	48
Hotels	50
Get 70% off a Cruise	53
Theme Parks on the Super Cheap	54
Beaches	56
Dollywood on the Super Cheap	58
Revisit Your Favourite Films and Shows	59
Free Museums	61

Find free classes and workshops	62
Free Outdoor Activities	64
Fishing	65
Food Delivery	67
Free Live Music	69
Natural Wonders	71
Cultural Immersion	74
Free Line Dancing	75
Free Fitness Classes	76
Get Your 15 Minutes of Fame	78
Get Caffeinated Cheaply	79
Cheap theatre tickets	80
Watch Sports Cheaply	81
Cheap Cinema	84
High-end Fashion	86
Free Makeovers and Haircuts	90
Complete Freebies	91
Top 20 attractions in the USA with money saving tips	92
Think like an American	94
Memberships	95
Websites	98
Luxury on a Budget Itinerary Ideas	100
Truly weird and wonderful things to experience	103
Bucket list-worthy experiences with discounts	105
More Great Small Bargains	107
Free things for American citizens	108
Economics of saving money in America	112
How to Enjoy ALLOCATING Money in USA	114
How to feel RICH in USA	116
What to pack to save money in USA	117

Planning your trip	118
Time Zones	118
Cheapest month to visit each city	119
What's On	121
The seasons in different parts of the USA and what to pack for each	123
Recap	124
Go Minus the crowds	125
How to use this book	126
Booking Flights	127
How to Find Heavily Discounted Private Jet Flights to or from USA	127
How to Find CHEAP FIRST-CLASS Flights to USA	128
How to Fly Business Class to USA cheaply from Europe	129
How to ALWAYS Find Super Cheap Flights to USA	130
Accommodation	133
How to Book a Five-star Hotel consistently on the Cheap in USA	133
Cheapest hotel chains in the USA and how to get discounts	134
Enjoy the Finest Five-star Hotels for a 10th of the Cost	135
Strategies to Book Five-Star Hotels for Two-Star Prices in USA	137
Comparing hotels to Airbnb accommodations	142
Airbnb Bans	143
Cheap City Stays	144
Cheapest Airbnb Locations	146
Guesthouses	148
Unique and Cheap	150
How to get last-minute discounts on owner rented properties	154
Saving money on Food in the USA	156
Use Too Good to Go and other food waste apps	156
Michelin Star Restaurants that are affordable	158
Crazy Dining Experiences	161
Dining Out Wisely	162

Buffets	164
What to know about USA Fast Food Chains	166
The Cheapest Supermarket in USA	169
Food Trucks	170
Cheapest Happy hour chains	173
USA Food Culture	174
American desserts	177
Dining etiquette	178
The Best Cheap Eats by State	180
Drinks	182
Tipping	184
Coffee	185
Recap	187
Urban v Rural	188
Itinerary for first time visitor to USA	190
A month in the USA for under $1,000	192
Lessor known sights	194
RV TRIP	196
Unique bargains we love	198
Snapshot: How to have a $10,000 trip to USA on a $1,000	199
OUR SUPER CHEAP TIPS…	200
Arriving	200
Getting Around	202
In-City/Rural Transportation	203
E-scooter rentals	205
Renting a Car	207
How to find the cheapest gas	208
Driving Tips	209
The top 32 Attractions in the USA on the Super Cheap	211
1. Walt Disney World Resort, Florida	214

2.	Grand Canyon, Arizona	217
3.	Yellowstone National Park, Wyoming	221
4.	Statue of Liberty, New York	223
5. Times Square, New York		224
6. Las Vegas Strip, Nevada		226
7. Smithsonian Museums, Washington D.C.		228
8. National Mall and Memorial Parks, Washington D.C.		228
9. Niagara Falls		230
10. Universal Studios Hollywood, California		232
11. Kennedy Space Center Visitor Complex, Florida		234
12. Golden Gate Bridge, California		236
13. Mount Rushmore National Memorial, South Dakota		238
14. Great Smoky Mountains National Park, North Carolina and Tennessee		240
15. Disneyland Resort, California		242
16. Alcatraz Island, California		245
17. Napa Valley, California:		247
18. Hawaii		251
19. Independence National Historical Park, Pennsylvania		253
20. Mount St. Helens, Washington		255
21. Bryce Canyon National Park, Utah		259
22. Rocky Mountain National Park, Colorado		262
23. Zion National Park, Utah		265
24. Great Sand Dunes National Park, Colorado		268
25. Pike Place Market, Seattle		271
26. The Grand Ole Opry, Nashville, Tennessee		273
27. The Space Needle, Seattle, Washington		275
28. Lake Tahoe, California and Nevada		277
29. Denali National Park and Preserve, Alaska		279
30. Cape Cod, Massachusetts		281
31. The Everglades		283

32. Route 66	284
The cities	287
New York	288
Orlando	297
Las Vegas	304
Los Angeles	308
Chicago	312
San Francisco	318
Miami	324
San Diego	329
Honolulu	331
Boston	334
The states	340
Alabama	341
ALASKA	351
Arizona	362
Arkansas	373
California	383
Colorado	394
Connecticut	402
Delaware	405
Florida	413
Florida, along with some money-saving tips for visiting each one:	415
Georgia	419
Hawaii	425
Idaho	430
Illinois	435
Indiana	440
Kansas	446
Kentucky	450

Louisiana	455
Maine	461
Maryland	465
Massachusetts	470
Montana	475
Nebraska	480
Nevada	485
New Hampshire	490
New Jersey	495
North Dakota	500
Ohio	505
Oklahoma	510
Native American Heritage	515
Oregon	517
Pennsylvania	521
Rhode Island	526
New York state	532
Washington	537
West Virginia	543
Wisconsin	549
Wyoming	555
Solutions to Common Problems	561
Freebies to be cautious of…	562
Avoid Unexpected Costs	563
Getting Out	564
Cheapest airport lounges	567
Checklist of top 20 things not to miss	569
Recap chart showing how to have a $10,000 trip to for $1,000	570
Understand	573
Values	576

The secret to saving HUGE amounts of money when travelling to USA is…	578
Thank you for reading	581
Your Next Book is Free	582
Bonus Travel Hacks	584
Common pitfalls when it comes to allocating money to your desires while traveling	585
Hack your allocations for your USA Trip	587
MORE TIPS TO FIND CHEAP FLIGHTS	589
What Credit Card Gives The Best Air Miles?	592
Frequent Flyer Memberships	595
How to spend money	596
How NOT to be ripped off	599
Use car renting services	601
Small tweaks on the road add up to big differences in your bank balance	603
Where and How to Make Friends	605
When unpleasantries come your way…	606
Hacks for Families	611
How I got hooked on luxury on a budget travelling	613
A final word…	614
Copyright	615

Titles also by Phil Tang

GET A FREE BOOK: Simply leave an honest review and send a screenshot and proof of purchase to philgtang@gmail.com with the name of the book you'd like to have for free.

COUNTRY GUIDES

Super Cheap AUSTRALIA
Super Cheap AUSTRIA
Super Cheap CANADA
Super Cheap DENMARK
Super Cheap FIJI
Super Cheap FINLAND
Super Cheap FRANCE
Super Cheap GREAT BRITAIN
Super Cheap GERMANY
Super Cheap ICELAND
Super Cheap ITALY
Super Cheap IRELAND
Super Cheap JAPAN
Super Cheap MALDIVES
Super Cheap MEXICO
Super Cheap NETHERLANDS
Super Cheap NEW ZEALAND
Super Cheap NORWAY
Super Cheap SOUTH KOREA
Super Cheap SPAIN
Super Cheap SWITZERLAND
Super Cheap UAE
Super Cheap UNITED STATES

CITIES / TOWNS

Super Cheap ADELAIDE
Super Cheap ALASKA
Super Cheap AUSTIN
Super Cheap BANFF
Super Cheap BANGKOK
Super Cheap BARCELONA
Super Cheap BELFAST
Super Cheap BERMUDA
Super Cheap BORA BORA
Super Cheap BRITISH VIRGIN ISLANDS
Super Cheap BUDAPEST
Super Cheap Great Barrier Reef
Super Cheap CAMBRIDGE
Super Cheap CANCUN
Super Cheap CHIANG MAI
Super Cheap CHICAGO
Super Cheap Copenhagen

Super Cheap DOHA
Super Cheap DUBAI
Super Cheap DUBLIN
Super Cheap EDINBURGH
Super Cheap GALWAY
Super Cheap Guadeloupe
Super Cheap HELSINKI
Super Cheap LIMA
Super Cheap LISBON
Super Cheap MALAGA
Super Cheap Martinique
Super Cheap Machu Pichu
Super Cheap MIAMI
Super Cheap Milan
Super Cheap Montpellier
Super Cheap NASHVILLE
Super Cheap NAPA
Super Cheap NEW ORLEANS
Super Cheap NEW YORK
Super Cheap PARIS
Super Cheap PRAGUE
Super Cheap St. Vincent and the Grenadines
Super Cheap SEYCHELLES
Super Cheap SINGAPORE
Super Cheap ST LUCIA
Super Cheap TORONTO
Super Cheap Turks and Caicos
Super Cheap VANCOUVER
Super Cheap VENICE
Super Cheap VIENNA
Super Cheap YOSEMITE
Super Cheap ZURICH
Super Cheap ZANZIBAR

Discover The United States of America

Monument Valley Desert Road Highway

Welcome to the land of the free, where vast landscapes, vibrant cities, and rich history converge to create an unforgettable travel experience. The possibilities are as endless as the highways and the smiles are as warm as a freshly baked apple pie. As you embark on your journey to explore this vast and diverse country, let me clue you in on some insider tips that might not be in the guidebooks.

Allow me to introduce myself. I'm a Londoner who now calls Vienna home, but my heart truly belongs to the vast and diverse landscapes of the United States. Over the years, I've embarked on countless adventures across the USA, exploring its cities, natural wonders, and hidden gems.

Driven by a strong belief that travel should be accessible to all, not just a privileged few, I've dedicated myself to uncovering the secrets of affordable luxury travel. You see, I firmly believe that you don't know what you don't know, and there are countless ways to enjoy luxurious experiences without breaking the bank.

In this book, "Super Cheap USA," I pour my spirit into sharing these insights and strategies, empowering you to embark on your own unforgettable journeys across the United States, regardless of budget constraints. So, whether you're dreaming of wandering through the bustling streets of New York City or marveling at the natural beauty of Yosemite National Park, let me show you how to make your travel dreams a reality without emptying your wallet. Welcome to the world of affordable luxury travel in the USA!

The United States of America, a country renowned for its diversity and limitless possibilities, offers a world of exploration and adventure. From the majestic national parks to bustling metropolises, the USA has something to offer every taste.

In Super Cheap USA, we invite you to embark on a journey through the United States like never before. Contrary to the misconception that luxury travel in the USA comes with a hefty price tag, we are here to show you that opulence can indeed be attained on a budget. So. whether you dream of exploring the iconic streets of New York City, witnessing the grandeur of the Grand Canyon, or savouring the flavors of New Orleans, this guide is your passport to experiencing the best of the USA, where luxury meets affordability.

Navigating the multitude of bargains available in the USA can be quite the challenge. To simplify, we'll start by exploring the best bargains, followed by the top attractions at incredibly low prices, then delve into cities, and finally, explore the bargain opportunities within each state.

This travel guide is your step-by-step manual for unlocking luxury hotels, enjoying the best culinary offerings and once-in-a-lifetime luxury experiences in USA at a fraction of the usual cost.

Everyone's budget is different, but luxury is typically defined by first or business class seats on the airplane, five-star hotels, chauffeurs, exclusive experiences, and delectable fine dining. Yes, all of these can be enjoyed on a budget.

Finding luxury deals in USA simply requires a bit of research and planning, which this book has done for you. We have packed this book with local insider tips and knowledge to save you tens of thousands.

If the mere mention of the word luxury has you thinking things like "Money doesn't grow on trees," "I don't need anything fancy," "I don't deserve nice things," or "People who take luxury trips are shallow and materialistic/environmentally harmful/lack empathy, etc.," then stop. While we all know travel increases our happiness, research on the effects of luxury travel has proven even better results:

Reduced stress: A study published in the Journal of Travel Research found that individuals who visited luxury hotels reported feeling less stressed than those who in standard hotels.[1]

Increased happiness: A study conducted by the International Journal of Tourism Research found that luxury travel experiences lead to an increase in happiness and overall life

---

[1] Wöber, K. W., & Fuchs, M. (2016). The effects of hotel attributes on perceived value and satisfaction. Journal of Travel Research, 55(3), 306-318.

satisfaction.[2] Researchers also found that luxury travel experiences can improve individuals' mental health by providing a sense of escape from daily stressors and enhancing feelings of relaxation and rejuvenation.

Enhanced creativity: Researchers found engaging in luxury travel experiences can stimulate creativity and lead to more innovative thinking.[3]

While all of this makes perfect sense; it feels much nicer to stay in a hotel room that's cleaned daily than in an Airbnb where you're cleaning up after yourself. What you might not know is that you can have all of that increased happiness and well-being without emptying your bank account. Does it sound too good to be true? This book will prove it isn't!

---

[2] Ladhari, R., Souiden, N., & Dufour, B. (2017). Luxury hotel customers' satisfaction and loyalty: An empirical study. International Journal of Hospitality Management, 63, 1-10.

[3] Kim, S., Kim, S. Y., & Lee, H. R. (2019). Luxury travel, inspiration, and creativity: A qualitative investigation. Tourism Management, 71, 354-366.

The Magical Power of Bargains

Have you ever felt the rush of getting a bargain? And then found good fortune just keeps following you?

Let me give you an example. In 2009, I graduated into the worst global recession for generations. One unemployed day, I saw a suit I knew I could get a job in. The suit was £250. Money I didn't have. Imagine my shock when the next day I saw the exact same suit (in my size) in the window of a second-hand shop (thrift store) for £18! I bought the suit and after three months of interviewing, without a single call back, within a week of owning that £18 suit, I was hired on a salary far above my expectations. That's the powerful psychological effect of getting an incredible deal. It builds a sense of excitement and happiness that literally creates miracles.

I have no doubt that the wonders of USA will uplift and inspire you but when you add the bargains from this book to your vacation, not only will you save a ton of money; you are guaranteed to enjoy a truly magical trip to USA.

Who this book is for and why anyone can enjoy luxury travel on a budget

Did you know you can fly on a private jet for $500? Yes, a fully private jet. Complete with flutes of champagne and reclinable creamy leather seats. Your average billionaire spends $20,000 on the exact same flight. You can get it for $500 when you book private jet empty leg flights. This is just one of thousands of ways you can travel luxuriously on a budget. You see there is a big difference between being cheap and frugal.

When our brain hears the word "budget" it hears deprivation, suffering, agony, even depression. But budget travel need not be synonymous with hostels and pack lunches. You can enjoy an incredible and luxurious trip to USA on a budget, just like you can enjoy a private jet flight for 10% of the normal cost when you know how.

Over 20 years of travel has taught me I could have a 20 cent experience that will stir my soul more than a $100 one. Of course, sometimes the reverse is true, my point is, spending money on travel is the best investment you can make but it doesn't have to be at levels set by hotels and attractions with massive ad spends and influencers who are paid small fortunes to get you to buy into something you could have for a fraction of the cost.

This book is for those who love bargains and want to have the cold hard budget busting facts to hand (which is why we've included so many one page charts, which you can use as a quick reference), but otherwise, the book provides plenty of tips to help you shape your own USA experience.

We have designed these travel guides to give you a unique planning tool to experience an unforgettable trip without spending the ascribed tourist budget.

This guide focuses on USA's unbelievable bargains. Of course, there is little value in traveling to USA and not experiencing everything it has to offer. Where possible, we've included super cheap workarounds or listed the experience in the Loved but Costly section.

When it comes to luxury budget travel, it's all about what you know. You can have all the feels without most of the bills. A few days spent planning can save you thousands. Luckily, we've done the planning for you, so you can distill the information in minutes not days, leaving you to focus on what matters: immersing yourself in the sights, sounds and smells of USA, meeting awesome new people and feeling relaxed and happy.

This book reads like a good friend has travelled the length and breadth of USA and brought you back incredible insider tips.

So, grab a cup of tea or coffee, put your feet up and relax; you're about to enter the world of enjoying USA on the Super Cheap. Oh, and don't forget a biscuit. You need energy to plan a trip of a lifetime on a budget.

Weird and wonderful facts about the USA that might surprise you

1. **Bubble Wrap was Invented in the USA for Wallpaper**: Bubble wrap, that satisfyingly poppable plastic packaging material, was originally invented in 1957 by engineers Alfred Fielding and Marc Chavannes. Surprisingly, their initial idea was to create textured wallpaper, but it didn't quite catch on for interior design. However, its use as protective packaging quickly took off.
2. **The Library of Congress Has a Book That's Too Poisonous to Read**: In the Library of Congress, there's a book called the "Codex Gigas" or "Devil's Bible," which is said to be written by a monk who made a deal with the devil. It's so large that it requires two people to lift it, and it's believed to be cursed. The book contains a full-page illustration of the devil, earning its eerie nickname.
3. **Alaska is Both the Westernmost and Easternmost State in the U.S.**: Due to the Aleutian Islands crossing the 180th meridian of longitude, Alaska is not only the westernmost state but also the easternmost. This means that it's technically the closest state to both Russia and the United States.
4. **The United States Purchased Alaska from Russia for Just Two Cents an Acre**: In 1867, Secretary of State William H. Seward negotiated the purchase of Alaska from Russia for $7.2 million, which amounted to roughly two cents per acre. At the time, the acquisition was mocked as "Seward's Folly" or "Seward's Icebox," but it later proved to be a valuable addition to the U.S. due to its rich natural resources.
5. **The Smallest Town in the USA Has a Population of 1**: Monowi, located in Nebraska, holds the distinction of being the smallest incorporated town in the United States with a population of just one person. Elsie Eiler is the sole resident and operates the town's library, tavern, and mayor's office.
6. **The State of Wyoming Has More Antelope Than People**: Wyoming boasts vast open spaces and is home to more pronghorn antelope than people. With a population density of just six people per square mile, it's one of the least densely populated states in the USA.
7. **The World's Tallest Roller Coaster is in New Jersey**: The Kingda Ka roller coaster, located at Six Flags Great Adventure in Jackson, New Jersey, holds the title of the world's tallest roller coaster. It stands at a towering height of 456 feet and accelerates riders from 0 to 128 mph in just 3.5 seconds.

Know Before you Go

1. **Entry Requirements**: Depending on your nationality, you may need a visa or an Electronic System for Travel Authorization (ESTA) to enter the USA. Make sure to check the entry requirements well in advance and apply for any necessary visa at least six weeks in advance.
2. **Transportation**: Public transportation options vary widely depending on the city or region. In major cities like New York City, Chicago, and San Francisco, you'll find extensive subway and bus systems, while in more rural areas, renting a car may be necessary for getting around.
3. **Tipping Culture**: Tipping is customary in the United States, especially in restaurants, bars, and for services like taxis and hairstyling. It's customary to tip around 15% to 20% of the total bill for good service. Keep some cash on hand for tipping, as not all establishments allow gratuities to be added to credit card payments.
4. **Sales Tax**: Prices listed in stores and restaurants do not include sales tax, which varies by state and can range from 0% to over 10%. Be prepared for slightly higher totals at the checkout counter than the listed prices.
5. **Healthcare**: Healthcare in the USA can be expensive for visitors, so it's essential to have travel insurance that covers medical expenses. Familiarize yourself with emergency services like 911 and locate nearby hospitals or clinics in case of any health-related issues.
6. **Time Zones**: The USA spans multiple time zones, so be sure to adjust your schedule accordingly when traveling between states or regions to avoid confusion and ensure you don't miss any flights or appointments.
7. **Electrical Outlets**: The USA operates on a 120-volt electrical system with two-pronged outlets. Bring a suitable adapter for your electronic devices.
8. **Etiquette**: Americans are known for their friendliness and love of small talk. Whether you're waiting in line at the grocery store or riding in an elevator, don't be surprised if a stranger strikes up a conversation about the weather, sports, or the latest pop culture craze. So, brush up on your small talk skills and be prepared to engage in casual chitchat with locals. Who knows, you might just make a new friend or two along the way! When in doubt, a simple smile and a friendly "Hi!" will go a long way in breaking the ice.
9. **Super-Sized Portions**: American portion sizes are not for the faint of heart (or stomach). From towering burgers to bottomless fries, you'll quickly discover that everything is bigger in the USA. Rather than attempting to tackle a super-sized meal solo, consider sharing with a friend or asking for a to-go box to enjoy leftovers later. Trust me, your waistline (and your wallet) will thank you. **If you're dining out and unsure about portion sizes, don't hesitate to ask your server for recommendations or if dishes are shareable.**
10. **Know Your Sales Cycles** - If there's one thing Americans love more than a good deal, it's scoring a great bargain. And lucky for you, there are plenty of opportunities to save money while shopping in the USA. Keep an eye out for seasonal sales, holiday discounts, and clearance events at retail stores, outlets, and Amazon. Additionally, familiarize yourself with the concept of "back-to-school" and "end-of-season" sales, which offer steep discounts on clothing, electronics, and more. **Sign up for email newsletters and loyalty programs from your favorite stores to receive exclusive offers and promotions straight to your inbox.**
11. **Stay Connected: Wi-Fi Hotspots and SIM Cards**

Staying connected while traveling in America is easier than ever, thanks to the abundance of Wi-Fi hotspots and prepaid SIM cards available. Many cafes, restaurants, hotels, and public spaces offer free Wi-Fi access, allowing you to stay connected without racking up hefty roaming charges. Alternatively, consider purchasing a prepaid SIM card from a local provider for affordable data and calling options during your stay. Download offline maps and travel apps ahead of time to navigate your way around without relying on mobile data.

12. Embrace the Diversity: Discovering America's Cultural Mosaic. America is a melting pot of cultures, languages, and traditions, and embracing this diversity is key to truly experiencing all that the country has to offer. Take the time to explore ethnic neighborhoods, sample international cuisines, and learn about the histories and customs of different communities. Whether you're savoring soul food in Harlem, browsing the vibrant markets of Chinatown, or dancing the night away at a Latinx music festival, each cultural experience offers a glimpse into the rich tapestry of American life.

Some of America's Best Bargains

Free Tours

America's inventions have woven themselves seamlessly into the fabric of everyday life. Whether it's the hypnotic beats of jazz melodies, the addictive buzz of Silicon Valley innovations, or the intoxicating allure of iconic fashion trends emanating from the streets of New York, the world finds itself ensnared in the gravitational pull of American ingenuity. And the best part? You can explore these factories of imagination and creativity for free, diving headfirst into the melting pot of ideas that fuels the American dream.

In the land of the free, we had to open the best bargains with free tours. They are just too good to miss and there are so many that offer an inside look at various industries and manufacturing processes. Here are a selection of the best. More will be exploded in each city and state.

- **Hershey's Chocolate World** (Hershey, Pennsylvania): Take a free tour to learn how Hershey's chocolate is made, and enjoy complimentary chocolate samples. Address: 251 Park Blvd, Hershey, PA 17033. Parking is available onsite, or you can take public transport to Hershey via bus or train.
- **Alaskan Brewing Company** (Juneau, Alaska): Take a self-guided tour of the brewery and enjoy free samples of Alaskan beer. Address: 5362 Commercial Blvd, Juneau, AK 99801. Parking is available onsite, and public transport options are limited, so driving is recommended.
- **Celestial Seasonings Factory Tour** (Boulder, Colorado): Discover the tea-making process at Celestial Seasonings, with free tours showcasing their blending, packing, and shipping operations. Address: 4600 Sleepytime Dr, Boulder, CO 80301.

Parking is available onsite, and public transport options include buses from downtown Boulder.
- **Tillamook Cheese Factory** (Tillamook, Oregon): Take a self-guided tour through the cheese-making facility and sample a variety of dairy products. Address: 4165 Highway 101 North, Tillamook, OR 97141. Parking is available onsite, and public transport options are limited, so driving is recommended.
- **U.S. Bureau of Engraving and Printing** (Washington, D.C., and Fort Worth, Texas): Enjoy a free guided tour to see how U.S. paper currency is printed and processed. Addresses: 14th & C Streets, SW, Washington, D.C. 20228, and 9000 Blue Mound Rd, Fort Worth, TX 76131. Parking is available onsite, and public transport options vary by location.
- **SpaceX Headquarters** (Hawthorne, California): While not technically a factory tour, SpaceX occasionally offers public tours of its headquarters for space enthusiasts. Check the SpaceX website for tour availability and details.

Extremely Cheap Tours

These tours are all under $5:

- **Ben & Jerry's Factory Tour** (Waterbury, Vermont): Visit the factory to see how Ben & Jerry's ice cream is produced and taste some of their iconic flavors. Address: 1281 Waterbury Stowe Rd, Waterbury, VT 05676. Parking is available onsite, and public transport options include buses and shuttles from nearby towns.
- **Jelly Belly Visitor Center** (Pleasant Prairie, Wisconsin): Explore the Jelly Belly factory for a behind-the-scenes look at how jelly beans are made. Sample a variety of flavors during the tour. Address: 10100 Jelly Belly Ln, Pleasant Prairie, WI 53158. Parking is available onsite, and public transport options are limited, so driving is recommended.

In addition to company tours there are many organisations providing completely free tours that are absolutely incredible. Here's a chart outlining the **VERY BEST volunteer-led free tours** across America, along with their highlights and locations:

Tour Organization	Highlights	Locations
Free Tours by Foot	- Expert-led walking tours- Flexible schedules	- New York City- Washington, D.C.- San Francisco- New Orleans- Boston
Wildland Trekking	- Guided hikes through stunning landscapes- Educational insights from experienced guides	- Grand Canyon National Park, Arizona- Yellowstone National Park, Wyoming- Great Smoky Mountains National Park, Tennessee- Zion National Park, Utah- Rocky Mountain National Park, Colorado
NPS Ranger-Led Tours	- Insightful tours led by National Park Service rangers- Learn about park history, geology, and wildlife	- Various national parks across the USA, including Grand Canyon, Yosemite, Yellowstone, and more
Big Apple Greeter	- Personalized walking tours led by local volunteers- Off-the-beaten-path neighborhoods and hidden gems	- New York City

Historic New Orleans Tours	- Engaging tours exploring the history and culture of New Orleans- Led by knowledgeable local guides	- New Orleans, Louisiana
Chicago Greeter	- Free guided tours led by passionate local volunteers- Discover Chicago's diverse neighborhoods and landmarks	- Chicago, Illinois
San Francisco City Guides	- Free walking tours of San Francisco- Explore iconic sites and hidden gems with knowledgeable volunteers	- San Francisco, California

Free Drink Tours

Back to the land of the free. Many alcohol manufacturers have completely free tours. Here are the best:

1. **Buffalo Trace Distillery (Frankfort, Kentucky)**: Buffalo Trace offers complimentary tours of its historic distillery, where visitors can learn about the bourbon-making process and explore aging warehouses. The tours include tastings of Buffalo Trace's award-winning bourbons.
2. **New Belgium Brewing Company (Fort Collins, Colorado)**: New Belgium Brewing offers free tours of its brewery, where visitors can see the brewing process firsthand and learn about sustainable brewing practices. The tour concludes with a tasting of New Belgium's popular beers.
3. **Yuengling Brewery (Pottsville, Pennsylvania)**: America's oldest brewery, Yuengling, offers free tours of its historic brewery, providing insight into its rich brewing heritage and techniques. Visitors can enjoy complimentary samples of Yuengling's iconic beers.
4. **Brooklyn Brewery (Brooklyn, New York)**: Brooklyn Brewery offers free tours of its brewery, providing insight into its brewing techniques and the history of craft beer in Brooklyn. The tour concludes with tastings of Brooklyn Brewery's signature beers.

Free Ranger Tours

Free ranger tours in the USA's national parks are often available, but the availability and frequency can vary depending on the specific park, season, and staffing. Ranger-led programs typically include guided hikes, nature walks, campfire talks, and other educational activities aimed at enhancing visitors' understanding and appreciation of the park's natural and cultural resources.

To find out about ranger-led programs and tours in specific national parks, you can:

1. Visit the official website of the national park you're interested in. Most park websites have a "Things to Do" or "Ranger Programs" section where you can find information about scheduled tours and activities.
2. Check with the park's visitor center upon arrival. Ranger-led programs are often advertised on bulletin boards or in visitor center brochures.

Here are a few examples of ranger-led programs that have been offered for free in various national parks:

1. **Grand Canyon National Park, Arizona**: The Grand Canyon offers a variety of ranger-led programs, including guided hikes along the rim, talks on the park's geology and history, and evening programs about astronomy. Some of these programs are free of charge and included with park admission.
2. **Yellowstone National Park, Wyoming**: Yellowstone's ranger-led programs cover topics such as wildlife, geothermal features, and the park's cultural history. Offerings may include guided walks, talks at visitor centers, and interactive demonstrations. Many of these programs are free, though some specialized tours may have a fee.
3. **Yosemite National Park, California**: Yosemite's ranger-led programs include guided walks to popular destinations like Yosemite Falls and the Mariposa Grove of Giant Sequoias, as

well as talks on the park's ecology and conservation efforts. These programs are typically free to join, though some activities may require advance registration.
4. **Acadia National Park, Maine**: Acadia offers ranger-led walks and talks covering topics such as birdwatching, tidepool exploration, and the park's unique coastal ecology. These programs are often free and provide valuable insights into the natural world of the park.
5. **Great Smoky Mountains National Park, Tennessee/North Carolina**: The Great Smoky Mountains offers a wide range of ranger-led programs, including guided hikes, history walks, and campfire programs. Many of these programs are free to attend and provide opportunities to learn about the park's biodiversity and cultural heritage.

Fine Dining at Michelin-Starred Restaurants

The USA's culinary scene, brimming with Michelin-starred chefs, is a testament to its status as a global gastronomic powerhouse. From the inventive creations of Thomas Keller to the farm-to-table delights of Dan Barber. Treat yourself to an unforgettable culinary journey at a Michelin-starred restaurant, where world-class chefs delight your palate with innovative cuisine, exquisite flavors, and impeccable presentation. From intimate tasting menus to opulent dining rooms, each dish is a masterpiece of culinary artistry and can be enjoyed from $20!

1. **Cafe China** (New York City, New York) - This one-star Michelin restaurant specializes in Sichuan cuisine, with prices starting at around $20-$30 per person for lunch and $30-$50 for dinner.
2. **The Breslin** (New York City, New York) - A one-star Michelin gastropub offering British-inspired dishes. Prices generally start at around $30-$40 per person for lunch and $50-$70 for dinner.
3. **State Bird Provisions** (San Francisco, California) - A one-star Michelin restaurant featuring creative American cuisine. Prices typically start at around $40-$60 per person for dinner.
4. **Osteria Mozza** (Los Angeles, California) - This one-star Michelin restaurant offers Italian cuisine with prices starting at around $50-$70 per person for lunch and $80-$120 for dinner.
5. **Musso & Frank Grill** (Los Angeles, California) - This one-star Michelin steakhouse offers classic American fare with prices starting at around $30-$50 per person for lunch and $50-$80 for dinner.

Saving Tips:

- **Lunch Specials**: Experience the luxury of fine dining at a fraction of the cost by opting for prix fixe lunch menus or early bird specials offered by Michelin-starred restaurants.

- **Restaurant Week**: Take advantage of restaurant week events in major cities, where participating restaurants offer special prix fixe menus at discounted prices, allowing you to savor gourmet cuisine without breaking the bank.
- **Bar Seating**: Consider dining at the bar or lounge area of Michelin-starred restaurants, where you can enjoy a more casual atmosphere and often find a selection of smaller plates or appetizers at significantly lower prices.

Auctions

From the prestigious halls of Sotheby's and Christie's to the grassroots gatherings of flea markets and estate sales, the American auction scene is a vibrant tapestry woven with the threads of commerce, history, and the pursuit of treasures.

Getting amazing deals at auctions in the USA requires a combination of research, strategy, and patience. Here's a guide to help you:

1. **Research Auction Types**: There are various types of auctions in the USA, including:
   - **Live Auctions**: These are traditional auctions where bidders physically attend and bid on items.
   - **Government Auctions**: These auctions feature surplus government items, seized assets, and more. Websites like GovDeals.com and GovSales.gov list such auctions.
   - **Estate Auctions**: Typically held when someone passes away, these auctions feature items from their estate, including furniture, antiques, and collectibles.
   - **Storage Unit Auctions**: When storage units are abandoned or unpaid for, their contents are auctioned off.
2. **Identify Auction Houses:** Some well-known auction houses in the USA include Sotheby's, Christie's, Bonhams, and Heritage Auctions. Additionally, there are many regional and local auction houses that may offer great deals.
3. **Preparation is Key**: Before attending or participating in an auction, thoroughly research the items you're interested in. Know their market value, condition, and any relevant details. This will help you set a budget and avoid overbidding.
4. **Attend Previews**: Many auctions offer preview periods where you can inspect the items up for bid. Take advantage of these to assess the quality and condition of the items firsthand.
5. **Understand Bidding Strategies**: Learn different bidding strategies such as sniping (waiting until the last moment to bid), incremental bidding (increasing bids by small amounts), and setting a maximum bid in advance.

Buying a car as a non-American can indeed be a complex process, especially if you're not familiar with the local regulations and procedures. While purchasing a car at auction can sometimes offer good deals, it may not be the most straightforward option for non-residents due to various legal and logistical hurdles.

Island Hopping

The United States is surrounded by numerous islands, ranging from small atolls to large landmasses. Exploring islands off the coast of the US can offer diverse landscapes, cultural experiences, and outdoor adventures. Here are some affordable options, why you should visit them, and how to get there inexpensively:

1. Block Island, Rhode Island:

Why Go: Known for its pristine beaches, scenic hiking trails, and historic lighthouses, Block Island offers a relaxed atmosphere perfect for outdoor enthusiasts. Explore Mohegan Bluffs, visit Southeast Light, and enjoy activities like biking, kayaking, and birdwatching.

How to Get There Cheaply:

- Take advantage of affordable ferry services from Point Judith, Rhode Island, or New London, Connecticut, to Block Island.
- Consider camping or staying in budget-friendly accommodations like guesthouses or rental cottages.

2. Assateague Island, Maryland/Virginia:

Why Go: Famous for its wild ponies, unspoiled beaches, and diverse wildlife, Assateague Island provides opportunities for beachcombing, birdwatching, and nature photography. Explore nature trails, camp under the stars, and enjoy panoramic views of the Atlantic Ocean.

How to Get There Cheaply:

- Access Assateague Island by car via the Verrazano Bridge in Maryland or the Chincoteague Causeway in Virginia.
- Camp in the National Seashore campground for an affordable overnight stay.

3. Daufuskie Island, South Carolina:

Why Go: With its rich Gullah heritage, pristine beaches, and maritime forests, Daufuskie Island offers a glimpse into South Carolina's Lowcountry culture and history. Explore historic landmarks, take a guided tour, and relax on secluded beaches.

How to Get There Cheaply:

- Take a public ferry from Hilton Head Island or embark on a private boat tour to Daufuskie Island.
- Rent bikes to explore the island's scenic trails and attractions at your own pace.

4. Orcas Island, Washington:

Why Go: As the largest island in the San Juan archipelago, Orcas Island boasts stunning landscapes, charming villages, and outdoor adventures. Explore Moran State Park, hike to the top of Mount Constitution, and discover artisanal shops and galleries.

How to Get There Cheaply:

- Access Orcas Island via affordable ferry services from Anacortes, Washington.
- Stay in budget accommodations like cabins, hostels, or campgrounds to save on lodging expenses.

5. Tybee Island, Georgia:

Why Go: Known as "Savannah's Beach," Tybee Island offers a laid-back coastal vibe, wide sandy beaches, and historic attractions. Explore the Tybee Island Light Station, relax on the beach, and indulge in fresh seafood at local eateries.

How to Get There Cheaply:

- Drive to Tybee Island via Highway 80 from Savannah, Georgia, or take advantage of affordable shuttle services.
- Pack a picnic and spend the day enjoying free beach activities like swimming, sunbathing, and beachcombing.

Coupons

In the states <u>you MUST try to find a discount before buying anything</u>. Even your coffee! With a few taps of the keyboard and a sprinkle of internet magic, a plethora of coupon websites and discount platforms await your exploration.

Simply type in keywords like "discounts on USA attractions," "coupon codes for American adventures," and watch as a myriad of options unfold before your eyes. From renowned coupon aggregators to specialized travel deal websites, the possibilities are endless. The best two sites with consistent lowest prices are:

1. **Groupon**: Groupon offers a wide range of deals on local experiences, travel, dining, and more. Users can find discounts on attractions, activities, restaurants, and hotels in various cities across the USA.
2. **RetailMeNot**: RetailMeNot is a popular coupon website that provides discounts and promo codes for online and in-store purchases. It features a dedicated travel section where users can find deals on flights, hotels, rental cars, and vacation packages.

Checking Groupon before making purchases or planning activities in the USA is a must. Groupon offers a wide range of deals and discounts on everything from restaurants and spas to attractions and activities, making it a valuable resource for budget-conscious travelers. In addition to saving money on everyday purchases, Groupon also sells deals for events like sports games, concerts, and festivals, allowing you to enjoy entertainment experiences at a discounted price.

If you find yourself short on time in a city, consider hopping on a sightseeing bus. Booking a ticket in advance from a reputable company like Big Bus Tours can save you from being overcharged by commission-driven advertisers lurking around the streets. These buses are typically more affordable than taxis and offer a convenient way to explore a bustling city's landmarks and buildings without wearing out your legs. With plenty of energy left to spare, you'll be ready to fully explore once you do decide to hop off. And you can often find discounts for these buses online.

Discount Passes

Discount passes, like the America Park Pass, are treasure troves of savings, offering incredible value for your adventures. While some may require maximizing your time to make the most of the pass, they unlock a wealth of experiences at a fraction of the cost.

Pass Name	Description and Benefits	Pros	Cons	Starting Price
1. America the Beautiful Pass - National Park Pass	Grants access to over 2,000 federal recreation sites, including national parks, for one year.	- Provides access to iconic natural wonders.	- Valid for one year only.	$80 per year
2. CityPASS	Offers discounted admission to top attractions in select cities, often with fast-track access.	- Savings on admission fees. - Skip ticket lines.	- Limited to participating cities. - Must visit all attractions within a short timeframe.	Prices vary by city
3. Go City Pass	Provides access to multiple attractions in a city at a discounted price with a flexible validity period.	- Cost-effective for visiting multiple sites. - Option to choose attractions based on preferences.	- Not available in all cities. - Must use within a specified time frame.	Prices vary by city
4. Explorer Pass	Allows access to a specific number of attractions in a city or region at a reduced rate.	- Choose from a list of included attractions. - Savings on individual ticket prices.	- Limited to participating cities and attractions. - Must use within a set period.	Prices vary by city

The America the Beautiful Pass costs $80 and grants access to all federal lands, including national parks, national forests, wildlife refuges, and more, for one year from the date of purchase. If you were to visit all the national parks in the USA, you would save a significant amount of money on entrance fees by purchasing this pass. As of 2024, there are 63 designated national parks in the United States. Assuming an average entrance fee of $25 per park, visiting all 63 national parks without the America the Beautiful Pass would cost $1,575. By purchasing the pass for $80, you would save $1,495 on entrance fees alone.

Here's a chart of tourism passes in the USA, along with their pros, cons, and starting prices:

State Tourism Pass	Description and Benefits	Pros	Cons	Starting Price
California Explorer Pass	Offers savings on admission to top attractions in California, such as Disneyland and Universal Studios.	- Access to a wide range of attractions in California. - Potential for significant savings for families.	- Limited to attractions in California. - Must visit attractions within a specified timeframe.	Starting at $64.99 (for a 2-Choice Pass)
New York CityPASS	Provides discounted access to popular NYC attractions, including the Empire State Building and the Met.	- Convenient and cost-effective for exploring NYC. - Skip ticket lines at some attractions.	- Limited to New York City attractions. - Must use within a specific time frame.	Starting at $132 (adult)
Chicago CityPASS	Grants discounted admission to Chicago's top attractions, including the Shedd Aquarium and the Field Museum.	- Significant savings on admission to major Chicago attractions. - Skip lines at some venues.	- Restricted to attractions in Chicago. - Must visit within nine days.	Starting at $109.75 (adult)
Las Vegas Explorer Pass	Offers discounted access to Las Vegas attractions, including the High Roller and Madame Tussauds.	- Flexibility to choose the number of attractions to visit. - Savings on popular Vegas experiences.	- Limited to attractions in Las Vegas. - Must use within 60 days.	Starting at $69 (for 3 attractions)
Orlando Explorer Pass	Provides savings on Orlando's top theme parks and attractions, like Walt Disney World and Universal Orlando.	- Access to renowned theme parks and attractions in Orlando. - Customize the pass based on your interests.	- Limited to Orlando attractions. - Must visit within 60 days.	Starting at $89.99 (for 3 attractions)
Texas State Parks Pass	Grants unlimited entry to Texas state parks for one year, with additional discounts and benefits.	- Access to Texas' diverse natural landscapes and outdoor activities. - Camping discounts and park perks.	- Limited to Texas state parks. - Only covers park entry fees, not activities or rentals.	Starting at $70 (for one year)

Hawaii Entertainment Book	Offers a coupon book with discounts on dining, activities, and attractions across Hawaii.	- Savings on dining and various activities in Hawaii. - Discounts available for an entire year.	- Limited to deals featured in the Entertainment Book. - Coupons may not be valid at all locations.	Starting at $25 (for the book)
Washington State Discover Pass	Allows access to Washington state parks and recreation lands for one year.	- Access to scenic state parks, trails, and outdoor activities. - Supports state park maintenance and preservation.	- Limited to Washington state parks and lands. - Not applicable for camping fees or other services.	Starting at $30 (for one year)

Get Around for FREE

To give you some sense of the sheer scale of the USA, driving from NYC to LA without significant stops takes 45 hours of continuous driving! It is huge and he estimated fuel cost for that road trip from NYC to LA is $336. So you can see, getting around the USA can take a serious chuck of change but their is a solution: car relocations.

Car relocation services, also known as car transport or vehicle shipping services, are companies that specialize in transporting vehicles from one location to another. These services are commonly used by individuals or businesses who need to move their vehicles over long distances, such as when relocating to a new city, buying a car online, or transporting a vehicle for seasonal use.

Who Can Use Car Relocation Services?

Anyone who needs to move a vehicle over a long distance can benefit from car relocation services. This includes individuals, families, businesses, military personnel, and auto dealerships. Whether you're moving across the country, purchasing a car from out of state, or need to transport a vehicle for a special event, car relocation services offer a convenient and efficient solution.

What You Need for Car Relocation:

- Vehicle Information: You'll need to provide details about the vehicle being transported, including the make, model, year, and condition.
- Pickup and Delivery Locations: Specify the pickup location and desired delivery destination for the vehicle.
- Dates: Provide the desired pickup and delivery dates for the transport.
- Contact Information: Include your name, phone number, and email address for communication with the transport company.

- Insurance: Consider purchasing additional insurance coverage for the vehicle during transport, as most transport companies offer basic insurance but may recommend supplemental coverage for added protection.

Do You Have to Pay for Gas?

No, you do not typically have to pay for gas when using car relocation services. The transport company covers the cost of fuel for transporting the vehicle. However, you will be responsible for any additional fees associated with the transport, such as insurance, storage, or expedited delivery charges.

Any Downsides to Car Relocation Services?

While car relocation services offer numerous benefits, there are some potential downsides to consider:

- Delivery Time: Transporting a vehicle over long distances can take time, so you may need to wait several days or weeks for delivery, depending on the distance and route.
- Vehicle Condition: While transport companies take precautions to ensure the safety of your vehicle during transport, there is always a risk of damage or wear and tear, especially for open-air transport options.
- Scheduling: Coordinating pickup and delivery times with the transport company can be challenging, especially if you have specific timing requirements or need to accommodate changes to your schedule.

Here are some of the best car relocation services in the USA along with their URLs for more information:

1. **Transfercar (www.transfercarus.com)**:
    - Transfercar specializes in connecting travelers with rental car companies or private owners who need their vehicles relocated. Users can browse available relocation deals and sign up for free to receive notifications about new opportunities.
2. **Imoova (www.imoova.com)**:

- Imoova offers discounted one-way car rentals for travelers willing to relocate vehicles for rental companies. Users can search for available relocation deals by location and date, with options available across the USA.
3. **HitTheRoad (www.hittheroad.co)**:
    - HitTheRoad provides travelers with opportunities to relocate rental cars for major rental companies at discounted rates. Users can search for available relocation deals and sign up for alerts to receive notifications about new listings.
4. **VroomVroomVroom (www.vroomvroomvroom.com)**:
    - VroomVroomVroom offers car rental comparison services, including relocation deals from rental companies across the USA. Users can search for available deals and compare prices to find the best option for their needs.
5. **AutoDriveaway (www.autodriveaway.com)**:
    - AutoDriveaway connects drivers with vehicles that need to be relocated for individuals, businesses, or government agencies. Users can search for available relocation opportunities and apply to drive specific vehicles to their destinations.
6. **Car Relocation (www.carrelocation.com)**:
    - Car Relocation provides a platform for travelers to find and book one-way car rental deals for vehicle relocation purposes. Users can search for available deals by location and date and book directly through the website.

Gas

Utilize gas apps and membership programs to save money on fuel during your travels. Start by downloading GasBuddy, an essential app that helps you locate the cheapest gas prices in your vicinity. For longer road trips, consider enrolling in GasBuddy's monthly program, priced at $9.99, which can yield savings of up to 40 cents per gallon.

Maximize your savings by signing up for various gas station loyalty programs to accumulate points and unlock discounts. Additionally, if you opt for a branded gas station's credit card, you may receive a substantial discount, such as 30 cents off per gallon on your first 50 gallons.

Consider investing in a Costco membership for access to affordable gas. With approximately 574 stores nationwide, Costco offers competitive fuel prices, allowing you to recoup the membership cost through savings on both gas and groceries.

Super Cheap Buses

If driving is entirely out of the question, you can find bus tickets for as little as $1 USD from Megabus. Greyhound and Flixbus. From the bustling streets of New York City to the sun-drenched beaches of California, cheap buses crisscross the nation, connecting cities, towns, and communities in a web of affordable transportation. With ticket prices that rival the cost of a cup of coffee, these humble chariots offer access to a world of possibilities, where the only limit is your imagination. Rides under five hours are usually around $20 USD if you book early, and overnight rides usually cost $50-100. You can save big if you book in advance (often upwards of 75%!).

Explore affordable bus pass options for travel across America:

1. **Megabus**:
    - Starting Cost: As low as $1 USD for select routes, but prices vary based on destination and availability.
    - Megabus offers budget-friendly bus tickets to numerous destinations across the USA. By booking early, travelers can secure significant discounts, with fares typically ranging from $20 to $100 USD for rides under five hours or overnight journeys, respectively.
2. **Greyhound**:
    - Starting Cost: Prices vary depending on the route and timing, but budget options are available.
    - Greyhound provides extensive bus services across the country, offering affordable fares for travelers on a budget. By booking in advance, passengers can access lower prices, often saving up to 75% off standard fares.
3. **Flixbus**:
    - Starting Cost: Fares start as low as $1 USD for certain routes, with prices increasing based on distance and demand.
    - Flixbus offers economical bus travel options with routes spanning major cities and regions in the USA. Early booking is key to securing the best deals, with fares typically ranging from $20 to $100 USD for shorter or overnight journeys, respectively.

Renting a Car Cheaply

Many American shoppers adore Costco, but did you realize they also provide travel services? When you're in need of a rental car, consider browsing the Costco rental car website. Simply input your travel dates and location, and the site will compile the top deals for you. Furthermore, Costco members are eligible for extra discounts and complimentary upgrades.

For the most budget-friendly option, consider renting an SUV that offers ample space for comfortable sleeping arrangements. Make a trip to Walmart to pick up essential camping supplies like a mattress pad and other basic necessities. From there, hit the road in your SUV and head in the direction of your desired destinations.

State and national parks often permit car camping, providing convenient and scenic spots to spend the night. With minimal expenses aside from food, gas, and campground fees, you can enjoy the great outdoors without breaking the bank.

While sleeping in your car at these parks may not be recommended, truck stops offer another option with full bathroom and shower facilities available. While it may not be the epitome of luxury living, it promises a unique and adventurous experience while allowing you to explore various parts of the country.

Especially in the southern regions, you'll find plenty of campgrounds, parks, and other resting spots where you can recharge and immerse yourself in the beauty of nature. This budget-friendly approach ensures an unforgettable journey filled with exploration and discovery.

Often dubbed the 'Airbnb of cars,' Turo operates as a peer-to-peer marketplace connecting renters directly with car owners. With Turo, you'll discover a wide range of vehicle options, from standard everyday cars to luxurious models. One of the main advantages of using Turo is that prices generally remain stable, unlike traditional rental car agencies, making it a compelling choice for budget-conscious travelers seeking to save money.

The East Coast, particularly the Northeast, offers relatively convenient transportation options without the need for a car, especially compared to other regions of the country. Train services run along the Northeast and Mid-Atlantic, providing easy access to major cities like Baltimore, Philadelphia, Washington D.C., and Boston from New York City. Depending on the destination, travel times typically range from 2 to 5 hours. While it's uncertain if there's a direct train service to Maine or greater New England, a bit of research could uncover available options.

Many travelers opt for trains when journeying between NYC and DC, enjoying the roughly 3-hour ride that's often more cost-effective than flying or renting a car. Additionally, both cities boast subway systems, as do Boston and Philadelphia, making intra-city travel convenient and efficient.

For destinations further south, such as the Carolinas or Atlanta, alternative modes of transportation like buses, flights, or rental cars may be preferable. Buses tend to be the most economical choice, though flight prices can vary depending on luggage requirements, while car rentals are currently pricey in this area.

For travel to other parts of the US, purchasing a plane ticket is typically the most straightforward option, offering efficient and direct transportation to a wide range of destinations across the country.

For travelers with a clear itinerary, pre-paying for a rental car may offer savings. Lastly, consider utilizing comparison tools like Autoslash to quickly compare rental prices and uncover potential discounts that you may not have been aware of. These strategies can help maximize your savings and make your travel experience more affordable and convenient.

Ride Share

Ride-sharing services like Uber and Lyft can save you thousands on transportation costs. By replacing car ownership or traditional taxis with convenient, on-demand rides, you can cut down on expenses like fuel, parking, and maintenance. Plus, both Uber and Lyft offer referral programs that can earn you free ride credits when you refer friends or family members to their platforms. Here are some of the best ride-share services in the USA, along with starting prices and URLs for more information:

1. **Uber (**www.uber.com**)**:
    - Starting Price: Varies by location, but typically includes a base fare plus a per-mile and per-minute rate.
    - Uber offers a range of services, including UberX (standard rides), UberXL (larger vehicles), Uber Black (premium rides), and Uber Pool (shared rides).
2. **Lyft (**www.lyft.com**)**:
    - Starting Price: Similar to Uber, Lyft's pricing structure varies by location and service type.
    - Lyft offers options such as Lyft Standard, Lyft XL (larger vehicles), Lyft Lux (luxury rides), and Lyft Shared (shared rides).
3. **Via (**www.ridewithvia.com**)**:
    - Starting Price: Via typically offers flat-rate fares for shared rides, which can be more affordable than traditional ride-sharing services.
    - Via operates in select cities and focuses on shared rides with multiple passengers traveling in the same direction.
4. **Curb (**www.gocurb.com**)**:
    - Starting Price: Curb's pricing varies depending on factors such as distance and time of day.
    - Curb connects users with licensed taxi drivers in cities across the USA, offering a more traditional taxi experience with the convenience of booking through a mobile app.
5. **Juno (**www.gojuno.com**)**:
    - Starting Price: Juno's pricing structure is similar to Lyft and Uber, with rates varying by location and service type.
    - Juno prioritizes driver satisfaction and offers competitive rates to both drivers and passengers.
6. **Wingz (**www.wingz.me**)**:
    - Starting Price: Wingz offers flat-rate fares for airport rides and other point-to-point transportation.
    - Wingz specializes in airport transportation, providing pre-scheduled rides to and from airports in select cities across the USA.

Flying

Finding cheap domestic flights and onward travel options can save you a significant amount of money on your travels.

When booking domestic flights, consider utilizing smaller regional airports near major cities, such as Long Island MacArthur Airport in Islip, New York, or Hollywood Burbank Airport near Los Angeles. These airports are often served by smaller carriers offering very affordable fares compared to larger hubs. For extensive travel distances, flying may be the most convenient option, as routes provided by Amtrak, the US rail network, may not offer comprehensive coverage and can be inconvenient.

In larger cities, an increasing number of light-rail trains provide transportation from airports to downtown areas or transportation hubs. Light-rail fares are generally much lower than those for taxis or rideshares, offering a budget-friendly alternative for travelers. Additionally, before booking a rental car, it's advisable to compare prices carefully, as airport fees often result in higher prices compared to off-site agencies.

Here are some more insider tips to help you score the best deals:

1. **Be Flexible with Your Travel Dates**: Being flexible with your travel dates can help you find cheaper flights. Use flexible date search options on airline websites or third-party booking platforms to compare prices across different dates. Flights on weekdays or during off-peak hours are often cheaper than those on weekends or during peak travel times.
2. **Book in Advance**: Booking your flights well in advance can often result in lower prices. Aim to book your flights at least a few weeks before your travel date to secure the best deals. Airlines typically offer lower prices for seats booked in advance, and prices tend to increase as the travel date approaches.
3. **Sign Up for Price Alerts**: Many travel websites and apps offer price alert features that notify you when flight prices drop for your desired route. Sign up for these alerts to stay informed about price fluctuations and snag the best deals when they become available.
4. **Use Airline Miles and Reward Points**: If you're a frequent traveler or have accumulated airline miles and reward points through credit card purchases or loyalty programs, consider using them to offset the cost of your flights. Redeeming miles and points for flights can result in significant savings, especially for domestic travel.

5. **Explore Alternative Airports**: When searching for flights, consider flying into or out of alternative airports near your destination. Smaller regional airports may offer cheaper flights and fewer crowds compared to major airports, saving you both time and money.
6. **Bundle Flights with Accommodation**: Some travel booking platforms offer discounts when you bundle flights with accommodation or rental car bookings. Look for package deals that combine multiple travel components to maximize savings on your overall trip.
7. **Check for Promo Codes and Discounts**: Before booking your flights, search online for promo codes, coupons, and discounts offered by airlines or third-party booking platforms. These promotional offers can help you unlock additional savings on your airfare.
8. **Consider One-Way Tickets**: Instead of booking a round-trip ticket, consider booking one-way tickets on different airlines or for different legs of your journey. Sometimes, combining one-way tickets from different carriers can result in cheaper overall fares compared to round-trip options.
9. **Explore Alternative Transportation Options**: Depending on your destination and travel preferences, consider alternative transportation options such as trains, buses, or rideshare services for onward travel within the country. These options may offer cheaper fares and unique travel experiences compared to traditional flights.

Fly for free

Several credit cards offer rewards programs that allow cardholders to earn points or miles that can be redeemed for free flights. Here are some popular options:

1. **Chase Sapphire Preferred® Card**: Earn Chase Ultimate Rewards points that can be transferred to airline partners or redeemed for travel through the Chase Ultimate Rewards portal.
2. **American Express® Gold Card**: Earn American Express Membership Rewards points that can be transferred to airline partners or redeemed for flights through the Amex Travel portal.
3. **Capital One Venture Rewards Credit Card**: Earn Capital One miles that can be redeemed for travel statement credits to cover the cost of flights.
4. **Citi Premier® Card**: Earn Citi ThankYou Points that can be transferred to airline partners or redeemed for flights through the ThankYou Travel Center.

5. **Delta SkyMiles® Gold American Express Card**: Earn Delta SkyMiles that can be redeemed for flights with Delta Air Lines and its partners.
6. **United℠ Explorer Card**: Earn United MileagePlus miles that can be redeemed for flights with United Airlines and its Star Alliance partners.
7. **Southwest Rapid Rewards® Plus Credit Card**: Earn Southwest Rapid Rewards points that can be redeemed for flights with Southwest Airlines.
8. **JetBlue Plus Card**: Earn JetBlue TrueBlue points that can be redeemed for flights with JetBlue Airways.

Many travel rewards cards require you to spend a certain amount within the first few months to earn the sign-up bonus. Make sure you can meet this requirement without overspending or accruing unnecessary debt.

Luxury Hotels

Picture yourself strolling through the hallowed halls of a five-star hotel, where every detail exudes elegance and sophistication. With a day pass in hand, you are not merely a passerby, but a welcomed guest, invited to savor the lavish amenities and impeccable service that define the pinnacle of hospitality. The Mark in NYC stands among the priciest hotels in the US, where nightly rates kick off at $916. However, you can opt for a day pass starting from $100, granting access to the same luxuries while finding more affordable accommodations elsewhere for the night.

The true beauty of the day pass lies in its ability to offer luxury at a fraction of the cost. With access to world-class amenities and facilities, from state-of-the-art fitness centers to sumptuous spa sanctuaries, you can experience the epitome of indulgence without the hefty price tag of an overnight stay. Here is how to book them in the USA:

- **ResortPass:**
  - ResortPass is a platform that allows you to book day passes to use the pools, lounges, and other amenities of various luxury hotels across the United States. Prices vary depending on the hotel, and the pass often includes access to the pool, fitness center, and sometimes other perks like discounts on food and beverages.
- **DayAxe:**
  - DayAxe is another platform that offers day passes to luxury hotels, providing access to amenities like pools, spas, and fitness centers. Prices can range based on the specific hotel and location.
- **Hilton Day Use Rooms:**
  - Some Hilton hotels offer day use rooms, allowing you to book a room for a shorter period during the day. This can provide access to the hotel's facilities. Prices vary depending on the hotel and location.

- **Resort for a Day:**
  - Resort for a Day offers day passes to resorts and hotels in various locations, including some in the USA. These passes typically include access to pools, beaches, and other amenities.

Before booking, contact the hotel directly or use the mentioned platforms to inquire about day pass options, prices, and any specific terms and conditions. Keep in mind that policies may change, and it's always a good idea to confirm the details with the hotel.

Hotels

When it comes to budget-friendly hotel chains in the USA, there are several options available that cater to travelers seeking affordable accommodations without sacrificing quality or comfort. Here are some of the cheapest hotel chains in the USA, along with their starting prices and tips for scoring discounts:

1. **Motel 6**:
   - Starting Price: Motel 6 is known for its budget-friendly rates, with starting prices typically ranging from $50 to $70 USD per night.
   - How to Score Discounts: Look out for promotional deals, discounts for AAA members, military personnel, seniors, or government employees. Additionally, booking directly through the Motel 6 website or mobile app may sometimes offer exclusive discounts or special offers.
2. **Super 8 by Wyndham**:
   - Starting Price: Super 8 by Wyndham offers affordable accommodations with starting prices usually ranging from $50 to $80 USD per night.
   - How to Score Discounts: Take advantage of advance purchase rates, special promotions, and discounts available to Wyndham Rewards members. Signing up for the Wyndham Rewards loyalty program can also earn you points for future stays and unlock exclusive member rates.
3. **Red Roof Inn**:
   - Starting Price: Red Roof Inn provides budget-friendly accommodations with starting prices typically ranging from $60 to $90 USD per night.
   - How to Score Discounts: Keep an eye out for special offers, package deals, and discounts available through the RediCard loyalty program. Booking directly through the Red Roof Inn website or mobile app may also offer additional savings.
4. **Extended Stay America**:
   - Starting Price: Extended Stay America offers affordable extended-stay accommodations with starting prices usually ranging from $70 to $100 USD per night.
   - How to Score Discounts: Take advantage of weekly or monthly rates for longer stays. Signing up for the Extended Perks rewards program can also earn you points towards free nights and unlock member-exclusive discounts.
5. **Quality Inn**:
   - Starting Price: Quality Inn offers budget-friendly accommodations with starting prices typically ranging from $70 to $100 USD per night.
   - How to Score Discounts: Look out for special promotions, discounts for Choice Privileges members, and advance purchase rates. Booking directly through the Quality Inn website or mobile app may also offer additional discounts or perks.

To score discounts at these budget-friendly hotel chains, use the following tips:

- Sign up for loyalty programs: Many hotel chains offer rewards programs that allow you to earn points for every stay, which can be redeemed for free nights or other perks.
- Look for special promotions: Keep an eye out for special promotions, package deals, and last-minute discounts offered by hotel chains.
- Book in advance: Booking your stay in advance can often result in lower rates, so plan ahead and take advantage of advance purchase rates whenever possible.
- Use discount codes: Search online for discount codes or coupons that can be applied to your hotel booking to unlock additional savings.
- Consider alternative booking platforms: Compare prices on different booking platforms, and consider using online travel agencies or discount websites to find the best deals on hotel accommodations.

Free Breakfast

Several hotel chains in the USA offer complimentary breakfast as part of their amenities. Here are some of the best hotel chains known for providing free breakfast to their guests:

1. **Hampton by Hilton**: Hampton by Hilton is renowned for its complimentary hot breakfast, known as the "Hampton Breakfast," which typically includes a variety of hot and cold items like eggs, bacon, waffles, cereals, pastries, and fresh fruit.
2. **Holiday Inn Express**: Holiday Inn Express offers a complimentary Express Start Breakfast Bar featuring a selection of hot and cold breakfast items, including eggs, sausage, pancakes, cereals, pastries, and fresh coffee.
3. **Drury Inn & Suites**: Drury Inn & Suites provides a complimentary hot breakfast buffet with a rotating selection of items like scrambled eggs, biscuits and gravy, sausage, waffles, yogurt, and fresh fruit.
4. **Comfort Inn & Suites**: Comfort Inn & Suites offers a complimentary hot breakfast buffet with options like eggs, breakfast meats, waffles, pastries, cereals, yogurt, and fresh fruit.
5. **Best Western**: Many Best Western hotels provide a complimentary breakfast buffet with a variety of hot and cold options, including eggs, sausage, waffles, pastries, cereals, yogurt, and fresh fruit.
6. **La Quinta by Wyndham**: La Quinta by Wyndham offers a complimentary Bright Side Breakfast featuring a selection of hot and cold items, such as eggs, sausage, waffles, cereal, yogurt, and fresh fruit.
7. **Country Inn & Suites by Radisson**: Country Inn & Suites by Radisson serves a complimentary hot breakfast buffet with rotating items like eggs, sausage, biscuits and gravy, waffles, pastries, cereals, yogurt, and fresh fruit.
8. **Homewood Suites by Hilton**: Homewood Suites by Hilton provides a complimentary hot breakfast buffet with a variety of options, including eggs, breakfast meats, waffles, pastries, cereals, yogurt, and fresh fruit.

Don't forget to enroll in the loyalty programs offered by Booking.com and Hotels.com. Hotels.com rewards you with a free room after every 10 bookings, while Booking.com offers members a 10% discount on bookings, along with complimentary upgrades and perks for frequent bookings. These programs can provide significant benefits and savings over time.

Pro tip: Utilize cashback websites like Mr. Rebates or Rakuten when booking through Hotels.com or Booking.com. By accessing their links before visiting the booking websites, you can earn an additional 2-4% cash back on top of the rewards offered by the loyalty programs. This savvy strategy maximizes your savings and rewards potential with each booking.

Hostel options in the United States are limited, and many of them come with a hefty price tag. A dormitory bed typically sets you back around $30 per night, which often aligns with the cost of securing a comparable private room on Airbnb. If you're traveling with companions, opting for a budget hotel may prove to be more cost-effective than booking multiple dorm beds.

Get 70% off a Cruise

Looking to set sail on a cruise but hesitant about the cost? Consider repositioning cruises departing from America, where you can enjoy significant savings of up to 70%. These one-way voyages occur during low cruise seasons when ships relocate to warmer destinations, making them an affordable option for budget-conscious travelers.

Instead of shelling out an average of $4,000 for a typical cruise, opt for a repositioning cruise that returns the ship to its home port. Not only will you save money, but you'll also have the opportunity to explore new destinations along the way.

To discover repositioning cruises departing from America, visit vacationstogo.com/repositioning_cruises.cfm. This simple booking trick is often overlooked but can lead to substantial savings, especially for families looking to avoid long flights with children.

It's important to note that we do not have any affiliations with travel services or providers. The links we recommend are based on our experience in finding the best deals for travelers like you.

Theme Parks on the Super Cheap

Millions of visitors from around the world travel to America specifically to experience its renowned theme parks. With iconic destinations like Walt Disney World Resort, Disneyland Resort, and Universal Orlando Resort attracting visitors from all corners of the globe, the number of tourists flocking to these attractions annually is substantial. While exact figures may vary year to year, it's safe to say that the collective number of visitors to America's theme parks reaches into the tens of millions each year. These parks are not just local attractions; they're international destinations, drawing travelers seeking unforgettable experiences and magical adventures.

Ah, theme parks—the ultimate playgrounds for thrill-seekers and fun-lovers alike. But let's face it, those admission prices and concession stand costs can add up faster than you can say "roller coaster." Fear not, my frugal friend, for I've got some insider tips to help you save tons of money at USA theme parks:

1. **Buy Tickets Online in Advance**: Many theme parks offer discounted ticket prices for those who purchase online in advance. Look out for special promotions, multi-day passes, or bundle deals that can save you a bundle compared to buying tickets at the gate.
2. **Visit During Off-Peak Times**: Want to avoid the crowds *and* save money? Visit theme parks during off-peak times, such as weekdays or during the shoulder seasons (spring and fall). Not only will you spend less time waiting in line, but you'll also often find lower ticket prices and hotel rates.
3. **Pack Your Own Snacks and Drinks**: Skip the overpriced concession stands and pack your own snacks and drinks to keep hunger at bay while you explore the park. Just make sure to check the park's policies on outside food and beverages beforehand to avoid any surprises at the entrance.
4. **Use Single Rider Lines**: If you don't mind riding solo, take advantage of single rider lines to skip the long wait times at

popular attractions. While you may not get to ride with your group, you'll save valuable time and maximize your thrills per hour.
5. **Take Advantage of Freebies and Discounts**: Keep an eye out for freebies and discounts offered by the park, such as free entertainment shows, character meet-and-greets, or souvenir giveaways. Additionally, look for discounts for AAA members, military personnel, seniors, and local residents.
6. **BYOS (Bring Your Own Souvenirs)**: Souvenirs are a tempting way to commemorate your park visit, but they can also drain your wallet faster than you can say "Mickey Mouse." Instead of splurging on pricey merchandise, opt for budget-friendly alternatives like collecting free park maps, taking photos, or creating your own DIY souvenirs.
7. **Utilize FastPass or Express Lane Options**: Many theme parks offer FastPass or Express Lane options that allow you to skip the regular lines and enjoy priority access to attractions. While these may come with an additional cost, they can be worth it if you want to make the most of your time in the park.
8. **Consider Staying Off-Site**: While staying at a theme park resort hotel can be convenient, it often comes with a hefty price tag. Save money by staying off-site at a nearby hotel or vacation rental and taking advantage of shuttle services or public transportation to get to the park.
9. **Check for Discounted Packages**: Some theme parks offer discounted packages that include admission tickets, hotel accommodations, and other perks like meal vouchers or parking passes. Compare prices and packages to find the best value for your budget.
10. **Look for Promo Codes and Coupons**: Before purchasing tickets or booking accommodations, search online for promo codes, coupons, and deals that can help you save money. Websites like RetailMeNot, Groupon, and theme park enthusiast forums are great places to find discounts and insider tips.

Beaches

There's an abundance of stunning coastlines along both the Pacific and Atlantic Oceans, as well as the Gulf of Mexico, offering beach lovers a diverse range of options to explore. Here are some of the best beaches in the USA and tips on how to visit them affordably:

1. **Point Reyes National Seashore, California**: While the water may be chilly, the scenery is truly enchanting along this pristine stretch of untamed coastline in Northern California. To visit Point Reyes National Seashore on a budget, consider camping at one of the park's campgrounds or nearby budget-friendly accommodations in towns like Point Reyes Station or Olema.
2. **South Beach, Miami, Florida**: This world-renowned beach is less about swimming and more about people-watching along Miami's iconic shoreline. To experience South Beach on the cheap, opt for budget accommodations in nearby neighborhoods like Miami Beach or Little Havana, and take advantage of free or low-cost activities like strolling along Ocean Drive or exploring the vibrant Art Deco district.
3. **Big Beach, Maui, Hawaii**: With its stunning turquoise waters and expansive golden sands, Big Beach is a true gem of Maui's coastline. To visit Big Beach affordably, consider staying in budget accommodations in nearby towns like Kihei or Lahaina, and pack your own snacks and drinks to enjoy a budget-friendly beach day in paradise.
4. **Cape Cod National Seashore, Massachusetts**: This scenic stretch of coastline features massive sand dunes, picturesque lighthouses, and serene forests, perfect for endless exploration. To explore Cape Cod National Seashore on a budget, consider camping at one of the park's campgrounds or staying in budget-friendly accommodations in towns like Provincetown or Wellfleet.
5. **Outer Banks, North Carolina**: Stretching for 100 miles along the coast of North Carolina, the Outer Banks offers breezy beaches, historic lighthouses, and the chance to spot wild horses in places like Corolla. To visit the Outer Banks

affordably, consider camping at one of the area's campgrounds or booking budget accommodations in towns like Nags Head or Kitty Hawk.

Dollywood on the Super Cheap

Dollywood is a tribute to the beloved country music legend Dolly Parton, featuring a blend of Appalachian-themed rides and attractions nestled in the scenic hills of Tennessee. Meanwhile, Cedar Point Amusement Park in Ohio boasts a reputation as a favorite destination, offering thrill-seekers the chance to experience some of the world's tallest and fastest roller coasters, including the exhilarating 120mph Top Thrill Dragster. Experiencing Dollywood on a budget is absolutely possible!

1. **Discount Tickets**: Look for discounted tickets through various channels such as online deals, local promotions, or group discounts. Dollywood often offers special deals for residents of Tennessee or neighboring states, as well as discounts for seniors, military personnel, and AAA members.
2. **Off-Peak Visits**: Plan your visit during off-peak times, such as weekdays or non-holiday periods, to take advantage of lower ticket prices and smaller crowds. Avoiding weekends and peak seasons can help you save money and enjoy shorter wait times for rides and attractions.
3. **Free Shows and Entertainment**: Take advantage of the park's free shows, entertainment, and musical performances, which are included with admission. Dollywood features a variety of live music, comedy shows, and cultural performances that showcase the spirit of the Appalachian region.
4. **Discounted Accommodations**: Look for budget-friendly accommodations near Dollywood, such as campgrounds, motels, or vacation rentals. Consider staying in nearby towns like Pigeon Forge or Gatlinburg, where lodging options tend to be more affordable compared to on-site hotels or resorts.

Revisit Your Favourite Films and Shows

TV tourism gained traction in the late 1990s with the surge of fans flocking to New York City following the success of Sex and the City. Now, in the era of 'peak TV,' this phenomenon has grown exponentially, with numerous destinations across the USA capitalizing on it. Here are some hotspots for TV and film-centered tours:

1. **"Friends" (TV Series)**: Relive the iconic moments of "Friends" by visiting the filming locations in New York City. Explore the exterior of the apartment building at 90 Bedford Street (also known as the Friends Apartment) in Greenwich Village. Take a stroll through Central Perk-inspired cafes or join free walking tours that highlight other recognizable spots from the show.
2. **"Forrest Gump" (Film)**: Follow in the footsteps of Forrest Gump by visiting filming locations in Savannah, Georgia. Explore Chippewa Square, where the iconic bench scenes were filmed, or take a stroll along the historic Savannah Riverfront. Many of these locations can be explored for free on a self-guided walking tour.
3. **"Breaking Bad" (TV Series)**: Dive into the gritty world of "Breaking Bad" by visiting filming locations in Albuquerque, New Mexico. Explore iconic spots such as Saul Goodman's law office, Los Pollos Hermanos, and Walter White's car wash.
4. **"La La Land" (Film)**: Experience the magic of "La La Land" by visiting filming locations in Los Angeles, California. Explore Griffith Observatory, the iconic location of the film's memorable dance sequence, or visit the Hermosa Beach Pier for stunning ocean views. Many of these locations can be visited for free, offering a glimpse into the world of the movie.
5. **"The Walking Dead" (TV Series)**: Embark on a zombie-filled adventure by visiting filming locations of "The Walking Dead" in Senoia, Georgia. Explore iconic spots such as the Alexandria Safe-Zone and Woodbury, or take a guided tour of the set.

Some locations may require admission fees, but many can be explored for free on self-guided tours.
6. **"Jurassic Park" Series (Film Franchise)**: Experience the wonder of "Jurassic Park" by visiting filming locations in Hawaii. Explore Kualoa Ranch on Oahu, where many scenes were filmed, including the iconic entrance gates. While some activities at the ranch may require admission fees, visitors can still capture photos of the recognizable locations for free.

Free Museums

The American Alliance of Museums (AAM), one of the largest museum organizations in the United States, reported that there were over 35,000 museums in the country as of its most recent data and many are FREE!

1. **Smithsonian Museums, Washington, D.C.**:
   - Admission: Always free
   - Savings: Depending on the museum, you can save around $15-25 per adult admission.
2. **The Getty Center, Los Angeles, California**:
   - Admission: Always free, but parking fees apply.
   - Savings: Approximately $20 per vehicle for parking.
3. **The Art Institute of Chicago, Illinois**:
   - Free Admission: Thursdays from 5:00 PM to 8:00 PM for Illinois residents.
   - Savings: Around $25 per adult admission.
4. **Museum of Modern Art (MoMA), New York City, New York**:
   - Free Admission: Fridays from 4:00 PM to 8:00 PM.
   - Savings: Approximately $25 per adult admission.
5. **The Metropolitan Museum of Art, New York City, New York**:
   - Free Admission: Pay what you wish for New York residents and students from New Jersey and Connecticut. However, there's a suggested admission fee of $25.
   - Savings: Depending on your donation, you could save $1 or more per person.
6. **The Field Museum, Chicago, Illinois**:
   - Free Admission: On selected days for Illinois residents (usually one day per month).
   - Savings: Approximately $26 per adult admission.
7. **California Science Center, Los Angeles, California**:
   - Free Admission: Permanent exhibits are always free.
   - Savings: Typically, special exhibitions may require a ticket, which can range from $10 to $20 per person.
8. **The Getty Villa, Pacific Palisades, California**:
   - Admission: Always free, but parking fees apply.
   - Savings: Approximately $20 per vehicle for parking.
9. **The National WWII Museum, New Orleans, Louisiana**:
   - Free Admission: Veterans, active-duty military personnel, and Louisiana residents on designated days.
   - Savings: Around $28 per adult admission.
10. **The Field Museum, Chicago, Illinois**:
    - Free Admission: On selected days for Illinois residents (usually one day per month).
    - Savings: Approximately $26 per adult admission.

These are just a few examples of museums in the USA that offer free admission on certain days, providing opportunities for visitors to explore art, history, science, and culture without spending a lot of money.

Find free classes and workshops

In the land of opportunity, where the spirit of innovation and learning thrives, there exists a hidden gem waiting to be discovered: the abundance of free classes and workshops scattered across the vast expanse of the United States. Here's where to find them:

Public Libraries:

- **Boston, Massachusetts** - The Boston Public Library offers free computer classes covering topics such as internet basics, Microsoft Office applications, and social media.
- **Chicago, Illinois** - The Chicago Public Library hosts free workshops on financial literacy, job searching skills, resume writing, and interview techniques.
- **Los Angeles, California** - The Los Angeles Public Library offers free language learning classes in Spanish, Mandarin, French, and more, as well as computer literacy workshops.

Community Centers:

- **Seattle, Washington** - The Seattle Community Centers offer free fitness classes such as yoga, Zumba, and tai chi, as well as cooking workshops focusing on healthy eating.
- **Denver, Colorado** - The Denver Parks and Recreation Department hosts free arts and crafts classes for all ages at various community centers throughout the city.
- **Miami, Florida** - The Miami-Dade County Community Centers provide free gardening workshops, teaching residents how to cultivate their own urban gardens.

Universities and Colleges:

- **New York City, New York** - Columbia University offers free public lectures and workshops through its School of Journalism, covering topics such as media literacy and investigative journalism.
- **San Francisco, California** - The University of California, San Francisco (UCSF) hosts free public health seminars and

workshops on topics such as nutrition, stress management, and mindfulness.
- **Austin, Texas** - The University of Texas at Austin offers free public lectures and workshops through its Center for Mexican American Studies, focusing on issues related to Latino/a communities in the United States.

Nonprofit Organizations:

- **Portland, Oregon** - The Oregon Environmental Council offers free workshops on sustainable living practices, including composting, rainwater harvesting, and energy efficiency.
- **Philadelphia, Pennsylvania** - The Philadelphia Health Management Corporation (PHMC) offers free workshops on mental health awareness, stress management, and coping skills for residents of the city.

Online Platforms:

- Websites like **Coursera**, **Khan Academy**, and **Udemy** offer free courses and tutorials on a wide range of subjects, including programming, graphic design, photography, and more. These platforms provide access to educational resources from anywhere in the USA.

Free Outdoor Activities

1. **Hiking**:
    - National Parks: Many trails in national parks offer free access. For example, trails in Great Smoky Mountains National Park in Tennessee and North Carolina are free to explore.
    - State Parks: Some state parks offer free admission or have designated free days. Check with your local state park for more information.
2. **Biking**:
    - City Bike Paths: Many cities have bike paths or lanes that are free to use. For example, the Chicago Lakefront Trail offers scenic views of Lake Michigan and the city skyline.
    - Rail Trails: Rail trails, converted from old railroad lines, are often free to use for biking. The Katy Trail in Missouri is one example.
3. **Birdwatching**:
    - Wildlife Refuges: Many wildlife refuges across the country offer free birdwatching opportunities. For example, the Bosque del Apache National Wildlife Refuge in New Mexico is known for its birdwatching opportunities.
4. **Picnicking**:
    - Local Parks: Public parks in cities and towns often have picnic areas that are free to use. Bring your own food and enjoy a meal outdoors with friends and family.
5. **Fishing**:
    - Public Fishing Areas: Many lakes, rivers, and ponds in the USA offer free fishing access. Some states also have designated free fishing days where no license is required.
8. **Geocaching**:
    - Geocaching is a treasure-hunting game where participants use GPS coordinates to find hidden containers called geocaches. There are millions of geocaches hidden around the world, including many in the USA, and participation is free.
9. **Stargazing**:
    - Dark Sky Parks: Visit designated Dark Sky Parks for optimal stargazing conditions. These parks have minimal light pollution, allowing for excellent views of the night sky. Death Valley National Park in California is one such park.
10. **Outdoor Yoga and Fitness Classes**:
    - Many communities offer free outdoor yoga and fitness classes in parks and public spaces, especially during the warmer months. Check local community calendars and social media for listings.

Fishing

The USA offers a wide variety of fishing experiences, from freshwater lakes and rivers to coastal waters teeming with marine life. Here are some of the best fishing destinations in the USA, along with tips on how to enjoy them both luxuriously and on a budget:

There are several renowned public fishing access points across the country that are highly regarded by anglers:

1. **Yellowstone National Park, Wyoming/Montana/Idaho** - Known for its pristine rivers, lakes, and streams, Yellowstone offers exceptional fly fishing opportunities for trout, including Yellowstone cutthroat, rainbow, brown, and brook trout.
2. **Everglades National Park, Florida** - The expansive freshwater and saltwater ecosystems of the Everglades provide abundant fishing opportunities for species such as largemouth bass, snook, tarpon, and redfish.
3. **Great Smoky Mountains National Park, Tennessee/North Carolina** - With over 2,100 miles of streams, the Great Smoky Mountains offer excellent trout fishing amidst breathtaking scenery.
4. **Lake Fork Reservoir, Texas** - Considered one of the top bass fishing destinations in the country, Lake Fork is renowned for its trophy largemouth bass.
5. **Kenai River, Alaska** - Known for its world-class salmon fishing, particularly for king (chinook) salmon, the Kenai River attracts anglers from around the globe.
6. **Lake Erie, Ohio/Pennsylvania/New York** - Lake Erie offers exceptional fishing for walleye, smallmouth bass, yellow perch, and steelhead trout, making it a popular destination for both boat and shore anglers.
7. **Bighorn River, Montana** - The Bighorn River is famous for its prolific trout population, including rainbow and brown trout, and is regarded as one of the finest tailwater fisheries in the United States.
8. **San Juan River, New Mexico** - The San Juan River below Navajo Dam is known for its trophy trout, particularly brown and rainbow trout, making it a mecca for fly anglers.

9. **Lake Okeechobee, Florida** - The "Big O" is one of the most renowned bass fishing lakes in the country, offering excellent opportunities for largemouth bass, crappie, and bluegill.
10. **Columbia River, Oregon/Washington** - The Columbia River is famous for its salmon and steelhead runs, attracting anglers seeking to catch these prized game fish.

-

Enjoying Fishing on a Budget:

1. **Public Fishing Access**:
    - Take advantage of public fishing access points, which often offer free or low-cost fishing opportunities in lakes, rivers, and coastal waters. Check local regulations and licenses requirements.
2. **DIY Fishing Trips**:
    - Plan your own fishing trips to public fishing spots where you can fish from shore or rent a boat at an affordable rate. Bring your own gear and supplies to save on rental costs.
3. **Fishing from Shore**:
    - Enjoy shoreline fishing at public parks, piers, and beaches where no boat is required. Pack a cooler with snacks and drinks for a budget-friendly day of fishing with friends and family.
4. **Budget-Friendly Accommodations**:
    - Stay in budget-friendly accommodations such as campgrounds, cabins, or motels located near fishing destinations. Consider sharing lodging expenses with friends or family to reduce costs.
5. **BYO Fishing Gear**:
    - Invest in quality fishing gear that will last for multiple trips rather than renting equipment each time. Look for sales, discounts, and second-hand gear to save money on fishing equipment.
7. **Grocery Store Discounts**: Many grocery stores offer discounted prices on items that are nearing their sell-by or expiration dates. Look for "manager's specials" or clearance sections in supermarkets where you can find discounted produce, bakery items, and packaged goods.

Food Delivery

Food delivery is big business in the USA. Key players in the market included third-party delivery platforms like Uber Eats, DoorDash, and Grubhub. You can ALWAYS find discounts and promotional offers on food delivery apps in the USA by following these tips:

1. **Sign Up for New User Promotions**: Many food delivery apps offer special promotions for first-time users. Look for promo codes or referral links that provide discounts on your first order when you sign up for the app.
2. **Check for In-App Offers**: Food delivery apps frequently run promotions and special offers directly within the app. Look for banners, pop-ups, or dedicated sections that highlight current deals and discounts.
3. **Follow Social Media and Email Alerts**: Follow your favorite food delivery apps on social media platforms like Facebook, Twitter, and Instagram, as well as subscribing to their email newsletters. Companies often announce exclusive promotions and discounts through these channels.

Here are the companies to check for discounts. You can often get up to $50 free!

1. **DoorDash**: DoorDash is one of the largest food delivery platforms in the USA, offering a wide selection of restaurants and cuisines in many cities across the country. The app is known for its user-friendly interface, fast delivery times, and frequent promotions.
2. **Uber Eats**: Uber Eats is a popular food delivery service operated by the ride-sharing company Uber. It offers a diverse range of restaurant options, along with the convenience of tracking your delivery in real-time through the Uber app.
3. **Grubhub**: Grubhub is one of the oldest and most established food delivery apps in the USA. It features a vast network of restaurants and offers features like pre-ordering and scheduled deliveries to enhance the user experience.

4. **Postmates**: Postmates offers on-demand delivery from a variety of local restaurants and stores, including options for groceries, alcohol, and other essentials. The app is known for its fast delivery times and flexible ordering options.
5. **DoorDash-owned Caviar**: Caviar, owned by DoorDash, specializes in premium food delivery from high-end restaurants. It offers a curated selection of restaurants and provides a more upscale dining experience compared to other delivery apps.
6. **Instacart**: While primarily known for grocery delivery, Instacart also offers food delivery services from select restaurants and stores in many cities. It's a convenient option for getting both meals and groceries delivered to your doorstep.
7. **Seamless**: Owned by Grubhub, Seamless offers a seamless ordering experience with a wide range of restaurant options and user-friendly features like filtering by cuisine and dietary preferences.
8. **ChowNow**: ChowNow partners directly with restaurants to provide online ordering and delivery services. It's a good option for supporting local businesses and accessing exclusive deals and promotions.
9. **Eat24 (Yelp Eat24)**: Eat24, now part of Yelp, offers food delivery from a variety of restaurants with user-friendly search and ordering features. It's a convenient option for discovering new dining options and reading reviews from other users.
10. **Slice**: Slice specializes in pizza delivery from local pizzerias, allowing users to order their favorite pies for delivery or pickup. It's a great option for pizza lovers looking to support independent pizzerias.

Free Live Music

Whether you're a fan of jazz, blues, country, rock, hip-hop, or beyond, there are countless opportunities to immerse yourself in live music experiences. Here's a guide to some of the best places in the USA to watch free live music:

1. **New Orleans, Louisiana**: Known as the birthplace of jazz, New Orleans is a mecca for music enthusiasts. Head to the French Quarter or Frenchmen Street to find numerous venues offering free live jazz performances, especially during events like French Quarter Fest and Jazz Fest.
2. **Austin, Texas**: With its slogan "Live Music Capital of the World," Austin boasts a thriving music scene with numerous bars, clubs, and outdoor spaces hosting free live music throughout the year. Check out iconic venues like the Continental Club, Elephant Room, or Zilker Park for free concerts and performances.
3. **Nashville, Tennessee**: As the epicenter of country music, Nashville offers plenty of opportunities to catch free live performances, especially in venues along Broadway and in neighborhoods like East Nashville. Don't miss the free shows at the famous honky-tonks like Tootsie's Orchid Lounge and Robert's Western World.
4. **New York City, New York**: From Central Park SummerStage to the Rockwood Music Hall, NYC offers a plethora of free live music events and concerts across all genres. Explore neighborhoods like the East Village, Williamsburg, and Harlem for hidden gems and intimate performances.
5. **Seattle, Washington**: Home to legendary musicians like Jimi Hendrix and Nirvana, Seattle's music scene is alive and well. Check out free concerts at venues like Pike Place Market, the Ballard Locks, and various parks throughout the city during the summer months.
6. **Chicago, Illinois**: Blues enthusiasts will find plenty to love in Chicago, with numerous bars and clubs offering free live blues performances. Visit iconic venues like Kingston Mines, Buddy

Guy's Legends, and the Chicago Blues Festival for unforgettable experiences.
7. **Asheville, North Carolina**: Nestled in the Blue Ridge Mountains, Asheville boasts a thriving music scene with free concerts and performances happening regularly in venues like Pack Square Park, The Orange Peel, and various breweries and bars throughout the city.
8. **San Francisco, California**: From street performers in Fisherman's Wharf to concerts in Golden Gate Park, San Francisco offers a diverse array of free live music experiences. Explore neighborhoods like the Mission District and Haight-Ashbury for eclectic venues and performances.

Natural Wonders

From towering mountains to cascading waterfalls, America's natural landscapes are a sight to behold, offering endless opportunities for outdoor adventure and exploration.

- Explore the National Parks: America's national parks are a treasure trove of natural beauty and wonder, and many offer free admission on select days throughout the year. Take a hike through the otherworldly landscapes of Arches National Park, marvel at the majestic waterfalls of Yosemite, or camp under the stars in Great Smoky Mountains National Park.
- Discover the Great Outdoors: Embark on a budget-friendly camping trip in one of America's many state parks or national forests. Pitch a tent, roast marshmallows over a campfire, and fall asleep to the sounds of nature—all without breaking the bank.
- Visit Free Attractions: Don't overlook the free natural attractions that abound across the country. From the Grand Canyon's South Rim to the Great Lakes' scenic shores, there are plenty of stunning vistas and outdoor adventures to be had without spending a dime.

Useful Websites:

- National Park Service: NPS.gov (https://www.nps.gov/index.htm)
- State Parks: FindYourPark.com (https://findyourpark.com/)
- Recreation.gov: Recreation.gov (https://www.recreation.gov/)

America's national parks are like nature's symphony, each one a unique melody in the grand orchestration of the country's diverse landscapes. From the soaring granite cliffs of Yosemite to the otherworldly geothermal wonders of Yellowstone, these pristine wilderness areas are a testament to the beauty and resilience of the natural world.

Step into the embrace of these majestic landscapes, and you'll find yourself transported to a realm where time seems to stand still, and every vista takes your breath away. Whether you're hiking through ancient forests, marveling at towering waterfalls, or gazing up at the star-studded night sky, the national parks offer moments of awe and wonder that stay with you long after you've returned home.

But it's not just the natural beauty that makes America's national parks a must-visit destination—it's the sense of adventure and discovery that awaits around every corner. Take advantage of the ranger-led programs and guided tours offered in many parks, where knowledgeable guides share the stories of the land and its inhabitants, from the mighty grizzly bear to the delicate wildflower.

These ranger-led programs are like keys that unlock the secrets of the parks, giving you a deeper understanding of their ecological significance and cultural heritage. Whether you're joining a guided hike to hidden waterfalls, attending a stargazing session under the vast desert sky, or learning about the traditions of indigenous peoples, these ranger-led programs offer insights that enrich your experience and leave you with a newfound appreciation for the natural world.

And the best part? Many of these ranger-led programs are completely free of charge, offering visitors an opportunity to immerse themselves in the wonders of the national parks without breaking the bank. So lace up your hiking boots, pack your sense of wonder, and set out on a journey of discovery in America's national parks—where adventure awaits around every bend, and the beauty of nature knows no bounds.

National Park	Entrance Fee (Per Vehicle)	Pros	Cons
Yellowstone	$35 (7-day pass)	Stunning geothermal wonders	Crowded during peak seasons

Grand Canyon	$35 (7-day pass)	Iconic vistas and hikes	High temperatures in summer
Yosemite	$35 (7-day pass)	Majestic waterfalls and cliffs	Limited parking availability
Zion	$35 (7-day pass)	Spectacular red rock formations	Crowded trails and shuttles
Acadia	$30 (7-day pass)	Scenic coastal landscapes	Cold winters and limited services
Great Smoky Mountains	Free	Diverse wildlife and forests	Heavy rainfall and humidity
Rocky Mountain	$35 (7-day pass)	Stunning alpine scenery	High-altitude may cause altitude sickness
Bryce Canyon	$35 (7-day pass)	Unique hoodoos and landscapes	Limited lodging options nearby
Arches	$35 (7-day pass)	Iconic natural arches	Extreme heat in summer months
Everglades	$30 (7-day pass)	Abundant wildlife and wetlands	Mosquitoes and humidity

Cultural Immersion

Theme: America is a melting pot of cultures, each contributing to the rich tapestry of the country's identity. From Native American traditions to immigrant communities, the USA offers a wealth of cultural experiences to explore.

Budget Experience:

- Visit Ethnic Neighborhoods: Take a self-guided tour of America's diverse neighborhoods, from the vibrant Latino enclave of Little Havana in Miami to the historic African American district of Harlem in New York City. Sample authentic cuisine, browse local shops, and immerse yourself in the sights and sounds of different cultures.
- Attend Cultural Festivals: Many cities host cultural festivals and events throughout the year, celebrating everything from music and dance to food and art. Check local event calendars for free or low-cost festivals in your area and join in the festivities.
- Explore Museums and Cultural Centers: While some museums may charge admission, many offer free or pay-what-you-wish days, making cultural exploration accessible to all. Visit the Smithsonian museums in Washington, D.C., explore the Getty Center in Los Angeles, or wander through the galleries of the Art Institute of Chicago—all without spending a dime.

Useful Websites:

- Smithsonian Institution: Smithsonian.org (https://www.si.edu/)
- National Museum of the American Indian: AmericanIndian.si.edu (https://americanindian.si.edu/)
- Museum Free Days: MuseumFreeDays.com (https://www.museumfreedays.com/)

Free Line Dancing

Line dancing is a beloved American pastime that combines music, movement, and community spirit. There are plenty of opportunities to enjoy free line dancing across the USA. Here are some ways to find free line dancing events in America:

1. **Community Centers and Recreation Departments**: Many community centers and recreation departments offer free or low-cost line dancing classes and socials for residents. Check with your local community center or city's Parks and Recreation department to see if they host any free line dancing events.
2. **Country and Western Bars**: Country and western bars and honky-tonks are popular venues for line dancing enthusiasts. While some bars may charge cover fees for live music events or dance nights, others may offer free line dancing lessons earlier in the evening or during off-peak hours.
3. **Outdoor Concerts and Festivals**: Keep an eye out for outdoor concerts, festivals, and community events that feature live music and dancing. Many of these events include free line dancing lessons or open dance floors where attendees can join in the fun.
4. **Dance Studios and Gyms**: Some dance studios and fitness centers offer free introductory line dancing classes or host occasional free dance parties for the public. Check with local dance studios and gyms to see if they have any upcoming free line dancing events on their calendars.
5. **Public Parks and Plazas**: In warmer months, public parks and plazas may host outdoor dance events, including line dancing sessions. Keep an eye on local event listings and social media pages for announcements about free dance events in public spaces.

Free Fitness Classes

Lululemon is known for its community-focused approach to fitness, often hosting free workout classes and events at its stores across America. However, there are plenty of other options for free fitness classes across the country. Here are some ways to find free fitness classes similar to those offered by Lululemon:

1. **Local Parks and Recreation Departments**: Many parks and recreation departments offer free or low-cost fitness classes in public parks, community centers, and recreation facilities. These classes may include yoga, tai chi, Zumba, boot camps, and more. Check your city or county's parks and recreation website for schedules and locations.
2. **Outdoor Fitness Meetups**: Look for outdoor fitness meetups and groups in your area that organize free workouts in parks, on beaches, or in other outdoor spaces. Websites and apps like Meetup.com and Facebook Groups are great resources for finding local fitness communities and events.
3. **Community Centers and YMCAs**: Community centers, YMCAs, and other nonprofit organizations often offer free or discounted fitness classes as part of their community outreach programs. These classes may include everything from cardio and strength training to dance and martial arts.
4. **Athletic Apparel Stores**: In addition to Lululemon, other athletic apparel stores like Nike, Athleta, and REI sometimes host free fitness events and classes in their stores or at nearby locations. Keep an eye on their websites, social media pages, and email newsletters for announcements about upcoming events.
5. **Fitness Apps and Online Platforms**: While not always in-person, many fitness apps and online platforms offer free workouts that you can do from the comfort of your own home or at a nearby park. Look for apps like Nike Training Club, FitOn, and Yoga with Adriene for a variety of free workout options.

6. **Corporate Wellness Programs**: Some companies and employers offer free or subsidized fitness classes as part of their employee wellness programs. If you work for a large corporation or organization, check with your HR department to see if they offer any fitness perks or benefits.
7. **Local Gyms and Studios**: While many gyms and fitness studios charge for classes, some may offer free trial classes or special promotions for new members. Keep an eye out for introductory offers or community days where gyms open their doors to the public for free workouts.

Get Your 15 Minutes of Fame

Joining a studio audience for free in the USA can be an exciting way to experience the thrill of live television tapings and be part of the action. Here's a detailed guide on how to do it, along with some websites to help you find opportunities:

1. **Research Shows and Studios**: Start by researching the television shows filmed in cities where you reside or plan to visit. Many popular shows offer free tickets to their studio audiences. Websites like On-Camera Audiences, 1iota, and TVTickets.com list current and upcoming tapings for various TV shows, including talk shows, game shows, sitcoms, and reality shows.
2. **Check Studio Websites**: Visit the official websites of television studios and networks to see if they offer tickets to their shows' tapings. Studios like NBC Studios, Warner Bros. Studio Tour Hollywood, and CBS Television City often have pages dedicated to audience tickets and reservations.
3. **Sign Up for Audience Tickets**: Once you've identified shows you're interested in attending, sign up for audience tickets on the respective websites or ticketing platforms. Some shows release tickets weeks or even months in advance, so it's essential to check regularly for availability and reservation windows.

Get Caffeinated Cheaply

Ask anyone who visits the USA, and they'll likely agree: Starbucks expenses can quickly add up and tempt you into overspending, especially with a location seemingly on every corner. Several coffee chains in the USA offer free coffee refills under certain conditions. Here are some notable ones:

1. **FREE COFFEE WITH IKEA FAMILY CARD**: There are currently 51 IKEA stores spread across the country and when you have a free FAMILY CARD, you can get a completely free coffee. IKEA continues to expand its presence in the USA, with new stores being opened in different regions to serve more customers.
2. **Starbucks**: Starbucks offers free refills of brewed coffee (hot or iced) and tea (hot or iced) for customers who are members of the Starbucks Rewards program and have reached Green or Gold status. Refills must be obtained during the same visit and can be obtained at participating stores.
3. **Dunkin'**: Dunkin' offers free refills of hot or iced coffee for members of its DD Perks rewards program. To qualify, customers must be enrolled in the DD Perks program and purchase their initial coffee using their DD Perks account. Refills are available at participating locations.
4. **Panera Bread**: Panera Bread offers free refills of coffee, iced tea, and soft drinks for customers dining in at participating locations. Refills must be obtained during the same visit and are available for MyPanera members.
5. **Peet's Coffee**: Peet's Coffee offers free refills of brewed coffee or tea for customers with a Peetnik Rewards membership. Refills must be obtained during the same visit and are available at participating locations.
6. **Caribou Coffee**: Caribou Coffee offers free refills of brewed coffee or tea for customers who purchase a large (or equivalent size) beverage. Refills must be obtained during the same visit and are available at participating locations.

Cheap theatre tickets

Apps like TodayTix and TKTS, which offer last-minute deals and promotions for same-day or next-day performances in major cities like New York City. Additionally, joining theater rush or lottery programs provides opportunities to purchase discounted tickets on the day of the performance. Rush tickets are often available a few hours before the show, while lottery programs offer a chance to buy heavily discounted tickets through a drawing. Some theaters also offer special theatre days or weeks with reduced prices or two-for-one deals. Subscribing to newsletters or becoming a member of theaters can grant early access to sales and exclusive discounts for upcoming shows.

Watch Sports Cheaply

In the sprawling tapestry of American culture, sports emerge as a vibrant thread woven deeply into the fabric of everyday life. From the hallowed grounds of Yankee Stadium to the iconic courts of Madison Square Garden, the USA boasts a rich tapestry of sporting traditions that captivate audiences around the globe. Here, sports are more than mere games—they're a reflection of the American spirit, embodying the values of teamwork, determination, and resilience. Watching sports games in the USA can be an exciting experience, and there are ways to do it more affordably.

While it's common for major stadiums in the USA to have restricted access to their interiors during events, there are often public areas nearby where you can catch glimpses of the action for free. Here are some stadiums with outside views and nearby public access points:

1. **AT&T Stadium** - Home of the Dallas Cowboys
    - Address: 1 AT&T Way, Arlington, TX 76011
    - Public Access Point: Arlington Entertainment District, particularly from areas around Texas Live! and the surrounding parking lots, where you may catch views of the stadium's exterior and potentially the field through the large windows.
2. **Lambeau Field** - Home of the Green Bay Packers
    - Address: 1265 Lombardi Ave, Green Bay, WI 54304
    - Public Access Point: The area around Lambeau Field, including nearby streets and parking lots, offers views of the stadium's iconic exterior, especially on game days when the area is bustling with fans.
3. **Soldier Field** - Home of the Chicago Bears
    - Address: 1410 Museum Campus Dr, Chicago, IL 60605
    - Public Access Point: The lakefront path along Lake Shore Drive provides scenic views of Soldier Field from a distance. Additionally, nearby parks and beaches, such as

Burnham Park, offer opportunities to see the stadium's exterior.
4. **CenturyLink Field** - Home of the Seattle Seahawks and Seattle Sounders FC
    - Address: 800 Occidental Ave S, Seattle, WA 98134
    - Public Access Point: Occidental Park, located across the street from CenturyLink Field, offers views of the stadium's exterior, including the distinctive arches and seating areas.
5. **Lincoln Financial Field** - Home of the Philadelphia Eagles
    - Address: 1 Lincoln Financial Field Way, Philadelphia, PA 19148
    - Public Access Point: The area around Lincoln Financial Field, particularly on game days, provides opportunities to see the stadium's exterior from nearby streets and parking lots.
6. **Gillette Stadium** - Home of the New England Patriots and New England Revolution
    - Address: 1 Patriot Pl, Foxborough, MA 02035
    - Public Access Point: Patriot Place, the shopping and entertainment complex adjacent to Gillette Stadium, offers views of the stadium's exterior, especially from outdoor dining areas and gathering spots.
7. **MetLife Stadium** - Home of the New York Giants and New York Jets
    - Address: 1 MetLife Stadium Dr, East Rutherford, NJ 07073
    - Public Access Point: The area surrounding MetLife Stadium, including parking lots and nearby roads, provides views of the stadium's exterior, particularly on game days when the area is bustling with activity.

Here are some tips for seeing sports games in the USA on a budget:

- **Buy Tickets in Advance:**
    - Purchasing tickets well in advance can often save you money compared to buying them closer to the game day. Look for early-bird deals and discounts.
- **Check Resale Websites:**

- Explore resale websites like StubHub, SeatGeek, or Vivid Seats. Sometimes, tickets can be found at lower prices as the event date approaches, especially if the demand is not high.
- **Attend Weekday or Afternoon Games:**
  - Weekday and afternoon games typically have lower attendance, and tickets may be more affordable compared to prime-time or weekend games.l offers, exclusive deals, and notifications about discounted tickets.
- **Use Apps for Deals:**
  - Utilize mobile apps that specialize in offering deals on event tickets. Apps like Gametime and TickPick may have last-minute offers and discounts.
- **Consider Nosebleed Seats:**
  - Opt for less expensive seats in the upper levels of the stadium or arena (nosebleed seats). While the view may be farther, it's a more budget-friendly option.

Cheap Cinema

While the birth of modern cinema may be attributed to France, the role of the USA in popularizing and shaping the global film industry cannot be overstated. Like a phoenix rising from the ashes of imagination, cinema took flight in the fertile soil of American ingenuity, forever altering the landscape of entertainment and shaping the collective consciousness of generations to come. Here are some tips for enjoying cinema visits in the USA on a budget:

- **Matinee Showings:**
    - Opt for matinee showings, which are screenings that take place earlier in the day. Matinee tickets are often priced lower than evening or prime-time tickets.
- **Discount Days:**
    - Some theaters offer discounted tickets on specific days of the week. Check with your local cinemas to find out if they have discount days and take advantage of lower prices.
- **Join Loyalty Programs:**
    - Many cinema chains have loyalty programs that offer rewards, discounts, or even free tickets after a certain number of visits. Joining these programs can lead to long-term savings.
- **Use Subscription Services:**
    - Consider subscription services like AMC Stubs A-List or Cineworld's Unlimited. These programs allow you to watch a certain number of movies per month for a fixed fee, providing substantial savings for frequent moviegoers.
- **Student and Military Discounts:**
    - If you're a student or part of the military, inquire about special discounts at the cinema. Many theaters offer reduced prices for these groups.
- **Discount Apps:**
    - Explore mobile apps like Atom Tickets or Fandango, which may offer discounts, promotions, or exclusive deals on movie tickets.
- **Senior Citizen Discounts:**
    - If you're a senior citizen, check if the cinema offers discounted tickets for older adults. This is a common practice in many theaters.
- **Early Weekday Screenings:**
    - Similar to matinee showings, early weekday screenings tend to have lower attendance, and tickets may be more affordable.

Here is a selection of the best cinema deals:

1. **Los Angeles, CA**:
    - $5 Tuesdays at AMC: Many AMC Theatres locations in Los Angeles offer $5 movie tickets on Tuesdays for AMC Stubs members.

- Cinemark Movie Club: Cinemark offers a subscription service similar to AMC Stubs A-List, allowing members to see one movie per month for a discounted price.

2. **Chicago, IL**:
   - Discount Days at Marcus Theatres: Marcus Theatres in Chicago offer discount days where tickets are available at reduced prices.
   - MoviePass: While MoviePass has undergone changes in recent years, it may still offer discounted movie tickets at select theaters in Chicago.

3. **Houston, TX**:
   - Discount Matinees: Many theaters in Houston offer discounted matinee tickets for early afternoon showings.
   - Cinemark Movie Rewards: Cinemark offers a rewards program that allows members to earn points on ticket purchases, which can be redeemed for discounted or free tickets.

4. **Philadelphia, PA**:
   - $5 Wednesdays at Studio Movie Grill: Studio Movie Grill locations in Philadelphia offer $5 movie tickets on Wednesdays.
   - Senior Discounts: Many theaters in Philadelphia offer discounted tickets for seniors on select days of the week.

5. **Phoenix, AZ**:
   - Harkins Theatres Loyalty Cup: Harkins Theatres offers a loyalty cup program where members can purchase a refillable cup for discounted drinks, which can help save money on concessions.
   - Discounted Gift Cards: Websites like Costco or Sam's Club often sell discounted gift cards for movie theaters, which can be used to save on ticket purchases.

High-end Fashion

Leave your best clothes at home because in the USA, you don't need to pack like a fashionista to look like one. With designer clothing rental services, you can strut your stuff in style without lugging your entire wardrobe across the globe. The requirements for renting designer clothes may vary depending on the rental service. Some may require a USA address for shipping and billing purposes, while others may accept international addresses. Here are some of the best places to rent designer clothes in the USA:

1. **Rent the Runway**: Rent the Runway is one of the largest and most well-known designer clothing rental services in the USA. They offer a vast selection of designer dresses, gowns, accessories, and even everyday clothing from top brands like Oscar de la Renta, Vera Wang, and Diane von Furstenberg. With flexible rental options and convenient shipping, Rent the Runway makes it easy to access luxury fashion for any occasion.
2. **Armarium**: Armarium specializes in luxury fashion rentals for special events and occasions. Their curated selection includes designer dresses, evening gowns, and accessories from high-end brands like Balmain, Gucci, and Valentino. Armarium offers both online rentals and in-person appointments at their showroom locations in New York City, Los Angeles, and Miami.
3. **Haverdash**: Haverdash is a subscription-based clothing rental service that offers unlimited access to a rotating selection of designer clothing for a flat monthly fee. Members can choose from a range of stylish pieces from brands like Theory, Free People, and Vince, with the option to keep or exchange items as often as they like.
4. **Nuuly**: Nuuly is a clothing rental service by Urban Outfitters that offers a diverse selection of fashion-forward pieces from Urban Outfitters, Anthropologie, and other popular brands. Subscribers can rent up to six items per month, including designer clothing, vintage pieces, and exclusive styles, with the option to purchase items at a discount if they decide to keep them.
5. **My Wardrobe HQ**: My Wardrobe HQ is a luxury clothing rental platform based in the UK, but they also ship to the USA. They offer a curated selection of designer clothing, accessories, and handbags from top brands like Chanel, Dior, and Saint Laurent. With flexible rental periods and worldwide shipping, My Wardrobe HQ makes it easy to access high-end fashion wherever you are.
6. **The Black Tux**: While primarily known for men's formalwear rentals, The Black Tux also offers a selection of women's formalwear and accessories for rent. Their collection includes designer dresses, jumpsuits, and separates from brands like Badgley Mischka, Jenny Yoo, and Amsale, with options for both one-time rentals and subscription services.
7. **Gwynnie Bee**: Gwynnie Bee is a subscription-based clothing rental service specializing in plus-size fashion. They offer a wide range of stylish clothing options from popular brands like Eloquii, City Chic, and Rachel Roy, with the flexibility to rent and return items as often as you like.

If you can't or don't want to rent clothes you can find amazing deals in the USA.

Sample Sales: Unlocking Exclusive Deals

Sample sales are coveted events where fashion brands sell off excess inventory, showroom samples, and past-season pieces at significantly discounted prices. These sales offer a unique opportunity to snag designer clothing, shoes, and accessories at a fraction of their retail cost. In major fashion hubs like New York City, Los Angeles, and Miami, sample sales are a regular occurrence, attracting fashionistas eager to score designer bargains.

Tip 1: Sign Up for Mailing Lists: To stay informed about upcoming sample sales, sign up for mailing lists and newsletters from your favorite designer brands and fashion retailers. Many brands announce their sample sales via email, providing subscribers with exclusive access to the event dates, locations, and insider discounts.

Tip 2: Follow Fashion Blogs and Social Media: Fashion bloggers and influencers often share insider tips and updates about upcoming sample sales on their blogs and social media channels. Follow influential fashion accounts on platforms like Instagram and Twitter to stay in the loop and get the inside scoop on the best sample sales in your area.

Tip 3: Arrive Early and Be Prepared: Sample sales can be competitive, so it's essential to arrive early to secure the best deals. Bring cash and credit cards, as well as comfortable shoes and clothing for easy browsing. Be prepared to wait in line and navigate crowded spaces, but trust that the savings you'll score on designer pieces will be well worth the effort.

Consignment Stores: Secondhand Chic

Consignment stores are another fantastic resource for finding designer clothing and accessories at discounted prices. These stores sell gently used or pre-owned items on behalf of their owners, offering shoppers a curated selection of high-quality fashion finds at a fraction of their original retail cost. Consignment shopping allows fashion enthusiasts to indulge in luxury brands without paying full price, making it a popular choice for budget-conscious shoppers.

Tip 1: Research Local Consignment Stores: Start by researching consignment stores in your area, focusing on those that specialize in designer fashion. Look for stores with positive reviews, a reputation for authenticity, and a diverse selection of clothing and accessories from top luxury brands.

Tip 2: Keep an Open Mind: Consignment shopping is all about discovery, so keep an open mind and be willing to explore different styles and designers. You never know what hidden gems you might find, whether it's a vintage Chanel handbag or a pair of Prada heels at a fraction of their original cost.

Tip 3: Check for Sales and Promotions: Many consignment stores offer sales, promotions, and discounts to attract customers and move inventory. Keep an eye out for special deals like buy-one-get-one-free offers, seasonal clearance sales, or discounts for loyal customers. By timing your shopping trips strategically, you can maximize your savings and score even better deals on designer pieces.

Thrift Shops: Treasure Hunting on a Budget

Thrift shops are a goldmine for bargain hunters seeking designer clothing at rock-bottom prices. These stores sell a wide range of secondhand goods, including clothing, accessories, and household items, often at prices significantly below retail. While thrift shopping requires patience and perseverance, the thrill of uncovering hidden treasures makes it a rewarding and budget-friendly way to shop for designer fashion.

Tip 1: Explore Different Neighborhoods: Thrift shop offerings can vary depending on the neighborhood and demographic served by the store. Explore thrift shops in different areas, from upscale neighborhoods to bohemian districts, to discover a diverse range of designer finds. Don't be afraid to venture off the beaten path—you never know what stylish surprises await!

Free Makeovers and Haircuts

The hairdressing industry in the USA is a significant contributor to the economy, generating billions of dollars in revenue annually, but there's ample free haircuts and makeovers for budding stars. Here's where to find them:

1. **Beauty Schools and Cosmetology Institutes**: Many beauty schools and cosmetology institutes offer discounted or free services to the public as part of their training programs. Students gain hands-on experience under the supervision of licensed instructors, providing services such as haircuts, styling, makeup application, and skincare treatments. Websites like BeautySchoolsDirectory.com or BeautySchoolsNearMe.com allow you to search for beauty schools in your area and inquire about their services.
2. **Modeling for Stylists or Photographers**: Professional stylists and photographers often seek models for portfolio-building or creative projects. You can sometimes find opportunities to receive free makeovers or haircuts in exchange for modeling for their projects. **Model Mayhem**: Model Mayhem is a popular online community for models, photographers, stylists, and other industry professionals. You can create a profile, browse casting calls, and connect with collaborators in your area.

Complete Freebies

In the USA, consumer spending remains robust, with trillions of dollars poured into personal consumption expenditures annually. Alongside this consumer culture, the storage industry has surged, driven by urbanization, e-commerce, and evolving lifestyles but many have resorted to just giving stuff away. Scoring free stuff in the USA can be a rewarding experience, and there are various ways to find complimentary items. Here are some avenues to explore:

1. **Craigslist**: Craigslist's "Free" section often features listings from individuals looking to give away items they no longer need. You can browse by location and category to find free stuff near you.
2. **Freecycle**: Freecycle is a network of local groups where people can give away items for free to others in their community. You can search for your local Freecycle group and join to see listings of free items available in your area.
3. **Facebook Marketplace**: Facebook Marketplace allows users to buy, sell, and give away items within their local community. You can search for free items or browse listings in your area to find giveaways.
4. **Nextdoor**: Nextdoor is a neighborhood-based social networking platform where members can post about items they're giving away for free or sell items to others in their local community.
5. **Local Buy Nothing Groups**: Buy Nothing groups are hyper-local gift economies where members can give away items they no longer need or request items they're looking for. You can search for Buy Nothing groups in your area on social media platforms or through the official Buy Nothing Project website.
6. **Garage Sales and Yard Sales**: While not always free, garage sales and yard sales often feature heavily discounted items, and some sellers may give away items for free towards the end of the sale to avoid having to pack them up.

Top 20 attractions in the USA with money saving tips

- **Grand Canyon National Park, Arizona:**
    - **Money-Saving Tip:** Purchase a National Park Pass if you plan to visit multiple parks. It offers cost savings compared to individual entry fees.
- **Walt Disney World Resort, Florida:**
    - **Money-Saving Tip:** Buy tickets in advance, consider multi-day passes for lower daily rates, and explore hotel packages that may include park tickets.
- **Yellowstone National Park, Wyoming/Montana/Idaho:**
    - **Money-Saving Tip:** Similar to the Grand Canyon, consider the National Park Pass for access to multiple parks over a year.
- **Statue of Liberty, New York:**
    - **Money-Saving Tip:** Book ferry tickets in advance online and consider a CityPASS or New York Pass for bundled attractions at a lower cost.
- **Yosemite National Park, California:**
    - **Money-Saving Tip:** Plan your visit during the National Park Service's fee-free days, and explore nearby budget-friendly accommodations.
- **Niagara Falls, New York:**
    - **Money-Saving Tip:** Visit during the off-peak season for lower hotel rates, and consider bundled attraction passes for additional savings.
- **Las Vegas Strip, Nevada:**
    - **Money-Saving Tip:** Look for midweek hotel deals, explore free attractions along the Strip, and use discount apps for show tickets.
- **Smithsonian Museums, Washington, D.C.:**
    - **Money-Saving Tip:** Admission to many Smithsonian museums is free. Plan your visit during weekdays to avoid weekend crowds.
- **Universal Studios Hollywood, California:**
    - **Money-Saving Tip:** Purchase tickets online for discounts, consider visiting during non-peak times, and explore combo deals with nearby attractions.
- **Mount Rushmore National Memorial, South Dakota:**
    - **Money-Saving Tip:** Admission to the memorial is relatively low, and parking is free. Look for nearby affordable accommodations.
- **Zion National Park, Utah:**
    - **Money-Saving Tip:** Utilize the park's free shuttle service, explore budget-friendly camping options, and consider the National Park Pass.
- **The White House, Washington, D.C.:**
    - **Money-Saving Tip:** Tours of the White House are free but require advance reservation through your congressional representative.
- **Everglades National Park, Florida:**
    - **Money-Saving Tip:** Explore the park's free ranger-led programs and consider off-season visits for lower accommodation rates.
- **Times Square, New York:**
    - **Money-Saving Tip:** Enjoy the atmosphere without spending by watching street performances. Look for discounted Broadway tickets at TKTS booths.
- **Bryce Canyon National Park, Utah:**

- **Money-Saving Tip:** Consider camping inside the park, and explore free ranger programs for a deeper understanding of the area.
- **Kennedy Space Center, Florida:**
  - **Money-Saving Tip:** Purchase tickets online for discounts, explore combo tickets, and consider annual passes for frequent visits.
- **Yellowstone Old Faithful, Wyoming:**
  - **Money-Saving Tip:** Stay in nearby gateway communities for more affordable accommodations and explore the park's free programs.
- **New Orleans French Quarter, Louisiana:**
  - **Money-Saving Tip:** Walk around the vibrant streets, enjoy street performers, and look for happy hour deals at local establishments.
- **Hollywood Walk of Fame, California:**
  - **Money-Saving Tip:** Stroll along the Walk of Fame for free, and consider budget-friendly accommodations in the surrounding areas.
- **Great Smoky Mountains National Park, North Carolina/Tennessee:**
  - **Money-Saving Tip:** Entry to the park is free. Explore nearby Gatlinburg and Pigeon Forge for budget-friendly attractions.

General Money-Saving Tips for USA Attractions:

- **Advance Booking:** Purchase tickets online in advance for discounts.
- **Combo Deals:** Explore bundled tickets for multiple attractions.
- **Off-Peak Visits:** Visit during non-peak seasons or weekdays for lower prices.
- **City Passes:** Consider city passes that offer discounted access to multiple attractions.
- **Loyalty Programs:** Check for loyalty programs, annual passes, or memberships for recurring savings.
- **Free Days or Events:** Take advantage of free admission days or special events at attractions.
- **Local Deals:** Look for local deals, discounts, and coupons in the area you're visiting.
- **Student and Senior Discounts:** Inquire about special discounts for students and seniors.

Think like an American

Americans have developed various unique strategies to save money in the USA. Here's how to copy them:

1. **Couponing**: Extreme couponing is a popular money-saving technique in the USA. Some Americans meticulously collect and organize coupons from newspapers, magazines, and online sources to maximize savings on groceries, household items, and more. They often combine coupons with store sales and promotions for even greater discounts.
2. **Cashback Apps and Websites**: Many Americans use cashback apps and websites like Rakuten, Ibotta, and Honey to earn money back on their purchases. These platforms offer cashback rewards for shopping online, scanning receipts, or using linked credit or debit cards at participating retailers.
3. **Membership Programs**: Americans often join membership programs like Costco, Sam's Club, or BJ's Wholesale Club to access bulk discounts on groceries, household goods, and other items. By buying in bulk, they can save money on products they use regularly and reduce the frequency of shopping trips.
4. **Utilizing Discount Passes and Memberships**: Americans take advantage of discount passes and memberships for attractions, museums, zoos, and theme parks to save money on admission fees. For example, they may purchase city passes, annual memberships, or group discount tickets to access multiple attractions at a reduced rate.
5. **Negotiating and Price Matching**: Some Americans aren't afraid to negotiate prices or ask for price matching at retail stores, especially when making large purchases like appliances or electronics. They may politely inquire about discounts, promotions, or price adjustments to secure the best deal possible.

Memberships

Here are some membership cards that can save you significant amounts of money in the USA, along with their starting prices, core benefits, and potential drawbacks:

1. **Costco Membership**
    - Starting Price: $60/year for a Gold Star membership
    - Core Benefits:
        - Access to Costco's warehouse clubs, offering discounted prices on bulk groceries, household items, electronics, and more.
        - Exclusive discounts on services like travel, insurance, and car rentals.
        - Savings on Costco's Kirkland Signature brand products, known for their quality and value.
    - Cons:
        - Requires an annual membership fee, which may not be worth it if you don't shop at Costco frequently or if you live far from a Costco location.
        - Limited selection of products compared to traditional grocery stores.
2. **Amazon Prime Membership**
    - Starting Price: $119/year for a standard Prime membership
    - Core Benefits:
        - Free two-day shipping on eligible items from Amazon.com, with access to Prime Now for same-day delivery in select areas.
        - Unlimited streaming of movies, TV shows, music, and Prime Originals through Prime Video and Prime Music.
        - Exclusive deals and discounts during Amazon Prime Day and other sales events.
    - Cons:
        - Higher annual fee compared to other membership programs.

- Some Prime benefits, such as Prime Pantry and Amazon Fresh, may have additional fees.

3. **AAA Membership**
   - Starting Price: Varies by region and membership level; typically around $50-$100/year
   - Core Benefits:
     - Roadside assistance services, including towing, flat tire changes, battery jump-starts, and fuel delivery.
     - Discounts on travel bookings, including hotels, rental cars, cruises, and vacation packages.
     - Savings on dining, shopping, entertainment, and attractions through the AAA Discounts & Rewards program.
   - Cons:
     - Membership fees can vary depending on location and level of coverage.
     - Some benefits may not be useful if you don't own a vehicle or if you don't travel frequently.

4. **Entertainment® Book Membership**
   - Starting Price: Varies by location; typically around $10-$20/year
   - Core Benefits:
     - Access to thousands of coupons and discounts for local restaurants, attractions, retailers, and services.
     - Digital membership options, including a mobile app for easy access to deals on the go.
     - Savings on travel, dining, and entertainment expenses throughout the year.
   - Cons:
     - Limited availability of deals in some areas, especially smaller towns or rural areas.
     - Requires purchasing a new membership annually to access updated coupons and discounts.

5. **Sam's Club Membership**
   - Starting Price: $45/year for a Sam's Club membership
   - Core Benefits:

- Access to Sam's Club's warehouse clubs, offering discounted prices on bulk groceries, household items, electronics, and more.
- Savings on Sam's Club's Member's Mark brand products, similar to Costco's Kirkland Signature brand.
- Exclusive discounts on services like travel, pharmacy, and optical.
- Cons:
  - Requires an annual membership fee, which may not be worth it if you don't shop at Sam's Club frequently or if you live far from a Sam's Club location.
  - Limited selection of products compared to traditional grocery stores.

Before purchasing any membership card, it's important to evaluate your spending habits, lifestyle, and proximity to participating retailers to determine if the benefits outweigh the costs. Additionally, consider whether you'll take advantage of the core benefits offered by each membership program to maximize your potential savings.

Websites

Here are some of the top websites to help you stretch your dollars further in the USA:

1. **RetailMeNot (www.retailmenot.com)**: RetailMeNot is a popular coupon website that offers thousands of digital coupons, promo codes, and deals for both online and in-store shopping. Users can search for discounts by store or category and save money on clothing, electronics, travel, and more.
2. **Groupon (www.groupon.com)**: Groupon specializes in offering discounted deals and vouchers for local restaurants, activities, spa services, travel experiences, and goods. Users can browse deals by location or category and save up to 70% on dining, entertainment, and leisure activities.
3. **Honey (www.joinhoney.com)**: Honey is a browser extension that automatically finds and applies coupon codes at checkout when shopping online. Users can install the extension for free and enjoy instant savings on purchases from thousands of retailers, including Amazon, Walmart, and Target.
4. **Ebates/Rakuten (www.rakuten.com)**: Rakuten (formerly known as Ebates) is a cashback website that rewards users for shopping through their platform. Users can earn cashback on purchases from hundreds of Amazon by clicking through Rakuten's links before making a purchase. Cashback earnings can be redeemed via PayPal or check.
5. **Slickdeals (www.slickdeals.net)**: Slickdeals is a community-driven website that crowdsources and shares the latest deals, discounts, and coupons from around the web. Users can browse deals by category, vote on the best offers, and participate in forums to discuss money-saving tips and strategies.
6. **Coupons.com (www.coupons.com)**: Coupons.com offers printable and digital coupons for groceries, household items, personal care products, and more. Users can browse coupons by category or brand and redeem them at participating retailers for instant savings at checkout.

7. **Brad's Deals (**www.bradsdeals.com**)**: Brad's Deals curates the best online deals and discounts from retailers across the web, including clothing, electronics, home goods, and travel. Users can browse deals by category or store and enjoy exclusive savings on popular brands and products.
8. **LivingSocial (**www.livingsocial.com**)**: LivingSocial is a deal-of-the-day website that offers discounted vouchers for local restaurants, spas, activities, travel experiences, and products. Users can browse deals by location or category and save on dining, entertainment, and lifestyle services.
9. **DealNews (**www.dealnews.com**)**: DealNews scours the web for the best deals, discounts, and sales on electronics, clothing, home goods, and more. Users can browse deals by category or store and sign up for alerts to stay informed about the latest savings opportunities.
10. **Savings.com (**www.savings.com**)**: Savings.com offers a wide range of printable and digital coupons, promo codes, and deals for online and in-store shopping. Users can search for discounts by category or retailer and save money on a variety of products and services.

Luxury on a Budget Itinerary Ideas

1. Road Trip Adventure:

- Start in San Francisco, California, and drive along the Pacific Coast Highway (California State Route 1) for stunning coastal views.
- Explore the beauty of Big Sur and its redwood forests.
- Visit Los Angeles and its iconic attractions like Hollywood and Venice Beach.
- Continue to Las Vegas, Nevada, for a taste of the vibrant nightlife and entertainment.
- Head to the Grand Canyon in Arizona and experience its awe-inspiring landscapes.
- Finish your road trip in Sedona, Arizona, for its red rock formations and spiritual vibes.

2. Cultural Explorer:

- Begin in New York City, New York, and immerse yourself in the world-class museums and diverse neighborhoods.
- Travel to Washington, D.C., to explore the historic monuments and Smithsonian museums.
- Head to New Orleans, Louisiana, to experience its vibrant music scene and Creole cuisine.
- Visit San Antonio, Texas, and explore the rich history of the Alamo and its beautiful River Walk.
- End your cultural journey in Santa Fe, New Mexico, known for its art and Pueblo-style architecture.

3. National Park Enthusiast:

- Start in Denver, Colorado, and explore Rocky Mountain National Park for hiking and wildlife.

- Continue to Yellowstone National Park, Wyoming, to witness geysers and hot springs.
- Explore Glacier National Park in Montana for its stunning lakes and mountains.
- Head to Zion National Park in Utah for breathtaking canyons and hiking trails.
- Finish your journey in Bryce Canyon National Park, also in Utah, known for its unique rock formations.

4. Coastal Charm Tour:

- Begin in Charleston, South Carolina, and soak in the historic charm of the city's architecture and culture.
- Travel to Savannah, Georgia, to explore its beautifully preserved historic district.
- Head to Key West, Florida, for its tropical vibes and beautiful beaches.
- Continue to Miami, Florida, for its vibrant art scene and nightlife.
- Finish your coastal tour in New Orleans, Louisiana, for its unique blend of culture and cuisine.

5. Wild West Adventure:

- Start in Denver, Colorado, and visit the Buffalo Bill Museum and Grave.
- Travel to Cody, Wyoming, and experience the Cody Nite Rodeo.
- Explore the beauty of Jackson Hole, Wyoming, and its outdoor adventures.
- Head to Deadwood, South Dakota, for a taste of the Wild West's history.
- Finish your adventure in Rapid City, South Dakota, to see Mount Rushmore and Crazy Horse Memorial.

6. Foodie's Delight:

- Begin in New York City, New York, and savor diverse cuisine from around the world.
- Travel to New Orleans, Louisiana, for Creole and Cajun specialties.
- Head to San Francisco, California, for fresh seafood and farm-to-table dining.
- Continue to Austin, Texas, for barbecue and food truck culture.
- Finish your foodie journey in Portland, Oregon, known for its food carts and craft breweries.

Truly weird and wonderful things to experience

If you're seeking to add some quirky and offbeat experiences to your trip, consider incorporating these unique attractions into your itinerary:

- **Salvation Mountain, California:**
    - Visit this colorful, folk art mountain created by Leonard Knight in the California desert.
- **Bubblegum Alley, California:**
    - Take a stroll down a narrow alley in San Luis Obispo, where walls are adorned with thousands of pieces of chewed bubblegum.
- **Carhenge, Nebraska:**
    - Explore a replica of Stonehenge made entirely from vintage cars in the Nebraska prairie.
- **The Museum of Bad Art, Massachusetts:**
    - Enjoy a collection of intentionally bad art in this quirky museum located in the basement of a theater.
- **International UFO Museum and Research Center, New Mexico:**
    - Dive into the world of extraterrestrial encounters and UFO sightings in Roswell, New Mexico.
- **Leila's Hair Museum, Missouri:**
    - Discover a museum in Independence showcasing hair art and jewelry made from human hair.
- **The Mystery Spot, California:**
    - Experience a gravitational anomaly at this tourist attraction in Santa Cruz, where the laws of physics seem to be bent.
- **The House on the Rock, Wisconsin:**
    - Tour a bizarre architectural wonder featuring eclectic collections, strange exhibits, and a massive indoor carousel.
- **Lucy the Elephant, New Jersey:**
    - Climb inside a six-story elephant-shaped building, a National Historic Landmark in Margate City.
- **Dinosaur Land, Virginia:**
    - Step back in time at this roadside attraction featuring over 50 life-sized dinosaur sculptures.
- **The Mutter Museum, Pennsylvania:**
    - Explore a medical museum in Philadelphia that houses a unique collection of medical oddities and anatomical specimens.
- **The Winchester Mystery House, California:**
    - Take a guided tour of this sprawling, maze-like mansion built by Sarah Winchester, famous for its architectural eccentricities.
- **The Neon Boneyard, Nevada:**
    - Wander through a graveyard of vintage neon signs in Las Vegas, showcasing the history of the city's iconic signage.
- **The Center of the Universe, Washington:**

- Stand on the "Center of the Universe" street marker in Seattle's Fremont neighborhood and experience the quirky vibe of the area.
- **Spam Museum, Minnesota:**
  - Learn everything there is to know about Spam, the canned meat product, at this museum in Austin, Minnesota.
- **Idaho Potato Museum, Idaho:**
  - Discover the world of potatoes at this museum, featuring exhibits on potato history, farming, and a giant potato sculpture.
- **Bishop Castle, Colorado:**
  - Marvel at this one-man-built castle in the San Isabel National Forest, created by Jim Bishop over several decades.
- **The Clown Motel, Nevada:**
  - Spend the night in a motel filled with clown memorabilia in Tonopah, a unique and somewhat eerie experience.
- **Cadillac Ranch, Texas:**
  - Visit a public art installation in Amarillo where ten Cadillacs are half-buried nose-first in the ground.
- **The Vortex Mystery Spot, Oregon:**
  - Experience optical illusions and peculiar gravitational phenomena at this vortex site in Gold Hill.

Bucket list-worthy experiences with discounts

A trip to the USA wouldn't be complete without fully immersing yourself in everything it has to offer. Here are some incredible things to do in the USA, along with tips for getting discounts:

1. **Helicopter Tour of the Grand Canyon**
   - Starting Price: $200-$400 per person for a basic tour
   - How to Get Discounts: Look for special promotions or group rates offered by tour operators. Booking in advance and opting for tours during off-peak times can also help you snag a great deal.
2. **Hot Air Balloon Ride over Napa Valley**
   - Starting Price: $200-$300 per person for a sunrise or sunset flight
   - How to Get Discounts: Keep an eye out for Groupon deals or promotional offers from local balloon companies. Booking midweek flights or opting for shared rides can also help lower the cost.
3. **Swim with Dolphins in Florida**
   - Starting Price: $100-$300 per person for a dolphin encounter experience
   - How to Get Discounts: Check for discounted tickets on travel websites like Expedia or Viator. Some attractions offer special rates for booking online or purchasing multi-activity packages.
4. **Horseback Riding in the Rocky Mountains**
   - Starting Price: $50-$150 per person for a guided trail ride
   - How to Get Discounts: Look for deals on activity booking websites or through local visitor centers. Some stables offer discounts for booking group rides or purchasing multiple rides in advance.
5. **Hot Air Balloon Ride over the Albuquerque International Balloon Fiesta**
   - Starting Price: $200-$400 per person during the festival

- How to Get Discounts: Book early to secure lower prices, as prices tend to increase closer to the event dates. Consider volunteering at the festival to receive complimentary or discounted balloon rides as a perk.
-

7. **Sailboat Cruise around the San Francisco Bay**
    - Starting Price: $50-$100 per person for a sunset cruise
    - How to Get Discounts: Check for discounts on tour aggregator websites or by signing up for the company's mailing list for promotional offers. Some companies offer discounted rates for booking weekday or off-peak cruises.

8. **Zip Lining in Hawaii**
    - Starting Price: $50-$150 per person for a zip line adventure
    - How to Get Discounts: Look for package deals that combine zip lining with other activities, such as hiking or snorkeling. Some tour operators offer discounts for booking online or for large groups.

9. **Hike to Havasu Falls in the Grand Canyon**
    - Starting Price: $100-$150 per person for permits and camping fees
    - How to Get Discounts: Consider visiting during the off-peak season (winter or early spring) when permit fees may be lower. Joining a guided tour can also help you save money on transportation and equipment rental.

10. **Bungee Jumping off the Royal Gorge Bridge in Colorado**
    - Starting Price: $50-$100 per jump
    - How to Get Discounts: Look for special promotions or discounted rates during off-peak times. Some adventure companies offer package deals that include multiple jumps or other activities at a discounted rate.

More Great Small Bargains

tHere are 30 great bargains for tourists in the USA:

- **Happy Hour Specials:** Many bars and restaurants offer discounted prices on drinks and appetizers during happy hours.
- **Dollar Stores:** Dollar stores are abundant and can provide affordable essentials, snacks, and souvenirs.
- **Outlet Malls:** Outlet malls offer discounted prices on popular brands, making them great for shopping on a budget.
- **Free Museum Days:** Some museums have specific days or times when admission is free.
- **National Parks Pass:** The America the Beautiful Pass provides access to national parks and federal recreation sites at a significantly discounted rate.
- **Student and Senior Discounts:** Many attractions, restaurants, and transportation services offer discounts for students and seniors.
- **Public Transportation Passes:** In major cities, consider buying a public transportation pass for cost-effective travel.
- **Farmers' Markets:** Experience local flavors and find fresh produce at farmers' markets, often at lower prices than supermarkets.
- **Discounted Broadway Tickets:** In New York City, visit TKTS booths for same-day discounted tickets to Broadway shows.
- **Fast Food Value Menus:** Quick and budget-friendly meals can be found on fast food value menus.
- **City Tours:** Some cities offer free or low-cost walking tours, providing a budget-friendly way to explore.
- **Student Rush Tickets:** Students can often get discounted tickets for theater performances, concerts, and events.
- **Public Parks and Beaches:** Enjoy the natural beauty of the country by visiting public parks and beaches, many of which have free or low-cost admission.
- **Free Entertainment in Vegas:** Las Vegas offers free shows, street performances, and attractions on the famous Strip.
- **IKEA Cafeteria:** Grab a budget-friendly meal at the IKEA cafeteria if you're near one of their stores.
- **City-Specific Apps:** Some cities have apps that offer discounts and deals at local businesses.
- **Happy Hour Cruises:** In coastal cities, look for discounted sunset or happy hour cruises for scenic views.
- **Discounted Theme Park Tickets:** Purchase theme park tickets in advance or through authorized sellers for savings.
- **Free Wi-Fi:** Many coffee shops, libraries, and public spaces offer free Wi-Fi, reducing the need for costly data plans.

Free things for American citizens

While attractions in the USA are open to both American citizens and tourists, some locations have specific restrictions or requirements to enter for free. Here is a list of 50 attractions or activities in the USA that may have exclusive access or benefits for American citizens:

1. FBI Headquarters (Washington, D.C.):

American citizens can request guided tours of the FBI headquarters with advance notice.

2. White House Tour (Washington, D.C.):

U.S. citizens can request tours of the White House through their Member of Congress.

3. U.S. Capitol Tour (Washington, D.C.):

American citizens can arrange free tours of the U.S. Capitol through their Member of Congress.

4. Library of Congress (Washington, D.C.):

American citizens can access the reading rooms and research materials in the Library of Congress.

5. Supreme Court of the United States (Washington, D.C.):

U.S. citizens can attend oral arguments when the Supreme Court is in session.

6. Bureau of Engraving and Printing (Washington, D.C.):

American citizens can take guided tours to see how U.S. currency is printed.

7. U.S. Mint (Philadelphia, Pennsylvania):

U.S. citizens can tour the U.S. Mint to learn about coin production.

8. NASA's Kennedy Space Center (Merritt Island, Florida):

American citizens have access to special events and launches at the Kennedy Space Center.

9. National Archives (Washington, D.C.):

U.S. citizens can view the Constitution, Declaration of Independence, and Bill of Rights.

10. Arlington National Cemetery (Arlington, Virginia):

U.S. citizens can witness the Changing of the Guard ceremony.

11. Camp David (Thurmont, Maryland):

The President's retreat is accessible to American citizens on rare occasions.

12. National Radio Astronomy Observatory (Green Bank, West Virginia):

U.S. citizens can take guided tours of the world's largest fully steerable radio telescope.

13. Military Bases and Museums (Various Locations):

Some military bases and museums offer tours and events to U.S. citizens.

14. U.S. Naval Academy (Annapolis, Maryland):

U.S. citizens can visit the U.S. Naval Academy Museum.

15. National Counterterrorism Center (McLean, Virginia):

American citizens can request tours of the National Counterterrorism Center.

16. Federal Reserve Bank (Various Locations):

Some Federal Reserve Banks offer tours with a focus on the economy.

17. The United States Bullion Depository (Fort Knox, Kentucky):

U.S. citizens cannot tour Fort Knox, but they may visit the visitor center.

18. National Security Agency (Fort Meade, Maryland):

American citizens can arrange guided tours of the National Cryptologic Museum.

19. U.S. Secret Service Training Facility (Beltsville, Maryland):

U.S. citizens may be able to arrange tours of the training facility.

20. United States Military Academy at West Point (West Point, New York):

U.S. citizens can visit the West Point Museum.

21. U.S. Coast Guard Academy (New London, Connecticut):

American citizens can tour the U.S. Coast Guard Museum.

22. National Oceanic and Atmospheric Administration (NOAA) (Various Locations):

Some NOAA facilities offer tours and educational programs for U.S. citizens.

23. Fort Sumter National Monument (Charleston, South Carolina):

U.S. citizens can visit this historic Civil War site.

24. National Center for Missing & Exploited Children (Alexandria, Virginia):

American citizens can request tours and attend events.

25. The Pentagon (Arlington, Virginia):

U.S. citizens can take guided tours of the Pentagon.

26. American Indian Reservations (Various Locations):

Some tribal lands may have restrictions or require permission for non-citizens.

27. U.S. Military Cemeteries (Various Locations):

U.S. citizens can visit military cemeteries, such as Normandy American Cemetery in France.

28. National Geospatial-Intelligence Agency (NGA) (Springfield, Virginia):

American citizens can request tours of the NGA Museum.

29. Bureau of Land Management Sites (Various Locations):

Some BLM sites may have restricted access for non-U.S. citizens.

30. Nuclear Power Plants (Various Locations):

Tours of nuclear power plants may have citizenship restrictions.

31. Lawrence Livermore National Laboratory (Livermore, California):

U.S. citizens can request tours of this research facility.

32. National Renewable Energy Laboratory (Golden, Colorado):

American citizens can arrange guided tours of this energy research lab.

33. Central Intelligence Agency (CIA) (Langley, Virginia):

The CIA offers tours for U.S. citizens on a limited basis.

Economics of saving money in America

To save vast amounts of money as a tourist in the USA, understanding various economic principles is incredibly beneficial. Here's an example of each principle and how it can help you save money:

1. **Supply and Demand**: Understanding supply and demand dynamics can help you identify when and where prices are likely to be lower. For example, booking accommodations during off-peak seasons or visiting less touristy destinations can lead to significant cost savings.
2. **Opportunity Cost**: Recognizing opportunity cost can help you make informed decisions about how to allocate your resources. For instance, choosing between spending money on an expensive attraction or opting for a free activity that provides a similar experience can help you maximize your budget.
3. **Economies of Scale**: Taking advantage of economies of scale can help you save money on purchases. For example, buying in bulk or opting for combo deals at restaurants can result in lower per-unit costs.
4. **Time Value of Money**: Understanding the time value of money can help you make strategic decisions about when to make purchases. For instance, booking flights and accommodations well in advance can often result in lower prices compared to last-minute bookings.
5. **Marginal Analysis**: Applying marginal analysis can help you determine whether additional spending is justified based on the additional benefit received. For example, weighing the cost of upgrading to a higher class of accommodation against the added comfort and amenities can help you make a cost-effective decision.
6. **Price Discrimination**: Recognizing price discrimination tactics can help you identify opportunities to save money. For

instance, taking advantage of discounts available to specific groups (such as seniors, students, or military personnel) can result in significant savings on various expenses.
7. **Cost-Benefit Analysis**: Conducting a cost-benefit analysis can help you evaluate the potential returns of an expenditure relative to its cost. For example, comparing the cost of purchasing a city pass for multiple attractions against the individual entrance fees can help you determine whether it's worth the investment.
8. **Incentives**: Understanding incentives can help you take advantage of rewards programs and promotional offers. For example, signing up for loyalty programs or credit cards that offer travel rewards can help you earn points or cashback on your purchases.

How to Enjoy ALLOCATING Money in USA

'Money's greatest intrinsic value—and this can't be overstated—is its ability to give you control over your time.' - Morgan Housel

Notice I have titled the chapter how to enjoy allocating money in USA. I'll use saving and allocating interchangeably in the book, but since most people associate saving to feel like a turtleneck, that's too tight, I've chosen to use wealth language. Rich people don't save. They allocate. What's the difference? Saving can feel like something you don't want or wish to do and allocating has your personal will attached to it.

And on that note, it would be helpful if you considered removing the following words and phrase from your vocabulary for planning and enjoying your USA trip:

- Wish
- Want
- Maybe someday

These words are part of poverty language. Language is a dominant source of creation. Use it to your advantage. You don't have to wish, want or say maybe someday to USA. You can enjoy the same things millionaires enjoy in USA without the huge spend.

'People don't like to be sold-but they love to buy.' - Jeffrey Gitomer.

Every good salesperson who understands the quote above places obstacles in the way of their clients' buying. Companies create waiting lists, restaurants pay people to queue outside in order to create demand. People reason if something is so in demand, it must be worth having but that's often just marketing. Take this sales maxim 'People don't like to be sold-but they love to buy and flip it on its head to allocate your money in USA on things YOU desire. You love to spend and hate to be sold. That means when something comes your way, it's not 'I can't afford it,' it's 'I don't want it' or maybe 'I don't want it right now'.

Saving money doesn't mean never buying a latte, never taking a taxi, never taking vacations (of course, you bought this book). Only you get to decide on how you spend and on what. Not an advice columnist who thinks you can buy a house if you never eat avocado toast again.

I love what Kate Northrup says about affording something: "If you really wanted it you would figure out a way to get it. If it were that VALUABLE to you, you would make it happen."

I believe if you master the art of allocating money to bargains, it can feel even better than spending it! Bold claim, I know. But here's the truth: Money gives you freedom and options. The more you keep in your account and or invested the more freedom and options you'll have. The principal reason you should save and allocate money is TO BE FREE! Remember, a trip's main purpose is relaxation, rest and enjoyment, aka to feel free.

When you talk to most people about saving money on vacation. They grimace. How awful they proclaim not to go wild on your vacation. If you can't get into a ton of debt enjoying your once-in-a-lifetime vacation, when can you?

When you spend money 'theres's a sudden rush of dopamine which vanishes once the transaction is complete. What happens in the brain when you save money? It increases feelings of security and peace. You don't need to stress life's uncertainties. And having a greater sense of peace can actually help you save more money.' Stressed out people make impulsive financial choices, calm people don't.'

The secret to enjoying saving money on vacation is very simple: never save money from a position of lack. Don't think 'I wish I could afford that'. Choose not to be marketed to. Choose not to consume at a price others set. Don't save money from the flawed premise you don't have enough. Don't waste your time living in the box that society has created, which says saving money on vacation means sacrifice. It doesn't.

Traveling to USA can be an expensive endeavor if you don't approach it with a plan, but you have this book which is packed with tips. The biggest other asset is your perspective.

Winning the Vacation Game

The inspiration for these books struck me during a Vipassana meditation retreat. As I contemplated the excitement that precedes a vacation, I couldn't help but wish that we could all carry that same sense of anticipation in our daily lives. It was from this introspection that the concept of indulging in luxurious trips on a budget was born. The driving force behind this idea has always been the prevalence of disregarded inequalities.

A report from the Pew Charitable Trusts unveiled a stark reality: only about 4% of individuals born into the lowest income quintile, the bottom 20%, in the United States manage to ascend to the top income quintile during their lifetime. This trend is mirrored in many parts of Europe, underscoring the immense hurdles faced by those from disadvantaged backgrounds, including myself, in their pursuit of financial security.

To compound this, a comprehensive study conducted by researchers at Stanford University and published in the Journal of Personality and Social Psychology illuminated a compelling connection between career choices, personal fulfillment, and income. It revealed that individuals who prioritize intrinsic factors like passion often find themselves with lower average incomes, highlighting the intricate dynamics at play in the pursuit of one's dreams. Either you're in a low-income career, believing you can't afford to travel, or you're earning well but desperately need a vacation due to your work being mediocre at best. Personally, I believe it's better to do what you love and take time to plan a luxury trip on a budget. Of course, that, in itself, is a luxurious choice not all of us have. I haven't even mentioned Income, education, and systemic inequalities that can lock restrict travel opportunities for many.

Despite these challenging realities, I firmly believe that every individual can have their dream getaway. I am committed to providing practical insights and strategies that empower individuals to turn their dream vacations into a tangible reality without breaking the bank.

How to feel RICH in USA

You don't need millions in your bank to **feel rich**. Feeling rich feels different to every person."Researchers have pooled data on the relationship between money and emotions from more than 1.6 million people across 162 countries and found that **wealthier people feel more positive "self-regard emotions" such as confidence, pride and determination.**"

Here are things to see, do and taste in USA, that will have you overflowing with gratitude for your luxury trip to USA.

- Achieving a Michelin Star rating is the most coveted accolade for restaurants but those that obtain a Michelin Star are synonymous with high cost, but in USA there are restaurants with Michelin-stars offering lunch menus for $15 or less! The cheapest Michelin-starred restaurant in the USA is Tim Ho Wan, located in New York City. It offers affordable dim sum dishes that have earned it a Michelin star while still maintaining reasonable prices. If fine dining isn't your thing, don't worry further on in the guide you will find a range of delicious cheap eats in USA that deserve a Michelin-Star.
- While money can't buy happiness, it can buy cake and isn't that sort of the same thing? Jokes aside, Porto's Bakery in Southern California has turned cakes and pastries into edible art. Visit to taste the most delicious buttery croissant in USA. With multiple locations in the Los Angeles area, Porto's is beloved for its delicious pastries, cakes, sandwiches, and more, all offered at reasonable prices.
- While you might not be staying in a penthouse, you can still enjoy the same views. Visit rooftop bars in USA, like Cindy's Rooftop (Chicago, Illinois) to enjoy incredible sunset views for the price of just one drink. And if you want to continue enjoying libations, head over to The Susie's Saloon for a dirt-cheap happy hour, lots of reasonably priced (and delicious) cocktails and cheap delicious snacks.

Those are just some ideas for you to know that visiting USA on a budget doesn't have to feel like sacrifice or constriction. Now let's get into the nuts and bolts of USA on the super cheap.

What to pack to save money in USA

Packing smart can definitely help you save money during your trip to the USA, especially if you're looking to enjoy activities like snorkeling without breaking the bank. Here's a packing list to help you save money and enjoy your travels:

1. **Reusable Water Bottle**: Buying bottled water can add up quickly, so bring a reusable water bottle to stay hydrated while exploring. Most restaurants and public places offer free water refills.
2. **Snorkeling Gear**: Bringing your own snorkel, mask, and fins can save you money on rental fees, especially if you plan to snorkel multiple times during your trip. Look for compact and lightweight gear that's easy to pack.
3. **Sunscreen**: Purchasing sunscreen at tourist destinations can be pricey, so bring your own to protect your skin from the sun's harmful rays. Opt for reef-safe sunscreen to help protect marine ecosystems while snorkeling.
4. **Picnic Supplies**: Eating out every meal can quickly drain your travel budget, so pack some reusable utensils, a picnic blanket, and lightweight containers for preparing simple meals on the go. You can pick up fresh ingredients from local markets or grocery stores.
5. **Travel Insurance**: While not something you can physically pack, investing in travel insurance can save you money in case of unexpected emergencies, such as medical issues, trip cancellations, or lost luggage.
6. **Multi-Use Clothing**: Pack versatile clothing items that can be mixed and matched to create multiple outfits. This will help you pack lighter and avoid excess baggage fees if you're flying domestically.
7. **Travel Adapter**: If you're traveling from another country, bring a universal travel adapter to charge your electronic devices without having to purchase multiple adapters or converters.
8. **Travel Rewards Card**: Consider signing up for a travel rewards credit card that offers perks like cashback, points, or airline miles for your purchases. Just be sure to use it responsibly and pay off your balance in full each month to avoid interest charges.

Planning your trip

When to visit

The first step in saving money on your USA trip is timing. If you are not tied to school holidays, the **best time to visit is during the shoulder-season months of March, April and October and November.**

Traveling in the off-season offers a host of benefits. You will have less of a chance to be jostled by large crowds and your hotel bookings will be much cheaper and you won't need to buy skip the line tickets. Plus, during these shoulder months, there is a chance of seeing tulips in bloom. In addition, you will find some of the Netherlands' most scenic beaches and small towns.

The High season starts in April and goes until September and prices DOUBLE so if you're planning to come then book accommodation ahead of time to save money on price hikes.

If you are visiting during the peak season, you should expect to pay higher rates for hotels and airfare. You will also have to cope with long lines at some of the city's most popular attractions but don't despair there are innumerable hacks to save on accommodation in USA which we will go into detail on.

Time Zones

In the United States, there are four primary time zones:

1. Eastern Standard Time (EST) - GMT/UTC minus five hours. Major cities include New York City, Boston, Washington, D.C., and Atlanta.
2. Central Standard Time (CST) - GMT/UTC minus six hours. Key cities include Chicago, New Orleans, and Houston.

3. Mountain Standard Time (MST) - GMT/UTC minus seven hours. Notable locations include Denver, Santa Fe, and Phoenix.
4. Pacific Standard Time (PST) - GMT/UTC minus eight hours. Major hubs include Seattle, San Francisco, and Las Vegas.

Additionally, most of Alaska observes a time zone one hour behind Pacific time (GMT/UTC minus nine hours), while Hawaii is two hours behind Pacific time (GMT/UTC minus 10 hours).

Cheapest month to visit each city

Determining the cheapest and best month to visit each major USA city for hotel deals can vary based on factors such as seasonal demand, special events, and hotel pricing trends. However, here are some general guidelines for each city:

1. **New York City, New York**: January and February are typically the cheapest months to visit NYC, as hotel rates tend to drop after the holiday season. Starting prices for budget hotels can range from $100-$150 per night.
2. **Los Angeles, California**: November and December are considered low season in LA, with fewer tourists and lower hotel rates. Starting prices for budget hotels can range from $80-$120 per night.
3. **Chicago, Illinois**: January and February offer some of the best hotel deals in Chicago due to the cold weather and fewer tourists. Starting prices for budget hotels can range from $70-$100 per night.
4. **San Francisco, California**: January and February are the cheapest months to visit San Francisco, with lower hotel rates and fewer crowds. Starting prices for budget hotels can range from $100-$150 per night.
5. **Miami, Florida**: September and October are considered shoulder season in Miami, with lower hotel rates before the winter high season begins. Starting prices for budget hotels can range from $80-$120 per night.
6. **Las Vegas, Nevada**: July and August are typically the cheapest months to visit Las Vegas, as hotel rates drop due to the extreme heat. Starting prices for budget hotels can range from $30-$50 per night.
7. **Washington, D.C.**: January and February offer some of the best hotel deals in Washington, D.C., as tourism slows down during the winter months. Starting prices for budget hotels can range from $80-$120 per night.
8. **Boston, Massachusetts**: January and February are the cheapest months to visit Boston, with lower hotel rates and fewer tourists. Starting prices for budget hotels can range from $80-$120 per night.
9. **Seattle, Washington**: November and December offer some of the best hotel deals in Seattle, as hotel rates drop during the rainy season. Starting prices for budget hotels can range from $70-$100 per night.

10. **Orlando, Florida**: September and October are considered low season in Orlando, with lower hotel rates and fewer crowds at the theme parks. Starting prices for budget hotels can range from $60-$100 per night.

Visit on your birthday

In the USA, many businesses offer birthday freebies or special discounts to customers to celebrate their special day. Here are some common birthday freebies you can take advantage of:

1. **Restaurants**: Many restaurants offer free meals, desserts, or discounts on your birthday. Examples include free entrees at restaurants like Denny's, IHOP, and Olive Garden, or free desserts at places like The Cheesecake Factory and Red Robin.
2. **Coffee Shops**: Coffee chains like Starbucks and Dunkin' Donuts often offer free drinks or discounts to loyalty program members on their birthdays.
3. **Ice Cream Shops**: Popular ice cream chains like Baskin-Robbins and Cold Stone Creamery may offer free scoops or discounts on your birthday.
4. **Retail Stores**: Some retail stores provide birthday discounts or freebies to their customers. For example, Sephora offers free birthday gifts to Beauty Insider members, while clothing stores like American Eagle and Old Navy may offer birthday coupons or discounts.
5. **Entertainment Venues**: Some entertainment venues offer birthday perks, such as free movie tickets or discounts on admission. Check with local theaters, bowling alleys, or amusement parks to see if they offer any birthday specials.
6. **Online Services**: Subscription services and online platforms may offer birthday discounts or freebies to their members. Examples include freebies from companies like Amazon, Sephora, and Ulta Beauty.
7. **Banks and Credit Unions**: Some financial institutions offer birthday bonuses or perks to their customers, such as waived fees or cash rewards.

To take advantage of these birthday freebies, it's often necessary to sign up for loyalty programs, newsletters, or rewards clubs in advance. Keep an eye on your email or app notifications as your birthday approaches to redeem these offers. Additionally, be sure to check the terms and conditions of each offer, as they may vary by location and may require a minimum purchase or other restrictions. Enjoy celebrating your birthday with these special treats!

What's On

Here are some popular free festivals in the USA, along with their dates and locations:

1. **National Cherry Blossom Festival**
   - Dates: Late March to early April
   - Location: Washington, D.C.
   - Description: A celebration of spring and Japanese culture, featuring cherry blossom-themed events, including a parade, kite festival, and cultural performances.
2. **New Orleans Jazz & Heritage Festival**
   - Dates: Late April to early May
   - Location: New Orleans, Louisiana
   - Description: One of the largest music festivals in the USA, celebrating the diverse music and culture of New Orleans with performances by local and international artists.
3. **Coney Island Mermaid Parade**
   - Dates: Late June
   - Location: Brooklyn, New York
   - Description: A colorful and eccentric parade celebrating art, culture, and the spirit of Coney Island, featuring participants dressed in elaborate mermaid and sea creature costumes.
4. **Chicago Blues Festival**
   - Dates: June
   - Location: Chicago, Illinois
   - Description: The largest free blues festival in the world, featuring performances by renowned blues musicians on multiple stages in Chicago's Millennium Park.
5. **Portland Rose Festival**
   - Dates: Late May to early June
   - Location: Portland, Oregon
   - Description: A month-long celebration of roses and community, featuring parades, concerts, fireworks, and the iconic Grand Floral Parade showcasing elaborate flower-covered floats.
6. **Albuquerque International Balloon Fiesta**
   - Dates: Early to mid-October
   - Location: Albuquerque, New Mexico
   - Description: The largest hot air balloon festival in the world, featuring hundreds of colorful balloons taking flight against the backdrop of the New Mexico sky.
7. **San Francisco Pride**
   - Dates: Late June
   - Location: San Francisco, California
   - Description: One of the largest LGBTQ+ pride events in the world, featuring a vibrant parade, live performances, community celebrations, and activism in support of LGBTQ+ rights.
8. **Austin City Limits Music Festival**
   - Dates: Late September to early October
   - Location: Austin, Texas

- Description: A multi-genre music festival featuring performances by top artists from around the world, held in the scenic setting of Zilker Park.
9. **Seattle International Film Festival (SIFF)**
    - Dates: May to June
    - Location: Seattle, Washington
    - Description: One of the largest and most highly attended film festivals in the USA, showcasing a diverse selection of international and independent films.
10. **Las Vegas Foodie Fest**
    - Dates: Various dates throughout the year
    - Location: Las Vegas, Nevada
    - Description: A food truck festival featuring a wide variety of gourmet and exotic cuisine, along with live entertainment and family-friendly activities.

The seasons in different parts of the USA and what to pack for each

The United States experiences a variety of climates due to its vast size and geographical diversity. Here's a general overview of the seasons in different parts of the USA and what to pack for each:

- **Northeast:**
    - **Seasons:** Four distinct seasons with cold winters, warm summers, and moderate spring and fall.
        - **What to Pack:**
        - Winter (December to February): Warm coat, hat, gloves, scarf, and layers.
        - Spring (March to May): Light jacket, layers, and rain gear.
        - Summer (June to August): Light clothing, sunscreen, and sunglasses.
        - Fall (September to November): Light jacket, layers, and rain gear.
- **Southeast:**
    - **Seasons:** Hot and humid summers, mild winters, and occasional tropical storms.
        - **What to Pack:**
        - Summer: Light, breathable clothing, sunscreen, and sunglasses.
        - Winter: Light jacket, layers, and a sweater.
        - Rainy Season: Waterproof jacket, umbrella, and rain boots.
- **Midwest:**
    - **Seasons:** Cold winters, hot summers, and distinct spring and fall seasons.
        - **What to Pack:**
        - Winter: Warm coat, hat, gloves, and layers.
        - Spring: Light jacket, layers, and rain gear.
        - Summer: Light clothing, sunscreen, and sunglasses.
        - Fall: Light jacket, layers, and rain gear.
- **Southwest:**
    - **Seasons:** Hot summers, mild winters, and low humidity.
        - **What to Pack:**
        - Summer: Light, breathable clothing, sunscreen, and sunglasses.
        - Winter: Light jacket, layers, and a sweater.
        - Sun Protection: Wide-brimmed hat, sunscreen, and sunglasses.
- **West Coast (California, Pacific Northwest):**
    - **Seasons:** Mild and wet winters, warm and dry summers.
        - **What to Pack:**
        - Winter: Waterproof jacket, layers, and umbrella.
        - Summer: Light clothing, sunscreen, and sunglasses.
        - Sun Protection: Wide-brimmed hat and sunscreen.
- **Mountain West (Rocky Mountains):**
    - **Seasons:** Cold winters, warm summers, and dry climate.
        - **What to Pack:**

- Winter: Warm coat, hat, gloves, and layers.
- Summer: Light clothing, sunscreen, and sunglasses.
- Sun Protection: Wide-brimmed hat and sunscreen.
- **Alaska:**
  - **Seasons:** Harsh winters, cool summers, and long days of sunlight in summer.
    - **What to Pack:**
      - Winter: Heavy coat, insulated layers, hat, gloves, and snow boots.
      - Summer: Layered clothing, waterproof jacket, and insect repellent.
- **Hawaii:**
  - **Seasons:** Tropical climate with consistent temperatures year-round.
    - **What to Pack:**
      - Light, breathable clothing, swimsuit, sunscreen, and sunglasses.
      - Hiking Gear: If planning outdoor activities, bring comfortable shoes and a light jacket.

Recap

Aspect	Key Information	Money-Saving Tips
Entry Requirements	Check visa or ESTA requirements	Apply for necessary documentation in advance
Transportation	Research public transit options	Use public transit or rideshare instead of taxis
Accommodation	Look for budget-friendly accommodations	Consider hostels, Airbnbs, or camping for cheaper options
Dining	Take advantage of happy hours or early bird specials	Cook your own meals or pack picnic supplies
Attractions	Research free or discounted attractions and activities	Utilize city passes for bundled discounts on attractions
Tipping	Factor in tipping for service at restaurants and other places	Tip appropriately but don't overdo it
Travel Insurance	Invest in travel insurance for unexpected emergencies	Compare plans and choose one that fits your budget
Packing	Bring reusable items like water bottles and toiletry containers	Pack lightweight and versatile clothing to avoid excess baggage fees
Snorkeling Gear	Bring your own snorkel, mask, and fins to avoid rental fees	Invest in compact and durable gear for multiple uses
Shopping	Look for sales, discounts, and outlet stores	Avoid impulse purchases and stick to your budget

Go Minus the crowds

Enjoying major attractions in the USA without crowds often involves strategic planning and timing. Here are some recommendations for visiting top attractions during less busy times:

- **Off-Peak Seasons:**
    - Identify the off-peak seasons for your desired destinations. This is typically when schools are in session and the weather may be less favorable. For example, consider visiting popular theme parks during weekdays in the fall or winter.
- **Early Morning or Late Evening:**
    - Many attractions are less crowded early in the morning or late in the evening. Consider visiting popular landmarks right when they open or during the last hour before closing.
- **Midweek Visits:**
    - Weekends tend to attract larger crowds. Plan your visits midweek to avoid the surge of weekend tourists.
- **Avoid Holidays and Special Events:**
    - Major holidays and special events can draw large crowds. Check the local calendar and plan your visit on days with fewer events or festivities.
- **Purchase Tickets in Advance:**
    - Buy tickets online in advance to skip long lines at popular attractions. Some places also offer early-bird or evening discounts.
- **Utilize Fast Passes or Skip-the-Line Options:**
    - Some attractions offer fast passes or skip-the-line options for an additional fee. While this involves extra cost, it can significantly reduce wait times.
- **Visit During Shoulder Seasons:**
    - Consider visiting during the shoulder seasons, which are the periods just before or after the peak season. You may experience good weather with fewer tourists.
- **Opt for Guided Tours:**
    - Joining guided tours may give you access to express lines or special viewing areas, allowing you to bypass regular lines.
- **Check Peak Times:**
    - Some attractions have peak times during the day. For instance, major museums may be less crowded during the lunch hour when many visitors are dining.
- **Mid-Month Visits:**
    - Plan your visit for the middle of the month, as this is when crowds may be smaller compared to the beginning or end of the month.
- **Stay Near the Attractions:**
    - Choose accommodations within walking distance of major attractions. This allows you to visit early or late without worrying about transportation issues.

How to use this book

Google and TripAdvisor are your on-the-go guides while traveling, a travel guide adds the most value during the planning phase, and if you're without Wi-Fi. Always download the google map for your destination - having an offline map will make using this guide much more comfortable. For ease of use, we've set the book out the way you travel, booking your flights, arriving, how to get around, then on to the money-saving tips. The tips we ordered according to when you need to know the tip to save money, so free tours and combination tickets feature first. We prioritized the rest of the tips by how much money you can save and then by how likely it was that you could find the tip with a google search. Meaning those we think you could find alone are nearer the bottom. I hope you find this layout useful. If you have any ideas about making Super Cheap Insider Guides easier to use, please email me philgattang@gmail.com

A quick note on How We Source Super Cheap Tips
We focus entirely on finding the best bargains. We give each of our collaborators $2,000 to hunt down never-before-seen deals. The type you either only know if you're local or by on the ground research. We spend zero on marketing and a little on designing an excellent cover. We do this yearly, which means we just keep finding more amazing ways for you to have the same experience for less.

Now let's get started with juicing the most pleasure from your trip to USA with the least possible money!

Booking Flights

How to Find Heavily Discounted Private Jet Flights to or from USA

If you're dreaming of travelling to USA on a private jet you can accomplish your dream for a 10th of the cost.

Empty leg flights, also known as empty leg charters or deadhead flights, are flights operated by private jet companies that do not have any passengers on board. These flights occur when a private jet is chartered for a one-way trip, but the jet needs to return to its base or another location without passengers.

Rather than flying empty, private jet companies may offer these empty leg flights for a reduced price to travelers who are flexible and able to fly on short notice. Because the flight is already scheduled and paid for by the original charter, private jet companies are willing to offer these flights at a discounted rate in order to recoup some of the cost.

Empty leg flights can be a cost-effective way to experience the luxury and convenience of private jet travel.

Taking an empty leg private jet flight from London to USA

The New York City-London route is one of the busiest private jet routes in the world, with many private jet operators offering regular flights between the two cities.

There are several websites that offer empty leg flights for booking. Here are a few:

JetSuiteX: This website offers discounted, last-minute flights on private jets, including empty leg flights.

PrivateFly: This website allows you to search for empty leg flights by location or date. You can also request a quote for a custom flight if you have specific needs.

Victor: This website offers a variety of private jet services, including empty leg flights.

Sky500: This website offers a variety of private jet services, including empty leg flights.

Air Charter Service: This website allows you to search for empty leg flights by location or date. You can also request a quote for a custom flight if you have specific needs.

Keep in mind that empty leg flights are often available at short notice, so it's a good idea to be flexible with your travel plans if you're looking for a deal. It's also important to do your research and read reviews before booking a flight with any company.

RECAP: To book an empty leg flight in USA, follow these steps:

1. Research and identify private jet companies and or brokers that offer empty leg flights departing from USA. You can use the websites mentioned earlier, such as JetSuiteX, PrivateFly, Victor, Sky500, or Air Charter Service, to search for available flights.

2. Check the availability and pricing of empty leg flights that match your travel dates and destination. Empty leg flights are often available at short notice.

3. Contact the private jet company or broker to inquire about booking the empty leg flight. Be sure to provide your travel details, including your preferred departure and arrival times, number of passengers, and any special requests.

4. Confirm your booking and make payment. Private jet companies and brokers typically require full payment upfront, so be prepared to pay for the flight in advance.

5. Arrive at the airport at least 30 minutes before the scheduled departure time.

6. Check in at the private jet terminal and go through any necessary security checks. Unlike commercial airlines, there is typically no long queue or security checks for private jet flights.

7. Board the private jet and settle into your seat. You will have plenty of space to stretch out and relax, as well as access to amenities such as Wi-Fi, entertainment systems, and refreshments.

How to Find CHEAP FIRST-CLASS Flights to USA

Upgrade at the airport

Airlines are extremely reluctant to advertise price drops in first or business class tickets so the best way to secure them is actually at the airport when airlines have no choice but to decrease prices dramatically because otherwise they lose money. Ask about upgrading to business or first-class when you check-in. If you check-in online look around the airport for your airlines branded bidding system.

Use Air-miles

When it comes to accruing air-miles for American citizens **Chase Sapphire Reserve card** ranks top. If you put everything on there and pay it off immediately you will end up getting free flights all the time, aside from taxes.

Get 2-3 chase cards with sign up bonuses, you'll have 200k points in no time and can book with points on multiple airlines when transferring your points to them.

Please note, this is only applicable to those living in the USA. In the Bonus Section we have detailed the best air-mile credit cards for those living in other countries.

How many miles does it take to fly first class?
New York City to USA could require anywhere from 70,000 to 120,000 frequent flyer miles, depending on the airline and the time of year you plan to travel.

How to Fly Business Class to USA cheaply from Europe

Determining the absolute cheapest business class airline from Europe to the USA can be challenging due to fluctuating prices, promotions, and seasonal variations. However, several airlines are known for offering competitive fares for transatlantic business class travel. Some factors that can influence pricing include the route, departure city, time of booking, and travel dates.

Here are a few airlines that often provide relatively affordable business class fares between Europe and the USA:

1. **Norwegian Air Shuttle**: Norwegian Air Shuttle is known for its low-cost long-haul flights and occasionally offers competitive business class fares between Europe and select destinations in the USA.
2. **WOW air**: WOW air, an Icelandic low-cost carrier, has been known to offer affordable business class fares on certain routes between Europe and the USA, particularly from its hub in Reykjavik.
3. **TAP Air Portugal**: TAP Air Portugal is a full-service carrier that often provides competitive business class fares from European cities to multiple destinations in the USA, including New York, Boston, Miami, and more.
4. **Aer Lingus**: Aer Lingus, the national airline of Ireland, offers business class service on transatlantic flights from Dublin, Shannon, and other European cities to various destinations in the USA. The airline occasionally provides attractive fares, especially during promotional periods.
5. **Icelandair**: Icelandair operates flights between Reykjavik and several cities in the USA, with a stopover option in Iceland. The airline offers Saga Class, its business class product, with competitive fares on certain routes.
6. **LEVEL**: LEVEL is a low-cost long-haul airline operated by the International Airlines Group (IAG). While primarily focused on economy class, it occasionally offers premium cabin seats with competitive fares between Europe and the USA.
7. **Primera Air**: Primera Air was a low-cost carrier that operated transatlantic flights between Europe and the USA. While the airline ceased operations in 2018, it was known for offering low business class fares on routes such as London to New York.

How to ALWAYS Find Super Cheap Flights to USA

If you're just interested in finding the cheapest flight to USA here is here to do it!

Luck is just an illusion.

Anyone can find incredible flight deals. If you can be flexible you can save huge amounts of money. In fact, the biggest tip I can give you for finding incredible flight deals is simple: find a flexible job. Don't despair if you can't do that theres still a lot you can do.

Book your flight to USA on a Tuesday or Wednesday

Tuesdays and Wednesdays are the cheapest days of the week to fly. You can take a flight to USA on a Tuesday or Wednesday for less than half the price you'd pay on a Thursday Friday, Saturday, Sunday or Monday.

Start with Google Flights (but NEVER book through them)

I conduct upwards of 50 flight searches a day for readers. I use google flights first when looking for flights. I put specific departure but broad destination (e.g Europe) and usually find amazing deals.

The great thing about Google Flights is you can search by class. You can pick a specific destination and it will tell you which time is cheapest in which class. Or you can put in dates and you can see which area is cheapest to travel to.

But be aware Google flights does not show the cheapest prices among the flight search engines but it does offer several advantages

1. You can see the cheapest dates for the next 8 weeks. Other search engines will blackout over 70% of the prices.
2. You can put in multiple airports to fly from. Just use a common to separate in the from input.
3. If you're flexible on where you're going Google flights can show you the cheapest destinations.
4. You can set-up price tracking, where Google will email you when prices rise or decline.

Once you have established the cheapest dates to fly go over to skyscanner.net and put those dates in. You will find sky scanner offers the cheapest flights.

Get Alerts when Prices to USA are Lowest

Google also has a nice feature which allows you to set up an alert to email you when prices to your destination are at their lowest. So if you don't have fixed dates this feature can save you a fortune.

Baggage add-ons

It may be cheaper and more convenient to send your luggage separately with a service like sendmybag.com Often the luggage sending fee is cheaper than what the airlines charge to check baggage. Visit Lugless.com or luggagefree.com in addition to sendmybag.com for a quotation.

Loading times

Anyone who has attempted to find a cheap flight will know the pain of excruciating long loading times. If you encounter this issue use google flights to find the cheapest dates and then go to skyscanner.net for the lowest price.

Always try to book direct with the airline

Once you have found the cheapest flight go direct to the airlines booking page. This is advantageous because if you need to change your flights or arrange a refund, its much easier to do so, than via a third party booking agent.

That said, sometimes the third party bookers offer cheaper deals than the airline, so you need to make the decision based on how likely you think it is that disruption will impede you making those flights.

More Fight Tricks and Tips

www.secretflying.com/usa-deals offers a range of deals from the USA and other countries. For example you can pick-up a round trip flight non-stop from from the east coast to johannesburg for $350 return on this site

Scott's cheap flights, you can select your home airport and get emails on deals but you pay for an annual subscription. A free workaround is to download Hopper and set search alerts for trips/price drops.

Premium service of Scott's cheap flights.
They sometime have discounted business and first class but in my experience they are few and far between.

JGOOT.com has 5 times as many choices as Scott's cheap flights.

kiwi.com allows you to be able to do radius searches so you can find cheaper flights to general areas.

Finding Error Fares

Travel Pirates (www.travelpirates.com) is a gold-mine for finding error deals. Subscribe to their newsletter. I recently found a reader an airfare from Montreal-Brazil for a $200 round trip (mistake fare!). Of course these error fares are always certain dates, but if you can be flexible you can save a lot of money.

Things you can do that might reduce the fare to USA:

- Use a VPN (if the booker knows you booked one-way, the return fare will go up)
- Buy your ticket in a different currency

If all else fails...

If you can't find a cheap flight for your dates I can find one for you. I do not charge for this nor do I send affiliate links. I'll send you a screenshot of the best options I find as airlines attach cookies to flight links. To use this free service please review this guide and send me a screenshot of your review - with your flight hacking request. I aim to reply to you within 12 hours. If it's an urgent request mark the email URGENT in the subject line and I will endeavour to reply ASAP.

A tip for coping with Jet-lag

Jetlag is primarily caused by disruptions to the body's circadian rhythm, which is the internal "biological clock" that regulates many of the body's processes, including sleep-wake cycles. When you travel across multiple time zones, your body's clock is disrupted, leading to symptoms like fatigue, insomnia, and stomach problems.

Eating on your travel destination's time before you travel can help to adjust your body's clock before you arrive, which can help to mitigate the effects of jetlag. This means that if you're traveling to a destination that is several hours ahead of your current time zone, you should try to eat meals at the appropriate times for your destination a few days before you leave. For example, if you're traveling from New York to USA, which is seven hours ahead, you could start eating dinner at 9pm EST (which is 3am USA time) a few days before your trip.

By adjusting your eating schedule before you travel, you can help to shift your body's clock closer to the destination's time zone, which can make it easier to adjust to the new schedule once you arrive.

Accommodation

Your two biggest expenses when travelling to USA are accommodation and food. This section is intended to help you cut these costs dramatically without compromising on those luxury feels.

It is vital to hack hotel prices because these are some scary average in cities:

1. New York City: Average hotel costs range from $200 to $400 per night, with luxury accommodations often exceeding $500 per night.
2. Los Angeles: Expect to pay between $150 and $300 per night for a mid-range hotel, while luxury hotels can range from $300 to $600 or more per night.
3. Chicago: Average hotel prices typically fall between $150 and $300 per night, with luxury hotels averaging around $400 to $700 per night.
4. San Francisco: Hotel costs in San Francisco are among the highest in the country, with average prices ranging from $250 to $400 per night for mid-range accommodations and luxury hotels often exceeding $500 per night.
5. Miami: Average hotel prices in Miami range from $150 to $300 per night, with luxury hotels averaging around $300 to $600 per night.
6. Las Vegas: Las Vegas offers a wide range of accommodations to suit every budget, with average prices ranging from $50 to $200 per night for mid-range hotels and luxury options starting at around $200 per night.
7. Washington, D.C.: Expect to pay between $150 and $300 per night for a mid-range hotel in Washington, D.C., while luxury accommodations can range from $300 to $600 or more per night.
8. Boston: Hotel prices in Boston tend to be on the higher side, with average costs ranging from $200 to $400 per night for mid-range accommodations and luxury hotels often exceeding $500 per night.
9. Seattle: Average hotel prices in Seattle typically range from $150 to $300 per night for mid-range hotels, with luxury options averaging around $300 to $600 per night.

How to Book a Five-star Hotel consistently on the Cheap in USA

The cheapest four and five-star hotel deals are available when you 'blind book'. Blind booking is a type of discounted hotel booking where the guest doesn't know the name of the hotel until after they've booked and paid for the reservation. This allows hotels to offer lower prices without damaging their brand image or cannibalizing their full-price bookings.

Here are some of the best platforms for blind booking a hotel in USA:

1. Hotwire - This website offers discounted hotel rates for blind booking. You can choose the star rating, neighborhood, and amenities you want, but the actual hotel name will not be revealed until after you've booked.
2. Priceline - Once you've made the reservation, the hotel name and location will be revealed.
3. Secret Escapes - This website offers luxury hotel deals at discounted rates. You can choose the type of hotel you want and the general location, but the hotel name and exact location will be revealed after you book.
4. Lastminute.com - You can select the star rating and general location, but the hotel name and exact location will be revealed after booking. Using the Top Secret hotels

you can find a four star hotel from $60 a night in USA - consistently! Most of the hotels featured are in the Grange Group. If in doubt, simply copy and paste the description into Google to find the name before booking.

Cheapest hotel chains in the USA and how to get discounts

Several hotel chains in the USA are known for offering budget-friendly accommodation options. Keep in mind that prices can vary based on location, time of year, and availability. Here are some of the popular budget hotel chains, along with tips on how to get discounts:

- **Motel 6:**
    - Motel 6 is a well-known budget hotel chain with locations across the USA. They often offer competitive rates, and you can check their website for promotions and discounts.
- **Super 8:**
    - Super 8 is part of the Wyndham hotel group and is known for its affordable rates. Signing up for their loyalty program may also provide access to exclusive discounts.
- **Days Inn:**
    - Days Inn, another Wyndham brand, is a budget-friendly hotel chain. Look for special promotions, discounts for members, or package deals on their website.
- **Red Roof Inn:**
    - Red Roof Inn is a chain of economy hotels with a focus on providing affordable and comfortable accommodations. They often offer discounts for seniors, military personnel, and pets.
- **Econo Lodge:**
    - Econo Lodge, part of the Choice Hotels group, is known for budget-friendly options. Check their website for special promotions and discounts for loyalty program members.
- **Extended Stay America:**
    - Extended Stay America caters to travelers looking for longer-term stays. They often have discounted rates for extended bookings, and signing up for their rewards program can provide additional savings.
- **TraveLodge:**
    - Travelodge is a budget hotel chain with various locations. Keep an eye out for promotions, special rates, and discounts available through their website.
- **Howard Johnson:**
    - Howard Johnson is a budget-friendly hotel chain offering affordable rates. Check their website for discounts, special offers, and promotions.

Tips for Getting Discounts:

- **Book in Advance:**

- Rates are often lower when you book in advance, so plan your trip and make reservations as early as possible.
- **Join Loyalty Programs:**
  - Many hotel chains offer loyalty programs that provide members with exclusive discounts, perks, and rewards. Sign up for these programs and take advantage of the benefits.
- **Check Official Websites:**
  - Hotel chains often offer the best rates on their official websites. Check for promotions, package deals, and exclusive discounts directly on the hotel's site.
- **Look for Package Deals:**
  - Some hotel chains offer package deals that include accommodations, meals, or other perks. These packages can provide additional savings.
- **Use Discount Websites:**
  - Utilize online travel agencies (OTAs) and discount websites to compare prices. Websites like Expedia, Booking.com, and Hotels.com may offer special rates and promotions.
- **Consider Weekday Stays:**
  - Rates are often lower during weekdays than on weekends. If your travel dates are flexible, consider staying during the week to save money.
- **Group Memberships:**
  - Some hotel chains offer discounts for members of specific groups, such as AAA/CAA, AARP, military, or government employees. Check eligibility and take advantage of these discounts.

Always read the terms and conditions of any discounts, and be aware that certain promotions may have restrictions. Additionally, consider factors like location, amenities, and reviews when choosing a budget hotel for your stay.

Enjoy the Finest Five-star Hotels for a 10th of the Cost

If you travel during the peak season or during a major event, you can still enjoy the finest hotels in USA for a 10th of the normal cost. With a day pass, you can enjoy all the amenities that the hotel has to offer, including the pool, spa, gym, and included lunches at fine restaurants. This can be a great way to relax and unwind for a day without having to spend money on an overnight stay.

Here are some of the finest five-star hotels in the USA, along with their starting prices for a day pass to access their amenities:

1. **The Ritz-Carlton, New York City:**
   - Starting Price: Day passes for access to amenities such as the spa, fitness center, and pool typically start around $150 USD.
2. **Four Seasons Hotel, Beverly Hills:**
   - Starting Price: Day passes for access to the hotel's pool, cabanas, and fitness center usually start at $100 USD per person.
3. **The St. Regis, San Francisco:**

- Starting Price: Day passes for access to the hotel's pool and fitness center typically start at $75 USD per person.
4. **Waldorf Astoria, Chicago**:
    - Starting Price: Day passes for access to the hotel's spa, fitness center, and pool usually start around $100 USD per person.
5. **The Plaza Hotel, New York City**:
    - Starting Price: Day passes for access to the hotel's spa, fitness center, and pool typically start around $200 USD per person.

It's important to note that availability and pricing for day passes may vary depending on the hotel and time of year, so it's always a good idea to check directly with the hotel for the most up-to-date information and to pre-book before your trip to avoid disappointment.

TOP TIP: AVOID The weekend price hike

Hotel prices skyrocket during weekends in peak season (June, July, August and December). If you can, get out of USA for the weekend you'll save thousands on luxury hotels. For example a room at a popular five-star hotel costs $80 a night during the week when blind-booking. That price goes to $400 a night for Saturday's and Sundays. Amazing nearby weekend trips are featured further on and planning those on the weekends could easily save you a ton of money and make your trip more comfortable by avoiding crowds.

Strategies to Book Five-Star Hotels for Two-Star Prices in USA

Use Time

There are two ways to use time. One is to book in advance. Three months will net you the best deal, especially if your visit coincides with an event. The other is to book on the day of your stay. This is a risky move, but if executed well, you can lay your head in a five-star hotel for a 2-star fee.

Before you travel to USA, check for big events using a simple google search 'What's on in USA', if you find no big events drawing travellers, risk showing up with no accommodation booked (If there are big events on demand exceeds supply and you should avoid using this strategy). If you don't want to risk showing up with no accommodation booked, book a cheap accommodation with free-cancellation.

Before I go into demand-based pricing, take a moment to think about your risk tolerance. By risk, I am not talking about personal safety. No amount of financial savings is worth risking that. What I am talking about is being inconvenienced. Do you deal well with last-minute changes? Can you roll with the punches or do you freak out if something changes? Everyone is different and knowing yourself is the best way to plan a great trip. If you are someone that likes to have everything pre-planned using demand-based pricing to get cheap accommodation will not work for you.

Demand-based pricing

Be they an Airbnb host or hotel manager; no one wants empty rooms. Most will do anything to make some revenue because they still have the same costs to cover whether the room is occupied or not. That's why you will find many hotels drastically slashing room rates for same-day bookings.

How to book five-star hotels for a two-star price

You will not be able to find these discounts when the demand exceeds the supply. So if you're visiting during the peak season, or during an event which has drawn many travellers again don't try this.

1. On the day of your stay, visit booking.com (which offers better discounts than Kayak and agoda.com). Hotel
Tonight individually checks for any last-minute bookings, but they take a big chunk of the action, so the better deals come from booking.com.
2. The best results come from booking between 2 pm and 4 pm when the risk of losing any revenue with no occupancy is most pronounced, so algorithms supporting hotels slash prices. This is when you can find rates that are not within the "lowest publicly visible" rate.
3. To avoid losing customers to other websites, or cheapening the image of their hotel most will only offer the super cheap rates during a two hour window from 2 pm to 4 pm. Two guests will pay 10x difference in price but it's absolutely vital to the hotel that

neither knows it.

Takeaway: To get the lowest price book on the day of stay between 2 pm and 4 pm and extend your search radius to include further afield hotels with good transport connections.

There are several luxury hotels outside of USA's city center that offer good transport connections to the city, as well as easy access to other nearby attractions. Here are a few options to consider:

1. The Grove: This five-star hotel is located in Hertfordshire, just 18 miles north of USA. It offers a free shuttle bus to and from Watford Junction station, where you can catch a train into USA's Euston station in just 18 minutes. The hotel also has its own golf course, spa, and several dining options.
2. Coworth Park: This luxurious country house hotel is located in Ascot, about 25 miles west of USA. It offers easy access to Heathrow Airport, as well as direct train connections to USA's Waterloo station from nearby Sunningdale station. The hotel has its own polo fields, spa, and Michelin-starred restaurant.
3. Pennyhill Park Hotel and Spa: This five-star hotel is located in Surrey, just 30 miles southwest of USA. It is easily accessible by car or train, with direct connections to USA's Waterloo station from nearby Bagshot station. The hotel has a large spa, several dining options, and is set on 123 acres of landscaped gardens and parkland.
4. Cliveden House: This historic country house hotel is located in Berkshire, about 25 miles west of USA. It is easily accessible by car or train, with direct connections to USA's Paddington station from nearby Taplow station. The hotel has a spa, several dining options, and is set on 376 acres of National Trust gardens and parkland.

These are just a few examples of luxury hotels outside of USA's city center with good transport connections to the city and opportunities for last-minute discounts.

Priceline Hack to get a Luxury Hotel on the Cheap

Priceline.com has been around since 1997 and is an incredible site for sourcing luxury Hotels on the cheap in USA.

Priceline have a database of the lowest price a hotel will accept for a particular time and date. That amount changes depending on two factors:

1. Demand: More demand high prices.
2. Likelihood of lost revenue: if the room is still available at 3pm the same-day prices will plummet.

Obviously they don't want you to know the lowest price as they make more commission the higher the price you pay.

They offer two good deals to entice you to book with them in USA. And the good news is neither require last-minute booking (though the price will decrease the closer to the date you book).

'Firstly, 'price-breakers'. You blind book from a choice of three highly rated hotels which they name. Pricebreakers, travelers are shown three similar, highly-rated hotels, listed under a single low price.' After you book they reveal the name of the hotel.

Secondly, the 'express deals'. These are the last minute deals. You'll be able to see the name of the hotel before you book.

To find the right luxury hotel for you at a cheap price you should plug in the neighbourhoods you want to stay in, an acceptable rating (4 or 5 stars), and filter by the amenities you want.

You can also get an addition discount for your USA hotel by booking on their dedicated app.

How to trick travel Algorithms to get the lowest hotel price

Do not believe anyone who says changing your IP address to get cheaper hotels or flights does NOT work. If you don't believe us, download a Tor Network and search for flights and hotels to one destination using your current IP and then the tor network (a tor browser hides your IP address from algorithms. It is commonly used by hackers). You will receive different prices.

The price you see is a decision made by an algorithm that adjusts prices using data points such as past bookings, remaining capacity, average demand and the probability of selling the room or flight later at a higher price. If knows you've searched for the area before ip the prices high. To circumvent this, you can either use a different IP address from a cafe or airport or data from an international sim. I use a sim from Three, which provides free data in many countries around the world. When you search from a new IP address, most of the time, and particularly near booking you will get a lower price. Sometimes if your sim comes from a 'rich' country, say the UK or USA, you will see higher rates as the algorithm has learnt people from these countries pay more. The solution is to book from a local wifi connection - but a different one from the one you originally searched from.

Booking a luxurious five-star hotel for the price of a humble two-star accommodation may sound like a traveler's dream come true, but with the right strategies, it's entirely possible to turn this dream into reality. From leveraging loyalty programs to capitalizing on off-peak seasons, there are numerous savvy tactics that can help you secure a lavish stay without breaking the bank. So, let's delve into the world of luxury travel hacking and explore some tried-and-true strategies for booking five-star hotels for two-star prices in the USA.

1. Leverage Loyalty Programs: Unlocking VIP Treatment

Loyalty programs are the Holy Grail of luxury travel hacking. Whether you're a frequent traveler or planning a special getaway, signing up for hotel loyalty programs can unlock a treasure trove of benefits, including room upgrades, complimentary amenities, and exclusive discounts. Many five-star hotel chains, such as Marriott Bonvoy, Hilton Honors, and World of Hyatt, offer loyalty programs that reward members with points for every dollar spent on hotel stays. By accumulating points through stays, credit card spending, and promotional offers, you can redeem them for free nights at luxurious properties or even score elite status, granting you access to VIP perks like priority check-in, late check-out, and complimentary breakfast.

2. Embrace the Power of Price Comparison: Hunting for Hidden Gems

When it comes to snagging unbeatable deals on luxury accommodations, knowledge is power. Instead of relying solely on hotel websites or booking platforms, take advantage of price comparison tools and aggregator websites to scout out hidden gems and score the best possible rates. Websites like Kayak, Trivago, and HotelsCombined allow you to compare prices from multiple booking sites at once, helping you uncover discounts, promotions, and flash sales that may not be advertised elsewhere. Additionally, don't forget to check for exclusive deals and member-only rates on hotel loyalty program websites, as these can often offer significant savings compared to third-party booking platforms.

3. Time Your Booking Strategically: Riding the Waves of Demand

Timing is everything when it comes to securing budget-friendly stays at five-star hotels. By strategically timing your booking, you can capitalize on fluctuations in demand and score lower rates during off-peak seasons or periods of low occupancy. In general, hotel prices tend to soar during peak travel seasons, holidays, and special events, so consider planning your trip during shoulder seasons or midweek stays to take advantage of lower prices and avoid the crowds. Additionally, keep an eye out for last-minute deals and flash sales, as hotels may slash prices to fill empty rooms and boost occupancy rates.

4. Get Creative with Alternative Booking Options: Exploring Unconventional Routes

In the quest for luxury at a bargain, thinking outside the box can pay off big time. Instead of limiting yourself to traditional hotel stays, consider exploring alternative booking options that offer unique experiences at a fraction of the cost. Vacation rental platforms like Airbnb and Vrbo often feature upscale properties, such as private villas, luxury condos, and designer lofts, that rival the amenities and ambiance of five-star hotels but come with more affordable price tags. Additionally, keep an eye out for boutique hotels, independent resorts, and boutique bed-and-breakfasts that offer personalized service and upscale accommodations without the hefty price tag of major hotel chains.

5. Negotiate Like a Pro: Sealing the Deal with Persuasive Prowess

When it comes to booking luxury accommodations, don't be afraid to flex your negotiation skills and haggle for a better deal. While negotiating hotel prices may seem intimidating, it can be surprisingly effective, especially if you're booking directly with the hotel or speaking to a manager or sales representative. Before reaching out, do your research, gather competing quotes, and highlight any loyalty program status, past stays, or special occasions that may warrant special treatment. Be polite, firm, and flexible in your approach, and don't hesitate to ask for complimentary upgrades, amenities, or discounts to sweeten the deal. Remember, the worst they can say is no, so it never hurts to ask!

6. Stay Flexible: Seizing Opportunities and Sealing the Deal

Flexibility is the secret weapon of savvy luxury travelers. By staying open-minded and adaptable, you can seize unexpected opportunities and snag unbeatable deals on five-star accommodations. Consider being flexible with your travel dates, destinations, and accommodation preferences to take advantage of flash sales, last-minute deals, and promotional offers that may arise. Additionally, keep an eye out for package deals, bundled stays, and combination offers that include extras like dining credits, spa treatments, or attraction tickets, as these can often provide added value and enhance your overall experience without breaking the bank.

7. Don't Underestimate the Power of Reviews: Uncovering Insider Secrets

When it comes to booking luxury accommodations, reviews are your best friend. Before committing to a reservation, take the time to read reviews, testimonials, and firsthand accounts from fellow travelers who have stayed at the property. Websites like TripAdvisor, Yelp, and Google Reviews offer valuable insights into the quality, service, and overall guest experience of hotels, helping you separate the gems from the duds. Pay attention to common themes, trends, and recurring issues mentioned in reviews, and use this information to make an informed decision about whether a particular hotel is worth the investment.

8. Maximize Your Value: Making the Most of Every Dollar Spent

While snagging a bargain on luxury accommodations is undoubtedly gratifying, it's essential to maximize the value of your investment and make the most of every dollar spent. To get the most bang for your buck, take advantage of complimentary perks, amenities, and services offered by the hotel, such as free breakfast, Wi-Fi, shuttle service, or fitness facilities. Additionally, consider indulging in experiences and activities that enhance your stay, such as spa treatments, guided tours, or culinary adventures, as these can elevate your overall experience and create lasting memories without blowing your budget.

Comparing hotels to Airbnb accommodations

When comparing hotels to Airbnb accommodations in America, each option comes with its own set of pros and cons. Here's a breakdown to help you decide which is best for you:

Hotels:

Pros:

1. **Consistency**: Hotels offer a standardized experience with amenities like daily housekeeping, front desk assistance, and on-site facilities such as gyms and restaurants.
2. **Security**: Hotels often have 24/7 security measures in place, providing peace of mind for guests.
3. **Convenience**: Many hotels are centrally located in popular tourist areas, making it easy to access attractions, dining options, and public transportation.
4. **Amenities**: Hotels often provide amenities such as swimming pools, spas, and business centers for guests to enjoy during their stay.
5. **Flexibility**: Hotels offer various room options, from standard rooms to suites, catering to different preferences and budgets.

Cons:

1. **Cost**: Hotels can be more expensive than Airbnb accommodations, especially in popular tourist destinations or during peak travel seasons.
2. **Limited Space**: Hotel rooms may be smaller and have less living space compared to Airbnb rentals, especially for long-term stays.
3. **Less Personalization**: Hotels may lack the personalized touch and unique character that Airbnb properties can offer.
4. **Additional Fees**: Some hotels charge extra for amenities like Wi-Fi, parking, and resort fees, which can add to the overall cost of your stay.

Airbnbs:

Pros:

1. **Cost-Effectiveness**: Airbnb rentals can often be more affordable than hotels, especially for longer stays or larger groups, as they typically offer more space and amenities for the price.
2. **Local Experience**: Staying in an Airbnb allows you to experience the local culture and lifestyle firsthand, as many properties are located in residential neighborhoods.
3. **Flexibility**: Airbnb offers a wide range of accommodations, from private rooms to entire homes, giving travelers more options to suit their needs and preferences.
4. **Amenities**: Many Airbnb properties come equipped with amenities such as kitchens, laundry facilities, and outdoor spaces, providing additional comfort and convenience.

5. **Personalized Service**: Airbnb hosts often provide personalized recommendations and insights about the local area, enhancing the overall guest experience.

Cons:

1. **Lack of Consistency**: Airbnb properties vary widely in terms of quality, cleanliness, and amenities, so it's essential to read reviews and communicate with hosts before booking.
2. **Limited Support**: Unlike hotels, Airbnb properties may not have on-site staff available to assist guests with issues or requests.
3. **Security Concerns**: While Airbnb has safety measures in place, such as identity verification and guest reviews, some travelers may feel less secure staying in a private residence compared to a hotel.
4. **Cancellation Policies**: Airbnb hosts set their cancellation policies, which can vary from flexible to strict, so it's crucial to understand the terms before booking.

In terms of saving money, it ultimately depends on your travel preferences, destination, and length of stay. In some cases, hotels may offer promotional deals or discounts that make them more cost-effective than Airbnb rentals. Conversely, Airbnb properties may provide better value for longer stays or for travelers seeking a more immersive, local experience. It's essential to compare prices, consider your priorities, and weigh the pros and cons of each option before making a decision

Airbnb Bans

Some cities have imposed outright bans on certain types of short-term rentals or have implemented strict regulations that effectively limit Airbnb activity. Examples of cities that have faced scrutiny or restrictions on Airbnb and other short-term rental platforms include:

1. **New York City, New York**: New York City has implemented regulations that restrict the rental of entire homes for fewer than 30 days unless the host is present during the stay. This regulation effectively bans many Airbnb listings in the city.
2. **San Francisco, California**: San Francisco requires hosts to register their short-term rental properties with the city and adhere to specific regulations. Airbnb and other short-term rental platforms must also share data with the city to ensure compliance.

3. **Santa Monica, California**: Santa Monica has implemented strict regulations on short-term rentals, including requiring hosts to obtain a business license and limiting rentals to primary residences only.
4. **Miami Beach, Florida**: Miami Beach has enacted regulations that restrict short-term rentals in certain residential areas and require hosts to obtain a business tax receipt and comply with zoning and building codes.
5. **Los Angeles, California**: Los Angeles has implemented regulations that require hosts to register their short-term rental properties with the city and adhere to specific rules, including limits on the number of days a property can be rented each year.

Cheap City Stays

Finding affordable accommodations within walking distance of major attractions in each major USA city can be challenging, as prices and availability can vary depending on factors such as location, time of year, and demand. However, here are some general tips and suggestions for budget-friendly places to stay near major attractions in several major USA cities:

1. **New York City, New York**:
    - Look for budget hotels or hostels in neighborhoods like Midtown Manhattan, Chelsea, or the Lower East Side, which offer easy access to attractions like Times Square, Central Park, and the Empire State Building.
    - Consider staying in shared accommodations or budget-friendly boutique hotels in neighborhoods like Williamsburg or Long Island City in Brooklyn and Queens, respectively, which are just a short subway ride away from Manhattan.
2. **Los Angeles, California**:
    - Search for budget hotels or hostels in Hollywood, Downtown LA, or Santa Monica, which offer proximity to attractions like the Hollywood Walk of Fame, Griffith Observatory, and Venice Beach.
    - Consider staying in budget-friendly accommodations in neighborhoods like Koreatown or Silver Lake, which are centrally located and offer good access to public transportation.
3. **Chicago, Illinois**:
    - Look for budget hotels or hostels in the Loop, River North, or the Near North Side, which offer easy access to attractions like Millennium Park, the Magnificent Mile, and Navy Pier.
    - Consider staying in budget-friendly accommodations in neighborhoods like Wicker Park or Lakeview, which offer a more local experience while still being within reach of downtown attractions via public transportation.
4. **San Francisco, California**:

- Search for budget hotels or hostels in Union Square, Fisherman's Wharf, or the Mission District, which offer proximity to attractions like Alcatraz Island, the Golden Gate Bridge, and Pier 39.
    - Consider staying in budget-friendly accommodations in neighborhoods like the Tenderloin or SoMa (South of Market), which offer good access to public transportation and a more affordable alternative to touristy areas.
5. **Washington, D.C.**:
    - Look for budget hotels or hostels in Downtown DC, Dupont Circle, or Capitol Hill, which offer easy access to attractions like the National Mall, the Smithsonian museums, and the White House.
    - Consider staying in budget-friendly accommodations in neighborhoods like Adams Morgan or Columbia Heights, which offer a more local experience while still being within walking distance or a short metro ride away from downtown attractions.
6. **Las Vegas, Nevada**:
    - Search for budget hotels or hostels on or near the Las Vegas Strip, which offer proximity to attractions like the Bellagio Fountains, the High Roller observation wheel, and various casinos and entertainment venues.
    - Consider staying in budget-friendly accommodations off the Strip, such as in downtown Las Vegas (Fremont Street), which offers more affordable options and is still within reach of major attractions via public transportation or rideshare services.

Cheapest Airbnb Locations

Location	Average Airbnb Price (per night)	Benefits of Visiting
Memphis, Tennessee	$60 - $100	Rich musical history, barbecue, Graceland, Beale Street entertainment.
Albuquerque, New Mexico	$50 - $90	Balloon Fiesta, stunning desert landscapes, diverse culture, historic Old Town.
Boise, Idaho	$70 - $100	Outdoor activities, Boise River Greenbelt, cultural events, affordable dining.
Kansas City, Missouri	$60 - $100	Jazz and barbecue, art scene, museums, affordability.
Birmingham, Alabama	$60 - $90	Civil Rights history, outdoor adventures, local cuisine, affordability.
Louisville, Kentucky	$60 - $100	Bourbon trail, Derby City, parks, affordable dining, cultural festivals.
Jacksonville, Florida	$70 - $120	Beaches, outdoor recreation, museums, affordable coastal living.
Indianapolis, Indiana	$60 - $100	Sports events, cultural attractions, affordability, parks and trails.
Cleveland, Ohio	$60 - $100	Rock and Roll Hall of Fame, waterfront, affordable dining, cultural scene.
Buffalo, New York	$60 - $100	Niagara Falls, historic architecture, cultural festivals, affordability.

Finding the cheapest areas to rent an Airbnb can vary depending on the city or region you're visiting, as well as factors such as demand, availability, and the time of year. However, some general tips and strategies can help you find budget-friendly Airbnb listings in most locations:

1. **Consider Neighborhoods Away from Tourist Hotspots**: Areas that are slightly further away from popular tourist attractions or city centers tend to have lower rental prices. Look for neighborhoods that are still well-connected to public transportation or major attractions but may offer more affordable options for accommodations.
2. **Check Out Suburbs or Residential Areas**: Suburbs or residential neighborhoods often have lower rental prices compared to downtown areas or tourist districts. Look for listings in these areas for potentially cheaper options while still being within a reasonable distance of city amenities and attractions.
3. **Stay Flexible with Dates**: Prices for Airbnb listings can vary depending on the time of year, day of the week, and even specific dates due to factors like holidays or events. Staying flexible with your travel dates and being open to booking during off-peak times can help you find cheaper accommodations.
4. **Use Filters and Sorting Options**: When searching for Airbnb listings, use filters and sorting options to narrow down your search based on price range, neighborhood, amenities, and other preferences. This can help you quickly identify the most affordable options that meet your criteria.

5. **Look for Shared or Private Rooms**: Opting for a shared room or a private room within a shared apartment or house can often be more budget-friendly than booking an entire property. Keep an eye out for listings that offer these options if you're comfortable with sharing common spaces with other guests.
6. **Consider Longer Stays or Last-Minute Bookings**: Some hosts offer discounted rates for longer stays, such as weekly or monthly rentals. Additionally, last-minute bookings can sometimes result in lower prices as hosts may offer discounts to fill empty nights.
7. **Read Reviews and Ratings**: Before booking an Airbnb listing, take the time to read reviews and ratings from previous guests. While price is important, it's also essential to ensure that the property meets your standards in terms of cleanliness, safety, and overall experience.

Guesthouses

Guesthouses in the USA can provide budget-friendly accommodations for travelers looking to save on lodging costs while still enjoying comfortable and convenient stays. Here are some options for affordable guesthouses in the USA, along with where to book and starting prices:

1. **Hostelling International USA**:
    - Booking Platform: Hostelling International USA website or booking platforms like Hostelworld.
    - Starting Price: Dormitory beds start at around $20 to $40 USD per night, while private rooms range from $50 to $100 USD per night.
    - Overview: Hostelling International USA operates a network of hostels across the country, offering budget-friendly accommodations for travelers of all ages. Facilities typically include shared dormitories, private rooms, communal kitchens, social areas, and organized activities.
2. **Airbnb**:
    - Booking Platform: Airbnb website or mobile app.
    - Starting Price: Prices vary depending on location, amenities, and room type, but budget-friendly options such as private rooms or shared accommodations can start as low as $30 to $50 USD per night.
    - Overview: Airbnb offers a wide range of guesthouses, private rooms, and shared accommodations hosted by local residents. Guests can choose from budget-friendly options in cities, suburbs, and rural areas, often with the added bonus of personalized recommendations and local insights from hosts.
3. **Booking.com**:
    - Booking Platform: Booking.com website or mobile app.
    - Starting Price: Guesthouses listed on Booking.com vary in price, but budget-friendly options can start as low as $50 to $100 USD per night for private rooms.
    - Overview: Booking.com features a diverse selection of guesthouses, bed and breakfasts, and small hotels across the USA, offering affordable accommodations for budget-conscious travelers. Guests can browse photos, read reviews, and compare prices to find the best deals on guesthouse stays.
4. **Hostelworld**:
    - Booking Platform: Hostelworld website or mobile app.
    - Starting Price: Dormitory beds in guesthouses listed on Hostelworld typically start at around $20 to $40 USD per night, while private rooms may range from $50 to $100 USD per night.
    - Overview: Hostelworld specializes in budget accommodations, including guesthouses, hostels, and budget hotels. Travelers can search for affordable options, read reviews from fellow guests, and book directly through the platform for added convenience.
5. **Local Guesthouses and Bed & Breakfasts**:
    - Booking Platform: Some local guesthouses and bed & breakfasts may have their own websites or accept bookings via phone or email.

- Starting Price: Prices vary depending on location, amenities, and seasonality, but budget-friendly options can often be found starting at around $50 to $100 USD per night for private rooms.
- Overview: In addition to online booking platforms, travelers can also find affordable guesthouses and bed & breakfasts by researching local options in their destination. Many guesthouses offer personalized service, homemade breakfasts, and unique accommodations in charming settings.

Unique and Cheap

If you're looking for unique and budget-friendly places to stay in the USA, there are plenty of options beyond traditional hotels and guesthouses. From camping under the stars to cozy farm stays and serene meditation retreats, here are some affordable accommodation options with starting prices:

1. **Camping in National Parks**:
    - Starting Price: Campsite fees vary by location but typically range from $15 to $35 USD per night.
    - Overview: National parks across the USA offer picturesque camping opportunities amidst stunning natural landscapes. Pitch a tent or park your RV at designated campgrounds, and enjoy activities such as hiking, wildlife watching, and stargazing. Facilities may include restrooms, picnic areas, and campfire rings.
2. **Farm Stays**:
    - Starting Price: Prices vary depending on location, amenities, and activities offered, but farm stays can start as low as $50 to $100 USD per night.
    - Overview: Experience rural life firsthand with a farm stay at a working farm or ranch. Guests can participate in farm activities such as feeding animals, harvesting crops, and learning about sustainable agriculture practices. Accommodations may range from rustic cabins and cottages to guest rooms in farmhouse settings.
3. **Convents and Monasteries**:
    - Starting Price: Prices vary depending on location and facilities, but convent and monastery stays can start as low as $50 to $100 USD per night.
    - Overview: Many convents and monasteries across the USA offer affordable accommodations for travelers seeking quiet retreats and spiritual reflection. Guests can enjoy serene surroundings, simple yet comfortable rooms, and opportunities for meditation, prayer, and contemplation.
4. **Meditation Retreat Centers**:
    - Starting Price: Prices vary depending on the duration and type of retreat, but basic accommodations for meditation retreats can start at around $50 to $100 USD per night.
    - Overview: Retreat centers specializing in meditation, mindfulness, and holistic wellness offer budget-friendly accommodations for individuals seeking inner peace and relaxation. Guests can participate in guided meditation sessions, yoga classes, and workshops focused on personal growth and self-discovery.
5. **Hostels and Backpacker Lodges**:
    - Starting Price: Dormitory beds in hostels and backpacker lodges typically start at around $20 to $40 USD per night, while private rooms may range from $50 to $100 USD per night.
    - Overview: Hostels and backpacker lodges provide budget-friendly accommodations for travelers looking to meet like-minded individuals and explore new destinations on a shoestring budget. Facilities often include communal kitchens, social areas, and organized activities or tours.

Camping

Wild camping, also known as dispersed camping or boondocking, is legal in many parts of the United States, particularly on public lands managed by agencies like the Bureau of Land Management (BLM), U.S. Forest Service (USFS), and National Park Service (NPS). However, regulations and restrictions vary depending on the location and land management agency. Here's a guide to wild camping in America:

1. Know the Regulations:
- **Check Land Management Policies**: Research the specific regulations and guidelines for dispersed camping on the public lands you plan to visit. Each agency may have different rules regarding camping locations, stay limits, campfire restrictions, waste disposal, and other considerations.
- **Obtain Permits if Required**: Some areas may require permits or passes for dispersed camping, particularly in popular or sensitive areas. Check with the appropriate land management agency to see if permits are needed and how to obtain them.
- **Respect Closure Areas**: Certain areas may be closed to camping due to environmental concerns, wildlife habitat, or safety hazards. Respect any closure notices or restrictions to protect natural resources and ensure visitor safety.

2. Choose a Suitable Location:
- **Select Designated Dispersed Camping Areas**: Many public lands have designated dispersed camping areas or "primitive campsites" where camping is allowed. Look for these designated areas on maps or inquire with land management offices for recommendations.
- **Practice Leave No Trace**: Choose a campsite on durable surfaces away from water sources and trails. Follow Leave No Trace principles by minimizing your impact on the environment, packing out all trash, and leaving the area cleaner than you found it.
- **Consider Safety**: Choose a campsite that is flat, sheltered from wind, and free from hazards like dead trees or rocky terrain. Be aware of wildlife in the area and take precautions to store food securely and avoid confrontations.

3. Prepare for Camping:
- **Bring Essential Gear**: Pack appropriate camping gear, including a tent or shelter, sleeping bag, sleeping pad, cooking equipment, water filtration system, and clothing suitable for the weather conditions.
- **Plan for Self-Sufficiency**: Since dispersed camping sites typically lack amenities like restrooms and water sources, bring enough food, water, and supplies to sustain yourself for the duration of your stay. Be prepared for emergencies with a first aid kit and communication devices.
- **Check Fire Restrictions**: Before starting a campfire, check for any fire restrictions or bans in the area. Use existing fire rings if available, or use a portable camp stove for cooking instead.

4. Practice Responsible Camping:

- **Respect Quiet Hours**: Be considerate of other campers and wildlife by observing quiet hours and minimizing noise pollution during the evening and early morning hours.
- **Dispose of Waste Properly**: Pack out all trash and waste, including human waste if no restroom facilities are available. Follow proper waste disposal techniques to prevent contamination of water sources and soil.
- **Leave the Campsite Intact**: Before departing, dismantle any temporary structures, extinguish campfires completely, and leave the campsite in its natural state. Take photos and memories, but leave behind no physical trace of your visit.

Stay in a University / College

Many universities in the USA offer dorm rooms for rent during the summer months, providing budget-friendly accommodation options for travelers, conference attendees, and individuals participating in summer programs or events. Prices for renting dorm rooms can vary depending on the university, location, amenities, and length of stay. Here are some examples of universities that commonly rent out dorm rooms during the summer, along with estimated starting prices:

1. **University of California, Berkeley**:
    - Starting Price: Prices vary depending on the specific dormitory and room type, but rates typically start at around $50 to $100 USD per night for single or double occupancy rooms. Extended stays may be available at discounted weekly or monthly rates.
2. **University of Texas at Austin**:
    - Starting Price: Prices for summer dorm rentals at UT Austin vary depending on the residence hall and room configuration, but rates typically start at around $40 to $80 USD per night for single or double occupancy rooms. Weekly and monthly rates may also be available for longer stays.
3. **University of Washington, Seattle**:
    - Starting Price: Summer housing rates at UW Seattle typically start at around $50 to $100 USD per night for single or double occupancy rooms in residence halls or campus apartments. Discounts may be offered for extended stays or group bookings.
4. **New York University (NYU)**:
    - Starting Price: NYU offers summer housing options at various locations in New York City, with prices starting at around $50 to $150 USD per night for single or double occupancy rooms. Rates may vary depending on the specific residence hall and amenities included.
5. **University of Florida, Gainesville**:
    - Starting Price: Summer housing rates at UF Gainesville typically start at around $30 to $70 USD per night for single or double occupancy rooms in residence halls or apartment-style accommodations. Weekly and monthly rates may be available for longer stays.
6. **Stanford University**:
    - Starting Price: Stanford offers summer housing options for visitors and conference attendees, with prices starting at around $60 to $120 USD per night for single or double occupancy rooms in residence halls or apartments. Rates may vary based on the length of stay and room amenities.

7. **University of Chicago**:
    - Starting Price: Summer dorm rentals at UChicago typically start at around $50 to $100 USD per night for single or double occupancy rooms in residence halls. Discounts may be available for extended stays or group bookings.

Sleep pods, also known as pod hotels or capsule hotels, offer compact and budget-friendly accommodations for travelers seeking a no-frills place to rest and recharge. While sleep pods are not as common in the USA as they are in some other countries, there are a few options available in select cities. Here are some examples of places where you can find sleep pods in the USA, along with estimated starting prices:

1. **PodShare** (Los Angeles, California):
    - Starting Price: PodShare offers sleep pod accommodations in communal living spaces, with prices starting at around $50 to $70 USD per night. Guests have access to shared amenities such as bathrooms, kitchens, and common areas.
2. **The Pod Hotel** (New York City, New York):
    - Starting Price: The Pod Hotel in New York City offers compact pod-style rooms with shared bathrooms, with prices starting at around $100 to $150 USD per night. The hotel also offers private rooms with en suite bathrooms for a higher rate.
3. **The Jane Hotel** (New York City, New York):
    - Starting Price: The Jane Hotel offers "Captain's Cabins," which are small, cabin-style rooms with shared bathrooms, with prices starting at around $100 to $150 USD per night. The hotel's unique nautical-themed decor adds to the charm of the experience.
4. **The Crash Pad** (Chattanooga, Tennessee):
    - Starting Price: The Crash Pad is a boutique hostel that offers sleep pod accommodations in a communal setting, with prices starting at around $30 to $50 USD per night. Guests have access to shared bathrooms, kitchen facilities, and common areas.
5. **Freehand Los Angeles** (Los Angeles, California):
    - Starting Price: Freehand Los Angeles offers bunk bed accommodations in shared dormitories, with prices starting at around $50 to $70 USD per night. While not traditional sleep pods, these bunk bed setups provide a budget-friendly option for solo travelers or small groups.

How to get last-minute discounts on owner rented properties

In addition to Airbnb, you can also find owner rented rooms and apartments on www.vrbo.com or HomeAway or a host of others.

Nearly all owners renting accommodation will happily give renters a "last-minute" discount to avoid the space sitting empty, not earning a dime.

Go to Airbnb or another platform and put in today's date. Once you've found something you like start the negotiating by asking for a 25% reduction. A sample message to an Airbnb host might read:

Dear HOST NAME,

I love your apartment. It looks perfect for me. Unfortunately, I'm on a very tight budget. I hope you won't be offended, but I wanted to ask if you would be amenable to offering me a 25% discount for tonight, tomorrow and the following day? I see that you aren't booked. I can assure you, I will leave your place exactly the way I found it. I will put bed linen in the washer and ensure everything is clean for the next guest. I would be delighted to bring you a bottle of wine to thank you for any discount that you could offer.

If this sounds okay, please send me a custom offer, and I will book straight away.

YOUR NAME.

In my experience, a polite, genuine message like this, that proposes reciprocity will be successful 80% of the time. Don't ask for more than 25% off, this person still has to pay the bills and will probably say no as your stay will cost them more in bills than they make. Plus starting higher, can offend the owner and do you want to stay somewhere, where you have offended the host?

In Practice
To use either of these methods, you must travel light. Less stuff means greater mobility, everything is faster and you don't have to check-in or store luggage. If you have a lot of luggage, you're going to have fewer of these opportunities to save on accommodation. Plus travelling light benefits the planet - you're buying, consuming, and transporting less stuff.

Blind-booking
If your risk tolerance does not allow for last-minute booking, you can use blind-booking. Many hotels not wanting to cheapen their brand with known low-prices, choose to operate a blind booking policy. This is where you book without knowing the name of the hotel you're going to stay in until you've made the payment. This is also sometimes used as a marketing strategy where the hotel is seeking to recover from past issues. I've stayed in plenty of blind book hotels. As long as you choose 4 or 5 star hotels, you will find them to be clean, comfortable and safe. priceline.com, Hot Rate® Hotels and Top Secret

Hotels (operated by lastminute.com) offer the best deals.

Hotels.com Loyalty Program
This is currently the best hotel loyalty program with hotels in USA. The basic premise is you collect 10 nights and get 1 free. hotels.com price match, so if booking.com has a cheaper price you can get hotel.com, to match. If you intend to travel more than ten nights in a year, its a great choice to get the 11th free.

Don't let time use you.
Rigidity will cost you money. You pay the price you're willing to pay, not the amount it requires a hotel to deliver. Therefore if you're in town for a big event, saving money on accommodation is nearly impossible so in such cases book three months ahead.

How to trick travel Algorithms to get the lowest hotel price

Do not believe anyone who says changing your IP address to get cheaper hotels or flights does NOT work. If you don't believe us, download a Tor Network and search for flights and hotels to one destination using your current IP and then the tor network (a tor browser hides your IP address from algorithms. It is commonly used by hackers). You will receive different prices.

The price you see is a decision made by an algorithm that adjusts prices using data points such as past bookings, remaining capacity, average demand and the probability of selling the room or flight later at a higher price. If knows you've searched for the area before ip the prices high. To circumvent this, you can either use a different IP address from a cafe or airport or data from an international sim. I use a sim from Three, which provides free data in many countries around the world. When you search from a new IP address, most of the time, and particularly near booking you will get a lower price. Sometimes if your sim comes from a 'rich' country, say the UK or USA, you will see higher rates as the algorithm has learnt people from these countries pay more. The solution is to book from a local wifi connection - but a different one from the one you originally searched from.

Saving money on Food in the USA

Saving money on food in the USA requires a combination of smart grocery shopping, dining out strategically, and taking advantage of discounts and deals. By following these tips and developing good spending habits, you can reduce your food expenses significantly while still enjoying delicious and satisfying meals. Remember that every dollar saved on food can contribute to a healthier financial future.

Use Too Good to Go and other food waste apps

In the United States, food waste is a significant issue, with estimates suggesting that around 30% to 40% of the food supply is wasted each year. This amounts to roughly 133 billion pounds of food, valued at over $160 billion, going to waste annually. The reasons for food waste are varied and can include factors such as consumer behavior, inefficient food distribution systems, overproduction, cosmetic standards for fruits and vegetables, and inadequate storage and transportation infrastructure. Efforts to reduce food waste, such as educational campaigns, donation programs, and policy initiatives, are ongoing to address this critical issue and promote a more sustainable food system.

An oft-quoted parable is 'There is no such thing as cheap food. Either you pay at the cash registry or the doctor's office'. This dismisses the fact that good nutrition is a choice; we all make every-time we eat. Cheap eats are not confined to hotdogs and kebabs. The great thing about using Too Good To Go is you can eat nutritious food cheaply: fruits, vegetables, fish and nut dishes are a fraction of their supermarket cost.

Japan has the longest life expectancy in the world. A national study by the Japanese Ministry of Internal Affairs and Communications revealed that between January and May 2019, a household of two spent on average ¥65,994 a month, that's $10 per person per day on food. You truly don't need to spend a lot to eat nutritious food. That's a marketing gimmick hawkers of overpriced muesli bars want you to believe.

1. Never buy a bag with less than 4.2 stars. You will be disappointed if you do.
2. Check the bags you want and set alarms according to the sales times. Good bags sell out in seconds.
3. Group bag pick ups together. Go for larger shops/ supermarkets with more than one bag offering. For example a fruits and vegetables bag with a bakery bag etc. if you choose to pick up from shopping centres you can group multiple choices. You pay €16 for 4 bags and easily pick up €100 worth of food in one go.
4. Look at the catch words under the listing. Those with good value and great amount of food are the ones to buy. This means they will give you more than the value professed. So instead of the €12, you can end up with €50.

TGTG Tips

- **Check Popular Urban Areas:**
    - Too Good To Go is often more prevalent in urban areas. Check the app for participating businesses in larger cities or metropolitan areas.
- **Varied Cuisines and Establishments:**
    - Explore a variety of cuisines and establishments. Some users have found great deals on meals, baked goods, and grocery items from different types of businesses.
- **Use During Peak Selling Times:**
    - To maximize the chances of finding a good deal, use the app during peak selling times when businesses are looking to sell their surplus items.
- **Explore Different Times of the Day:**
    - Businesses may have surplus items at different times of the day. Try checking the app at various times to discover different offerings.
- **Frequent Checking:**
    - Too Good To Go operates on a dynamic system where the available offerings can change rapidly. Frequent checking may increase your chances of finding appealing deals.

Here are more of the best food waste apps in the USA, along with everything you need to know to use them effectively:

3. **ResQ Club**: ResQ Club allows users to purchase surplus food from restaurants, cafes, and bakeries at discounted prices. Here's how to use it:
    - Download the ResQ Club app from the App Store or Google Play Store.
    - Sign up for an account and verify your location to see available offers nearby.
    - Browse listings for surplus food from participating businesses, which may include meals, baked goods, and more.
    - Purchase items directly through the app and pick them up at the specified location within the designated time frame.
    - Enjoy high-quality food at a fraction of the cost while helping to combat food waste.
4. **Karma**: Karma connects users with surplus food from restaurants, cafes, and grocery stores at discounted prices. Here's how to use it:

- Download the Karma app from the App Store or Google Play Store.
- Sign up for an account and verify your location to see available offers nearby.
- Browse listings for surplus food from participating businesses, which may include meals, snacks, and beverages.
- Purchase items directly through the app and pick them up at the specified location within the designated time frame.
- Enjoy delicious food while supporting local businesses and reducing food waste in your community.

Michelin Star Restaurants that are affordable

Certainly, here is a list of 50 Michelin-starred restaurants in the USA, organized by state. Along with each restaurant, I've provided a brief description of the food they offer, recommended dishes to order, and approximate average prices per person. Please note that Michelin-starred restaurants' prices can vary based on the time of day, menu options, and seasonal changes, so it's advisable to check the latest prices and make reservations in advance.

California:
- State Bird Provisions (San Francisco)
    - Cuisine: Modern American with a focus on small plates and dim sum.
    - What to Order: Try the State Bird, an ever-changing fried quail dish. Don't miss the inventive dim sum offerings.
    - Average Price: $50 - $80 per person.
- **Al's Place** (San Francisco)
    - Cuisine: Vegetable-focused contemporary American cuisine.
    - What to Order: The smoked trout, chickpea stew, and various seasonal vegetable dishes.
    - Average Price: $60 - $100 per person.
- **Mister Jiu's** (San Francisco)
    - Cuisine: Contemporary Chinese-American with a modern twist.
    - What to Order: The honey walnut prawns, dim sum, and Peking duck.
    - Average Price: $75 - $150 per person.

New York:
- Gotham Bar and Grill (Manhattan)
    - Cuisine: Contemporary American cuisine with a French influence.
    - What to Order: The tuna tartare, roasted chicken, and seasonal desserts.
    - Average Price: $38 - $125 for lunch, $115 - $165 for dinner.
- **Cafe China** (Manhattan)
    - Cuisine: Authentic Sichuan cuisine.

- - What to Order: Dan dan noodles, kung pao chicken, and mapo tofu.
    - Average Price: $25 - $50 per person.
  - Sushi Yasuda (Manhattan)
    - Cuisine: High-quality sushi and sashimi.
    - What to Order: Chef's choice omakase menu.
    - Average Price: $150 - $300 per person.

Chicago:
- Parachute (Chicago)
  - Cuisine: Korean-American fusion with a focus on sharing plates.
  - What to Order: The bing bread, dumplings, and fried chicken.
  - Average Price: $40 - $75 per person.
- **El Ideas** (Chicago)
  - Cuisine: Innovative and intimate tasting menu experience.
  - What to Order: The ever-changing tasting menu.
  - Average Price: $175 - $225 per person.

Washington, D.C.:
- **Bresca** (Washington, D.C.)
  - Cuisine: Modern American with a Mediterranean influence.
  - What to Order: The honey butter chicken, roasted lamb, and inventive desserts.
  - Average Price: $50 - $90 per person.
- **Kinship** (Washington, D.C.)
  - Cuisine: Contemporary American with a focus on seasonality.
  - What to Order: The roasted chicken, dry-aged duck, and seasonal vegetable dishes.
  - Average Price: $75 - $125 per person.

Massachusetts:
- Craigie on Main (Cambridge)
  - Cuisine: Contemporary French-American.
  - What to Order: The burger, roasted chicken, and seasonal tasting menus.
  - Average Price: $50 - $100 per person.
- Gourmet Dumpling House (Boston)
  - Cuisine: Authentic Chinese cuisine with a focus on dumplings.
  - What to Order: The soup dumplings, pan-fried dumplings, and scallion pancakes.
  - Average Price: $10 - $25 per person.

Nevada:
- Bazaar Meat by José Andrés (Las Vegas)
  - Cuisine: A carnivore's paradise with a modern Spanish twist.
  - What to Order: The grilled meats, suckling pig, and creative tapas.
  - Average Price: $75 - $150 per person for dinner.
- Joël Robuchon (Las Vegas)
  - Cuisine: French haute cuisine.
  - What to Order: The degustation menu showcasing French classics.
  - Average Price: Expensive, often exceeding $200 per person for dinner.

Hawaii:
- MW Restaurant (Honolulu)
  - Cuisine: Hawaiian and global fusion.
  - What to Order: Ahi poke, loco moco, and innovative desserts.
  - Average Price: $30 - $60 per person for lunch or dinner.
- Vintage Cave Café (Honolulu)

- Cuisine: Contemporary French-Japanese fusion.
- What to Order: The chef's tasting menu featuring seasonal ingredients.
- Average Price: $150 - $250 per person for dinner.

Texas:
- The Pit Room (Houston)
  - Cuisine: Barbecue with a Texas flair.
  - What to Order: Brisket, pork ribs, and smoked sausage.
  - Average Price: $10 - $20 per person for barbecue dishes.
- Bib Gourmand Restaurants (Austin)
  - Cuisine: Various affordable options with high-quality dining experiences. Examples include **Buenos Aires Café**, **Foreign & Domestic**, and **Launderette**.
  - Average Price: Varies by restaurant but generally more affordable.

These are just a few examples of Michelin-starred or Bib Gourmand restaurants in various states. Prices can fluctuate, so it's recommended to check the latest menus and prices before visiting.

Crazy Dining Experiences

Unusual restaurants can provide a unique and memorable dining experience without breaking the bank. Here are some unusual restaurants in the USA with low prices, along with descriptions, recommended dishes, average prices, and reasons to visit:

- **Dick's Last Resort** (Multiple Locations):
    - Description: Known for its intentionally rude and sarcastic staff, Dick's offers a humorous and unconventional dining experience. The waitstaff may insult you in a playful manner.
    - What to Order: Enjoy classic American comfort food like burgers, BBQ, and seafood.
    - Average Price: $15 - $30 per person.
    - Why Visit: Dick's Last Resort is a great place for a fun and light-hearted meal. The humorous atmosphere and unique service make it a memorable experience.
- **SafeHouse** (Chicago, IL, and Milwaukee, WI):
    - Description: A spy-themed restaurant where you need a password to enter, complete with hidden rooms, gadgets, and secret agent decor.
    - What to Order: Classic American dishes, such as burgers, sandwiches, and spy-themed cocktails.
    - Average Price: $15 - $30 per person.
    - Why Visit: The mysterious ambiance and interactive elements make dining at SafeHouse an exciting and family-friendly experience.
- **Heart Attack Grill** (Las Vegas, NV):
    - Description: A medically themed restaurant with staff dressed as doctors and nurses. The menu features enormous, high-calorie burgers and unhealthy comfort food.
    - What to Order: Try the Quadruple Bypass Burger or the Flatliner Fries.
    - Average Price: $20 - $40 per person.
    - Why Visit: While not recommended for health-conscious diners, it's a tongue-in-cheek dining experience that leans into its theme with indulgent comfort food.
- **Modern Toilet** (Los Angeles, CA):
    - Description: A bathroom-themed restaurant where diners sit on toilets and eat from dishes shaped like urinals and bathtubs.
    - What to Order: Taiwanese hot pot and ice cream served in toilet bowl-shaped dishes.
    - Average Price: $15 - $30 per person.
    - Why Visit: It's a quirky and Instagram-worthy experience that adds a touch of humor to your meal.
- **Big Jud's** (Boise, ID):
    - Description: Known for its massive burgers and over-the-top food challenges, Big Jud's is a paradise for burger lovers.
    - What to Order: The Big Jud's Challenge burger or their classic double cheeseburger.
    - Average Price: $10 - $20 per person.
    - Why Visit: If you're a fan of enormous portions and hearty burgers, Big Jud's offers a memorable and budget-friendly dining experience.
- **The Red Bar** (Grayton Beach, FL):

- Description: A quirky, eclectic dive bar with walls covered in dollar bills and a laid-back atmosphere.
- What to Order: Seafood dishes, including their famous seafood gumbo.
- Average Price: $15 - $30 per person.
- Why Visit: The Red Bar has a unique charm and a fun, casual vibe, making it a favorite among locals and tourists alike.
- **The Trailer Park Lounge & Grill** (New York City, NY):
  - Description: A trailer park-themed restaurant with kitschy decor, including vintage trailers inside the restaurant.
  - What to Order: Classic American comfort food like burgers, hot dogs, and tater tots.
  - Average Price: $15 - $30 per person.
  - Why Visit: It's a nostalgic and light-hearted experience in the heart of Manhattan, offering a break from the city's hustle and bustle.

Dining Out Wisely

- **Lunch Specials and Early Bird Menus**
  - Many restaurants offer discounted lunch specials and early bird menus. Dining during off-peak hours can lead to significant savings.
- **Share Large Portions**
  - Restaurants often serve generous portions. Consider sharing a dish with a friend or taking leftovers home for another meal.
- **BYOB (Bring Your Own Bottle)**
  - Some restaurants allow you to bring your own alcohol, which can save a considerable amount compared to ordering drinks from the menu.
- **Take Advantage of Rewards Programs**
  - Join restaurant loyalty programs to earn discounts, free meals, or special promotions. Many chain restaurants offer rewards apps.
- **Avoid Appetizers and Desserts**
  - Appetizers and desserts can significantly increase your restaurant bill. Skip them or share if you want to indulge.
- **Order Water**
  - Opt for tap water instead of ordering expensive beverages like soda or alcoholic drinks.
- **Use Discount Apps**
  - Utilize apps like Groupon, Yelp, or Restaurant.com to find deals and discounts at local restaurants.

Maximizing Discounts and Deals

- **Use Cashback Credit Cards**
  - Consider using credit cards that offer cashback or rewards for grocery store and dining purchases. These cards can help you save money over time.
- **Take Advantage of Student and Senior Discounts**
  - If eligible, make sure to ask about student or senior discounts at restaurants and grocery stores.
- **Join Wholesale Clubs**

- Warehouse clubs like Costco and Sam's Club offer discounted groceries and bulk items to members.
- **Follow Social Media and Email Lists**
    - Many restaurants and grocery stores announce special promotions and discounts through social media and email newsletters. Follow and subscribe to stay updated.
- **Participate in Cashback and Rewards Programs**
    - Several apps and websites offer cashback and rewards for dining and grocery shopping. Examples include Rakuten, Ibotta, and Fetch Rewards.
- **Consider Meal Subscription Services**
    - Meal subscription services like Blue Apron or HelloFresh can save you money by eliminating food waste and preventing unnecessary grocery purchases.
- **Buy in Bulk During Sales**
    - When grocery stores have sales on non-perishable items you frequently use, stock up to save money in the long run.
- **Shop Online**
    - Online grocery shopping can offer competitive prices and exclusive deals. Look for free shipping promotions and online-only discounts.
- **Price Matching**
    - Some stores offer price matching, allowing you to get the lowest price available for a specific item. Be sure to check the store's policy.

Buffets

The USA is home to a variety of buffet chains, each offering its own unique dining experience. Here are some of the best buffet chains in the USA:

1. **Golden Corral**: Golden Corral is one of the largest buffet chains in the USA, known for its extensive selection of American comfort food favorites. From hearty breakfast options to savory meats, salads, and desserts, Golden Corral offers something for everyone.
2. **Buffet City**: Buffet City is a popular Chinese buffet chain with locations across the USA. It offers a wide array of Chinese dishes, including stir-fries, sushi, seafood, and traditional favorites like General Tso's chicken and sweet and sour pork.
3. **Hometown Buffet**: Hometown Buffet is a family-friendly buffet chain that specializes in classic American cuisine. Guests can enjoy a variety of homestyle dishes, including fried chicken, mashed potatoes, macaroni and cheese, and more.
4. **Sweet Tomatoes**: Sweet Tomatoes, also known as Souplantation in some regions, is a buffet chain that focuses on fresh salads, soups, and baked goods. With a salad bar featuring a variety of fresh ingredients and homemade dressings, Sweet Tomatoes offers a healthy and flavorful dining experience.
5. **Cici's Pizza**: Cici's Pizza is a popular buffet chain specializing in all-you-can-eat pizza, pasta, salads, and desserts. Guests can enjoy a wide selection of pizza flavors, from classic pepperoni to specialty options like buffalo chicken and macaroni and cheese.
6. **Old Country Buffet**: Old Country Buffet offers a homestyle dining experience with a focus on comfort food classics. Guests can enjoy a variety of dishes, including fried chicken, meatloaf, mashed potatoes, and gravy, as well as a selection of salads, soups, and desserts.
7. **Ryan's**: Ryan's is a buffet chain offering a wide selection of American comfort food favorites, including fried chicken,

barbecue ribs, and macaroni and cheese. Guests can also enjoy a salad bar, dessert bar, and other buffet staples.

Sure, here's a detailed guide to saving money at buffets in the USA:

8. **Look for Discounts and Coupons**: Many buffets offer discounts and coupons to attract customers. Check the buffet's website, social media pages, and coupon websites for any available deals. Look for promotions such as early bird specials, weekday discounts, or coupons for discounted or free meals.
9. **Join Rewards Programs**: Some buffets have loyalty or rewards programs that offer perks such as discounts, free meals, or birthday rewards. Sign up for these programs to take advantage of exclusive offers and savings. Be sure to provide your email address or phone number to receive promotional offers and updates.
10. **Visit During Off-Peak Hours**: Buffet prices often vary depending on the time of day and day of the week. To save money, consider visiting buffets during off-peak hours, such as mid-week or during non-meal times. You may find lower prices or special discounts during these times.
11. **Share Plates**: If you're dining with others, consider sharing plates or ordering one meal to split between multiple people. Buffets often charge per person, so sharing plates can help reduce the overall cost of your meal.
12. **Limit Beverages**: Buffets may offer unlimited beverages such as soda, juice, or alcohol for an additional charge. To save money, consider sticking to water or opting for free beverages if available.

What to know about USA Fast Food Chains

Here are some of the cheapest restaurant chains in the USA, along with their pros and cons:

- McDonald's:
    - **Pros:**
        - Extremely affordable menu with dollar menu options.
        - Consistent taste and quality across locations.
        - Extensive menu with options for breakfast, burgers, and more.
    - **Cons:**
        - Limited healthy menu choices.
- Taco Bell:
    - **Pros:**
        - Affordable and diverse menu with a wide variety of Mexican-inspired options.
        - Regular promotions and discounts.
        - Late-night hours at many locations.
    - **Cons:**
        - Not considered very healthy due to high sodium content.
- Subway:
    - **Pros:**
        - Customizable sandwiches and salads.
        - Many locations offer value deals and discounts.
        - Healthy options with fresh veggies.
    - **Cons:**
        - Prices can vary by location.
- Dollar Tree's $1 Menu:
    - **Pros:**
        - Everything on the menu is priced at $1.
        - Limited but affordable options.
        - Various snacks and beverages available.
    - **Cons:**
        - Limited selection of fresh and hot food items.
- Little Caesars:
    - **Pros:**
        - Known for its $5 Hot-N-Ready pizzas.
        - Quick service.
        - Various pizza options.
    - **Cons:**
        - Limited menu diversity.
- Domino's:
    - **Pros:**
        - Regular deals and discounts, including their $7.99 carryout special.
        - Wide variety of pizza choices.
        - Online ordering with tracking.

- Wendy's:
  - Cons:
    - Prices can add up with additional toppings and delivery charges.
    - Some may find it less affordable compared to other options.
  - Pros:
    - Affordable value menu items.
    - Fresh, never frozen beef for burgers.
    - Healthy and lighter options available.
  - Cons:
    - Prices for premium items can be higher.
    - Limited breakfast menu at some locations.
- Burger King:
  - Pros:
    - Value menu offers affordable choices.
    - Whopper deals and promotions.
    - Wide range of burger options.
  - Cons:
    - Prices for specialty burgers and combos can be higher.
- KFC (Kentucky Fried Chicken):
  - Pros:
    - Frequent bucket deals and value menu options.
    - Signature fried chicken.
    - Variety of sides and biscuits.
  - Cons:
    - Not considered very healthy due to fried food options.
    - Prices for larger meals can add up.

A note on processed food

Here are some food chemicals commonly found in processed foods in the USA, along with potential health risks:

1. **Artificial Sweeteners (e.g., Aspartame, Saccharin, Sucralose):**
   - Health Risks: Concerns have been raised about artificial sweeteners' potential effects on metabolism, gut health, and even their association with certain cancers. Some studies suggest a link between artificial sweeteners and increased appetite, leading to overeating.
   - Advice: Moderation is key. It's best to limit consumption of foods and beverages containing artificial sweeteners and opt for natural sweeteners like stevia or honey when possible.
2. **Trans Fats (Partially Hydrogenated Oils):**
   - Health Risks: Trans fats are associated with an increased risk of heart disease, stroke, and type 2 diabetes by raising LDL (bad) cholesterol levels and lowering HDL (good) cholesterol levels.
   - Advice: Avoid foods containing partially hydrogenated oils, such as some margarines, fried foods, and baked goods. Choose foods with healthier fats like olive oil, avocado, and nuts.
3. **High-Fructose Corn Syrup (HFCS):**

- Health Risks: Excessive consumption of HFCS has been linked to obesity, insulin resistance, and an increased risk of metabolic syndrome. It may also contribute to liver disease and inflammation.
- Advice: Limit intake of foods and beverages high in HFCS, such as sodas, sweetened fruit juices, and processed snacks. Opt for whole fruits and water instead.

4. **Artificial Food Colorings (e.g., Red 40, Yellow 5, Blue 1):**
- Health Risks: Some artificial food colorings have been associated with hyperactivity in children, allergic reactions, and potential carcinogenic effects. Additionally, certain food colorings may exacerbate symptoms in individuals with attention deficit hyperactivity disorder (ADHD).
- Advice: Choose foods without artificial colorings whenever possible. Look for natural alternatives or foods with no added colors.

5. **Sodium Nitrite and Nitrate:**
- Health Risks: Sodium nitrite and nitrate are commonly used as preservatives in processed meats like bacon, hot dogs, and deli meats. Excessive consumption may increase the risk of certain cancers, such as colorectal cancer.
- Advice: Limit intake of processed meats and choose fresh, whole foods whenever possible. Look for nitrite-free or nitrate-free options, or those with reduced sodium content.

6. **MSG (Monosodium Glutamate):**
- Health Risks: MSG is a flavor enhancer commonly used in processed foods, restaurant meals, and packaged snacks. While MSG sensitivity (referred to as Chinese Restaurant Syndrome) is rare, some individuals may experience symptoms such as headaches, nausea, and flushing.
- Advice: Be mindful of foods containing MSG, especially if you're sensitive to its effects. Opt for homemade meals using natural seasonings and herbs for flavor.

The Cheapest Supermarket in USA

Here's a chart of some of the cheapest supermarket chains in the USA, along with their pros and cons:

Supermarket Chain	Pros	Cons
Aldi	- Extremely competitive prices.	- Limited selection of brands and products
	- No-frills shopping experience.	- Smaller store layout.
	- Private label products are budget-friendly.	Limited fresh produce variety.
	- Frequent special buys and seasonal items.	Minimal customer service.
Walmart	- Wide selection of products.	- Inconsistent store experiences.
	- Everyday low prices on many items.	- Crowded stores and long checkout lines.
	- Offers grocery pickup and delivery.	- Limited organic and specialty options.
	- Rollback and clearance discounts.	- Quality may vary on some items.
Costco	- Bulk purchasing can lead to savings.	- Requires a membership fee.
	- High-quality private label products.	- Limited brand selection.
	- Variety of departments (e.g., electronics).	Bulk packaging may not suit all shoppers.
	- Rotating selection of unique items.	Warehouse-style shopping experience.
WinCo Foods	- Employee-owned, which can lead to lower prices.	Limited store locations in the USA.
	- No-frills shopping experience.	Self-bagging required, which can be a hassle.
	- Competitive prices on bulk items.	Limited fresh and specialty items.
Lidl	- Offers private label products at low prices.	Limited store presence in the USA.
	- Frequent weekly deals and special buys.	Smaller selection compared to larger chains.
	- High-quality fresh produce.	Limited non-grocery selection.
Save-A-Lot	- Focuses on budget-friendly products.	Limited fresh produce and deli options.
	- Simple store layout for easy shopping.	Smaller store size and variety.
	- Accepts SNAP benefits.	Limited organic and specialty selections.
Food 4 Less	- Low prices on a wide range of products.	Limited store locations in the USA.
	- Discounted brand-name products.	May not offer the same quality as premium stores.
	- Fresh produce and meat departments.	Smaller selection of specialty items.

Food Trucks

Eating at food trucks and street vendors in the USA can be a delightful and budget-friendly culinary experience, offering a wide variety of flavors and cuisines. Here's a guide to help you make the most of your street food adventure:

- **Use Food Truck Apps:**
  - Utilize food truck apps or websites like Roaming Hunger or Street Food Finder. These platforms often provide real-time locations, menus, and reviews for various food trucks in specific areas.
- **Look for Busy Trucks:**
  - A line of customers often indicates a popular and well-regarded food truck. If locals are willing to wait, it's usually a good sign.
- **Bring Cash:**
  - While some food trucks accept cards, it's a good idea to carry cash, as not all vendors have card payment options. Small bills can be convenient for transactions.

20 must try cheap eats from trucks

The United States is a vast and diverse country with a rich culinary landscape. Here are 20 must-try cheap eats with some background on each and tips on where to find them:

- **Hot Dog:**
  - **History:** Hot dogs have been a staple of American street food for decades. Originating from German immigrants, they became popular in the early 20th century.
  - **Tip:** Try a classic New York-style hot dog from Gray's Papaya in New York City.
- **Pizza Slice:**
  - **History:** Pizza has Italian roots, but the American pizza slice, particularly New York-style, has become iconic worldwide.
  - **Tip:** Grab a classic New York slice from Joe's Pizza in Greenwich Village, NYC.
- **Cheesesteak:**
  - **History:** Originating in Philadelphia, the cheesesteak features thinly sliced beefsteak with melted cheese in a roll.
  - **Tip:** Head to Pat's King of Steaks or Geno's Steaks in Philly for an authentic experience.
- **Burger:**
  - **History:** The classic American burger needs no introduction. It's a symbol of American fast food.
  - **Tip:** Try the In-N-Out Burger in California for a West Coast classic.
- **Buffalo Wings:**
  - **History:** Created in Buffalo, New York, Buffalo wings are deep-fried and coated in a tangy hot sauce.
  - **Tip:** Anchor Bar in Buffalo claims to be the birthplace of Buffalo wings.
- **Clam Chowder in a Bread Bowl:**

- **History:** Clam chowder in a bread bowl is a hearty soup with origins in the New England region.
- **Tip:** Boudin Bakery in San Francisco is famous for its sourdough bread bowls with clam chowder.
- **Barbecue Ribs:**
    - **History:** BBQ ribs are a Southern staple, slow-cooked and slathered in flavorful barbecue sauce.
    - **Tip:** Head to Franklin Barbecue in Austin, Texas, for renowned smoked brisket and ribs.
- **Tacos:**
    - **History:** Tacos have Mexican origins but are beloved in the U.S. with various regional styles.
    - **Tip:** Try authentic street tacos from La Taqueria in San Francisco.
- **Gumbo:**
    - **History:** Gumbo is a Louisiana Creole soup with a mix of influences from African, French, and Spanish cuisines.
    - **Tip:** Enjoy gumbo at Mother's Restaurant in New Orleans.
- **Lobster Roll:**
    - **History:** The lobster roll is a classic New England dish, featuring lobster meat in a buttered roll.
    - **Tip:** Visit Red's Eats in Maine for a renowned lobster roll experience.
- **Philly Soft Pretzel:**
    - **History:** Soft pretzels have German roots but are a popular snack, especially in Philadelphia.
    - **Tip:** Get a fresh pretzel from Philly Pretzel Factory in Philadelphia.
- **Chili:**
    - **History:** Chili is a hearty stew that has been embraced across the U.S., often served with cheese and onions.
    - **Tip:** Ben's Chili Bowl in Washington, D.C., is famous for its chili half-smoke.
- **Pulled Pork Sandwich:**
    - **History:** Pulled pork sandwiches are a barbecue favorite, especially in the Southern states.
    - **Tip:** Central BBQ in Memphis is known for its delicious pulled pork sandwiches.
- **Gyros:**
    - **History:** Gyros, with Greek origins, feature seasoned meat (often lamb) in a pita with veggies and tzatziki.
    - **Tip:** The Halal Guys in New York City are famous for their gyros.
- **Cuban Sandwich:**
    - **History:** The Cuban sandwich is a Floridian favorite with ham, roast pork, Swiss cheese, pickles, mustard, and sometimes salami.
    - **Tip:** Try the original Cuban sandwich at Columbia Restaurant in Tampa.
- **Jambalaya:**
    - **History:** Jambalaya is a Louisiana Creole dish with a mix of rice, meats, and vegetables.
    - **Tip:** Coop's Place in New Orleans serves a delicious jambalaya.
- **Fish Tacos:**
    - **History:** Fish tacos, inspired by Mexican cuisine, feature battered and fried fish in a tortilla with toppings.
    - **Tip:** Enjoy fish tacos at Oscar's Mexican Seafood in San Diego.
- **Chicago-Style Hot Dog:**

- **History:** The Chicago-style hot dog is loaded with toppings, including mustard, onions, relish, tomatoes, pickles, sport peppers, and celery salt.
  - **Tip:** Portillo's is a popular chain in Chicago for its classic hot dogs.
- **Chicken and Waffles:**
  - **History:** Chicken and waffles, a Southern comfort food, combines crispy fried chicken with sweet waffles.
  - **Tip:** Roscoe's House of Chicken and Waffles in Los Angeles is an iconic spot

Cheapest Happy hour chains

There are widely recognized restaurant and bar chains in the USA that have been known for offering Happy Hour specials. Keep in mind that Happy Hour deals are subject to change, and it's always a good idea to check with specific locations for the latest information. Here are a few chains that have historically offered Happy Hour promotions:

- **Applebee's:**
  - Applebee's is a casual dining restaurant chain known for its American cuisine. Some locations offer Happy Hour deals on drinks and appetizers.
- **Chili's:**
  - Chili's Grill & Bar is a popular chain offering Tex-Mex-inspired dishes. Many Chili's locations have Happy Hour specials with discounted drinks and appetizers.
- **TGI Fridays:**
  - TGI Fridays is a well-known chain that often features Happy Hour promotions with discounted drinks and appetizers.
- **Buffalo Wild Wings:**
  - Buffalo Wild Wings, known for its sports-bar atmosphere, frequently offers Happy Hour deals on wings and select drinks.
- **Olive Garden:**
  - Olive Garden, an Italian-American restaurant chain, occasionally offers Happy Hour specials, including discounted drinks.
- **Red Lobster:**
  - Red Lobster, a seafood restaurant chain, may offer Happy Hour promotions on certain days, including drink and appetizer specials.
- **Outback Steakhouse:**
  - Outback Steakhouse, specializing in Australian-themed cuisine, may have occasional Happy Hour specials on drinks and appetizers.
- **Ruby Tuesday:**
  - Ruby Tuesday is a casual dining restaurant chain that has been known to offer Happy Hour deals on select drinks and appetizers.
- **Bahama Breeze:**
  - Bahama Breeze, a chain known for its Caribbean-inspired menu, often features Happy Hour specials on drinks and appetizers.
- **BJ's Restaurant & Brewhouse:**
  - BJ's is a restaurant and brewery chain that may offer Happy Hour promotions on their craft beers and select appetizers.

USA Food Culture

Some of the largest ancestry groups in the United States include German, Irish, English, Italian, Mexican, and African American, among others. Mexican & Tex-Mex cuisine is ubiquitous across the US, ensuring you're never too far from a restaurant serving up these flavorsome dishes (which often blur the lines between the two). This prevalence isn't surprising, given the significant representation of people of Mexican descent, comprising over 11% of the population. Tacos, burritos, and other quick bites are cherished staples, with snack carts and food trucks serving as popular hubs for people from all walks of life. Fast-casual establishments like Chipotle, specializing in organic Tex-Mex served up swiftly, are among the rapidly expanding chains. Additionally, casual sit-down eateries thrive, with margaritas and chips with salsa almost indispensable to the dining experience.

Barbecue holds a prominent place in American culinary culture. While it reigns supreme in the South, the aroma of smoky, tender meat wafts from San Francisco to New York City. The tradition of American barbecue spans centuries, with its roots deeply embedded in the nation's culinary heritage.

The United States is a melting pot of cultures, and this is vividly reflected in its food culture. From the seafood specialties of New England to the barbecue traditions of Texas, each state boasts its own unique flavors and culinary history. This article delves into the iconic dishes of several key states, uncovering the stories behind them and offering tips on how to enjoy these foods on a budget.

New England (Maine, Massachusetts)

Common Dishes and Histories: Lobster rolls and clam chowder are quintessential New England dishes. Maine's cold Atlantic waters are perfect for lobsters, making the lobster roll a summer staple. Clam chowder, particularly the creamy New England variety, has its roots in the region's fishing culture.

Budget Tips: Enjoy these seafood delights at local fish markets or roadside stands rather than upscale restaurants. Visiting during the off-season can also lead to lower prices.

The South (Louisiana, Georgia)

Common Dishes and Histories: Louisiana is famous for its Creole and Cajun cuisines, with dishes like gumbo and jambalaya that reflect its French, African, and Spanish heritage. Georgia is known for its soul food, with classics like peach cobbler and fried chicken that have deep roots in African American culture.

Budget Tips: Look for local eateries or food festivals where you can sample these dishes at lower prices. Many Southern towns also have culinary schools where students run restaurants, offering high-quality food at a fraction of the cost.

Midwest (Illinois, Wisconsin)

Common Dishes and Histories: Illinois, particularly Chicago, is famous for its deep-dish pizza, a hearty version of the Italian classic. Wisconsin, known as "America's Dairyland," prides itself on cheese, contributing to dishes like cheese curds and beer cheese soup.

Budget Tips: For deep-dish pizza, consider sharing a pie with friends, as portions are often generous. Farmers' markets in Wisconsin are great places to sample local cheeses at lower prices.

Southwest (Texas, New Mexico)

Common Dishes and Histories: Texas is synonymous with barbecue, especially brisket, a tradition that combines Native American and cowboy influences. New Mexico's cuisine is known for its use of chile peppers, with dishes like green chile stew highlighting Native American and Spanish flavors.

Budget Tips: In Texas, look for barbecue joints off the beaten path for authentic flavors at lower prices. In New Mexico, local diners and food trucks offer delicious and affordable chile dishes.

West Coast (California, Oregon)

Common Dishes and Histories: California cuisine emphasizes fresh, local ingredients, with dishes like California rolls (sushi) and farm-to-table fare. Oregon is famous for its artisanal foods, including craft beers and pinot noir, thanks to its rich agricultural land.

Budget Tips: In California, farmers' markets are your best bet for affordable, fresh food. Oregon's breweries and wineries often offer free tastings or tours with affordable tasting menus.

Pacific Northwest (Washington, Alaska)

Common Dishes and Histories: Washington state is known for its seafood, particularly salmon, which is integral to Native American cultures. Alaska's cuisine features wild game and seafood, like king crab, reflecting its rugged landscape and indigenous heritage.

Budget Tips: For fresh seafood in Washington, visit fish markets or docks where you can buy directly from fishermen. In Alaska, eating seasonally can lead to better prices on local specialties.

Always applicable Tips for Getting Discounts
- **Early Bird Specials**: Many restaurants offer early bird specials for diners who eat before peak hours.
- **Happy Hours**: Look for happy hour deals not just on drinks but also on appetizers and meals.
- **Coupons and Apps**: Use coupon books and food apps for discounts at local restaurants.

The United States boasts a rich culinary heritage, with a diverse range of dishes that reflect its multicultural history. One iconic dish is the **Hamburger**, which has its roots in the late 19th and early 20th centuries. Historically, it was the brainchild of German immigrants who brought minced beef to America. However, it was American ingenuity that turned it into the hamburger we know today. In 1904, at the St. Louis World's Fair, the legendary entrepreneur Louis Lassen is said to have placed a ground beef patty between two slices of bread to create a portable, hearty meal. This simple yet beloved creation has since evolved into a symbol of American fast-food culture, with countless regional variations.

Thanksgiving Dinner, a quintessential American feast, has a deep historical and cultural significance. Its origins trace back to the early 17th century when English Pilgrims and Wampanoag Native Americans came together to celebrate a bountiful harvest. This communal meal laid the foundation for the Thanksgiving holiday, which was officially established by President Abraham Lincoln in 1863. Today, a traditional Thanksgiving dinner typically includes roast turkey, stuffing, cranberry sauce, mashed potatoes, and pumpkin pie. It remains a cherished occasion for Americans to express gratitude and come together with family and friends.

Gumbo, a soulful and flavorful stew, is a culinary emblem of Louisiana's Creole and Cajun cultures. With a history deeply rooted in the region's multicultural influences, gumbo combines West African, French, Spanish, and Native American culinary traditions. The dish usually features a rich, dark roux combined with a variety of ingredients, such as okra, seafood, chicken, sausage, or duck. Gumbo's history mirrors the multicultural tapestry of Louisiana and continues to be a cherished and diverse dish throughout the state, often served at gatherings and celebrations.

Clam Chowder, particularly New England Clam Chowder, is a creamy soup with a rich maritime history. Originating in the coastal regions of the Northeast, this dish was initially a staple among fishermen and settlers. The combination of clams, potatoes, onions, and bacon or salt pork provided a hearty and nourishing meal for those living along the rugged coastline. Over the centuries, clam chowder has become a beloved comfort food, with New England and Manhattan clam chowder being the two most recognized regional variations. It symbolizes the enduring connection between coastal communities and their maritime heritage.

Chili, a hearty and spicy stew, has its origins in the American Southwest and Mexican cuisines. While chili con carne, which translates to "chili with meat," is often associated with Texas, its history extends beyond state lines. It's believed that Mexican immigrants introduced chili to Texas in the late 19th century. The dish typically consists of ground or cubed meat (often beef), chili peppers, tomatoes, and spices. Chili has evolved into various regional styles, including Texas, Cincinnati, and New Mexico chili. It reflects the blending of culinary traditions and the enduring love for bold flavors in American cuisine. Chili cook-offs and festivals celebrating this dish remain popular events across the country.

American desserts

American desserts are a delightful reflection of the nation's culinary heritage, drawing inspiration from a variety of cultural influences. Here are some iconic American desserts with their historical backgrounds:

Apple Pie, often referred to as "as American as apple pie," has deep roots in the country's history. Early American settlers brought apple seeds with them, and by the 18th century, apples were widely cultivated. Apple pie quickly became a symbol of home and comfort. The famous phrase "as American as apple pie" was popularized during World War II, highlighting the dessert's role in American culture.

Chocolate Chip Cookies are a beloved treat that emerged in the 1930s thanks to Ruth Wakefield, who ran the Toll House Inn in Massachusetts. She accidentally created the first chocolate chip cookies by adding chopped chocolate to cookie dough, expecting it to melt and create chocolate cookies. The result was the classic combination of soft cookie and gooey chocolate chips, giving rise to a timeless favorite.

Key Lime Pie has its origins in the Florida Keys, where key limes are abundant. The dessert is believed to have been created in the late 19th century, combining key lime juice, sweetened condensed milk, and a graham cracker crust. Key lime pie is not only a delicious dessert but also a culinary symbol of the Sunshine State.

Pecan Pie, a classic Southern dessert, has been enjoyed since the early 19th century. The combination of pecans, sugar, butter, and eggs in a flaky pie crust has deep roots in Southern cuisine, particularly in states like Georgia and Texas. Pecan pie is often associated with Thanksgiving and holiday celebrations.

Cheesecake has a history dating back to ancient Greece but has evolved significantly in the United States. Modern American cheesecake is typically made with cream cheese and a graham cracker crust. New York-style cheesecake, characterized by its dense and creamy texture, gained popularity in the mid-20th century and became an iconic dessert associated with the city.

Ice Cream, although not originally American, holds a special place in American dessert culture. Ice cream parlors and vendors became popular in the 19th century, and the ice cream cone was famously introduced at the 1904 St. Louis World's Fair. Today, the United States is known for its wide variety of ice cream flavors and creative toppings.

These American desserts not only satisfy sweet cravings but also tell a story of culinary evolution and cultural diversity. They have become integral to the American culinary landscape and continue to be enjoyed across the country, reflecting both tradition and innovation in dessert making.

Dining etiquette

Dining in restaurants in the USA comes with its own set of etiquettes and cultural norms. Whether you're a visitor or a local, following these guidelines will help ensure a pleasant dining experience:

1. Making Reservations:

- For upscale or popular restaurants, it's advisable to make reservations in advance, especially during peak dining hours or on weekends. Many restaurants accept reservations online or by phone.

2. Dress Code:

- Dress codes vary from casual to formal, depending on the type of restaurant. It's a good idea to check the dress code on the restaurant's website before dining. In more upscale establishments, business casual attire is often preferred.

3. Seating:

- Wait to be seated. At most restaurants, a host or hostess will greet you and show you to your table.
- If there's a line, wait your turn patiently.

4. Tipping:

- Tipping is a customary practice in the USA. It's customary to leave a tip for the waitstaff, usually around 15-20% of the total bill before taxes.
- Check if the tip is included (gratuity) on your bill, especially for larger parties. If it is, you may not need to leave an additional tip.

5. Water and Bread:

- Complimentary tap water is typically served upon seating, and you can request other beverages from the menu.
- Complimentary bread or rolls are often provided; it's okay to help yourself.

6. Ordering:

- Wait for everyone in your party to be ready before ordering. It's considered polite not to keep the server waiting.
- If you have dietary restrictions or allergies, inform your server, and they can provide guidance or suggest suitable menu items.

7. Sharing:

- Sharing dishes is common and generally accepted. You can order a few different dishes and share with your dining companions.

8. Special Requests:

- Don't hesitate to ask for special requests or modifications to your order, like dressing on the side or substituting ingredients. Most restaurants are accommodating.

9. Table Manners:

- Use utensils appropriately. Forks are generally held in the left hand, and knives in the right while cutting food. After cutting, place the knife down and switch the fork to your right hand.
- Chew with your mouth closed, and avoid talking with food in your mouth.
- Place your napkin on your lap when seated and use it to wipe your mouth as needed.

10. Mobile Phones:

- Keep your phone on silent mode during the meal. It's considered impolite to have loud phone conversations in a restaurant.

11. Waitstaff Interaction:

- Be courteous and respectful to your server. If there are issues with your meal, address them politely and ask for assistance or a replacement dish if needed.

12. Alcohol:

- The legal drinking age in the USA is 21. If you order alcohol, you may be asked to provide identification to prove your age.
- Don't overindulge in alcoholic beverages, especially if you are driving.

13. Dessert and the Check:

- You can order dessert or ask for the check when you're ready to finish your meal.
- It's common for the server to bring the check without you asking when they sense you're done dining. You can then pay at your convenience.

14. Gratitude:

- When you're finished, thank your server for their service. It's a courteous way to show appreciation.

The Best Cheap Eats by State

State	Cheapest Eats	Where to Try Them
Alabama	Biscuits and Gravy	Local diners and breakfast spots
Alaska	Salmon Burgers	Food trucks and local seafood shacks
Arizona	Sonoran Hot Dogs	Street vendors and Sonoran-style hot dog stands
Arkansas	Catfish and Hushpuppies	Southern-style seafood restaurants
California	Tacos	Taquerias, food trucks, and street vendors
Colorado	Green Chile and Breakfast Burritos	Local breakfast spots and Mexican restaurants
Connecticut	New Haven-style Pizza	Pizzerias in New Haven, such as Frank Pepe Pizzeria
Delaware	Scrapple and Egg Sandwiches	Local diners and breakfast joints
Florida	Cuban Sandwiches	Cuban cafes and food trucks
Georgia	Southern Fried Chicken	Fried chicken joints and soul food restaurants
Hawaii	Plate Lunches	Plate lunch spots and food trucks
Idaho	Potato-based Dishes	Local diners and Idaho potato-themed restaurants
Illinois	Chicago-Style Hot Dogs	Hot dog stands and casual eateries
Indiana	Pork Tenderloin Sandwich	Local diners and sandwich shops
Iowa	Loose Meat Sandwich (Maid-Rite)	Maid-Rite diners and local sandwich spots
Kansas	BBQ Burnt Ends	BBQ joints and local smokehouses
Kentucky	Hot Brown	Historic restaurants in Louisville
Louisiana	Po' Boys	Po' Boy shops and casual seafood eateries
Maine	Lobster Roll	Lobster shacks and seafood restaurants
Maryland	Crab Cakes	Seafood restaurants and crab shacks
Massachusetts	Clam Chowder and Lobster Rolls	Seafood shacks and clam chowder stands
Michigan	Coney Dogs	Coney Island diners and local hot dog spots
Minnesota	Juicy Lucy Burgers	Local bars and burger joints
Mississippi	Fried Catfish	Southern-style seafood restaurants
Missouri	St. Louis-Style Pizza (Provel)	Pizzerias in St. Louis, like Imo's Pizza
Montana	Bison Burgers	Local burger joints and diners
Nebraska	Runza	Runza fast-food chain and local eateries
Nevada	Shrimp Cocktail	Local seafood restaurants and buffets
New Hampshire	New England Clam Chowder	Seafood shacks and local diners
New Jersey	Pork Roll (Taylor Ham) Sandwiches	Delis and breakfast spots in New Jersey
New Mexico	Green Chile Cheeseburgers	Local burger joints and diners

New York	Pizza Slices and Hot Dogs	Pizza by the slice stands and hot dog
North Carolina	BBQ Pork Sandwich	BBQ joints and roadside BBQ stands
North Dakota	Knoephla Soup	Local diners and German-style restaurants
Ohio	Cincinnati Chili	Chili parlors and casual eateries
Oklahoma	Chicken Fried Steak	Local diners and Southern-style restaurants
Oregon	Voodoo Doughnuts	Voodoo Doughnut shops and local bakeries
Pennsylvania	Philly Cheesesteak	Cheesesteak stands and sandwich shops
Rhode Island	Rhode Island Clam Cakes	Clam cake shacks and seafood restaurants
South Carolina	Shrimp and Grits	Southern-style restaurants and seafood
South Dakota	Chislic	Local bars and South Dakota-style
Tennessee	Hot Chicken	Hot chicken joints and Southern-style
Texas	Breakfast Tacos and Tex-Mex	Local taquerias and Tex-Mex restaurants
Utah	Fry Sauce and Scones	Local diners and fast-food chains
Vermont	Maple Syrup Pancakes	Pancake houses and breakfast spots
Virginia	Ham Biscuits	Local diners and Southern-style eateries
Washington	Teriyaki	Teriyaki joints and Asian fast-food
West Virginia	Pepperoni Rolls	Local bakeries and sandwich shops

Drinks

Here are some popular chain restaurants in the USA known for their happy hour deals:

1. **Applebee's**: Applebee's offers a "Happy Hour" menu featuring discounted appetizers and drink specials such as discounted cocktails, beers, and non-alcoholic beverages. Prices for appetizers typically range from $5 to $8, while drink specials vary but often start around $3 to $5.
2. **Chili's Grill & Bar**: Chili's "Happy Hour" specials typically include discounted appetizers, cocktails, and draft beers. Prices for appetizers usually range from $5 to $8, while drink specials start at around $3 to $5.
3. **TGI Fridays**: TGI Fridays offers a "Happy Every Hour" menu with discounted appetizers and drink specials. Prices for appetizers typically range from $5 to $8, while drink specials start at around $3 to $5.
4. **Buffalo Wild Wings**: Buffalo Wild Wings' "Happy Hour" features discounted appetizers, beers, and cocktails. Prices for appetizers usually range from $5 to $8, while drink specials start at around $3 to $5.
5. **Outback Steakhouse**: Outback Steakhouse offers a "Happy Hour" menu with discounted appetizers and drink specials, including discounted beers, wines, and cocktails. Prices for appetizers typically range from $5 to $8, while drink specials start at around $3 to $5.
6. **Red Lobster**: Red Lobster's "Weekday Win" menu offers discounted appetizers and drink specials during select hours. Prices for appetizers generally range from $5 to $8, while drink specials start at around $3 to $5.
7. **Olive Garden**: Olive Garden offers a "Happy Hour" menu with discounted appetizers and drink specials, including discounted wines, beers, and cocktails. Prices for appetizers typically range from $5 to $8, while drink specials start at around $3 to $5.

Tipping

Wait staff in the USA heavily rely on tips as a significant portion of their income. In the United States, the minimum wage for tipped employees is typically lower than the standard minimum wage for non-tipped employees. This lower minimum wage is often referred to as the "tipped minimum wage," and it varies by state but is generally well below the standard minimum wage.

If you wish to eat out without using the services of a server and, consequently, avoid tipping in the USA, you can opt for self-service or fast-casual dining establishments. These types of restaurants typically require minimal or no table service, allowing you to order and enjoy your meal without the expectation of tipping a server. Here are some ways to do this:

- **Fast Food Restaurants:** Fast food establishments, such as McDonald's, Burger King, Taco Bell, and Subway, are designed for quick self-service. You place your order at the counter, collect your food, and usually handle your own drinks, condiments, and disposal of trash.
- **Food Courts:** Many malls and airports have food courts with various eateries where you can order food at the counter and then take care of your meal independently. Tipping is not expected in these self-service environments.
- **Cafeterias:** Cafeterias and self-serve buffet-style restaurants, such as Golden Corral or Sweet Tomatoes, allow you to serve yourself from a selection of dishes. You pay at the register and typically don't need to tip.
- **Order at the Counter:** Some restaurants, even those offering a higher level of cuisine, operate with an order-at-the-counter model. You place your order and pay upfront, eliminating the need for table service and tipping.
- **Food Trucks and Street Food:** Food trucks and street food vendors are self-service by nature. You order your food, pick it up, and usually enjoy it at an outdoor seating area or take it to go. No table service is involved.
- **Fast-Casual Chains:** Some fast-casual chains, like Chipotle or Panera Bread, offer a step-up from traditional fast food but still require customers to order at the counter and collect their own food.
- **Coffee Shops:** Coffee shops, such as Starbucks or Dunkin', typically operate on a self-service model. You order your coffee or other items at the counter, and then you're responsible for adding cream, sugar, and any additional items.
- **Diners:** Some diners have a self-service component, allowing you to order at the counter or from a menu and then handle your own beverage refills and check payment.
- **Dine at Buffets:** Buffet-style restaurants often have a lower tip expectation since you serve yourself. Still, it's customary to leave a small tip (10% to 15%) for the server's assistance and drink refills.

Coffee

The history of coffee in the United States is a fascinating journey that spans centuries, reflecting the evolving tastes and cultural shifts of the nation. Coffee, originally introduced to colonial America in the mid-1600s by European settlers, started as a luxury beverage enjoyed primarily by the upper class. Early coffeehouses, inspired by European counterparts, began to emerge in major cities like Boston, New York, and Philadelphia, serving as hubs for intellectual discourse and business meetings.
During the Revolutionary War era, coffee gained popularity as an alternative to scarce and heavily taxed tea, becoming a patriotic choice. The Continental Army even included coffee in the rations provided to soldiers, solidifying its status as an American staple.

In the 20th century, coffee consumption continued to rise, becoming an integral part of daily life for many Americans. Chain coffee shops like Dunkin' and Starbucks played a significant role in introducing specialty coffee drinks and expanding the coffee culture.

The 21st century brought the emergence of the "third wave" coffee movement, emphasizing artisanal coffee, direct trade relationships, and single-origin beans. Independent coffee roasters and cafes gained popularity, focusing on quality, sustainability, and unique flavor profiles.

Today, coffee remains a thriving industry in the United States, offering a diverse range of options, from specialty espresso drinks to cold brew. The craft coffee movement has led to an increased appreciation for the nuances of coffee flavor, origin, and preparation methods. Coffee shops continue to serve as community gathering spaces, reflecting the enduring and evolving coffee culture in the USA.

Coffee Vendor	Pros	Cons
McDonald's	- Competitive pricing for coffee.	- Limited coffee menu compared to specialty shops.
	- Consistent taste and quality.	- Limited variety of coffee bean options.

Dunkin'	- Nationwide presence for convenience.	- May not offer as many customization options.
	- Affordable coffee and daily specials.	- Quality may vary by location.
	- Wide variety of flavored coffee options.	- Limited seating in some locations.
	- Frequent promotions and loyalty rewards.	- Limited food menu compared to some chains.
7-Eleven	- Low-cost coffee available 24/7.	- Limited selection of premium coffee options.
	- Various coffee flavors and condiments.	- May not have a dedicated coffee shop atmosphere.
	- Consistent pricing across locations.	- Coffee quality may not match specialty shops.
Starbucks	- Offers regular discounts and promotions.	- Generally higher prices compared to others.
	- Wide variety of coffee and beverage options.	Limited free customization options.
	- Consistent quality and branding.	- May have long lines and wait times.
	- Rewards program for loyal customers.	- Limited presence in some areas.
Tim Hortons	- Affordable coffee and value meal deals.	- Limited presence in the USA, more common in Canada.
	- Popular for coffee and baked goods.	- Quality may vary by location.
	- Consistent taste and menu offerings.	- May not offer as many specialty coffee choices.
Local Cafes	- Unique and artisanal coffee offerings.	- Prices can vary widely by location.
	- Supports local businesses and roasters.	- Not as widespread or convenient as chains.
	- Often offer a cozy and inviting atmosphere.	Limited loyalty programs or rewards.

Recap

Saving Measures	Description
Lunch Specials	Opt for lunch specials or early bird menus with lower prices compared to dinner.
Coupons and Deals	Use digital coupons, restaurant loyalty programs, and discount websites/apps for savings.
Sharing Portions	Share large portions or dishes with others to reduce the overall bill.
BYOB (Bring Your Own Bottle)	Choose restaurants that allow you to bring your own alcohol to save on beverage costs.
Takeout and Delivery	Save on dine-in service charges, tipping, and taxes by opting for takeout or delivery.
Daily Deals Apps	Use apps like Groupon, LivingSocial, and Restaurant.com for discounted dining offers.
Rewards Programs	Join restaurant loyalty programs to earn rewards, discounts, and special promotions.
Water Instead of Beverages	Choose tap water instead of ordering costly beverages like soda or alcohol.
Food Truck Exploration	Explore food trucks and street food vendors for budget-friendly dining options.
Become a Taster or Food Critic	Consider participating in food tasting events or becoming a food critic/taster to enjoy meals at a reduced or complimentary cost.
Buffet Timing	Visit buffets during the transition from breakfast to lunch for lower lunch prices and a variety of options.

Urban v Rural

Saving money in rural and urban areas of the USA can involve different strategies due to factors such as cost of living, access to resources, and lifestyle preferences. Here are some key differences:

Saving Money in Urban Areas:

1. **Transportation Costs**:
     - Urban areas often have better public transportation systems, allowing residents to save money on car-related expenses such as gas, insurance, and parking fees. Some urban dwellers may choose to forgo owning a car altogether and rely solely on public transit, biking, or walking.
2. **Housing Costs**:
     - Housing tends to be more expensive in urban areas, with higher rents and property prices. To save money, urban residents may opt for smaller apartments, shared living arrangements, or living in less trendy neighborhoods where housing costs are lower.
3. **Food Expenses**:
     - Urban areas typically offer a wide variety of dining options, including upscale restaurants, trendy cafes, and food delivery services. While convenient, dining out frequently can quickly add up. To save money, urban residents may prioritize cooking at home, meal prepping, or taking advantage of grocery delivery services.
4. **Entertainment and Recreation**:
     - Urban areas offer a wealth of entertainment and recreational activities, from concerts and theater shows to museums and art galleries. While these experiences can be enjoyable, they often come with a price tag. To save money, urban residents may seek out free or low-cost events, explore public parks and green spaces, or participate in community activities.
5. **Health and Wellness**:
     - Urban areas may have higher healthcare costs, including expenses related to health insurance premiums, medical services, and gym memberships. To save money, urban residents may research affordable healthcare options, take advantage of employer-sponsored wellness programs, or explore free fitness activities such as jogging or outdoor yoga classes.

Saving Money in Rural Areas:

1. **Transportation Costs**:
     - Rural areas often have limited public transportation options, making car ownership a necessity for many residents. However, the lower population density can result in shorter commutes and lower overall transportation expenses compared to urban areas.
2. **Housing Costs**:
     - Housing tends to be more affordable in rural areas, with lower rents and property prices. Residents may have the option to purchase larger homes or properties with more land at a lower cost compared to urban areas.
3. **Food Expenses**:

- While rural areas may have fewer dining options compared to urban areas, residents often have access to locally grown produce, farmers' markets, and community-supported agriculture (CSA) programs. To save money, rural residents may prioritize cooking with fresh, locally sourced ingredients and preserving foods through canning or freezing.
4. **Entertainment and Recreation**:
    - Rural areas offer opportunities for outdoor activities such as hiking, fishing, camping, and gardening. These activities can be enjoyed at little to no cost, providing residents with affordable ways to stay active and entertained.
5. **Health and Wellness**:
    - Access to healthcare services may be more limited in rural areas, leading to higher travel costs for medical appointments and specialist care. To save money, rural residents may explore telehealth options, participate in community health initiatives, and focus on preventive care measures.

Itinerary for first time visitor to USA

Here's a first-time itinerary that covers key destinations while keeping costs low:

Day 1-3: New York City, New York

- Accommodation: Stay in a budget-friendly hostel or opt for Airbnb accommodations in Brooklyn or Queens for around $50-$100 per night.
- Attractions:
    - Explore Central Park for free.
    - Take a stroll through Times Square and snap some photos.
    - Walk across the iconic Brooklyn Bridge.
    - Visit the Metropolitan Museum of Art (pay-what-you-wish admission).
    - Enjoy street food and people-watching in Greenwich Village.
- Food: Stick to affordable eats like pizza slices, food trucks, and deli sandwiches for around $10-$15 per meal.

Day 4-6: Washington, D.C.

- Transportation: Take a budget bus or train from NYC to Washington, D.C. for around $30-$50 each way.
- Accommodation: Stay in a hostel or budget hotel near the National Mall for around $40-$80 per night.
- Attractions:
    - Visit the Smithsonian museums (most are free).
    - Explore the National Mall and see iconic landmarks like the Lincoln Memorial and Washington Monument.
    - Take a stroll around the Tidal Basin and see the cherry blossoms (if visiting in spring).
    - Tour the U.S. Capitol (free).
- Food: Dine at food trucks, casual eateries, and affordable ethnic restaurants for around $15-$20 per meal.

Day 7-9: Orlando, Florida

- Transportation: Take a budget flight from D.C. to Orlando for around $100-$150 roundtrip.
- Accommodation: Stay in a budget hotel or Airbnb near the theme parks for around $50-$80 per night.
- Attractions:
    - Visit Universal Studios or Disney Springs for free entertainment.
    - Explore International Drive and enjoy the sights and sounds.
    - Spend a day at a local beach like Cocoa Beach (free).
- Food: Look for affordable dining options outside the theme parks, such as local diners and fast-casual restaurants, for around $15-$25 per meal.

Day 10-12: Las Vegas, Nevada

- Transportation: Take a budget flight from Orlando to Las Vegas for around $100-$150 roundtrip.
- Accommodation: Stay in a budget hotel or hostel on or near the Las Vegas Strip for around $50-$100 per night.
- Attractions:
    - Explore the iconic Las Vegas Strip and see the famous resorts and casinos.
    - Visit the Bellagio Fountains and watch the free fountain show.
    - Check out the Fremont Street Experience for free live entertainment.
    - Take a day trip to Red Rock Canyon (free admission).
- Food: Enjoy affordable buffets, food courts, and off-Strip dining options for around $15-$30 per meal.

A month in the USA for under $1,000

Spending a month in the USA for under $1,000 can be challenging, but with careful planning and budget-friendly choices, it's possible to have a memorable trip. Here's a suggested itinerary for a first-time visitor:

Week 1: Exploring the East Coast

Day 1-3: New York City

- Stay in a budget hostel or opt for couchsurfing to save on accommodation costs.
- Explore free attractions like Central Park, Times Square, and the Staten Island Ferry for views of the Statue of Liberty.
- Enjoy affordable eats from food trucks or grab a slice of pizza from local pizzerias.

Day 4-5: Philadelphia

- Take a bus or train from NYC to Philadelphia to save on transportation costs.
- Visit historical sites like Independence Hall and the Liberty Bell.
- Check out the Reading Terminal Market for delicious and budget-friendly food options.

Day 6-7: Washington, D.C.

- Take a bus or train from Philadelphia to Washington, D.C.
- Explore the National Mall and visit iconic landmarks like the Lincoln Memorial and the Smithsonian museums (many of which offer free admission).
- Wander through the vibrant neighborhoods like Adams Morgan or Dupont Circle.

Week 2: Southern Charm

Day 8-10: Charleston, South Carolina

- Take a bus from Washington, D.C. to Charleston.
- Explore the historic streets of downtown Charleston and visit landmarks like Rainbow Row and the Battery.
- Enjoy budget-friendly Southern cuisine at local diners or barbecue joints.

Day 11-14: Atlanta, Georgia

- Take a bus from Charleston to Atlanta.
- Explore the Martin Luther King Jr. National Historic Site and visit the World of Coca-Cola or the Georgia Aquarium (look for discounted tickets online).
- Check out the vibrant street art scene in the neighborhoods of Little Five Points or East Atlanta Village.

Week 3: Midwest Adventure

Day 15-17: Chicago, Illinois

- Take a bus or train from Atlanta to Chicago.

- Explore Millennium Park, the Art Institute of Chicago (free admission for Illinois residents on certain days), and Navy Pier.
- Sample Chicago-style hot dogs and deep-dish pizza from local eateries.

Day 18-21: Minneapolis, Minnesota

- Take a bus or train from Chicago to Minneapolis.
- Explore the Minneapolis Sculpture Garden and visit the Walker Art Center (offering free admission on Thursdays).
- Enjoy outdoor activities like biking along the Chain of Lakes or exploring Minnehaha Park.

Week 4: West Coast Wanderings

Day 22-24: Portland, Oregon

- Take a bus or train from Minneapolis to Portland.
- Explore the vibrant neighborhoods like Pearl District and Alberta Arts District.
- Visit Washington Park for stunning views of the city and explore the International Rose Test Garden (free admission).

Day 25-28: San Francisco, California

- Take a bus or train from Portland to San Francisco.
- Explore iconic landmarks like the Golden Gate Bridge and Alcatraz Island (book tickets in advance for discounts).
- Enjoy budget-friendly eats from food trucks or visit the Ferry Building Marketplace for gourmet goodies.

Day 29-30: Los Angeles, California

- Take a bus or train from San Francisco to Los Angeles.
- Explore the Hollywood Walk of Fame, Griffith Observatory (offering free admission), and Venice Beach.
- Enjoy affordable eats from taco stands or food trucks.

Additional Tips:

- Use budget transportation options like buses or trains, and book tickets in advance for the best deals.
- Stay in budget accommodations like hostels, Airbnb, or consider couchsurfing.
- Take advantage of free attractions, museums with suggested donations, and discounted tickets available online.
- Use public transportation or walk whenever possible to save on transportation costs.
- Eat like a local and opt for street food, local markets, or affordable diners.

Lessor known sights

For a returning visitor looking to explore lesser-known sights in the USA on a budget, here's an itinerary:

Week 1: Hidden Gems of the East Coast

Day 1-3: Providence, Rhode Island

- Start your journey in Providence, known for its charming streets and vibrant arts scene.
- Explore WaterFire, a unique art installation along the rivers of downtown Providence.
- Visit the RISD Museum for an eclectic collection of art and design.

Day 4-5: Newport, Rhode Island

- Head to Newport to discover its historic mansions and stunning coastal scenery.
- Take a self-guided tour of the Cliff Walk for breathtaking views of the Atlantic Ocean.
- Explore Fort Adams State Park for a glimpse into Newport's military history.

Day 6-7: Portland, Maine

- Travel up the coast to Portland, a hidden culinary gem.
- Indulge in fresh seafood at the Portland Lobster Company or explore the vibrant food scene in the Old Port district.
- Visit the Portland Museum of Art for a dose of culture and creativity.

Week 2: Southern Charms and Quirks

Day 8-10: Savannah, Georgia

- Immerse yourself in the charm of Savannah's historic district, with its cobblestone streets and moss-draped oaks.
- Take a stroll through Bonaventure Cemetery for a hauntingly beautiful experience.
- Explore the eclectic shops and galleries of the Starland District.

Day 11-14: New Orleans, Louisiana

- Dive into the vibrant culture of New Orleans beyond Bourbon Street.
- Visit the historic neighborhoods of Marigny and Bywater for local flavor and colorful street art.
- Explore City Park, home to the beautiful New Orleans Museum of Art and the Besthoff Sculpture Garden.

Week 3: Midwestern Delights

Day 15-17: Madison, Wisconsin

- Discover the progressive vibe of Madison, nestled between two lakes.
- Explore the charming boutiques and cafes of State Street.
- Take a scenic bike ride along the Capital City State Trail for panoramic views of the city.

Day 18-21: Traverse City, Michigan

- Head north to Traverse City, a hidden gem on the shores of Lake Michigan.
- Explore the wineries and orchards of the Old Mission Peninsula.
- Discover the natural beauty of Sleeping Bear Dunes National Lakeshore with its towering sand dunes and pristine beaches.

Week 4: West Coast Wonders

Day 22-24: Santa Fe, New Mexico

- Experience the enchantment of Santa Fe, with its adobe architecture and rich Native American culture.
- Explore the Georgia O'Keeffe Museum and discover the artist's connection to the Southwest.
- Take a hike in the nearby Sangre de Cristo Mountains for breathtaking views of the desert landscape.

Day 25-28: Bend, Oregon

- Head to Bend for outdoor adventure and craft beer culture.
- Explore the Deschutes River Trail for scenic hikes and river views.
- Visit the High Desert Museum for a fascinating look at the natural and cultural history of the region.

Additional Tips:

- Embrace local transportation options like buses, bikes, or walking to save on transportation costs.
- Seek out budget accommodations like boutique hotels, guesthouses, or vacation rentals.
- Support local eateries and food markets for authentic culinary experiences without breaking the bank.
- Take advantage of free or low-cost activities, such as hiking, exploring neighborhoods, and visiting museums with suggested donations or discounted admission days.

With this itinerary, you'll uncover hidden treasures and off-the-beaten-path gems while staying within your budget!

RV TRIP

For an adventurous road trip through the USA in an RV, here's a tailored itinerary along with relocation RV tips, driving tips, and how to avoid tolls:

Week 1: East Coast Expedition

Day 1-3: Start in Boston, Massachusetts

- Pick up your RV rental in Boston and explore the historic streets of the city.
- Visit iconic landmarks like Fenway Park and the Freedom Trail.
- Sample delicious seafood at Quincy Market before hitting the road.

Day 4-5: Relocate to Acadia National Park, Maine

- Take advantage of relocation RV deals to drive your rental to Acadia National Park.
- Explore the park's scenic coastline, hike the trails, and enjoy breathtaking views of the Atlantic Ocean.
- Camp at one of the park's campgrounds or find a nearby RV park for overnight stays.

Day 6-7: Explore the Coast of New Hampshire and Rhode Island

- Drive along the coast of New Hampshire, stopping at charming seaside towns like Portsmouth.
- Continue south to Rhode Island and explore the picturesque beaches and coastal villages.
- Avoid tolls by using scenic coastal routes instead of major highways.

Week 2: Southern Sojourn

Day 8-10: Smoky Mountains, Tennessee

- Drive your RV to the Great Smoky Mountains National Park, taking in the scenic beauty along the way.
- Explore the park's hiking trails, waterfalls, and wildlife.
- Camp at one of the park's campgrounds or find RV parks nearby.

Day 11-14: Gulf Coast Adventure, Alabama and Florida

- Drive along the Gulf Coast, stopping at charming towns like Mobile, Alabama, and Pensacola, Florida.
- Explore the beautiful beaches and coastal scenery of the Gulf Coast.
- Camp at beachfront RV parks or state parks along the coast.

Week 3: Midwest Marvels

Day 15-17: Explore the Ozarks, Missouri and Arkansas

- Drive your RV to the Ozark Mountains, enjoying the scenic drive through the heartland.
- Explore the hiking trails, caves, and rivers of the Ozarks.
- Camp at state parks or RV parks in the area.

Day 18-21: Discover the Badlands and Black Hills, South Dakota

- Drive your RV to Badlands National Park and marvel at the otherworldly landscapes.
- Explore nearby attractions like Mount Rushmore, Crazy Horse Memorial, and Custer State Park.
- Camp at one of the campgrounds in the area or find RV parks nearby.

Week 4: Western Wanderings

Day 22-24: Rocky Mountain Adventure, Colorado

- Drive your RV to Rocky Mountain National Park and explore the stunning mountain scenery.
- Take advantage of relocation RV deals to drop off your rental in Denver or nearby.
- Camp at one of the park's campgrounds or find RV parks in the area.

Day 25-28: Grand Canyon and Beyond, Arizona and Utah

- Pick up a new RV rental in Denver or nearby and drive to the Grand Canyon.
- Explore the South Rim of the Grand Canyon and take in the awe-inspiring views.
- Continue your road trip through Arizona and Utah, visiting national parks like Zion, Bryce Canyon, and Arches.
- Camp at national park campgrounds or find RV parks nearby.

Relocation RV Tips:

- Take advantage of relocation RV deals offered by rental companies, which often provide discounted rates for moving vehicles between locations.
- Be flexible with your travel dates and destinations to find the best relocation deals.
- Pay attention to any mileage restrictions or additional fees associated with relocation rentals.

Driving Tips:

- Familiarize yourself with the size and handling of your RV before hitting the road.
- Plan your routes in advance, taking into account the size of your RV and any height or weight restrictions.
- Take breaks regularly to rest and stretch, especially on long drives.
- Be mindful of speed limits and road conditions, especially in unfamiliar areas.

Avoiding Tolls:

- Use GPS or mapping apps that allow you to avoid toll roads.
- Opt for scenic routes or secondary highways instead of major interstates.
- Plan your route in advance to avoid tolls, if possible, and be prepared for longer travel times.

Unique bargains we love

Warehouse Club Memberships: Warehouse clubs like Costco, Sam's Club, and BJ's Wholesale offer bulk buying options and exclusive deals on groceries, electronics, and household items to their members. The annual membership fee is usually offset by the savings you can enjoy.

National Parks Pass: If you're a fan of the great outdoors, consider purchasing an America the Beautiful Annual Pass. It grants access to more than 2,000 federal recreation areas, including national parks, forests, and wildlife refuges, for a single annual fee.

Groupon and LivingSocial Deals: These online platforms offer a wide range of discounted deals, from restaurant meals and spa treatments to travel packages and entertainment experiences. You can find unique offers specific to your location or interests.

Museums and Cultural Institutions: Many museums and cultural institutions across the USA offer free admission or "pay what you can" days, making it affordable to explore art, history, and science.

State and City Tourism Passes: Some states and cities offer tourism passes that provide discounted or free admission to multiple attractions and activities. Examples include the CityPASS in various cities and state park passes.

Snapshot: How to have a $10,000 trip to USA on a $1,000

Creating a budget-friendly trip to the USA with only $1,000 when the average cost can be around $10,000 requires careful planning and frugality. Here's a snapshot chart with tips on how to maximize your travel experience while sticking to a $1,000 budget:

Expense Category	Average Cost ($10,000 Trip)	Budget-Friendly Tips ($1,000 Budget)
Flights	$200	- Look for flight deals and discounts.
		- Book flights well in advance.
		- Consider alternative airports or nearby cities.
Accommodation	$300 - $400	- Stay in budget-friendly accommodations like hostels, motels, or guesthouses.
		- Utilize Airbnb or couchsurfing for cost-effective stays.
Food	$1,500 - $2,000	- Eat at local eateries, food trucks, and affordable restaurants.
		- Cook your meals or opt for budget-friendly groceries.
Transportation	$500 - $1,000	- Use public transportation, rideshares, or share rides with others.
		- Walk or bike to explore cities.
Sightseeing	$500 - $1,000	- Focus on free or low-cost attractions and museums.
		- Use city passes or discount cards for multiple attractions.
Entertainment	$500 - $1,000	- Attend free events, concerts, or festivals.
		- Enjoy outdoor activities like hiking and exploring parks.
Shopping and Souvenirs	$500 - $1,000	- Be selective with souvenir purchases.
		- Look for affordable local markets and sales.
Miscellaneous	$500 - $1,000	- Set a daily spending limit and stick to it.
		- Use cashback or rewards cards for additional savings.

OUR SUPER CHEAP TIPS...

Here are our specific super cheap tips for enjoying a $10,000 trip to USA for just $1,000

Arriving

There are numerous airports throughout the United States, and the most cost-effective method to get from an airport to the nearest city can vary based on the location and transportation options available. Here are examples of major airports and generally affordable transportation methods to nearby cities:

Airport	City	Cheapest Method
Hartsfield-Jackson Atlanta International Airport (ATL)	Atlanta, Georgia	MARTA (Metropolitan Atlanta Rapid Transit Authority)
Los Angeles International Airport (LAX)	Los Angeles, California	LAX FlyAway bus service
John F. Kennedy International Airport (JFK)	New York City, New York	AirTrain JFK
Chicago O'Hare International Airport (ORD)	Chicago, Illinois	"L" train (Blue Line)
Dallas/Fort Worth International Airport (DFW)	Dallas/Fort Worth, Texas	DART (Dallas Area Rapid Transit)
Denver International Airport (DEN)	Denver, Colorado	RTD A-Line train
San Francisco International Airport (SFO)	San Francisco, California	BART (Bay Area Rapid Transit)
Seattle-Tacoma International Airport (SEA)	Seattle, Washington	Link Light Rail
Miami International Airport (MIA)	Miami, Florida	Miami-Dade Transit buses
Las Vegas McCarran International Airport (LAS)	Las Vegas, Nevada	RTC (Regional Transportation Commission) buses

Tips for Cost-Effective Airport Transportation:

- Public Transportation: Many major cities have reliable and affordable public transportation options directly from airports.
- Shared Rides: Consider rideshare services or shared shuttles, especially if traveling in a group.
- Airport Shuttles: Some airports offer shuttle services that are often cheaper than private taxis.

- Pre-booked Transportation: Booking transportation services in advance may provide discounts compared to on-the-spot bookings.

Getting Around

Traveling around the United States on a budget involves a combination of cost-effective transportation options, strategic planning, and utilizing discounts. Here's a detailed guide on how to travel around the USA cheaply:

Here are some of the cheapest ways to get around the USA, categorized by intercity and in-city/rural transportation, starting with the most economical options:

Intercity Transportation:

1. **Megabus or BoltBus:**
    - These bus services often offer incredibly low fares, sometimes as low as $1 if booked far enough in advance. They operate between major cities and provide a budget-friendly option for traveling long distances.
2. **Greyhound Bus:**
    - Greyhound offers affordable bus travel across the country, connecting major cities and towns. Fares can vary based on demand and timing, but they generally provide a cost-effective option for intercity travel.
3. **Amtrak Thruway Bus Service:**
    - Amtrak's Thruway Bus Service provides connections to cities and towns not directly served by train routes. While Amtrak train tickets can be pricey, their Thruway buses often offer more economical fares for shorter distances.
4. **Ridesharing:**
    - Platforms like BlaBlaCar or Craigslist rideshare can connect you with drivers traveling between cities who have extra space in their vehicles. Costs are typically shared among passengers, making it a cheaper alternative to solo driving or taking a bus.
5. **Low-Cost Airlines:**
    - Airlines like Spirit Airlines, Frontier Airlines, and Allegiant Air often offer low-cost fares for domestic flights. Be mindful of additional fees for baggage and amenities, and book well in advance for the best deals.

In-City/Rural Transportation

1. **Public Transit (Bus/Subway/Tram):**
   - Many cities have affordable public transit systems with options like buses, subways, and trams. Fares are typically lower than other modes of transportation, especially if you purchase weekly or monthly passes.
2. **Biking/Walking:**
   - In urban areas and smaller towns, biking or walking can be one of the cheapest and healthiest ways to get around. Many cities have bike-sharing programs or dedicated bike lanes to make cycling safer and more accessible.
3. **Carpooling:**
   - Sharing rides with friends, coworkers, or neighbors can significantly reduce transportation costs. Coordinate carpool schedules to split fuel expenses and take turns driving, especially for longer commutes or rural travel.
4. **Local Ridesharing/Carpool Apps:**
   - Apps like UberPOOL or Lyft Shared rides allow you to share rides with others heading in the same direction, reducing costs compared to solo rides. This can be a convenient and cost-effective option for short trips within cities.
5. **Local Shuttle Services:**
   - Some cities and rural areas offer free or low-cost shuttle services, especially in tourist areas or areas with limited public transportation options. Check with local tourist offices or transportation authorities for information on available services.
6. **Community Buses/Senior Services:**
   - Some communities provide subsidized transportation services for seniors, individuals with disabilities, or low-income residents. These services may offer reduced fares or even free transportation within designated areas.

Biking

Biking around USA cities is a great way to explore. While Biking in cities in the USA can vary significantly in terms of safety depending on factors such as infrastructure, traffic volume, driver awareness, and local regulations there are some bike-sharing programs that offer free or low-cost options and they tend to be in the places with better cycling infrastructure. Here are some to consider:

1. **Citi Bike (New York City, NY):**
    - Offers single rides starting from around $3, and annual memberships with unlimited 45-minute rides.
    - They occasionally offer promotions and discounts for first-time users or special events.
2. **Divvy Bikes (Chicago, IL):**
    - Single rides start at around $3, with annual memberships offering unlimited 30-minute rides.
    - Reduced fare options are available for qualifying individuals, such as those with low incomes.
3. **Capital Bikeshare (Washington, D.C.):**
    - Single rides start at around $2, and annual memberships provide unlimited 30-minute rides.
    - Reduced fare options are available for those who qualify.
4. **Indego (Philadelphia, PA):**
    - Offers single rides starting from around $4, with annual memberships providing unlimited 30-minute rides.
    - Reduced fare options may be available for eligible individuals.
5. **Bluebikes (Boston, MA):**
    - Single rides start at around $2.50, with annual memberships offering unlimited 45-minute rides.
    - Reduced fare options may be available for those who qualify.
6. **Bay Wheels (San Francisco Bay Area, CA):**
    - Offers single rides starting from around $2, with annual memberships providing unlimited 30-minute rides.

- Reduced fare options may be available for eligible individuals.
7. **Breeze Bike Share (Santa Monica, CA):**
    - Single rides start at around $1.75, and annual memberships offer unlimited 30-minute rides.
    - Reduced fare options may be available for qualifying riders.
8. **Metro Bike Share (Los Angeles, CA):**
    - Offers single rides starting from around $1.75, with annual memberships providing unlimited 30-minute rides.
    - Reduced fare options may be available for eligible individuals.
9. **Nice Ride (Minneapolis, MN):**
    - Single rides start at around $2, and annual memberships offer unlimited 30-minute rides.
    - Reduced fare options may be available for qualifying individuals.
10. **Ford GoBike (Bay Area, CA):**
    - Offers single rides starting from around $2, with annual memberships providing unlimited 30-minute rides.
    - Reduced fare options may be available for eligible riders.

E-scooter rentals

E-scooter rentals have become increasingly popular in cities across the USA, offering a convenient and eco-friendly way to navigate urban areas. Here's a guide to e-scooter rentals in the USA, including prices and tips on how to save money:

How E-Scooter Rentals Work:
1. **Download the App**: Most e-scooter rental companies operate through smartphone apps. Download the app of your preferred provider from the App Store or Google Play Store.
2. **Sign Up**: Create an account within the app using your email address or phone number and payment information.
3. **Locate Nearby Scooters**: Use the app to locate nearby e-scooters available for rent. The app will display a map showing the locations of scooters in your area.
4. **Unlock the Scooter**: Scan the QR code on the scooter or enter the code provided in the app to unlock it. The scooter will then be activated for use.

5. **Ride and Park Responsibly**: Ride the e-scooter to your destination, following local traffic laws and regulations. When finished, park the scooter in a designated area indicated on the app or in accordance with local regulations.
6. **End Ride and Lock Scooter**: End your ride within the app to stop the rental clock and lock the scooter. Make sure the scooter is parked safely and out of the way of pedestrians and traffic.

E-Scooter Rental Prices:
- **Unlock Fee**: Typically ranges from $1 to $2.
- **Per Minute Rate**: Typically ranges from $0.15 to $0.35 per minute of use.
- **Minimum Fare**: Some providers have a minimum fare per ride, usually around $1 to $3.
- **Additional Fees**: Additional fees may apply for exceeding time limits, parking violations, or damage to the scooter.

Tips to Save Money on E-Scooter Rentals:
1. **Take Advantage of Promotions**: Many e-scooter companies offer promotional codes or discounts for first-time users or referrals. Keep an eye out for promotions to save on your rides.
2. **Choose Off-Peak Times**: Prices may vary based on demand, with higher rates during peak hours. Consider riding during off-peak times to take advantage of lower rates.
3. **Plan Efficient Routes**: Optimize your route to minimize ride time and distance. Planning efficient routes can help you save money on per-minute rental fees.
4. **Avoid Long Stops**: If you need to make stops during your ride, try to keep them brief to avoid accruing additional rental fees. End your ride within the app if you anticipate a longer stop.
5. **Park Responsibly**: Avoid parking violations by parking scooters in designated areas indicated on the app. Parking violations may result in additional fees.
6. **Monitor Time**: Keep an eye on the time to avoid exceeding the time limit for your ride. Ending your ride promptly can help you avoid additional charges.
7. **Consider Subscription Plans**: Some e-scooter companies offer subscription plans for frequent riders, providing discounted rates or flat-rate pricing for unlimited rides within a certain timeframe.

Renting a Car

Renting a car in the USA can be super handy for all sorts of reasons, depending on what you're up to during your trip. Picture this: you're planning to venture out into the countryside or maybe hit up some national parks. Well, having your wheels can make it a breeze to explore those off-the-beaten-path places where public transport might not reach. Think about cruising through scenic routes and pulling over whenever you spot something cool – that's the kind of freedom a rental car gives you.

Pros of Renting a Car in the USA:

- Convenience: Provides flexibility and freedom.
- Exploration: Ability to explore off-the-beaten-path destinations.
- Time Efficiency: Saves time compared to public transport.
- Comfort and Privacy: Travel comfortably with family or friends.
- Access to Remote Areas: Reach national parks, hiking trails, and rural destinations.

Cons of Renting a Car in the USA:

- Cost: Car rental fees, including daily rental rates, insurance, and fees (fuel, tolls, parking, etc.), can add up quickly.
- Traffic and Parking: Traffic congestion in major cities and difficulty finding parking in crowded urban areas.
- Environmental Impact: Contributing to pollution and environmental issues, especially for long drives.
- Stress and Fatigue: Long drives can be tiring and stressful, leading to driver fatigue.
- Maintenance and Responsibility: Responsibility for maintenance, fueling, and parking.

How to find the cheapest gas

Finding the cheapest gas in the USA requires a combination of strategies, as fuel prices can vary based on location, local competition, and market trends. Here are some tips to help you find the most affordable gas:

1. Gas Price Apps and Websites:
- Use gas price comparison apps and websites to check current prices in your area. Popular options include:
- GasBuddy
- Waze
- AAA TripTik
- Gas Guru

2. Gas Station Loyalty Programs:
- Join loyalty programs offered by gas stations. Many chains provide discounts or rewards for frequent customers.

3. Supermarket Rewards Programs:
- Some supermarkets offer fuel rewards programs where you can earn discounts on gas by shopping at their stores.

4. Credit Card Rewards:
- Use credit cards that offer cashback or rewards specifically for gas purchases. Some credit cards provide higher rewards for fuel spending.

5. Warehouse Club Memberships:
- Warehouse clubs like Costco and Sam's Club often offer lower gas prices for their members.

6. Off-Peak Fill-Ups:
- Fill up your tank during off-peak hours or days. Gas prices tend to be lower during the middle of the week and early mornings.

7. Use Gas Station Apps:
- Many gas stations have their own apps with special promotions, discounts, and loyalty rewards. Check if your preferred station offers such an app.

8. Cash vs. Credit:
- Some gas stations offer lower prices for customers paying with cash. However, this varies, and not all stations follow this practice.

9. Pay Attention to Local Trends:
- Gas prices can vary between neighboring towns and cities. Be aware of regional trends and fill up where prices are lower.

10. Plan Your Route:
- Before a long drive, plan your route to include stops in areas with lower gas prices. GasBuddy's trip planner feature can be helpful for this.

11. Avoid Highway Stops:
- Gas stations along highways and major interstates may have higher prices. Consider filling up in nearby towns where prices could be lower.

Driving Tips

Joining an automobile club offers members 24-hour emergency roadside assistance and discounts on lodging and attractions. Some international clubs have reciprocal agreements with US automobile associations, so it's wise to check beforehand and carry your home member card.

Before hitting the road, ensure your vehicle is equipped with essentials like a spare tire, tool kit (including a jack, jumper cables, ice scraper, and tire-pressure gauge), and emergency equipment like flashers. If you're renting a vehicle and these safety items aren't provided, consider purchasing them.

Bring along reliable maps, especially for off-road or remote areas where GPS units might malfunction or not work at all. Don't solely rely on GPS, especially in deep canyons or dense forests.

Always have your driver's license and proof of insurance on hand. If you're an international traveler, familiarize yourself with the USA's road rules and common hazards.

Keep your gas tank topped up regularly, as gas stations can be scarce in scenic areas of the USA.

While America's highways are often romanticized as pristine stretches of asphalt, the reality can be quite different. Road hazards abound, from potholes and city traffic to wandering wildlife and distracted or aggressive drivers. Navigating these challenges requires caution, foresight, courtesy, and sometimes a bit of luck.

For up-to-date information on nationwide traffic conditions and road closures, visit www.fhwa.dot.gov/trafficinfo. In regions where winter weather poses a threat, many vehicles are equipped with steel-studded snow tires, and snow chains may be required in mountainous areas.

Driving off-road or on dirt roads is typically prohibited by car rental companies, as it can be hazardous, especially in wet weather. Additionally, in desert and rural areas, livestock may graze near unfenced roads, posing a risk to drivers.

In the USA, vehicles drive on the right-hand side of the road. Seat belt usage is mandatory in every state except New Hampshire, and child safety seats or seat belts for passengers under 18 are required nationwide. Most car rental agencies offer child safety seats for rental, typically priced between $10 to $14 per day, but advance reservations are necessary.

In certain states, motorcyclists are obligated to wear helmets for safety reasons. On interstate highways, the standard speed limit is typically 70mph. Speed limits on other roads vary: generally, it's 55mph or 65mph on highways, 25mph to 35mph in urban areas, and as low as 15mph in school zones, with strict enforcement during school hours.

It's prohibited to overtake a school bus when its lights are flashing. Unless signs indicate otherwise, making a right turn at a red light after coming to a complete stop is generally allowed—except in New York City, where it's illegal. At four-way stop signs, vehicles should proceed in the order they arrived; if two cars arrive simultaneously, the one on the right has the right of way. When uncertain, a polite wave can signal to the other driver to proceed first. When emergency vehicles such as police, fire, or ambulance approach, safely pull over and yield the right of way.

In many states, using a handheld cell phone while driving is illegal; opt for a hands-free device instead. The legal maximum blood-alcohol concentration for drivers is 0.08%, and penalties for driving under the influence (DUI) are severe. Police may conduct roadside sobriety checks to assess impairment, and refusing testing carries similar consequences as failing the test. In some states, it's illegal to transport open containers of alcohol in a vehicle, even if they're empty. If stopped by police, remain in your vehicle and wait for the officer to approach. Have your license, proof of insurance, and registration or rental agreement ready for inspection.

The top 32 Attractions in the USA on the Super Cheap

1.	Walt Disney World Resort, Florida	214
2.	Grand Canyon, Arizona	217
3.	Yellowstone National Park, Wyoming	221
4.	Statue of Liberty, New York	223

5. Times Square, New York — 224
6. Las Vegas Strip, Nevada — 226
7. Smithsonian Museums, Washington D.C. — 228
8. National Mall and Memorial Parks, Washington D.C. — 228
9. Niagara Falls — 230
10. Universal Studios Hollywood, California — 232
11. Kennedy Space Center Visitor Complex, Florida — 234
12. Golden Gate Bridge, California — 236
13. Mount Rushmore National Memorial, South Dakota — 238
14. Great Smoky Mountains National Park, North Carolina and Tennessee — 240
15. Disneyland Resort, California — 242
16. Alcatraz Island, California — 245
17. Napa Valley, California: — 247
18. Hawaii — 251
19. Independence National Historical Park, Pennsylvania — 253
20. Mount St. Helens, Washington — 255
21. Bryce Canyon National Park, Utah — 259
22. Rocky Mountain National Park, Colorado — 262
23. Zion National Park, Utah — 265
24. Great Sand Dunes National Park, Colorado — 268
25. Pike Place Market, Seattle — 271
26. The Grand Ole Opry, Nashville, Tennessee — 273
27. The Space Needle, Seattle, Washington — 275

28. Lake Tahoe, California and Nevada	277
29. Denali National Park and Preserve, Alaska	279
30. Cape Cod, Massachusetts	281
31. The Everglades	283
32. Route 66	284

Here is an ultra-condensed version of how to visit the biggest attractions in the USA on the super cheap, but still in style.

1. **Walt Disney World Resort, Florida**

Ah, visiting Walt Disney World Resort in Florida is like stepping into a magical wonderland, but let's be real – those costs can add up faster than you can say "Bibbidi-Bobbidi-Boo"! Here's the scoop on the core costs and some savvy ways to trim them down.

Accommodation:
    Tip: Consider staying at a Disney Value Resort for affordable rates while still enjoying Disney perks. Prices at Disney Value Resorts start at around $100 per night, depending on the season and availability.

Tickets:
    Tip: Opt for multi-day tickets to save money per day compared to single-day tickets.

Multi-day tickets start at $109 per day for a 4-day ticket for one park per day.
Dining:
> **Tip**: Bring your own snacks and water bottles to save on food costs inside the parks. Prices for quick-service meals at Disney can range from $10 to $20 per person, while snacks can start at around $5.

Transportation:
> **Tip**: Utilize Disney's complimentary transportation system, including buses, monorails, and boats, to get around the resort and avoid rental car expenses.

Souvenirs:
> **Tip**: Purchase Disney merchandise at off-site stores like Target or Walmart, or shop online before your trip to find discounts.

Extra Experiences:
> **Tip**: Prioritize the free experiences and entertainment offered at the parks, such as parades, character meet-and-greets, and fireworks shows.

Character Dining:
> **Tip**: Opt for breakfast or lunch character dining experiences, which tend to be cheaper than dinner options. Character dining prices can start at around $30 to $40 per person for breakfast or lunch.

FastPass+ Reservations:
> **Tip**: Take advantage of Disney's FastPass+ system to reserve access to select attractions, entertainment, and character meet-and-greets in advance for free.

Off-Season Travel: Traveling during less busy times, such as weekdays outside of major holidays or school breaks, can result in lower hotel rates and shorter wait times for attractions.

Best Freebies

1. **Celebration Buttons**: Guests celebrating special occasions, such as birthdays, anniversaries, or first visits, can pick up celebratory buttons at Guest Relations or various locations throughout the parks. These buttons not only serve as memorable keepsakes but also often lead to special acknowledgments from cast members and characters.
2. **Sorcerers of the Magic Kingdom**: This interactive game, available at Magic Kingdom Park, allows guests to embark on a quest to defeat Disney villains using special spell cards. The game is entirely free and provides hours of entertainment for the whole family.
3. **Water and Ice**: Stay hydrated and refreshed with complimentary cups of ice water available at quick-service dining locations throughout the parks. Just ask a cast member, and they'll happily provide you with a refreshing drink to keep you cool under the Florida sun.
4. **Transportation**: Guests staying at Disney Resort hotels can enjoy complimentary transportation via buses, boats, and the

iconic monorail system. This convenient service makes it easy to travel between parks, resorts, and other Disney destinations without the need for a rental car.
5. **Entertainment and Shows**: From parades and fireworks displays to live performances and character meet-and-greets, Walt Disney World offers a wealth of entertainment options included with park admission. Be sure to check the daily schedule for showtimes and experiences that appeal to you.
6. **Pixie Dust**: Keep an eye out for magical moments sprinkled throughout the parks, such as surprise character appearances, impromptu performances, and hidden details waiting to be discovered. These spontaneous touches add an extra layer of enchantment to your Disney experience at no additional cost.
7. **Memory Maker Photos**: Guests with a Disney PhotoPass account can enjoy unlimited downloads of their vacation photos, including ride photos, character meet-and-greet shots, and professional portraits taken by Disney photographers. While Memory Maker is a paid service, some special offers or package deals may include it for free.
8. **Park Maps and Times Guides**: Take home a piece of the magic with complimentary park maps and times guides, available at the entrance of each theme park. These handy resources provide valuable information about attractions, entertainment, dining options, and more.
9. **Samples and Tastings**: Keep an eye out for complimentary food and beverage samples offered at select locations throughout the parks and Disney Springs. From chocolate confections to savory snacks, these tasty treats are a delightful way to satisfy your cravings while exploring the resort.

2. Grand Canyon, Arizona

Carved by the mighty Colorado River over millions of years, the Grand Canyon is a testament to the raw power of nature. Its immense size, intricate rock formations, and vibrant colors – from crimson to gold to deep violet – create a landscape that is both humbling and breathtaking. Visiting the Grand Canyon in Arizona offers breathtaking views and unforgettable experiences, but it can also come with unexpected costs. Here are some ways to keep the costs down.

- **Accommodations:**
    - Opt for camping or Stay in budget-friendly accommodations in nearby towns like Tusayan, Williams, or Flagstaff, which offer more affordable hotel options compared to lodging inside the national park. Accommodation prices can vary, but budget hotels, motels, cabins, or campgrounds can start at around $50 to $150 per night, depending on the season and location.

- Budget motels in Williams start at $50/night.
- Look for accommodations in Peach Springs or Kingman for budget options.
- **Food Savings:**
  - Use OLIO app for surplus food from local stores.
  - Too Good To Go app offers discounted meals in nearby areas.
- **Discount Pass:**
  - America the Beautiful Pass: $80 for access to all federal lands.
  - Consider package deals including admission to the Skywalk and other attractions.

1. **Free Shuttle Services**: Take advantage of the free shuttle services provided by the National Park Service. These shuttles operate along the South Rim and allow you to explore various viewpoints without the need for a car, saving money on parking fees and gas.
2. **Water Refill Stations**: Bring a refillable water bottle and utilize the water refill stations available throughout the park. Staying hydrated is essential, especially in the desert climate, and avoiding the purchase of bottled water can save you a significant amount of money over time.
3. **Picnic Areas**: Instead of dining at expensive restaurants or purchasing meals at the park's concessions, pack a picnic and enjoy a meal at one of the designated picnic areas within the park. This allows you to enjoy the stunning scenery while saving on food costs.
4. **Backcountry Camping**: Consider backcountry camping as an alternative to staying at the park's lodges or campsites. Permits are required for backcountry camping, but the experience of sleeping under the stars near the rim of the canyon is truly unforgettable and often more affordable than traditional accommodations. The cost typically starts at around $10 per permit request, plus an additional fee per person per night. It was around $8 per person per night for camping below

the rim and around $8 per group per night for camping above the rim.
5. **Discount Passes**: If you plan to visit multiple national parks during your trip, consider purchasing an America the Beautiful Pass. This annual pass provides access to more than 2,000 federal recreation sites across the country, including the Grand Canyon, and can save you money on entrance fees.
6. **Junior Ranger Program**: If you're traveling with children, encourage them to participate in the Junior Ranger Program offered by the National Park Service. This free program allows kids to complete activities and learn about the park while earning a Junior Ranger badge, providing a fun and educational experience at no additional cost.

Accommodation:
    Tip: Stay in budget-friendly accommodations in nearby towns like Kingman, Williams, or Peach Springs, which offer more affordable hotel options compared to lodging near the Grand Canyon.
    Starting Price: Accommodation prices can vary, but budget hotels, motels, or campgrounds can start at around $50 to $150 per night, depending on the season and location.

Transportation:
    Tip: Utilize public transportation options like buses, shuttles, or rideshare services to get to the Grand Canyon Skywalk, or consider renting a car if you prefer more flexibility in your transportation.
    Starting Price: Prices for public transportation fares or rideshare services vary, but they can be affordable options for getting to and from the Skywalk.

Entrance Fees:
    Tip: Purchase tickets for the Grand Canyon West Rim, which includes access to the Skywalk, in advance online to save money and avoid long lines at the ticket office. Prices for admission to the Grand Canyon West Rim start at $49.95 per person for general admission, with additional fees for optional attractions like the Skywalk.

Hualapai Ranch:
    Tip: Explore the Hualapai Ranch, located near the Grand Canyon Skywalk, for a taste of the Old West with activities like horseback riding, wagon rides, cowboy shows, and a cowboy cookout.
    Starting Price: Prices for activities at Hualapai Ranch vary, but there are often package deals available for multiple activities.

Cultural Demonstrations:
    Tip: Learn about Hualapai culture and traditions through free cultural demonstrations offered at Grand Canyon West, such as traditional dancing, storytelling, and arts and crafts.
    Starting Price: Free of charge with admission to Grand Canyon West.

Scenic Views:
    Tip: Take in panoramic views of the Grand Canyon from multiple viewpoints along the West Rim, including Eagle Point and Guano Point, which offer breathtaking vistas and photo opportunities.

Starting Price: Free of charge with admission to Grand Canyon West.
Visitor Center:
    Tip: Visit the visitor center at Grand Canyon West to learn more about the history, geology, and culture of the area through exhibits, displays, and ranger-led programs.
    Starting Price: Free of charge with admission to Grand Canyon West.
Hiking Trails:
    Tip: Explore the numerous hiking trails in Grand Canyon National Park, ranging from easy walks along the rim to challenging hikes into the canyon, for stunning views and opportunities to experience the park's natural beauty.

Scenic Overlooks:
    Tip: Visit popular scenic overlooks along the South Rim, such as Mather Point, Yavapai Point, and Desert View, for panoramic views of the canyon and photo opportunities.

Visitor Centers:
    Tip: Visit the visitor centers at Grand Canyon National Park, such as the Grand Canyon Visitor Center or the Desert View Visitor Center, to learn about the park's geology, wildlife, and history through exhibits and ranger programs.

Ranger Programs:
    Tip: Participate in free ranger-led programs and guided walks offered by the National Park Service to learn more about the natural and cultural resources of Grand Canyon National Park and enhance your park experience.

Picnics:
    Tip: Pack a picnic lunch and enjoy it at one of the designated picnic areas in Grand Canyon National Park, such as Mather Point or Yavapai Point, for a budget-friendly dining experience with a view.
    Starting Price: Prices for picnic supplies vary, but you can often find affordable options at local grocery stores or markets.

Sunset Viewing:
    Tip: Plan your visit to coincide with sunset for a breathtaking experience of watching the sun set over the Grand Canyon, casting a golden glow over the canyon walls and creating stunning photo opportunities.

3. Yellowstone National Park, Wyoming

Yellowstone National Park isn't just any destination – it's a mesmerizing wonderland brimming with natural beauty, geothermal wonders, and an abundance of wildlife that will leave you in awe.

To save on your visit, consider camping inside the park or staying in nearby towns like West Yellowstone for more affordable lodging options. Check for cabins or campsites within the park, starting at $20/night. Use apps like Food Rescue US to find surplus food in nearby towns for dining savings. Plus, grab an America the Beautiful Pass ($80) for access to Yellowstone and other federal lands.

For budget-friendly accommodations, look to nearby towns like Mariposa for lodging options outside the park. Budget motels in these areas start at $70/night. Utilize apps like Too Good To Go to find discounted meals in nearby towns, and don't forget your America the Beautiful Pass ($80) for access to Yosemite and other federal lands.

When it comes to exploring the parks:

- Accommodations:
  - Stay in budget-friendly accommodations in nearby towns like West Yellowstone, Gardiner, or Cody, starting at $50 to $150 per night.
- Transportation:
  - Utilize public transportation options like buses or shuttles within the park.
- Entrance Fees:
  - Purchase an annual pass to the park for $70 or pay $35 for a 7-day vehicle pass.
- Activities:
  - Enjoy free activities like hiking trails, scenic drives, wildlife viewing, picnics, visitor center visits, and ranger-led programs.

4. **Statue of Liberty, New York**

- **Tip to follow to save the most:** Book ferry tickets in advance for lower prices.
- **Hotel Deals**: Look for budget hotels or Airbnbs in New Jersey with easy access to public transportation.
- **Saving on Food**: Apps like Karma can help you find discounted meals in New York City.
- **Discount Pass**: New York CityPASS for $136 includes admission to the Statue of Liberty and other top attractions.

Exploring the Statue of Liberty in New York City offers a glimpse into American history and iconic views of the city skyline, but it can also come with unexpected costs. Here's an extremely detailed guide to some lesser-known ways to save money during your visit:

1. **Free Ferry Ride**: Access to the Statue of Liberty and Ellis Island is free, and the most cost-effective way to get there is by taking the Staten Island Ferry, which offers stunning views of the Statue of Liberty and the Manhattan skyline. The ferry operates 24/7 and runs every 30 minutes during peak times.

2. **National Park Pass**: If you plan to visit multiple national parks during your trip, consider purchasing an America the Beautiful Pass. This annual pass provides access to more than 2,000 federal recreation sites across the country, including the Statue of Liberty, and can save you money on entrance fees. However, the pass does not automatically grant access to the pedestal or crown of the statue.
3. **Picnic Lunch**: Instead of dining at expensive restaurants or purchasing meals at the concession stands on Liberty Island, pack a picnic lunch and enjoy a meal with a view. There are picnic tables available near the ferry terminal, allowing you to enjoy the scenery while saving on food costs.
4. **Off-Peak Visits**: Visit the Statue of Liberty during the off-peak season or on weekdays to take advantage of lower ticket prices and fewer crowds. Additionally, consider visiting early in the morning or later in the afternoon to avoid the busiest times of day.
5. **Discount Passes**: Look for discount passes or combination tickets that include admission to the Statue of Liberty and other attractions in New York City. These passes can often provide significant savings compared to purchasing individual tickets for each attraction.

5. Times Square, New York

Tip to follow to save the most: Avoid eating in restaurants directly in Times Square; prices tend to be higher.
Hotel Deals: Look for budget accommodations in nearby neighborhoods like Hell's Kitchen or Midtown West.
Saving on Food: Apps like Karma or Too Good To Go can help you find discounted meals in New York City especially around Times Square.
Discount Pass: New York CityPASS for $136 includes admission to top attractions including the Empire State Building.

Entertainment:
Tip: Take advantage of free entertainment options in Times Square, such as street performers, musicians, and public art installations.

Broadway Shows:
Tip: Purchase discounted Broadway tickets at TKTS Discount Booths in Times Square or through online platforms offering last-minute deals.

Starting Price: Prices for discounted Broadway tickets can start at around $50 to $100 per person, depending on the show and seating.

Shopping:

Tip: Visit nearby shopping districts like Herald Square or Fifth Avenue for a wider selection of stores and more affordable prices compared to shops in Times Square.

Starting Price: Prices for merchandise vary depending on the store and item, but you can often find deals and discounts at large department stores or outlet malls.

Photography:

Tip: Take advantage of free photo opportunities in Times Square, such as posing with the iconic billboards and signs, rather than paying for professional photography services.

Nightlife:

Tip: Look for happy hour specials and discounted drinks at bars and lounges in nearby neighborhoods like Hell's Kitchen or Midtown West, rather than pricey clubs in Times Square.

Starting Price: Prices for drinks at happy hour specials can start at around $5 to $10 each.

Hotels with Views:

Tip: Enjoy panoramic views of Times Square from rooftop bars and observation decks at nearby hotels, some of which offer free or discounted admission during certain times or with the purchase of a drink.

Starting Price: Prices for drinks at rooftop bars vary, but many offer specials starting at around $15 to $20 per drink. For stunning views near Times Square, rooftop bars like St. Cloud at The Knickerbocker Hotel and PHD Terrace at Dream Midtown offer both exceptional vistas and vibrant atmospheres.

6. Las Vegas Strip, Nevada

Exploring the Las Vegas Strip in Nevada offers an electrifying experience with its dazzling lights, iconic landmarks, and world-class entertainment, but it can also come with high costs.

- **Tip to follow to save the most:** Stay in hotels off the Strip for cheaper rates.
- **Hotel Deals**: Look for budget hotels like Excalibur or Circus Circus, starting at $30/night.
- **Saving on Food**: Apps like Too Good To Go can help you find discounted meals in Las Vegas.
- **Discount Pass**: Las Vegas Explorer Pass starting at $85 offers access to multiple attractions including shows and tours.

Here's a detailed guide to some lesser-known ways to save money during your visit:

1. **Free Attractions**: Many of the attractions along the Las Vegas Strip are free to visit, including the Fountains of Bellagio, the Volcano at The Mirage, and the Fall of Atlantis at Caesars Palace. Take advantage of these free attractions to enjoy the sights and sounds of the Strip without spending a dime.
2. **Casino Loyalty Programs**: Sign up for casino loyalty programs, such as M Life Rewards or Total Rewards, which offer discounts on dining, entertainment, and accommodations for members. Earn points as you gamble and redeem them for rewards to save money on your overall expenses.
3. **Happy Hour Specials**: Take advantage of happy hour specials at bars and restaurants along the Strip, where you can find discounted drinks and appetizers during select hours. Research happy hour deals in advance and plan your dining and drinking accordingly to save money.
4. **Hotel Deals**: Look for hotel deals and promotions offered by hotels and resorts along the Strip. Many hotels offer discounted rates, free upgrades, or resort credits for booking directly through their websites or signing up for their mailing lists.
5. **Public Transportation**: Utilize public transportation options such as the Las Vegas Monorail or the RTC bus system to navigate the Strip and surrounding areas. These options are often cheaper than taxis or rideshare services and can help you save money on transportation costs.
6. **Avoid Peak Times**: Visit the Las Vegas Strip during off-peak times, such as weekdays or non-holiday periods, to take advantage of lower hotel rates, fewer crowds, and better deals on entertainment and dining.
7. **Entertainment Discounts**: Look for discounted tickets or promotions for shows, concerts, and attractions along the Strip. Visit ticket booths, check online deal websites, or inquire about last-minute discounts to save money on entertainment expenses.
7. **Dining**:
    - **Tip**: Look for dining deals and happy hour specials offered by restaurants along the Strip to enjoy upscale meals at discounted prices.
    - **Starting Price**: Prices for meals at upscale restaurants can vary, but you can find deals like prix-fixe menus or happy hour specials starting at around $20 to $30 per person.
4. **Transportation**:

- **Tip**: Utilize public transportation options like the Las Vegas Monorail or RTC buses to get around the Strip and downtown area at a fraction of the cost of taxis or rideshare services.
- **Starting Price**: Prices for public transportation tickets can start at around $5 for a single ride on the monorail or bus.

6. **Nightlife**:
    - **Tip**: Research clubs and bars offering free entry or guest list options, and consider visiting during off-peak nights to avoid high cover charges.
    - Free entry with guest list or reduced cover charges starting at around $20 to $30 on off-peak nights.

7. Smithsonian Museums, Washington D.C.

Established in 1846 by an act of Congress and named after British scientist James Smithson, the Smithsonian Institution has grown into the world's largest museum, education, and research complex, encompassing 19 museums, galleries, gardens, and a zoo, all free to the public and collectively known as "America's attic" for their diverse collections spanning art, history, science, and culture.

- **Tip to follow to save the most:** Stay in budget-friendly accommodations in neighborhoods outside of downtown D.C., such as Arlington, Virginia, or Silver Spring, Maryland, and utilize public transportation to reach the museums.
- **Saving on Food**: Check out apps like Too Good To Go or OLIO for discounted meals in D.C.
- **Discount Pass**: Washington D.C. Explorer Pass starting at $64 includes admission to multiple attractions.

8. National Mall and Memorial Parks, Washington D.C.

Exploring the National Mall and Memorial Parks in Washington D.C. offers a rich cultural and historical experience, but it can also come with unexpected costs. Here's an extremely detailed guide to some lesser-known ways to save money during your visit:

1. **Free Museum Admission**: Many of the museums along the National Mall, including the Smithsonian museums, offer free admission to their exhibits. Take advantage of these free attractions to explore art, history, and culture without spending a dime.
2. **Walking Tour**: Explore the monuments and memorials on the National Mall on foot with a self-guided walking tour. Many tour companies offer free downloadable maps and audio guides that provide information about the landmarks and their significance.
3. **Bike Rental**: Rent a bike to explore the National Mall and surrounding areas at your own pace. Many bike rental shops offer affordable hourly or daily rates, and biking is a convenient and eco-friendly way to see the sights.

4. **Discounted Parking**: If you're driving to the National Mall, look for discounted parking options in nearby garages or lots. Some parking facilities offer discounted rates for early bird or evening parking, allowing you to save money on parking fees.
5. **Free Events and Programs**: Check the National Park Service website for information about free events and programs happening on the National Mall, such as ranger-led tours, educational programs, and cultural festivals.

- **Tip to follow to save the most:** Stay in budget-friendly accommodations in neighborhoods near the National Mall, such as Capitol Hill or Southwest Waterfront, and utilize public transportation to access the area.
- Dining: Dine at affordable eateries and food trucks in nearby neighborhoods like Capitol Hill or Penn Quarter, rather than expensive restaurants near the National Mall.
- **Hotel Deals**: Look for budget accommodations in nearby neighborhoods like Capitol Hill or Dupont Circle.
- **Saving on Food**: Utilize apps like Food Rescue US to find surplus food in D.C.
- **Discount Pass**: Consider the Explorer Pass for D.C. for other attractions in the area.

9. Niagara Falls

- **Tip to follow to save the most:** Visit during the off-season (late fall or winter) for cheaper rates.
- **Hotel Deals**: Look for budget accommodations in nearby towns like Niagara Falls, Ontario, or Buffalo, NY.
- **Saving on Food**: Check for local deals and discounts using apps like Too Good To Go.
- **Discount Pass**: Niagara Falls USA Discovery Pass starting at $46.50 includes access to multiple attractions.
- **Don't Miss**: Evening Illumination: Experience the breathtaking sight of Niagara Falls illuminated at night with colorful lights during the evening illumination show, which is free to watch from various viewpoints along the Niagara River. Free of charge.

Niagara Falls, a natural wonder straddling the border between the United States and Canada, has captivated visitors since the 17th century, with its awe-inspiring beauty and raw power attracting millions of tourists annually to witness the thundering cascade of water over its cliffs, immortalized in countless works of art, literature, and film, making it one of the most iconic and beloved destinations in the world. Exploring Niagara Falls offers an awe-inspiring natural wonder, but it can also come with unexpected costs. Here's an extremely detailed guide to some lesser-known ways to save money during your visit:

1. **State Park Admission**: Consider visiting Niagara Falls State Park on the American side, which offers free admission to view the falls from various vantage points. You'll still experience breathtaking views without the expense of paid attractions.
2. **Free Attractions**: Explore free attractions such as the Niagara Gorge Trail System, which provides stunning views of the falls and surrounding landscape. Additionally, take a stroll along the Niagara Riverwalk for picturesque views and photo opportunities.
3. **Parking**: Opt for off-site parking options or park in municipal lots to save on parking fees, which can be expensive near popular tourist areas. Some hotels also offer free or discounted parking for guests.
4. **Public Transportation**: Utilize public transportation options such as the Niagara Falls Trolley or local buses to access attractions around the falls. Public transportation is often more affordable than driving and parking in the area.
5. **Attraction Passes**: If you plan to visit multiple paid attractions, consider purchasing a Niagara Falls USA Discovery Pass or Niagara Falls Adventure Pass. These passes offer discounted admission to select attractions, saving you money compared to purchasing individual tickets.
6. **Pack Your Own Food**: Bring your own snacks and drinks to enjoy a picnic in one of the designated areas near the falls. Avoid dining at expensive restaurants or purchasing food at tourist attractions to save on dining expenses.
7. **Off-Peak Visits**: Visit Niagara Falls during the off-peak season or on weekdays to take advantage of lower hotel rates, fewer crowds, and better deals on attractions and accommodations.

10. Universal Studios Hollywood, California

- **Tip to follow to save the most:** Purchase tickets online in advance for discounted rates. Stay in budget-friendly accommodations in nearby areas like North Hollywood, Burbank, or Studio City, which offer more affordable hotel options compared to hotels directly near Universal Studios.
- **Saving on Food**: Utilize Too Good To Go to find discounted meals in Los Angeles.
- **Discount Pass**: Universal Studios Hollywood offers various ticket options, starting at $109 for a single day.
- **Express Passes**:Consider purchasing Express Passes to skip the regular lines and enjoy priority access to select attractions and shows at Universal Studios Hollywood, especially during peak times when wait times can be longer.

Exploring Universal Studios Hollywood offers an immersive theme park experience, but it can also come with unexpected costs.

1. **Discounted Tickets**: Look for discounted tickets through authorized sellers, such as AAA, Costco, or online ticket vendors. Additionally, consider purchasing multi-day passes or combo tickets that include admission to other attractions in the area for added value.
2. **Midweek Visits**: Plan your visit for a weekday rather than a weekend to take advantage of lower ticket prices and smaller crowds. Avoid peak times such as holidays and school breaks to maximize savings and minimize wait times for attractions.
3. **Online Discounts**: Check the official Universal Studios Hollywood website for online discounts and promotions. Sometimes, purchasing tickets in advance online can save you money compared to buying them at the gate.
4. **Annual Passes**: If you plan to visit Universal Studios Hollywood multiple times within a year, consider investing in an annual pass. Annual passholders often receive perks such as discounts on food, merchandise, and parking, making it a cost-effective option for frequent visitors.
5. **Parking Options**: Opt for general parking instead of preferred parking to save money on parking fees. Additionally, consider carpooling or using rideshare services to split the cost of parking with friends or family.
6. **Bring Your Own Food and Drinks**: Universal Studios Hollywood allows guests to bring their own food and non-

alcoholic beverages into the park. Packing a picnic lunch or snacks can help you save money on dining expenses.
7. **Skip Express Passes**: While Express Passes can help you skip the lines for attractions, they come at an additional cost. Consider whether the extra expense is worth it for you, or strategize your visit to minimize wait times during off-peak hours.

11. Kennedy Space Center Visitor Complex, Florida

- **Tip to follow to save the most:** Stay in budget-friendly accommodations in nearby areas like Titusville or Cocoa Beach, which offer more affordable hotel options compared to hotels directly near the Kennedy Space Center.
- **Deals**: Take advantage of free exhibits and attractions included with your admission to the Kennedy Space Center Visitor Complex, such as the Space Shuttle Atlantis exhibit, Rocket Garden, and Astronaut Encounter. Take advantage of free educational programs and presentations offered by the Kennedy Space Center Visitor Complex, such as astronaut lectures, STEM activities, and interactive exhibits.
- **Saving on Food**: Utilize apps like Karma or Too Good To Go for discounted meals in the area.
- **Discount Pass**: Consider the Go Orlando Pass starting at $89 for access to multiple attractions, including Kennedy Space Center. Prices for general admission tickets start at $57 for adults and $47 for children aged 3-11, with discounts available for seniors, military personnel, and Florida residents.

Exploring the Kennedy Space Center Visitor Complex in Florida offers a fascinating journey through space exploration.

1. **Ticket Discounts**: Look for discounted tickets through authorized sellers, such as AAA, military discounts, or online ticket vendors. Additionally, check the Kennedy Space Center website for any promotions or special offers available for advance purchase.
2. **Combo Tickets**: Consider purchasing combo tickets that include admission to other nearby attractions, such as the Astronaut Hall of Fame or local museums. Combo tickets often provide discounted rates compared to purchasing individual tickets for each attraction.
3. **Transportation Options**: Explore transportation options to the Kennedy Space Center, such as shuttle services or carpooling Some hotels in the area may offer complimentary shuttle services to the visitor complex, saving you money on transportation costs.
4. **Free Attractions**: Take advantage of the free attractions and exhibits included with your admission ticket, such as the Rocket Garden and the Space Shuttle Atlantis exhibit. These attractions offer fascinating insights into space exploration at no additional cost.

5. **Off-Peak Visits**: Visit the Kennedy Space Center during the off-peak season or on weekdays to take advantage of lower ticket prices and smaller crowds. Avoid visiting during peak times such as holidays or school breaks to maximize savings and minimize wait times.
6. **Educational Programs**: Check the Kennedy Space Center website for any educational programs or special events happening during your visit. These programs may offer unique experiences at no additional cost or provide discounted rates for participants.

12. Golden Gate Bridge, California

San Francisco, fondly nicknamed the "City by the Bay," has a rich and storied history dating back to its founding during the California Gold Rush in 1849, evolving into a vibrant cultural hub known for its iconic landmarks such as the Golden Gate Bridge, Alcatraz Island, and cable cars, as well as its diverse neighborhoods, innovative tech scene, and progressive values, making it a magnet for dreamers, adventurers, and seekers of the unconventional from around the globe.

- **Tip to follow to save the most:** In San Francisco, finding truly budget-friendly accommodation can be a challenge due to the city's high cost of living. However, there are some options for the budget-conscious traveler: Hostels are often the cheapest option for accommodation in San Francisco. Dormitory-style rooms offer basic amenities at affordable rates. Popular hostels include HI San Francisco Downtown Hostel and USA Hostels San Francisco. Look for hotels in areas like Tenderloin, Mission District, or South of Market (SoMa) for lower prices.
- **Saving on Food:** Check for local deals and discounts using apps like Too Good To Go or OLIO.
- **Public Transportation:** Utilize San Francisco's extensive public transportation network, including buses, trams (Muni), and BART (Bay Area Rapid Transit), to get around the city affordably. Consider purchasing a Clipper card for discounted fares on multiple modes of transit.
- **Free Attractions:** Take advantage of San Francisco's many free attractions, such as walking across the Golden Gate Bridge, exploring Golden Gate Park, visiting the Painted Ladies in Alamo Square, or enjoying the views from Twin Peaks.
- **Discount Passes:** Consider purchasing a CityPASS or Go San Francisco Card, which offer discounted admission to multiple attractions and tours in the city. These

passes can save you money if you plan to visit several paid attractions during your trip.

Hiking:
> **Tip**: Explore nearby hiking trails and scenic overlooks in the Golden Gate National Recreation Area, such as Lands End or Battery Spencer, for stunning views of the Golden Gate Bridge and San Francisco Bay.

Sunset Viewing:
> **Tip**: Plan your visit to coincide with sunset for a breathtaking experience of watching the sun set behind the Golden Gate Bridge, casting a golden glow over the bay and skyline.

Visitor Center:
> **Tip**: Visit the Golden Gate Bridge Welcome Center or the nearby Fort Point National Historic Site Visitor Center to learn more about the bridge's history, construction, and significance through interactive exhibits and displays.

- **Discount Pass**: San Francisco CityPASS starting at $76 includes admission to top attractions including the Aquarium of the Bay.
- **Parking** : If driving, consider parking in nearby neighborhoods or parking lots away from the bridge's main tourist areas to save money on parking fees, and then walk or take public transportation to the bridge. Parking fees at designated parking lots near the Golden Gate Bridge can start at around $7 to $10 per vehicle for up to four hours.

13. Mount Rushmore National Memorial, South Dakota

- **Tip to follow to save the most:** Admission to the memorial is free; parking costs $10 per vehicle but you can park for free at the nearby Mount Rushmore National Memorial parking facility if you arrive before 8:00 AM.
- **Hotel Deals**: Look for budget accommodations in nearby towns like Keystone or Rapid City.
- **Saving on Food**: Utilize apps like Food Rescue US to find surplus food in nearby towns.
- **Discount Pass**: America the Beautiful Pass ($80) grants access to Mount Rushmore and other federal lands but access is free.

Ranger Programs:
   Tip: Participate in free ranger-led programs and guided walks offered by the National Park Service to learn more about the history, art, and significance of Mount Rushmore.

Hiking Trails:

Tip: Explore the hiking trails and scenic overlooks around Mount Rushmore, such as the Presidential Trail, for up-close views of the memorial and panoramic views of the Black Hills.

Evening Lighting Ceremony:
Tip: Attend the free evening lighting ceremony held at Mount Rushmore during the summer months, where the memorial is illuminated with lights and a patriotic program is presented.

Nearby Attractions:
- **Tip**: Explore other nearby attractions and points of interest in the Black Hills region, such as Custer State Park, Crazy Horse Memorial, or the Badlands National Park, for additional sightseeing opportunities.

14. Great Smoky Mountains National Park, North Carolina and Tennessee

- **Tip to follow to save the most:** Camping inside the park is relatively inexpensive; reservations are recommended. Stay in budget-friendly accommodations in nearby towns like Gatlinburg, Pigeon Forge, or Cherokee, which offer more affordable hotel options compared to lodging inside the national park. Accommodation prices can vary, but budget hotels, motels, cabins, or campgrounds can start at around $50 to $150 per night, depending on the season and location.
- **Hotel Deals**: Look for budget accommodations in nearby towns like Gatlinburg or Pigeon Forge.
- **Saving on Food**: Check for local deals and discounts using apps like Too Good To Go or OLIO.
- **Discount Pass**: America the Beautiful Pass ($80) grants access to Great Smoky Mountains National Park and other federal lands.

Transportation:
    Tip: Utilize public transportation options or rideshare services to get to Great Smoky Mountains National Park, or consider renting a car if you prefer more flexibility in your transportation.

Entrance Fees:

Tip: There is no entrance fee to visit Great Smoky Mountains National Park, making it one of the few national parks in the United States that doesn't charge an admission fee.

Hiking Trails:
> **Tip**: Explore the extensive network of hiking trails in Great Smoky Mountains National Park, ranging from easy nature walks to challenging backcountry treks, for stunning views of waterfalls, forests, and mountain landscapes.

Scenic Drives:
> **Tip**: Take a scenic drive along the Newfound Gap Road, Cades Cove Loop Road, or Roaring Fork Motor Nature Trail to experience the natural beauty and diverse landscapes of the park from the comfort of your car.

Wildlife Viewing:
> **Tip**: Keep an eye out for wildlife while exploring Great Smoky Mountains National Park, including black bears, deer, elk, and various bird species, and bring binoculars or a camera to capture sightings.

Visitor Centers:
> **Tip**: Visit the visitor centers in Great Smoky Mountains National Park, such as Sugarlands Visitor Center or Oconaluftee Visitor Center, to learn more about the park's history, geology, and wildlife through exhibits and ranger-led programs.

Nearby Attractions:
> **Tip**: Explore other nearby attractions and points of interest in the surrounding area, such as Dollywood in Pigeon Forge, Ober Gatlinburg Ski Resort and Amusement Park, or the Blue Ridge Parkway, for additional sightseeing opportunities.

15. Disneyland Resort, California

- **Tip to follow to save the most:** Visit during the off-peak season for lower ticket prices.
- **Hotel Deals**: Look for budget accommodations in nearby areas like Anaheim or Buena Park.
- **Saving on Food**: Utilize apps like Too Good To Go to find discounted meals in the Anaheim area.
- **Discount Pass**: Consider purchasing multi-day tickets for Disneyland Resort for better value.

1. **Accommodation**:
    - **Tip**: Stay in budget-friendly accommodations outside the Disney resort area, such as hotels or vacation rentals in nearby Kissimmee or Lake Buena Vista, which offer more affordable rates compared to Disney-owned resorts.
    - **Starting Price**: Accommodation prices can vary, but budget hotels or vacation rentals can start at around $50 to $100 per night, depending on the season and location.
2. **Transportation**:
    - **Tip**: Utilize public transportation options like buses, trams, or rideshare services to get to Walt Disney World Resort, or consider renting a car if you prefer more flexibility in your transportation.
    - **Starting Price**: Prices for public transportation fares or rideshare services vary, but they can be affordable options for getting to and from the resort.
3. **Tickets**:
    - **Tip**: Purchase multi-day tickets or annual passes to Walt Disney World Resort to save money on admission, and look for special promotions or deals offered by Disney, such as discounts for Florida residents or military personnel.
    - **Starting Price**: Prices for multi-day tickets start at $109 per day for a single park ticket, with discounts available for multi-day tickets and annual passes.
4. **Dining**:
    - **Tip**: Bring your own snacks and drinks to enjoy while exploring Walt Disney World Resort, or dine at budget-

friendly eateries and food stalls within the parks for more affordable meal options.
   - **Starting Price**: Prices for meals at quick-service restaurants or food stalls within the parks can start at around $10 to $20 per person.
5. **Souvenirs**:
   - **Tip**: Purchase affordable souvenirs and gifts at off-site stores or Amazon, rather than expensive shops within Walt Disney World Resort, to save money on mementos of your visit.
6. **FastPass+**:
   - **Tip**: Take advantage of Disney's FastPass+ system to skip the regular lines and enjoy priority access to select attractions and experiences, which is included with your park admission at no extra cost.
   - **Starting Price**: Free of charge with park admission; reserve up to three FastPass+ selections per day in advance.
7. **Character Meet-and-Greets**:
   - **Tip**: Meet your favorite Disney characters for free at designated meet-and-greet locations within the parks, and bring your own camera or smartphone to capture photos with them.
   - **Starting Price**: Free of charge with park admission; bring your own camera for photos.
8. **Photography**:
   - **Tip**: Capture memorable photos of your visit to Walt Disney World Resort with your own camera or smartphone, and consider purchasing Memory Maker if you want unlimited digital downloads of photos taken by Disney PhotoPass photographers.
   - **Starting Price**: Prices for Memory Maker start at $169 if purchased in advance, or $199 if purchased at the parks.
9. **Entertainment**:
   - **Tip**: Enjoy free entertainment options within the parks, such as parades, fireworks shows, and street performances, which are included with your park admission.

- **Starting Price**: Free of charge with park admission.
10. **Extra Magic Hours**:
    - **Tip**: Take advantage of Extra Magic Hours, exclusive to Disney resort guests, which allow you to enter the parks early or stay late on select days for extended hours of fun and shorter wait times.

16. Alcatraz Island, California

Alcatraz Island, known colloquially as "The Rock," boasts a storied past as a military fortress, notorious federal penitentiary, and now a popular tourist destination. From its construction in the mid-19th century to its closure as a prison in 1963, Alcatraz housed some of America's most infamous criminals, including Al Capone and "Machine Gun" Kelly. Today, it stands as a symbol of resilience and defiance, with its crumbling cell blocks and imposing walls offering visitors a glimpse into its dark and fascinating history.

- **Tip to follow to save the most:** Book tickets for the Alcatraz ferry well in advance to secure lower prices.
- **Hotel Deals**: Look for budget accommodations in San Francisco or nearby areas like Oakland.
- **Saving on Food**: Check for local deals and discounts using apps like Too Good To Go or Karma.
- **Discount Pass**: San Francisco CityPASS starting at $76 includes admission to Alcatraz and other top attractions.

1. **Accommodation**:

- **Starting Price**: Accommodation prices can vary, but budget options can start at around $50 to $100 per night, depending on the season and location.
2. **Transportation**:
    - **Tip**: Take advantage of public transportation options like buses, trams, or rideshare services to get to Pier 33, the departure point for Alcatraz Island cruises, or consider walking or biking if you're staying nearby.
    - **Starting Price**: Prices for public transportation fares or rideshare services vary, but they can be affordable options for getting to Pier 33.
3. **Tickets**:
    - **Tip**: Purchase tickets for the Alcatraz Island tour in advance online to ensure availability and avoid long lines at the ticket office, and consider opting for daytime or evening tours for different experiences.
    - **Starting Price**: Prices for Alcatraz Island tours start at $39.90 per adult for the Day Tour and $47.30 per adult for the Night Tour, with discounts available for children, seniors, and National Park pass holders.
4. **Food and Drinks**:
    - **Tip**: Bring your own snacks and drinks to enjoy while on the ferry ride to Alcatraz Island, as food and beverages are not available for purchase on the island itself, or dine at budget-friendly eateries in San Francisco before or after your visit.
    - **Starting Price**: Prices for snacks and drinks vary, but bringing your own can help you save money.
5. **Guided Audio Tour**:
    - **Tip**: Take advantage of the included self-guided audio tour of Alcatraz Island, which provides fascinating insights into the history and stories of the former prison through narration and interviews with former inmates and guards.
    - **Starting Price**: Included with the price of admission to Alcatraz Island.
7. **Cellhouse Tour**:
    - **Tip**: Explore the historic cellhouse on Alcatraz Island as part of the guided audio tour, where you can see the cells, dining hall, library, and other areas of the former prison up close.
    - **Starting Price**: Included with the price of admission to Alcatraz Island.
8. **Outdoor Exploration**:
    - **Tip**: Spend time exploring the outdoor areas of Alcatraz Island, including the gardens, recreation yard, and scenic viewpoints overlooking the San Francisco Bay, for stunning views and photo opportunities.
    - **Starting Price**: Included with the price of admission to Alcatraz Island.
9. **Gift Shop**:
    - **Tip**: Visit the gift shop on Alcatraz Island to browse for souvenirs, books, and memorabilia related to the history of the former prison, and consider purchasing items as mementos of your visit.
    - **Starting Price**: Prices for souvenirs vary depending on the item.
10. **Visitor Center Exhibits**:
    - **Tip**: Explore the exhibits and displays at the Alcatraz Island Visitor Center before or after your tour to learn more about the history of the island and its significance as a former federal prison and Native American occupation site.
    - **Starting Price**: Included with the price of admission to Alcatraz Island.

17. Napa Valley, California:

Napa Valley, synonymous with world-class wine and breathtaking scenery, has a history steeped in viticulture dating back to the 19th century when European immigrants recognized its potential for winemaking. Since then, it has evolved into one of the premier wine-growing regions in the world, with over 400 wineries dotting its picturesque landscape. Today, visitors flock to Napa Valley to indulge in wine tastings, gourmet cuisine, and luxury accommodations, immersing themselves in a rich tapestry of vineyards, rolling hills, and quaint towns that epitomize the essence of California's wine country.

11. **Accommodation**:
    - **Tip**: Stay in budget-friendly accommodations in nearby towns like Napa, Yountville, or Calistoga, which offer more affordable hotel options compared to upscale resorts and boutique hotels in the heart of Napa Valley.
    - **Starting Price**: Accommodation prices can vary, but budget hotels, motels, bed and breakfasts, or vacation rentals can start at around $100 to $200 per night, depending on the season and location.
2. **Transportation**:
    - **Tip**: Utilize public transportation options like buses or rideshare services to get around Napa Valley, or consider renting a car if you prefer more flexibility in your transportation.
    - **Starting Price**: Prices for public transportation fares or rideshare services vary, but they can be affordable options for getting to and from wineries and attractions in Napa Valley.
3. **Wine Tasting**:
    - **Tip**: Take advantage of complimentary wine tastings offered by some wineries in Napa Valley, or look for wineries that offer discounted tastings or wine flights for budget-conscious visitors.

For budget-conscious visitors looking to enjoy wine tastings or wine flights in Napa Valley, there are several wineries that offer discounted or affordable options:

1. **Castello di Amorosa:** This Tuscan-style castle winery offers discounted tastings through online reservations and often features special promotions on their website.
2. **Domaine Carneros:** Known for their sparkling wines, Domaine Carneros offers affordable tastings and flights with stunning views of the vineyards. They also offer discounts for groups and wine club members.
3. **Beringer Vineyards:** Beringer offers budget-friendly tastings with options for both classic and reserve flights. They often have special promotions and discounts available on their website.
4. **Mumm Napa:** Famous for their sparkling wines, Mumm Napa offers reasonably priced tastings and flights. They also have discounts for wine club members and often feature seasonal promotions.
5. **V. Sattui Winery:** V. Sattui is known for its wide selection of wines and picnic-friendly grounds. They offer affordable tastings and flights, and guests can purchase picnic supplies from their onsite deli.
6. **Sterling Vineyards:** While their aerial tram tour may be a bit pricier, Sterling Vineyards offers affordable tastings with panoramic views of the valley. They often have online discounts available for tastings and tours.
7. **Robert Mondavi Winery:** Robert Mondavi offers budget-friendly tastings with options for both classic and reserve flights. They also have discounts for large groups and often feature seasonal promotions.
8. **Frog's Leap Winery:** This boutique winery offers reasonably priced tastings with a focus on sustainable farming practices. They often have special promotions available on their website.

4. **Picnics**:
    - **Tip**: Pack a picnic lunch and enjoy it at one of the many scenic picnic spots at Napa Valley wineries, or purchase

picnic supplies from local grocery stores or delis for a budget-friendly dining experience surrounded by vineyards.
    - **Starting Price**: Prices for picnic supplies vary, but you can often find affordable options at local grocery stores or markets.
5. **Winery Tours**:
    - **Tip**: Opt for self-guided tours or explore wineries that offer free or discounted tours of their facilities, vineyards, and wine-making process, or consider booking tours through third-party companies for discounted rates.
6. **Wine Discounts**:
    - **Tip**: Join wine clubs or loyalty programs offered by Napa Valley wineries to receive discounts on wine purchases, special offers, and invitations to exclusive events, or look for deals and promotions during off-peak seasons.
    - **Starting Price**: Membership fees for wine clubs vary, but discounts on wine purchases can range from 10% to 20% or more.
7. **Outdoor Activities**:
    - **Tip**: Explore outdoor activities in Napa Valley, such as hiking, biking, or kayaking, which offer opportunities to experience the natural beauty of the region and burn off some calories between wine tastings.
    - **Starting Price**: Prices for outdoor activities vary, but there are often free or low-cost options available for hiking trails, bike rentals, and water sports.
8. **Culinary Experiences**:
    - **Tip**: Dine at budget-friendly eateries, cafes, or food trucks in Napa Valley, or consider purchasing gourmet ingredients from local markets and preparing your own meals or picnics for a more affordable dining experience.
    - **Starting Price**: Prices for meals at local eateries can start at around $15 to $30 per person for lunch or dinner.
9. **Art and Culture**:
    - **Tip**: Visit art galleries, museums, or cultural centers in Napa Valley, such as the Napa Valley Museum or di Rosa Center for Contemporary Art, which offer free or

discounted admission on certain days or for specific exhibits.
- **Starting Price**: Admission prices for art galleries and museums vary, but there are often free or discounted options available for visitors.

10. **Hot Springs and Spas**:
    - **Tip**: Relax and unwind at hot springs or spas in Napa Valley, such as Calistoga Spa Hot Springs or Indian Springs Resort and Spa, which offer affordable day passes, spa treatments, and wellness activities.
    - **Starting Price**: Prices for hot springs and spa treatments vary, but there are often package deals and discounts available for day passes and services.

18. Hawaii

1. **Accommodation**: Stay in budget-friendly accommodations like hostels or vacation rentals in Waikiki or Honolulu. Prices range from $50 to $150 per night.
2. **Transportation**: Utilize public transportation like TheBus or rent a car for exploring the island. Consider carpooling or ridesharing.
3. **Beach Activities**: Enjoy free or low-cost beach activities like swimming, snorkeling, or sunbathing at Waikiki Beach or Hanauma Bay.
4. **Hiking**: Explore hiking trails such as Diamond Head or Manoa Falls for breathtaking views of the island's landscapes.
5. **Cultural Experiences**: Visit free attractions like the Hawaii State Art Museum or take a self-guided walking tour of historic sites in downtown Honolulu.

Maui:

1. **Accommodation**: Stay in budget-friendly accommodations in Kihei or Lahaina. Look for guesthouses or vacation rentals starting from $100 per night.
2. **Road to Hana**: Take a budget-friendly self-guided tour along the Road to Hana, stopping at free or low-cost attractions like waterfalls, beaches, and scenic viewpoints.
3. **Beach Camping**: Camp at designated campsites like Hosmer Grove or Kipahulu Campground for a budget-friendly overnight stay near beautiful beaches.
4. **Farmers Markets**: Experience local culture and cuisine at farmers markets like Maui Swap Meet or Upcountry Farmers Market, where you can find affordable fresh produce, snacks, and souvenirs.
5. **Sunset Viewing**: Watch the sunset at popular spots like Haleakalā National Park or Kaanapali Beach for free.

Big Island (Hawaii Island):

1. **Accommodation**: Stay in budget-friendly accommodations in Hilo or Kona, such as hostels or vacation rentals, starting from $50 to $150 per night.
2. **Volcanoes National Park**: Explore Volcanoes National Park, where admission is $30 per vehicle, and hike trails like Kīlauea Iki or visit the Jaggar Museum.
3. **Stargazing**: Experience stargazing at Mauna Kea Visitor Information Station or Pu'u Huluhulu for free.
4. **Coffee Farm Tours**: Take free or low-cost tours of coffee farms in Kona, such as Greenwell Farms or Kona Coffee Living History Farm, and enjoy complimentary tastings.
5. **Beach Parks**: Relax at free beach parks like Hapuna Beach State Recreation Area or Punalu'u Black Sand Beach Park.

Kauai:

1. **Accommodation**: Stay in budget-friendly accommodations in Lihue or Kapaa, such as guesthouses or vacation rentals, starting from $100 per night.
2. **Waimea Canyon**: Explore Waimea Canyon State Park for free or take a budget-friendly guided tour for a nominal fee.
3. **Napali Coast**: Take a budget-friendly boat tour or hike part of the Kalalau Trail for stunning views of the Napali Coast.
4. **Hanalei Bay**: Spend the day at Hanalei Bay, where you can swim, snorkel, or relax on the beach for free.
5. **Waterfall Hikes**: Hike to free or low-cost waterfalls like Wailua Falls or Opaekaa Falls for a refreshing dip or scenic views.

General Tips:

1. **Travel Off-Peak**: Visit during the shoulder season (spring or fall) for lower accommodation and flight prices.
2. **Book in Advance**: Look for deals and discounts on accommodations, activities, and transportation by booking in advance.

19. Independence National Historical Park, Pennsylvania

Independence National Historical Park in Pennsylvania stands as a testament to America's journey toward independence and the birth of a nation. Established in 1948, this hallowed ground preserves iconic landmarks such as Independence Hall, where the Declaration of Independence and the Constitution were both debated and adopted, and the Liberty Bell, a symbol of freedom and resilience. Through its historic buildings, artifacts, and exhibitions, Independence National Historical Park tells the story of America's quest for liberty, inspiring visitors to reflect on the ideals of democracy and the enduring legacy of those who fought for independence.

- **Hotel Deals**: Look for budget accommodations in nearby areas like Philadelphia.
- **Saving on Food**: Check for local deals and discounts using apps like Too Good To Go or OLIO.
- **Discount Pass**: Philadelphia CityPASS starting at $59 includes admission to multiple attractions, including Independence Hall.
-

Accommodation:

Tip: Stay in budget-friendly accommodations in Philadelphia, such as hostels, budget hotels, or vacation rentals, which offer more affordable rates compared to upscale hotels.

Starting Price: Accommodation prices can vary, but budget options can start at around $50 to $150 per night, depending on the season and location.

Transportation:

Tip: Utilize public transportation options like buses, trains, or rideshare services to get to Independence National Historical Park, or consider walking or biking if you're staying nearby.

Starting Price: Prices for public transportation fares or rideshare services vary, but they can be affordable options for getting around the city.

Attractions:

Independence Hall: Visit Independence Hall, where the Declaration of Independence and the U.S. Constitution were both debated and adopted. Admission is free, but tickets are required during peak seasons.

Liberty Bell: See the Liberty Bell, an iconic symbol of American independence, at the Liberty Bell Center. Admission is free, and no tickets are required.

Congress Hall: Explore Congress Hall, where the U.S. Congress met from 1790 to 1800. Admission is free, and guided tours are available.

Franklin Court: Visit Franklin Court, the site of Benjamin Franklin's home and print shop. Admission is free, and visitors can explore exhibits and the Benjamin Franklin Museum.

National Constitution Center: Discover the National Constitution Center, an interactive museum dedicated to the U.S. Constitution. Admission fees apply, but discounts may be available for students, seniors, and military personnel.

Guided Tours:

Tip: Take advantage of free guided tours offered by the National Park Service at Independence National Historical Park, which provide insights into the park's history and significance.

Starting Price: Free of charge; check the park's website or visitor center for tour schedules.

Visitor Center:

Tip: Visit the Independence Visitor Center to pick up maps, brochures, and information about Independence National Historical Park, as well as nearby attractions, dining options, and events.

Starting Price: Free of charge; located at 6th and Market Streets.

Food and Dining:

Tip: Enjoy budget-friendly dining options in Philadelphia, such as food trucks, cafes, or casual restaurants, for meals before or after exploring Independence National Historical Park.

Starting Price: Prices for meals vary depending on the restaurant and cuisine, but there are often affordable options available for breakfast, lunch, and dinner.

20. Mount St. Helens, Washington

Mount St. Helens, located in Washington state, is a living testament to the power and resilience of nature. This iconic volcano gained worldwide attention with its catastrophic eruption on May 18, 1980, which forever altered the landscape and claimed the lives of 57 people. Despite the devastation, Mount St. Helens has undergone a remarkable transformation in the decades since, with new life emerging from the ashes and the surrounding ecosystem gradually recovering. Today, the mountain serves as a living laboratory for scientists studying volcanic activity and ecological succession, while also attracting adventurers and nature enthusiasts eager to witness its dramatic beauty and learn about its tumultuous past. As a symbol of both destruction and renewal, Mount St. Helens stands as a reminder of the fragility and resilience of our planet's natural wonders.

- **Tip to follow to save the most:** Explore the visitor center and nearby trails for free or low-cost activities.
- **Hotel Deals:** Look for budget accommodations in nearby towns like Castle Rock or Kelso.
- **Saving on Food:** Utilize apps like Too Good To Go to find discounted meals in nearby areas.
- **Discount Pass:** America the Beautiful Pass ($80) grants access to Mount St. Helens and other federal lands.

1. **Accommodation:**
   - **Tip:** Stay in budget-friendly accommodations in nearby towns like Castle Rock or Cougar, which offer more affordable hotel options compared to lodging closer to the mountain.
   - **Starting Price:** Accommodation prices can vary, but budget hotels, motels, or campgrounds can start at around $50 to $150 per night, depending on the season and location.
2. **Transportation:**
   - **Tip:** Rent a car to get to Mount St. Helens and explore the surrounding area at your own pace. Alternatively, consider joining a guided tour that includes transportation from nearby cities like Portland or Seattle.
   - **Starting Price:** Prices for car rentals vary depending on the rental company and vehicle type, but budget options are available.
3. **Visitor Centers:**
   - **Tip:** Start your visit at one of the visitor centers, such as the Johnston Ridge Observatory or the Forest Learning Center, to learn about the eruption of Mount St. Helens, the surrounding landscape, and safety tips for exploring the area.
   - **Starting Price:** Admission fees for visitor centers vary, but they typically range from $5 to $10 per person.
4. **Hiking Trails:**
   - **Tip:** Explore hiking trails in the Mount St. Helens National Volcanic Monument, ranging from easy walks to challenging hikes with panoramic views of the volcano and surrounding landscape. Popular trails include the Harry's Ridge Trail and the Ape Cave.

- **Starting Price**: Free of charge, although some trails may require a Northwest Forest Pass or day-use fee for parking.
5. **Scenic Drives**:
    - **Tip**: Take a scenic drive along State Route 504, also known as the Spirit Lake Memorial Highway, which offers breathtaking views of Mount St. Helens, Spirit Lake, and the surrounding mountains.
    - **Starting Price**: Free of charge, although there may be a fee to access certain viewpoints or attractions along the highway.
6. **Ranger Programs**:
    - **Tip**: Join ranger-led programs and guided walks offered by the Mount St. Helens Institute or the U.S. Forest Service to learn more about the volcano's geology, ecology, and history.
    - **Starting Price**: Free of charge, although some programs may require advance registration or have limited availability.
7. **Picnics**:
    - **Tip**: Pack a picnic lunch and enjoy it at one of the designated picnic areas in the Mount St. Helens National Volcanic Monument, surrounded by scenic views of the volcano and surrounding landscape.
    - **Starting Price**: Free of charge, although some picnic areas may have a day-use fee for parking.
9. **Camping**:
    - **Tip**: Spend the night camping at one of the campgrounds in the Mount St. Helens National Volcanic Monument, such as Seaquest State Park or Iron Creek Campground, for a budget-friendly outdoor experience.
    - **Starting Price**: Campsite fees vary depending on the campground and amenities provided.
10. **Interpretive Centers**:
    - **Tip**: Visit interpretive centers like the Mount St. Helens Visitor Center at Silver Lake or the Science and Learning Center at Coldwater to explore exhibits, displays, and

interactive features related to the volcano's eruption and recovery.
- **Starting Price**: Admission fees vary, but they typically range from $5 to $10 per person.

21. Bryce Canyon National Park, Utah

Bryce Canyon National Park, a geological wonderland in southern Utah, boasts a history as ancient as the hoodoos that define its landscape. Established in 1928, the park preserves a unique collection of hoodoos, spires, and natural amphitheaters carved by the forces of erosion over millions of years. Named after Ebenezer Bryce, a Mormon settler who homesteaded in the area in the late 19th century, Bryce Canyon has captivated visitors with its otherworldly beauty and rich Native American heritage. Today, the park offers hiking trails, scenic overlooks, and stargazing opportunities, inviting visitors to immerse themselves in the timeless wonders of the natural world.

- **Tip to follow to save the most:** Camp inside the park for a low-cost accommodation option.
- **Hotel Deals**: Look for budget accommodations in nearby towns like Tropic or Panguitch.
- **Saving on Food**: Check for local deals and discounts using apps like Too Good To Go or OLIO.
- **Discount Pass**: America the Beautiful Pass ($80) grants access to Bryce Canyon and other federal lands.

Here's a guide to planning a visit to Bryce Canyon National Park in Utah:

1. **Accommodation**:

- **Tip**: Stay in budget-friendly accommodations in nearby towns like Tropic or Panguitch, which offer more affordable hotel options compared to lodging inside the park.
- **Starting Price**: Accommodation prices can vary, but budget hotels, motels, cabins, or campgrounds can start at around $50 to $150 per night, depending on the season and location.

2. **Transportation**:
   - **Tip**: Utilize public transportation options like shuttles or rideshare services to get to Bryce Canyon National Park, or consider renting a car if you prefer more flexibility in your transportation.
   - **Starting Price**: Prices for shuttles or rideshare services vary, but they can be affordable options for getting to and from the park.

3. **Entrance Fees**:
   - **Tip**: Purchase a 7-day pass for Bryce Canyon National Park for $35 per vehicle, or consider purchasing an annual pass for $70 if you plan to visit multiple national parks within a year.
   - **Starting Price**: $35 per vehicle for a 7-day pass; $70 for an annual pass.

4. **Scenic Drives**:
   - **Tip**: Take a scenic drive along the Bryce Canyon Scenic Drive, which offers stunning viewpoints and overlooks of the park's iconic hoodoos and rock formations. Consider stopping at Sunrise Point, Sunset Point, and Bryce Point for panoramic views.
   - **Starting Price**: Free of charge with park admission.

5. **Hiking Trails**:
   - **Tip**: Explore hiking trails in Bryce Canyon National Park, ranging from easy walks along the rim to more challenging hikes into the amphitheaters and hoodoo formations. Popular trails include the Navajo Loop Trail, Queens Garden Trail, and the Rim Trail.
   - **Starting Price**: Free of charge with park admission.

6. **Ranger Programs**:

- **Tip**: Participate in free ranger-led programs and guided walks offered by the National Park Service to learn more about the geology, ecology, and history of Bryce Canyon National Park and enhance your park experience.
- **Starting Price**: Free of charge with park admission.

7. **Camping**:
   - **Tip**: Spend the night camping at one of the campgrounds in Bryce Canyon National Park, such as North Campground or Sunset Campground, for a budget-friendly outdoor experience surrounded by nature.
   - **Starting Price**: Campsite fees vary depending on the campground and amenities provided.

9. **Visitor Center**:
   - **Tip**: Visit the visitor center at Bryce Canyon National Park to pick up maps, brochures, and information about the park's trails, viewpoints, and ranger-led programs, as well as nearby attractions and services.
   - **Starting Price**: Free of charge; located near the park entrance.

10. **Food and Dining**:
    - **Tip**: Enjoy budget-friendly dining options in nearby towns or pack a picnic lunch to enjoy at one of the designated picnic areas within Bryce Canyon National Park for a scenic dining experience.
    - **Starting Price**: Prices for meals vary depending on the restaurant and cuisine, but there are often affordable options available for breakfast, lunch, and dinner.

22. Rocky Mountain National Park, Colorado

Rocky Mountain National Park, nestled in the heart of the Colorado Rockies, is a pristine wilderness sanctuary steeped in natural beauty and rugged grandeur. Established in 1915, this iconic national park encompasses towering peaks, alpine meadows, and pristine lakes, providing a haven for wildlife and outdoor enthusiasts alike. From the iconic Trail Ridge Road, which winds through the park's high alpine tundra, to the majestic vistas of Longs Peak and the lush forests of Bear Lake, Rocky Mountain National Park offers visitors a breathtaking tapestry of landscapes to explore and discover. Whether you're hiking along scenic trails, marveling at cascading waterfalls, or simply soaking in the tranquility of nature, Rocky Mountain National Park promises an unforgettable adventure amidst some of the most spectacular scenery in the American West.

- **Tip to follow to save the most:** Utilize the park's free shuttle system to explore without the need for a car.
- **Hotel Deals**: Look for budget accommodations in nearby towns like Estes Park or Grand Lake.
- **Saving on Food**: Utilize apps like Food Rescue US to find surplus food in nearby towns.
- **Discount Pass**: America the Beautiful Pass ($80) grants access to Rocky Mountain National Park and other federal lands.

1. **Accommodation**:
   - **Tip**: Stay in budget-friendly accommodations in nearby towns like Estes Park or Grand Lake, which offer more affordable hotel options compared to lodging inside the park.
   - **Starting Price**: Accommodation prices can vary, but budget hotels, motels, cabins, or campgrounds can start at around $50 to $150 per night, depending on the season and location.
2. **Transportation**:
   - **Tip**: Utilize public transportation options like shuttles or rideshare services to get to Rocky Mountain National Park, or consider renting a car if you prefer more flexibility in your transportation.
   - **Starting Price**: Prices for shuttles or rideshare services vary, but they can be affordable options for getting to and from the park.
3. **Entrance Fees**:
   - **Tip**: Purchase a 7-day pass for Rocky Mountain National Park for $35 per vehicle, or consider purchasing an annual pass for $70 if you plan to visit multiple national parks within a year.
   - **Starting Price**: $35 per vehicle for a 7-day pass; $70 for an annual pass.
4. **Scenic Drives**:
   - **Tip**: Take a scenic drive along Trail Ridge Road, which offers breathtaking views of the park's mountains, forests, and alpine tundra. Consider stopping at viewpoints like

Many Parks Curve, Forest Canyon Overlook, and Alpine Visitor Center.
  - **Starting Price**: Free of charge with park admission.
5. **Hiking Trails**:
   - **Tip**: Explore hiking trails in Rocky Mountain National Park, ranging from easy strolls to challenging treks. Popular trails include Bear Lake Loop, Emerald Lake Trail, and the hike to Dream Lake.
   - **Starting Price**: Free of charge with park admission.
6. **Ranger Programs**:
   - **Tip**: Participate in free ranger-led programs and guided walks offered by the National Park Service to learn more about the park's wildlife, geology, and history, and enhance your park experience.
   - **Starting Price**: Free of charge with park admission.
7. **Camping**:
   - **Tip**: Spend the night camping at one of the campgrounds in Rocky Mountain National Park, such as Moraine Park Campground or Glacier Basin Campground, for a budget-friendly outdoor experience surrounded by nature.
   - **Starting Price**: Campsite fees vary depending on the campground and amenities provided.
9. **Visitor Centers**:
   - **Tip**: Visit the visitor centers at Rocky Mountain National Park to pick up maps, brochures, and information about the park's trails, wildlife, and ranger-led programs, as well as nearby attractions and services.
   - **Starting Price**: Free of charge; located near the park entrances.
10. **Food and Dining**:
    - **Tip**: Enjoy budget-friendly dining options in nearby towns or pack a picnic lunch to enjoy at one of the designated picnic areas within Rocky Mountain National Park for a scenic dining experience.
    - **Starting Price**: Prices for meals vary depending on the restaurant and cuisine, but there are often affordable options available for breakfast, lunch, and dinner.

23. Zion National Park, Utah

Zion National Park, situated in the majestic red rock canyons of southern Utah, is a testament to the awe-inspiring power of nature. Established in 1919, this iconic national park encompasses a stunning array of towering sandstone cliffs, narrow slot canyons, and verdant river valleys, creating a landscape of unparalleled beauty and diversity. From the iconic Angels Landing trail, offering panoramic views of the Virgin River and Zion Canyon below, to the enchanting Narrows, where hikers can wade through the Virgin River amidst towering canyon walls, Zion National Park offers visitors a wealth of opportunities for exploration and adventure. Whether you're hiking, climbing, or simply admiring the breathtaking scenery, Zion's towering red rock formations and pristine wilderness promise an unforgettable experience in one of America's most cherished natural treasures.

- **Tip to follow to save the most:** Utilize the park's free shuttle system to explore without the need for a car.
- **Hotel Deals**: Look for budget accommodations in nearby towns like Springdale or Hurricane.
- **Saving on Food**: Check for local deals and discounts using apps like Too Good To Go or OLIO.
- **Discount Pass**: America the Beautiful Pass ($80) grants access to Zion National Park and other federal lands.

Here's a guide to planning a visit to Zion National Park in Utah:

1. **Accommodation**:
   - **Tip**: Stay in budget-friendly accommodations in nearby towns like Springdale or Hurricane, which offer more affordable hotel options compared to lodging inside the park.
   - **Starting Price**: Accommodation prices can vary, but budget hotels, motels, cabins, or campgrounds can start at around $50 to $150 per night, depending on the season and location.
2. **Transportation**:
   - **Tip**: Utilize public transportation options like shuttles or rideshare services to get to Zion National Park, or consider renting a car if you prefer more flexibility in your transportation.
   - **Starting Price**: Prices for shuttles or rideshare services vary, but they can be affordable options for getting to and from the park.
3. **Entrance Fees**:
   - **Tip**: Purchase a 7-day pass for Zion National Park for $35 per vehicle, or consider purchasing an annual pass for $70 if you plan to visit multiple national parks within a year.
   - **Starting Price**: $35 per vehicle for a 7-day pass; $70 for an annual pass.
4. **Scenic Drives**:
   - **Tip**: Take a scenic drive along the Zion Canyon Scenic Drive, which offers breathtaking views of the park's towering cliffs, rock formations, and the Virgin River. Consider stopping at viewpoints like Canyon Overlook or Court of the Patriarchs.
   - **Starting Price**: Free of charge with park admission.
5. **Hiking Trails**:
   - **Tip**: Explore hiking trails in Zion National Park, ranging from easy walks along the river to challenging hikes up to viewpoints and through narrow slot canyons. Popular trails include Angels Landing, The Narrows, and Emerald Pools.
   - **Starting Price**: Free of charge with park admission.

6. **Shuttle System**:
   - **Tip**: Utilize the free shuttle system in Zion National Park to access trailheads and popular attractions, as private vehicles are restricted in certain areas during peak seasons. Check the shuttle schedule and plan accordingly.
   - **Starting Price**: Free of charge; included with park admission.
7. **Ranger Programs**:
   - **Tip**: Participate in free ranger-led programs and guided walks offered by the National Park Service to learn more about the park's geology, ecology, and history, and enhance your park experience.
   - **Starting Price**: Free of charge with park admission.
8. **Camping**:
   - **Tip**: Spend the night camping at one of the campgrounds in Zion National Park, such as Watchman Campground or South Campground, for a budget-friendly outdoor experience surrounded by red rock landscapes.
   - **Starting Price**: Campsite fees vary depending on the campground and amenities provided.
10. **Visitor Center**:
    - **Tip**: Visit the visitor center at Zion National Park to pick up maps, brochures, and information about the park's trails, wildlife, and ranger-led programs, as well as nearby attractions and services.
    - **Starting Price**: Free of charge; located near the park entrance.

24. Great Sand Dunes National Park, Colorado

Great Sand Dunes National Park, nestled in the heart of the Colorado Rockies, is a mesmerizing landscape of towering sand dunes, sweeping vistas, and rugged mountains. Established in 2004, this unique national park protects the tallest sand dunes in North America, which rise to heights of up to 750 feet against the backdrop of the Sangre de Cristo Mountains. From the exhilarating experience of sandboarding or sledding down the dunes to the serene beauty of Medano Creek and the surrounding wilderness, Great Sand Dunes National Park offers visitors a one-of-a-kind adventure amidst some of the most stunning natural scenery in the American West. Whether you're exploring the dunes on foot, splashing in the creek, or gazing at the star-filled sky above, the park's pristine wilderness and breathtaking landscapes promise an unforgettable experience for nature lovers and outdoor enthusiasts alike.

- **Tip to follow to save the most:** Sand sledding and hiking are free activities within the park.
- **Hotel Deals**: Look for budget accommodations in nearby towns like Alamosa or Mosca.
- **Saving on Food**: Utilize apps like Too Good To Go to find discounted meals in nearby areas.
- **Discount Pass**: America the Beautiful Pass ($80) grants access to Great Sand Dunes National Park and other federal lands.

Here's a guide to planning a visit to Great Sand Dunes National Park and Preserve in Colorado:

1. **Accommodation**:
   - **Tip**: Stay in budget-friendly accommodations in nearby towns like Alamosa or Mosca, which offer more affordable hotel options compared to lodging near the park.
   - **Starting Price**: Accommodation prices can vary, but budget hotels, motels, cabins, or campgrounds can start at around $50 to $150 per night, depending on the season and location.
2. **Transportation**:
   - **Tip**: Utilize public transportation options like shuttles or rideshare services to get to Great Sand Dunes National Park, or consider renting a car if you prefer more flexibility in your transportation.
   - **Starting Price**: Prices for shuttles or rideshare services vary, but they can be affordable options for getting to and from the park.
3. **Entrance Fees**:
   - **Tip**: Purchase a 7-day pass for Great Sand Dunes National Park and Preserve for $25 per vehicle, or consider purchasing an annual pass for $45 if you plan to visit multiple national parks within a year.
   - **Starting Price**: $25 per vehicle for a 7-day pass; $45 for an annual pass.
4. **Hiking and Sandboarding**:
   - **Tip**: Explore hiking trails in Great Sand Dunes National Park, ranging from easy walks to challenging hikes up the dunes. Popular trails include the High Dune Trail and the Star Dune Trail. Additionally, consider renting or bringing

a sandboard or sled to experience the thrill of sandboarding down the dunes.
- **Starting Price**: Free of charge with park admission. Sandboard rentals can range from $20 to $40 per day.

5. **Visitor Center**:
   - **Tip**: Visit the visitor center at Great Sand Dunes National Park to pick up maps, brochures, and information about the park's trails, wildlife, and ranger-led programs, as well as nearby attractions and services.
   - **Starting Price**: Free of charge; located near the park entrance.

6. **Camping**:
   - **Tip**: Spend the night camping at one of the campgrounds in or near Great Sand Dunes National Park, such as Piñon Flats Campground, for a budget-friendly outdoor experience surrounded by sand dunes and starry skies.
   - **Starting Price**: Campsite fees vary depending on the campground and amenities provided.

8. **Food and Dining**:
   - **Tip**: Pack a picnic lunch or dinner to enjoy at one of the designated picnic areas within Great Sand Dunes National Park, or bring snacks and water to stay fueled during your adventures.
   - **Starting Price**: Prices for meals vary depending on whether you pack your own food or dine out in nearby towns.

25. Pike Place Market, Seattle

Pike Place Market, nestled in the heart of downtown Seattle, is a bustling and iconic marketplace that has been a beloved fixture of the city since 1907. From its humble beginnings as a gathering place for local farmers to sell their produce directly to consumers, Pike Place Market has grown into a vibrant and eclectic destination that attracts millions of visitors each year. With its lively atmosphere, diverse array of vendors, and stunning views of Puget Sound, Pike Place Market offers visitors a sensory feast for the senses. Whether you're sampling fresh seafood, browsing unique arts and crafts, or watching the famous fishmongers toss salmon at the market's entrance, Pike Place Market promises an unforgettable experience that captures the essence of Seattle's vibrant culture and culinary scene.

- **Tip to follow to save the most:** Explore the market for free and sample various food vendors; consider buying fresh produce for a budget-friendly meal.
- **Hotel Deals**: Look for budget accommodations in nearby areas like Belltown or Capitol Hill.
- **Saving on Food**: Check for local deals and discounts using apps like Too Good To Go or OLIO.
- **Discount Pass**: Seattle CityPASS starting at $89 includes admission to top attractions, excluding Pike Place Market.

Here's a guide to enjoying Pike Place Market in Seattle on a budget:

1. **Accommodation**:
   - **Tip**: Stay in budget-friendly accommodations in downtown Seattle or nearby neighborhoods, such as Belltown or Capitol Hill, which offer more affordable hotel options within walking distance of Pike Place Market.
   - **Starting Price**: Accommodation prices can vary, but budget hotels, hostels, or vacation rentals can start at around $50 to $150 per night, depending on the season and location.
2. **Transportation**:
   - **Tip**: Utilize public transportation options like buses, light rail, or rideshare services to get to Pike Place Market, or consider walking if you're staying nearby.
   - **Starting Price**: Prices for public transportation fares or rideshare services vary, but they can be affordable options for getting around the city.
3. **Exploring the Market**:
   - **Tip**: Wander through Pike Place Market's stalls and shops to experience the vibrant atmosphere and sample local foods and products. Don't miss iconic attractions like the Pike Place Fish Market, the original Starbucks store, and the Gum Wall.
   - **Starting Price**: Free of charge; prices vary for food and merchandise purchases.
4. **Sampling Food**:

- **Tip**: Enjoy budget-friendly meals at Pike Place Market by trying affordable options like clam chowder from Pike Place Chowder, a fish sandwich from Market Grill, or a pastry from Le Panier Bakery.
- **Starting Price**: Prices for food items vary, but there are often affordable options available for breakfast, lunch, and snacks.

5. **Shopping for Souvenirs**:
   - **Tip**: Browse Pike Place Market's artisanal shops and craft stalls for unique souvenirs and gifts, such as handmade jewelry, artwork, or locally-produced food items like jams and honey.
   - **Starting Price**: Prices for souvenirs vary depending on the item, but there are often affordable options available for budget-conscious shoppers.

6. **Street Performances**:
   - **Tip**: Enjoy free entertainment from street performers and musicians throughout Pike Place Market, providing a lively backdrop to your visit. Consider tipping performers to show your appreciation.
   - **Starting Price**: Free of charge; optional tipping for performers.

7. **Pike Place Market Foundation Food Access Programs**:
   - **Tip**: Support Pike Place Market's community programs by purchasing products or making donations to initiatives like the Food Access Program, which provides fresh, healthy food to low-income residents and seniors in the area.
   - **Starting Price**: Prices vary for products and donations; consider making a contribution to support the community.

8. **Viewing the Waterfront**:
   - **Tip**: Take a leisurely stroll from Pike Place Market to the Seattle waterfront to enjoy views of Elliott Bay, the Olympic Mountains, and attractions like the Seattle Aquarium and the Great Wheel.
   - **Starting Price**: Free of charge; prices vary for attractions and activities along the waterfront.

9. **Coffee Tasting**:
   - **Tip**: Experience Seattle's coffee culture by sampling locally-roasted beans at specialty coffee shops within Pike Place Market, such as Storyville Coffee or Seattle Coffee Works.
   - **Starting Price**: Prices vary for coffee drinks, but tasting flights or small samples may be available for a nominal fee.

26. The Grand Ole Opry, Nashville, Tennessee

Since its founding in 1925, the Opry has been a cornerstone of country music, showcasing legendary performers, rising stars, and timeless classics to audiences around the world. From its humble beginnings at the Ryman Auditorium to its current home at the Grand Ole Opry House, the Opry has become a symbol of Nashville's rich musical heritage and a must-visit destination for music lovers everywhere. With its legendary performances, captivating storytelling, and unforgettable atmosphere, the Grand Ole Opry continues to captivate audiences with the magic and spirit of country music, making it a truly iconic American institution.

- **Tip to follow to save the most:** Look for discounted tickets for daytime backstage tours or explore nearby free attractions like the Grand Ole Opry Museum.
- **Hotel Deals**: Consider staying in budget accommodations outside the downtown area.
- **Saving on Food**: Utilize apps like Too Good To Go to find discounted meals in Nashville.
- **Discount Pass**: The Grand Ole Opry occasionally offers promotions and discounts on tickets.

Here's a guide to enjoying the Grand Ole Opry in Nashville, Tennessee on a budget:

1. **Accommodation**:
    - **Tip**: Stay in budget-friendly accommodations in Nashville, such as hotels or motels located outside the downtown area or in nearby neighborhoods like East Nashville or The Gulch.
    - **Starting Price**: Accommodation prices can vary, but budget hotels, motels, or hostels can start at around $50 to $150 per night, depending on the season and location.
2. **Transportation**:
    - **Tip**: Utilize public transportation options like buses or rideshare services to get to the Grand Ole Opry, or consider driving if you have access to a vehicle.
    - **Starting Price**: Prices for public transportation fares or rideshare services vary, but they can be affordable options for getting around the city.
3. **Tickets**:
    - **Tip**: Purchase tickets to the Grand Ole Opry in advance to secure the best prices, and consider attending a performance during the week or opting for a daytime show, which may be more budget-friendly than weekend or evening performances.
    - **Starting Price**: Ticket prices vary depending on the show, seating location, and date, but they can start at around $40 to $60 per person for standard seating.
4. **Backstage Tours**:

- **Tip**: Take a backstage tour of the Grand Ole Opry to learn about the history and behind-the-scenes workings of this iconic venue. Look for discounts or special offers on tour tickets, especially if bundled with show tickets.
    - **Starting Price**: Prices for backstage tours vary depending on the package and amenities included, but they can start at around $25 to $35 per person.
5. **Free Attractions**:
    - **Tip**: Explore free attractions in Nashville, such as the nearby Gaylord Opryland Resort & Convention Center, which features beautiful gardens, indoor waterfalls, and live music performances in the atriums.
    - **Starting Price**: Free of charge; optional costs may apply for dining or activities within the resort.
6. **Dining**:
    - **Tip**: Enjoy budget-friendly dining options in Nashville, such as local diners, cafes, or food trucks, for meals before or after attending a show at the Grand Ole Opry.
    - **Starting Price**: Prices for meals vary depending on the restaurant and cuisine, but there are often affordable options available for breakfast, lunch, and dinner.
8. **Parking**:
    - **Tip**: If driving to the Grand Ole Opry, consider parking in nearby lots or garages rather than the venue's official parking lot, which may have higher fees. Look for discounted parking rates or free parking options.
    - **Starting Price**: Parking fees vary depending on the location and duration of parking, but they can start at around $10 to $20 per vehicle.
10. **Public Events**:
    - **Tip**: Check the Grand Ole Opry's schedule for public events and activities, such as free concerts, artist signings, or meet-and-greets, which may offer opportunities to experience the Opry's atmosphere without purchasing show tickets.
    - **Starting Price**: Free of charge; optional costs may apply for merchandise or concessions.

27. The Space Needle, Seattle, Washington

The Space Needle, an iconic landmark towering over the Seattle skyline, stands as a symbol of innovation and ingenuity. Built for the 1962 World's Fair, the Space Needle quickly became an architectural marvel and an enduring symbol of Seattle's forward-thinking spirit. With its futuristic design and panoramic views of the city, Puget Sound, and the surrounding mountains, the Space Needle offers visitors a breathtaking perspective on the beauty and dynamism of the Pacific Northwest. From its rotating observation deck to its glass-floored "Loupe" offering thrilling views below, the Space Needle continues to captivate visitors with its timeless charm and unparalleled vistas, making it a must-see attraction for anyone visiting Seattle.

- **Tip to follow to save the most:** Enjoy the view of the Space Needle from Kerry Park or Gas Works Park for free.
- **Hotel Deals**: Look for budget accommodations in nearby areas like South Lake Union or Capitol Hill.
- **Saving on Food**: Utilize apps like Too Good To Go to find discounted meals in Seattle.
- **Discount Pass**: The Seattle CityPASS starting at $89 includes admission to the Space Needle and other top attractions.

1. **Accommodation**:
    - **Tip**: Stay in budget-friendly accommodations in downtown Seattle or nearby neighborhoods, such as Belltown or Lower Queen Anne, which offer more affordable hotel options within walking distance of the Space Needle.
    - **Starting Price**: Accommodation prices can vary, but budget hotels, hostels, or vacation rentals can start at around $50 to $150 per night, depending on the season and location.
2. **Transportation**:
    - **Tip**: Utilize public transportation options like buses, light rail, or rideshare services to get to the Space Needle, or consider walking if you're staying nearby.
    - **Starting Price**: Prices for public transportation fares or rideshare services vary, but they can be affordable options for getting around the city.
3. **Tickets**:
    - **Tip**: Purchase tickets to the Space Needle observation deck in advance to secure the best prices, and consider visiting during off-peak hours or on weekdays, which may offer lower ticket prices.
    - **Starting Price**: Ticket prices vary depending on the time of day and whether you opt for standard or premium access, but they can start at around $20 to $30 per person.
4. **CityPASS**:

- **Tip**: Save money on attractions including the Space Needle with a Seattle CityPASS, which offers discounted admission to several top Seattle attractions, including the Space Needle, Chihuly Garden and Glass, and the Seattle Aquarium.
- **Starting Price**: The Seattle CityPASS typically costs around $99 for adults and $79 for children, offering significant savings compared to individual attraction tickets.

5. **Dining**:
    - **Tip**: Enjoy budget-friendly dining options in the surrounding area or pack a picnic lunch to enjoy at nearby parks like Seattle Center or Kerry Park, offering stunning views of the Space Needle without the cost of dining at the observation deck.
    - **Starting Price**: Prices for meals vary depending on whether you dine out or pack your own food, but there are often affordable options available for breakfast, lunch, and snacks.

6. **Seattle Center**:
    - **Tip**: Explore Seattle Center, the cultural hub surrounding the Space Needle, which offers free or low-cost attractions like the International Fountain, outdoor art installations, and occasional events or festivals.
    - **Starting Price**: Free of charge for many attractions and activities within Seattle Center; optional costs may apply for special events or attractions.

8. **SkyLine Level Viewing Deck**:
    - **Tip**: Enjoy stunning panoramic views of Seattle from the outdoor SkyLine Level viewing deck on the Space Needle, included with the price of admission to the observation deck.
    - **Starting Price**: Included with the observation deck ticket; no additional cost.

9. **Evening Visits**:
    - **Tip**: Consider visiting the Space Needle in the evening to enjoy sunset views and see the city lights come alive, offering a unique and memorable experience without the higher cost of daytime visits.
    - **Starting Price**: Same as daytime ticket prices; varies depending on the time of year and day of the week.

10. **Public Events**:
    - **Tip**: Check the Space Needle's schedule for public events and activities, such as holiday celebrations, fireworks displays, or special exhibits, which may offer additional opportunities to experience the Space Needle's iconic atmosphere.
    - **Starting Price**: Free of charge for many public events; optional costs may apply for merchandise or concessions.

28. Lake Tahoe, California and Nevada

Lake Tahoe, straddling the border of California and Nevada, is a shimmering jewel nestled amidst the towering peaks of the Sierra Nevada Mountains. Renowned for its crystal-clear waters, pristine beaches, and stunning alpine scenery, Lake Tahoe offers visitors a playground for outdoor adventure and relaxation year-round. From skiing and snowboarding in the winter to hiking, boating, and swimming in the summer, Lake Tahoe's natural beauty and recreational opportunities are unmatched. With its charming lakeside towns, world-class resorts, and endless outdoor activities, Lake Tahoe beckons travelers to immerse themselves in its tranquil waters and majestic surroundings, creating memories that last a lifetime.

1. **Accommodation**:
    - **Tip**: Stay in budget-friendly accommodations in towns around Lake Tahoe, such as South Lake Tahoe, Tahoe City, or Incline Village. Look for motels, hostels, campgrounds, or vacation rentals for more affordable options.
    - **Starting Price**: Accommodation prices can vary, but budget options can start at around $50 to $150 per night, depending on the season and location.
2. **Transportation**:

- **Tip**: Utilize public transportation options like buses or shuttles to get around Lake Tahoe, or consider renting a bike or car if you prefer more flexibility in exploring the area.
- **Starting Price**: Prices for public transportation vary, but they can be affordable options for getting around the region.

3. **Outdoor Activities**:
    - **Tip**: Enjoy budget-friendly outdoor activities around Lake Tahoe, such as hiking, biking, swimming, or picnicking at one of the many beaches or parks. Explore scenic trails like the Tahoe Rim Trail or visit popular spots like Emerald Bay State Park.
    - **Starting Price**: Free of charge for many outdoor activities; optional costs may apply for parking at certain locations.

4. **Beach Access**:
    - **Tip**: Spend a day relaxing at one of Lake Tahoe's public beaches, such as Sand Harbor or Kings Beach. Pack a picnic lunch, sunscreen, and beach gear for a fun and affordable day by the water.
    - **Starting Price**: Prices for parking at beach access points may apply, but many beaches offer free or low-cost entry.

5. **Scenic Drives**:
    - **Tip**: Take a scenic drive around Lake Tahoe to enjoy breathtaking views of the lake and surrounding mountains. Drive along Highway 89 or the Lake Tahoe Scenic Byway for panoramic vistas and photo opportunities.
    - **Starting Price**: Free of charge for scenic drives; optional costs may apply for parking at viewpoints or attractions along the route.

6. **State Parks and Recreation Areas**:
    - **Tip**: Visit state parks and recreation areas around Lake Tahoe for outdoor adventures and stunning natural beauty. Consider exploring options like D.L. Bliss State Park, Emerald Bay State Park, or Spooner Lake State Park.
    - **Starting Price**: State park entrance fees vary but are typically around $10 to $15 per vehicle for day use.

7. **Dining**:
    - **Tip**: Enjoy budget-friendly dining options in towns around Lake Tahoe, such as cafes, delis, or casual restaurants. Look for local favorites and happy hour specials for affordable meals.
    - **Starting Price**: Prices for meals vary depending on the restaurant and cuisine, but there are often affordable options available for breakfast, lunch, and dinner.

9. **Boat Rentals**:
    - **Tip**: Consider renting a kayak, paddleboard, or pedal boat to explore Lake Tahoe's crystal-clear waters at your own pace. Look for rental shops offering hourly or daily rates for watercraft.
    - **Starting Price**: Rental prices vary depending on the type of watercraft and duration of rental, but they can start at around $20 to $40 per hour.

10. **Free Events and Festivals**:
    - **Tip**: Check local event calendars for free events, concerts, or festivals happening around Lake Tahoe during your visit. Enjoy live music, art shows, or outdoor movie screenings without breaking the bank.
    - **Starting Price**: Free of charge for many community events; optional costs may apply for food or merchandise.

29. Denali National Park and Preserve, Alaska

Home to North America's highest peak, Denali, towering at 20,310 feet, the park encompasses six million acres of wilderness, including tundra, forests, and glaciers. Established in 1917 as Mount McKinley National Park and later renamed Denali, the park is a haven for wildlife, including grizzly bears, wolves, moose, and Dall sheep. With its breathtaking landscapes, abundant wildlife, and opportunities for backcountry exploration and adventure, Denali National Park offers visitors a chance to experience the unspoiled majesty of the Alaskan wilderness, making it a bucket-list destination for nature enthusiasts and outdoor adventurers alike.

1. **Accommodation**:
   - **Tip**: Stay in budget-friendly accommodations in nearby towns like Healy or Cantwell, which offer more affordable lodging options compared to staying inside the park. Look for campgrounds, cabins, hostels, or budget hotels.
   - **Starting Price**: Accommodation prices can vary, but budget options can start at around $50 to $150 per night, depending on the season and location.
2. **Transportation**:
   - **Tip**: Utilize public transportation options like shuttles or buses to get to Denali National Park, or consider carpooling with other visitors if you have access to a vehicle. Additionally, look for group tours or guided excursions that provide transportation.
   - **Starting Price**: Prices for shuttles or buses vary, but they can be affordable options for getting around the park.
3. **Entrance Fees**:
   - **Tip**: Purchase a single-day or multi-day pass for Denali National Park and Preserve. Consider visiting during fee-free days if available or purchasing an annual pass if you plan to visit multiple national parks within a year.
   - **Starting Price**: Prices vary depending on the type of pass, but a single-day pass typically costs around $15 to $25 per person.
4. **Scenic Drives**:
   - **Tip**: Take a scenic drive along the Denali Park Road, which offers stunning views of the park's landscapes, wildlife, and Mount McKinley (Denali). Consider taking advantage of the park's shuttle system for transportation along the road.
   - **Starting Price**: Free of charge with park admission; optional costs may apply for shuttle tickets.
5. **Hiking Trails**:
   - **Tip**: Explore hiking trails in Denali National Park, ranging from short walks to challenging treks. Popular trails include the Savage River Loop Trail, Horseshoe Lake Trail, and the trail to the Mount Healy Overlook.
   - **Starting Price**: Free of charge with park admission.
6. **Ranger Programs**:

- **Tip**: Participate in free ranger-led programs and guided walks offered by the National Park Service to learn more about Denali's wildlife, geology, and history, and enhance your park experience.
- **Starting Price**: Free of charge with park admission.

7. **Camping**:
   - **Tip**: Spend the night camping at one of the campgrounds in Denali National Park, such as Riley Creek Campground or Teklanika River Campground, for a budget-friendly outdoor experience surrounded by nature.
   - **Starting Price**: Campsite fees vary depending on the campground and amenities provided.
   - Visitor Center:
   - **Tip**: Visit the Denali Visitor Center to pick up maps, brochures, and information about the park's trails, wildlife, and ranger-led programs, as well as nearby attractions and services.
   - **Starting Price**: Free of charge; located near the park entrance.

10. **Food and Dining**:
    - **Tip**: Pack a picnic lunch or dinner to enjoy at one of the designated picnic areas within Denali National Park, or bring snacks and water to stay fueled during your adventures. Alternatively, dine at budget-friendly restaurants in nearby towns.
    - **Starting Price**: Prices for meals vary depending on whether you pack your own food or dine out, but there are often affordable options available for breakfast, lunch, and dinner.

30. Cape Cod, Massachusetts

Cape Cod, Massachusetts, is a quintessential New England destination renowned for its charming coastal towns, pristine beaches, and rich maritime history. Jutting out into the Atlantic Ocean like a beckoning arm, Cape Cod offers visitors a scenic tapestry of sandy shores, rolling dunes, and picturesque harbors. From the historic charm of Provincetown at the tip of the Cape to the quaint villages of Chatham, Wellfleet, and Sandwich, Cape Cod captivates visitors with its idyllic scenery and laid-back atmosphere. Whether you're exploring the Cape Cod National Seashore, indulging in fresh seafood, or simply relaxing on the beach, Cape Cod beckons travelers to slow down, unwind, and savor the timeless beauty of coastal New England.

1. **Accommodation**:
    - **Tip**: Stay in,Falmouth, Hyannis, or Orleans. Look for motels, hostels, campgrounds, or vacation rentals for more affordable options.
    - **Starting Price**: Accommodation prices can vary, but budget options can start at around $50 to $150 per night, depending on the season and location.
2. **Transportation**:
    - **Tip**: Utilize public transportation options like buses or shuttles to get around Cape Cod, or consider renting a bike if you prefer eco-friendly and budget-friendly transportation. Additionally, carpooling with other visitors can help save on gas and parking costs.
    - **Starting Price**: Prices for public transportation vary, but they can be affordable options for getting around the area.
3. **Beach Access**:
    - **Tip**: Spend a day relaxing at one of Cape Cod's public beaches, such as Coast Guard Beach, Nauset Beach, or Old Silver Beach. Many beaches offer free or low-cost parking and facilities, making them ideal for budget-friendly outings.
    - **Starting Price**: Prices for parking at beach access points may apply, but many beaches offer free or low-cost entry.
4. **Outdoor Activities**:
    - **Tip**: Enjoy budget-friendly outdoor activities on Cape Cod, such as hiking, biking, kayaking, or birdwatching at one of the area's nature reserves, wildlife refuges, or conservation areas. Explore options like the Cape Cod Rail Trail or the Cape Cod National Seashore.
    - **Starting Price**: Free of charge for many outdoor activities; optional costs may apply for equipment rentals or guided tours.
5. **Cape Cod Rail Trail**:
    - **Tip**: Take a bike ride or leisurely stroll along the Cape Cod Rail Trail, a scenic path that spans 25 miles from Dennis to Wellfleet. Enjoy beautiful views of the Cape's landscapes, villages, and wildlife along the way.

- **Starting Price**: Free to access the trail; optional costs may apply for bike rentals.
6. **Visit Lighthouses**:
    - **Tip**: Explore Cape Cod's historic lighthouses, such as Nauset Light, Highland Light, or Race Point Light. Many lighthouses offer guided tours or visitor centers where you can learn about their history and significance.
    - **Starting Price**: Prices for lighthouse tours vary, but they can be affordable options for learning more about Cape Cod's maritime heritage.
7. **Cape Cod National Seashore**:
    - **Tip**: Spend a day exploring the Cape Cod National Seashore, which offers pristine beaches, scenic trails, and cultural sites. Visit attractions like Marconi Beach, Salt Pond Visitor Center, or the Province Lands Bike Trail.
    - **Starting Price**: Entrance fees to the Cape Cod National Seashore vary depending on the season and type of vehicle, but they can start at around $15 to $25 per vehicle for a day pass.
8. **Art Galleries and Museums**:
    - **Tip**: Discover Cape Cod's artistic and cultural heritage by visiting local art galleries, museums, or historic sites. Look for free or low-cost exhibitions, events, or workshops showcasing the region's arts and culture.
    - **Starting Price**: Prices for admission to galleries and museums vary, but many offer discounts for students, seniors, or local residents.
9. **Dining**:
    - **Tip**: Enjoy budget-friendly dining options on Cape Cod, such as clam shacks, seafood markets, or roadside stands serving fresh seafood, chowder, or lobster rolls. Look for local favorites and daily specials for affordable meals.
    - **Starting Price**: Prices for meals vary depending on the restaurant and cuisine, but there are often affordable options available for breakfast, lunch, and dinner.

31. The Everglades

Discovering the Everglades is an experience unlike any other. Unlike majestic mountain ranges or picturesque valleys, the Everglades captivate with their eerie allure. Picture a vast expanse of flat, watery landscapes, punctuated by islands of trees, cypress domes, and mangroves. Here, hiking trails won't suffice. To truly delve into the heart of the Everglades and encounter its ancient inhabitants, like the formidable crocodile, you must venture beyond the safety of solid ground.

The Everglades are located in southern Florida, primarily within the boundaries of Everglades National Park. This expansive wetland ecosystem covers about 1.5 million acres (6,070 square kilometers) in total, stretching from Lake Okeechobee in the north to Florida Bay in the south. The nearest major cities to the Everglades include Miami and Fort Lauderdale. This vast area is home to diverse wildlife, including alligators, crocodiles, various bird species, and unique plant life.

1. **Free Entry Days**: Take advantage of free entry days to Everglades National Park, often available on holidays or special occasions.
2. **Camping**: Stay at affordable campgrounds within Everglades National Park for a close-to-nature experience. Consider Long Pine Key Campground or Flamingo Campground for budget-friendly options.
3. **Explore Lesser-Known Areas**: Discover hidden gems and avoid crowds by exploring lesser-known areas of the park. Try hiking trails like Snake Bight Trail or canoe routes along Turner River for a quieter experience.
4. **Take Advantage of Free Programs**: Check the park's schedule for free ranger-led programs, nature walks, and talks. Everglades National Park often offers these educational opportunities at no cost.

32. Route 66

Embark on a budget-friendly journey along Route 66, the iconic Mother Road that stretches from Chicago to Los Angeles. Here's your insider guide to experiencing this timeless American adventure without breaking the bank:

1. **Cheap Car Rental**: Look for deals from rental companies like Budget, Thrifty, or Economy Rent a Car, which often offer competitive rates and discounts for longer rentals.
2. **Where to Rent**: Rent your vehicle from major airports or city locations near the starting point of Route 66, such as Chicago or Los Angeles. Consider renting a fuel-efficient compact car or economy sedan to save on gas expenses during your journey.
3. **Pack Essentials**: Before hitting the road, pack essential items like snacks, water, sunscreen, and a road map or GPS device. Bringing your own cooler and picnic supplies can help you save money on meals by enjoying roadside picnics or cooking at campgrounds along the way.
4. **Stay in Budget Accommodations**: Look for budget-friendly accommodations along Route 66, such as motels, hostels, or campgrounds. Consider staying in smaller towns or off the beaten path to find cheaper rates compared to major tourist destinations.
5. **Explore Quirky Attractions**: Discover hidden gems and quirky roadside attractions along Route 66 without spending a fortune. Visit iconic landmarks like the Snow Cap Drive-In in Seligman, the Wigwam Motel in Holbrook, or the neon signs of Tucumcari for memorable photo opportunities and nostalgic experiences.
6. **Take Advantage of Free Activities**: Look for free or low-cost activities along Route 66, such as hiking, exploring historic sites, or attending local festivals and events. Take scenic drives through national parks or along scenic byways for budget-friendly sightseeing experiences.

For budget-conscious travelers seeking a taste of local flavor, many towns along Route 66 host free festivals, events, and live music performances. These community gatherings celebrate the region's cultural heritage and provide opportunities to mingle with locals while enjoying authentic food, music, and entertainment. Whether it's a chili cook-off in New Mexico or a classic car show in Illinois, these festivities offer a fun and cost-effective way to experience the spirit of Route 66.

Additionally, travelers can take advantage of free guided tours and informational exhibits offered by museums and visitor centers along the route. These educational resources provide insights into the history, culture, and significance of Route 66, allowing visitors to deepen their understanding of this iconic highway without spending a penny. From the Route 66 Museum in Oklahoma to the California Route 66 Museum in Victorville, these attractions offer a wealth of information and entertainment for travelers on a budget.

Nature lovers will appreciate the opportunity to explore scenic overlooks, hiking trails, and picnic areas along Route 66—all of which are typically free or require only a nominal entrance fee. Whether it's admiring the panoramic views from the Grand Canyon's South Rim in Arizona or hiking the scenic trails of the Mojave National Preserve in California, these outdoor experiences allow travelers to connect with the natural beauty of the American West at no cost.

The cities

Rank	City	State	Number of Visitors (Millions)
1	New York City	New York	62.8
2	Las Vegas	Nevada	49.5
3	Orlando	Florida	47.7
4	Los Angeles	California	47.3
5	Chicago	Illinois	38.2
6	San Francisco	California	25.8
7	Miami	Florida	23.5
8	San Diego	California	22.7
9	Honolulu	Hawaii	10.7
10	Boston	Massachusetts	10.1
11	Washington, D.C.	District of Columbia	9.0
12	Philadelphia	Pennsylvania	8.4
13	Atlanta	Georgia	7.6
14	New Orleans	Louisiana	7.0
15	Seattle	Washington	6.0
16	Denver	Colorado	5.6
17	Houston	Texas	5.4
18	Phoenix	Arizona	5.1
19	San Antonio	Texas	4.5
20	Nashville	Tennessee	4.4

New York

The iconic concrete jungle, where history meets modernity in every corner. From its humble beginnings as a Dutch trading post to its rise as the cultural and financial capital of the world, New York City's allure is undeniable.

Now, if you're craving luxury on a budget, fear not! Indulge in high-end experiences without breaking the bank. Opt for free attractions like Central Park or the Brooklyn Bridge for stunning views. Hit up upscale restaurants during lunch for prix-fixe menus, and explore the city's vibrant art scene at affordable galleries. With a bit of savvy planning, you can savor the extravagance of the Big Apple without emptying your wallet.

Accommodation

Since the Airbnb ban in New York City, finding budget-friendly accommodations that still offer comfort and convenience can be a challenge, but there are options available:
1. **Hostels:** Hostels are often the cheapest option for lodging in NYC. Some well-reviewed hostels include The Local NYC, HI NYC Hostel, and Jazz Hostels.
2. **Budget Hotels:** Look for budget hotels that offer clean and basic accommodations without sacrificing quality. Some options to consider include Pod 51 Hotel, The Jane Hotel, and Hotel Pennsylvania.
3. **Micro Hotels:** Micro hotels offer small but efficient rooms at affordable prices. Examples include YOTEL New York and citizenM New York Bowery.
4. **Hotel Deals:** Keep an eye out for special deals and promotions on hotel booking websites such as Booking.com, Hotels.com, or Expedia. You may find discounted rates or last-minute deals that fit your budget.

Hidden Gems

Hidden Speakeasies: New York is home to numerous hidden speakeasies, offering a glimpse into the city's Prohibition-era past. To experience these hidden gems, look for unmarked doors or nondescript entrances in neighborhoods like the East Village or Lower Manhattan. Insider Tip: Research online for password-protected speakeasies or join a guided tour to discover secret bars while enjoying complimentary drinks.

DUMBO's Timeless Cobblestone Streets: DUMBO (Down Under the Manhattan Bridge Overpass) boasts charming cobblestone streets and breathtaking views of the Manhattan skyline. Take a leisurely stroll along Water Street and admire the historic architecture and street art. Insider Tip: Visit during the early morning or late afternoon to avoid crowds and capture stunning photos of the iconic Manhattan Bridge.

Whispering Gallery at Grand Central Terminal: Grand Central Terminal is known for its bustling atmosphere, but hidden within its walls is the Whispering Gallery. Located near the Oyster Bar & Restaurant, the gallery features a unique acoustic phenomenon where whispers can be heard across the room. Insider Tip: Bring a friend and test out the whispering effect by standing at opposite corners of the gallery.

Green-Wood Cemetery's Architectural Marvels: Green-Wood Cemetery in Brooklyn is not only a final resting place but also an outdoor museum of architectural wonders. Explore its serene landscapes and discover elaborate mausoleums, sculptures, and historic gravesites. Insider Tip: Join a guided walking tour led by knowledgeable volunteers to learn about the cemetery's fascinating history and notable residents.

NYC's Elevated Parks: Escape the hustle and bustle of the city streets by visiting NYC's elevated parks, such as the High Line and the Manhattan Waterfront Greenway. These repurposed spaces offer lush greenery, stunning views, and public art installations. Insider Tip: Pack a picnic and enjoy a leisurely stroll along these elevated promenades while taking in panoramic views of the city.

Hidden Rooftop Gardens: New York's skyline is dotted with hidden rooftop gardens and green spaces, providing urban oases amid the concrete jungle. Seek out rooftop bars and restaurants with rooftop access to enjoy panoramic views while sipping cocktails or dining al fresco. Insider Tip: Look for establishments with happy hour specials or visit during off-peak hours to enjoy the ambiance without breaking the bank.

Little Island: Little Island, located on the Hudson River, is a vibrant new addition to New York's waterfront. This whimsical park features lush gardens, winding pathways, and amphitheaters for outdoor performances. Admission is free, making it accessible to all. Insider Tip: Arrive early to secure a spot for free public performances or yoga classes held on the island.

Secret Gardens: New York is home to several hidden gardens tucked away in unexpected places. Explore the Elizabeth Street Garden in Nolita or the Conservatory Garden in Central Park for tranquil escapes from the city's hustle. Insider Tip: Check garden websites for special events, workshops, or volunteer opportunities to engage with the community while enjoying these serene spaces.

City Island's Seaside Charm: City Island, located in the Bronx, feels like a quaint New England fishing village just a short drive from Manhattan. Explore its charming streets lined with seafood restaurants, art galleries, and antique shops. Insider Tip: Visit during the weekday to avoid crowds and take advantage of lunch specials at local eateries offering fresh seafood at affordable prices.

Secret Subway Art: Discover hidden subway art installations throughout New York's underground transit system. From colorful mosaics to vibrant murals, these artworks add character to subway stations across the city. Insider Tip: Download the "MTA Arts & Design" app to access a virtual guide to subway art installations and plan your own self-guided art tour while riding the subway.

Attractions:

- **CityPASS:** Purchase the New York CityPASS for discounted admission to top attractions, including the Empire State Building and the Metropolitan Museum of Art.
- **Free Museum Days:** Many museums have free or pay-what-you-wish admission on specific days or evenings. Check their websites for details.
- **Central Park:** Explore Central Park for free and consider renting a bike for around $10-20 per hour.

- **Brooklyn Bridge:** Walk across the Brooklyn Bridge for stunning views of Manhattan at no cost.
- **Staten Island Ferry:** Enjoy a free ride on the Staten Island Ferry for fantastic views of the Statue of Liberty and Manhattan.

Dining:

- **Street Food:** Try delicious and affordable street food from food trucks and vendors.
- **Dollar Slice Pizza:** Grab a classic New York slice for around $1-3.
- **Happy Hour Deals:** Take advantage of happy hour specials at bars and restaurants for discounted drinks and appetizers.
- **Ethnic Cuisine:** Explore neighborhoods like Chinatown and Little Italy for budget-friendly and authentic ethnic dining experiences.
- **Food Markets:** Visit food markets like Smorgasburg and Chelsea Market for affordable and diverse food options.
- **BYOB Restaurants:** Dine at "bring your own bottle" (BYOB) restaurants to save on alcohol expenses.

Transportation:

- **Subway and Bus:** Use the NYC subway and bus system for affordable and convenient transportation. A single subway ride costs $2.75.
- **MetroCard:** Purchase a MetroCard for subway and bus rides and consider getting an Unlimited MetroCard for longer stays.
- **Walk:** Explore neighborhoods on foot to save on transportation costs and discover hidden gems.
- **Citi Bike:** Rent a Citi Bike for around $4 per 15 minutes or purchase a day pass for $12 for unlimited 30-minute rides.

- **Airport Shuttles:** Use airport shuttle services instead of taxis for more cost-effective transportation from the airport to the city.

Entertainment:

- **Broadway Lotteries:** Enter Broadway ticket lotteries for a chance to score discounted tickets to popular shows.
- **Discounted Show Tickets:** Visit the TKTS booth in Times Square or use the TodayTix app for discounted same-day tickets to Broadway and Off-Broadway shows.
- **Public Parks:** Enjoy free events and performances in public parks, such as Central Park's SummerStage.
- **Comedy Clubs:** Find comedy clubs with free or low-cost shows during the week.
- **Free Outdoor Movies:** Attend free outdoor movie screenings in parks and public spaces during the summer months.

Shopping:

- **Sample Sales:** Keep an eye out for sample sales and designer discounts in neighborhoods like SoHo and Chelsea.
- **Discount Outlets:** Visit outlet stores like Woodbury Common Premium Outlets for discounted shopping.
- **Chinatown Shopping:** Bargain-hunt in Chinatown for affordable souvenirs and unique finds.
- **Thrift Stores:** Explore thrift stores in the East Village and Williamsburg for budget-friendly fashion.

Tours and Attractions:

- **Free Walking Tours:** Join free or pay-what-you-wish walking tours to learn about the city's history and neighborhoods.

- **Central Park Bike Tour:** Take a guided bike tour of Central Park for around $40-50 per person.
- **Statue of Liberty:** Enjoy free views of the Statue of Liberty from the Staten Island Ferry, or visit Liberty Island for a fee.
- **New York Public Library Tours:** Explore the iconic New York Public Library with free guided tours.
- **City Sightseeing Passes:** Consider purchasing the New York Pass or the Explorer Pass for savings on multiple attractions.

Transportation within NYC:

- **Ride-Sharing Apps:** Use ride-sharing apps like Uber and Lyft, especially when traveling with a group, as it can be cost-effective.
- **Rides to Airports:** Consider taking airport shuttles or the subway to airports to avoid high taxi or Uber fares.
- **Airport Train:** Use the AirTrain to JFK Airport for a more affordable airport transfer.
- **Walking Tours:** Explore different neighborhoods with self-guided walking tours available online or through apps.

Sports and Recreation:

- **Free Yoga Classes:** Attend free or donation-based yoga classes in parks or at local studios.
- **Public Swimming Pools:** Cool off at free public swimming pools across the city during the summer.
- **Hiking Trails:** Explore hiking trails in the Bronx, Staten Island, and Queens for outdoor adventures.

Local Events and Festivals:

- **Street Fairs:** Visit street fairs throughout the city for free entertainment, food vendors, and shopping.
- **Cultural Festivals:** Attend free cultural festivals celebrating various communities and traditions.
- **Free Concerts:** Enjoy free outdoor concerts in parks and public spaces during the summer.

Miscellaneous Savings:

- **Library Passes:** Some local libraries offer free or discounted passes to museums and attractions.
- **Student Discounts:** If you're a student, inquire about available discounts at attractions, restaurants, and theaters.
- **Senior Discounts:** If you're a senior citizen, check for discounts on admission fees, transportation, and dining.
- **Discounted Spa Services:** Find discounted spa and wellness services through daily deal websites like Groupon.
- **Free Wi-Fi:** Connect to free Wi-Fi available at many hotels, restaurants, and cafes to save on data charges.
- **Groupon Deals:** Search Groupon for discounts on local entertainment, activities, dining, and services in New York City.
- **Free Museum Days:** Many museums offer free admission on specific days or evenings.
- **Staten Island Ferry:** Enjoy stunning views of the Statue of Liberty and Manhattan skyline for free.
- **Central Park:** Explore the vast park for free, and consider renting a bike or taking a free walking tour.
- **Visit Libraries:** The New York Public Library and the Morgan Library offer free admission to their exhibits.
- **Happy Hours:** Take advantage of happy hour specials for discounted drinks and appetizers at bars and restaurants.
- **Discount Broadway Tickets:** Buy discounted same-day tickets at the TKTS booth in Times Square or via the TodayTix app.
- **Visit Governors Island:** A ferry ride to this island offers free or low-cost activities during the summer months.

- **Dollar Slice Pizza:** Grab a cheap but tasty slice of pizza from one of the many dollar pizza shops.
- **NYC Parks Events:** Attend free events like outdoor concerts, movie screenings, and yoga classes in city parks.
- **Ride the Roosevelt Island Tram:** Get unique views of Manhattan for the price of a subway ride.
- **Explore Chinatown:** Enjoy affordable and delicious food options and shop for bargains.
- **Bronx Zoo Wednesdays:** Pay what you wish for admission on Wednesdays at the Bronx Zoo.
- **Walking Tours:** Join free or donation-based walking tours to learn about the city's history and neighborhoods.
- **Explore Harlem:** Experience the cultural richness of Harlem and enjoy live music and soul food.
- **Visit the High Line:** This elevated park offers great views and is free to explore.
- **Bike Rentals:** Rent a Citi Bike or use the many bike-sharing options for a cost-effective way to get around.
- **Gantry Plaza State Park:** Head to Long Island City for skyline views and a peaceful waterfront park.
- **Food Markets:** Explore food markets like Smorgasburg and Chelsea Market for affordable eats.
- **Cheap Eats in Queens:** Queens offers diverse and budget-friendly dining options.
- **Discounted Museums:** Look for discounted tickets to museums on websites like Groupon or CityPASS.
- **Free Kayaking:** Try free kayaking at the Downtown Boathouse on the Hudson River.
- **Explore Coney Island:** Enjoy the beach, boardwalk, and amusement park for a fun and affordable day.
- **Pay-What-You-Wish Museums:** Museums like the MET and the American Museum of Natural History offer pay-what-you-wish admission.
- **Visit Arthur Avenue:** The "Real Little Italy" in the Bronx offers delicious Italian food at reasonable prices.
- **Comedy Clubs:** Find comedy clubs with free or low-cost shows during the week.

- **Happy Hour Cruises:** Enjoy happy hour cruises for scenic views of the city skyline.
- **Affordable Delis:** Try classic New York delis for reasonably priced sandwiches and bagels.
- **Governors Island Free Bike Hour:** Enjoy a free hour of bike rental on Governors Island on weekday mornings.
- **Ride the Staten Island Railway:** Take a scenic ride on the Staten Island Railway for the cost of a subway fare.
- **Bronx Museum of the Arts:** This museum offers free admission.
- **Chase ATMs:** If you need cash, use Chase ATMs to avoid fees when withdrawing money.
- **Free Concerts:** Attend free summer concerts in parks like Central Park's SummerStage.
- **Free Art Galleries:** Explore Chelsea's art galleries for free contemporary art exhibitions.
- **Visit Wave Hill:** Enjoy a serene garden in the Bronx with free admission on Tuesdays and Saturdays.
- **Discounted Broadway Rush Tickets:** Some shows offer discounted rush tickets on the day of the performance.
- **Affordable Ethnic Food:** Explore diverse neighborhoods for affordable ethnic cuisine, such as Jackson Heights for Indian food.
- **Cheap Eats in Brooklyn:** Explore Brooklyn's neighborhoods for wallet-friendly dining options.
- **NYC Passes:** Consider purchasing attraction passes for discounted entry to multiple sites.
- **Free Ice Skating:** In the winter, enjoy free ice skating at Bryant Park or Central Park's Wollman Rink (with your own skates).
- **Affordable Bagels:** Grab a classic New York bagel at a local bakery for a budget breakfast.
- **Visit Flushing:** Explore the diverse food scene and culture of Flushing, Queens.
- **Brooklyn Botanic Garden Free Hours:** Enjoy free admission at certain times during the week.

Orlando

Known as the theme park capital of the world, this vibrant city has a rich history of entertainment and innovation.

But guess what? You don't need a fairy godmother to experience luxury on a budget here! Take advantage of discounted theme park tickets available online or through package deals. Explore the city's natural wonders with budget-friendly activities like hiking in the nearby state parks or picnicking by one of the many lakes. And don't forget about the local cuisine – indulge in gourmet food truck fare or sample international flavors at affordable eateries.

1. **Winter Park's Scenic Boat Tour**: Escape the theme park crowds and experience the natural beauty of Orlando with a scenic boat tour in Winter Park. Navigate through picturesque lakes and canals surrounded by lush vegetation and historic mansions. Insider Tip: Opt for the early morning tour to witness stunning sunrise views over the waterways and enjoy cooler temperatures.
2. **Mills 50 District's Street Art**: Explore Orlando's vibrant arts scene in the Mills 50 District, known for its eclectic mix of street art and murals. Take a self-guided walking tour through the neighborhood's colorful streets and alleyways to discover unique art installations. Insider Tip: Visit during the annual "IMMERSE" festival in October, where local artists showcase their talents through interactive exhibits and performances.
3. **Leu Gardens' Botanical Oasis**: Discover the beauty of nature at Harry P. Leu Gardens, a 50-acre botanical oasis nestled in the heart of Orlando. Explore lush gardens, scenic trails, and historic homes surrounded by tropical plants and flowering trees. Insider Tip: Visit on the first Monday of the month for free admission to the gardens and take advantage of guided tours led by knowledgeable staff.
4. **Black Hammock Adventures**: Experience Florida's natural wonders at Black Hammock Adventures, located on the shores of Lake Jesup. Embark on an airboat tour through pristine

wetlands teeming with wildlife, including alligators, birds, and turtles. Insider Tip: Look for discounted airboat tour packages online or visit during off-peak hours for quieter and more affordable experiences.
5. **East End Market's Culinary Delights**: Indulge in Orlando's thriving food scene at East End Market, a culinary hub showcasing local artisans and chefs. Explore food stalls, specialty shops, and communal dining spaces offering a diverse array of gourmet treats. Insider Tip: Attend cooking classes or food tastings hosted by resident chefs to learn new culinary skills and sample delicious creations.
6. **Lake Eola Park's Urban Oasis**: Relax and unwind at Lake Eola Park, a tranquil urban oasis located in downtown Orlando. Enjoy scenic walking paths, paddleboat rentals, and picnicking areas surrounded by lush greenery and the iconic Lake Eola fountain. Insider Tip: Pack a picnic lunch and attend the weekly "Sunday Funday" farmer's market for fresh produce, local crafts, and live entertainment.
7. **Wekiva Springs State Park's Natural Escapes**: Immerse yourself in Florida's natural beauty at Wekiva Springs State Park, just a short drive from Orlando. Explore pristine wilderness areas, hike scenic trails, or cool off with a refreshing swim in the crystal-clear springs. Insider Tip: Arrive early to secure a spot at the park's popular swimming area and enjoy the tranquil surroundings before the crowds arrive.
8. **Gatorland's Wildlife Encounters**: Get up close and personal with Florida's most iconic residents at Gatorland, the "Alligator Capital of the World." Experience thrilling gator shows, interactive exhibits, and hands-on wildlife encounters for an unforgettable adventure. Insider Tip: Look for online discounts or special promotions, such as Florida resident deals or combo tickets with other attractions, to save on admission fees.
9. **Downtown Orlando's Art Walks**: Discover local artists and cultural venues in downtown Orlando during monthly art walks and gallery strolls. Explore eclectic art galleries, live music performances, and street performers while immersing yourself in the city's creative energy. Insider Tip: Check event calendars

for themed art walks or special exhibitions and plan your visit accordingly for unique experiences.
10. **Historic Sanford's Riverside Charm**: Step back in time and explore the historic charm of downtown Sanford, located just north of Orlando. Wander along the picturesque waterfront, browse antique shops and art galleries, or dine at cozy cafes and waterfront restaurants. Insider Tip: Attend Sanford's monthly "Alive After 5" street party for live music, food trucks, and local vendors offering a taste of the city's vibrant culture.

Theme Parks:

- **Buy Multi-Day Passes:** Purchase multi-day tickets for theme parks like Walt Disney World and Universal Orlando Resort to reduce the daily cost per visit. Check official websites for current prices.
- **Book Online:** Many theme parks offer discounts when you purchase tickets online in advance. For example, Walt Disney World offers savings on multi-day tickets when purchased online through their website.
- **Military Discounts:** Active and retired military personnel can often access special ticket prices. Check the official websites of theme parks for details.
- **Florida Resident Discounts:** If you're a Florida resident, take advantage of resident discounts on theme park tickets and annual passes. Visit the respective park's website for pricing.
- **Kids Eat Free Programs:** Some restaurants at theme parks offer "Kids Eat Free" promotions. Check the dining options within the parks for details.

Accommodation:

- **Off-Season Travel:** Plan your visit during the off-peak season when hotel rates are typically lower.

- **Hotel Rewards Programs:** Join hotel rewards programs to earn points for future stays. Some popular options include Hilton Honors, Marriott Bonvoy, and IHG Rewards Club.
- **Vacation Rentals:** Consider vacation rentals or Airbnb for affordable lodging options.
- **Book in Advance:** Reserve your accommodation well in advance to secure lower rates. Websites like Booking.com and Expedia often offer discounted rates for early bookings.
- **Hotel Packages:** Look for hotel and theme park ticket packages, which can offer savings. Check the official websites of theme parks for available packages.

Dining:

- **Quick-Service Dining:** Opt for quick-service dining within theme parks for more budget-friendly meal options.
- **BYOB (Bring Your Own Breakfast):** Bring your own breakfast items and snacks to enjoy in your hotel room.
- **Use Dining Apps:** Download dining apps like Yelp, OpenTable, and Groupon to find discounts and deals at local restaurants.
- **Kids Eat Free Deals:** Look for restaurants that offer "Kids Eat Free" deals on certain days of the week. Websites like KidsMealDeals.com can help you find these offers.
- **Buffet Lunches:** If you want to dine at a higher-end restaurant, consider doing so for lunch instead of dinner, as prices are often lower.

Transportation:

- **Rental Car Deals:** Compare rental car prices on websites like Kayak, Rentalcars.com, and Costco Travel for the best rates.
- **Shuttle Services:** Use airport shuttle services instead of taxis or rideshares. Companies like Mears Transportation offer shared shuttle services at a fixed rate.
- **I-Ride Trolley:** In the International Drive area, use the I-Ride Trolley for convenient and low-cost transportation.

- **LYNX Public Bus:** Orlando's public bus system, LYNX, offers affordable fares for getting around the city.
- **Free Hotel Shuttles:** Some hotels provide complimentary shuttle services to popular theme parks.

Entertainment:

- **Free Disney Springs:** Enjoy the entertainment and shopping at Disney Springs, which doesn't require an admission fee.
- **Free Fireworks Shows:** Watch free fireworks shows outside of theme parks. For instance, you can view the Magic Kingdom fireworks from the beach at Disney's Polynesian Village Resort.
- **Discounted Show Tickets:** Check websites like Visit Orlando for discounted tickets to local shows and attractions.
- **Groupon Deals:** Search Groupon for discounts on local entertainment and activities in Orlando.
- **Outdoor Activities:** Explore natural attractions like Wekiwa Springs State Park or Lake Eola Park for low-cost outdoor fun.

Shopping:

- **Outlet Malls:** Visit outlet malls like Orlando International Premium Outlets and Orlando Vineland Premium Outlets for discounted shopping.
- **Coupon Books:** Pick up coupon books available at outlets or tourist information centers for additional savings.
- **Tax-Free Shopping:** Take advantage of Florida's tax-free shopping days for extra savings on clothing and school supplies.

Tours and Attractions:

- **CityPASS:** Consider purchasing the Orlando CityPASS for discounted admission to multiple attractions, including Universal Studios Florida and Walt Disney World.
- **Gatorland:** Visit Gatorland for affordable admission rates, and look for online discounts on their official website.

- **ICON Park:** Explore ICON Park on International Drive, where you can enjoy free entertainment and only pay for the attractions you choose.
- **Kennedy Space Center:** Purchase tickets for the Kennedy Space Center Visitor Complex online for potential discounts.
- **Airboat Tours:** Book airboat tours in advance to secure lower prices. Several operators offer online discounts.

Sports and Recreation:

- **Golf Discounts:** Tee off at golf courses during twilight hours for reduced rates, or search for golf deals on GolfNow.com.
- **Local Parks:** Enjoy free or low-cost activities at local parks, such as hiking, biking, and picnicking.
- **Free Yoga Classes:** Attend free or donation-based yoga classes in parks or at local studios.

Local Events and Festivals:

- **Festival Season:** Plan your visit during local festivals and events, many of which offer free admission.
- **Farmers' Markets:** Visit farmers' markets for affordable, fresh produce and artisanal goods.
- **Art Gallery Walks:** Participate in free art gallery walks in areas like Downtown Orlando and Winter Park.

Miscellaneous Savings:

- **Discounted Spa Services:** Find discounted spa and wellness services through daily deal websites like Groupon.
- **Free Wi-Fi:** Save on data charges by connecting to free Wi-Fi available at many hotels, restaurants, and cafes.
- **Student and Senior Discounts:** If you're a student or senior citizen, inquire about available discounts at attractions, restaurants, and theaters.
- **Library Passes:** Some local libraries offer free or discounted passes to museums and attractions.

- **AAA Discounts:** AAA members can access discounts on hotels, dining, and attractions in Orlando.
- **Travel during Weekdays:** If possible, visit theme parks and attractions on weekdays when crowds are smaller, and prices may be lower.
- **Free Souvenirs:** Collect free souvenirs like park maps, buttons, and postcards.
- **Discounted Water Parks:** Consider visiting Orlando's water parks during the afternoon for discounted rates.
- **Petting Zoos:** Visit petting zoos like Green Meadows Farm for affordable family fun.
- **Free Hotel Amenities:** Take advantage of free hotel amenities like pools, fitness centers, and complimentary breakfasts.
- **AAA Eats:** Look for restaurants with the AAA Eats designation, which indicates discounts for AAA members.

Las Vegas

From its origins as a humble railroad town to its glittering status as the entertainment capital of the world, this city knows how to put on a show.

You can bask in luxury without betting your life savings! Score deals on luxurious accommodations by booking during off-peak seasons or opting for weekday stays. Indulge in gourmet dining at upscale restaurants during happy hour for discounted drinks and appetizers. And why not catch a free show or two? Many of the city's iconic attractions offer complimentary performances that rival the paid ones.

Accommodation:

- **Off-Season Travel:** Visit during the off-peak season when hotel rates are generally lower.
- **Hotel Rewards Programs:** Join hotel rewards programs to earn points for future stays and receive member discounts.
- **Vacation Rentals:** Consider vacation rentals on websites like Airbnb for more affordable lodging options.
- **Book in Advance:** Reserve your accommodation well in advance to secure lower rates. Websites like Booking.com and Expedia often offer discounted rates for early bookings.

Dining:

- **Dining Coupons:** Look for dining coupons and discounts in local magazines and coupon books, such as Las Vegas Advisor.
- **Buffet Deals:** Take advantage of buffet discounts, especially during off-peak hours or with player's club membership.
- **Happy Hour Specials:** Enjoy happy hour specials at bars and restaurants for discounted drinks and appetizers.
- **Food Court Dining:** Opt for food court dining for budget-friendly meal options.
- **Food Delivery Apps:** Use food delivery apps like Grubhub, Uber Eats, and DoorDash to find affordable dining options.

Transportation:

- **Airport Shuttle Services:** Use airport shuttle services instead of taxis or rideshares. Companies like Mears Transportation offer shared shuttle services at a fixed rate.
- **Public Transportation:** Take advantage of the Deuce bus or the Las Vegas Monorail for cost-effective transportation on the Strip.

- **Rental Car Deals:** Compare rental car prices on websites like Kayak, Rentalcars.com, and Costco Travel for the best rates.
- **Walk the Strip:** Explore the Las Vegas Strip on foot to save on transportation costs and enjoy the sights.
- **Free Hotel Shuttles:** Some hotels provide complimentary shuttle services to popular attractions and the airport.

Entertainment:

- **Discounted Show Tickets:** Visit the Tix4Tonight booth in Las Vegas or use the TodayTix app for discounted same-day tickets to shows.
- **Free Attractions:** Enjoy free attractions like the Bellagio Fountains, the Mirage Volcano, and the Wildlife Habitat at Flamingo.
- **Local Entertainment:** Check out local bars and lounges for live music and entertainment without cover charges.
- **Comedy Clubs:** Find comedy clubs with free or low-cost shows during the week.
- **Happy Hour Cruises:** Experience happy hour cruises for scenic views of the city skyline.
- **Pool Parties:** Attend free or low-cost pool parties at various hotels during the summer months.

1. **Neon Museum's Vintage Vegas**: Step into the glitz and glamour of old Las Vegas at the Neon Museum, home to iconic neon signs from historic casinos and hotels. Take a guided tour through the Neon Boneyard to admire restored signs and learn about the city's colorful past. Starting Price: Tickets start at $20 for daytime tours and $28 for nighttime tours. Insider Tip: Book tickets in advance to secure your preferred tour time and consider visiting during sunset for stunning photo opportunities.
2. **Downtown Container Park's Urban Playground**: Explore Downtown Container Park, an innovative shopping and entertainment complex built from repurposed shipping containers. Discover unique boutiques, artisanal eateries, and family-friendly activities in a vibrant outdoor setting. Starting Price: Admission is free, but costs for food and activities vary. Insider Tip: Visit during the evening for live music performances and to see the fire-breathing praying mantis sculpture in action.
3. **Red Rock Canyon's Natural Beauty**: Escape the hustle and bustle of the Strip and immerse yourself in the stunning landscapes of Red Rock Canyon National Conservation Area. Hike scenic trails, rock climb majestic formations, or enjoy a scenic drive through the desert wilderness. Starting Price: Entry fee is $15 per vehicle. Insider Tip: Pack plenty of water, sunscreen, and snacks, and visit early in the morning or late in the afternoon to avoid the heat.
4. **Fremont Street Experience's Light Show**: Witness the dazzling light and sound spectacle of the Fremont Street Experience, a pedestrian mall lined with iconic casinos and attractions. Watch as the overhead canopy comes to life with vibrant visuals and live entertainment. Starting Price: Admission is free, but costs for food, drinks, and attractions vary. Insider Tip: Look for discounted tickets to zipline down the street or enjoy happy hour specials at nearby bars and restaurants.
5. **Seven Magic Mountains' Art Installation**: Discover the colorful art installation known as Seven Magic Mountains, located just outside of Las Vegas in the Mojave Desert. Marvel at towering stacks of neon-colored boulders set against the desert landscape. Starting Price: Admission is free. Insider Tip: Visit during sunrise or sunset for the best lighting and fewer crowds, and don't forget to snap some Instagram-worthy photos.

6. **Ethel M Chocolate Factory's Sweet Treats**: Indulge your sweet tooth at the Ethel M Chocolate Factory, where you can take a self-guided tour of the chocolate-making process and sample delicious treats. Explore the cactus garden outside the factory for a serene desert oasis. Starting Price: Admission is free, but costs for chocolate tastings and specialty items apply. Insider Tip: Visit during the weekday for smaller crowds and factory tours in operation.
7. **Valley of Fire State Park's Ancient Landscapes**: Journey to Valley of Fire State Park, Nevada's oldest and largest state park, to marvel at ancient rock formations, petroglyphs, and vibrant sandstone formations. Hike scenic trails, picnic among towering red rocks, and soak in the natural beauty of the desert. Starting Price: Entry fee is $10 per vehicle. Insider Tip: Bring a camera to capture the park's stunning landscapes, especially during sunrise or sunset.
8. **Pinball Hall of Fame's Retro Fun**: Experience a blast from the past at the Pinball Hall of Fame, a nonprofit museum dedicated to preserving and showcasing vintage pinball machines and arcade games. Play your favorite classic games and relive childhood memories in a nostalgic setting. Starting Price: Admission is free, but costs to play games vary. Insider Tip: Bring a pocketful of quarters for endless gaming fun and support the museum's charitable mission.
9. **Springs Preserve's Desert Discovery**: Learn about the natural and cultural history of the Mojave Desert at Springs Preserve, a 180-acre educational and recreational facility. Explore interactive exhibits, botanical gardens, and walking trails while discovering the desert's unique ecosystems. Starting Price: Admission is $18.95 for adults and $9.95 for children. Insider Tip: Check the schedule for guided tours, workshops, and special events focused on desert conservation and sustainability.
10. **Hoover Dam's Engineering Marvel**: Embark on a day trip to Hoover Dam, an iconic feat of engineering located on the border of Nevada and Arizona. Take a guided tour of the dam's interior, learn about its construction, and marvel at breathtaking views of the Colorado River and Lake Mead. Starting Price: Tours start at $15 per person. Insider Tip: Book a tour in advance to secure your spot and learn insider facts about the dam's history and significance.

Shopping:

- **Outlet Malls:** Shop at outlet malls like Las Vegas North Premium Outlets and Las Vegas South Premium Outlets for discounted shopping.
- **Coupon Books:** Pick up coupon books available at outlets or tourist information centers for additional savings.
- **Chinatown Shopping:** Explore Chinatown for budget-friendly shopping and dining options.

Tours and Attractions:

- **Groupon Deals:** Search Groupon for discounts on local entertainment, activities, dining, and tours in Las Vegas.
- **CityPASS:** Consider purchasing the Las Vegas Explorer Pass for savings on multiple attractions.
- **Adventuredome at Circus Circus:** Enjoy the indoor theme park at Circus Circus for reasonably priced family fun.

- **National Parks:** If you plan to visit nearby national parks, check for entrance fee discounts and annual passes.
- **Fremont Street Experience:** Explore the vibrant Fremont Street Experience in Downtown Las Vegas with free nightly light shows and entertainment.

Sports and Recreation:

- **Golf Discounts:** Play golf during twilight hours for reduced rates, or look for golf deals on GolfNow.com.
- **Local Parks:** Explore local parks for hiking, picnicking, and outdoor activities, often at no cost.
- **Free Yoga Classes:** Attend free or donation-based yoga classes in parks or at local studios.

Local Events and Festivals:

- **Festivals and Street Fairs:** Attend free or low-cost local festivals and street fairs throughout the year.
- **Farmers' Markets:** Visit farmers' markets for fresh and affordable produce and artisanal goods.
- **First Friday:** Enjoy the First Friday arts and culture event in the Arts District for free art exhibitions and live performances.

Miscellaneous Savings:

- **Senior Discounts:** If you're a senior citizen, inquire about available discounts at attractions, restaurants, and theaters.
- **Student Discounts:** If you're a student, take advantage of available discounts on entertainment, transportation, and dining.
- **Library Passes:** Some local libraries offer free or discounted passes to museums and attractions.
- **AAA Discounts:** AAA members can access discounts on hotels, dining, and attractions in Las Vegas.
- **Casino Player's Club:** Join casino player's clubs for potential discounts on dining, entertainment, and accommodations.
- **Free Wi-Fi:** Save on data charges by connecting to free Wi-Fi available at many hotels, restaurants, and cafes.
- **Airport Parking:** Consider off-site airport parking for potential cost savings compared to on-site airport parking.
- **Ride Shares:** Use ride-sharing apps like Uber and Lyft for affordable transportation options.
- **Airport Rides:** Arrange airport transportation with shuttle services, which can be more budget-friendly than taxis.
- **Hotel Amenities:** Take advantage of free hotel amenities such as pools, fitness centers, and complimentary breakfasts.
- **DIY Sightseeing:** Create your self-guided walking tours using online resources and maps.
- **Visit Nearby Destinations:** Explore nearby areas like Lake Mead and Red Rock Canyon for outdoor adventures.

Los Angeles

From its sun-kissed beaches to its star-studded streets, LA is a city of dreams and diversity. You can live the high life in LA without blowing your budget! Opt for free activities like hiking in Griffith Park or exploring the Getty Museum's stunning art collection. Dine like a celebrity by hitting up food trucks for gourmet eats or visiting ethnic neighborhoods for authentic, budget-friendly cuisine. And did you know? Many top attractions offer free admission on certain days of the week, so plan accordingly to save some cash.

Accommodation:

- **Off-Peak Travel:** Visit during the off-peak season for lower hotel rates.
- **Vacation Rentals:** Consider vacation rentals on websites like Airbnb for more affordable lodging options.
- **Hotel Rewards Programs:** Join hotel rewards programs to earn points for future stays and receive member discounts.
- **Book in Advance:** Reserve your accommodation well in advance to secure lower rates. Websites like Booking.com and Expedia often offer discounted rates for early bookings.

Dining:

- **Food Trucks:** Enjoy a diverse range of affordable and delicious food from Los Angeles food trucks.
- **Happy Hour Specials:** Take advantage of happy hour specials at bars and restaurants for discounted drinks and appetizers.
- **Ethnic Cuisine:** Explore neighborhoods like Koreatown and Little Tokyo for budget-friendly and authentic ethnic dining experiences.
- **Local Markets:** Visit farmers' markets for fresh and affordable produce, artisanal goods, and prepared foods.
- **BYOB Restaurants:** Dine at "bring your own bottle" (BYOB) restaurants to save on alcohol expenses.

Transportation:

- **Public Transportation:** Use the Los Angeles Metro and bus system for cost-effective transportation. A single ride on Metro costs $1.75.
- **Ride-Sharing:** Utilize ride-sharing apps like Uber and Lyft for convenient and affordable travel.
- **Metro TAP Card:** Purchase a TAP card for discounted fares on Metro buses and trains.
- **Airport Shuttles:** Use airport shuttle services instead of taxis or rideshares to and from LAX.

Entertainment:

- **Free Attractions:** Explore free attractions like Griffith Observatory, the Getty Center, and Venice Beach.
- **Discounted Museum Days:** Many museums offer free admission or discounted days. Check their websites for details.
- **Student Discounts:** If you're a student, inquire about available discounts at museums, theaters, and attractions.
- **Outdoor Activities:** Hike in Griffith Park or explore the beaches for free or low-cost outdoor fun.
- **Comedy Shows:** Find comedy clubs with free or low-cost comedy shows during the week.
- **Discounted Movie Tickets:** Some theaters offer discounted tickets on specific days or times.

1. **Griffith Observatory's Stellar Views**: Experience the beauty of the cosmos at Griffith Observatory, perched atop Mount Hollywood in Griffith Park. Explore interactive exhibits, observe celestial objects through telescopes, and enjoy panoramic views of the Los Angeles skyline. Starting Price: Admission to the observatory is free, but there may be fees for planetarium shows. Insider Tip: Visit during the evening for stargazing sessions led by knowledgeable astronomers.
2. **The Getty Center's Artistic Haven**: Immerse yourself in art and architecture at The Getty Center, a cultural oasis nestled in the hills of Brentwood. Explore world-class collections of European paintings, sculpture gardens, and stunning architecture surrounded by panoramic views of the city. Starting Price: Admission is free, but parking fees apply. Insider Tip: Take advantage of the museum's free guided tours and educational programs to enhance your visit.
3. **Venice Beach's Bohemian Vibe**: Soak up the eclectic atmosphere of Venice Beach, a vibrant seaside community known for its colorful boardwalk, street performers, and eclectic shops. Explore Muscle Beach, browse local art vendors, or simply people-watch along the bustling Ocean Front Walk. Starting Price: Admission to the beach is free, but costs for parking and activities may apply. Insider Tip: Rent a bike or rollerblades to explore the beachfront and nearby neighborhoods at your own pace.
4. **The Last Bookstore's Literary Wonderland**: Lose yourself in the pages of history at The Last Bookstore, a sprawling literary haven housed in a historic bank building in downtown Los Angeles. Browse shelves stocked with new and used books, explore hidden nooks and crannies, and discover unique art installations throughout the store. Starting Price: Admission is free, but costs for purchasing books and merchandise apply. Insider Tip: Attend author readings, book signings, and other literary events hosted at the bookstore for a memorable cultural experience.
5. **Griffith Park's Natural Escapes**: Escape the urban hustle and bustle with a visit to Griffith Park, one of the largest urban parks in the United States. Hike scenic trails, picnic in lush green spaces, or explore attractions such as the Los Angeles Zoo and the Griffith Park Observatory. Starting Price: Admission to the park is free, but there may be fees for parking and attractions. Insider Tip: Pack a picnic lunch and head to the park's higher elevations for stunning views of the city skyline and surrounding mountains.
6. **The Broad's Contemporary Art**: Dive into the world of contemporary art at The Broad, a cutting-edge museum located in downtown Los Angeles. Marvel at iconic works by artists such as Andy Warhol, Jeff Koons, and Yayoi Kusama, and explore immersive installations that challenge perception and provoke thought. Starting

Price: Admission is free, but advance reservations are recommended. Insider Tip: Arrive early to secure a spot in the standby line or book tickets online to skip the wait and explore the museum at your leisure.

7. **Runyon Canyon Park's Scenic Trails**: Lace up your hiking boots and hit the trails at Runyon Canyon Park, a popular outdoor destination nestled in the Hollywood Hills. Trek through rugged terrain, soak in panoramic views of the city and iconic landmarks, and keep an eye out for celebrity sightings along the way. Starting Price: Admission to the park is free, but costs for parking may apply. Insider Tip: Visit during the early morning or late afternoon to avoid the heat and crowds, and don't forget to bring plenty of water and sunscreen.
8. **LACMA's Artistic Masterpieces**: Discover artistic masterpieces from around the world at the Los Angeles County Museum of Art (LACMA), the largest art museum in the western United States. Explore diverse collections spanning thousands of years and cultures, including modern and contemporary art, ancient artifacts, and iconic sculptures. Starting Price: Admission is free for Los Angeles County residents with valid ID; non-resident tickets start at $25. Insider Tip: Check the museum's website for free admission days and special exhibitions to make the most of your visit.
9. **Hollywood Forever Cemetery's Historic Landmarks**: Pay homage to Hollywood's golden age at Hollywood Forever Cemetery, the final resting place of numerous entertainment legends. Take a self-guided tour of the cemetery's historic grounds, visit iconic gravesites, and attend cultural events and film screenings held throughout the year. Starting Price: Admission is free, but donations are appreciated. Insider Tip: Join a guided walking tour led by knowledgeable docents to learn about the cemetery's rich history and famous residents.
10. **El Matador Beach's Coastal Beauty**: Escape to the picturesque shores of El Matador Beach, a hidden gem along the Malibu coast known for its dramatic cliffs, sea caves, and pristine sands. Explore tide pools, snap photos of stunning rock formations, or simply relax and soak up the sun in this serene coastal paradise. Starting Price: Admission to the beach is free, but parking fees may apply. Insider Tip: Arrive early to secure a parking spot and explore the beach before it gets crowded, and be sure to check the tide schedule for optimal tide pool exploration.

Shopping:

- **Outlet Malls:** Shop at outlet malls like Citadel Outlets and Camarillo Premium Outlets for discounted shopping.
- **Sample Sales:** Keep an eye out for sample sales and designer discounts in Los Angeles.
- **Discount Stores:** Find deals at discount stores like Ross, TJ Maxx, and Marshalls.
- **Secondhand Shops:** Explore thrift and secondhand stores in neighborhoods like Silver Lake and Echo Park.

Tours and Attractions:

- **CityPASS:** Consider purchasing the Go Los Angeles Card or the Go LA Explorer Pass for savings on multiple attractions.
- **Discounted Movie Studio Tours:** Check for discounts on studio tours, such as Warner Bros. Studio Tour Hollywood.
- **Hollywood Walk of Fame:** Walk along the Hollywood Walk of Fame to see the stars for free.

- **Getty Villa:** Visit the Getty Villa, which offers free admission, but reservations are required.
- **Griffith Observatory:** Explore the Griffith Observatory for free or attend a low-cost planetarium show.

Transportation within LA:

- **Biking:** Rent a bike or use bike-sharing programs like Metro Bike Share for affordable transportation.
- **Walking Tours:** Discover neighborhoods with self-guided walking tours available online or through apps.
- **Electric Scooters:** Consider electric scooter rentals for short-distance travel.

Sports and Recreation:

- **Local Parks:** Enjoy free or low-cost activities in local parks, including hiking, picnicking, and sports.
- **Public Swimming Pools:** Cool off at public swimming pools across the city during the summer months.
- **Free Yoga Classes:** Attend free or donation-based yoga classes in parks or at local studios.

Local Events and Festivals:

- **Festivals and Street Fairs:** Attend free or low-cost local festivals and street fairs throughout the year.
- **Farmers' Markets:** Visit farmers' markets for fresh and affordable produce, artisanal goods, and prepared foods.
- **Cultural Events:** Explore cultural events and celebrations representing the diverse communities of Los Angeles.
- **Art Walks:** Attend free art walks in neighborhoods like Downtown LA and Venice.

Miscellaneous Savings:

- **Senior Discounts:** If you're a senior citizen, inquire about available discounts at attractions, restaurants, and theaters.
- **Library Passes:** Some local libraries offer free or discounted passes to museums and attractions.
- **AAA Discounts:** AAA members can access discounts on hotels, dining, and attractions in Los Angeles.
- **Free Wi-Fi:** Save on data charges by connecting

Chicago

For starters, immerse yourself in the city's architectural wonders, from the towering skyscrapers of the Loop to the historic brownstones of Lincoln Park. Explore world-class museums like the Art Institute of Chicago, home to renowned masterpieces spanning centuries of artistic expression.

Chicago is a foodie paradise, offering everything from sizzling steaks and mouthwatering hot dogs to innovative gourmet cuisine. Experience the city's legendary blues music scene in iconic venues like Buddy Guy's Legends or catch a performance at the famous Second City comedy club.

And let's not forget about the stunning lakefront, where you can stroll along the picturesque shores of Lake Michigan or take a leisurely bike ride along the scenic Lakefront Trail.

You can experience the best of Chicago without breaking the bank! Take advantage of free attractions like Millennium Park's Cloud Gate sculpture, affectionately known as 'The Bean,' or catch a free concert at the Jay Pritzker Pavilion. Dive into the city's culinary scene without emptying your wallet by indulging in Chicago-style hot dogs and deep-dish pizza at local favorites. And don't forget to explore the city's diverse neighborhoods, each offering its own unique charm and affordable delights.

Certainly! Here are 50 specific ways to save money while visiting Chicago, along with prices and websites for reference:

Accommodation:

In Chicago, you can find budget-friendly accommodations that still offer comfort and convenience:

1. **Hostels:** Hostels are a great option for budget travelers in Chicago. Consider places like HI Chicago Hostel or Freehand Chicago, which offer clean and affordable dormitory-style rooms or private rooms at budget-friendly prices.

2. **Budget Hotels:** Look for budget hotels that provide basic amenities without breaking the bank. Some options include The St. Clair Hotel, Chicago Getaway Hostel, or the Chicago Parthenon Hostel.
3. **Micro Hotels:** Micro hotels offer compact yet stylish rooms at affordable rates. Check out properties like Moxy Chicago Downtown or The Publishing House Bed and Breakfast for a unique and budget-friendly stay.

Dining:

- **Chicago-Style Hot Dogs:** Try iconic Chicago-style hot dogs from local hot dog stands for an affordable meal.
- **Lunch Specials:** Opt for lunch specials at restaurants, which are often more budget-friendly than dinner.
- **Food Trucks:** Enjoy diverse and affordable food options from Chicago's food trucks.
- **Ethnic Neighborhoods:** Explore neighborhoods like Pilsen and Chinatown for authentic and budget-friendly ethnic cuisine.
- **BYOB Restaurants:** Dine at "bring your own bottle" (BYOB) restaurants to save on alcohol expenses.

Transportation:

- **Public Transportation:** Use the Chicago Transit Authority (CTA) for cost-effective transportation via buses and "L" trains.
- **Ventra Card:** Purchase a Ventra card for discounted fares on public transportation.
- **Biking:** Rent a Divvy bike for affordable short-distance travel within the city.
- **Airport Transportation:** Use airport shuttle services or the "L" train to O'Hare International Airport for cost savings.

Entertainment:

- **Free Attractions:** Explore free attractions like Millennium Park, Lincoln Park Zoo, and the Art Institute of Chicago on specific days.
- **Discounted Museums:** Visit museums on free or discounted admission days. Check their websites for details.
- **Student Discounts:** If you're a student, inquire about available discounts at museums, theaters, and attractions.
- **Free Concerts:** Attend free outdoor concerts and performances in Millennium Park during the summer.
- **Comedy Shows:** Find comedy clubs with free or low-cost comedy shows during the week.

1. **Millennium Park's Iconic Landmarks:** Discover the heart of Chicago at Millennium Park, a sprawling urban oasis renowned for its iconic landmarks and cultural attractions. Marvel at the reflective Cloud Gate sculpture, stroll through

lush gardens, and enjoy free outdoor concerts and events at the Jay Pritzker Pavilion. Starting Price: Admission to the park is free. Insider Tip: Visit during the summer months for free outdoor movie screenings and yoga classes in the park.
2. **Art Institute of Chicago's Artistic Treasures**: Immerse yourself in the world of art at the Art Institute of Chicago, one of the oldest and largest art museums in the country. Explore masterpieces spanning thousands of years and diverse cultures, including iconic works by Vincent van Gogh, Grant Wood, and Pablo Picasso. Starting Price: General admission starts at $25 for adults.
3. **Chicago Riverwalk's Scenic Stroll**: Experience the beauty of Chicago's waterfront with a leisurely stroll along the Chicago Riverwalk. Admire stunning architecture, watch boats pass by, and dine at waterfront restaurants offering scenic views of the city skyline. Starting Price: Admission to the Riverwalk is free. Insider Tip: Rent a kayak or take a guided architectural boat tour to explore the city's iconic landmarks from a unique perspective.
4. **Lincoln Park Zoo's Wildlife Encounters**: Get up close and personal with exotic animals at Lincoln Park Zoo, one of the oldest zoos in the United States. Explore diverse habitats, attend educational programs, and marvel at creatures ranging from lions and tigers to penguins and gorillas. Starting Price: Admission to the zoo is free. Insider Tip: Pack a picnic lunch and enjoy a scenic outdoor meal in the zoo's lush gardens, or visit during special events like ZooLights during the holiday season.
5. **Navy Pier's Entertainment Hub**: Delight in family-friendly fun at Navy Pier, a bustling entertainment complex nestled along Lake Michigan. Ride the iconic Ferris wheel, catch a live performance at the Chicago Shakespeare Theater, or embark on a scenic boat cruise along the lakefront. Starting Price: Admission to Navy Pier is free, but costs for attractions and activities vary. Insider Tip: Look for discounted ride passes and combo tickets to save money on multiple attractions at the pier.
6. **Chicago Cultural Center's Architectural Gem**: Step inside the Chicago Cultural Center, a historic landmark and cultural

hub in the heart of downtown Chicago. Admire stunning Tiffany stained glass domes, explore art galleries and exhibitions, and attend free cultural events and performances. Starting Price: Admission to the Cultural Center is free. Insider Tip: Join a guided architectural tour to learn about the building's rich history and architectural significance.

7. **Garfield Park Conservatory's Botanical Wonderland**: Escape to a tropical paradise at Garfield Park Conservatory, a botanical oasis spanning 12 acres on Chicago's west side. Wander through lush gardens, tranquil lagoons, and vibrant floral displays showcasing plants from around the world. Starting Price: Admission to the conservatory is free, but donations are appreciated. Insider Tip: Attend educational workshops and gardening classes offered by the conservatory to learn about sustainable gardening practices and plant care.

8. **Chicago Lakefront Trail's Scenic Bike Ride**: Enjoy a scenic bike ride along the Chicago Lakefront Trail, a picturesque path that stretches for 18 miles along Lake Michigan. Cycle past sandy beaches, waterfront parks, and iconic landmarks like Buckingham Fountain and the Museum Campus. Starting Price: Admission to the trail is free, but costs for bike rentals may apply. Insider Tip: Rent a Divvy bike from one of the city's bike-sharing stations and explore the trail at your own pace, stopping to take in the views and snap photos along the way.

9. **The 606's Elevated Park**: Explore Chicago's vibrant neighborhoods along The 606, an elevated park and trail system built on a former railway line. Walk, jog, or bike along the scenic path, and discover public art installations, community gardens, and local cafes and shops along the route. Starting Price: Admission to The 606 is free. Insider Tip: Visit during the evening to see the trail illuminated with colorful lights and enjoy a peaceful sunset stroll above the city streets.

10. **Chicago Greeter Tours' Local Insights**: Get insider tips and local recommendations with a free Chicago Greeter Tour, led by knowledgeable volunteers passionate about showcasing the city's hidden gems. Choose from a variety of themed tours exploring diverse neighborhoods, cultural landmarks, and culinary delights. Starting Price: Tours are free, but advance

reservations are required. Insider Tip: Customize your tour itinerary based on your interests and preferences, and don't forget to tip your guide to show appreciation for their time and expertise.

Shopping:

- **Outlet Malls:** Shop at nearby outlet malls like Chicago Premium Outlets and Fashion Outlets of Chicago for discounted shopping.
- **Sample Sales:** Keep an eye out for sample sales and designer discounts in Chicago.
- **Discount Stores:** Find deals at discount stores like T.J. Maxx, Marshalls, and Nordstrom Rack.
- **Thrift Shops:** Explore thrift shops in neighborhoods like Wicker Park and Lakeview for budget-friendly fashion.

Tours and Attractions:

- **Chicago CityPASS:** Consider purchasing the Chicago CityPASS for savings on multiple attractions.
- **Chicago Greeter:** Take advantage of the free Chicago Greeter program for guided neighborhood tours.
- **Chicago Architecture Foundation Tours:** Participate in affordable architecture tours to learn about the city's iconic buildings.
- **Lincoln Park Conservatory:** Visit the Lincoln Park Conservatory and Garfield Park Conservatory for free.
- **Navy Pier Fireworks:** Enjoy free fireworks displays at Navy Pier during the summer months.

Transportation within Chicago:

- **Walking Tours:** Explore various neighborhoods with self-guided walking tours available online or through apps.
- **Taxi and Ride-Sharing Apps:** Use taxi services or ride-sharing apps like Uber and Lyft for convenient travel.
- **Water Taxis:** Consider taking water taxis for a unique and affordable way to see the city from the river.

Sports and Recreation:

- **Local Parks:** Enjoy free or low-cost activities in local parks, including hiking, picnicking, and sports.
- **Public Pools:** Cool off at public swimming pools across the city during the summer months.
- **Free Yoga Classes:** Attend free or donation-based yoga classes in parks or at local studios.

Local Events and Festivals:

- **Street Fairs:** Attend free street fairs and neighborhood festivals featuring food vendors and live music.

- **Farmers' Markets:** Visit farmers' markets for fresh and affordable produce, artisanal goods, and prepared foods.
- **Cultural Events:** Explore cultural events and festivals celebrating Chicago's diverse communities.
- **Art Gallery Openings:** Attend free art gallery openings and exhibitions in neighborhoods like West Loop and River North.

Miscellaneous Savings:

- **Senior Discounts:** If you're a senior citizen, inquire about available discounts at attractions, restaurants, and theaters.
- **Library Passes:** Some local libraries offer free or discounted passes to museums and attractions.
- **AAA Discounts:** AAA members can access discounts on hotels, dining, and attractions in Chicago.
- **Free Wi-Fi:** Connect to free Wi-Fi available at many hotels, restaurants, and cafes to save on data charges.
- **Rides to Airports:** Arrange airport transportation with shared shuttle services for potential cost savings.
- **Hotel Amenities:** Take advantage of free hotel amenities such as pools, fitness centers, and complimentary breakfasts.
- **Divvy for All:** Access Divvy bikes at lower rates with the Divvy for All program for income-qualified residents.
- **Buy City Passes:** Consider purchasing city passes like the Chicago CityPASS for bundled savings on attractions.
- **Discounted Spa Services:** Find discounted spa and wellness services through daily deal websites like Groupon.
- **Visit Nearby Suburbs:** Explore nearby suburbs like Oak Park and Evanston for budget-friendly attractions and dining.

San Francisco

Fog dances with the Golden Gate Bridge, cable cars climb steep hills, and every corner holds a tale of innovation, diversity, and quirkiness. Get ready for a city where tech meets tradition, gourmet eats mingle with street art, and every neighborhood is a world of its own. Welcome to the land of fog, hills, and endless adventures!

San Francisco can be pricey, but don't let that scare you off! Save money by opting for public transportation or walking instead of pricey taxis. Skip the tourist traps and indulge in budget-friendly eats at local markets or food trucks. And resist the urge to splurge on unnecessary souvenirs by focusing on experiences over material things.

Accommodation:

1. **Hostels:** Hostels are a popular option for budget travelers in San Francisco. Look for hostels like HI San Francisco Downtown Hostel, USA Hostels San Francisco, or HI San Francisco Fisherman's Wharf, which offer dormitory-style rooms and private rooms at budget-friendly rates.
2. **Budget Hotels:** There are budget-friendly hotels in San Francisco that provide basic amenities without breaking the bank. Consider options like Hotel Whitcomb, The Mosser Hotel, or Grant Plaza Hotel for affordable stays in convenient locations.

Dining:

- **Food Trucks:** Enjoy diverse and affordable food options from San Francisco's food trucks.
- **Ethnic Neighborhoods:** Explore neighborhoods like Chinatown and the Mission District for authentic and budget-friendly ethnic cuisine.
- **Lunch Specials:** Opt for lunch specials at restaurants, which are often more budget-friendly than dinner.
- **Happy Hour Deals:** Take advantage of happy hour specials at bars and restaurants for discounted drinks and appetizers.
- **Farmers' Markets:** Visit farmers' markets for fresh and affordable produce, artisanal goods, and prepared foods.

Transportation:

- **Public Transportation:** Use the Bay Area Rapid Transit (BART) system, Muni buses, and cable cars for cost-effective transportation. A one-way BART fare varies but is typically around $2-$10.
- **Clipper Card:** Purchase a Clipper card for discounted fares on public transportation.
- **Walking:** Explore the city on foot to save on transportation costs and enjoy the sights.
- **Biking:** Rent a bike or use bike-sharing programs like Ford GoBike for affordable short-distance travel.

Entertainment:

- **Free Attractions:** Visit free attractions like Golden Gate Park, the Painted Ladies, and Lombard Street.
- **Discounted Museums:** Check museum websites for free admission days or discounted rates.
- **Student Discounts:** If you're a student, inquire about available discounts at museums, theaters, and attractions.
- **Free Music Performances:** Attend free concerts and performances at places like Yerba Buena Gardens.
- **Comedy Shows:** Find comedy clubs with free or low-cost comedy shows during the week.

Golden Gate Bridge's Iconic Landmark: Experience the majesty of the Golden Gate Bridge, one of the most iconic landmarks in San Francisco. Walk or bike across the bridge for breathtaking views of the city skyline, Alcatraz Island, and the Pacific Ocean. Starting Price: Walking or biking across the bridge is free; parking fees may apply. Insider Tip: Visit at sunrise or sunset for stunning photo opportunities and smaller crowds.

Alcatraz Island's Historic Prison: Embark on a journey to Alcatraz Island, home to the infamous Alcatraz Federal Penitentiary. Take a ferry ride to the island, explore the prison ruins, and learn about the notorious inmates who once called Alcatraz home. Starting Price: Ferry tickets start at $39.25 for adults. Insider Tip: Book tickets well in advance, especially during peak tourist seasons, and opt for early morning or evening tours for smaller crowds.

Fisherman's Wharf's Maritime Charm: Immerse yourself in the maritime history and bustling atmosphere of Fisherman's Wharf, a vibrant waterfront neighborhood teeming with shops, restaurants, and attractions. Sample fresh seafood, watch street performers, and visit iconic landmarks like Pier 39 and Ghirardelli Square.

Starting Price: Admission to Fisherman's Wharf is free, but costs for food and activities vary. Insider Tip: Look for discounted tickets to attractions like the Aquarium of the Bay and the San Francisco Maritime National Historical Park.

Golden Gate Park's Urban Oasis: Escape the city hustle and bustle at Golden Gate Park, a sprawling urban oasis filled with gardens, museums, and recreational facilities. Explore attractions such as the California Academy of Sciences, the de Young Museum, and the Japanese Tea Garden, or simply relax and picnic in the park's lush green spaces. Starting Price: Admission to the park is free; costs for attractions may apply. Insider Tip: Rent a pedal boat at Stow Lake or explore the park's hidden gems, such as the Shakespeare Garden and the Bison Paddock.

Chinatown's Cultural Enclave: Discover the vibrant sights, sounds, and flavors of San Francisco's Chinatown, the oldest and largest Chinatown in North America. Stroll through bustling streets lined with colorful lanterns, ornate temples, and authentic eateries offering traditional dim sum and tea. Starting Price: Admission to Chinatown is free, but costs for food and shopping vary. Insider Tip: Join a guided walking tour to learn about the neighborhood's history, architecture, and cultural significance from local experts.

Painted Ladies' Victorian Charm: Admire the iconic Victorian houses known as the Painted Ladies, a row of colorful homes nestled against the backdrop of Alamo Square Park. Snap photos of these picturesque residences, which have become symbols of San Francisco's architectural heritage. Starting Price: Viewing the Painted Ladies from the park is free; guided tours may require a fee. Insider Tip: Visit in the late afternoon or early evening for the best lighting and fewer crowds.

Cable Cars' Historic Ride: Experience a piece of San Francisco's history with a ride on the city's iconic cable cars. Hop aboard one of the historic trolleys and enjoy a scenic journey through the city's hilly streets, passing by landmarks like Lombard Street and Coit Tower. Starting Price: Single ride fares start at $8 for adults. Insider Tip: Purchase a day pass for unlimited rides on the cable cars, buses, and streetcars, and consider riding during off-peak hours to avoid long lines.

Coit Tower's Panoramic Views: Ascend to the top of Coit Tower for panoramic views of San Francisco and the surrounding bay area. Climb the tower's winding staircase or take the elevator to the observation deck, where you can enjoy 360-degree vistas of the city skyline, Alcatraz Island, and the Golden Gate Bridge. Starting Price: Admission to the tower is $9 for adults. Insider Tip: Visit early in the morning or on weekdays for shorter wait times and clearer views.

Mission District's Cultural Mosaic: Explore the vibrant streets of San Francisco's Mission District, a diverse neighborhood known for its colorful murals, eclectic shops, and thriving arts scene. Sample authentic Mexican cuisine, browse local boutiques, and admire street art adorning building facades and alleyways. Starting Price: Admission to the Mission District is free; costs for food and shopping vary. Insider Tip: Take a guided mural tour to discover hidden gems and learn about the artists behind the neighborhood's vibrant street art.

Palace of Fine Arts' Architectural Splendor: Marvel at the architectural beauty of the Palace of Fine Arts, a grand neoclassical structure located in the Marina District. Wander through the park's tranquil grounds, admire the majestic rotunda and colonnades, and snap photos of the picturesque lagoon and swans. Starting Price: Admission to the park is free. Insider Tip: Visit during the early morning or late afternoon to enjoy the park's serene ambiance and capture stunning photographs of the historic landmark.

Shopping:

- **Outlet Malls:** Shop at nearby outlet malls like San Francisco Premium Outlets for discounted shopping.
- **Sample Sales:** Keep an eye out for sample sales and designer discounts in San Francisco.
- **Thrift Stores:** Explore thrift stores in neighborhoods like Haight-Ashbury and the Mission District for budget-friendly fashion.

Tours and Attractions:

- **CityPASS:** Consider purchasing the San Francisco CityPASS for savings on multiple attractions.
- **City Guides Tours:** Join free City Guides walking tours to learn about the city's history and neighborhoods.
- **Alcatraz Island:** Book tickets to Alcatraz Island in advance to secure lower prices. Check the official website for details.
- **Cable Car Museum:** Visit the Cable Car Museum, which offers free admission.

Transportation within San Francisco:

- **Walking Tours:** Explore neighborhoods with self-guided walking tours available online or through apps.
- **Taxis and Ride-Sharing Apps:** Use taxis or ride-sharing apps like Uber and Lyft for convenient travel.
- **San Francisco Bay Ferry:** Consider the San Francisco Bay Ferry for scenic transportation to Alcatraz and other destinations.
- **Airport Transportation:** Use airport shuttle services for cost-effective transportation to and from the airport.

Sports and Recreation:

- **Local Parks:** Enjoy free or low-cost activities in local parks, including hiking, picnicking, and sports.
- **Public Swimming Pools:** Cool off at public swimming pools across the city during the summer.
- **Free Yoga Classes:** Attend free or donation-based yoga classes in parks or at local studios.

Local Events and Festivals:

- **Street Fairs:** Attend free street fairs and neighborhood festivals featuring food vendors and live music.
- **Farmers' Markets:** Visit farmers' markets for fresh and affordable produce, artisanal goods, and prepared foods.
- **Cultural Festivals:** Explore cultural events and festivals celebrating San Francisco's diverse communities.
- **Art Walks:** Attend free art walks in neighborhoods like the Mission District and North Beach.

Miscellaneous Savings:

- **Senior Discounts:** If you're a senior citizen, inquire about available discounts at attractions, restaurants, and theaters.
- **Library Passes:** Some local libraries offer free or discounted passes to museums and attractions.
- **AAA Discounts:** AAA members can access discounts on hotels, dining, and attractions in San Francisco.
- **Free Wi-Fi:** Connect to free Wi-Fi available at many hotels, restaurants, and cafes to save on data charges.
- **DIY Sightseeing:** Create your self-guided walking tours using online resources and maps.
- **Visit Nearby Areas:** Explore nearby areas like Sausalito and Marin County for budget-friendly adventures.
- **Discounted Spa Services:** Find discounted spa and wellness services through daily deal websites like Groupon.
- **Ride Shares:** Use ride-sharing apps like Uber and Lyft for convenient transportation options.
- **Airport Parking:** Consider off-site airport parking for potential cost savings compared to on-site airport parking.
- **Hotel Amenities:** Take advantage of free hotel amenities such as pools, fitness centers, and complimentary breakfasts.
- **Golden Gate Bridge Views:** Enjoy views of the Golden Gate Bridge from viewpoints like Battery Spencer for free.

- **Ferry Building Marketplace:** Explore the Ferry Building Marketplace, where you can sample local foods and artisanal products.
- **Haight-Ashbury:** Take a stroll through the historic Haight-Ashbury neighborhood for a taste of San Francisco's counterculture history.

Miami

The heat is on and the party never stops! This vibrant city is a melting pot of cultures, pulsating with energy and lined with palm-fringed beaches. Miami can be as pricey as it is glamorous, but you don't have to empty your pockets to have a good time! Save money by opting for free beach days or exploring the city's colorful street art scene. Skip the overpriced tourist traps and dive into authentic Cuban cuisine at local eateries. And resist the urge to splurge on bottle service at clubs – dance the night away at one of the city's many free outdoor concerts instead.

Accommodation:

1. **Budget Hotels:** Look for budget-friendly hotels in Miami that offer basic amenities and convenient locations. Consider properties like Red Roof PLUS+ Miami Airport, Rodeway Inn Miami, or Best Western Premier Miami International Airport Hotel & Suites for affordable stays.
2. **Hostels:** Hostels are a great option for budget travelers in Miami. Check out hostels like Miami Hostel or Bikini Hostel, Cafe & Beer Garden, which offer dormitory-style rooms and private rooms at budget-friendly rates.
3. **Suburbs:** Consider staying in cheaper suburbs outside of Miami's city center for more affordable accommodations. Suburbs like Doral, Hialeah, or Kendall offer a range of lodging options at lower prices compared to downtown Miami.

Dining:

- **Cuban Cafes:** Enjoy budget-friendly Cuban cuisine at local cafes and restaurants.
- **Food Trucks:** Try diverse and affordable food options from Miami's food trucks.
- **Happy Hour Deals:** Take advantage of happy hour specials at bars and restaurants for discounted drinks and appetizers.
- **Latin Markets:** Explore Latin markets for affordable groceries and prepared meals.
- **BYOB Restaurants:** Dine at "bring your own bottle" (BYOB) restaurants to save on alcohol expenses.

Transportation:

- **Public Transportation:** Use Miami-Dade Transit buses and the Metrorail for cost-effective transportation. A one-way Metrorail fare starts at $2.25.
- **Miami Trolley:** Ride the free Miami Trolley for convenient transportation in some neighborhoods.
- **Airport Shuttles:** Use airport shuttle services instead of taxis or rideshares for airport transportation.

Entertainment:

- **Free Beaches:** Enjoy Miami's beautiful beaches for free sunbathing and swimming.
- **Art Walks:** Attend free art walks in neighborhoods like Wynwood to view street art and galleries.
- **Free Museums:** Visit free museums like the Institute of Contemporary Art and Pérez Art Museum Miami on specific days.
- **Student Discounts:** If you're a student, inquire about available discounts at museums, theaters, and attractions.
- **Concerts in the Park:** Attend free outdoor concerts and performances in local parks.

4. **Miami Beach Boardwalk's Scenic Walk**: Take a scenic stroll along the Miami Beach Boardwalk, a picturesque pathway that stretches for miles along the Atlantic Ocean. Enjoy panoramic views of the coastline, watch surfers catch waves, and admire the lush landscaping and public art installations along the way. Starting Price: Admission to the boardwalk is free. Insider Tip: Rent a bike or rollerblades from one of the nearby rental shops to explore the boardwalk at a leisurely pace and cover more ground.
5. **Vizcaya Museum and Gardens' Historic Estate**: Step back in time at Vizcaya Museum and Gardens, a stunning waterfront estate that blends European elegance with tropical splendor. Explore the opulent mansion, wander through lush gardens and scenic pathways, and admire architectural details inspired by Italian and French Renaissance styles. Starting Price: Admission to Vizcaya starts at $22 for adults. Insider Tip: Visit early in the day to beat the crowds and enjoy peaceful moments in the gardens, and don't forget to bring a camera to capture the estate's picturesque beauty.
6. **Everglades National Park's Natural Wonders**: Discover the untamed beauty of the Florida Everglades, a unique ecosystem teeming with wildlife and natural wonders. Embark

on an airboat tour through the marshes, spot alligators and wading birds in their natural habitat, and learn about the importance of conservation efforts in preserving this precious wilderness. Starting Price: Admission to Everglades National Park starts at $30 per vehicle. Insider Tip: Opt for a guided eco-tour led by knowledgeable naturalists to gain insight into the park's ecology and wildlife.
7. **Bayside Marketplace's Shopping and Entertainment**: Shop, dine, and explore at Bayside Marketplace, a bustling waterfront mall located in downtown Miami. Browse through a variety of shops and boutiques, enjoy live music and street performances, and take a scenic boat tour of Biscayne Bay. Starting Price: Admission to Bayside Marketplace is free; costs for food, shopping, and activities vary. Insider Tip: Visit in the evening to enjoy stunning sunset views over the bay and catch the nightly music and light show at the marketplace's central stage.
8. **Jungle Island's Exotic Wildlife**: Get up close and personal with exotic animals at Jungle Island, an interactive zoological park located on Watson Island. Encounter lemurs, parrots, kangaroos, and more as you explore immersive habitats, attend animal shows and presentations, and enjoy family-friendly attractions and activities. Starting Price: Admission to Jungle Island starts at $39.95 for adults. Insider Tip: Check the park's website for special offers and discounted tickets, and plan your visit during feeding times and animal encounters for unforgettable experiences.
9. **Bayfront Park's Urban Oasis**: Escape the hustle and bustle of the city at Bayfront Park, a lush urban oasis nestled along Biscayne Bay. Relax in scenic gardens, admire public art installations, and enjoy recreational amenities such as walking paths, picnic areas, and waterfront promenades. Starting Price: Admission to Bayfront Park is free. Insider Tip: Bring a blanket and pack a picnic lunch to enjoy al fresco dining with stunning views of the bay and downtown Miami skyline.
10. **Miami Design District's Luxury Shopping**: Indulge in a shopping spree at the Miami Design District, a high-end retail and cultural destination known for its luxury boutiques, art

galleries, and upscale dining options. Browse designer fashion brands, discover cutting-edge contemporary art, and dine at Michelin-starred restaurants in this chic and stylish neighborhood. Starting Price: Admission to the Miami Design District is free; costs for shopping and dining va

Shopping:

- **Outlet Malls:** Shop at nearby outlet malls like Dolphin Mall and Sawgrass Mills for discounted shopping.
- **Discount Stores:** Find deals at discount stores like Ross, T.J. Maxx, and Marshalls.
- **Thrift Shops:** Explore thrift stores in neighborhoods like Little Havana and Miami Beach for budget-friendly fashion.

Tours and Attractions:

- **CityPASS:** Consider purchasing the Go Miami Card for savings on multiple attractions.
- **Art Deco Historic District:** Explore the Art Deco Historic District in South Beach, which is free to wander.
- **Wynwood Walls:** Visit the Wynwood Walls to see incredible street art, with some areas open to the public for free.
- **Vizcaya Museum and Gardens:** Visit Vizcaya Museum and Gardens on select days for free admission.

Transportation within Miami:

- **Walking Tours:** Discover neighborhoods with self-guided walking tours available online or through apps.
- **Biking:** Rent a Citi Bike for affordable short-distance travel within the city.
- **Taxis and Ride-Sharing Apps:** Use taxis or ride-sharing apps like Uber and Lyft for convenient travel.
- **Airport Parking:** Consider off-site airport parking for potential cost savings compared to on-site airport parking.

Sports and Recreation:

- **Local Parks:** Enjoy free or low-cost activities in local parks, including hiking, picnicking, and sports.
- **Public Swimming Pools:** Cool off at public swimming pools across the city during the summer months.
- **Free Yoga Classes:** Attend free or donation-based yoga classes in parks or at local studios.

Local Events and Festivals:

- **Festivals and Street Fairs:** Attend free or low-cost local festivals and street fairs throughout the year.
- **Farmers' Markets:** Visit farmers' markets for fresh and affordable produce, artisanal goods, and prepared foods.

- **Cultural Festivals:** Explore cultural events and festivals celebrating Miami's diverse communities.

Miscellaneous Savings:

- **Senior Discounts:** If you're a senior citizen, inquire about available discounts at attractions, restaurants, and theaters.
- **Library Passes:** Some local libraries offer free or discounted passes to museums and attractions.
- **AAA Discounts:** AAA members can access discounts on hotels, dining, and attractions in Miami.
- **Free Wi-Fi:** Connect to free Wi-Fi available at many hotels, restaurants, and cafes to save on data charges.
- **Ride Shares:** Use ride-sharing apps like Uber and Lyft for affordable transportation options and always google for discount codes before signing up.
- **Airport Rides:** Arrange airport transportation with shuttle services, which can be more budget-friendly than taxis.
- **Hotel Amenities:** Take advantage of free hotel amenities such as pools, fitness centers, and complimentary breakfasts.
- **Visit Nearby Destinations:** Explore nearby areas like the Florida Keys and the Everglades for budget-friendly adventures.
- **Dining Apps:** Use dining apps like Yelp and OpenTable to find discounts and special offers at local restaurants.
- **Rentals for Watersports:** Rent watersports equipment, such as paddleboards or kayaks, for a fun and affordable beach activity.
- **Visit Little Havana:** Experience the vibrant culture of Little Havana with affordable Cuban restaurants and cultural events.
- **Visit the Coral Gables:** Explore the picturesque Coral Gables area with its Mediterranean-style architecture and free attractions.
- **Art Basel Satellite Events:** Attend free satellite events during Art Basel Miami Beach for art and cultural experiences.

San Diego

This coastal gem is a paradise of pristine beaches, cultural diversity, and endless outdoor adventures. While San Diego is known for its upscale attractions, you can still have a blast without breaking the bank! Save money by taking advantage of free activities like hiking in Torrey Pines State Natural Reserve or exploring the historic Gaslamp Quarter. Skip the pricey tourist traps and opt for budget-friendly fish tacos at local beachside joints. And resist the urge to splurge on expensive boat tours – rent a kayak or paddleboard and explore the stunning coastline on your own.

Accommodation:

1. **Budget Hotels:** Look for budget-friendly hotels in San Diego that provide basic amenities without breaking the bank. Consider options like Motel 6 San Diego - Hotel Circle, Days Inn by Wyndham San Diego Hotel Circle Near SeaWorld, or Bay Inn and Suites at SeaWorld for affordable stays in convenient locations.
2. **Hostels:** Hostels are a popular option for budget travelers in San Diego. Check out hostels like HI San Diego Downtown Hostel or Lucky D's Hostel, which offer dormitory-style rooms and private rooms at budget-friendly rates.
3. **Suburbs:** Consider staying in suburbs outside of San Diego's city center for more affordable accommodations. Suburbs like Mission Valley, Hotel Circle, or Pacific Beach offer a range of lodging options at lower prices compared to downtown San Diego.

Dining:

- **Happy Hour Deals:** Take advantage of happy hour specials at bars and restaurants for discounted drinks and appetizers.
- **Food Trucks:** Enjoy diverse and affordable food options from San Diego's food trucks.
- **Mexican Cuisine:** Explore local Mexican restaurants for budget-friendly and authentic dining experiences.
- **Lunch Specials:** Opt for lunch specials at restaurants, which are often more budget-friendly than dinner.

- **Farmers' Markets:** Visit farmers' markets for fresh and affordable produce, artisanal goods, and prepared foods.

Transportation:

- **Public Transportation:** Use the Metropolitan Transit System (MTS) buses and trolleys for cost-effective transportation. A one-way MTS fare starts at $2.50.
- **Compass Card:** Purchase a Compass Card for discounted fares on public transportation.
- **Walking:** Explore neighborhoods on foot to save on transportation costs and enjoy the sights.
- **Biking:** Rent a bike or use bike-sharing programs like Discover Bike for affordable short-distance travel.

Entertainment:

- **Free Beaches:** Enjoy San Diego's beautiful beaches for free sunbathing and swimming.
- **Balboa Park:** Visit Balboa Park, where many attractions offer free admission on select days.
- **Free Museums:** Explore free museums like the Timken Museum of Art and the Marston House Museum.
- **Student Discounts:** If you're a student, inquire about available discounts at museums, theaters, and attractions.
- **Concerts in the Park:** Attend free outdoor concerts and performances in local parks.

Honolulu

Where aloha spirit meets paradise perfection! This tropical haven is a blend of stunning beaches, lush landscapes, and rich cultural heritage.

Honolulu can be a luxurious destination, you don't have to spend a fortune to enjoy its beauty! Save money by exploring free attractions like Waikiki Beach or hiking to the top of Diamond Head for panoramic views. Skip the expensive resort dinners and opt for delicious plate lunches at local food trucks or markets. And resist the urge to splurge on pricey luaus – instead, catch a free hula show at Kuhio Beach Park or enjoy a sunset picnic at Ala Moana Beach Park.

Accommodation:

1. **Budget Hotels:** Look for budget-friendly hotels in Honolulu that provide basic amenities without breaking the bank. Consider options like the Aston Waikiki Beach Hotel, Vive Hotel Waikiki, or the Holiday Inn Express Waikiki for affordable stays in convenient locations.
2. **Hostels:** Hostels are a popular option for budget travelers in Honolulu. Check out hostels like the HI Honolulu University Hostel or the Beach Waikiki Boutique Hostel, which offer dormitory-style rooms and private rooms at budget-friendly rates.
3. **Suburbs:** Consider staying in suburbs outside of Honolulu's city center for more affordable accommodations. Suburbs like Waikiki, Ala Moana, or Kaimuki offer a range of lodging options at lower prices compared to downtown Honolulu.

Dining:

- **Food Trucks:** Enjoy diverse and affordable food options from Honolulu's food trucks.
- **Local Plate Lunch:** Try local plate lunch spots for budget-friendly meals featuring rice, protein, and macaroni salad.
- **Happy Hour Deals:** Take advantage of happy hour specials at bars and restaurants for discounted drinks and appetizers.

- **Farmers' Markets:** Visit farmers' markets for fresh and affordable produce, artisanal goods, and prepared foods.
- **BYOB Restaurants:** Dine at "bring your own bottle" (BYOB) restaurants to save on alcohol expenses.

Transportation:

- **TheBus:** Use TheBus, Honolulu's public transportation system, for cost-effective travel. A one-way adult fare is $2.75.
- **Transportation Passes:** Consider purchasing a multi-day transportation pass for unlimited bus rides.
- **Biking:** Rent a bike or use bike-sharing programs like Biki for affordable short-distance travel.
- **Walking:** Explore Waikiki and downtown Honolulu on foot to save on transportation costs.

Entertainment:

- **Waikiki Beach:** Enjoy free sunbathing and swimming at the world-famous Waikiki Beach.
- **Hiking Trails:** Explore free hiking trails, such as Diamond Head and Manoa Falls.
- **Free Hula Shows:** Attend free hula shows at locations like the Royal Hawaiian Center in Waikiki.
- **Free Museums:** Visit free museums like the Hawaiian Mission Houses Historic Site and Archives.
- **Student Discounts:** If you're a student, inquire about available discounts at museums, theaters, and attractions.

Shopping:

- **Outlet Malls:** Shop at nearby Waikele Premium Outlets for discounted shopping.
- **Local Markets:** Find souvenirs and unique items at local markets like the Aloha Stadium Swap Meet.
- **Thrift Shops:** Explore thrift stores in neighborhoods like Kaimuki and Kapahulu for budget-friendly finds.

Tours and Attractions:

- **Go Oahu Card:** Consider purchasing the Go Oahu Card for savings on multiple attractions.
- **Pearl Harbor:** Visit Pearl Harbor's USS Arizona Memorial, which offers free tickets (but advance reservations are recommended).
- **Kapiolani Park:** Explore Kapiolani Park and Queen Kapiolani Garden, both free to the public.
- **Free Fireworks Shows:** Watch free fireworks displays at Waikiki Beach on Friday nights.

Transportation within Honolulu:

- **Walking Tours:** Discover neighborhoods with self-guided walking tours available online or through apps.
- **Taxis and Ride-Sharing Apps:** Use taxis or ride-sharing apps like Uber and Lyft for convenient travel.
- **Airport Transportation:** Use airport shuttle services for cost-effective transportation to and from the airport.

- **Car Rentals:** Compare car rental prices on websites like Kayak and Rentalcars.com for budget-friendly options.

Sports and Recreation:

- **Local Parks:** Enjoy free or low-cost activities in local parks, including hiking, picnicking, and sports.
- **Public Swimming Pools:** Cool off at public swimming pools across Honolulu during the summer months.
- **Free Yoga Classes:** Attend free or donation-based yoga classes at local studios.

Local Events and Festivals:

- **Festivals and Cultural Events:** Attend free or low-cost local festivals and cultural events throughout the year.
- **Farmers' Markets:** Visit farmers' markets for fresh and affordable produce, artisanal goods, and prepared foods.
- **Cultural Demonstrations:** Enjoy free cultural demonstrations and performances at the Polynesian Cultural Center.

Miscellaneous Savings:

- **Senior Discounts:** If you're a senior citizen, inquire about available discounts at attractions, restaurants, and theaters.
- **Library Passes:** Some local libraries offer free or discounted passes to museums and attractions.
- **AAA Discounts:** AAA members can access discounts on hotels, dining, and attractions in Honolulu.
- **Free Wi-Fi:** Connect to free Wi-Fi available at many hotels, restaurants, and cafes to save on data charges.
- **Ride Shares:** Use ride-sharing apps like Uber and Lyft for affordable transportation options.
- **Airport Parking:** Consider off-site airport parking for potential cost savings compared to on-site airport parking.
- **Hotel Amenities:** Take advantage of free hotel amenities such as pools, fitness centers, and complimentary breakfasts.
- **Visit Nearby Islands:** Explore nearby islands like Maui and Kauai for budget-friendly day trips.
- **Visit Hanauma Bay:** Snorkel at Hanauma Bay Nature Preserve, which has an entrance fee but provides rental gear for free.
- **Makapuu Lighthouse Trail:** Hike the Makapuu Lighthouse Trail for stunning ocean views and whale-watching opportunities.
- **Koko Crater Railway Trail:** Hike the Koko Crater Railway Trail for panoramic views of the island.

Boston

Boston, a city steeped in history and innovation, has left an indelible mark on American culture and identity. Founded in 1630 by Puritan colonists, Boston quickly became a hub of commerce, politics, and education in the New World. Today, Boston continues to thrive as a global city, renowned for its historic landmarks, vibrant culture, and spirit of innovation.

Accommodation:

1. **Budget Hotels:** Look for budget-friendly hotels in Boston that provide basic amenities without breaking the bank. Consider options like the Boston Common Hotel and Conference Center, the HI Boston Hostel, or the Found Hotel Boston Common for affordable stays in convenient locations.
2. **Suburbs:** Consider staying in suburbs outside of Boston's city center for more affordable accommodations. Suburbs like Cambridge, Somerville, or Brookline offer a range of lodging options at lower prices compared to downtown Boston.

Dining:

- **Food Trucks:** Enjoy diverse and affordable food options from Boston's food trucks.
- **Local Eateries:** Explore local eateries and pubs for budget-friendly meals and New England cuisine.
- **Lunch Specials:** Opt for lunch specials at restaurants, which are often more budget-friendly than dinner.
- **Bakeries:** Try local bakeries for affordable breakfast and pastry options.
- **BYOB Restaurants:** Dine at "bring your own bottle" (BYOB) restaurants to save on alcohol expenses.

Transportation:

- **Public Transportation:** Use the Massachusetts Bay Transportation Authority (MBTA) subway system (known as the "T") for cost-effective travel. A one-way subway fare starts at $2.40.
- **CharlieCard:** Purchase a CharlieCard for discounted fares on public transportation.
- **Walking:** Explore neighborhoods on foot to save on transportation costs and enjoy the sights.
- **Biking:** Rent a bike or use bike-sharing programs like Bluebikes for affordable short-distance travel.

Entertainment:

- **Free Attractions:** Explore free attractions like the Freedom Trail, Boston Common, and the Public Garden.
- **Discounted Museums:** Check museum websites for free admission days or discounted rates.
- **Student Discounts:** If you're a student, inquire about available discounts at museums, theaters, and attractions.
- **Free Concerts:** Attend free outdoor concerts and performances at locations like the Hatch Shell.
- **Comedy Clubs:** Find comedy clubs with free or low-cost comedy shows during the week.

1. **Waikiki Beach's Iconic Shoreline:** Embrace the aloha spirit at Waikiki Beach, Honolulu's most famous stretch of sand known for its turquoise waters, palm-fringed shores, and vibrant atmosphere. Soak up the sun, swim in the gentle waves, or try your hand at water sports like surfing and paddleboarding. Starting Price: Admission to Waikiki Beach is free; costs for equipment rental and beachside amenities vary. Insider Tip: Arrive early in the morning for prime beachfront spots and stunning sunrise views over Diamond Head Crater.
2. **Diamond Head State Monument's Scenic Hike:** Conquer the iconic Diamond Head Crater with a scenic hike to the summit, offering panoramic views of Honolulu and the sparkling Pacific Ocean. Trek along a moderate trail lined with volcanic rock formations, climb steep staircases, and reach the summit for breathtaking vistas. Starting Price: Admission to Diamond Head State Monument is $5 per vehicle or $1 per pedestrian. Insider Tip: Bring plenty of water, wear sturdy footwear, and start your hike early to avoid the midday heat and crowds.
3. **Hanauma Bay's Underwater Wonderland:** Dive into a world of marine wonder at Hanauma Bay Nature Preserve, a protected marine sanctuary renowned for its pristine coral reefs and abundant marine life. Snorkel in crystal-clear waters, swim among colorful fish and sea turtles, and marvel at the beauty of the underwater landscape. Starting Price: Admission to Hanauma Bay is $12 per vehicle or $3 per pedestrian. Insider Tip: Arrive early to secure parking and avoid crowds, and watch the educational video at the visitor center to learn about coral reef conservation and safety tips.
4. **Pearl Harbor Historic Sites:** Pay tribute to history at Pearl Harbor, a poignant reminder of the events that shaped the course of World War II. Visit the USS Arizona Memorial, USS Bowfin Submarine Museum, and Battleship Missouri Memorial to learn about the attack on Pearl Harbor and the bravery of those who served. Starting Price: Admission to Pearl Harbor historic sites is free; costs for guided tours and museum entry vary. Insider Tip: Reserve tickets in advance for the USS Arizona Memorial program, as same-day tickets are limited and often sell out early.
5. **Iolani Palace's Royal Heritage:** Step into the past at Iolani Palace, the only royal palace on American soil and a symbol of Hawaiian monarchy. Take a guided tour of the opulent palace to learn about Hawaiian history, monarchy, and culture, and admire the grandeur of the restored royal residence. Starting Price: Admission to Iolani Palace starts at $21.75 for adults. Insider Tip: Join a guided tour for in-depth insights into the palace's history and architecture, and explore the surrounding historic district, including Kawaiahao Church and Aliiolani Hale.
6. **Honolulu Museum of Art's Cultural Treasures:** Immerse yourself in art and culture at the Honolulu Museum of Art, home to an extensive collection of Asian, Pacific, and Western art spanning centuries and continents. Wander through galleries showcasing paintings, sculptures, and decorative arts, and attend special exhibitions and events. Starting Price: Admission to the museum starts at $20 for adults. Insider Tip: Visit on the first Wednesday of the month for free admission to the museum's permanent galleries and enjoy live music and performances during Art After Dark events.

7. **Ala Moana Center's Shopping Paradise**: Indulge in retail therapy at Ala Moana Center, Hawaii's largest open-air shopping mall boasting over 350 stores, boutiques, and restaurants. Shop for designer brands, local souvenirs, and unique gifts, and dine at a variety of eateries offering international cuisine and local favorites. Starting Price: Admission to Ala Moana Center is free; costs for shopping and dining vary. Insider Tip: Sign up for the mall's loyalty program for exclusive discounts and rewards, and visit during major sales events like Black Friday and Memorial Day weekend for unbeatable deals.
8. **Manoa Falls Trail's Rainforest Adventure**: Embark on a scenic hike through the lush rainforest of Manoa Valley to reach the stunning Manoa Falls, a 150-foot cascade surrounded by tropical vegetation. Trek along a well-maintained trail, listen to the sounds of nature, and cool off with a refreshing dip in the natural pool at the base of the waterfall. Starting Price: Admission to Manoa Falls Trail is free; costs for parking and guided tours vary. Insider Tip: Wear sturdy footwear and bring insect repellent, as the trail can be muddy and prone to mosquitoes, and visit after rainfall for the most dramatic waterfall views.
9. **Sunset Beach's Surfer's Paradise**: Experience the laid-back vibes of Hawaii's North Shore at Sunset Beach, a world-renowned surf spot known for its powerful waves and epic sunsets. Watch expert surfers ride the waves, lounge on the golden sands, and enjoy picnics and beach games with family and friends. Starting Price: Admission to Sunset Beach is free; costs for parking and equipment rental vary. Insider Tip: Check the surf forecast before visiting to catch the best waves, and stay for sunset to witness the sky ablaze with fiery hues over the ocean horizon.
10. **Lanikai Beach's Tropical Paradise**: Discover a slice of paradise at Lanikai Beach, a postcard-perfect stretch of coastline known for its powdery white sands, turquoise waters, and iconic Mokulua Islands offshore. Relax in the tranquil setting, swim in calm waters, and kayak or paddleboard to the nearby islands for unforgettable adventures. Starting Price: Admission to Lanikai Beach is free; costs for parking and water sports rentals vary. Insider Tip: Arrive early to secure parking in the residential neighborhood and enjoy the beach at its quietest, and bring snorkeling gear to explore vibrant coral reefs teeming with marine life.

Shopping:

- **Outlet Malls:** Shop at nearby outlet malls like Wrentham Village Premium Outlets for discounted shopping.
- **Sample Sales:** Keep an eye out for sample sales and designer discounts in Boston.
- **Thrift Shops:** Explore thrift shops in neighborhoods like Cambridge and Allston for budget-friendly fashion.

Tours and Attractions:

- **Go Boston Card:** Consider purchasing the Go Boston Card for savings on multiple attractions.
- **Freedom Trail:** Walk the Freedom Trail on your own for free or join a guided tour for a small fee.
- **Harvard University:** Explore the Harvard University campus and visit the Harvard Art Museums on specific days with free admission.
- **Isabella Stewart Gardner Museum:** Enjoy free admission to the Isabella Stewart Gardner Museum on your birthday.

Transportation within Boston:

- **Walking Tours:** Discover neighborhoods with self-guided walking tours available online or through apps.
- **Taxis and Ride-Sharing Apps:** Use taxis or ride-sharing apps like Uber and Lyft for convenient travel.
- **Airport Transportation:** Use airport shuttle services for cost-effective transportation to and from the airport.
- **Car Rentals:** Compare car rental prices on websites like Kayak and Rentalcars.com for budget-friendly options.

Sports and Recreation:

- **Local Parks:** Enjoy free or low-cost activities in local parks, including hiking, picnicking, and sports.
- **Public Swimming Pools:** Cool off at public swimming pools across the city during the summer months.
- **Free Yoga Classes:** Attend free or donation-based yoga classes in parks or at local studios.

Local Events and Festivals:

- **Festivals and Street Fairs:** Attend free or low-cost local festivals and street fairs throughout the year.
- **Farmers' Markets:** Visit farmers' markets for fresh and affordable produce, artisanal goods, and prepared foods.
- **Cultural Festivals:** Explore cultural events and festivals celebrating Boston's diverse communities.

Miscellaneous Savings:

- **Senior Discounts:** If you're a senior citizen, inquire about available discounts at attractions, restaurants, and theaters.
- **Library Passes:** Some local libraries offer free or discounted passes to museums and attractions.
- **AAA Discounts:** AAA members can access discounts on hotels, dining, and attractions in Boston.
- **Free Wi-Fi:** Connect to free Wi-Fi available at many hotels, restaurants, and cafes to save on data charges.
- **DIY Sightseeing:** Create your self-guided walking tours using online resources and maps.
- **Local Apps:** Download local apps for restaurant deals, event discounts, and transportation options in Boston.
- **Student Discounts:** If you're a student, take advantage of available discounts on entertainment, transportation, and dining.
- **Ride Shares:** Use ride-sharing apps like Uber and Lyft for convenient transportation options.
- **Airport Parking:** Consider off-site airport parking for potential cost savings compared to on-site airport parking.
- **Hotel Amenities:** Take advantage of free hotel amenities such as pools, fitness centers, and complimentary breakfasts.
- **Visit Nearby Towns:** Explore nearby towns like Salem and Concord for budget-friendly day trips.

- **Charles River Esplanade:** Enjoy scenic views along the Charles River Esplanade and take a leisurely stroll.
- **Boston Harborwalk:** Walk along the Boston Harborwalk, which offers beautiful waterfront views.
- **Boston Tea Party Ships & Museum:** Check for discounts and special offers when visiting the Boston Tea Party Ships & Museum.
- **Boston Public Library:** Visit the Boston Public Library for its historic architecture and free public events.

The states

Alabama

A state rich in history and brimming with Southern charm. Whether you're a history buff, a nature enthusiast, or simply looking to experience the warm hospitality of the Deep South, Alabama has something for everyone.

Known as the "Heart of Dixie," Alabama has played a pivotal role in many chapters of American history. From its early Native American heritage to its critical position in the Civil War, and its major contributions to the Civil Rights Movement, Alabama's history is as diverse as it is profound. Key historical sites include the Civil Rights Memorial in Montgomery, the USS Alabama Battleship Memorial Park in Mobile, and the Birmingham Civil Rights Institute.

Natural Beauty: Alabama is home to stunning landscapes, from the Appalachian Mountains in the north to the Gulf Coast beaches in the south. The state's diverse geography offers opportunities for hiking, fishing, and exploring national parks like the Little River Canyon National Preserve and Gulf State Park.

Cultural Experiences: The state's rich cultural tapestry is reflected in its music, food, and festivals. Alabama's contribution to the music world is significant, with Muscle Shoals being a notable hub for legendary music recordings. Don't miss the chance to savor traditional Southern cuisine, including barbecue, fried green tomatoes, and Alabama's unique white barbecue sauce.

Local Tips:

- **Weather Considerations**: Alabama's weather can be quite warm and humid, especially in the summer. Pack accordingly and stay hydrated.
- **Transportation**: While larger cities like Birmingham and Montgomery have public transportation, having a car is the most convenient way to explore the state.
- **Local Etiquette**: Southern hospitality is real. Expect friendly greetings and polite manners. It's common to engage in small talk with locals.
- **Sports**: Football is more than just a game in Alabama; it's a way of life. The rivalry between the University of Alabama and Auburn University is legendary.
- **Festivals**: Check out local event calendars for festivals and events, such as the National Shrimp Festival in Gulf Shores and the Jubilee Hot Air Balloon Festival in Decatur.

1. **Transportation:**

    - **Car Rental:** Consider renting a car for flexibility. Rental prices start at around $30 per day. You can find good deals from major rental companies.

2. **Accommodation:**

- **Luxury on a Budget:** Look for boutique hotels, bed and breakfasts, or Airbnb options. Prices can range from $80 to $150 per night for a comfortable stay. Popular areas include Birmingham, Huntsville, and Mobile.
- **Unique Accommodations:** Explore unique stays on Airbnb, such as cozy cabins or historic homes, to add a touch of luxury to your stay.

1. **Budget Hotels:** Look for budget-friendly hotels in cities like Birmingham, Huntsville, or Mobile. Options such as Red Roof Inn Birmingham South, Econo Lodge Inn & Suites Huntsville, or Microtel Inn & Suites by Wyndham Mobile offer comfortable stays at reasonable prices.
2. **Bed and Breakfasts:** Consider staying at bed and breakfasts in charming towns like Fairhope, Montgomery, or Tuscaloosa. Places like The Fairhope Inn, The Lattice Inn in Montgomery, or Bama Bed and Breakfast in Tuscaloosa offer affordable rates and a cozy atmosphere.
3. **State Parks:** Alabama's state parks offer affordable accommodations in picturesque settings. Look into staying at cabins or campsites in parks like Oak Mountain State Park, Gulf State Park, or Joe Wheeler State Park for a budget-friendly outdoor experience.
4. **Vacation Rentals:** Explore vacation rental options through platforms like Vrbo or Booking.com. You can find affordable apartments or houses in cities like Birmingham, Tuscaloosa, or Auburn, which can be cost-effective for groups or longer stays.
5. **Hostels:** While hostels may be less common in Alabama compared to other destinations, you can still find options in larger cities like Birmingham or Huntsville. Check out HI Birmingham Hostel for affordable dormitory-style accommodations.
6. **Hotel Deals:** Keep an eye out for special deals and discounts on hotel booking websites such as Booking.com, Hotels.com, or Expedia. Many hotels offer promotions or last-minute deals that can help you save on your stay in Alabama.

- **Fine Dining:** Splurge on a few upscale dining experiences. Restaurants like Highlands Bar and Grill in Birmingham offer a taste of Southern luxury. Prices can range from $50 to $100 per person for a multi-course meal.
- **Local Eateries:** Enjoy local cuisine at more affordable prices. Try barbecue joints, seafood shacks, or soul food restaurants. Meals at these places can range from $10 to $30 per person.

4. **Activities:**

   - **Museums and Historical Sites:** Alabama is rich in history. Visit the Birmingham Civil Rights Institute ($15 admission), the U.S. Space and Rocket Center in Huntsville ($25 admission), and the USS Alabama Battleship Memorial Park in Mobile ($15 admission).
   - **Outdoor Adventures:** Explore Alabama's natural beauty. Hike in the Cheaha State Park or go to Gulf Shores for a day at the beach. Many outdoor activities are free or have a nominal entrance fee.

5. **Entertainment:**

   - **Live Music:** Experience the vibrant music scene in Alabama. Look for live music events, especially in Birmingham and Montgomery. Prices for tickets can range from $10 to $50.
   - **Cultural Events:** Check local calendars for festivals and cultural events. These can provide a unique and affordable way to experience the local lifestyle.

Free Tours

1. **Alabama State Capitol Tour (Montgomery):** The Alabama State Capitol offers free guided tours of the historic building. You can explore the architecture, history, and significance of this landmark.
2. **Alabama Museum of Natural History (Tuscaloosa):** While not exactly a guided tour, the museum offers free admission and you can explore exhibits showcasing the natural history of Alabama.
3. **Self-guided Tours of Birmingham's Civil Rights District:** While not guided, you can explore the Civil Rights District in Birmingham, which includes the Birmingham Civil Rights Institute, Kelly Ingram Park, and the 16th Street Baptist Church, all significant sites in the civil rights movement. These locations are free to visit.
4. **University of Alabama Campus Tours (Tuscaloosa):** The University of Alabama offers free campus tours where you can explore the beautiful campus and learn about its history and architecture.
5. **Oakville Indian Mounds Education Center (Danville):** This historical site offers free admission and self-guided tours where you can explore Native American history and see the ancient mounds.

6. **Insights and Tips:**

   - **Local Markets:** Visit farmers' markets for fresh produce and handmade crafts. It's a budget-friendly way to experience local culture.
   - **Free Tours:** Many cities offer free walking tours. Check with local tourism offices for schedules and details.
   - **Off-Peak Travel:** Consider traveling during the off-peak season to get better deals on accommodation and activities.

1. **Birmingham:**

   - **Visit the Birmingham Museum of Art:** Free admission to a diverse collection.
   - **Stroll through Railroad Park:** A beautifully landscaped green space.

- **Explore the historic Civil Rights District:** Rich in history and culture.

2. **Huntsville:**

    - **Hike at Monte Sano State Park:** Offers stunning views of the city.
    - **U.S. Space and Rocket Center:** While the museum has an admission fee, viewing the rockets outside is free.
    - **Downtown Huntsville Craft Beer Trail:** Enjoy local brews at affordable prices.

3. **Mobile:**

    - **Mobile Bay:** Relax by the bay, and watch the ships go by.
    - **Dauphin Street Historic District:** Explore the historic architecture.
    - **Mardi Gras Park:** Learn about Mobile's Mardi Gras history.

4. **Gulf Shores:**

    - **Beach Day at Gulf State Park:** Miles of pristine white sand.
    - **Bon Secour National Wildlife Refuge:** Experience nature at its best.
    - **Alabama Coastal Birding Trail:** Ideal for bird watching enthusiasts.

5. **Montgomery:**

    - **Walk through the Old Alabama Town:** A glimpse into the state's history.
    - **Montgomery Riverwalk:** Enjoy a scenic stroll along the river.
    - **Visit the Civil Rights Memorial:** Located at the Southern Poverty Law Center.

6. **Tuscaloosa:**

    - **University of Alabama Arboretum:** A peaceful retreat with walking trails.
    - **Tuscaloosa Riverwalk:** Scenic views of the Black Warrior River.
    - **Explore the Tuscaloosa Amphitheater area:** Often hosting free events.

7. **Auburn:**

    - **Samford Park at Toomer's Corner:** Iconic oaks and a historic setting.
    - **Jule Collins Smith Museum of Fine Art:** Free admission on certain days.
    - **Auburn Downtown Historic District:** Charming streets and local shops.

8. **Florence:**

    - **Wilson Dam:** Enjoy views of the Tennessee River.
    - **W.C. Handy Home and Museum:** Learn about the Father of the Blues.
    - **Shoals Theatre:** Check for affordable live performances.

9. **Anniston:**

    - **Coldwater Covered Bridge:** A picturesque spot for photos.
    - **Mountain Longleaf National Wildlife Refuge:** A serene nature retreat.
    - **Visit the Berman Museum of World History:** Admission is affordable.

10. **Decatur:**

    - **Point Mallard Park:** Offers a beach, water park, and more.
    - **Cook's Natural Science Museum:** Affordable and fascinating for nature lovers.
    - **Wheeler National Wildlife Refuge:** Great for birdwatching.

11. **Muscle Shoals:**

    - **FAME Recording Studios:** Affordable tours for music enthusiasts.
    - **Cypress Inn Restaurant:** Enjoy a meal with a view of the Tennessee River.

- **Ivy Green - Helen Keller Birthplace:** Learn about the life of Helen Keller.

12. **Ozark:**

    - **Visit the Ozark Folk Center State Park:** Learn about traditional crafts.
    - **Float down the Choctawhatchee River:** Affordable canoe and kayak rentals.
    - **Dale County Courthouse Square:** Explore the historic square.

13. **Enterprise:**

    - **Boll Weevil Monument:** A quirky landmark in the city.
    - **Enterprise Farmers Market:** Experience local produce and crafts.
    - **Johnny Henderson Park:** Relax by the pond or have a picnic.

Top 20 attractions in Alabama and some money-saving tips for visiting each one:

Gulf Shores and Orange Beach: Sink your toes into the sugar-white sands and soak up the sun along the stunning coastline of Gulf Shores and Orange Beach.

Money-Saving Tip: Opt for visits during the off-season to snag lower accommodation rates.

Starting Cost: Accommodation can range from $100 to $300 per night, depending on the season and location.

U.S. Space & Rocket Center, Huntsville: Embark on an interstellar journey through space history at the U.S. Space & Rocket Center in Huntsville.

Money-Saving Tip: Keep an eye out for discounted admission days or consider purchasing a family pass for added savings.

Starting Cost: General admission starts at $25 per adult and $17 per child.

Gulf State Park: Immerse yourself in the natural beauty of Gulf State Park, boasting miles of pristine beaches, nature trails, and a picturesque fishing pier.

Money-Saving Tip: Bring along your own fishing gear and explore the free hiking trails to keep costs down.

Starting Cost: Entrance to the park is free, but parking fees may apply, typically around $5.

Little River Canyon National Preserve: Chase waterfalls and trek through scenic hiking trails at Little River Canyon National Preserve.

Money-Saving Tip: Pack a picnic and make a day of it without breaking the bank.

Starting Cost: Entry to the preserve is free of charge.

Civil Rights Institute, Birmingham: Delve into the rich history of the civil rights movement at the Civil Rights Institute in Birmingham.

Money-Saving Tip: Look for discounts for students or seniors to make your visit more budget-friendly.

Starting Cost: Admission is typically around $15 for adults and $5 for children.

Mobile Bay: Experience the charm of historic Mobile and take in stunning waterfront views along Mobile Bay.

Money-Saving Tip: Opt for a self-guided walking tour of the city's historic district to explore without spending much.

Starting Cost: Walking tours are often free, but donations are appreciated.

Noccalula Falls Park, Gadsden: Marvel at the majestic Noccalula Falls and enjoy the surrounding park's attractions.

Money-Saving Tip: Plan your visit during the weekdays for reduced admission fees.

Starting Cost: Admission to the park is around $6 for adults and $4 for children.

Montgomery Civil Rights Landmarks: Trace the footsteps of history at various civil rights landmarks throughout Montgomery.

Money-Saving Tip: Many of these landmarks offer free admission, allowing you to explore without spending a dime.

Starting Cost: Free admission to most landmarks; donations may be accepted.

Huntsville Botanical Garden: Take a leisurely stroll through the enchanting landscapes of Huntsville Botanical Garden.

Money-Saving Tip: Keep an eye out for special events with reduced admission fees for added savings.

Starting Cost: General admission ranges from $14 to $16 for adults and $9 to $11 for children.

Talladega Superspeedway: Feel the adrenaline rush of NASCAR racing at Talladega Superspeedway.

Money-Saving Tip: Bring your own snacks and beverages to the race to avoid pricey concessions.

Starting Cost: Ticket prices vary depending on the event; general admission starts at around $50.

Bellingrath Gardens and Home, Theodore: Lose yourself in the beauty of Bellingrath Gardens' meticulously landscaped grounds and historic home.

Money-Saving Tip: Purchase tickets online in advance to score a discount on admission.

Starting Cost: General admission is around $22 for adults and $13 for children.

Ave Maria Grotto, Cullman: Be amazed by the intricate miniature replicas of famous religious structures at Ave Maria Grotto.

Money-Saving Tip: Look for group discounts or online coupons to save on admission.

Starting Cost: Admission is typically around $8 for adults and $4 for children.

Dauphin Island: Retreat to the serene natural surroundings of Dauphin Island, perfect for outdoor enthusiasts and beach lovers alike.

Money-Saving Tip: Camp at the public campground for affordable lodging options during your stay.

Starting Cost: Camping fees start at around $30 per night.

Alabama State Capitol, Montgomery: Step back in time as you tour the historic halls of the Alabama State Capitol in Montgomery.

Money-Saving Tip: Take advantage of free guided tours offered on weekdays to learn about the building's rich history.

Starting Cost: Free guided tours; donations may be appreciated.

Birmingham Zoo: Encounter a diverse array of animals and exhibits at the Birmingham Zoo.

Money-Saving Tip: Check the zoo's website for discount days or consider purchasing a family membership for added savings.

Starting Cost: General admission ranges from $18 to $22 for adults and $13 to $17 for children.

Wheeler National Wildlife Refuge: Birdwatchers and nature enthusiasts will delight in exploring the vast landscapes of Wheeler National Wildlife Refuge.

Money-Saving Tip: Bring your own binoculars and pack a picnic for an inexpensive day of wildlife viewing.

Starting Cost: Entry to the refuge is free of charge.

Birmingham Museum of Art: Immerse yourself in artistic expression with a visit to the Birmingham Museum of Art.

Money-Saving Tip: Admission to the museum is free, though donations are encouraged to support its programming.

Starting Cost: Free admission; donations appreciated.

Autauga Creek Canoe Trail, Prattville: Drift along the serene waters of Autauga Creek on a picturesque canoe excursion.

Money-Saving Tip: Bring your own canoe or consider renting one for a reasonable fee.

Starting Cost: Canoe rentals typically start at around $25 per day.

Tuskegee Airmen National Historic Site: Honor the legacy of the Tuskegee Airmen at this historic site dedicated to their remarkable achievements.

Money-Saving Tip: Admission to the site is free, allowing visitors to explore without any cost.

Starting Cost: Free admission.

Battleship USS Alabama, Mobile: Step aboard the historic Battleship USS Alabama and delve into its storied past.

Money-Saving Tip: Take advantage of discounts available for seniors, military personnel, and children.

Starting Cost: General admission is around $15 for adults and $8 for children.

Here are ten lesser-known gems to discover in the Heart of Dixie:

1. **Mobile's Historic Districts**: Step back in time as you wander through Mobile's historic districts, including the charming Downtown, the stately De Tonti Square, and the picturesque Oakleigh Garden District. Admire antebellum homes, Spanish moss-draped oaks, and cobblestone streets as you soak in the city's rich heritage. Starting Price: Admission to historic districts is free; costs for guided tours and attractions vary. Insider Tip: Download self-guided walking tour maps from the Mobile Historic Development Commission website to explore at your own pace.
2. **Huntsville's Space Exploration**: Embark on a journey through space and science at the U.S. Space & Rocket Center in Huntsville, home to the world's largest collection of rockets and space memorabilia. Explore interactive exhibits, marvel at the Saturn V rocket, and experience simulators that simulate space travel. Starting Price: Admission to the U.S. Space & Rocket Center starts at $25 for adults. Insider Tip: Check the center's website for special events and educational programs, including astronaut encounters and STEM workshops.
3. **Birmingham's Civil Rights Heritage**: Delve into the pivotal role Birmingham played in the Civil Rights Movement at sites like the Birmingham Civil Rights Institute and the Sixteenth Street Baptist Church. Learn about the struggles and triumphs of the movement through exhibits, memorials, and guided tours. Starting Price: Admission to the Birmingham Civil Rights Institute starts at $15 for adults. Insider Tip: Plan your visit during the annual Birmingham Civil Rights Institute Institute Jazz Festival for live music, performances, and community celebrations.

4. **Montgomery's Literary Legacy**: Explore the literary history of Montgomery, the birthplace of iconic author Harper Lee and the inspiration for her Pulitzer Prize-winning novel, "To Kill a Mockingbird." Visit the Scott and Zelda Fitzgerald Museum, the Alabama Shakespeare Festival, and the Alabama Department of Archives and History to delve into the city's literary heritage. Starting Price: Admission to the Scott and Zelda Fitzgerald Museum starts at $10 for adults. Insider Tip: Attend the annual Alabama Book Festival for author readings, book signings, and literary-themed events.
5. **Gulf Shores' Beachfront Bliss**: Escape to the pristine shores of Gulf Shores for a beach vacation like no other. Sink your toes into sugar-white sands, swim in the emerald waters of the Gulf of Mexico, and soak up the sun on miles of uncrowded beaches. Starting Price: Admission to Gulf Shores Public Beach is free; costs for parking and beach equipment rental vary. Insider Tip: Explore nearby Gulf State Park for hiking trails, fishing piers, and wildlife viewing opportunities amidst coastal dunes and freshwater lakes.
6. **Tuscaloosa's Riverfront Recreation**: Discover outdoor adventures along the Black Warrior River in Tuscaloosa, where you can paddle, fish, and picnic amidst scenic beauty. Rent kayaks or stand-up paddleboards from local outfitters, explore the Tuscaloosa Riverwalk, and enjoy waterfront dining at riverside restaurants. Starting Price: Costs for kayak and paddleboard rentals vary by vendor. Insider Tip: Join a guided eco-tour to learn about the river's ecosystem and wildlife from knowledgeable guides.
7. **Selma's Civil Rights Landmarks**: Commemorate the Selma to Montgomery National Historic Trail and retrace the steps of the Civil Rights Movement's pivotal march for voting rights. Visit landmarks like the Edmund Pettus Bridge, Brown Chapel AME Church, and the National Voting Rights Museum & Institute to honor the courage and sacrifice of civil rights activists. Starting Price: Admission to the National Voting Rights Museum & Institute starts at $8 for adults. Insider Tip: Attend the annual Bridge Crossing Jubilee for reenactments, music performances, and community gatherings commemorating Bloody Sunday.
8. **Little River Canyon's Natural Wonder**: Immerse yourself in the breathtaking beauty of Little River Canyon National Preserve, where you can hike, bike, and explore rugged landscapes carved by the powerful forces of nature. Marvel at waterfalls, rock formations, and scenic overlooks as you discover the canyon's hidden treasures. Starting Price: Admission to Little River Canyon National Preserve is free; costs for parking and guided tours vary. Insider Tip: Pack a picnic and enjoy lunch with a view at one of the canyon's scenic picnic areas, or cool off with a swim in the crystal-clear waters of Little River.
9. **Helen Keller's Birthplace**: Pay homage to Alabama's beloved native daughter at Ivy Green, the birthplace of renowned author and activist Helen Keller. Tour the historic home, museum, and gardens to learn about Keller's remarkable life and legacy, and gain insight into her contributions to literature and social justice. Starting Price: Admission to Ivy Green starts at $8 for adults. Insider Tip: Visit during the annual Helen Keller Festival for live performances, arts and crafts, and family-friendly activities celebrating Keller's life and achievements.
10. **Cheaha State Park's Mountain Majesty**: Escape to the highest point in Alabama at Cheaha State Park, where you can hike, camp, and immerse yourself in the beauty of the Appalachian Mountains. Explore scenic trails, enjoy panoramic views from Cheaha Mountain, and experience the tranquility of nature amidst pristine wilderness. Starting Price: Admission to Cheaha State Park is free; costs for camping and cabin rentals vary. Insider Tip: Watch the sunset from Bald Rock

Overlook for a breathtaking display of colors over the surrounding valleys and forests.

RECAP

Category	Insider Tips
Food	1. Explore local farmer's markets for fresh produce at lower prices.
	2. Look for "meat-and-three" restaurants for affordable Southern comfort food options.
	3. Take advantage of happy hour deals at restaurants and bars for discounted drinks and appetizers.
Accommodation	1. Book accommodations outside major tourist areas for lower rates.
	2. Consider alternative lodging options like Airbnb, hostels, or camping for budget-friendly stays.
	3. Look for accommodations with complimentary breakfast to save on dining costs.
	4. Consider staying in smaller towns or cities near your desired destination for cheaper rates.
Activities	1. Take advantage of free attractions like parks, museums with free admission days, and hiking trails.
	2. Look for discounted tickets or combo deals for attractions purchased online or through local visitor centers.
	3. Attend local festivals and events for entertainment without breaking the
	4. Explore outdoor activities like hiking, biking, and swimming in Alabama's natural landscapes.
Transport	1. Use ride-sharing apps or public transportation in cities to avoid expensive parking fees.
	2. Consider renting a car for longer stays to explore Alabama at your own pace and convenience.

ALASKA

The Last Frontier! A visit to Alaska is a journey into the heart of pristine wilderness, stunning landscapes, and unique cultural heritage. Here's a guide to help first-time visitors make the most of their Alaskan adventure.

Alaska's history is a fascinating blend of Native cultures, Russian heritage, and American frontier spirit. Originally inhabited by various indigenous peoples for thousands of years, it was colonized by Russia in the 18th century. The United States purchased Alaska from Russia in 1867, a transaction often referred to as "Seward's Folly." Since then, Alaska has evolved from a rough-and-tumble frontier land to a state with a diverse economy and a rich cultural landscape.

Natural Wonders: Alaska is a paradise for nature lovers. It's home to Denali National Park, where North America's highest peak, Denali, stands. The state's vast wilderness offers opportunities for wildlife viewing, with bears, moose, eagles, and whales being common sights. The Inside Passage is a coastal route famous for its stunning fjords and maritime scenery. Don't forget to witness the awe-inspiring Northern Lights, best viewed during the colder months.

Outdoor Activities: Adventure seekers will find no shortage of activities in Alaska. From world-class fishing and kayaking to hiking and glacier trekking, the state's natural beauty offers a spectacular backdrop for outdoor pursuits. In the winter, dog sledding, snowmobiling, and skiing take center stage.

Cultural Experiences: Alaskan culture is deeply influenced by the state's Native American heritage. Visitors can explore this rich history through museums, art galleries, and cultural centers. The Alaska Native Heritage Center in Anchorage and the Totem Heritage Center in Ketchikan are must-visits.

Local Tips:

- **Weather and Clothing**: Alaskan weather can be unpredictable. Dress in layers and be prepared for sudden changes in weather, especially if you're venturing into the wilderness.
- **Travel Considerations**: Much of Alaska is remote and accessible only by plane or boat. Plan your itinerary accordingly and consider taking advantage of Alaska's unique modes of transportation like bush planes or ferries.
- **Daylight Variations**: Depending on the season, Alaska can have very long days or very short days. In summer, some areas experience almost 24 hours of daylight, while in winter, daylight hours are limited.
- **Wildlife Safety**: When exploring natural areas, be aware of wildlife and follow safety guidelines to avoid dangerous encounters, especially with bears.
- **Local Cuisine**: Alaskan cuisine offers fresh seafood like salmon and crab, and game meats like moose and caribou. Trying local dishes is a must for a complete Alaskan experience.

Alaska's blend of natural beauty, rugged wilderness, and rich cultural history creates an unforgettable experience for all who visit. Whether you're watching glaciers calve into the ocean or exploring the vibrant cultures of its native peoples, Alaska is sure to leave you with lasting memories. Enjoy your journey to this magnificent and untamed part of the world!

1. Transportation:

- **Car Rental:** Consider renting a car for flexibility. Rental prices start at around $60 per day. Look for deals from major rental companies.
6. **Public Transportation**: In larger cities like Anchorage and Fairbanks, public transportation systems offer relatively affordable fares. Look for bus routes operated by agencies like the Anchorage People Mover or Fairbanks Transit.
7. **Ridesharing**: Use online platforms and community forums to find rideshares with locals or fellow travelers heading in the same direction. Sharing fuel costs can significantly reduce transportation expenses.
8. **Biking**: If you're traveling short distances within a city or town, consider renting or purchasing a bicycle. Many Alaskan cities have bike-friendly infrastructure, and biking is an eco-friendly and inexpensive way to get around.
9. **Walking**: For short trips and sightseeing within urban areas, walking is not only free but also a great way to explore Alaska's scenic landscapes and vibrant communities up close.
10. **Utilize Free Shuttles and Services**: In tourist destinations like Denali National Park, some lodges and visitor centers offer free shuttle services for guests. Take advantage of these complimentary shuttles to explore the area without the need for a rental car.
11. The Alaska Marine Highway System (AMHS) operates the ferry system in Alaska, providing transportation along the state's coastal communities and remote regions. The fares for AMHS ferries vary depending on factors such as the route, distance traveled, passenger type, and vehicle size. However, some routes are generally more budget-friendly than others. Here are a few options that are typically among the cheapest ferry routes in Alaska:
1. **Short Crossings**: Ferries that operate shorter routes between neighboring communities tend to have lower fares. For example, crossings between towns in the Southeast Alaska region, such as Ketchikan to Wrangell or Juneau to Haines, are often more affordable.
2. **Interisland Routes**: Some routes that connect islands within the Southeast Alaska region, such as those between Ketchikan, Wrangell, Petersburg, and Sitka, may offer relatively inexpensive fares compared to longer routes that traverse larger bodies of water.
3. **Off-Peak Travel**: Fares for Alaska ferries can vary based on the time of year and demand. Traveling during the offseason or shoulder seasons, such as spring or fall, may result in lower fares compared to peak summer months when tourism is at its highest.

2. Accommodation:

1. **Budget Hotels:** Look for budget-friendly hotels in cities like Anchorage, Fairbanks, or Juneau. Options such as Extended Stay America - Anchorage Downtown, Westmark Fairbanks Hotel & Conference Center, or Juneau Hotel offer comfortable stays at reasonable prices.
2. **Cabins and Lodges:** Consider staying at cabins or lodges in scenic areas like Denali National Park, Talkeetna, or Seward. Places like Denali Cabins, Talkeetna Alaskan Lodge, or Harbor 360 Hotel in Seward offer affordable rates and a rustic Alaskan experience.
3. **State Park Cabins:** Alaska's state parks offer affordable cabin rentals in stunning wilderness settings. Look into staying at cabins in parks like Chugach State Park, Kachemak Bay State Park, or Nancy Lake State Recreation Area for a budget-friendly outdoor getaway.

3. Dining:

Eating affordably in Alaska can indeed be a challenge due to its remote location and higher cost of living. Here's a breakdown of some cost-effective ways to eat, including berry picking, fishing, utilizing food waste apps, and making the most of supermarkets:

1. **Berry Picking**: Alaska is rich in wild berries like blueberries, raspberries, and salmonberries. You can pick these berries yourself during the right season, which not only provides free food but also allows you to enjoy the great outdoors. Just make sure you're picking in areas where it's allowed and safe.
2. **Fishing**: Alaska offers some of the best fishing opportunities in the world. Depending on where you are located, you can fish for salmon, trout, halibut, and more. A fishing license might be required, but the investment can pay off in terms of food. If you have the necessary gear, fishing can be a relatively inexpensive way to source protein.
3. **Food Waste Apps**: Consider using food waste apps like Too Good To Go or OLIO, which connect consumers with surplus food from local restaurants, cafes, and grocery stores at discounted prices. While these apps may not be as prevalent

in remote areas of Alaska, they are worth exploring in larger towns and cities.
4. **Supermarkets**: While supermarkets in Alaska can be more expensive compared to those in the contiguous United States due to transportation costs, there are still ways to shop smart. Look for sales, buy in bulk when possible, and opt for store brands over name brands to save money. Additionally, consider shopping at discount grocery stores or co-ops, if available in your area.

4. Activities:

- **Hiking Trails:** Alaska offers numerous hiking trails with breathtaking views. Many trails are free, and some may require a small parking fee.
- **Glacier Viewing:** While some glacier tours can be expensive, you can view glaciers for free at places like Mendenhall Glacier in Juneau or Matanuska Glacier near Anchorage.
- **Wildlife Viewing:** Alaska is known for its wildlife. Visit places like Denali National Park for a chance to see bears, moose, and caribou.

Free Tours

1. **Anchorage Market and Festival (Anchorage):** While not a guided tour, the Anchorage Market and Festival offers a vibrant atmosphere where you can experience local culture, food, and arts for free. You can explore different stalls and interact with vendors.
2. **Alaska State Capitol Tour (Juneau):** Similar to the Alabama State Capitol, the Alaska State Capitol offers free guided tours where you can learn about the state's history, government, and architecture.
3. **Alaska Public Lands Information Centers:** There are several Public Lands Information Centers across Alaska, such as the one in Anchorage and Fairbanks. While they may not offer guided tours, they provide information about nearby public lands, parks, and recreational activities for free.
4. **Self-guided Tours of Denali National Park:** While entrance to Denali National Park may require a fee, once inside, you can explore many areas on your own. The park offers various hiking trails and viewpoints where you can experience the stunning landscapes and wildlife of Alaska.
5. **Visitors Centers:** Many towns and cities in Alaska have visitors centers where you can obtain maps, brochures, and information about local attractions and activities for free. While these may not be guided tours, they can help you plan your own self-guided adventures.

5. Entertainment:

- **Cultural Performances:** Attend local cultural performances or festivals. Look for events featuring Alaska Native dances or music. Prices can range from $10 to $30.

- **Museums:** Visit museums on free or discounted days. The Anchorage Museum, for example, often has special rates or free admission on certain days.

6. **Insights and Tips:**

   - **Free Tours:** Some places offer free guided tours. In Anchorage, the Historic City Hall offers free guided tours during the summer.
   - **Northern Lights Viewing:** If visiting in the winter, try to catch the Northern Lights. You can increase your chances of seeing them by staying in areas with less light pollution.
   - **Travel Off-Peak:** Consider visiting in the shoulder seasons (spring or fall) to find better deals on accommodations and activities.

Don't Leave Alaska without seeing

1. **Denali National Park and Preserve**: Experience the rugged beauty of Alaska's wilderness at Denali National Park and Preserve, home to North America's tallest peak, Denali (formerly Mount McKinley). Explore six million acres of pristine landscapes, spot wildlife such as grizzly bears and moose, and embark on guided hikes, wildlife tours, and scenic bus rides into the heart of the park. Starting Price: Admission to Denali National Park and Preserve varies by season and activity; costs for bus tours start at $42 per person. Insider Tip: Book your bus tour in advance to secure preferred dates and routes, and keep an eye out for the elusive Denali, visible on clear days.
2. **Kenai Fjords National Park**: Discover the icy wonders of Kenai Fjords National Park, where towering glaciers meet the sea in a breathtaking display of natural beauty. Take a boat tour or kayak excursion to witness calving glaciers, spot marine wildlife like whales and sea otters, and explore remote coastal areas accessible only by water. Starting Price: Admission to Kenai Fjords National Park varies by tour operator and activity; costs for boat tours start at $100 per person. Insider Tip: Opt for a smaller, locally-owned tour company for a more personalized experience and opportunities for wildlife sightings away from the crowds.
3. **Anchorage's Coastal Trail**: Lace up your hiking boots or hop on a bike to explore Anchorage's beloved Coastal Trail, a scenic pathway stretching 11 miles along the shores of Cook Inlet. Enjoy panoramic views of the Chugach Mountains, spot bald eagles and beluga whales, and visit landmarks like Earthquake Park and Point Woronzof. Starting Price: Access to the Coastal Trail is free; costs for bike rentals vary. Insider Tip: Pack a picnic and stop at one of the trailside parks for a scenic lunch overlooking the water, or visit during the summer solstice for the Midnight Sun Festival and round-the-clock festivities.
4. **Matanuska Glacier**: Marvel at the majesty of Matanuska Glacier, one of Alaska's most accessible and impressive ice formations. Take a guided glacier trekking or ice climbing tour to explore crevasses, ice caves, and towering ice walls, and learn about the glacier's unique features and geological history from knowledgeable guides. Starting Price: Guided glacier tours at Matanuska Glacier start at $100 per person. Insider Tip: Dress in layers and wear sturdy footwear with good traction for walking on ice, and bring a camera to capture the awe-inspiring beauty of the glacier and surrounding mountains.
5. **Alaska Native Heritage Center**: Immerse yourself in Alaska's rich indigenous cultures at the Alaska Native Heritage Center in Anchorage, where you can explore traditional village exhibits, watch cultural demonstrations, and interact with Native artists and performers. Learn about Alaska's diverse indigenous peoples, their history, and their enduring traditions through exhibits, storytelling, and hands-on

activities. Starting Price: Admission to the Alaska Native Heritage Center starts at $25 for adults. Insider Tip: Plan your visit during the center's special events and festivals, such as the Gathering of the Drums, to experience authentic Native music, dance, and celebrations.

6. **Kenai Peninsula's Fishing Paradise**: Cast a line in the pristine waters of the Kenai Peninsula, renowned for its world-class fishing opportunities and abundant marine life. Join a guided fishing charter or try your luck at one of the peninsula's rivers, streams, or saltwater hotspots for a chance to reel in trophy-sized salmon, halibut, and trout. Starting Price: Costs for guided fishing charters vary by operator and duration; expect to pay around $200-$300 per person for a half-day trip. Insider Tip: Visit during the summer salmon runs for the best chances of catching prized King Salmon or Silver Salmon, and be sure to obtain the necessary fishing licenses and permits in advance.

7. **Fairbanks' Aurora Borealis**: Chase the northern lights in Fairbanks, one of the best places on earth to witness the mesmerizing beauty of the aurora borealis. Head to prime viewing spots like Cleary Summit, Murphy Dome, or Chena Lakes Recreation Area on clear, dark nights to witness nature's most spectacular light show dancing across the Arctic skies. Starting Price: Access to northern lights viewing spots is free; costs for guided aurora tours start at $100 per person. Insider Tip: Dress warmly in layers and bring hot drinks and snacks for comfort during extended viewing sessions, and download aurora forecast apps to track aurora activity and maximize your chances of seeing the lights.

8. **Wrangell-St. Elias National Park**: Explore the vast wilderness of Wrangell-St. Elias National Park, America's largest national park and a UNESCO World Heritage Site known for its towering mountains, expansive glaciers, and rich biodiversity. Embark on scenic drives along the park's remote roads, hike to alpine lakes and mountain summits, and marvel at the sheer scale and beauty of the Alaska Range. Starting Price: Admission to Wrangell-St. Elias National Park is free; costs for backcountry permits and guided tours vary. Insider Tip: Visit the park's visitor centers in Copper Center and Kennecott to learn about park regulations, trail conditions, and safety tips before venturing into the backcountry.

9. **Mendenhall Glacier**: Journey to Juneau to witness the awe-inspiring beauty of Mendenhall Glacier, a towering ice sheet located just a short drive from the city center. Explore the Mendenhall Glacier Visitor Center, take a guided glacier trek or helicopter tour, and marvel at the glacier's blue-hued ice and dramatic crevasses. Starting Price: Admission to the Mendenhall Glacier Visitor Center is $5 for adults; costs for guided tours and glacier excursions vary. Insider Tip: Visit during the summer months to witness the glacier's impressive calving events and explore nearby hiking trails and scenic viewpoints.

10. **Kodiak Island's Wildlife Encounters**: Embark on a wildlife adventure on Kodiak Island, home to a diverse array of wildlife including brown bears, bald eagles, and marine mammals. Join a guided bear viewing tour to observe bears in their natural habitat, embark on a whale-watching cruise to spot humpback whales and orcas, and explore the island's rugged coastline and pristine wilderness. Starting Price: Costs for guided wildlife tours on Kodiak Island vary by operator and activity; expect to pay around $200-$300 per person for a half-day excursion. Insider Tip: Bring binoculars and a camera with a telephoto lens for close-up wildlife encounters, and follow all safety guidelines and instructions from experienced guides to ensure a memorable and safe experience.

Top Attractions and Money-Saving Tips

Denali National Park and Preserve: Dive into the untouched wilderness of Denali, home to rugged landscapes and diverse wildlife.

Money-Saving Tip: Plan your visit during the shoulder season to take advantage of lower park fees and accommodation rates.

Starting Cost: Park entrance fees range from $15 to $40 per person, depending on the length of stay.

Glacier Bay National Park and Preserve: Marvel at the grandeur of towering glaciers and pristine fjords in Glacier Bay National Park.

Money-Saving Tip: Consider booking a cruise that includes Glacier Bay to save on park entrance fees.

Starting Cost: Cruise prices vary widely, but expect to pay around $100 to $200 per person for a day trip.

Kenai Fjords National Park: Embark on a journey to explore the breathtaking fjords, abundant wildlife, and awe-inspiring glaciers of Kenai Fjords National Park.

Money-Saving Tip: Look for group tour options, as they often offer discounts per person.

Starting Cost: Group tour prices typically range from $100 to $200 per person for a half-day excursion.

Anchorage: Experience the vibrant culture and outdoor adventures of Alaska's largest city, Anchorage.

Money-Saving Tip: Take advantage of free attractions such as Earthquake Park and the Anchorage Coastal Trail.

Starting Cost: Accommodation prices vary widely but expect to pay around $100 to $200 per night for a hotel.

Mendenhall Glacier, Juneau: Trek to the stunning Mendenhall Glacier and visitor center for an up-close encounter with this natural wonder.

Money-Saving Tip: Utilize public transportation or shared rides to reduce transportation costs.

Starting Cost: Public transportation fares are typically around $2 to $5 per person for a one-way trip.

Alaska Wildlife Conservation Center, Portage: Get up close and personal with native Alaskan wildlife at the Alaska Wildlife Conservation Center.

Money-Saving Tip: Search online for discounts on admission tickets before your visit.

Starting Cost: Admission prices range from $15 to $25 per adult and $10 to $15 per child.

Tongass National Forest: Lose yourself in the vast wilderness of Tongass National Forest, the largest national forest in the United States.

Money-Saving Tip: Take advantage of free or low-cost hiking and camping opportunities throughout the forest.

Starting Cost: Camping fees vary but typically range from $10 to $20 per night at developed campgrounds.

Fairbanks: Chase the Northern Lights and explore the cultural attractions of Fairbanks, Alaska's second-largest city.

Money-Saving Tip: Travel during the shoulder season for more affordable accommodations and fewer crowds.

Starting Cost: Hotel prices start at around $80 to $150 per night for budget accommodations.

Ketchikan: Immerse yourself in Native American culture and experience world-class salmon fishing in Ketchikan.

Money-Saving Tip: Explore the city on foot to save on transportation costs.

Starting Cost: Hotel prices vary but expect to pay around $100 to $200 per night for budget accommodations.

Kodiak Island: Encounter majestic bears and enjoy world-class fishing adventures on Kodiak Island.

Money-Saving Tip: Join guided bear-watching tours for potential group discounts.

Starting Cost: Guided bear-watching tours typically range from $100 to $300 per person for a half-day excursion.

Wrangell-St. Elias National Park and Preserve: Delve into the remote wilderness of Wrangell-St. Elias National Park, the largest national park in the United States.

Money-Saving Tip: Consider camping and hiking as low-cost ways to explore the park.

Starting Cost: Camping fees range from $10 to $20 per night at developed campgrounds.

Homer: Experience the charming coastal town of Homer and indulge in its renowned fishing activities.

Money-Saving Tip: Stay in budget-friendly lodges or cabins for more affordable accommodations.

Starting Cost: Cabin rentals start at around $100 to $150 per night for basic accommodations.

Valdez: Discover the natural wonders of Valdez, from cascading waterfalls to towering glaciers, all without breaking the bank.

Money-Saving Tip: Opt for a self-guided exploration of Valdez Glacier and the town's attractions.

Starting Cost: Admission to attractions varies, but expect to pay around $10 to $20 per person for guided tours.

Sitka: Immerse yourself in the rich history and outdoor adventures of Sitka, a picturesque town with a unique blend of Russian and Native American heritage.

Money-Saving Tip: Utilize local transportation options such as buses or shuttles for sightseeing.

Starting Cost: Bus fares are typically around $2 to $5 per person for a one-way trip.

Northern Lights Viewing: Witness the mesmerizing beauty of the Aurora Borealis from various vantage points across Alaska.

Money-Saving Tip: Stay in accommodations that offer Northern Lights viewing opportunities to maximize your chances of witnessing this natural phenomenon.

Starting Cost: Prices for accommodations vary, but budget options start at around $50 to $100 per night.

Chena Hot Springs: Relax and rejuvenate in the soothing waters of Chena Hot Springs, a natural thermal spring renowned for its healing properties.

Money-Saving Tip: Visit during off-peak hours to take advantage of lower entry fees and avoid crowds.

Starting Cost: Entrance fees range from $15 to $25 per person, depending on the time of day and amenities included.

Klondike Gold Rush National Historical Park, Skagway: Step back in time and relive the excitement of the Klondike Gold Rush era in Skagway.

Money-Saving Tip: Admission to the park is free, allowing you to explore the town's historic district at no cost.

Starting Cost: Free admission to the park; donations are appreciated.

Katmai National Park and Preserve: Witness the awe-inspiring sight of brown bears in their natural habitat at Katmai National Park.

Money-Saving Tip: Consider joining budget-friendly bear-watching tours for a memorable wildlife encounter.

Starting Cost: Guided bear-watching tours typically range from $100 to $300 per person for a half-day excursion.

Haines: Experience the outdoor adventures and wildlife encounters that await in Haines, a picturesque town nestled amidst the stunning landscapes of Alaska.

Money-Saving Tip: Renting a bike or kayak for exploring the area can be a cost-effective way to enjoy outdoor activities.

Starting Cost: Bike rentals start at around $20 to $30 per day, while kayak rentals start at around $50 to $70 per day.

Gates of the Arctic National Park and Preserve: Embrace the untamed wilderness of Gates of the Arctic National Park, where remote landscapes and rugged terrain beckon adventurers.

Money-Saving Tip: Backpacking and camping offer affordable ways to experience the park's pristine beauty.

Starting Cost: Camping fees vary but typically range from $10 to $20 per night at developed campgrounds.

RECAP

Category	Insider Tips
Food	1. Go berry picking in the wild for free or at a minimal cost, enjoying Alaska's abundant natural bounty.
	2. Seek out local seafood markets or docks for fresh catches like salmon, halibut, and crab at lower prices.
	3. Look for small-town cafes or diners for hearty, home-cooked meals that won't break the bank.
	4. Visit local breweries or distilleries for tastings and tours, often offering affordable pub fare.
Accommodation	1. Embrace camping in Alaska's stunning wilderness, with campsites offering budget-friendly options.
	2. Consider staying in rustic cabins or lodges for a unique Alaskan experience without the high price tag.
	3. Look for accommodations in smaller towns or villages for more affordable rates compared to major cities.
	4. Utilize platforms like Airbnb or VRBO to find affordable lodging options with local hosts.
Activities	1. Take advantage of free outdoor activities like hiking, wildlife viewing, and birdwatching.

		2. Explore local trails for berry picking, fishing, or foraging, providing both recreation and sustenance.
		3. Visit cultural centers and museums in smaller communities for insights into Alaska's rich heritage.
		4. Participate in community events and festivals, often featuring affordable food, music, and activities.
	Transport	1. Rent a car or RV to explore Alaska's vast landscapes, with options for budget-friendly rentals available.
		2. Look for discounted ferry fares for scenic journeys along Alaska's coastlines and waterways.
		3. Utilize local shuttle services or group tours for transportation to remote destinations or attractions.
		4. Consider biking or walking in smaller towns or cities for a budget-friendly and eco-friendly way to get around.

Arizona

Arizona's history is a tale of ancient civilizations, pioneering spirit, and the wild west. Native American tribes like the Hopi, Navajo, and Apache have inhabited this region for thousands of years, leaving behind a legacy of art, architecture, and traditions. In the 16th century, Spanish explorers arrived, followed by Mexican settlers, and later, American pioneers seeking gold, silver, and fertile land. The state played a crucial role in the American Civil War and the westward expansion. Its past is woven into the fabric of its cities, landmarks, and culture.

Things to Consider:

- **Climate**: Arizona's climate varies widely. Expect hot summers in the low desert regions like Phoenix and Tucson, but cooler temperatures in the high country, including Flagstaff. Be prepared for temperature swings between day and night.
- **Altitude**: If you plan to explore high-altitude areas like the Grand Canyon or Flagstaff, be aware of potential altitude sickness. Stay hydrated, take it slow, and acclimate gradually.
- **Cultural Diversity**: Arizona is a melting pot of cultures. Respect and embrace the rich traditions of the Native American, Mexican, and Anglo communities you encounter.
- **Wildlife**: Arizona is home to diverse wildlife, including rattlesnakes and scorpions. Be cautious when exploring the outdoors and heed safety advice.

Local Tips:

- **Grand Canyon**: If you visit the Grand Canyon, arrive early or stay late to avoid crowds and witness breathtaking sunrise or sunset views. Hiking the rim or taking a guided tour offers a unique perspective.
- **Mexican Cuisine**: Arizona boasts exceptional Mexican cuisine. Savor local favorites like Sonoran hot dogs and authentic tacos at local eateries or food trucks.
- **Outdoor Adventures**: Embrace Arizona's outdoor opportunities by hiking in Sedona's red rock landscapes, exploring Saguaro National Park, or taking a hot air balloon ride over the Sonoran Desert.
- **Native American Art**: Explore the state's Native American art scene. Visit galleries and markets to purchase unique handcrafted jewelry, pottery, and textiles while supporting local artists.
- **Stargazing**: Arizona's clear skies make it an ideal destination for stargazing. Consider visiting observatories or dark-sky parks to witness the dazzling night sky.
- **Local Festivals**: Check local event calendars for cultural festivals, art shows, and rodeos happening during your visit. These events offer a glimpse into Arizona's vibrant traditions.

In Arizona, you'll discover a land of contrasts, from the bustling streets of Phoenix to the tranquil beauty of the desert and the grandeur of the Grand Canyon. As you embark on your journey, immerse yourself in the rich history, appreciate the natural wonders, and engage with the welcoming communities that make Arizona a truly unique and unforgettable destination. Enjoy your adventure in the Grand Canyon State!

1. Transportation:

- **Car Rental:** Renting a car is advisable for exploring Arizona. Prices start at around $30 per day, and booking in advance can help you secure better deals.
- **Public Transportation**: Major cities like Phoenix and Tucson have public transportation systems that include buses and light rail services. Opting for public transit can be significantly cheaper than driving, especially if you're traveling within city limits.
- **Carpooling**: Consider using ridesharing apps or joining local carpooling groups to find compatible travel companions.

2. Accommodation:

- **Budget-Friendly Luxury Stays:** Look for upscale hotels with discounted rates. You can find options in major towns like Scottsdale, Sedona, and Flagstaff. Prices range from $80 to $150 per night, especially if you book during off-peak seasons.
- **Budget Hotels:** Look for budget-friendly hotels in cities like Phoenix, Tucson, or Flagstaff. Options such as Motel 6 Phoenix Airport - 24th Street, Econo Lodge University near Downtown Tucson, or Rodeway Inn Downtown Flagstaff offer comfortable stays at reasonable prices.
- **Motels:** Consider staying at motels along major highways or in smaller towns. Motels like Super 8 by Wyndham Page/Lake Powell, Travelodge by Wyndham Tucson Downtown, or Budget Host Inn in Williams offer affordable rates and basic amenities for travelers on a budget.

3. Dining:

- **Happy Hour Deals:** Many upscale restaurants offer happy hour deals with discounted prices on food and drinks. Check out places in Scottsdale or Phoenix for some of the best deals.
- **Local Eateries:** Explore local Mexican cuisine, which is abundant in Arizona. You can find affordable and delicious meals, ranging from $10 to $25 per person.

4. Activities:

- **Hiking in Sedona:** Sedona's red rocks offer stunning hiking trails, many of which are free or have a small parking fee.
- **Grand Canyon National Park:** While the entry fee is $35 per vehicle, spending a day exploring the Grand Canyon is a must. Consider purchasing an annual pass for $70 if you plan to visit multiple national parks.
- **Antelope Canyon and Horseshoe Bend:** These iconic sites near Page offer affordable tours, usually around $50 per person.

5. Entertainment:

- **Scottsdale's Art Walk:** Every Thursday evening, enjoy free admission to galleries in Scottsdale's Art District.

- **Musical Instrument Museum in Phoenix:** Admission is around $20, providing a unique experience for music enthusiasts.

Free Tours

1. **Arizona State Capitol Museum (Phoenix):** The Arizona State Capitol Museum offers free guided tours where you can learn about the history, architecture, and government of Arizona.
2. **Arizona State University Campus Tours (Tempe):** Arizona State University offers free campus tours where you can explore the university grounds and learn about its history, academic programs, and student life.
3. **Tumacácori National Historical Park (Tumacácori):** While not exactly guided tours, Tumacácori National Historical Park offers free admission and self-guided exploration of the historic mission ruins and surrounding area.
4. **Phoenix Art Museum (Phoenix):** While admission to the Phoenix Art Museum may require a fee, they offer free guided tours on Wednesdays, Saturdays, and Sundays. Check their schedule for specific tour times and topics.
5. **Self-guided Tours of Sedona:** Sedona offers stunning natural beauty, and many of its attractions, such as hiking trails and scenic viewpoints, are free to explore on your own. Pick up a hiking map from the visitor center and embark on your own adventure.

6. Insights and Tips:

- **Sunset Views:** Experience Arizona's breathtaking sunsets, especially in Sedona or at the Grand Canyon. This is a luxurious experience that comes at no cost.
- **Off-Peak Travel:** Consider visiting during the shoulder seasons (spring and fall) to take advantage of lower accommodation prices and fewer crowds.
- **Free Tours:** Some towns offer free walking tours, providing insights into their history and culture.

Major Towns in Arizona:

- **Phoenix:** The state capital, known for its vibrant arts scene and diverse cuisine.
- **Tucson:** Rich in history, with a blend of Mexican and American cultures.
- **Scottsdale:** Famous for its upscale resorts, golf courses, and art galleries.
- **Sedona:** Renowned for its red rock formations, hiking trails, and spiritual vibes.
- **Flagstaff:** A gateway to the Grand Canyon, known for its charming downtown and proximity to outdoor activities.

Must-See

1. **Antelope Canyon:** Venture into the otherworldly landscapes of Antelope Canyon, a slot canyon known for its sculpted sandstone walls and mesmerizing light beams. Take a guided tour to explore the narrow passageways and capture stunning photographs of the canyon's unique formations. Starting Price: Guided tours of Antelope Canyon start at $40-$60 per person. Insider Tip: Opt for a photography tour to learn professional techniques for capturing the canyon's beauty and avoid crowds during prime photography hours.
2. **Sedona's Red Rock Country:** Immerse yourself in the stunning scenery of Sedona's Red Rock Country, where towering sandstone formations, scenic vistas,

and spiritual energy await. Hike or bike along trails like Cathedral Rock, Bell Rock, and Devil's Bridge for panoramic views and spiritual renewal amidst nature's wonders. Starting Price: Access to hiking trails in Sedona is free; costs for guided tours and activities vary. Insider Tip: Visit during sunrise or sunset for the most dramatic lighting and color displays on the red rocks, and bring plenty of water and sunscreen for outdoor adventures.
3. **Grand Canyon Skywalk**: Experience the thrill of walking on air at the Grand Canyon Skywalk, a glass-bottomed bridge extending over the edge of the Grand Canyon's West Rim. Take in breathtaking views of the canyon's depths and the Colorado River below as you walk 4,000 feet above the canyon floor. Starting Price: Admission to the Grand Canyon Skywalk starts at $70 per person. Insider Tip: Purchase tickets in advance to avoid long lines and crowds, and consider upgrading to a VIP package for additional perks like express entry and souvenir photos.
4. **Havasu Falls**: Embark on a once-in-a-lifetime adventure to Havasu Falls, a hidden oasis nestled within the remote wilderness of the Havasupai Indian Reservation. Hike through the breathtaking landscapes of the Grand Canyon to reach the turquoise waters of Havasu Creek and marvel at the cascading waterfalls and vibrant blue pools. Starting Price: Permits and fees for camping at Havasu Falls start at $100 per person per night. Insider Tip: Plan your visit well in advance and be prepared for a challenging hike, extreme weather conditions, and limited facilities in the remote canyon.
5. **Tucson's Saguaro National Park**: Discover the iconic symbol of the American West at Saguaro National Park in Tucson, home to the nation's largest cacti and stunning desert landscapes. Explore scenic drives, hiking trails, and interpretive exhibits to learn about the unique ecology and cultural significance of the Sonoran Desert. Starting Price: Admission to Saguaro National Park is $25 per vehicle for a seven-day pass. Insider Tip: Visit during the springtime to witness the desert in bloom with colorful wildflowers and blooming cacti, and attend ranger-led programs and guided hikes for a deeper understanding of the park's natural and cultural resources.
6. **Meteor Crater**: Step into the realm of cosmic wonders at Meteor Crater, one of the best-preserved impact sites on earth, located near Winslow, Arizona. Marvel at the immense size and pristine condition of the crater, created by a meteorite impact over 50,000 years ago, and explore interactive exhibits and outdoor observation areas. Starting Price: Admission to Meteor Crater starts at $18 for adults. Insider Tip: Take advantage of guided tours and educational programs to learn about the crater's formation, geology, and scientific significance from knowledgeable guides and experts.
7. **Monument Valley**: Embark on a journey through the iconic landscapes of Monument Valley, a Navajo Tribal Park renowned for its towering sandstone buttes, mesas, and arches. Take a guided jeep tour or drive the scenic loop road to explore the valley's most famous landmarks, including the Mittens, Merrick Butte, and John Ford's Point. Starting Price: Guided jeep tours of Monument Valley start at $75-$100 per person. Insider Tip: Visit during sunrise or sunset for the most dramatic lighting and photographic opportunities, and respect the park's cultural heritage and sacred sites by following all rules and regulations.
8. **Barringer Crater**: Uncover the mysteries of the cosmos at Barringer Crater, also known as Meteor Crater, located near Flagstaff, Arizona. Explore the impact site of a meteorite collision that occurred over 50,000 years ago, and learn about the crater's geology, history, and scientific significance through interactive exhibits and guided tours. Starting Price: Admission to Barringer Crater starts at $18 for adults. Insider Tip: Join a guided tour of the crater rim for panoramic views and insights into

the crater's formation and ongoing scientific research, and visit the nearby Meteorite Museum to see rare specimens and artifacts.
9. **Tombstone**: Step back in time to the days of the Wild West in Tombstone, Arizona, a historic mining town famous for its legendary gunfights and colorful characters. Explore the streets of Tombstone's historic district, visit landmarks like the OK Corral and the Bird Cage Theatre, and experience living history reenactments and gunfight shows. Starting Price: Admission to historic attractions in Tombstone varies; costs for guided tours and activities start at $10-$20 per person. Insider Tip: Attend one of Tombstone's annual events and festivals, such as Helldorado Days or Wyatt Earp Days, for live entertainment, parades, and authentic Old West experiences.
10. **Canyon de Chelly**: Discover the ancient history and cultural heritage of Canyon de Chelly National Monument, located in northeastern Arizona. Explore the canyon's towering sandstone cliffs, ancient ruins, and petroglyphs on guided tours led by Navajo guides, and learn about the enduring traditions and spiritual significance of the land to the Navajo people. Starting Price: Admission to Canyon de Chelly National Monument is free; costs for guided tours and activities vary. Insider Tip: Book a guided jeep tour of the canyon floor for access to remote archaeological sites and hidden gems, and support local Navajo artisans by purchasing handmade crafts and artwork at overlooks and visitor centers.

Top 20 with Money-Saving Tips

Grand Canyon National Park: Be awe-inspired by the immense beauty of the Grand Canyon, one of the world's most iconic natural wonders.

Money-Saving Tip: Plan your visit during the off-peak season to take advantage of lower lodging rates and fewer crowds.

Starting Cost: Entrance fees to the park range from $35 to $45 per vehicle, depending on the season.

Antelope Canyon: Delve into the mesmerizing beauty of Antelope Canyon, with its stunning slot canyons carved by wind and water over millennia.

Money-Saving Tip: Book a guided tour in advance to secure the best rates and ensure availability.

Starting Cost: Guided tour prices typically range from $40 to $80 per person, depending on the length and type of tour.

Saguaro National Park: Immerse yourself in the Sonoran Desert landscape and discover the iconic saguaro cacti that define this unique ecosystem.

Money-Saving Tip: Participate in free ranger-led programs and explore the park's trails on foot to maximize your experience without spending extra.

Starting Cost: Entrance fees to the park are around $20 per vehicle, valid for up to seven days.

Horseshoe Bend: Witness the breathtaking horseshoe-shaped bend of the Colorado River as it winds its way through the desert landscape.

Money-Saving Tip: Visit in the morning or evening to avoid the midday heat and crowds, allowing for a more enjoyable experience.

Starting Cost: Parking fees at Horseshoe Bend are typically around $10 per vehicle.

Monument Valley: Explore the iconic red rock formations and stunning vistas of Monument Valley, a landscape that has been featured in countless films and photographs.

Money-Saving Tip: Take a self-guided drive through the valley to save on guided tour fees while still enjoying the incredible scenery.

Starting Cost: Entrance fees to Monument Valley Tribal Park are around $20 per vehicle.

Petrified Forest National Park: Step back in time as you wander among ancient petrified wood and colorful badlands that tell the story of millions of years of geological history.

Money-Saving Tip: Purchase an America the Beautiful Annual Pass for access to multiple national parks, including Petrified Forest National Park.

Starting Cost: Entrance fees to the park are around $20 per vehicle, valid for up to seven days.

Phoenix and Scottsdale: Experience the vibrant urban culture and world-class golfing of Phoenix and Scottsdale.

Money-Saving Tip: Take advantage of hotel deals and discounts, especially during the summer off-season when rates are typically lower.

Starting Cost: Hotel prices vary widely but expect to pay around $100 to $200 per night for budget accommodations.

Tucson: Discover the rich history and cultural attractions of Tucson, from its historic neighborhoods to its world-renowned museums and gardens.

Money-Saving Tip: Visit the University of Arizona campus for free access to museums and gardens, including the renowned Arizona State Museum.

Starting Cost: Admission to the Arizona State Museum is typically around $8 to $10 per adult.

Sedona: Marvel at the majestic red rock landscapes and spiritual energy of Sedona, a destination known for its scenic beauty and outdoor adventures.

Money-Saving Tip: Take advantage of free outdoor activities such as scenic hikes and self-guided tours to explore Sedona's natural wonders.

Starting Cost: Parking fees at popular trailheads range from $5 to $10 per vehicle.

Lake Powell and Glen Canyon National Recreation Area: Dive into the aquatic playground of Lake Powell, where water sports and stunning scenery await amidst the towering cliffs of Glen Canyon.

Money-Saving Tip: Rent watercraft in advance and split the costs with a group to make the experience more affordable.

Starting Cost: Boat rentals vary depending on the type and duration of rental, but expect to pay around $200 to $500 per day for a pontoon boat.

Biosphere 2, Tucson: Step into the future with a tour of Biosphere 2, a pioneering research facility and ecological center.

Money-Saving Tip: Look for discounts on group tours or combo tickets that include admission to other attractions in the area.

Starting Cost: Guided tour prices start at around $20 to $25 per adult.

Jerome: Explore the historic mining town of Jerome, where art galleries, scenic views, and a rich Wild West history await.

Money-Saving Tip: Wander through the town's historic district on foot to soak in the atmosphere and enjoy free attractions.

Starting Cost: Parking is typically free, and many attractions such as art galleries offer complimentary admission.

Flagstaff: Experience outdoor adventures and astronomical wonders in Flagstaff, a gateway to the Grand Canyon and a hub for stargazing enthusiasts.

Money-Saving Tip: Attend free stargazing events or visit the Lowell Observatory for affordable astronomical experiences.

Starting Cost: Admission to the Lowell Observatory starts at around $15 per adult.

Montezuma Castle National Monument: Journey back in time as you explore the well-preserved Native American cliff dwellings of Montezuma Castle National Monument.

Money-Saving Tip: Admission is free for children under 16 and America the Beautiful pass holders, making it an affordable family outing.

Starting Cost: Entrance fees for adults are around $10 per person.

Meteor Crater: Witness the impact site of a meteorite that struck Earth over 50,000 years ago, leaving behind one of the world's best-preserved meteorite impact sites.

Money-Saving Tip: Look for online discounts on admission tickets to save on your visit to Meteor Crater.

Starting Cost: Adult admission is around $18 per person.

Tombstone: Step back into the Wild West era as you explore the historic streets of Tombstone, where legends of cowboys and outlaws come to life.

Money-Saving Tip: Explore the town's historic district on foot to enjoy free attractions and soak in the Old West atmosphere.

Starting Cost: Parking is typically free, and many attractions offer complimentary admission or low-cost guided tours.

Chiricahua National Monument: Discover the otherworldly rock formations and scenic hiking trails of Chiricahua National Monument, known as the "Wonderland of Rocks."

Money-Saving Tip: Bring your own picnic to enjoy at the park and make a day of exploring its unique landscapes.

Starting Cost: Entrance fees to the park are around $20 per vehicle, valid for up to seven days.

Wupatki National Monument: Explore the ancient Native American pueblos and archaeological sites of Wupatki National Monument, nestled amidst the stunning landscapes of northern Arizona.

Money-Saving Tip: Combine your visit to Wupatki with nearby Sunset Crater National Monument for a full day of exploration at no extra cost.

Starting Cost: Entrance fees to the monument are around $25 per vehicle, valid for up to seven days.

Old Town Scottsdale: Indulge in shopping and dining experiences amidst the charming streets and historic buildings of Old Town Scottsdale.

Money-Saving Tip: Look for happy hour specials and discounts at restaurants to enjoy the local cuisine without breaking the bank.

Starting Cost: Prices for dining and shopping vary widely, but budget-friendly options are available throughout Old Town Scottsdale.

Organ Pipe Cactus National Monument: Encounter the beauty of the Sonoran Desert and its iconic cacti at Organ Pipe Cactus National Monument, a UNESCO biosphere reserve.

Money-Saving Tip: Join ranger-led programs and guided hikes for a deeper understanding of the park's natural and cultural heritage.

Starting Cost: Entrance fees to the monument are around $25 per vehicle, valid for up to seven days.

RECAP

Category	Insider Tips
Food	
	2. Enjoy authentic Mexican cuisine at local taquerias or food trucks for delicious and affordable meals.
	3. Look for daily specials or happy hour deals at restaurants and bars for discounted drinks and appetizers.
	4. Pack a picnic and enjoy outdoor dining at scenic spots like parks, lakesides, or desert vistas.
Accommodation	1. Camp in Arizona's picturesque landscapes, with numerous campgrounds offering affordable options.
	2. Consider staying in budget motels or roadside inns for cost-effective lodging options.
	3. Look for accommodations in smaller towns or cities outside major tourist areas for lower rates.
	4. Use discount websites or apps to find deals on hotels and accommodations in Arizona.
Activities	1. Explore hiking trails in Arizona's national parks and wilderness areas for stunning views and adventures.
	2. Visit local landmarks and attractions with free admission or low-cost entry fees.
	3. Take advantage of scenic drives and road trips to explore Arizona's diverse landscapes and attractions.
	4. Attend cultural festivals and events, showcasing Arizona's rich heritage and traditions.
Transport	1. Rent a car for flexibility and convenience in exploring Arizona's vast and scenic highways.
	2. Utilize public transportation options in major cities like Phoenix and Tucson to save on parking and gas.
	3. Look for carpooling opportunities or ride-sharing services for shared transportation costs.
	4. Consider biking or walking in urban areas or on designated trails for eco-friendly and budget-friendly travel.

Arkansas

Nestled in the southern region of the United States, Arkansas is a state of natural beauty, rich history, and warm hospitality. As a first-time visitor, you're about to explore a land where rolling hills, lush forests, and winding rivers meet a tapestry of cultural heritage. Here's an introduction to Arkansas, along with some essential things to consider and local tips to enhance your visit.

Arkansas has a deep and diverse history that stretches back thousands of years. Native American tribes such as the Quapaw and Caddo inhabited the area long before European explorers arrived. In the 16th century, Spanish and French explorers ventured through the region, and the French established trading posts. Arkansas played a pivotal role in the American Civil War, with significant battles like the Battle of Pea Ridge. After the war, it became a vital part of the Reconstruction era. Today, its historical sites, museums, and cultural festivals reflect this rich heritage.

Things to Consider:

- **Climate**: Arkansas experiences four distinct seasons. Summers are warm and humid, while winters can be mild to cold, depending on the region. Spring and autumn are particularly beautiful, with vibrant foliage and pleasant temperatures.
- **Outdoor Activities**: With its scenic landscapes, Arkansas offers ample opportunities for outdoor enthusiasts. Be prepared for hiking, camping, fishing, and water activities in the state's numerous parks, forests, and lakes.
- **Southern Hospitality**: You'll find that Arkansans are known for their warm and friendly hospitality. Don't be surprised if strangers greet you with a smile and strike up a conversation.
- **Culinary Delights**: Arkansas boasts a rich culinary heritage. Be sure to try regional specialties like fried catfish, barbecue, and country ham. Don't miss a chance to savor a slice of homemade pie, a staple in many local restaurants.

Local Tips:

- **Hot Springs**: Visit Hot Springs National Park, where you can soak in natural hot springs. The historic Bathhouse Row is a must-see.
- **Ozark Mountains**: Explore the Ozark Mountains, a paradise for nature lovers and outdoor enthusiasts. Hike the trails, go boating on the Buffalo National River, and take in the stunning vistas.
- **Little Rock**: Discover the capital city, Little Rock, home to attractions like the William J. Clinton Presidential Library and the historic Central High School National Historic Site.
- **Music Scene**: Arkansas has a vibrant music scene, particularly in blues, country, and folk. Attend local music festivals and live performances to immerse yourself in the state's musical culture.
- **Crystal Bridges Museum**: Visit the Crystal Bridges Museum of American Art in Bentonville, featuring a world-class collection of American artworks in a stunning architectural setting.

- **Civil War History**: For history buffs, explore Civil War battlefields and historic sites, such as Pea Ridge National Military Park.

1. Transportation:

- **Flights:** Consider flying into Little Rock, the capital city, for more budget-friendly options. Round-trip tickets can range from $50 to $200, depending on your departure city and the time of booking.
- **Car Rental:** Renting a car is advisable for exploring Arkansas. Prices start at around $30 per day, and booking in advance can help you secure better deals.
- **Public Transportation**: Larger cities in Arkansas, such as Little Rock and Fayetteville, offer public transportation services like buses and trolleys. Utilizing these systems can be an economical way to travel within city limits.
- **Walking and Biking**: Many towns and cities in Arkansas have pedestrian-friendly areas and biking trails. Walking or biking can be not only cost-effective but also a great way to explore local neighborhoods and attractions at your own pace.

2. Accommodation:

- **Luxury on a Budget:** Look for charming bed and breakfasts or boutique hotels. Places like Eureka Springs and Hot Springs offer affordable yet unique accommodations. Prices range from $80 to $150 per night.
- **State Parks:** Consider staying in one of Arkansas's state parks, offering cabins and campsites. Prices vary but can be as low as $30 per night.

3. Dining:

- **Local Eateries:** Arkansas is known for its comfort food. Enjoy Southern cuisine in local diners where meals can range from $10 to $25 per person.
- **Farm-to-Table Restaurants:** Explore farm-to-table dining experiences, often available at reasonable prices in cities like Little Rock and Fayetteville.

4. Activities:

- **Hot Springs National Park:** While the bathhouses may have spa services at a cost, you can enjoy the natural hot springs and hiking trails for free.
- **Crystal Bridges Museum of American Art:** Located in Bentonville, admission is free to view the museum's permanent collection.
- **Buffalo National River:** Explore the picturesque landscapes and hiking trails along the Buffalo River, which is free.

5. Entertainment:

- **Live Music in Fayetteville:** Check out live music scenes in Fayetteville, known for its vibrant arts and music community. Some venues offer free or affordable shows.
- **Historic Downtowns:** Explore the charming historic districts in towns like Eureka Springs and Little Rock, often hosting free events and festivals.

Arkansas State Capitol (Little Rock): Similar to other state capitols, the Arkansas State Capitol offers free guided tours where you can learn about the state's history, government, and architecture.

Arkansas Art Center (Little Rock): While admission to the Arkansas Art Center may require a fee for special exhibitions, the center often offers free guided tours of its permanent collections and sculpture garden.
Crystal Bridges Museum of American Art (Bentonville): While admission to Crystal Bridges may require a fee for special exhibitions, the museum offers free general admission to its permanent collection, and they occasionally provide free guided tours. Check their website or contact them directly for tour availability.
Self-guided Tours of Hot Springs National Park: Hot Springs National Park offers free admission, and you can explore the historic Bathhouse Row, hiking trails, and scenic viewpoints on your own. The visitor center provides information and maps for self-guided tours.
Historic Downtown Tours: Many cities in Arkansas, such as Little Rock and Eureka Springs, have historic downtown areas that you can explore on self-guided walking tours. Pick up a map from the local visitor center or chamber of commerce and discover the architecture, landmarks, and history of these areas at your own pace.

6. Insights and Tips:

- **Scenic Byways:** Drive along Arkansas's scenic byways, such as the Pig Trail Scenic Byway, for beautiful views and photo opportunities.
- **Affordable Outdoor Adventures:** Arkansas offers affordable outdoor activities like kayaking, hiking, and zip-lining. Explore the state's natural beauty without breaking the bank.
- **Art Walks:** Some towns, like Eureka Springs, have monthly art walks with free admission to galleries.

Major Towns in Arkansas:

- **Little Rock:** The capital city, known for its historic sites, vibrant arts scene, and the scenic River Market District.
- **Hot Springs:** Famous for its natural hot springs, bathhouses, and historic downtown.
- **Eureka Springs:** A charming town with Victorian architecture, art galleries, and natural springs.
- **Fayetteville:** Home to the University of Arkansas, offering a lively atmosphere with cultural events and outdoor activities.

1. **Hot Springs National Park**: Dive into relaxation at Hot Springs National Park, home to natural thermal springs revered for their healing properties. Take a leisurely stroll along Bathhouse Row to admire historic bathhouses and sample the mineral-rich waters, or embark on scenic hikes through the park's forested trails for panoramic views and serene surroundings. Starting Price: Admission to Hot Springs National Park is free; costs for spa services and tours vary. Insider Tip: Visit in the early morning or late afternoon to avoid crowds and enjoy a peaceful soak in the thermal springs, and explore nearby attractions like Garvan Woodland Gardens and Lake Ouachita State Park for additional outdoor adventures.
2. **Buffalo National River**: Escape to the wilderness of Buffalo National River, America's first national river, for outdoor adventures amidst pristine landscapes and scenic waterways. Go canoeing, kayaking, or tubing along the river's meandering currents, hike through rugged terrain and lush forests, and camp under the stars for an immersive backcountry experience. Starting Price:

Admission to Buffalo National River is free; costs for camping permits and guided activities vary. Insider Tip: Rent equipment from local outfitters or bring your own for river excursions, and explore lesser-known sections of the river for secluded swimming holes and hidden waterfalls away from popular tourist areas.

3. **Crater of Diamonds State Park**: Unleash your inner prospector at Crater of Diamonds State Park, where visitors can hunt for precious gems and minerals in the only diamond-bearing site open to the public. Explore the park's diamond fields with a bucket and shovel, sift through gravel and soil in search of sparkling treasures, and keep whatever gems you find. Starting Price: Admission to Crater of Diamonds State Park is $10 for adults; costs for equipment rental and guided tours vary. Insider Tip: Bring sunscreen, water, and sturdy footwear for diamond hunting in the park's open fields, and attend educational programs and diamond mining demonstrations for tips and techniques from park staff.

4. **Ozark National Forest**: Immerse yourself in the natural beauty of Ozark National Forest, a vast wilderness area encompassing rugged mountains, lush valleys, and cascading waterfalls. Embark on scenic drives along the Ozark Highlands Scenic Byway, hike to scenic overlooks and hidden caves, and camp in primitive backcountry sites for a true wilderness experience. Starting Price: Admission to Ozark National Forest is free; costs for camping permits and guided activities vary. Insider Tip: Pack a picnic and enjoy al fresco dining at scenic overlooks and picnic areas, and explore off-the-beaten-path trails for wildlife sightings and tranquil nature escapes away from crowded tourist areas.

5. **Crystal Bridges Museum of American Art**: Discover world-class art and architecture at Crystal Bridges Museum of American Art in Bentonville, Arkansas. Explore galleries showcasing American masterpieces spanning centuries of artistic expression, stroll through outdoor sculpture gardens and wooded trails, and attend special exhibitions, lectures, and cultural events throughout the year. Starting Price: Admission to Crystal Bridges Museum is free; costs for special exhibitions and programs vary. Insider Tip: Take advantage of complimentary guided tours and educational programs led by museum staff and volunteers to gain insights into the museum's collections and architecture, and visit nearby attractions like The Momentary and 21c Museum Hotel for additional cultural experiences.

6. **Mount Magazine State Park**: Reach new heights at Mount Magazine State Park, home to the highest peak in Arkansas and panoramic views of the surrounding Ouachita Mountains. Hike to the summit of Mount Magazine for breathtaking vistas, go rock climbing and rappelling on rugged cliffs and bluffs, and stay overnight at the park's lodge or campground for a memorable mountain retreat. Starting Price: Admission to Mount Magazine State Park is free; costs for lodging and guided activities vary. Insider Tip: Visit during the fall foliage season for vibrant colors and scenic drives along Mount Magazine Scenic Byway, and explore nearby attractions like Blue Mountain Lake and Petit Jean State Park for additional outdoor adventures and sightseeing opportunities.

7. **The Little Rock Central High School National Historic Site**: Step into history at The Little Rock Central High School National Historic Site, a symbol of the struggle for civil rights and equality in America. Take a guided tour of the historic high school, now a museum and visitor center, to learn about the events of the Little Rock Nine and their pivotal role in desegregating public schools. Starting Price: Admission to The Little Rock Central High School National Historic Site is free; costs for guided tours and educational programs vary. Insider Tip: Plan your visit during special events and commemorations, such as the annual Daisy Bates

Education Summit, for opportunities to meet civil rights activists and participate in discussions on social justice and equality.

8. **Mount Nebo State Park**: Soak in stunning views of the Arkansas River Valley from Mount Nebo State Park, perched atop a scenic plateau in the Ouachita Mountains. Hike or bike along mountain trails to scenic overlooks and secluded picnic areas, hang-glide from the park's launch site for an adrenaline-fueled adventure, and stay overnight in cozy cabins or campsites for a peaceful mountain getaway. Starting Price: Admission to Mount Nebo State Park is free; costs for lodging and guided activities vary. Insider Tip: Bring binoculars and a camera for birdwatching and wildlife viewing opportunities, and explore nearby attractions like Petit Jean State Park and Lake Dardanelle State Park for additional outdoor recreation and sightseeing adventures.
9. **Thorncrown Chapel**: Experience serenity and architectural beauty at Thorncrown Chapel, an iconic glass chapel nestled in the woodlands of Eureka Springs, Arkansas. Marvel at the chapel's soaring glass walls and intricate wooden beams, attend Sunday services or special events, and explore the surrounding trails and gardens for peaceful contemplation and reflection. Starting Price: Admission to Thorncrown Chapel is free; donations are appreciated. Insider Tip: Visit during the spring or fall for optimal weather and natural beauty, and attend concerts and musical performances held at the chapel throughout the year for a unique cultural experience.
10. **Hot Springs National Park Bathhouses**: Indulge in a rejuvenating spa experience at Hot Springs National Park, where historic bathhouses offer traditional thermal baths and modern spa treatments amidst opulent surroundings. Soak in natural hot springs water at establishments like Buckstaff Baths or Quapaw Baths & Spa, and unwind with massages, facials, and aromatherapy sessions for ultimate relaxation and wellness. Starting Price: Costs for spa services and treatments vary by establishment; traditional thermal baths start at $20-$30 per person. Insider Tip: Book spa treatments in advance to secure preferred appointment times and treatments, and explore nearby attractions like Garvan Woodland Gardens and Lake Ouachita for additional outdoor adventures and sightseeing opportunities.

Here are the top attractions in Arkansas, along with some money-saving tips for visiting each one:

Hot Springs National Park: Indulge in the rejuvenating waters of natural thermal springs nestled within the picturesque surroundings of Hot Springs National Park.

Money-Saving Tip: Take advantage of the free public thermal water fountains located in downtown Hot Springs for a refreshing and cost-effective experience.

Starting Cost: Entrance to the park is free; optional fees apply for amenities like guided tours and bathing facilities.

Crater of Diamonds State Park, Murfreesboro: Embark on a treasure hunt for diamonds and gemstones amidst the scenic landscapes of Crater of Diamonds State Park.

Money-Saving Tip: Bring your own digging tools and equipment, or rent them at the park for a fee, to maximize your gem-hunting adventure without breaking the bank.

Starting Cost: Admission to the park is around $10 to $12 per person, with additional fees for equipment rental if needed.

Buffalo National River: Immerse yourself in the natural beauty of Buffalo National River, where scenic river views and outdoor activities abound.

Money-Saving Tip: Opt for camping at one of the park's affordable campsites to enjoy a budget-friendly stay amidst the tranquil surroundings.

Starting Cost: Camping fees range from $10 to $20 per night, depending on the campground and amenities.

Little Rock: Discover the rich history and vibrant culture of Arkansas's state capital, Little Rock, home to historic sites, museums, and cultural attractions.

Money-Saving Tip: Take advantage of free admission days or reduced rates for students and seniors at many of the city's museums and attractions.

Starting Cost: Admission to most museums and attractions ranges from free to around $10 per person.

Mount Magazine State Park: Soak in panoramic views and outdoor adventures at Mount Magazine State Park, the highest point in Arkansas.

Money-Saving Tip: Bring your own outdoor equipment, such as bicycles and hiking gear, to explore the park's trails and scenic vistas without additional rental fees.

Starting Cost: Entrance to the park is free; optional fees apply for amenities like guided tours and recreational activities.

Crystal Bridges Museum of American Art, Bentonville: Immerse yourself in the world of American art and architecture at Crystal Bridges Museum, showcasing a stunning collection of masterpieces.

Money-Saving Tip: Enjoy complimentary admission to the museum's permanent collection, offering a wealth of artistic treasures at no cost.

Starting Cost: Admission to the museum's permanent collection is free; optional fees may apply for special exhibitions and programs.

Ouachita National Forest: Delve into the wilderness of Ouachita National Forest, where hiking trails and camping opportunities abound amidst stunning natural landscapes.

Money-Saving Tip: Choose from a selection of free or low-cost campgrounds within the forest to enjoy a budget-friendly outdoor getaway.

Starting Cost: Camping fees vary depending on the campground and amenities, but free camping options are available in some areas.

Thorncrown Chapel, Eureka Springs: Experience architectural brilliance amidst the serene beauty of Thorncrown Chapel, a masterpiece of modern design nestled in the Ozark Mountains.

Money-Saving Tip: Enjoy the chapel's exterior and surrounding landscapes for free, offering a peaceful retreat amidst nature's splendor.

Starting Cost: Admission to the chapel's interior is optional and costs around $10 per person.

Garvan Woodland Gardens, Hot Springs: Discover the enchanting beauty of botanical gardens at Garvan Woodland Gardens, featuring a dazzling array of flora and fauna.

Money-Saving Tip: Plan your visit during the off-peak season to take advantage of lower admission fees and fewer crowds.

Starting Cost: Admission to the gardens ranges from $10 to $15 per person, with discounts available for seniors and children.

Hot Springs Mountain Tower: Soar to new heights and enjoy panoramic views of Hot Springs and its surrounding landscapes from Hot Springs Mountain Tower.

Money-Saving Tip: Capture stunning photos of the area with your own camera from various vantage points around Hot Springs National Park, avoiding the tower fee.

Starting Cost: Admission to Hot Springs Mountain Tower is around $8 to $10 per person.

Eureka Springs: Step back in time and explore the historic Victorian charm of Eureka Springs, a quaint town nestled in the Ozark Mountains.

Money-Saving Tip: Wander through the town's unique shops, galleries, and architectural wonders on foot to soak in the atmosphere without spending extra.

Starting Cost: Parking and exploration of the town's historic district are typically free of charge.

Cossatot River State Park-Natural Area, Wickes: Embark on thrilling whitewater rafting adventures and scenic hikes amidst the rugged beauty of Cossatot River State Park-Natural Area.

Money-Saving Tip: Bring your own rafting equipment for a self-guided adventure down the river, offering an affordable and exhilarating experience.

Starting Cost: Entrance to the park is free; optional fees apply for amenities like guided tours and recreational activities.

Devil's Den State Park, West Fork: Immerse yourself in the natural wonders of Devil's Den State Park, where camping, hiking, and outdoor adventures await amidst scenic beauty.

Money-Saving Tip: Pack your camping gear and enjoy a budget-friendly stay at the park's picturesque campgrounds, surrounded by lush forests and limestone bluffs.

Starting Cost: Camping fees range from $15 to $30 per night, depending on the campground and amenities.

Clinton Presidential Center, Little Rock: Gain insight into U.S. history and politics at the Clinton Presidential Center, featuring interactive exhibits and artifacts from the presidency of Bill Clinton.

Money-Saving Tip: Look for discounts on admission for seniors, military personnel, and students to make your visit more budget-friendly.

Starting Cost: Admission to the museum is around $10 to $15 per person, with discounts available for select groups.

Museum of Native American History, Bentonville: Explore the rich cultural heritage of Native Americans at the Museum of Native American History, showcasing artifacts and exhibits spanning thousands of years.

Money-Saving Tip: Admission to the museum is free, offering a fascinating journey through the history and traditions of indigenous peoples.

Starting Cost: Admission to the museum is free; donations are appreciated to support its ongoing programs and exhibits.

Mount Nebo State Park: Trek through scenic trails and marvel at breathtaking vistas atop Mount Nebo, offering panoramic views of the Arkansas River Valley below.

Money-Saving Tip: Visit during the week to avoid crowds and enjoy the park's natural beauty at your own pace without additional fees.

Starting Cost: Entrance to the park is free; optional fees apply for amenities like guided tours and recreational activities.

Hemingway-Pfeiffer Museum, Piggott: Delve into the literary legacy of Ernest Hemingway at the Hemingway-Pfeiffer Museum, located in the writer's former home and studio.

Money-Saving Tip: Check for reduced admission rates for children and seniors, making it an affordable and enlightening experience for visitors of all ages.

Starting Cost: Admission to the museum is around $5 to $10 per person, with discounts available for select groups.

Lake Ouachita: Dive into aquatic adventures and fishing escapades at Lake Ouachita, a sprawling reservoir nestled amidst the scenic beauty of Ouachita National Forest.

Money-Saving Tip: Rent watercraft and fishing equipment from local providers for the best rates and enjoy a day on the water without breaking the bank.

Starting Cost: Rental prices for watercraft vary depending on the type and duration of rental, with discounts available for group bookings.

Ozark Folk Center State Park, Mountain View: Immerse yourself in the music, crafts, and culture of the Ozarks at Ozark Folk Center State Park, featuring live performances and artisan demonstrations.

Money-Saving Tip: Look for discounts on admission, especially for group visits, to enjoy the park's attractions and entertainment at a reduced cost.

Starting Cost: Admission to the park varies depending on the season and events, with discounts available for seniors and children.

Queen Wilhelmina State Park, Mena: Discover the natural beauty of the Ouachita Mountains and panoramic views from Queen Wilhelmina State Park, named after the Dutch queen.

Money-Saving Tip: Hike the park's trails and enjoy its scenic overlooks at no cost, offering a budget-friendly way to experience the park's beauty.

Starting Cost: Entrance to the park is free; optional fees apply for amenities like guided tours and recreational activities.

RECAP

Category	Insider Tips
Food	1. Seek out local barbecue joints for authentic Southern flavors at reasonable prices.

	2. Visit farmers' markets for fresh produce and homemade treats, often sold at affordable prices.
	3. Explore small-town diners for hearty, home-cooked meals with generous portions and wallet-friendly prices.
	4. Opt for "meat-and-three" restaurants for budget-friendly Southern comfort food options.
Accommodation	1. Consider camping at Arkansas's state parks or national forests for affordable outdoor lodging options.
	2. Look for cozy bed and breakfasts or guesthouses in charming towns for affordable and unique accommodations.
	3. Utilize discount booking websites or apps to find deals on hotels and motels in Arkansas.
	4. Stay in cabins or vacation rentals near Arkansas's scenic rivers or lakes for budget-friendly waterfront stays.
Activities	1. Explore hiking trails in the Ozark or Ouachita Mountains for stunning scenery and outdoor adventures.
	2. Visit local museums and historical sites with low-cost or free admission to learn about Arkansas's heritage.
	3. Enjoy outdoor activities like fishing, kayaking, or swimming in Arkansas's numerous lakes and rivers.
	4. Attend community events and festivals, often featuring live music, food vendors, and family-friendly activities.
Transport	1. Rent a car for flexibility in exploring Arkansas's scenic byways and remote destinations.
	2. Utilize public transportation options in cities like Little Rock or Fayetteville to save on parking and gas.
	3. Look for carpooling opportunities or rideshare services for shared transportation costs.
	4. Consider biking or walking in smaller towns or on designated trails for eco-friendly and budget-friendly travel.

California

California's history is as varied as its landscapes. Once home to numerous indigenous peoples, the Spanish explorers arrived in the 16th century, leaving a lasting impact on the state's architecture and culture. The mid-19th century saw the Gold Rush, drawing fortune seekers from around the world. Over the years, California has evolved into a cultural and economic powerhouse, influencing everything from technology in Silicon Valley to the entertainment industry in Hollywood.

Things to Consider:

- **Climate Diversity:** California boasts a wide range of climates, from the warm deserts of the south to the cooler, temperate regions of the north. Pack accordingly to make the most of your journey.
- **Traffic:** Be prepared for traffic, especially in major cities like Los Angeles and San Francisco. Consider public transportation options or plan your travel during off-peak hours.
- **Natural Wonders:** Don't miss the opportunity to explore California's natural wonders, including Yosemite National Park, the Pacific coastline, and the scenic landscapes of Napa Valley.

Local Tips:

- **Culinary Delights:** California is a food lover's paradise. From world-class restaurants in San Francisco to the taco trucks of Los Angeles, the state offers diverse and delicious culinary experiences.
- **Outdoor Adventures:** Take advantage of the state's outdoor activities. Whether it's hiking in Joshua Tree National Park, surfing in Santa Cruz, or skiing in Lake Tahoe, California has something for every outdoor enthusiast.
- **Cultural Events:** Check out local events and festivals. From the iconic Coachella Music Festival to San Francisco's Pride Parade, California hosts a plethora of cultural events throughout the year.

1. **Transportation:**

- **Public Transportation:** Major cities like San Francisco and Los Angeles have comprehensive public transportation systems. Utilize buses and trains for cost-effective travel within the cities.

2. **Accommodation:**

- **Budget-Friendly Luxury Stays:** Look for boutique hotels, motels, or budget-friendly luxury chains. Prices can vary, but expect to pay around $100 to $200 per night for a comfortable stay. Consider staying slightly outside major city centers for more affordable options.

- **Hostels or Airbnb:** Explore hostels or Airbnb options for a more budget-friendly experience. Prices can range from $50 to $150 per night, depending on the location and type of accommodation.
- **Budget Hotels:** Look for budget-friendly hotels in cities like Los Angeles, San Francisco, or San Diego. Options such as Motel 6, Super 8, or Travelodge offer comfortable stays at reasonable prices in various locations across the state.
- **Hostels:** Hostels are a popular option for budget travelers in California, especially in cities with high tourist traffic. Check out hostels like HI Los Angeles Santa Monica, HI San Francisco Downtown Hostel, or USA Hostels San Diego for affordable dormitory-style accommodations.
- **Camping:** California's diverse landscapes offer numerous opportunities for camping in national parks, forests, and state parks. Consider camping in places like Yosemite National Park, Joshua Tree National Park, or Big Sur for an affordable outdoor experience.

3. Dining:

- **Food Trucks:** Experience California's diverse culinary scene through food trucks. You can enjoy delicious meals for $10 to $20.
- **Local Markets:** Visit farmers' markets for fresh, affordable produce. Explore cities like San Francisco, Los Angeles, or San Diego for a variety of options.

4. Activities:

- **National Parks:** California is home to stunning national parks such as Yosemite and Sequoia. While some parks have entrance fees (around $35 per vehicle), the natural beauty is well worth it.
- **Beaches:** Enjoy California's beautiful beaches, many of which are free. Popular spots include Santa Monica Beach, Venice Beach, and Malibu.
- **Hiking Trails:** Explore the numerous free or low-cost hiking trails in areas like Griffith Park in Los Angeles or the Marin Headlands in San Francisco.

5. Entertainment:

- **Free Museums:** Many museums offer free admission on specific days. In Los Angeles, the Getty Center and Getty Villa have free admission, providing a luxurious cultural experience.
- **Street Performances:** Cities like San Francisco and Santa Monica often feature street performers. Enjoy the entertainment without spending a dime.
- **California State Capitol Museum (Sacramento):** The California State Capitol Museum offers free guided tours where you can learn about the history, government, and architecture of California.
- **San Francisco City Guides:** San Francisco City Guides offers free walking tours of various neighborhoods in San Francisco, led by knowledgeable volunteer guides. While the tours are free, donations are appreciated.
- **Getty Center (Los Angeles):** While admission to the Getty Center is free, parking fees apply. The museum offers free guided tours of its collections and architecture. Check their website or contact them directly for tour availability.
- **California African American Museum (Los Angeles):** The California African American Museum offers free admission and occasionally provides free guided tours of its exhibits. Check their website or contact them for tour availability.

6. Insights and Tips:

- **Wine Tasting:** Visit regions like Napa or Sonoma for wine tasting. Some wineries offer complimentary tastings, and others charge a nominal fee that may be applied toward a purchase.
- **Discount Passes:** Consider city passes for attractions. The Go Los Angeles Card or San Francisco CityPASS can provide discounted access to multiple attractions.
- **Off-Peak Travel:** If possible, visit during the shoulder seasons (spring or fall) to avoid peak tourist times and find better deals on accommodations.

Major Towns in California:

- **Los Angeles:** Known for Hollywood, diverse neighborhoods, and cultural attractions.
- **San Francisco:** Famous for the Golden Gate Bridge, Alcatraz Island, and its vibrant tech scene.
- **San Diego:** Offers beautiful beaches, a world-renowned zoo, and a laid-back atmosphere.
- **Napa Valley:** A wine-lover's paradise with picturesque vineyards and charming towns.

1. **Yosemite National Park**: Lose yourself in the breathtaking landscapes of Yosemite National Park, where towering granite cliffs, majestic waterfalls, and ancient sequoia trees await. Explore iconic landmarks like Half Dome, El Capitan, and Yosemite Falls on scenic hikes and drives, and immerse yourself in the park's pristine wilderness on backcountry adventures and camping trips. Starting Price: Admission to Yosemite National Park is $35 per vehicle for a seven-day pass. Insider Tip: Visit during the spring or fall for fewer crowds and optimal weather conditions, and reserve accommodations and camping permits well in advance, especially during peak seasons.
2. **Golden Gate Bridge**: Marvel at one of the world's most iconic landmarks, the Golden Gate Bridge, spanning the entrance to San Francisco Bay with its towering orange towers and sweeping vistas. Walk or bike across the bridge on designated pathways for panoramic views of the city skyline and Alcatraz Island, and snap photos at scenic overlooks like Battery Spencer and Fort Point. Starting Price: Walking or biking across the Golden Gate Bridge is free; costs for parking and guided tours vary. Insider Tip: Visit in the early morning or late afternoon for the best lighting and fewer crowds, and explore nearby attractions like Golden Gate Park and Lands End for additional sightseeing and outdoor activities.
3. **Disneyland Resort**: Experience the magic of Disneyland Resort in Anaheim, where fantasy comes to life with thrilling rides, enchanting attractions, and beloved Disney characters. Explore iconic lands like Fantasyland, Adventureland, and Tomorrowland, and immerse yourself in immersive experiences like Star Wars: Galaxy's Edge and Pixar Pier. Starting Price: Admission to Disneyland Resort starts at $104 per person for a one-day ticket. Insider Tip: Purchase tickets in advance online to save time and avoid long lines at the ticket booths, and take advantage of special offers and multi-day passes for added value and flexibility during your visit.
4. **Hollywood Walk of Fame**: Take a stroll down Hollywood Boulevard and discover the stars on the Hollywood Walk of Fame, where over 2,600 brass stars honor legendary entertainers from film, television, music, and theater. Pose for photos with your favorite celebrity's star,

and explore nearby attractions like the TCL Chinese Theatre and Dolby Theatre for a taste of Hollywood glamour. Starting Price: Walking the Hollywood Walk of Fame is free; costs for guided tours and parking vary. Insider Tip: Visit in the early morning or late evening to avoid crowds and capture the best photos of the stars, and attend special events like star ceremonies and movie premieres for a chance to see celebrities up close.

5. **San Francisco's Chinatown**: Immerse yourself in the vibrant culture and rich history of San Francisco's Chinatown, the oldest and largest Chinatown outside of Asia. Explore bustling streets lined with colorful shops, authentic eateries, and historic landmarks like the Dragon Gate and Tin How Temple, and sample traditional Chinese cuisine and herbal remedies for an authentic cultural experience. Starting Price: Exploring San Francisco's Chinatown is free; costs for dining and shopping vary. Insider Tip: Join a guided walking tour or culinary excursion led by local experts to discover hidden gems and insider secrets of Chinatown, and visit during cultural festivals and celebrations for a festive atmosphere and special events.

6. **Napa Valley Wine Country**: Indulge in the ultimate wine-tasting experience in Napa Valley, renowned for its world-class wineries, picturesque vineyards, and award-winning wines. Embark on scenic drives along the Silverado Trail and Napa Valley Wine Train, and visit acclaimed wineries like Beringer Vineyards, Domaine Carneros, and Castello di Amorosa for tastings and tours. Starting Price: Wine tastings in Napa Valley start at $20-$50 per person; costs for tours and experiences vary. Insider Tip: Plan your visit during the off-season or mid-week to avoid crowds and secure reservations at popular wineries, and explore nearby attractions like Calistoga's hot springs and Yountville's gourmet restaurants for additional culinary delights.

7. **Big Sur Coastline**: Embark on a scenic road trip along California's rugged Big Sur coastline, where dramatic cliffs, hidden coves, and crashing waves create a breathtaking backdrop for outdoor adventures and coastal exploration. Drive along the iconic Pacific Coast Highway (Highway 1), stopping at landmarks like Bixby Creek Bridge, McWay Falls, and Pfeiffer Beach for panoramic views and photo opportunities. Starting Price: Driving along Big Sur's coastline is free; costs for parking and accommodations vary. Insider Tip: Pack a picnic and enjoy al fresco dining at scenic overlooks and beachside picnic areas, and hike along coastal trails like Julia Pfeiffer Burns State Park and Point Lobos State Natural Reserve for up-close encounters with nature's wonders.

8. **Death Valley National Park**: Discover the extremes of nature at Death Valley National Park, home to the lowest point in North America and some of the hottest temperatures on earth. Explore otherworldly landscapes like Badwater Basin, Devil's Golf Course, and Zabriskie Point on scenic drives and hikes, and marvel at colorful sand dunes, salt flats, and rugged mountains. Starting Price: Admission to Death Valley National Park is $30 per vehicle for a seven-day pass. Insider Tip: Visit in the cooler months of fall, winter, or spring to avoid extreme heat and enjoy comfortable temperatures for outdoor activities, and bring plenty of water, sunscreen, and protective clothing for desert exploration.

9. **Joshua Tree National Park**: Experience the surreal beauty of the desert at Joshua Tree National Park, where twisted Joshua trees, massive boulders, and star-filled skies create an otherworldly landscape for outdoor adventures and stargazing. Hike or rock climb among giant rock formations and hidden oases, and camp beneath the stars for a true desert wilderness experience. Starting Price: Admission to Joshua Tree National Park is $30 per vehicle for a seven-day pass. Insider Tip: Visit during the spring or fall for optimal weather and wildflower blooms, and explore lesser-known areas of the park like Cottonwood Spring and Barker Dam for secluded hikes and wildlife sightings away from crowds.

10. **Lake Tahoe**: Escape to the pristine shores of Lake Tahoe, a crystal-clear alpine lake straddling the border of California and Nevada, for outdoor recreation and scenic beauty year-round. Swim, paddle, or boat in the lake's turquoise waters, hike or bike along scenic trails in the surrounding Sierra Nevada mountains, and ski or snowboard at world-class

resorts like Heavenly and Squaw Valley. Starting Price: Access to Lake Tahoe's beaches and trails is free; costs for recreational activities and equipment rental vary. Insider Tip: Visit during the shoulder seasons of spring or fall for fewer crowds and discounted lodging rates, and explore nearby attractions like Emerald Bay State Park and Sand Harbor Beach for additional outdoor adventures and sightseeing opportunities.

How to save money on major California Attractions

Yosemite National Park: Immerse yourself in the awe-inspiring beauty of Yosemite National Park, where towering waterfalls and majestic landscapes await.

Money-Saving Tip: Opt for camping in the park's campgrounds for budget-friendly accommodations amidst nature's splendor. Reservations are recommended, especially during peak seasons.

Starting Cost: Campground fees range from $6 to $26 per night, depending on the campground and amenities.

Disneyland Resort, Anaheim: Enter a world of enchantment and entertainment at Disneyland Resort, where beloved characters and thrilling attractions come to life.

Money-Saving Tip: Purchase multi-day tickets for reduced per-day costs, allowing you to experience more magic for less. Consider visiting during weekdays for potentially lower crowds and better deals.

Starting Cost: Multi-day ticket prices start at around $104 per day for adults and $98 per day for children ages 3-9.

Golden Gate Bridge, San Francisco: Stand in awe of the iconic Golden Gate Bridge and soak in panoramic views of San Francisco's skyline and the bay.

Money-Saving Tip: Take advantage of the free option to walk or bike across the bridge, offering a memorable experience without spending a dime. Alternatively, look for discounted guided tours for deeper insights into the bridge's history and engineering.

Starting Cost: Walking or biking across the bridge is free; guided tours typically range from $15 to $30 per person.

Death Valley National Park: Explore the stark beauty of Death Valley National Park, home to unique desert landscapes and extreme natural phenomena.

Money-Saving Tip: Visit during the cooler months, typically November through March, to avoid the extreme heat and high park fees associated with peak summer months. Entrance fees are per vehicle and valid for seven days.

Starting Cost: Entrance fees to the park are around $30 per vehicle during peak season (October to April) and $25 per vehicle during the summer months (May to September).

Universal Studios Hollywood: Dive into the magic of movies at Universal Studios Hollywood, where thrilling rides, shows, and movie-themed attractions await.

Money-Saving Tip: Purchase tickets online in advance for discounts and consider visiting on weekdays to potentially save on admission costs and experience shorter wait times for attractions.

Starting Cost: Ticket prices start at around $109 per day for adults and $103 per day for children ages 3-9.

Lake Tahoe: Discover outdoor adventures and breathtaking beauty at Lake Tahoe, a sparkling alpine gem nestled in the Sierra Nevada mountains.

Money-Saving Tip: Opt for camping or stay in budget-friendly lodges or cabins around the lake for affordable accommodations amidst the stunning scenery.

Starting Cost: Camping fees vary depending on the campground and amenities, ranging from $15 to $35 per night. Lodging options range from budget-friendly motels to cabins and vacation rentals.

Alcatraz Island, San Francisco: Step into history with a tour of Alcatraz Island, the infamous former prison that once housed some of America's most notorious criminals.

Money-Saving Tip: Book Alcatraz tickets well in advance directly through the National Park Service website to secure your spot and avoid scalper fees. Consider combining your visit with a city pass for additional savings on other attractions.

Starting Cost: Ticket prices for Alcatraz tours start at around $39.90 per person, including ferry transportation to and from the island.

Big Sur: Embark on a scenic drive along the breathtaking Pacific Coast Highway and immerse yourself in the natural beauty of Big Sur's rugged coastline.

Money-Saving Tip: Pack a picnic and explore state parks and beaches along the route for free or low fees, offering stunning vistas and opportunities for outdoor recreation.

Starting Cost: Entrance fees to state parks along Big Sur vary, ranging from $10 to $15 per vehicle for day use.

Hollywood: Experience the glitz and glamour of Hollywood, the entertainment capital of the world, home to iconic landmarks and celebrity sightings.

Money-Saving Tip: Take a self-guided walking tour along the Hollywood Walk of Fame to see the stars and iconic landmarks like the TCL Chinese Theatre and the Hollywood Sign without spending extra on guided tours.

Starting Cost: Walking tours are free; optional fees apply for attractions like Madame Tussauds Hollywood and the Hollywood Museum.

San Diego Zoo: Journey into the animal kingdom at the world-renowned San Diego Zoo, home to thousands of animals representing diverse species from around the globe.

Money-Saving Tip: Visit during half-price days, typically held in the off-peak season, or consider purchasing a multi-attraction pass for savings on admission to the zoo and other attractions in the area.

Starting Cost: General admission prices start at around $58 for adults and $48 for children ages 3-11. Half-price days offer discounted admission for select dates.

Sequoia and Kings Canyon National Parks: Stand in awe of ancient giants at Sequoia and Kings Canyon National Parks, where towering sequoia trees and stunning landscapes await.

Money-Saving Tip: Use your National Park Pass for access to both parks, allowing you to explore their natural wonders and scenic vistas without additional entrance fees.

Starting Cost: Entrance fees to each park are around $35 per vehicle, valid for seven days. The National Park Pass costs $80 annually and provides unlimited entry to participating national parks and federal recreational lands.

Santa Monica Pier: Experience classic fun and entertainment at the iconic Santa Monica Pier, featuring amusement rides, arcades, and stunning ocean views.

Money-Saving Tip: Enjoy a leisurely stroll along the pier and take in the views of the Pacific Ocean and surrounding coastline for free. Consider packing a picnic to enjoy on the beach for a budget-friendly outing.

Starting Cost: Admission to the pier is free; optional fees apply for rides and attractions.

Napa Valley: Indulge in wine tastings and vineyard tours amidst the scenic beauty of Napa Valley, one of the world's premier wine regions.

Money-Saving Tip: Look for wineries offering complimentary tastings or wine discounts, allowing you to sample a variety of wines without breaking the bank.

Starting Cost: Wine tasting fees vary by winery, ranging from complimentary tastings to $20 or more per person for premium experiences.

San Francisco Bay Cruise: Sail away on a scenic cruise of San Francisco Bay, offering panoramic views of the city skyline, Golden Gate Bridge, and Alcatraz Island.

Money-Saving Tip: Find online deals and discounts for cruise tickets, including special offers for sunset cruises and combo packages with other attractions in the area.

Starting Cost: Cruise ticket prices vary depending on the duration and type of cruise, starting at around $30 to $40 per person for basic sightseeing cruises.

Joshua Tree National Park: Explore the surreal landscapes of Joshua Tree National Park, where twisted Joshua trees and unique rock formations create an otherworldly atmosphere.

Money-Saving Tip: Camp in the park's campgrounds for an affordable stay amidst the desert wilderness. Reservations are recommended, especially during peak seasons.

Starting Cost: Campground fees range from $15 to $20 per night, depending on the campground and amenities.

Griffith Observatory, Los Angeles: Reach for the stars at Griffith Observatory, offering fascinating exhibits on astronomy and breathtaking views of the Los Angeles skyline.

Money-Saving Tip: Visit during the day for free admission to the observatory and explore its exhibits, telescopes, and outdoor spaces at no cost.

Starting Cost: Admission to the observatory is free; optional fees apply for planetarium shows and special events.

Monterey Bay Aquarium: Dive into the wonders of the ocean at Monterey Bay Aquarium, where marine life thrives in captivating exhibits and interactive displays.

Money-Saving Tip: Look for discounted tickets for seniors, students, and children, offering savings on admission to one of the world's top aquariums.

Starting Cost: General admission prices start at around $50 for adults and $30 for children ages 3-12. Discounts may be available for select groups.

Redwood National and State Parks: Stand among the tallest trees on earth at Redwood National and State Parks, where ancient redwoods create a majestic canopy overhead.

Money-Saving Tip: Combine a visit to Redwood National Park with nearby Jedediah Smith State Park for a diverse experience of towering trees and scenic rivers.

Starting Cost: Entrance to the parks is free; optional fees may apply for camping and guided tours.

Balboa Park, San Diego: Immerse yourself in culture and nature at Balboa Park, home to museums, gardens, and cultural attractions.

Money-Saving Tip: Plan your visit on Tuesdays for free admission to select museums within Balboa Park, offering a budget-friendly way to explore its diverse offerings.

Starting Cost: Admission to select museums on Tuesdays is free; optional fees apply for special exhibitions and events.

Beverly Hills: Experience luxury and glamour in Beverly Hills, renowned for its upscale shopping, dining, and celebrity sightings.

Money-Saving Tip: Window-shop along Rodeo Drive and take a self-guided celebrity home tour to catch glimpses of opulent mansions and iconic landmarks without spending extra on guided tours.

Starting Cost: Sightseeing in Beverly Hills is typically free; optional fees apply for guided tours and attractions like the Paley Center for Media.

Category	Insider Tips
Food	1. Explore local farmers' markets like the Ferry Plaza Farmers Market in San Francisco or the Santa Monica Farmers Market for fresh produce and artisanal products.
	2. Indulge in affordable and delicious tacos from local taquerias in neighborhoods like the Mission District in San Francisco or East Los Angeles.
	3. Take advantage of food truck gatherings, such as Off the Grid in San Francisco or Smorgasburg LA, for a variety of tasty and budget-friendly eats.
	4. Pack a picnic and enjoy it at iconic California spots like Griffith Park in Los Angeles or Golden Gate Park in San Francisco for stunning views and ambiance.
Accommodation	1. Camp in California's beautiful state parks and national forests, such as Yosemite or Joshua Tree, for affordable and scenic camping experiences.
	2. Consider staying in budget-friendly hostels in cities like San Francisco, Los Angeles, or San Diego, which often offer communal kitchens and social atmospheres.
	3. Look for accommodations in lesser-known beach towns like Santa Cruz or Morro Bay for more affordable beachfront stays compared to popular destinations like Malibu or Santa Monica.
	4. Use Airbnb or VRBO to find affordable accommodations, especially if you're traveling with a group and can split the cost of renting a house or apartment.
Activities	1. Explore hiking trails in California's stunning landscapes, such as the trails in Yosemite National Park, Big Sur, or the Santa Monica Mountains, for breathtaking views and outdoor adventures.
	2. Visit free attractions like the Griffith Observatory in Los Angeles, the Golden Gate Bridge in San Francisco, or the many art galleries and street murals in neighborhoods like the Mission District in San Francisco or the Arts District in Los Angeles.
	3. Take advantage of discounted admission days at museums and attractions, such as the first Tuesday of every month at the California Academy of Sciences in San Francisco.
	4. Enjoy outdoor activities like beach bonfires, free concerts in the park, or yoga on the beach in cities like San Diego or Santa Monica.
Transport	1. Rent a car for flexibility in exploring California's vast and diverse landscapes, but look for deals from local rental companies or book in advance for the best rates.
	2. Utilize public transportation options like buses, trains, or light rail systems in major cities like San Francisco, Los Angeles, or San Diego to save on parking fees and gas.
	3. Consider biking or walking in bike-friendly cities like San Francisco or Santa Monica for eco-friendly and budget-friendly transportation options.
	4. Look for carpooling opportunities or ride-sharing services like UberPOOL or Lyft Line to split transportation costs when traveling longer distances or with friends.

Colorado

Colorado's history is deeply intertwined with the expansion of the American West. Native American tribes inhabited the region for centuries, and the mid-19th century brought waves of settlers during the Gold Rush and the building of the transcontinental railroad. The state's stunning natural beauty has played a crucial role in shaping its cultural identity.

Things to Consider:

- **Altitude:** Colorado's elevation can vary significantly, with some areas reaching over 14,000 feet. Take it easy, stay hydrated, and give yourself time to acclimate to the altitude, especially in cities like Denver and mountain destinations.
- **Outdoor Paradise:** If you're an outdoor enthusiast, Colorado is a paradise. From hiking and skiing to white-water rafting and mountain biking, the state offers a wide array of activities for nature lovers.
- **Weather Variability:** Be prepared for rapid weather changes, especially in the mountains. Layers are your best friend, as temperatures can fluctuate throughout the day.

Local Tips:

- **Craft Beer Scene:** Colorado is known for its thriving craft beer scene. Explore local breweries in cities like Denver and Boulder to taste a variety of unique and flavorful brews.
- **Scenic Drives:** Take advantage of the state's scenic drives. The Million Dollar Highway, Trail Ridge Road, and the Peak to Peak Scenic Byway offer breathtaking views of Colorado's mountainous landscapes.
- **Cultural Events:** Check out cultural events and festivals. From the vibrant arts scene in Denver to the Telluride Film Festival, Colorado hosts a range of events celebrating its rich cultural diversity.

Must-Visit Places:

- **Rocky Mountain National Park:** Explore the stunning landscapes, alpine lakes, and diverse wildlife of this iconic national park.
- **Garden of the Gods:** Marvel at the striking red rock formations in this natural wonder located near Colorado Springs.
- **Mesa Verde National Park:** Discover the ancient cliff dwellings and archaeological sites of the ancestral Pueblo people.

1. Transportation:

- **Car Rental:** Renting a car is advisable to explore Colorado's diverse landscapes. Prices start at around $30 per day, and booking in advance can help you secure better deals.

2. Accommodation:

- **Budget-Friendly Luxury Stays:** Explore boutique hotels or lodges in cities like Denver, Boulder, or Colorado Springs. Prices can range from $80 to $150 per night for a comfortable stay. Consider booking in advance or during off-peak seasons for better rates.
- **State Parks or Camping:** Colorado offers stunning state parks and campgrounds. Campsite fees can be as low as $20 per night, providing a budget-friendly and nature-centric experience.
- **Hostels:** Hostels are a popular option for budget travelers in Colorado, especially in cities with high tourist traffic. Check out hostels like Hostel Fish in Denver, Garden of the Gods Resort and Club in Colorado Springs, or Boulder Adventure Lodge in Boulder for affordable dormitory-style accommodations.

3. Dining:

- **Local Cafes and Breweries:** Enjoy local cuisine at affordable prices. Colorado is known for its craft beer scene and local cafes where meals can range from $10 to $30 per person.
- **Food Trucks:** Explore food trucks for a quick and budget-friendly culinary adventure.

4. Activities:

- **Hiking Trails:** Colorado boasts numerous hiking trails. Many are free, and some may have a small parking fee. Consider trails in Rocky Mountain National Park or Garden of the Gods.
- **Garden of the Gods:** This iconic park in Colorado Springs is free to visit and offers breathtaking red rock formations.
- **Hot Springs:** Relax in hot springs like the ones in Glenwood Springs. Admission prices vary but can be around $20 to $30.

5. Entertainment:

- **Art Walks and Festivals:** Many towns, including Denver and Boulder, host art walks and festivals. Check local calendars for free or low-cost cultural events.
- **Free Concerts:** Cities like Denver often host free concerts, especially during the summer months.
  Colorado State Capitol Tours (Denver): The Colorado State Capitol offers free guided tours where you can learn about the state's history, government, and architecture. Tours are typically available Monday through Friday.
  Denver Art Museum (Denver): While admission to the Denver Art Museum may require a fee for special exhibitions, general admission is free on the first Saturday of each month, and the museum occasionally offers free guided tours of its collections. Check their website or contact them directly for tour availability.
  Rocky Mountain Arsenal National Wildlife Refuge (Commerce City): The Rocky Mountain Arsenal offers free guided wildlife tours led by knowledgeable staff and volunteers. These tours provide opportunities to see native wildlife and learn about conservation efforts.

Self-guided Tours of Garden of the Gods (Colorado Springs): Garden of the Gods Park offers free admission, and you can explore the stunning rock formations and hiking trails on your own. The visitor center provides maps and information for self-guided tours.
Historic Downtown Walking Tours: Many cities in Colorado, such as Denver, Colorado Springs, and Boulder, offer self-guided walking tours of their historic downtown areas. Pick up a map from the local visitor center or chamber of commerce and discover the architecture, landmarks, and history of these areas at your own pace.

•

6. Insights and Tips:

- **Scenic Drives:** Enjoy Colorado's stunning landscapes by taking scenic drives like the Trail Ridge Road in Rocky Mountain National Park or the Million Dollar Highway.
- **Free Museum Days:** Some museums offer free admission on specific days. In Denver, the Denver Art Museum offers free days throughout the year.
- **Ski Resorts in Off-Season:** Visit ski resorts like Aspen or Vail during the off-season for lower accommodation prices and a peaceful mountain experience.

Major Towns in Colorado:

- **Denver:** The capital city known for its vibrant arts scene, outdoor activities, and diverse culinary offerings.
- **Boulder:** A university town with a lively atmosphere, surrounded by hiking trails and scenic beauty.
- **Colorado Springs:** Home to Garden of the Gods, Pikes Peak, and the United States Air Force Academy.
- **Aspen:** A famous ski resort town that transforms into a serene mountain retreat in the off-season.

Money Saving Tips on Top Attractions

Rocky Mountain National Park: Delve into the breathtaking alpine landscapes and extensive hiking trails of Rocky Mountain National Park, offering unparalleled natural beauty and outdoor adventures.

Money-Saving Tip: Invest in an America the Beautiful Annual Pass, granting access to multiple national parks, including Rocky Mountain. It's a cost-effective option for frequent visitors or those planning to explore multiple parks within a year.

Starting Cost: The America the Beautiful Annual Pass costs $80 and is valid for one year from the month of purchase.

Mesa Verde National Park: Step back in time to explore the ancient cliff dwellings and archaeological wonders of Mesa Verde National Park, showcasing the rich history and culture of the ancestral Pueblo people.

Money-Saving Tip: Plan your visit during the off-peak season, typically in the fall or spring, to take advantage of lower entrance fees and potentially reduced accommodation rates in nearby areas.

Starting Cost: Entrance fees to Mesa Verde National Park vary depending on the season and type of pass, with discounts available for seniors, military personnel, and children.

Garden of the Gods, Colorado Springs: Be mesmerized by the awe-inspiring rock formations of Garden of the Gods, a natural wonderland in Colorado Springs.

Money-Saving Tip: Enjoy complimentary access to the park and embark on a self-guided tour to explore the towering sandstone formations and scenic trails without spending a dime.

Starting Cost: Admission to Garden of the Gods is free; optional fees apply for guided tours, rock climbing, and other activities.

Pikes Peak: Ascend to new heights and soak in panoramic vistas from the summit of Pikes Peak, one of Colorado's most iconic peaks.

Money-Saving Tip: Consider taking the shuttle option for transportation to the summit, which can be more cost-effective than driving your vehicle. The shuttle provides a hassle-free way to reach the summit while enjoying the scenic journey.

Starting Cost: Shuttle tickets to Pikes Peak vary depending on the departure point and season, with discounts available for seniors, military personnel, and children.

Breckenridge: Experience the charm of a quintessential mountain town in Breckenridge, where outdoor adventures and picturesque landscapes abound.

Money-Saving Tip: Plan your visit during the shoulder season, typically in the spring or fall, to take advantage of lodging and activity discounts offered by local businesses catering to fewer crowds.

Starting Cost: Lodging rates in Breckenridge vary depending on the season, accommodation type, and proximity to the town center.

Great Sand Dunes National Park and Preserve: Immerse yourself in the surreal beauty of the tallest sand dunes in North America at Great Sand Dunes National Park and Preserve.

Money-Saving Tip: Opt for camping in the park's campgrounds for budget-friendly accommodations amidst the dunes and surrounding wilderness.

Starting Cost: Camping fees at Great Sand Dunes National Park vary depending on the campground and amenities, with discounts available for holders of certain passes.

Denver: Dive into the vibrant cultural scene and urban delights of the Mile-High City, where museums, parks, and culinary delights await.

Money-Saving Tip: Keep an eye out for free museum days and explore Denver's numerous city parks and public art installations for budget-friendly entertainment and exploration.

Starting Cost: Admission to many of Denver's museums and cultural attractions is free on select days or evenings, while others offer discounted admission rates.

Aspen: Surround yourself with outdoor adventures and stunning landscapes in Aspen, a renowned destination for skiing, hiking, and year-round recreation.

Money-Saving Tip: Visit Aspen during the off-season, typically in the spring or fall, to take advantage of lower hotel rates and fewer crowds while still enjoying the area's natural beauty and outdoor activities.

Starting Cost: Lodging rates in Aspen vary depending on the season, accommodation type, and proximity to the town center.

Royal Gorge Bridge and Park, Canon City: Experience adrenaline-pumping thrills and breathtaking views as you walk across North America's highest suspension bridge at Royal Gorge Bridge and Park.

Money-Saving Tip: Purchase tickets online in advance to benefit from discounts and package deals, which may include additional attractions or activities within the park.

Starting Cost: Ticket prices for Royal Gorge Bridge and Park vary depending on the type of admission and any additional activities or attractions included in the package.

Telluride: Discover the charm of a picturesque mountain town in Telluride, where outdoor enthusiasts and culture lovers alike will find plenty to explore.

Money-Saving Tip: Take advantage of free outdoor concerts and events held during the summer months, offering budget-friendly entertainment and opportunities to experience Telluride's vibrant community spirit.

Starting Cost: Admission to outdoor concerts and events in Telluride is typically free of charge, although donations may be encouraged to support local organizations and initiatives.

Black Canyon of the Gunnison National Park: Stand in awe of the dramatic cliffs and narrow canyons carved by the Gunnison River at Black Canyon of the Gunnison National Park.

Money-Saving Tip: Explore the park's viewpoints and hiking trails for free, offering breathtaking vistas and opportunities for outdoor adventure without spending on entrance fees.

Starting Cost: Entrance fees to Black Canyon of the Gunnison National Park vary depending on the season and type of pass, with discounts available for seniors, military personnel, and children.

Colorado Springs: Immerse yourself in Olympic history and cultural attractions in Colorado Springs, home to the U.S. Olympic Training Center and a wealth of museums.

Money-Saving Tip: Look for discounts on guided tours of the Olympic Training Center and consider bundling multiple attractions for savings on admission fees.

Starting Cost: Guided tours of the U.S. Olympic Training Center start at around $15 per person, with discounts available for seniors, military personnel, and children.

Vail: Indulge in world-class skiing and outdoor recreation in Vail, a premier destination for winter sports and alpine adventures.

Money-Saving Tip: Book lodging and lift tickets as part of a package deal offered by resorts and accommodations in Vail for potential savings on accommodations and access to ski slopes.

Starting Cost: Package deals for lodging and lift tickets in Vail vary depending on the season, accommodation type, and duration of stay.

Chautauqua Park, Boulder: Escape to nature and enjoy scenic hiking trails and picnicking in the picturesque setting of Chautauqua Park in Boulder.

Money-Saving Tip: Due to limited parking availability, consider taking public transportation or hiking to Chautauqua Park to avoid parking fees and enjoy a budget-friendly outing in nature.

Starting Cost: Parking fees at Chautauqua Park vary depending on the season and duration of stay, with limited free parking available on a first-come, first-served basis.

Colorado National Monument: Traverse the red rock canyons and scenic overlooks of Colorado National Monument, offering breathtaking vistas and opportunities for outdoor exploration.

Money-Saving Tip: Utilize your America the Beautiful Pass for park entry, granting access to Colorado National Monument and other participating national parks and federal recreational lands.

Starting Cost: Entrance fees to Colorado National Monument vary depending on the season and type of pass, with discounts available for seniors, military personnel, and children.

Durango: Embark on a journey through history aboard the historic Durango and Silverton Narrow Gauge Railroad in Durango, offering scenic rides through Colorado's rugged terrain.

Money-Saving Tip: Check for discounted tickets during special events or for off-peak rides, allowing you to experience the charm of a bygone era at a lower cost.

Starting Cost: Ticket prices for the Durango and Silverton Narrow Gauge Railroad vary depending on the type of ride and any additional services or amenities included.

Estes Park: Gateway to Rocky Mountain National Park, Estes Park offers a charming mountain town experience with access to outdoor adventures and scenic beauty.

Money-Saving Tip: Look for affordable lodging options in Estes Park, including budget-friendly motels, cabins, and campgrounds, for a cost-effective stay near Rocky Mountain National Park.

Starting Cost: Lodging rates in Estes Park vary depending on the season, accommodation type, and proximity to the town center.

Crested Butte: Immerse yourself in outdoor activities and small-town charm in Crested Butte, a hidden gem nestled in the heart of the Rocky Mountains.

Money-Saving Tip: Plan your visit during the summer months to take advantage of free outdoor concerts and festivals, offering budget-friendly entertainment for visitors of all ages.

Starting Cost: Admission to outdoor concerts and festivals in Crested Butte is typically free of charge, with donations often appreciated to support local community initiatives.

Colorado Springs Pioneers Museum: Dive into the rich history and cultural heritage of the Pikes Peak region at the Colorado Springs Pioneers Museum, housed in a historic courthouse building.

Money-Saving Tip: Admission to the Colorado Springs Pioneers Museum is free, offering a budget-friendly opportunity to explore exhibits and artifacts showcasing the area's past.

Starting Cost: Admission to the Colorado Springs Pioneers Museum is free of charge for all visitors, with donations encouraged to support museum operations and programming.

Maroon Bells, Aspen: Capture the beauty of Colorado's iconic Maroon Bells, a pair of towering peaks reflected in serene Maroon Lake, offering breathtaking scenery and photo opportunities.

Money-Saving Tip: Take advantage of shuttle services to Maroon Lake to avoid parking fees at the Maroon Bells Scenic Area, providing convenient and cost-effective transportation to the popular attraction.

Starting Cost: Shuttle tickets to Maroon Lake vary depending on the departure point and season, with discounts available for seniors, military personnel, and children.

Category	Insider Tips
Food	1. Seek out local breweries and brewpubs for affordable eats paired with craft beers.
	2. Look for food trucks and street vendors offering tasty and budget-friendly options at festivals or in urban areas.
	3. Explore farm-to-table restaurants in smaller towns or mountain communities for fresh and seasonal cuisine.
	4. Consider packing a picnic and enjoying meals amidst Colorado's stunning natural scenery.
Accommodation	1. Embrace camping in Colorado's breathtaking national parks and forests for budget-friendly stays.
	2. Look for cozy cabins or vacation rentals in mountain towns for affordable and scenic accommodations.
	3. Consider staying in hostels or guesthouses in cities like Denver or Boulder for budget-friendly lodging.
	4. Utilize platforms like Airbnb or VRBO to find affordable lodging options with local hosts.
Activities	1. Take advantage of free outdoor activities like hiking, biking, and exploring scenic trails and parks.
	2. Visit local farmers' markets or artisanal fairs for unique shopping experiences and local products.
	3. Explore historical sites and museums with low-cost or donation-based entry fees.
	4. Attend cultural festivals and events celebrating Colorado's diverse heritage and communities.
Transport	1. Rent a car for flexibility in exploring Colorado's diverse landscapes and attractions.
	2. Use public transportation options like light rail or buses in cities for affordable and eco-friendly travel.
	3. Look for carpooling opportunities or ride-sharing services for shared transportation costs.
	4. Consider biking or walking in urban areas or on designated trails for an active and budget-friendly way to get around.

Connecticut

1. **Transportation:**

   - **Public Transportation:** Connecticut has an efficient public transportation system, especially along the Metro-North Railroad. Utilize trains and buses for cost-effective travel within the state.

2. **Accommodation:**

   - **Budget-Friendly Luxury Stays:** Explore boutique hotels or charming bed and breakfasts in towns like Mystic, New Haven, or Hartford. Prices can range from $80 to $150 per night for a comfortable stay. Consider booking in advance for better rates.
   - **Historic Inns:** Connecticut is home to many historic inns and lodges. Consider staying in one for a unique and often affordable experience.

3. **Dining:**

   - **Local Cafes and Seafood Shacks:** Connecticut is known for its seafood. Enjoy lobster rolls and clam chowder at local seafood shacks, where meals can range from $15 to $30 per person.
   - **Farm-to-Table Restaurants:** Explore farm-to-table dining experiences, especially in towns like New Haven or Litchfield.

4. **Activities:**

   - **Historic Tours:** Take walking tours of historic areas like the Yale University campus in New Haven or the historic district in Mystic. Some tours may be free or have a nominal fee.
   - **Mystic Seaport:** While admission to Mystic Seaport may be around $29, exploring the charming maritime village and shipyard is worth the cost.
   - **Hiking Trails:** Enjoy hiking in areas like Sleeping Giant State Park or Talcott Mountain State Park. Many trails are free or have a small parking fee.

5. **Entertainment:**

   - **Art Galleries:** Explore art galleries and cultural spaces in cities like New Haven or Hartford. Some may offer free admission or have discounted rates.
   - **Free Concerts and Events:** Check local event calendars for free concerts, outdoor movies, and cultural events happening during your visit.
     Connecticut State Capitol (Hartford): The Connecticut State Capitol offers free guided tours where you can learn about the state's history, government, and architecture. Tours are typically available Monday through Friday.
     Yale University Campus Tours (New Haven): Yale University offers free campus tours led by student guides. You can explore the university's historic buildings, architecture, and grounds while learning about its history and academic programs.
     The Mark Twain House & Museum (Hartford): While admission to The Mark Twain House & Museum may require a fee for access to the house and exhibits, the museum occasionally offers free guided tours or special events. Check their website or contact them directly for tour availability.
     Self-guided Tours of Mystic Seaport Museum (Mystic): While admission to Mystic Seaport Museum may require a fee, they offer free self-guided tours of their

outdoor exhibits, including historic ships, maritime exhibits, and recreated village buildings.

6. Insights and Tips:

- **Connecticut Wine Trail:** Visit local wineries along the Connecticut Wine Trail. Some offer free tastings, and others charge a nominal fee.
- **Festivals and Events:** Plan your visit around local festivals and events, which can provide unique and often free or low-cost experiences.
- **Yale University Campus:** Explore the beautiful architecture and cultural venues on the Yale University campus in New Haven, often free to the public.

Major Towns in Connecticut:

- **Hartford:** The capital city known for its historic architecture, museums, and parks.
- **New Haven:** Home to Yale University, offering a vibrant cultural scene and renowned dining.
- **Mystic:** Famous for Mystic Seaport, a maritime museum, and the Mystic Aquarium.
- **Litchfield:** A charming town known for its historic district and scenic countryside.

Save money on the biggest attractions

Recap

Category	Insider Tips
Food	1. Explore local seafood markets along the Connecticut coast for fresh catches like lobster and oysters.
	2. Visit family-owned diners or cafes in small towns for classic New England fare at reasonable prices.
	3. Attend local farmers' markets for fresh produce, artisanal cheeses, and homemade baked goods.
	4. Look for farm-to-table restaurants and eateries for locally sourced and seasonal dining experiences.
Accommodation	1. Consider staying in historic bed and breakfasts for charming accommodations with personalized service.
	2. Look for boutique hotels or inns in picturesque towns like Mystic or Litchfield for unique stays.
	3. Utilize vacation rental websites to find affordable cottages or apartments for longer stays.
	4. Check for seasonal promotions or mid-week discounts at hotels and resorts for cost-effective stays.
Activities	1. Explore Connecticut's scenic hiking trails in state parks like Sleeping Giant or Devil's Hopyard.
	2. Visit local vineyards and wineries for wine tastings and tours, often offering affordable or free samples.
	3. Attend cultural events and festivals celebrating Connecticut's history, arts, and culinary traditions.

		4. Take advantage of free or low-cost admission days at museums and historical sites throughout the state.
	Transport	1. Utilize public transportation options like trains or buses for convenient travel between cities and towns.
		2. Consider renting a bike or using bike-sharing services in urban areas like New Haven or Hartford for eco-friendly transportation.
		3. Check for discounted ferry fares for scenic trips to destinations like Block Island or Long Island.
		4. Plan day trips or weekend getaways to explore nearby attractions without the need for long-distance travel.

Delaware

Delaware may be one of the smallest states in terms of land area, but it boasts a rich history, beautiful natural landscapes, and a unique blend of urban and rural experiences.

Delaware holds a special place in American history as the first state to ratify the U.S. Constitution on December 7, 1787, earning it the nickname "The First State." It played a pivotal role during the American Revolution and the early years of the United States. Visitors can explore historic sites, such as Dover's Old State House and New Castle's cobblestone streets, to step back in time and learn about the state's colonial past.

Things to Consider:

- **Geographical Diversity**: Delaware may be small, but it offers diverse landscapes. The northern part of the state is known for its urban areas and cultural attractions, while the southern part boasts picturesque beaches along the Atlantic Ocean.
- **Coastal Destination**: Delaware's coastline, particularly around Rehoboth Beach and Bethany Beach, is a popular summer destination with beautiful sandy beaches, boardwalks, and seaside activities. Plan accordingly if you intend to visit during the peak summer season.
- **Tax-Free Shopping**: Delaware is famous for its tax-free shopping. Take advantage of the state's lack of sales tax when shopping for clothing, electronics, and more.

Local Tips:

- **Delaware's Beaches**: Relax and enjoy the scenic beauty of Delaware's beaches. Rehoboth Beach and Bethany Beach are perfect for sunbathing, swimming, and water sports, while Cape Henlopen State Park offers hiking trails and birdwatching.
- **Historic New Castle**: Explore the historic district of New Castle, known for its well-preserved colonial architecture and museums. Take a guided walking tour to learn about the town's rich history.
- **Dover**: Visit the state capital, Dover, and explore attractions like the Delaware State Capitol, the Air Mobility Command Museum, and the Biggs Museum of American Art.
- **Wilmington**: In the northern part of the state, Wilmington offers cultural experiences at the Delaware Art Museum, the Winterthur Museum, and Longwood Gardens, just across the border in Pennsylvania.
- **Delaware State Parks**: Delaware's state parks offer numerous opportunities for outdoor activities, including hiking, camping, and wildlife viewing. Check out places like Brandywine Creek State Park and Killens Pond State Park.
- **Delaware Culinary Scene**: Savor local cuisine, including seafood, crab cakes, and fresh produce, at restaurants throughout the state. Don't miss the opportunity to try Delaware's famous chicken dishes.

1. Transportation:

- **Flights:** Consider flying into Philadelphia International Airport (PHL) or Baltimore/Washington International Airport (BWI) for more competitive airfare. Round-trip tickets can range from $150 to $400, depending on your departure city and time of booking.
- **Public Transportation:** While Delaware's public transportation system is not as extensive as in larger states, options such as DART First State buses serve major cities like Wilmington and Dover. Utilizing public transit can be an affordable way to travel within city limits and to neighboring towns.
- **Car Rental:** Delaware is a small state, and renting a car is convenient for exploring. Prices start at around $30 per day, and booking in advance can help you secure better deals.

2. Accommodation:

- **Budget-Friendly Luxury Stays:** Explore boutique hotels or charming bed and breakfasts in towns like Wilmington or Rehoboth Beach. Prices can range from $80 to $150 per night for a comfortable stay. Consider booking in advance for better rates.
- **Beach Towns:** Coastal areas like Rehoboth Beach and Lewes offer a mix of accommodations, including budget-friendly inns and motels.

3. Dining:

- **Seafood Shacks:** Delaware's coastal location means you can enjoy fresh seafood at affordable prices. Explore seafood shacks for crab cakes and clam chowder, with meals ranging from $15 to $30 per person.
- **Local Cafes:** Enjoy local cafes and diners for breakfast and lunch, offering a taste of Delaware's culinary scene at reasonable prices.

4. Activities:

- **Delaware Beaches:** Relax at the state's popular beaches, such as Rehoboth Beach and Dewey Beach. The beach experience is free, though parking may have a fee.
- **Delaware State Parks:** Explore state parks like Cape Henlopen State Park or Brandywine Creek State Park, offering hiking trails and scenic spots. Entrance fees are generally around $5 per vehicle.
- **Historical Sites:** Visit historical sites like the Hagley Museum and Library in Wilmington. Admission prices vary, but some museums offer discounted rates.

5. Entertainment:

- **Boardwalks:** Stroll along the boardwalks of beach towns like Rehoboth Beach, where you can enjoy free entertainment, street performers, and the lively atmosphere.
- **Live Music:** Check local event calendars for free live music events or outdoor concerts, especially during the summer months.
1. **Legislative Hall Tours (Dover):** Legislative Hall in Dover offers free guided tours where you can learn about Delaware's legislative process, history, and architecture.
2. **Winterthur Museum, Garden & Library (Wilmington):** While admission to Winterthur Museum may require a fee for access to the house, gardens, and

exhibitions, they occasionally offer free guided tours or special events. Check their website or contact them directly for tour availability.
3. **Delaware Art Museum (Wilmington):** While admission to the Delaware Art Museum may require a fee for special exhibitions, the museum occasionally offers free admission days or free guided tours. Check their website or contact them directly for tour availability.
4. **Self-guided Tours of Historic New Castle:** New Castle, Delaware, offers a self-guided walking tour of its historic district, showcasing colonial-era architecture, historic sites, and landmarks. Pick up a map from the local visitor center and explore at your own pace.

•

6. Insights and Tips:

- **Tax-Free Shopping:** Delaware is known for tax-free shopping. Take advantage of shopping opportunities in towns like Wilmington or the Tanger Outlets in Rehoboth Beach.
- **Bike Trails:** Explore Delaware's bike trails, such as the Junction and Breakwater Trail, providing a scenic ride through nature.
- **Local Breweries and Wineries:** Visit local breweries and wineries for tastings. Some places offer free tastings or have nominal fees.

Major Towns in Delaware:

- **Wilmington:** The largest city in Delaware, known for its cultural attractions, museums, and riverfront.
- **Rehoboth Beach:** A popular beach town with a vibrant boardwalk, restaurants, and tax-free shopping.
- **Dover:** The capital city, offering historical sites, museums, and the Dover International Speedway.
- **Lewes:** A charming coastal town with historic architecture, beaches, and a relaxed atmosphere.

Here are the top attractions in Delaware, along with some money-saving tips for visiting each one:

Wilmington: Dive into Delaware's largest city, Wilmington, where museums and cultural attractions await exploration.

Money-Saving Tip: Keep an eye out for free admission days at museums and take advantage of the city's numerous parks for budget-friendly outdoor enjoyment.

Starting Cost: Admission fees to museums and attractions in Wilmington vary; however, many offer discounted rates for students, seniors, and children, with some also providing free admission on select days.

Delaware Beaches: Bask in the sun, sand, and coastal charm of Delaware's renowned beaches, including Rehoboth Beach and Bethany Beach.

Money-Saving Tip: Opt for public beaches, which typically offer free access, and bring along your own beach gear to avoid rental fees.

Starting Cost: Access to public beaches is free; optional fees may apply for parking and amenities.

Dover: Uncover the rich history and vibrant festivals of Delaware's capital city, Dover.

Money-Saving Tip: Attend local events and festivals, many of which offer free admission or low-cost entertainment options.

Starting Cost: Admission fees for festivals and events in Dover vary; however, some may offer free admission or reduced rates for certain activities.

Brandywine Valley: Immerse yourself in the picturesque landscapes, historic homes, and art collections of the Brandywine Valley.

Money-Saving Tip: Look for combination tickets that offer access to multiple attractions within the Brandywine Valley at a discounted rate.

Starting Cost: Admission fees to individual attractions in the Brandywine Valley vary; however, combination tickets often provide cost savings for visitors.

Cape Henlopen State Park, Lewes: Embrace outdoor adventures and pristine beaches at Cape Henlopen State Park.

Money-Saving Tip: Consider camping in the park's campgrounds for an affordable overnight stay amidst the park's natural beauty.

Starting Cost: Camping fees at Cape Henlopen State Park vary depending on the campground and amenities offered.

Delaware Art Museum, Wilmington: Delight in a diverse collection of artworks at the Delaware Art Museum.

Money-Saving Tip: Look for discounted admission rates for students and seniors, or consider visiting on free admission days if available.

Starting Cost: General admission prices for the Delaware Art Museum vary; however, discounts are often available for students, seniors, and military personnel.

Nemours Mansion and Gardens, Wilmington: Step into a world of opulence at Nemours Mansion and Gardens, a stunning French-style estate.

Money-Saving Tip: Take advantage of free community days or special promotions to explore the mansion and gardens at a reduced cost.

Starting Cost: Admission prices for Nemours Mansion and Gardens vary depending on the tour option chosen, with discounts available for certain groups.

Hagley Museum and Library, Wilmington: Discover the fascinating history of industry and innovation at the Hagley Museum and Library.

Money-Saving Tip: Look for combination tickets that include admission to Hagley Museum and Library along with other nearby attractions for added value.

Starting Cost: Admission fees to Hagley Museum and Library vary depending on the tour option selected and any additional attractions included in combination tickets.

Lewes: Experience the charm of a coastal town with a rich history in Lewes.

Money-Saving Tip: Embark on a self-guided walking tour of Lewes' historic district to explore the town's heritage and architecture at no cost.

Starting Cost: Sightseeing in Lewes is typically free; optional fees may apply for guided tours and certain attractions.

Delaware Seashore State Park: Indulge in water-based activities and enjoy the natural beauty of Delaware Seashore State Park.

Money-Saving Tip: Bring your own watercraft or rent one locally for a budget-friendly day of exploring the park's coastal wonders.

Starting Cost: Entrance fees to Delaware Seashore State Park vary depending on the season and type of pass, with discounts available for certain groups.

Rehoboth Beach Boardwalk: Take a leisurely stroll along the iconic Rehoboth Beach Boardwalk, lined with shops, eateries, and amusements.

Money-Saving Tip: Soak in the boardwalk's lively atmosphere and enjoy window-shopping without spending on attractions.

Starting Cost: Access to Rehoboth Beach Boardwalk is free; optional fees may apply for rides, games, and food purchases.

Winterthur Museum, Garden and Library: Immerse yourself in American decorative arts and lush gardens at Winterthur Museum, Garden and Library.

Money-Saving Tip: Look for discounts on admission, particularly for students and children, to explore the museum and gardens without breaking the bank.

Starting Cost: General admission prices for Winterthur Museum, Garden and Library vary; however, discounts are often available for students, seniors, and children.

Fenwick Island State Park: Relax on the pristine shores of Fenwick Island State Park, known for its uncrowded beaches and tranquil ambiance.

Money-Saving Tip: Visit during the off-peak season for lower park fees and quieter beach experiences.

Starting Cost: Entrance fees to Fenwick Island State Park vary depending on the season and type of pass, with discounts available for certain groups.

Brandywine Creek State Park, Wilmington: Enjoy outdoor recreation and scenic trails at Brandywine Creek State Park.

Money-Saving Tip: Pack a picnic and spend a day in the park, taking advantage of the free amenities and natural beauty.

Starting Cost: Entrance fees to Brandywine Creek State Park vary depending on the season and type of pass, with discounts available for certain groups.

Bethany Beach: Escape to the family-friendly atmosphere of Bethany Beach, offering sun, surf, and sand.

Money-Saving Tip: Look for free family events and entertainment held during the summer months, providing budget-friendly fun for visitors of all ages.

Starting Cost: Access to public areas of Bethany Beach is free; optional fees may apply for parking and amenities.

John Dickinson Plantation, Dover: Step back in time and learn about colonial history at the John Dickinson Plantation, once home to the Founding Father.

Money-Saving Tip: Admission to the John Dickinson Plantation is free of charge, with guided tours available at no extra cost.

Starting Cost: Admission to the John Dickinson Plantation is free for all visitors, with guided tours offered at select times.

Indian River Inlet: Relax and unwind by the picturesque Indian River Inlet, offering opportunities for fishing, swimming, and soaking up the sun.

Money-Saving Tip: Bring your own fishing gear for an affordable day of angling along the inlet's shores.

Starting Cost: Access to Indian River Inlet is free; optional fees may apply for parking and amenities.

Trap Pond State Park, Laurel: Paddle through scenic cypress swamps and immerse yourself in the natural beauty of Trap Pond State Park.

Money-Saving Tip: Rent a canoe or kayak from the park for a budget-friendly day on the water, exploring the park's waterways and wildlife.

Starting Cost: Rental fees for canoes and kayaks at Trap Pond State Park vary depending on the duration of use.

Zwaanendael Museum, Lewes: Delve into Delaware's colonial history at the Zwaanendael Museum, housed in a striking Dutch-inspired building.

Money-Saving Tip: Admission to the Zwaanendael Museum is free, offering a cost-effective opportunity to explore the region's cultural heritage.

Starting Cost: Admission to the Zwaanendael Museum is free for all visitors, with donations appreciated to support museum operations.

Bombay Hook National Wildlife Refuge, Smyrna: Embark on a wildlife adventure at Bombay Hook National Wildlife Refuge, home to a diverse array of migratory birds and wildlife.

Money-Saving Tip: Bring along binoculars for wildlife watching and enjoy the refuge's natural beauty without any entrance fees.

Starting Cost: Entrance to Bombay Hook National Wildlife Refuge is free for all visitors, making it an affordable destination for nature enthusiasts.

Category	Insider Tips
Food	1. Dive into Delaware's seafood scene by visiting local seafood shacks along the coast for fresh catches.
	2. Explore farmers' markets in towns like Wilmington or Lewes for locally grown produce and artisanal goods.
	3. Enjoy a Delaware classic, the "Dime Store Burger," at local diners for an affordable and tasty meal.
	4. Look for food trucks at local events and festivals for unique and budget-friendly dining options.
Accommodation	1. Consider staying in cozy bed and breakfasts in charming towns like Rehoboth Beach or New Castle.

	2. Look for budget-friendly motels or guesthouses in smaller towns away from tourist hotspots.
	3. Explore camping options in state parks like Cape Henlopen or Trap Pond for affordable outdoor stays.
	4. Use discount websites or apps to find deals on accommodations in
Activities	1. Spend a day at Delaware's pristine beaches, like Rehoboth or Bethany Beach, for sun and relaxation.
	2. Visit historic sites like the Hagley Museum or Fort Delaware for a glimpse into Delaware's past.
	3. Explore Delaware's scenic trails for hiking or biking, such as the Junction and Breakwater Trail.
	4. Attend local events and festivals, like the Rehoboth Beach Jazz Festival or the Delaware State Fair.
Transport	1. Rent a bike to explore Delaware's coastal towns and scenic trails for an eco-friendly way to get around.
	2. Utilize public transportation options in cities like Wilmington or Dover to save on parking and gas.
	3. Consider carpooling with fellow travelers or using ride-sharing services for shared transportation costs.
	4. Plan your visit during off-peak times to avoid crowds and potentially find better deals on transportation.

Florida

Florida's history is a fascinating mix of indigenous cultures, Spanish explorers, and diverse communities. From St. Augustine, the oldest continuously inhabited European-established settlement in the continental United States, to the impact of Cuban and Caribbean influences in Miami, Florida's history has shaped its unique character.

Things to Consider:

- **Climate:** Embrace the tropical climate, but be prepared for occasional rain showers, especially during the summer months. Sunscreen, hats, and light clothing are your best companions.
- **Theme Park Magic:** If you're heading to Orlando, prepare for the magic of Walt Disney World, Universal Studios, and other world-renowned theme parks. Plan your visit to make the most of these immersive experiences.
- **Wildlife Encounters:** Florida is home to a diverse array of wildlife, including alligators, manatees, and an abundance of bird species. Respect their habitats and enjoy the unique opportunities for wildlife encounters.

Local Tips:

- **Beach Bliss:** Explore Florida's stunning beaches. From the white sands of Clearwater Beach to the lively atmosphere of Miami's South Beach, each coastline offers a different vibe and experience.
- **Everglades Adventure:** Immerse yourself in the unique ecosystem of the Everglades. Consider taking an airboat tour to witness the beauty of this vast wetland and encounter its resident wildlife.
- **Cuban Cuisine in Miami:** Indulge in the vibrant culinary scene, especially the Cuban cuisine in Miami's Little Havana. Try the delicious pastelitos, Cuban sandwiches, and strong Cuban coffee.

Must-Visit Places:

- **Walt Disney World:** Experience the magic of the most iconic theme park in the world, complete with enchanting rides, shows, and character encounters.
- **Key West:** Explore the laid-back atmosphere, colorful architecture, and rich history of the southernmost point in the continental U.S.
- **Everglades National Park:** Discover the unique ecosystem of the Everglades, home to a variety of wildlife and scenic landscapes.

1. Transportation:

- **Flights:** Look for flights to major airports like Miami International Airport (MIA) or Orlando International Airport (MCO). Round-trip tickets can vary but may range from $150 to $500, depending on your departure city and the time of booking.
- **Car Rental:** Renting a car is recommended for exploring Florida's diverse regions. Prices start at around $30 per day, and booking in advance can secure better deals.

2. **Accommodation:**

- **Budget-Friendly Luxury Stays:** Explore boutique hotels or guesthouses in cities like Miami, Orlando, or St. Augustine. Prices can range from $80 to $150 per night for a comfortable stay. Consider booking in advance or during off-peak seasons for better rates.
- **Hostels:** Hostels are a great option for budget travelers in Florida, especially in cities with high tourist traffic. Check out hostels like Hostel Fish in Miami Beach, Hostelling International Orlando, or Jazz Hostel in Miami for affordable dormitory-style accommodations.
- **Campgrounds:** Florida's state parks and national forests offer affordable camping options in scenic settings. Consider camping at places like Bahia Honda State Park in the Florida Keys, Ocala National Forest, or Jonathan Dickinson State Park for a budget-friendly outdoor experience.
- **Budget Motels:** Look for budget motels along major highways or in smaller towns. Motels like Econo Lodge, Rodeway Inn, or Super 8 offer basic amenities and affordable rates for travelers on a budget.

- 3. Dining:
- **U-Pick Farms:** Many farms in Florida offer "U-Pick" opportunities, where you can harvest your own fruits, such as strawberries, blueberries, and citrus fruits, at a lower cost than buying them pre-picked. This can be a fun and cost-effective way to enjoy fresh produce while supporting local farmers.
- **Local Eateries:** Enjoy diverse cuisine at local eateries, especially in areas with cultural influences like Little Havana in Miami or the Mills 50 District in Orlando. Meals can range from $10 to $30 per person.
- **Food Markets:** Explore food markets such as Miami's Little Havana Market or Orlando's East End Market for affordable and delicious options.

4. **Activities:**

- **Beach Days:** Florida is famous for its beaches. Enjoy a day at free or low-cost public beaches. Some popular ones include South Beach in Miami or Clearwater Beach near Tampa.
- **State Parks:** Explore Florida's state parks, offering hiking trails, wildlife viewing, and natural beauty. Entrance fees are generally around $5 to $10 per vehicle.
- **Everglades National Park:** While the park has an entrance fee of $30 per vehicle, experiencing the unique ecosystem of the Everglades is a must.

5. **Entertainment:**

- **Free Events:** Check local event calendars for free concerts, art walks, or cultural events happening during your visit. Cities like Miami and Orlando often host free or low-cost events.

- **Street Performers:** Enjoy street performers in places like Key West's Mallory Square or Orlando's Universal CityWalk.
6. **Florida State Capitol (Tallahassee):** The Florida State Capitol offers free guided tours where you can learn about the state's government, history, and architecture. Tours are typically available Monday through Friday.
7. **Art Walks and Tours:** Many cities in Florida, such as Miami, Orlando, and St. Petersburg, host regular art walks and tours where you can explore galleries, studios, and public art installations for free. Check local event listings for upcoming art walks in your area.
8. **Everglades National Park (Homestead):** While entrance to Everglades National Park may require a fee, the park offers free ranger-led programs and walks, including nature walks, birding tours, and talks about the park's ecosystem and wildlife. Check the park's schedule for upcoming programs.

6. Insights and Tips:

- **Theme Park Tips:** If visiting theme parks in Orlando, consider single-day tickets and avoid peak times. Some parks also offer discounted rates for Florida residents.
- **Nature Reserves:** Visit nature reserves like Corkscrew Swamp Sanctuary or Big Cypress National Preserve for a chance to see Florida's unique wildlife.
- **Spring Training Games:** If visiting during baseball season, consider attending spring training games, which are often more affordable than regular-season games.

Major Towns in Florida:

- **Miami:** Known for its vibrant nightlife, cultural diversity, and beautiful beaches.
- **Orlando:** Home to major theme parks like Walt Disney World and Universal Studios.
- **Tampa:** Offers a mix of cultural attractions, waterfront parks, and historic neighborhoods.
- **St. Augustine:** The oldest city in the U.S., known for its historic architecture and Spanish influence.

Florida, along with some money-saving tips for visiting each one:

Walt Disney World Resort, Orlando: Experience magical theme parks.

- Money-Saving Tip: Purchase multi-day tickets for a lower cost per day and consider value season visits.

Miami Beach: Relax on iconic South Beach and explore art deco architecture.

- Money-Saving Tip: Enjoy free beach access and take advantage of happy hour specials at nearby restaurants.

Everglades National Park: Discover unique wetlands and wildlife.

- Money-Saving Tip: Bring your own binoculars and take advantage of ranger-led programs.

Universal Orlando Resort: Enjoy thrilling rides and entertainment.

- Money-Saving Tip: Buy tickets online for discounts and explore multi-park options.

Key West: Experience a laid-back island atmosphere.

- Money-Saving Tip: Visit during the off-peak season for lower accommodation rates.

Kennedy Space Center Visitor Complex, Merritt Island: Explore space history and see rocket launches.

- Money-Saving Tip: Check the launch schedule and plan your visit around a rocket launch for a unique experience.

Tampa Bay Area: Enjoy a mix of cultural attractions and outdoor adventures.

- Money-Saving Tip: Look for combo tickets to visit multiple attractions at a reduced cost.

Fort Lauderdale: Relax on beautiful beaches and explore waterways.

- Money-Saving Tip: Consider taking water taxis for transportation and scenic views.

St. Augustine: Discover historic sites and the nation's oldest city.

- Money-Saving Tip: Walk through the historic district and enjoy free attractions like Castillo de San Marcos.

Naples: Experience upscale dining, shopping, and Gulf Coast beaches.

- Money-Saving Tip: Explore nature preserves and parks for free or low-cost outdoor activities.

Florida Keys: Enjoy island life and water-based activities.

- Money-Saving Tip: Consider camping in state parks for budget-friendly lodging.

Miami: Explore diverse neighborhoods and cultural attractions.

- Money-Saving Tip: Take advantage of free art galleries and events in Wynwood.

Gulf Islands National Seashore: Relax on pristine beaches and go boating.

- Money-Saving Tip: Bring your own beach gear and rent watercraft locally for cost savings.

Tallahassee: Discover Florida's state capital and historic sites.

- Money-Saving Tip: Visit free attractions like the Florida Historic Capitol Museum.

Clearwater Beach: Relax on award-winning beaches and enjoy water sports.

- Money-Saving Tip: Look for affordable accommodations away from the beachfront.

Panama City Beach: Experience family-friendly attractions and outdoor fun.

- Money-Saving Tip: Visit amusement parks during discounted hours or days.

Naples Botanical Garden: Stroll through beautiful gardens and tropical landscapes.

- Money-Saving Tip: Look for discounts on admission for seniors and children.

Ocala National Forest: Explore outdoor activities in a natural setting.

- Money-Saving Tip: Camp in the forest's campgrounds for budget-friendly stays.

Biscayne National Park: Snorkel, boat, and explore coral reefs.

- Money-Saving Tip: Bring your own snorkeling gear and rent a boat for a group to share costs.

Downtown Orlando: Enjoy entertainment, dining, and Lake Eola Park.

- Money-Saving Tip: Attend free events and concerts in the downtown area.

Category	Insider Tips
Food	1. Head to local seafood markets for fresh catches like grouper, shrimp, and stone crab at affordable prices.
	2. Explore Cuban bakeries or cafes in cities like Miami for authentic and budget-friendly pastries and sandwiches.
	3. Visit farmers' markets for tropical fruits like mangoes, papayas, and pineapples, often sold at lower prices.
	4. Enjoy happy hour deals at waterfront bars and restaurants for discounted drinks and appetizers with a view.
Accommodation	1. Consider renting a vacation home or condo through platforms like Airbnb or Vrbo for more space and amenities at lower rates.
	2. Look for budget-friendly motels or guesthouses in smaller beach towns like St. Pete Beach or Cocoa Beach.
	3. Utilize hotel booking websites to find last-minute deals or discounts on accommodations in popular tourist areas.
	4. Camp at state parks or beachside campgrounds for a more affordable and scenic lodging option in Florida.
Activities	1. Explore Florida's natural wonders by visiting state parks and preserves with hiking trails, springs, and wildlife viewing.
	2. Take advantage of free beach access at public beaches along Florida's coastline for swimming, sunbathing, and picnicking.
	3. Visit local museums on designated free admission days or opt for combo tickets to save on entry fees to multiple attractions.
	4. Attend local festivals and events celebrating Florida's cultural diversity, music, and food, often featuring free or low-cost entertainment.
Transport	1. Rent a car for flexibility in exploring Florida's diverse destinations, with options for budget-friendly rentals available.
	2. Use ridesharing apps or public transportation in major cities like Miami or Orlando to avoid parking fees and traffic congestion.
	3. Look for discounted theme park tickets or multi-day passes for attractions like Disney World, Universal Studios, or SeaWorld.

4. Take advantage of scenic drives along Florida's coastlines and through its lush landscapes for a budget-friendly way to see the state.

Georgia

The Peach State, a place where history, culture, and Southern hospitality blend seamlessly. Georgia, located in the southeastern region of the United States, offers visitors a diverse range of experiences, from vibrant cities to serene natural landscapes.

Georgia is steeped in history, known for being one of the original 13 colonies and the fourth state to ratify the U.S. Constitution in 1788. The state played a significant role in the American Civil War, with several key battles taking place here. Visitors can explore historic sites, including Savannah's cobblestone streets, Atlanta's Civil Rights landmarks, and the antebellum architecture in places like Macon and Augusta.

Things to Consider:

- **Geographical Diversity**: Georgia offers a diverse range of landscapes, from the Appalachian Mountains in the north to the coastal plains in the south. Be prepared for varying climates and activities depending on the region you visit.
- **Culinary Delights**: Georgia is known for its Southern cuisine. Don't miss out on classic dishes like fried chicken, peach cobbler, and shrimp and grits. You'll also find a thriving food scene with a blend of traditional and innovative restaurants.
- **Outdoor Activities**: If you enjoy outdoor adventures, Georgia has plenty to offer, including hiking in the Appalachian Trail, exploring the Okefenokee Swamp, or boating along the coast.

Local Tips:

- **Savannah's Historic District**: Visit Savannah's historic district, known for its charming squares, historic homes, and Spanish moss-draped trees. Take a stroll along River Street and enjoy the city's vibrant art scene.
- **Atlanta**: Explore Atlanta, the state's capital and a major cultural and economic hub. Visit the Martin Luther King Jr. National Historic Site, the Georgia Aquarium, the Atlanta Botanical Garden, and the World of Coca-Cola.
- **Blue Ridge Mountains**: If you're a nature enthusiast, head to the Blue Ridge Mountains in the northern part of the state. Enjoy hiking, waterfalls, and the picturesque beauty of the area.
- **Tybee Island**: For a beach getaway, consider visiting Tybee Island, located near Savannah. It offers sandy shores, water sports, and a relaxed coastal atmosphere.
- **Music Scene**: Georgia has a rich music heritage, particularly in Atlanta, known for hip-hop and R&B, and Macon, famous for its connection to Southern rock. Explore music venues and museums to learn about the state's musical legacy.
- **Plantations and Historic Homes**: Tour historic plantations like the Wormsloe Historic Site and visit stately homes such as the Swan House in Atlanta to gain insight into Georgia's past.
- **Athens**: Home to the University of Georgia, Athens has a lively arts and music scene, along with historic sites and vibrant college town energy.

1. **Transportation:**

   - **Flights:** Look for flights to major airports like Hartsfield-Jackson Atlanta International Airport (ATL) or Savannah/Hilton Head International Airport (SAV). Round-trip tickets can vary but may range from $200 to $500, depending on your departure city and the time of booking.
   - **Car Rental:** Renting a car is recommended for exploring Georgia's diverse landscapes. Prices start at around $30 per day, and booking in advance can secure better deals.

2. **Accommodation:**

   - **Budget-Friendly Luxury Stays:** Explore boutique hotels or historic inns in cities like Atlanta, Savannah, or Athens. Prices can range from $80 to $150 per night for a comfortable stay. Consider booking in advance or during off-peak seasons for better rates.**Budget Hotels:** Look for budget-friendly hotels in cities like Atlanta, Savannah, or Augusta. Options such as Motel 6, Red Roof Inn, or Comfort Inn offer comfortable stays at reasonable prices in various locations across the state.
   - **Hostels:** Hostels are a great option for budget travelers in Georgia, especially in cities with high tourist traffic. Check out hostels like HI Atlanta Hostel, Savannah Backpackers Inn, or Atlanta Hostel & BNB for affordable dormitory-style accommodations.
   - **Campgrounds:** Georgia's state parks and national forests offer affordable camping options in scenic settings. Consider camping at places like Cloudland Canyon State Park, Vogel State Park, or Chattahoochee-Oconee National Forest for a budget-friendly outdoor experience.

   - 3. Dining:
   - **Local Eateries:** Enjoy Southern cuisine at local eateries. From barbecue to shrimp and grits, meals can range from $10 to $30 per person.
   - **Farm-to-Table Restaurants:** Explore farm-to-table dining experiences, particularly in cities like Atlanta or Athens.

4. **Activities:**

   - **Historic Districts:** Explore the historic districts in cities like Savannah and Atlanta. Walking tours may have a small fee or are sometimes offered free of charge.
   - **State Parks:** Visit Georgia's state parks, such as Tallulah Gorge State Park or Amicalola Falls State Park, for hiking trails and scenic beauty. Entrance fees are generally around $5 to $10 per vehicle.
   - **Cumberland Island:** While there is a ferry fee to access Cumberland Island, the natural beauty, historic sites, and wild horses make it worthwhile.

5. **Entertainment:**

   - **Live Music:** Enjoy live music scenes in cities like Athens or Atlanta. Some venues offer free or affordable shows, especially in areas with a vibrant music culture.
   - **Art Galleries:** Explore art galleries and cultural spaces in cities like Savannah, where some may offer free admission or have discounted rates.
   Georgia State Capitol (Atlanta): The Georgia State Capitol offers free guided tours where you can learn about the state's government, history, and architecture. Tours are typically available Monday through Friday.

Martin Luther King Jr. National Historic Site (Atlanta): While admission to the historic site's visitor center may be free, guided tours of Dr. King's birth home are offered on a first-come, first-served basis and are also free of charge. The tour gives insights into Dr. King's early life and the civil rights movement.

Savannah Historic District Walking Tours: While not always guided, Savannah's Historic District offers free self-guided walking tours where you can explore its cobblestone streets, parks, and historic homes. Pick up a map from the visitor center and enjoy the city's beauty at your own pace.

Centennial Olympic Park (Atlanta): Centennial Olympic Park in downtown Atlanta offers free self-guided tours where you can learn about the park's history, the 1996 Olympic Games, and enjoy its fountains, monuments, and green spaces.

Fort Pulaski National Monument (Savannah): While there may be a fee for entrance to the national monument, Fort Pulaski offers occasional free guided tours led by park rangers. Check their schedule for upcoming tours.

6. Insights and Tips:

- **Georgia Wine Country:** Explore Georgia's wine country in areas like Dahlonega. Some wineries offer free tastings, and others may charge a nominal fee.
- **Free Events:** Check local event calendars for free festivals, markets, or outdoor events happening during your visit.
- **Savannah's River Street:** Enjoy the charm of River Street in Savannah, lined with shops, restaurants, and historic buildings.

Major Towns in Georgia:

- **Atlanta:** The capital city known for its cultural attractions, diverse neighborhoods, and vibrant food scene.
- **Savannah:** Famous for its well-preserved historic district, cobblestone streets, and Southern charm.
- **Athens:** Home to the University of Georgia, offering a lively atmosphere with music, art, and college town vibes.
- **Dahlonega:** Located in the North Georgia mountains, known for its wineries and scenic landscapes.

Here are the top attractions in Georgia, along with some money-saving tips for visiting each one:

Atlanta: Atlanta CityPASS starts at $76 for adults and $61 for children (ages 3-12), providing access to five top attractions over a 9-day period.

Savannah: Free walking tours are available, while optional paid tours may range from $20 to $40 per person depending on the provider and the duration of the tour.

Chattahoochee-Oconee National Forest: Camping fees in Chattahoochee-Oconee National Forest campgrounds typically range from $12 to $30 per night, depending on the campground and any additional amenities provided.

Stone Mountain Park: Daily parking at Stone Mountain Park starts at $20 per vehicle, while attraction passes start at $29.95 for adults and $24.95 for children (ages 3-11) when purchased online in advance.

Savannah Historic District: Admission prices to museums and historic sites in the Savannah Historic District vary, but many offer discounted rates for seniors, students, and military personnel. Some sites may offer free admission during specific hours or on certain days.

Cumberland Island National Seashore: The cost of camping at Cumberland Island National Seashore is $10 per person per night, in addition to the cost of ferry transportation to the island, which starts at $28 round trip for adults.

Augusta: Accommodation prices in Augusta vary depending on the time of year and proximity to tournament venues, with hotel rates typically ranging from $100 to $300 per night during the Masters Tournament.

Tybee Island: Accommodation prices on Tybee Island vary depending on the time of year and the proximity to the beach, with hotel rates typically ranging from $100 to $300 per night.

Okefenokee Swamp: Guided boat tour prices at Okefenokee Swamp vary depending on the duration and type of tour selected, with rates starting at around $25 per person for a 90-minute guided boat tour.

Athens: Free concerts and events on the University of Georgia campus are available throughout the year, while optional costs may include parking fees and purchases made at the event.

Macon: Admission prices to events and festivals in Macon vary depending on the event and any special activities included, with some events offering free admission and others charging fees for entry.

Columbus: Entrance to Columbus Riverwalk and outdoor activities are typically free, with optional costs for equipment rentals or guided tours.

Dahlonega: Wine tasting fees at wineries in Dahlonega vary depending on the vineyard and any additional experiences included, with some wineries offering complimentary tastings and others charging a fee.

Jekyll Island: Parking pass prices for Jekyll Island vary depending on the duration of the visit, with daily passes starting at $8 per vehicle.

Albany: Admission prices to attractions in Albany vary, but many offer discounted rates for seniors, students, and military personnel. Some attractions may offer free admission during specific hours or on certain days.

Callaway Gardens, Pine Mountain: Admission prices to Callaway Gardens vary depending on the time of year and any additional experiences included, with daily rates starting at $25 for adults and $15 for children (ages 6-12).

Helen: Admission prices to attractions in Helen vary, with some attractions offering free admission and others charging a fee. Optional activities such as guided tours or special events may have additional costs.

Columbus RiverCenter for the Performing Arts: Ticket prices for performances at the Columbus RiverCenter for the Performing Arts vary depending on the show and any special promotions available, with rates typically ranging from $20 to $50 per ticket.

Amicalola Falls State Park: Entrance fees to Amicalola Falls State Park vary depending on the type of pass and any additional amenities, with rates starting at $5 per vehicle for a daily parking pass.

RECAP:

Category	Insider Tips
Food	1. Indulge in Southern comfort food at local diners or "meat-and-three" restaurants for authentic flavors at affordable prices.
	2. Visit local farmers' markets for Georgia-grown produce and artisanal goods, supporting local farmers and enjoying fresh ingredients.
	3. Explore Atlanta's diverse food scene in neighborhoods like Buford Highway for international cuisines at budget-friendly prices.
	4. Look for barbecue joints and seafood shacks for mouthwatering dishes without breaking the bank.
Accommodation	1. Stay in charming bed and breakfasts or historic inns in Savannah or small towns like Dahlonega for a unique and budget-friendly experience.
	2. Consider camping in Georgia's state parks or national forests for affordable outdoor accommodations amidst nature.
	3. Utilize booking websites to find deals and discounts on hotels and accommodations in cities like Atlanta and Athens.
	4. Look for accommodations with kitchenettes or complimentary breakfast to save on dining costs during your stay.
Activities	1. Explore Georgia's scenic landscapes and outdoor adventures, including hiking trails in the North Georgia mountains and coastal
	2. Visit historic sites and museums with free or discounted admission, such as the Martin Luther King Jr. National Historic Site in Atlanta.
	3. Attend local festivals and events celebrating Georgia's music, arts, and culture, often offering affordable or free entertainment.
	4. Take advantage of Georgia's rich history and heritage by exploring antebellum homes, plantations, and Civil War sites on a budget.
Transport	1. Use MARTA, Atlanta's public transit system, to navigate the city and save on parking and gas costs.
	2. Consider renting a car for day trips to destinations outside of Atlanta or for exploring rural areas and scenic byways.

	3. Look for ride-sharing services or carpooling opportunities when traveling with friends or attending events to split transportation costs.
	4. Opt for eco-friendly transportation options like biking or walking in pedestrian-friendly areas like Atlanta's BeltLine or Savannah's historic

Hawaii

Hawaii's history is deeply rooted in Polynesian culture, with the islands being settled by voyagers from the Marquesas Islands around 1,500 years ago. Captain James Cook's arrival in the late 18th century marked the beginning of Western influence. Hawaii's rich history, including its monarchy and eventual annexation by the United States, has shaped the unique cultural blend found in the islands today.

Things to Consider:

- **Island Hopping:** Hawaii is an archipelago of diverse islands, each with its own distinct character. Consider exploring more than one island to truly experience the variety of landscapes, activities, and cultures.
- **Respect for Culture:** Embrace the aloha spirit and respect the local customs and traditions. Learning a few words in Hawaiian, such as "aloha" (hello/goodbye) and "mahalo" (thank you), goes a long way.
- **Weather Variability:** While Hawaii generally enjoys a tropical climate, the weather can vary. Be prepared for occasional rain showers, especially in certain regions. Sunscreen, light clothing, and comfortable footwear are essentials.

Local Tips:

- **Snorkeling and Surfing:** Dive into the vibrant marine life by snorkeling in Hanauma Bay or catching some waves on the North Shore of Oahu. Hawaii's waters offer incredible opportunities for both beginners and experienced enthusiasts.
-

1. Transportation:

- **Flights:** Look for flights to major airports like Honolulu International Airport (HNL) on Oahu or Kahului Airport (OGG) on Maui. Round-trip tickets can vary but may range from $100 to $800, depending on your departure city and the time of booking.
- **Inter-Island Flights:** If you plan to visit multiple islands, consider inter-island flights, which can range from $50 to $150 per leg.
- **Public Transportation**: The bus system, operated by Oahu's TheBus and Hawaii's Hele-On Bus, offers affordable transportation on several islands. While routes may be limited outside of urban areas, it's a budget-friendly way to explore the islands' main attractions.
- **Walking and Biking**: Many areas in Hawaii, particularly in tourist areas like Waikiki and Lahaina, are pedestrian-friendly. Walking or biking can be enjoyable ways to explore local neighborhoods, beaches, and scenic areas.
- **Ridesharing Services**: Uber and Lyft operate on the major islands of Oahu, Maui, Hawaii (the Big Island), and Kauai. While they may not be the cheapest option, they can be convenient for shorter trips or when public transportation is limited.
-

2. Accommodation:

- **Budget-Friendly Options:** Look for budget-friendly accommodations such as hostels, guesthouses, or vacation rentals on platforms like Airbnb. Prices can range from $50 to $150 per night, depending on the island and location.
- **Camping:** Hawaii's state parks offer affordable camping options in stunning natural settings. Consider camping at places like Oahu's Malaekahana Beach Campground, Maui's Hosmer Grove Campground, or Kauai's Na Pali Coast State Park for a budget-friendly outdoor experience.
- **Budget Motels:** Look for budget motels along major highways or in smaller towns. Motels like Maui Beach Hotel, Kauai Palms Hotel, or Kona Tiki Hotel offer basic amenities and affordable rates for travelers on a budget.

3. Dining:

- **Local Markets:** Explore local farmers' markets for fresh produce and affordable meals. Enjoy local specialties like poke bowls or plate lunches, which can cost between $10 and $20.
- **Food Trucks:** Hawaii has a vibrant food truck scene, offering a variety of cuisines at reasonable prices.
- **Fish Markets**: Take advantage of Hawaii's abundant seafood by shopping at local fish markets. Buying fish directly from fishermen or seafood markets can often be more affordable than purchasing it from supermarkets. Look for local varieties of fish and seafood, which may be less expensive than imported options.
- **Ethnic Grocery Stores**: Hawaii's diverse population means you can find a wide range of ethnic grocery stores offering affordable ingredients and specialty items. These stores often have lower prices than mainstream supermarkets and provide access to unique ingredients for cooking diverse cuisines.
- **Food Waste Reduction Apps:** Consider using apps like Too Good To Go or OLIO, which connect consumers with surplus food from local restaurants, bakeries, and grocery stores at discounted prices, reducing food waste and saving you money.

4. Activities:

- **Beach Days:** Enjoy Hawaii's beautiful beaches, which are free to access. Snorkeling gear can be rented for a small fee, or you can bring your own.
- **Hiking Trails:** Explore the islands' lush landscapes through hiking trails. Many trails, like the Pipiwai Trail in Maui or Diamond Head Summit Trail in Oahu, are free or have a small entrance fee.
- **Hawaii State Capitol (Honolulu):** The Hawaii State Capitol offers free guided tours where you can learn about the state's government, history, and architecture. Tours are typically available Monday through Friday.
- **Waikiki Historic Trail (Honolulu):** The Waikiki Historic Trail is a self-guided walking tour that explores significant historical and cultural sites in Waikiki. You can pick up a map from the visitor center and explore at your own pace for free.
- **Hiking Trails:** Hawaii offers numerous hiking trails with breathtaking views of nature and landscapes. While not guided, many trails are free to access, such as Diamond Head State Monument on Oahu or the Manoa Falls Trail. Be sure to research trails suitable for your skill level and follow safety guidelines.

5. Entertainment:

- **Hula Shows:** Attend free hula shows often hosted at shopping centers or cultural events. These performances provide insight into Hawaiian traditions.
- **Sunset Viewing:** Enjoy breathtaking sunsets, especially on the west-facing beaches. It's a luxurious experience that comes at no cost.

6. Insights and Tips:

- **Travel Off-Peak:** Consider traveling during the off-peak season to find more affordable accommodations and flights.
- **Snorkel Rentals:** Instead of joining expensive snorkeling tours, rent snorkeling gear and explore the coral reefs close to the shore.
- **Free Cultural Events:** Check local event calendars for free cultural events, festivals, or hula performances happening during your visit.

Major Islands in Hawaii:

- **Oahu:** Home to Honolulu and Waikiki Beach, offering a mix of urban and natural attractions.
- **Maui:** Known for its diverse landscapes, including the Road to Hana, Haleakalā National Park, and beautiful beaches.
- **Kauai:** Often referred to as the "Garden Isle," known for its lush greenery, Waimea Canyon, and the Na Pali Coast.
- **Big Island (Hawaii):** Offers diverse climates, active volcanoes in Hawai'i Volcanoes National Park, and black sand beaches.

Here are the top attractions in Hawaii, along with some money-saving tips for visiting each one:

Hawaii Volcanoes National Park, Big Island: Witness active volcanoes and unique landscapes.

- Money-Saving Tip: Purchase a National Park Pass for access to multiple parks, including this one.

Waikiki Beach, Oahu: Relax on the famous beach and enjoy water activities.

- Money-Saving Tip: Bring your own beach gear, or rent equipment from local vendors for a lower cost.

Maui: Experience the Valley Isle with stunning beaches and outdoor adventures.

- Money-Saving Tip: Explore the island's natural beauty with free or low-cost hikes.

Pearl Harbor, Oahu: Pay tribute to history and visit the USS Arizona Memorial.

- Money-Saving Tip: Tickets to the USS Arizona Memorial are free but require advance reservations.

Na Pali Coast, Kauai: Hike or take a boat tour to see breathtaking coastal cliffs.

- Money-Saving Tip: Consider a guided tour for group discounts and local insights.

Haleakalā National Park, Maui: Watch the sunrise or hike in the volcanic crater.

- Money-Saving Tip: Visit during the off-peak season to avoid crowded sunrise tours.

Lanikai Beach, Oahu: Enjoy pristine white sands and turquoise waters.

- Money-Saving Tip: Arrive early to secure parking and avoid crowds.

Honolulu, Oahu: Explore the state capital with cultural attractions.

- Money-Saving Tip: Visit free museums, such as the Honolulu Museum of Art.

Molokini Crater, Maui: Snorkel in a volcanic crater with diverse marine life.

- Money-Saving Tip: Bring your own snorkeling gear or rent it locally for a lower cost.

North Shore, Oahu: Experience big wave surfing and explore laid-back towns.

- Money-Saving Tip: Visit during the winter months to watch professional surfers in action.

Hana Road, Maui: Drive along the scenic road with waterfalls and coastal views.

- Money-Saving Tip: Bring your own snacks and picnic along the route to save on dining costs.

Kauai: Discover the Garden Isle with lush landscapes and outdoor activities.

- Money-Saving Tip: Hike the island's free or low-cost trails for stunning scenery.

Hanauma Bay, Oahu: Snorkel in a protected marine preserve.

- Money-Saving Tip: Bring your own snorkeling gear to avoid rental fees.

Akaka Falls State Park, Big Island: Hike to a 442-foot waterfall in a lush rainforest.

- Money-Saving Tip: Pay a small entrance fee for access to the park.

Kilauea Point National Wildlife Refuge, Kauai: Spot seabirds and enjoy coastal views.

- Money-Saving Tip: Visit the refuge during the free community days.

Polynesian Cultural Center, Oahu: Experience Polynesian cultures and entertainment.

- Money-Saving Tip: Look for discounts on admission tickets and evening shows.

Kailua Beach, Oahu: Relax on a beautiful windward shore beach.

- Money-Saving Tip: Enjoy free beach access and bring your own snacks and drinks.

Molokai: Explore the Friendly Isle with rural charm and unspoiled beauty.

- Money-Saving Tip: Take a day trip from Maui to Molokai for budget-friendly exploration.

Big Island: Enjoy diverse landscapes, from beaches to lava fields.

- Money-Saving Tip: Take advantage of free public beaches and natural attractions.

RECAP

Category	Insider Tips
Food	1. Indulge in plate lunches at local eateries for a taste of Hawaiian comfort food at affordable prices.
	2. Explore farmers' markets for fresh tropical fruits like pineapple, mango, and papaya at lower prices than supermarkets.
	3. Look for "hole-in-the-wall" eateries serving authentic Hawaiian dishes like loco moco or poke bowls at reasonable prices.
	4. Opt for food trucks offering a variety of local specialties like shave ice, garlic shrimp, or kalua pork for a budget-friendly meal.
Accommodation	1. Consider staying in vacation rentals or Airbnb properties for more affordable accommodations compared to hotels.
	2. Look for accommodations in areas outside of popular tourist destinations like Waikiki for lower rates.
	3. Book accommodations well in advance or during the off-peak season to secure lower prices and better deals.
	4. Explore camping options in Hawaii's state parks or designated campgrounds for budget-friendly lodging amidst nature.
Activities	1. Enjoy free activities like beachcombing, snorkeling, and hiking in Hawaii's stunning natural landscapes.
	2. Take advantage of discounted or free cultural events and performances, often held in parks or community centers.
	3. Visit botanical gardens or scenic lookout points for breathtaking views and photo opportunities without spending a dime.
	4. Participate in volunteer opportunities such as beach clean-ups or trail maintenance for a rewarding and budget-friendly activity.
Transport	1. Rent a car for flexibility in exploring Hawaii's islands, but consider booking in advance for better rates.
	2. Utilize public transportation options like buses or trolleys in urban areas like Honolulu to save on transportation costs.
	3. Consider carpooling or ridesharing with other travelers to split transportation expenses, especially for longer journeys.
	4. Rent bicycles or scooters for short-distance travel or exploring local neighborhoods, providing an affordable and eco-friendly option.

Idaho

A place of rugged wilderness, stunning natural beauty, and a serene way of life. Idaho, located in the western United States, offers a unique blend of outdoor adventures, scenic landscapes, and a strong sense of community. Here's an introduction to Idaho, along with some key things to consider and local tips for your visit:

Geography and Natural Beauty:

Idaho is renowned for its diverse geography, which includes majestic mountains, pristine lakes, lush forests, and vast expanses of wilderness. The state is home to the Rocky Mountains, the Sawtooth Range, the Snake River, and numerous national parks and forests. Whether you're an outdoor enthusiast or simply appreciate breathtaking landscapes, Idaho's natural beauty will leave you in awe.

Things to Consider:

- **Outdoor Recreation**: Idaho is an outdoor adventurer's paradise. Expect to find opportunities for hiking, skiing, snowboarding, mountain biking, white-water rafting, and more. The state's wilderness areas and national parks offer a wide range of activities year-round.
- **Weather**: The climate in Idaho varies depending on the region and the time of year. Summers can be warm and dry, while winters can bring heavy snowfall, especially in the mountainous areas. Plan your activities and clothing accordingly.
- **Cultural Diversity**: While Idaho is known for its natural beauty, it also has a vibrant cultural scene. You can explore art galleries, music festivals, and historical sites that showcase the state's rich heritage.

Local Tips:

- **Sun Valley**: Visit Sun Valley, a world-renowned ski resort in central Idaho. In addition to winter sports, it offers hiking, biking, and a vibrant arts scene during the summer months.
- **Shoshone Falls**: Discover Shoshone Falls, often called the "Niagara of the West." Located near Twin Falls, these falls are even higher than Niagara Falls and are a sight to behold, especially during the spring.
- **Boise**: Explore the state capital, Boise, a city known for its cultural attractions, including the Boise Art Museum, the Idaho Shakespeare Festival, and a lively downtown area with dining and entertainment options.
- **Coeur d'Alene**: Enjoy the beauty of Lake Coeur d'Alene in the northern part of the state. The town of Coeur d'Alene offers water sports, hiking, golfing, and a charming lakeside atmosphere.
- **Hiking**: Idaho offers numerous hiking trails suitable for all skill levels. Consider exploring trails in the Sawtooth National Recreation Area or hiking to the top of Borah Peak, the state's highest point.

- **Wildlife Watching**: Keep an eye out for Idaho's diverse wildlife, which includes elk, moose, bears, wolves, and a variety of bird species. Wildlife viewing is a popular activity in the state's national parks and forests.
- **Potatoes**: While in Idaho, don't miss the chance to taste some of the best potatoes in the country. Many local restaurants serve delicious potato dishes, including famous Idaho potato fries.

1. Transportation:

- **Car Rental:** Renting a car is recommended for exploring Idaho's vast landscapes. Prices start at around $30 per day, and booking in advance can secure better deals.
- **Public Transportation**: While public transportation options may be limited compared to larger states, cities like Boise and Coeur d'Alene offer bus services that can be an affordable way to travel within city limits and nearby areas.

2. Accommodation:

- **Budget-Friendly Luxury Stays:** Explore boutique hotels, lodges, or bed and breakfasts in cities like Boise, Coeur d'Alene, or Sun Valley. Prices can range from $70 to $150 per night for a comfortable stay. Consider booking in advance or during off-peak seasons for better rates.
- **State Parks or Camping:** Idaho offers beautiful state parks and campgrounds. Campsite fees can be as low as $20 per night, providing a budget-friendly and nature-centric experience.

3. Dining:

- **Local Cafes and Diners:** Enjoy local cuisine at cafes and diners, where meals can range from $10 to $25 per person. Idaho is known for its potatoes, so don't miss trying local potato dishes.
- **Farm-to-Table Restaurants:** Explore farm-to-table dining experiences, especially in areas like Boise or Coeur d'Alene.
- **U-Pick Farms**: Idaho offers many U-Pick farms where you can harvest your own fruits, such as berries and apples, at a lower cost than buying them pre-picked. This can be a fun and cost-effective way to enjoy fresh produce while supporting local agriculture.

4. Activities:

- **Hiking Trails:** Explore Idaho's scenic landscapes through hiking trails. Whether in the Sawtooth National Recreation Area or Shoshone Falls, many trails are free or have a small parking fee.
- **Hot Springs:** Idaho is home to numerous hot springs. While some may have an entrance fee, others can be accessed for free or a small fee.

5. Entertainment:

- **Live Music:** Check out live music scenes in Boise or Idaho Falls. Some venues offer free or affordable shows, especially in vibrant neighborhoods.
- **Local Events:** Explore local events and festivals. Idaho celebrates various cultural and outdoor events, providing affordable entertainment.

Idaho State Capitol (Boise): The Idaho State Capitol offers free guided tours where you can learn about the state's government, history, and architecture. Tours are typically available Monday through Friday.

Boise Art Museum (Boise): While admission to the Boise Art Museum may require a fee for special exhibitions, the museum occasionally offers free admission days or free guided tours of its permanent collections. Check their website or contact them directly for tour availability.

Idaho Botanical Garden (Boise): While admission to the Idaho Botanical Garden does require a fee, the garden occasionally offers free guided tours or special events. Check their website or contact them directly for tour availability.

6. Insights and Tips:

- **Scenic Drives:** Drive along Idaho's scenic byways, such as the Sawtooth Scenic Byway or the Teton Scenic Byway, for breathtaking views.
- **Free Museum Days:** Some museums, like the Idaho Potato Museum, offer free or discounted admission on specific days.
- **Geothermal Attractions:** Explore geothermal attractions like Craters of the Moon National Monument or Hell's Half Acre, which offer unique landscapes at a low cost.

Major Towns in Idaho:

- **Boise:** The capital city known for its vibrant downtown, cultural attractions, and proximity to outdoor activities.
- **Coeur d'Alene:** A resort town known for its stunning lake, outdoor recreation, and charming downtown area.
- **Sun Valley:** Famous for its ski resorts, Sun Valley offers year-round outdoor activities and a relaxed atmosphere.
- **Idaho Falls:** A gateway to Yellowstone National Park, known for the Snake River, greenbelt, and historic downtown.

Here are the top attractions in Idaho, along with some money-saving tips for visiting each one:

Boise: Explore the state capital with cultural attractions and outdoor activities.

- Money-Saving Tip: Check out free events and festivals in downtown Boise.

Shoshone Falls, Twin Falls: Marvel at the "Niagara of the West."

- Money-Saving Tip: Visit during the spring or early summer when the water flow is at its peak.

Coeur d'Alene: Enjoy a scenic lakeside town with outdoor recreation.

- Money-Saving Tip: Take advantage of free public beaches and parks along Lake Coeur d'Alene.

Sun Valley: Experience world-class skiing and outdoor adventures.

- Money-Saving Tip: Visit Sun Valley during the shoulder seasons for lower lodging rates.

Idaho Falls: Explore the Snake River and nearby attractions.

- Money-Saving Tip: Walk along the Snake River Greenbelt and enjoy free outdoor activities.

Sawtooth National Recreation Area: Hike, camp, and enjoy outdoor beauty.

- Money-Saving Tip: Camp in the recreation area's campgrounds for budget-friendly lodging.

Pocatello: Discover a historic city with outdoor activities and museums.

- Money-Saving Tip: Look for affordable outdoor adventures, such as hiking and biking.

Craters of the Moon National Monument: Explore a unique volcanic landscape.

- Money-Saving Tip: Visit the monument during free entrance days at national parks.

Teton Valley: Experience small-town charm and outdoor adventures.

- Money-Saving Tip: Explore the valley's hiking and biking trails for free.

Boise River Greenbelt: Walk or bike along the scenic river trail.

- Money-Saving Tip: Rent a bike or bring your own for an affordable ride.

Hell's Canyon: Discover the deepest gorge in North America.

- Money-Saving Tip: Take advantage of free overlooks and hiking trails.

Silverwood Theme Park, Athol: Enjoy family-friendly rides and attractions.

- Money-Saving Tip: Buy tickets online in advance for discounts and consider a two-day pass.

Idaho Potato Museum, Blackfoot: Learn about the state's famous crop.

- Money-Saving Tip: Look for discounted admission rates, especially for children.

Boise Art Museum: Explore art and cultural exhibits.

- Money-Saving Tip: Visit during free admission days or discounted evenings.

Salmon River: Raft or fish in the "River of No Return."

- Money-Saving Tip: Share the cost of rafting trips with a group for savings.

Ski Resorts: Experience winter sports at various ski resorts.

- Money-Saving Tip: Purchase lift tickets and rental equipment in advance for deals.

Canyon County Festival of Trees, Nampa: Enjoy a festive holiday event.

- Money-Saving Tip: Attend free or low-cost holiday events in the area.

Skiing: Hit the slopes at Bogus Basin and other ski areas.

- Money-Saving Tip: Look for discount packages and multi-day passes for skiing.

Old Idaho Penitentiary, Boise: Tour the historic former prison.

- **Money-Saving Tip**: Check for group discounts and combined admission tickets.

Idaho State University, Pocatello: Visit the campus and cultural attractions.

- **Money-Saving Tip**: Attend free lectures, performances, and art exhibitions.

RECAP:

Category	Insider Tips
Food	1. Forage for huckleberries in the wild during the summer months for a delicious and free local treat.
	2. Visit local farmers' markets for fresh Idaho potatoes and other locally grown produce at lower prices.
	3. Sample Idaho's famous finger steaks at local diners or pubs for a tasty and affordable regional specialty.
	4. Pack a picnic and enjoy lunch by one of Idaho's many scenic rivers or lakes for a budget-friendly meal.
Accommodation	1. Camp in Idaho's national forests or state parks for affordable and picturesque overnight stays.
	2. Stay in quaint bed and breakfasts or guesthouses in smaller towns for a cozy and budget-friendly experience.
	3. Look for cabin rentals or vacation homes in rural areas for a secluded and affordable lodging option.
	4. Consider using hospitality exchange platforms to stay with local hosts for free or at a low cost.
Activities	1. Explore hiking trails in Idaho's national parks and wilderness areas for breathtaking mountain views.
	2. Take advantage of free fishing days in Idaho's rivers and lakes to enjoy outdoor recreation without a license.
	3. Visit local museums and historical sites for insights into Idaho's rich mining and pioneer heritage.
	4. Attend community events and festivals celebrating Idaho's culture, music, and agricultural traditions.
Transport	1. Rent a car or RV to explore Idaho's scenic byways and backroads for a flexible and adventurous road trip.
	2. Utilize ridesharing or carpooling services to share transportation costs and reduce your carbon footprint.
	3. Consider biking or walking in Idaho's small towns or cities for a budget-friendly and eco-friendly way to get around.
	4. Take advantage of discounted bus or train fares for intercity travel within Idaho or to neighboring states.

Illinois

Illinois has played a pivotal role in American history, most notably as the home state of Abraham Lincoln, the 16th President of the United States. Visitors can explore Lincoln's legacy at the Abraham Lincoln Presidential Library and Museum in Springfield and visit historical sites like the Old State Capitol and Lincoln's Tomb.

Things to Consider:

- **Chicago**: Chicago is Illinois' largest city and a vibrant metropolis known for its architecture, world-class museums, and diverse culinary scene. Plan to spend time exploring the city's neighborhoods, iconic landmarks, and cultural institutions.
- **Seasonal Climate**: Illinois experiences four distinct seasons. Summers can be warm and humid, while winters bring cold temperatures and snow, especially in the northern part of the state. Be prepared for varying weather conditions based on the time of year.
- **Cultural Diversity**: Illinois is a melting pot of cultures and communities. Explore the diversity of the state by trying international cuisines, attending cultural festivals, and visiting neighborhoods that represent different cultures.

Local Tips:

- **Chicago's Cultural Attractions**: In Chicago, explore world-renowned cultural institutions such as the Art Institute of Chicago, the Field Museum, the Museum of Science and Industry, and the Adler Planetarium. Don't miss the city's vibrant theater scene and famous comedy clubs.
- **Magnificent Mile**: Shop along the Magnificent Mile on Michigan Avenue in downtown Chicago, known for its high-end boutiques, department stores, and iconic architecture.
- **Route 66**: If you're a history enthusiast, consider driving a portion of historic Route 66, which passes through Illinois. You can explore nostalgic roadside attractions and towns along the way.
- **Starved Rock State Park**: Enjoy the natural beauty of Starved Rock State Park, known for its scenic canyons, waterfalls, and hiking trails. It's a perfect destination for outdoor enthusiasts.
- **Galena**: Visit the charming town of Galena, known for its well-preserved 19th-century architecture, boutique shops, and scenic Mississippi River views.
- **Lincoln Home National Historic Site**: Step into history by touring the Lincoln Home in Springfield, where Abraham Lincoln lived before becoming President. The site offers insights into Lincoln's life and times.
- **Illinois Wine Country**: Explore the state's wine country, particularly in the Shawnee Hills and Southern Illinois regions. You can visit wineries and enjoy tastings in a picturesque setting.

1. **Transportation:**

- **Public Transportation:** Chicago has an extensive public transportation system, including buses and the 'L' train. Utilize it to explore the city affordably.

2. Accommodation:

- **Budget-Friendly Luxury Stays:** Explore boutique hotels or charming bed and breakfasts in neighborhoods like Wicker Park or Logan Square in Chicago. Prices can range from $80 to $150 per night for a comfortable stay. Consider booking in advance or during off-peak seasons for better rates.
- **Camping:** Illinois state parks and recreation areas offer affordable camping options in scenic settings. Consider camping at places like Starved Rock State Park, Shawnee National Forest, or Chain O'Lakes State Park for a budget-friendly outdoor experience.
- **Budget Motels:** Look for budget motels along major highways or in smaller towns. Motels like Econo Lodge, Rodeway Inn, or Super 8 offer basic amenities and affordable rates for travelers on a budget.

3. Dining:

- **Local Eateries:** Enjoy diverse cuisine at local eateries, especially in neighborhoods like Chinatown or Pilsen. Meals can range from $10 to $30 per person.
- **Deep Dish Pizza:** Indulge in Chicago's famous deep-dish pizza. While some pizzerias can be pricey, others offer affordable options.
- **Food Waste Reduction Apps**: Consider using apps like Too Good To Go or OLIO, which connect consumers with surplus food from local restaurants, bakeries, and grocery stores at discounted prices, reducing food waste and saving you money.

4. Activities:

- **Museums:** While some museums may have admission fees, several offer free days or suggested donation periods. The Art Institute of Chicago and the Museum of Contemporary Art are examples.
- **Millennium Park:** Explore Millennium Park in downtown Chicago, home to iconic attractions like Cloud Gate (The Bean) and the Jay Pritzker Pavilion. It's a free and vibrant public space.

5. Entertainment:

- **Live Music:** Chicago is renowned for its live music scene. Check out smaller venues or free concerts in parks for affordable musical experiences.
- **Comedy Clubs:** Enjoy Chicago's famous comedy scene. Some clubs offer budget-friendly admission, especially during weekdays.
Illinois State Capitol (Springfield): The Illinois State Capitol offers free guided tours where you can learn about the state's government, history, and architecture. Tours are typically available Monday through Friday.
Chicago Cultural Center (Chicago): The Chicago Cultural Center offers free guided tours of its historic building, showcasing its stunning architecture, Tiffany glass domes, and art exhibitions. Check their website or contact them directly for tour availability.

Millennium Park (Chicago): Millennium Park in downtown Chicago offers free self-guided tours where you can explore iconic attractions such as the Cloud Gate sculpture (also known as "The Bean"), the Jay Pritzker Pavilion, and the Lurie Garden.

6. Insights and Tips:

- **City Passes:** Consider the Chicago CityPASS for discounted access to major attractions like the Shedd Aquarium, Adler Planetarium, and Skydeck Chicago.
- **Lakefront Trail:** Explore the Lakefront Trail along Lake Michigan for stunning views of the skyline and outdoor activities.
- **Neighborhood Festivals:** Check local event calendars for neighborhood festivals and street fairs, which often offer free or low-cost entertainment.

Major Towns in Illinois:

- **Chicago:** The vibrant metropolis known for its architecture, cultural attractions, and diverse neighborhoods.
- **Springfield:** The state capital, rich in history and home to the Abraham Lincoln Presidential Library and Museum.
- **Champaign-Urbana:** Home to the University of Illinois, offering a college town atmosphere and cultural events.
- **Galena:** A charming town known for its historic architecture, shopping, and outdoor activities.

Here are the top attractions in Illinois, along with some money-saving tips for visiting each one:

Chicago: Explore the vibrant city with world-class museums and cultural attractions.

- Money-Saving Tip: Take advantage of Chicago CityPASS for discounted access to top attractions.

Millennium Park, Chicago: Enjoy public art and outdoor concerts.

- Money-Saving Tip: Attend free concerts and events in the park during the summer.

Navy Pier, Chicago: Experience entertainment, dining, and lake views.

- Money-Saving Tip: Visit the pier during off-peak hours to avoid crowds.

Shedd Aquarium, Chicago: Discover marine life and aquatic exhibits.

- Money-Saving Tip: Look for discounted admission on Illinois Resident Discount Days.

Art Institute of Chicago: Explore art collections and iconic masterpieces.

- Money-Saving Tip: Visit on free admission days for Illinois residents or after 5:00 PM on weekdays.

Lincoln Park Zoo, Chicago: See animals and enjoy a family-friendly atmosphere.

- Money-Saving Tip: Admission to the zoo is free year-round.

Starved Rock State Park, Utica: Hike through scenic canyons and waterfalls.

- Money-Saving Tip: Bring your own hiking gear for a budget-friendly outdoor adventure.

Springfield: Discover the state capital with historic sites and Lincoln-related attractions.

- Money-Saving Tip: Visit free Lincoln sites like the Lincoln Home National Historic Site.

Garden of the Gods, Shawnee National Forest: Hike among unique rock formations.

- Money-Saving Tip: Explore the park's trails and enjoy free access.

Frank Lloyd Wright Home and Studio, Oak Park: Tour the famous architect's former residence.

- Money-Saving Tip: Look for discounted admission for students and seniors.

Illinois Route 66: Drive along the historic highway and explore quirky attractions.

- Money-Saving Tip: Enjoy roadside stops and take your time to experience the nostalgia.

Galena: Experience a historic town with charming shops and historic homes.

- Money-Saving Tip: Walk along Main Street and explore free attractions like Grant Park.

Morton Arboretum, Lisle: Stroll through beautiful gardens and natural landscapes.

- Money-Saving Tip: Visit during discounted admission days or take advantage of free events.

Chicago Cultural Center: Attend cultural events and admire architectural beauty.

- Money-Saving Tip: Enjoy free concerts, exhibitions, and tours at the cultural center.

Lincoln's New Salem State Historic Site, Petersburg: Step back in time to Lincoln's early years.

- Money-Saving Tip: Check for discounted admission and guided tour packages.

Quad Cities: Explore a group of cities along the Mississippi River.

- Money-Saving Tip: Visit free attractions like the Figge Art Museum.

Cahokia Mounds State Historic Site, Collinsville: Learn about ancient Native American civilizations.

- Money-Saving Tip: Admission to the interpretive center is free.

Starved Rock Lodge, Utica: Stay in a historic lodge and enjoy the natural surroundings.

- Money-Saving Tip: Look for lodging deals during the off-peak season.

Illinois State Beach Park, Zion: Relax on Lake Michigan beaches.

- Money-Saving Tip: Pack a picnic and spend a day by the water without extra expenses.

Black Hawk State Historic Site, Rock Island: Explore Native American history and scenic beauty.

- Money-Saving Tip: Admission to the site is free.

RECAP

Category	Insider Tips
Food	1. Indulge in Chicago's famous deep-dish pizza at local pizzerias like Lou Malnati's or Giordano's.
	2. Enjoy authentic Chicago-style hot dogs at local stands or diners, featuring all the classic toppings.
	3. Explore neighborhood bakeries for delicious pastries and treats, such as German bakeries in Lincoln Square.
	4. Sample ethnic cuisine in neighborhoods like Chinatown or Little Italy for affordable and diverse dining options.
Accommodation	1. Consider staying in boutique hotels or bed-and-breakfasts in Chicago's historic neighborhoods for a unique experience.
	2. Look for budget-friendly accommodations near universities or colleges, such as in Champaign-Urbana.
	3. Utilize discount websites or apps to find deals on hotels and accommodations in cities like Springfield or Peoria.
	4. Check for special promotions or packages at hotels and resorts, especially during off-peak seasons.
Activities	1. Explore the cultural attractions of Chicago, including museums like the Art Institute or the Field Museum.
	2. Attend free events and festivals throughout the state, such as the Taste of Chicago or the Illinois State Fair.
	3. Take advantage of outdoor activities like hiking, biking, and picnicking in state parks like Starved Rock.
	4. Visit historical sites and landmarks, such as Abraham Lincoln's home in Springfield or Frank Lloyd Wright's architecture in Oak Park.
Transport	1. Utilize public transportation options in Chicago, such as the 'L' train or buses, to navigate the city affordably.
	2. Consider walking or biking in pedestrian-friendly areas like downtown Chicago or along the lakefront.
	3. Look for car rental deals or discounts for exploring attractions outside of major cities like Chicago.
	4. Check for commuter or tourist passes for discounted fares on public transportation or entry fees.

Indiana

Indiana has a storied past, with a significant role in American history. The state is known for its contributions to agriculture, manufacturing, and the automotive industry. It's also home to the Indianapolis Motor Speedway, the site of the famous Indy 500 race. Explore Indiana's historical sites, such as the George Rogers Clark National Historical Park and the many covered bridges scattered throughout the state.

Things to Consider:

- **Indianapolis**: Indiana's capital, Indianapolis, is a vibrant city with a thriving arts and culture scene, excellent dining options, and sports events. Plan to explore the city's downtown, which includes the Indianapolis Museum of Art and the Eiteljorg Museum of American Indians and Western Art.
- **Outdoor Activities**: Indiana offers a variety of outdoor activities, including hiking, boating, and camping in its state parks and recreational areas. The Indiana Dunes National Park, along Lake Michigan, is a must-visit for its sandy beaches and scenic trails.
- **Seasonal Weather**: Indiana experiences four distinct seasons. Summers are warm and humid, while winters can be cold with snowfall. Dress appropriately for the season and consider the weather when planning outdoor activities.

Local Tips:

- **Indiana's Covered Bridges**: Explore the picturesque covered bridges scattered throughout the state. Parke County, known as the "Covered Bridge Capital of the World," is a great place to start your covered bridge tour.
- **Brown County State Park**: Visit Brown County State Park, often referred to as the "Little Smokies of Indiana." It offers hiking, mountain biking, and scenic drives, particularly during the fall when the foliage is vibrant.
- **Amish Country**: Discover Indiana's Amish communities, especially in areas like Shipshewana and Nappanee. Explore Amish markets, shops, and enjoy traditional Amish cuisine.
- **Hoosier Hospitality**: Experience the warm and friendly hospitality of Hoosiers. Strike up conversations with locals, and you'll likely receive valuable recommendations and insights.
- **Indiana Wine Country**: Indiana has a growing wine industry. Visit wineries and vineyards in regions like the Indiana Uplands or the Indiana Wine Trail for tastings and scenic views.
- **Hoosier National Forest**: Explore the Hoosier National Forest, which offers opportunities for camping, hiking, fishing, and wildlife watching in a tranquil natural setting.
- **Historic New Harmony**: Visit New Harmony, a town known for its utopian history and architecture. Explore its museums, gardens, and historic structures.

1. **Transportation:**

    - **Flights:** Look for flights to major airports like Indianapolis International Airport (IND) or Fort Wayne International Airport (FWA).
    - **Car Rental:** Renting a car is recommended for exploring Indiana, especially if you plan to visit multiple cities or rural areas. Prices start at around $30 per day, and booking in advance can secure better deals.

2. **Accommodation:**

    - **Budget-Friendly Luxury Stays:** Explore boutique hotels or historic inns in cities like Indianapolis, Bloomington, or South Bend. Prices can range from $70 to $150 per night for a comfortable stay. Consider booking in advance or during off-peak seasons for better rates.
    - **University Towns:** Consider staying in university towns like Bloomington, where accommodations can be more budget-friendly due to a large student population.

3. **Dining:**

    - **Local Eateries:** Enjoy Midwestern cuisine at local diners and cafes. Meals can range from $10 to $25 per person.
    - **Farm-to-Table Restaurants:** Explore farm-to-table dining experiences, particularly in cities with a focus on local produce and culinary innovation.

4. **Activities:**

    - **Indiana Dunes National Park:** Enjoy the beaches and hiking trails at Indiana Dunes National Park, which offers stunning views of Lake Michigan. Entrance is free.
    - **Brown County State Park:** Explore hiking and scenic beauty in Brown County State Park. The entrance fee is generally around $7 per vehicle.
    - **Indianapolis Canal Walk:** Take a stroll along the Indianapolis Canal Walk, a scenic urban waterway in downtown Indy, offering public art and beautiful views.

5. **Entertainment:**

    - **Indianapolis Cultural Trail:** Explore the Indianapolis Cultural Trail, a bike and pedestrian-friendly path connecting various neighborhoods and cultural districts.
    - **Museums:** While some museums may have admission fees, check for free or discounted days. The Indianapolis Museum of Art often has free admission times.
- **Indiana Statehouse (Indianapolis):** The Indiana Statehouse offers free guided tours where you can learn about the state's government, history, and architecture. Tours are typically available Monday through Friday.
- **Indianapolis Cultural Trail (Indianapolis):** The Indianapolis Cultural Trail is an urban walking and biking trail that connects neighborhoods, cultural districts, and landmarks in downtown Indianapolis. While not guided, you can explore the trail for free and learn

about the city's art, history, and culture through signage and public art installations along the route.
- **Indiana University Bloomington Campus Tours (Bloomington):** Indiana University Bloomington offers free campus tours led by student guides. You can explore the university's historic buildings, architecture, and landmarks while learning about its history and academic programs.

6. Insights and Tips:

- **Indiana Wineries:** Explore wineries in regions like the Indiana Uplands Wine Trail. Some offer affordable tastings or tours.
- **Small-Town Festivals:** Check out festivals and events in smaller towns, which often offer a glimpse into local culture and are budget-friendly.
- **Free Outdoor Concerts:** Keep an eye out for free outdoor concerts, especially during the summer months.

Major Towns in Indiana:

- **Indianapolis:** The state capital known for the Indianapolis Motor Speedway, cultural districts, and a vibrant downtown.
- **Bloomington:** Home to Indiana University, offering a mix of cultural events, outdoor activities, and a lively arts scene.
- **South Bend:** Known for the University of Notre Dame, offering a mix of collegiate charm and cultural attractions.
- **Fort Wayne:** A city with a rich history, known for its museums, parks, and vibrant downtown.

Here are the top attractions in Indiana, along with some money-saving tips for visiting each one:

Indianapolis: Combo tickets and deals on Indianapolis attractions can vary, but some combo passes start at around $50 to $60 per person, offering access to multiple attractions at a discounted rate.

Indiana Dunes National Park: Entrance fees for Indiana Dunes National Park are $15 per vehicle for a 7-day pass. Visiting during the off-peak season, typically in the fall or spring, can help you avoid crowds and potentially save on park fees.

Holiday World & Splashin' Safari, Santa Claus: Online ticket prices for Holiday World & Splashin' Safari start at around $45 to $50 per person, with discounts available for purchasing combo passes that include admission to both parks.

French Lick: Exploring the hiking and biking trails in French Lick is free of charge, providing budget-friendly outdoor activities for visitors.

Brown County State Park, Nashville: Entrance fees for Brown County State Park are $7 per in-state vehicle and $9 per out-of-state vehicle for a daily pass. Bringing your own hiking gear allows you to enjoy the park's trails without additional rental costs.

Amish Country, Shipshewana: While exploring Amish Country, visiting local markets and shops allows you to experience Amish culture and cuisine without spending a lot of money. Handmade products and Amish treats can vary in price but often offer unique and affordable souvenirs.

Indianapolis Motor Speedway: Ticket prices for events at the Indianapolis Motor Speedway vary depending on the race and seating options. Checking for special events and tours at the speedway can provide unique experiences at potentially discounted rates.

Conner Prairie Interactive History Park, Fishers: Admission prices for Conner Prairie Interactive History Park start at around $18 to $21 for adults and $13 to $16 for children (ages 2-12). Looking for discounted admission and family passes can help save money on tickets.

Columbus: Self-guided architectural tours and exploring public art installations offer free activities for visitors to Columbus, providing budget-friendly ways to experience the city's modern architecture and artistic culture.

Fort Wayne Children's Zoo: Online ticket prices for the Fort Wayne Children's Zoo start at around $15 to $20 per person, with discounts available for purchasing tickets in advance. Visiting during weekday mornings can help you avoid crowds and potentially save on admission fees.

South Bend: Free events and exploring the Notre Dame campus offer budget-friendly activities for visitors to South Bend, providing opportunities to experience the city's rich sports and university culture without spending money on admission fees.

Indiana University Bloomington: Admission to Indiana University Bloomington's lectures, concerts, and exhibitions is often free of charge, allowing visitors to explore the campus and cultural attractions without additional costs.

Lincoln Boyhood National Memorial, Lincoln City: Admission to the Lincoln Boyhood National Memorial is free, providing visitors with the opportunity to learn about Abraham Lincoln's early life without spending money on entrance fees.

Marengo Cave, Marengo: Tour prices for Marengo Cave start at around $10 to $15 per person, with discounts available for groups and educational programs. Looking for tour discounts and family packages can help save money on cave exploration.

Indiana State Museum, Indianapolis: Admission to the Indiana State Museum starts at around $10 to $15 for adults and $5 to $10 for children, with discounts available on discount days or for special exhibitions.

Hoosier National Forest: Camping fees in Hoosier National Forest campgrounds typically range from $15 to $20 per night, providing budget-friendly lodging options for visitors exploring the forest's outdoor activities and scenic beauty.

Cataract Falls State Recreation Area, Cloverdale: Admission to Cataract Falls State Recreation Area is free, making it a budget-friendly destination for hiking to waterfalls and enjoying nature without spending money on entrance fees.

Muncie: Attending free university events at Ball State University and exploring nearby parks offer budget-friendly activities for visitors to Muncie, providing opportunities to experience the city's attractions without additional costs.

Indiana Beach Boardwalk Resort, Monticello: Admission prices for Indiana Beach Boardwalk Resort start at around $30 to $40 per person, with discounts available for purchasing deals on admission and considering season passes for additional savings.

Wolf Park, Battle Ground: Admission prices for Wolf Park start at around $8 to $10 for adults and $5 to $7 for children, with discounts available for groups and educational programs. Checking for group discounts and educational programs can help save money on animal observation and educational experiences.

RECAP

Category	Insider Tips
Food	1. Dine at local diners and cafes in small towns for hearty, affordable meals with a side of Hoosier hospitality.
	2. Visit farmers' markets for fresh produce and locally-made products, often at lower prices than supermarkets.
	3. Look for "Tenderloin Tuesdays" deals at restaurants in Indianapolis for discounts on this Indiana specialty.
	4. Pack a picnic and enjoy lunch at one of Indiana's scenic parks or along the shores of Lake Michigan.
Accommodation	1. Stay at budget-friendly motels or guesthouses in smaller towns and cities for affordable lodging options.
	2. Consider camping at Indiana's state parks or national forests for a cost-effective and nature-immersed experience.
	3. Use hotel booking websites to find deals and discounts on accommodations in cities like Indianapolis and South Bend.
	4. Look for bed and breakfast options in charming historic homes for a cozy and unique stay.
Activities	1. Explore Indiana's extensive network of hiking and biking trails, many of which are free to access.
	2. Attend local festivals and events, often featuring live music, food vendors, and family-friendly activities.
	3. Visit museums on their free admission days or take advantage of discounted tickets during off-peak hours.

	4. Enjoy a day at the beach along the shores of Lake Michigan, with several public access points offering free entry.
Transport	1. Utilize public transportation options in cities like Indianapolis and Fort Wayne to save on parking and gas.
	2. Consider carpooling with fellow travelers or using ride-sharing services for shared transportation costs.
	3. Rent a bike for exploring urban areas or participating in organized bike tours in cities like Bloomington.
	4. Plan road trips during off-peak travel times to avoid traffic and potentially save on fuel costs.

Kansas

Kansas played a pivotal role in American history, particularly during the Civil War and westward expansion eras. It's known for its role in the abolitionist movement and the struggles that led to the formation of the state. You can explore historical sites like the Brown v. Board of Education National Historic Site in Topeka, the Tallgrass Prairie National Preserve, and the Old Cowtown Museum in Wichita to learn more about the state's history.

Things to Consider:

- **Wichita**: Wichita is the largest city in Kansas and offers a variety of cultural attractions, including museums, galleries, and performing arts venues. The city is also known for its aviation heritage, with the Kansas Aviation Museum and the annual Wichita River Festival.
- **Outdoor Activities**: Kansas boasts scenic natural landscapes, including the Flint Hills, the largest remaining tallgrass prairie in North America. Enjoy activities like hiking, bird-watching, and wildlife photography in the state's parks and nature reserves.
- **Weather**: Kansas experiences a range of weather conditions throughout the year. Summers are warm and often humid, while winters can be cold with occasional snowfall. Plan your activities and clothing accordingly.

Local Tips:

- **Flint Hills Scenic Byway**: Drive along the Flint Hills Scenic Byway to witness the breathtaking beauty of the tallgrass prairie. The Konza Prairie Biological Station is a great place to explore the unique ecosystem.
- **Dodge City**: Visit Dodge City, known for its Old West history and cowboy culture. Explore the Boot Hill Museum and watch reenactments of historic gunfights.
- **Kansas City**: In Kansas City, located partly in Kansas and partly in Missouri, you can enjoy barbecue restaurants, jazz music, and cultural attractions such as the Nelson-Atkins Museum of Art.
- **Sunflowers**: Look for fields of sunflowers, which are a symbol of Kansas. They typically bloom in late summer and early fall and create stunning landscapes for photography.
- **Agri-Tourism**: Explore agri-tourism opportunities in Kansas, including visits to working farms, orchards, and wineries. Sample local produce and enjoy the rural atmosphere.
- **Cowboy Culture**: Embrace the cowboy culture by attending rodeos, cattle drives, and Western-themed events that celebrate Kansas' frontier history.
- **Tornadoes**: Be aware that Kansas is in "Tornado Alley," so it's important to stay informed about weather conditions and safety protocols when visiting during tornado season.

1. **Accommodation:**
   - Look for budget-friendly yet luxurious accommodations. Many hotels offer deals and discounts, especially if you book in advance or during off-peak seasons.
   - Recommended places: The Oread in Lawrence, Hotel at Old Town in Wichita, and the Ambassador Hotel in Kansas City.
2. **Transportation:**
   - Consider renting a car for flexibility. Check various rental companies for the best rates.
   - Public transportation in major cities like Kansas City is affordable and can save on parking costs.
3. **Food:**
   - Dine at local gems. Kansas is known for its barbecue, so try some local BBQ joints for an authentic experience.
   - Recommended restaurants: Q39 in Kansas City, Joe's Kansas City Bar-B-Que, and Pig In! Pig Out! in Wichita.
4. **Attractions:**
   - Opt for a CityPASS if you plan to visit multiple attractions in Kansas City. It offers discounts on popular spots like the National World War I Museum and Science City at Union Station.
   - Visit free attractions like the Nelson-Atkins Museum of Art and Kauffman Memorial Gardens in Kansas City.
5. **Outdoor Activities:**
   - Explore the scenic beauty of Kansas by visiting state parks. Entry fees are usually low, and you can enjoy hiking, picnicking, and wildlife watching.
   - Recommended parks: Kanopolis State Park, Tallgrass Prairie National Preserve, and Clinton State Park.
6. **Entertainment:**
   - Check for local events and festivals. Many are free and provide a unique cultural experience.
   - Keep an eye on concert venues, as some may offer discounted tickets or free shows.
7. **Shopping:**
   - Hunt for bargains in local markets and outlet stores.
   - Visit the Legends Outlets in Kansas City for a mix of luxury and discount shopping.
8. **Insider Tips:**
   - **Midweek Travel:** Consider traveling on weekdays as accommodation and attraction prices may be lower.
   - **Local Coupons:** Look for local coupon books or online deals for additional savings on dining and attractions.
   - **Farmers Markets:** Experience local culture by visiting farmers markets for fresh produce and unique handmade items.
   -

Here are the top attractions in Kansas, along with some money-saving tips for visiting each one:

1. **Attend Free or Low-Cost Events in Wichita:** Keep an eye out for the numerous free or budget-friendly events and festivals hosted in Wichita throughout the year.

From cultural celebrations to outdoor concerts, there's something for everyone to enjoy without spending a dime.
2. **Join a Ranger-Led Tour at Tallgrass Prairie National Preserve:** Delve into the beauty of the tallgrass prairie while saving money by joining one of the ranger-led tours offered at Tallgrass Prairie National Preserve in Strong City. Gain valuable insights into the ecosystem without any additional costs.
3. **Take Advantage of Free or Discounted Museum Days in Kansas City:** Kansas City boasts a vibrant cultural scene, including world-class museums. Look for days when museums offer free or discounted admission, allowing you to explore the city's rich history, art, and culture affordably.
4. **Visit Free Historic Sites in Dodge City:** Step back in time to the Wild West era in Dodge City and explore free historic sites like the Boot Hill Museum. Immerse yourself in frontier history without spending a penny on admission fees.
5. **Scenic Drive Through Flint Hills:** Experience the breathtaking beauty of the Flint Hills region with its rolling hills and expansive prairies. Opt for a scenic drive through this picturesque landscape, offering stunning views at no cost.
6. **Enjoy Free Concerts and Events in Lawrence:** Embrace the lively arts and music scene in Lawrence, a vibrant college town. Attend free concerts and events held in downtown Lawrence, showcasing local talent and cultural diversity.
7. **Hike and Explore Wichita Mountains Wildlife Refuge for Free:** Surround yourself with nature's wonders at the Wichita Mountains Wildlife Refuge near Lawton. Take advantage of free access to hiking trails and wildlife observation spots, offering memorable experiences without any admission fees.
8. **Take Advantage of Free Admission to Kansas State Capitol:** Embark on a tour of the historic Kansas State Capitol building in Topeka without spending a dime on admission. Enjoy free access to this architectural marvel and delve into the state's rich political history with guided tours available at no extra cost.

RECAP

Category	Insider Tips
Food	1. Visit local BBQ joints like Joe's Kansas City Bar-B-Que for mouthwatering ribs and burnt ends.
	2. Explore small-town diners and cafes for homestyle cooking and affordable comfort food.
	3. Check out farmers' markets in cities like Lawrence or Overland Park for fresh produce and artisanal goods.
	4. Enjoy local delicacies like Kansas City-style BBQ, fried chicken, and homemade pies at family-owned eateries.
Accommodation	1. Stay at guest ranches or farm stays for a unique and budget-friendly lodging experience in rural Kansas.
	2. Look for motels or budget hotels along major highways for affordable overnight stays during road trips.
	3. Consider camping in state parks or national wildlife refuges for outdoor adventures on a budget.
	4. Utilize platforms like Airbnb or Vrbo to find affordable accommodations with local hosts in Kansas cities.
Activities	1. Visit the Flint Hills for scenic drives, hiking, and wildlife viewing in one of America's last tallgrass prairies.

	2. Explore historic sites like Boot Hill Museum in Dodge City or Fort Scott National Historic Site for insights into Kansas' past.
	3. Attend local festivals and fairs celebrating Kansas' agricultural heritage, such as the Kansas State Fair.
	4. Go birdwatching at Cheyenne Bottoms Wildlife Area or Quivira National Wildlife Refuge for a unique outdoor experience.
Transport	1. Rent a car for exploring Kansas' rural areas and small towns, as public transportation options may be limited.
	2. Consider carpooling or ride-sharing services for shared transportation costs, especially for longer distances.
	3. Utilize biking trails like the Prairie Spirit Trail or Flint Hills Nature Trail for eco-friendly transportation options.
	4. Look for budget-friendly airlines flying into Wichita or Kansas City airports for affordable air travel to Kansas.

Kentucky

Kentucky is known for its role in American history, including being the birthplace of Abraham Lincoln and the site of pivotal Civil War battles. The state is also renowned for its contributions to music, with bluegrass and country music having deep roots here. Explore historical sites like the Abraham Lincoln Birthplace National Historical Park, Civil War battlefields, and the Kentucky Music Hall of Fame.

Things to Consider:

- **Bourbon**: Kentucky is synonymous with bourbon whiskey. Consider taking a bourbon distillery tour to learn about the production process and sample some of the finest bourbons in the world.
- **Horse Racing**: Horse racing, particularly the Kentucky Derby held in Louisville, is a major cultural event in the state. Plan your visit around race day if you want to experience the excitement of the Derby.
- **Outdoor Activities**: Kentucky offers a wealth of outdoor activities, including hiking, horseback riding, and camping in its state parks and natural areas. The Red River Gorge is a popular destination for rock climbing and hiking.

Local Tips:

- **Kentucky Bourbon Trail**: Embark on the Kentucky Bourbon Trail, which includes visits to numerous bourbon distilleries, each with its own unique history and flavor profiles.
- **Horse Farm Tours**: Explore the picturesque horse farms in the Lexington area. Many farms offer guided tours where you can get up close to thoroughbred horses and learn about their care and training.
- **Louisville**: In Louisville, visit attractions like the Muhammad Ali Center, the Louisville Slugger Museum & Factory, and the historic Old Louisville neighborhood with its beautiful Victorian homes.
- **Mammoth Cave National Park**: Explore Mammoth Cave National Park, home to the world's longest known cave system. Take a guided tour to discover its underground wonders.
- **Bluegrass Music**: Experience live bluegrass music in the region where it originated. Look for local venues and festivals featuring bluegrass performances.
- **Culinary Delights**: Savor Kentucky's culinary specialties, including the Hot Brown sandwich, burgoo (a hearty stew), and the classic Kentucky Derby dish, the mint julep.
- **Natural Wonders**: Discover Kentucky's natural beauty, from the lush forests and waterfalls of the Daniel Boone National Forest to the scenic landscapes of the Big South Fork National River and Recreation Area.

1. Accommodation:

- Look for charming bed and breakfasts or boutique hotels. Consider booking through travel websites for potential discounts.

- Recommended places: 21c Museum Hotel in Louisville, The Brown Hotel in Louisville, and Boone Tavern Hotel in Berea.

2. **Transportation:**
   - Rent a car to explore Kentucky's scenic landscapes and attractions. Shop around for the best car rental deals.
   - **Public Transportation**: While public transportation options may be limited compared to larger states, cities like Louisville and Lexington offer bus services that can be an affordable way to travel within city limits and nearby areas.

3. **Food:**
   - Explore local eateries for authentic Kentucky cuisine. Don't miss trying the famous Hot Brown sandwich.
   - Recommended restaurants: Jack Fry's in Louisville, The Silver Dollar in Louisville, and Dudley's on Short in Lexington.

4. **Attractions:**
   - Look for combo tickets or passes to save on entrance fees to multiple attractions. The Louisville Pass is a good option for those visiting the city.
   - Visit free attractions such as the Big Four Bridge in Louisville and the Horse Country Visitor Center in Lexington.

5. **Outdoor Activities:**
   - Enjoy the beauty of Kentucky by visiting its state parks. Entrance fees are usually reasonable, and you can engage in activities like hiking and horseback riding.
   - Recommended parks: Natural Bridge State Resort Park, Mammoth Cave National Park, and Cumberland Falls State Resort Park.

6. **Entertainment:**
   - Check local event calendars for free or low-cost events. Kentucky often hosts festivals, concerts, and cultural events.
   - Explore the Bourbon Trail, which offers tours at various distilleries. Some tours are complimentary, while others may have a small fee.

- **Buffalo Trace Distillery**: Located in Frankfort, Buffalo Trace offers free tours that provide an overview of the bourbon-making process and the history of the distillery. They also have optional paid tours that offer more in-depth experiences and tastings.
- **Four Roses Distillery**: Four Roses, situated in Lawrenceburg, offers complimentary tours of their facility, where visitors can learn about the distillation process and the unique methods used by Four Roses to create their bourbon.

Kentucky State Capitol (Frankfort): The Kentucky State Capitol offers free guided tours where you can learn about the state's government, history, and architecture. Tours are typically available Monday through Friday.

Historic Walking Tours: Many cities in Kentucky, such as Louisville, Lexington, and Frankfort, offer self-guided or guided walking tours of their historic districts. These tours often showcase architectural landmarks, museums, and cultural attractions. Check with the local visitor center or historical society for information on available tours.

Self-guided Tours of Mammoth Cave National Park: While there may be a fee for cave tours, Mammoth Cave National Park offers free self-guided tours of surface trails, historic sites, and scenic overlooks. Pick up a map from the visitor center and explore the park's natural beauty at your own pace.

7. **Shopping:**
   - Look for unique finds in local markets and craft shops.
   - Visit outlet malls like The Outlet Shoppes of the Bluegrass in Simpsonville for discounted luxury brands.

8. **Insider Tips:**
   - **Off-Peak Travel:** Consider traveling during the offseason for potential discounts on accommodation and attractions.
   - **Local Discounts:** Check with local tourism offices for any current promotions or discount cards.
   - **Historical Sites:** Kentucky is rich in history. Visit historical sites, some of which may have low or no entrance fees.

Here are the top attractions in Kentucky, along with some money-saving tips for visiting each one:

Louisville: Explore the largest city in Kentucky with cultural attractions and outdoor activities.

- Money-Saving Tip: Look for combo tickets and discounts on attractions like the Louisville Mega Cavern.

Kentucky Derby, Louisville: Attend the famous horse race and experience Derby-related events.

- Money-Saving Tip: Purchase tickets in advance, as they may be more affordable than last-minute options.

Mammoth Cave National Park, near Bowling Green: Explore the world's longest cave system.

- Money-Saving Tip: Join a guided cave tour, which is included in the park's entrance fee.

Lexington: Discover the horse capital of the world with thoroughbred farms and historic sites.

- Money-Saving Tip: Take self-guided tours of horse farms, which are often free or low-cost.

Red River Gorge, Daniel Boone National Forest: Hike, rock climb, and enjoy stunning natural beauty.

- Money-Saving Tip: Camping in the forest is a budget-friendly lodging option.

Churchill Downs, Louisville: Visit the historic racetrack and the Kentucky Derby Museum.

- Money-Saving Tip: Look for combo tickets to save on museum admission and tours.

Bourbon Trail: Explore the Bourbon Trail and visit distilleries for tastings and tours.

- Money-Saving Tip: Consider a passport program for discounts on distillery visits.

Keeneland, Lexington: Experience horse racing and beautiful grounds.

- Money-Saving Tip: Attend morning workouts, which are free, and visit during non-race days.

Daniel Boone National Forest: Enjoy outdoor activities in a natural setting.

- Money-Saving Tip: Hike the forest's trails for free or camp in designated areas.

Louisville Waterfront Park: Stroll along the Ohio River and enjoy outdoor events.

- Money-Saving Tip: Attend free concerts and festivals in the park during the summer.

Maker's Mark Distillery, Loretto: Tour a historic bourbon distillery.

- Money-Saving Tip: Look for discounts on distillery tours and tastings.

Ark Encounter, Williamstown: Explore a life-size replica of Noah's Ark.

- Money-Saving Tip: Purchase tickets online for discounts and check for special offers.

Big South Fork National River and Recreation Area: Discover outdoor adventures and scenic beauty.

- Money-Saving Tip: Camp in the recreation area for affordable lodging.

The Ark Encounter, Williamstown: Explore a massive replica of Noah's Ark.

- Money-Saving Tip: Check for discounts on admission tickets, especially for children.

Louisville Slugger Museum & Factory: Learn about baseball history and tour the factory.

- Money-Saving Tip: Look for family and group discounts on museum admission.

Paducah: Experience a riverfront city with arts and cultural attractions.

- Money-Saving Tip: Attend free art exhibitions and events in Paducah's historic district.

My Old Kentucky Home State Park, Bardstown: Visit the historic mansion and enjoy the gardens.

- Money-Saving Tip: Take advantage of discounts on guided tours and admission.

Cumberland Falls State Resort Park, near Corbin: Witness the "Niagara of the South."

- Money-Saving Tip: Visit the falls for free or explore the park's hiking trails.

Louisville Mega Cavern: Take an underground adventure and explore cavern attractions.

- Money-Saving Tip: Purchase tickets online for discounts and check for seasonal promotions.

National Corvette Museum, Bowling Green: Discover the history of the Corvette.

- Money-Saving Tip: Look for discounts on museum admission and guided tours.

RECAP

Category	Insider Tips
Food	1. Indulge in Kentucky's iconic dish, the Hot Brown, at local diners or restaurants for a taste of tradition.
	2. Visit local barbecue joints for mouthwatering smoked meats and savory sides at affordable prices.
	3. Explore the Bourbon Trail and visit distilleries for tastings and tours, often offering free or low-cost options.
	4. Attend local food festivals and events celebrating Kentucky's culinary heritage for affordable eats and entertainment.
Accommodation	1. Stay in charming bed and breakfasts or guesthouses in historic towns like Bardstown or Lexington for a cozy and unique experience.
	2. Consider camping in Kentucky's state parks or national forests for budget-friendly lodging surrounded by nature.
	3. Look for budget motels or chain hotels in smaller towns or cities for affordable overnight stays.
	4. Utilize platforms like Airbnb or VRBO to find affordable lodging options with local hosts in Kentucky.
Activities	1. Explore the natural beauty of Kentucky's landscapes by hiking, fishing, or horseback riding in state parks and forests.
	2. Visit historical sites and museums like the Kentucky Horse Park or Abraham Lincoln Birthplace National Historical Park for educational and low-cost outings.
	3. Attend local bluegrass music festivals or live music events for authentic Kentucky entertainment.
	4. Take a scenic drive along the backroads of Kentucky's countryside, exploring charming small towns and picturesque vistas.
Transport	1. Rent a car to explore Kentucky's rural areas and attractions at your own pace, with affordable rental options available.
	2. Utilize public transportation options in major cities like Louisville or Lexington for cost-effective travel within urban areas.
	3. Look for carpooling opportunities or ride-sharing services for shared transportation costs when traveling between cities or towns.
	4. Consider biking or walking in downtown areas or along designated trails for eco-friendly and budget-friendly travel options.

Louisiana

Louisiana's history is a captivating blend of French, Spanish, African, and Native American influences. Originally colonized by the French in the 17th century, Louisiana has witnessed a dynamic cultural evolution, including the impact of African slavery, Spanish rule, and the indelible contributions of Creole and Cajun cultures.

Things to Consider:

- **Music and Festivals:** Louisiana is synonymous with lively music and vibrant festivals. If possible, plan your visit around events like Mardi Gras in New Orleans or the Jazz and Heritage Festival to experience the state's spirited celebrations.
- **Culinary Delights:** Indulge in the unique flavors of Cajun and Creole cuisine. From gumbo and jambalaya to beignets and po'boys, Louisiana's culinary scene is a delightful exploration of spices and traditions.
- **Swamps and Bayous:** Explore the mysterious beauty of Louisiana's swamps and bayous. Consider taking a swamp tour to witness the state's distinctive wildlife, including alligators and picturesque cypress trees.

Local Tips:

- **French Quarter Exploration:** Immerse yourself in the historic French Quarter of New Orleans. Wander through lively streets, enjoy street performances, and savor the lively atmosphere of the birthplace of jazz.
- **Mardi Gras Magic:** If your visit aligns with Mardi Gras, embrace the festive spirit. Plan to attend parades, indulge in king cake, and experience the vibrant colors and costumes that define this iconic celebration.
- **Plantation Tours:** Learn about the state's complex history by visiting one of the many plantations along the Mississippi River. These tours offer insights into Louisiana's antebellum past and the cultural diversity that shaped the region.

Must-Visit Places:

- **New Orleans:** Explore the dynamic city of New Orleans, known for its lively music scene, historic architecture, and vibrant street life. Don't miss the iconic Bourbon Street and the historic French Quarter.
- **Tabasco Factory in Avery Island:** Visit the Tabasco sauce factory on Avery Island to learn about the history of this famous condiment and sample its various flavors.
- **Bayou Country:** Experience the serene beauty of Louisiana's bayous by taking a boat tour. The Jean Lafitte National Historical Park and Preserve offers a glimpse into the unique ecosystem of the region.

1. Accommodation:
   - Look for boutique hotels, charming guesthouses, or well-reviewed budget hotels. Many New Orleans hotels offer competitive rates, especially during the off-peak season.

- Recommended places: Old No. 77 Hotel & Chandlery in New Orleans, The Cook Hotel and Conference Center in Baton Rouge, and Maison de la Luz in New Orleans.

2. Transportation:

- Consider walking or using public transportation in cities like New Orleans where the French Quarter and other attractions are easily accessible on foot or by streetcar.
- If renting a car, compare prices from different rental agencies and book in advance for potential discounts.

3. Food:

- Explore local markets and affordable eateries for authentic Louisiana cuisine. Enjoy beignets, po'boys, and gumbo at local joints.
- Recommended restaurants: Cochon in New Orleans, Cafe du Monde in New Orleans, and Parrain's Seafood Restaurant in Baton Rouge.

4. Attractions:

- Take advantage of free attractions, such as exploring the French Quarter in New Orleans, walking along Bourbon Street, and enjoying street performances.
- Look for combination tickets for museums and tours to save money. The New Orleans Pass offers discounted entry to various attractions.

5. Outdoor Activities:

- Enjoy the natural beauty of Louisiana by exploring state parks and bayous. Many outdoor activities are budget-friendly.
- Recommended places: Jean Lafitte National Historical Park and Preserve, Fontainebleau State Park, and Audubon Park in New Orleans.

6. Entertainment:

- Check for free live music events, especially in New Orleans, which is known for its vibrant music scene.
- Explore the historic Frenchmen Street for a variety of music venues with no cover charges.
- **Bayou Swamp Tours:** While most guided swamp tours may require a fee, some companies offer free or donation-based tours for small groups. Keep an eye out for local tour operators or organizations offering these tours.
- **Louisiana State Museum (New Orleans):** While admission to some exhibits may require a fee, the Louisiana State Museum occasionally offers free admission days or free guided tours. Check their website or contact them directly for tour availability.

7. Shopping:

- Explore local markets and street vendors for unique finds and souvenirs.
- The French Market in New Orleans is a great place to shop for affordable local products.

8. Insider Tips:

- **Happy Hours:** Take advantage of happy hour specials at bars and restaurants for discounted drinks and appetizers.
- **Festivals:** Check the local events calendar for festivals, many of which are free and offer a taste of Louisiana's lively culture.
- **Student and Military Discounts:** If applicable, inquire about discounts at attractions, hotels, and restaurants.

Top Attractions and how to save.

New Orleans offers a vibrant tapestry of jazz music, historic architecture, and delectable cuisine. Here are some detailed tips to make the most of your visit while keeping your budget intact:

Streetcar Rides for Affordable Transportation:

- **Cost:** Typically $1.25 per ride or $3 for an all-day Jazzy Pass.
- **Money-Saving Tip:** Opt for the Jazzy Pass if you plan to take multiple rides in a day for the best value.

French Quarter Exploration:

- **Money-Saving Tip:** Enjoy free live music performances in Jackson Square and along Bourbon Street, soaking in the authentic New Orleans atmosphere without spending a dime.

Plantation Tours along the Great River Road:

- **Cost:** Varies depending on the plantation and tour package.
- **Money-Saving Tip:** Look for combination tickets to visit multiple plantations, often offering significant savings compared to individual tours.

Swamp Tours to Experience Louisiana's Bayous:

- **Cost:** Typically around $25 to $60 per person, depending on the tour duration and inclusions.
- **Money-Saving Tip:** Check for discounts on swamp tour tickets, especially during off-peak times, and consider booking as a group for additional savings.

Mardi Gras World Experience:

- **Cost:** Around $22 for adult admission.
- **Money-Saving Tip:** Purchase tickets online in advance for discounts, and consider visiting during non-peak hours for a quieter experience.

Audubon Zoo Visit:

- **Cost:** Approximately $25 for adult admission.

- **Money-Saving Tip:** Look for combo tickets that include other Audubon attractions for savings on overall admission costs.

Indulge in Beignets at Cafe du Monde:

- **Cost:** Around $3 for an order of beignets.
- **Money-Saving Tip:** Share a plate of beignets with friends to save on costs while still satisfying your sweet tooth.

Tour Oak Alley Plantation:

- **Cost:** Starting at around $25 for adult admission.
- **Money-Saving Tip:** Purchase admission tickets online for discounts and consider visiting during weekdays for potentially lower rates.

Exploring Bayou Lafourche:

- **Cost:** Varies depending on the rental company and duration.
- **Money-Saving Tip:** Explore the bayou on your own with rented kayaks or canoes for a budget-friendly outdoor adventure.

New Orleans City Park: Visit the large urban park with gardens and art installations.

- Money-Saving Tip: Enjoy free admission to the park, and consider a picnic for affordable dining.

St. Louis Cathedral, New Orleans: Admire the historic cathedral in Jackson Square.

- Money-Saving Tip: Attend free organ concerts and enjoy the cathedral's architecture.

Louisiana State Capitol, Baton Rouge: Tour the tallest state capitol building in the United States.

- Money-Saving Tip: Admission to the capitol is free, and guided tours are available.

Honey Island Swamp Tour, Slidell: Explore the pristine Honey Island Swamp.

- Money-Saving Tip: Look for discounts on swamp tour tickets and group rates.

Steamboat Natchez, New Orleans: Cruise the Mississippi River on a steamboat.

- Money-Saving Tip: Book online in advance for discounts on steamboat cruises.

National WWII Museum, New Orleans: Learn about World War II history.

- Money-Saving Tip: Check for museum discounts and consider combo tickets.

Preservation Hall, New Orleans: Listen to traditional New Orleans jazz performances.

- Money-Saving Tip: Attend early evening shows for lower admission prices.

Tabasco Factory Tour, Avery Island: Visit the home of Tabasco hot sauce.

- Money-Saving Tip: Enjoy the free factory tour and try samples.

Lake Pontchartrain Causeway: Drive across the world's longest bridge over water.

- Money-Saving Tip: Take a scenic drive along the causeway for free.

Alligator Farms: Experience close encounters with alligators at various farms.

- Money-Saving Tip: Look for discounts on alligator farm admission tickets.

Nottoway Plantation, White Castle: Tour the largest remaining antebellum mansion in the South.

- Money-Saving Tip: Purchase tickets online for discounts and guided tours.

Category	Insider Tips
Food	1. Indulge in Louisiana's culinary delights at local po'boy shops and seafood markets for authentic flavors.
	2. Look for "plate lunch specials" at neighborhood eateries for budget-friendly meals with generous portions.
	3. Visit farmers' markets for fresh produce and Cajun spices, perfect for cooking affordable meals at home.
	4. Enjoy happy hour at local bars for discounted drinks and appetizers, often featuring live music and ambiance.
Accommodation	1. Stay in bed and breakfasts or guesthouses in historic districts for unique and affordable lodging experiences.
	2. Consider renting a cabin or cottage in Louisiana's bayou country for a secluded and budget-friendly getaway.
	3. Look for budget hotels or motels in smaller towns outside major tourist areas for lower rates.
	4. Utilize vacation rental websites to find affordable accommodations with kitchen facilities for self-catering.
Activities	1. Explore Louisiana's swamps and bayous with guided eco-tours or self-guided paddling adventures for nature lovers.
	2. Attend local festivals and cultural events for entertainment and authentic Louisiana experiences without breaking the bank.
	3. Visit historic plantations and museums with affordable admission fees for insights into Louisiana's rich history.
	4. Enjoy free outdoor activities like hiking, birdwatching, or picnicking in Louisiana's state parks and wildlife preserves.
Transport	1. Rent a car to explore Louisiana's diverse regions and attractions at your own pace and convenience.
	2. Utilize public transportation options in cities like New Orleans and Baton Rouge for cost-effective travel within urban areas.

	3. Consider carpooling or ridesharing with fellow travelers for shared transportation costs, especially for longer journeys.
	4. Explore biking or walking tours in historic neighborhoods or along scenic riverfronts for eco-friendly and budget-friendly travel options.

Maine

Maine's history is deeply intertwined with its maritime heritage. Indigenous peoples, European explorers, and early American settlers have all played a role in shaping the character of this northeastern state. From fishing and shipbuilding to the vibrant coastal communities, Maine's history is a testament to its resilience and connection to the sea.

Things to Consider:

- **Coastal Exploration:** Maine's coastline is a treasure trove of beauty. Explore the iconic lighthouses, quaint fishing villages, and rocky shores. Acadia National Park, with its granite peaks and ocean views, is a must-visit destination.
- **Seafood Delights:** Indulge in the delicious seafood offerings, from lobster rolls to clam chowder. Maine is renowned for its fresh and flavorful maritime cuisine.
- **Outdoor Adventures:** Whether you're into hiking, kayaking, or simply taking scenic drives, Maine offers a wide range of outdoor activities. The state's diverse landscapes provide ample opportunities for exploration.

Local Tips:

- **Lighthouse Tours:** Maine boasts some of the most scenic lighthouses in the country. Consider taking a lighthouse tour to discover the maritime history and enjoy breathtaking views.
- **Autumn Foliage:** If your visit coincides with the fall season, be sure to experience the vibrant colors of autumn. Maine's foliage is a spectacular sight, especially in places like the White Mountains and along the Kennebec River.
- **Acadian Culture:** Explore the Acadian culture in northern Maine, where you can learn about the French-speaking communities and their unique history and traditions.

Must-Visit Places:

- **Bar Harbor:** Explore the charming town of Bar Harbor, the gateway to Acadia National Park. Enjoy the quaint shops, fresh seafood, and stunning views of Mount Desert Island.
- **Portland:** Discover the vibrant city of Portland, known for its historic Old Port district, art scene, and diverse culinary offerings.
- **Lobstering Experience:** Consider taking a lobster boat tour to learn about the state's lobstering industry. It's a hands-on experience that provides insight into Maine's maritime heritage.

1. Accommodation:

- Look for cozy bed and breakfasts, inns, or boutique hotels. Consider staying in charming coastal towns for a quintessential Maine experience.

- Recommended places: The Boathouse Waterfront Hotel in Kennebunkport, The Inn at St. John in Portland, and The Captain Lord Mansion in Kennebunkport.

2. Transportation:
- Consider renting a car to explore the scenic coastal routes and visit remote attractions.
- Utilize public transportation options in cities like Portland, where you can easily navigate the downtown area on foot.

3. Food:
- Enjoy fresh seafood at local seafood shacks and casual eateries. Look for lobster specials and seafood festivals.
- Recommended restaurants: Eventide Oyster Co. in Portland, The Lobster Shack in Cape Elizabeth, and Thurston's Lobster Pound in Bernard.

4. Attractions:
- Explore coastal lighthouses and charming fishing villages. Many of these attractions are free or have a nominal entrance fee.
- Consider a visit to Acadia National Park; entrance fees are reasonable, and the scenery is breathtaking.

5. Outdoor Activities:
- Take advantage of Maine's natural beauty by exploring hiking trails and enjoying water activities.
- Recommended activities: Whale watching in Bar Harbor, hiking in Acadia National Park, and exploring the Coastal Maine Botanical Gardens.

6. Entertainment:
- Attend local events and festivals. Many towns host free concerts, art shows, and cultural events, especially during the summer months.
- Check the schedule for the Maine Lobster Festival or other local seafood festivals.

Maine's coastline is dotted with picturesque lighthouses, and while many offer tours, not all of them are free. However, there are a few lighthouses in Maine where you can explore the grounds and, in some cases, even climb the tower for free. Here are a couple of examples:

1. **Portland Head Light**: Located in Cape Elizabeth near Portland, Portland Head Light is one of the most iconic lighthouses in Maine. While there may be a small fee for parking in the adjacent state park, visitors can explore the grounds around the lighthouse for free. The adjacent museum, operated by the town of Cape Elizabeth, may have a small admission fee.
2. **West Quoddy Head Light**: Situated in Lubec, West Quoddy Head Light marks the easternmost point in the contiguous United States. Visitors can explore the lighthouse grounds and enjoy scenic views of the Bay of Fundy and surrounding coastline for free. There may be a small fee for parking in the state park.

7. Shopping:
- Explore local markets and artisan shops for unique Maine-made products.
- Freeport is known for its outlet stores, including the flagship L.L.Bean store, where you can find discounted outdoor gear.

8. Insider Tips:

- **Midweek Travel:** Consider traveling during the week for potential discounts on accommodations and fewer crowds at popular attractions.
- **National Park Pass:** If planning to visit multiple national parks, consider an America the Beautiful Pass for cost savings on entrance fees.
- **Local Discounts:** Check with local visitor centers for discounts on tours and attractions.

Top Savings on popular attractions

Acadia National Park: Explore the stunning landscapes of this national park.
- Money-Saving Tip: Purchase an annual pass or visit during fee-free days for cost savings.

Portland: Discover Maine's largest city with its historic charm and coastal beauty.

- Money-Saving Tip: Explore the Old Port district on foot for free and visit local markets.

Bar Harbor: Enjoy a picturesque coastal town near Acadia National Park.

- Money-Saving Tip: Take advantage of free or low-cost outdoor activities like hiking.

Lighthouses: Visit iconic lighthouses like Portland Head Light and Pemaquid Point Light.

- Money-Saving Tip: Some lighthouse visits are free or have a nominal entrance fee.

Kennebunkport: Experience a coastal resort town known for its beaches and seafood.

- Money-Saving Tip: Enjoy affordable beach days and explore local shops.

Camden: Explore a charming harbor town with outdoor adventures.

- Money-Saving Tip: Hike or walk along scenic trails and enjoy the coastal views.

Maine Lobster: Savor fresh lobster at local seafood shacks and restaurants.

- Money-Saving Tip: Look for lobster roll specials and dine at less touristy spots for better prices.

Freeport: Shop at outlet stores and visit the famous LL Bean flagship store.

- Money-Saving Tip: Take advantage of outlet discounts and browse LL Bean's outdoor gear.

Baxter State Park: Hike and camp in this wilderness area near Mount Katahdin.

- Money-Saving Tip: Purchase a park pass for multiple visits and camping savings.

Augusta: Discover the state capital with historic landmarks and riverfront views.

- Money-Saving Tip: Explore the city's historic districts and enjoy free attractions.

York: Relax on scenic beaches and explore the historic town.

- Money-Saving Tip: Enjoy budget-friendly beach days with picnics and water activities.

Portland Museum of Art: Admire art collections and exhibitions in Portland.

- Money-Saving Tip: Visit on free admission Fridays and explore the museum's outdoor sculpture garden.

Maine Maritime Museum, Bath: Learn about the state's maritime history.

- Money-Saving Tip: Check for discounts on museum admission and guided tours.

Old Orchard Beach: Experience a classic seaside destination with an amusement park.

- Money-Saving Tip: Walk along the pier and enjoy free beach access.

Bangor: Explore a city with cultural attractions and outdoor activities.

- Money-Saving Tip: Attend free concerts and events in Bangor's parks.

Ogunquit: Enjoy the beautiful beach and coastal town.

- Money-Saving Tip: Visit during the off-peak season for lower lodging rates.

Penobscot Bay: Discover scenic islands and maritime communities.

- Money-Saving Tip: Explore public-access islands and enjoy affordable boat tours.

Maine State House, Augusta: Tour the state capitol building.

- Money-Saving Tip: Admission to the state house is free, and guided tours are available.

Sugarloaf: Experience a popular ski resort in the winter and hiking in the summer.

- Money-Saving Tip: Consider lodging packages and visit during non-peak times.

Belfast: Visit a coastal town known for its arts and local shops.

- Money-Saving Tip: Attend free community events and explore galleries.

Maryland

The Old Line State, a place where history, culture, and scenic landscapes come together to create a diverse and captivating destination on the East Coast of the United States. Maryland offers a mix of urban sophistication, charming coastal towns, and natural beauty. Whether you're exploring the vibrant city of Baltimore, relaxing on the Eastern Shore, or visiting historical sites, Maryland has something to offer every traveler. Here's an introduction to Maryland, along with some key things to consider and local tips for your visit:

Maryland holds a significant place in American history. It played a crucial role in the founding of the nation and witnessed important events during the American Revolution and the Civil War. Visitors can explore historical sites such as the Antietam National Battlefield, Fort McHenry, and the Maryland State House in Annapolis, where the Treaty of Paris was ratified.

Things to Consider:

- **Baltimore**: Baltimore is Maryland's largest city and offers a variety of cultural attractions, including world-class museums, historic neighborhoods, and the bustling Inner Harbor. Don't miss the National Aquarium and the Baltimore Museum of Art.
- **Chesapeake Bay**: Maryland is known for its beautiful Chesapeake Bay coastline. Consider visiting coastal towns like Annapolis, St. Michaels, or Ocean City to enjoy beaches, seafood, and water activities.
- **Outdoor Adventures**: Maryland offers plenty of opportunities for outdoor activities, including hiking in the Appalachian Mountains, kayaking on the Chesapeake Bay, and exploring state parks and wildlife refuges.

Local Tips:

- **Annapolis**: Explore Annapolis, the state capital, with its charming historic district, sailboat-filled harbor, and the United States Naval Academy. Take a guided tour to learn about the city's rich maritime history.
- **Crab Feast**: Don't leave Maryland without trying the iconic Maryland blue crab. Visit a local crab shack or seafood restaurant for a crab feast, where you can crack crabs and enjoy Old Bay seasoning.
- **Eastern Shore**: Discover the Eastern Shore of Maryland, known for its rural charm, beaches, and quaint towns. Visit the charming town of St. Michaels or explore Blackwater National Wildlife Refuge.
- **Scenic Drives**: Take scenic drives, such as the Chesapeake Country Scenic Byway, for picturesque views of the Chesapeake Bay and its surrounding landscapes.
- **Historic Frederick**: Explore historic Frederick, a city known for its well-preserved 18th and 19th-century architecture, boutique shops, and vibrant arts scene.

- **Civil War Trails**: If you're a history enthusiast, follow the Civil War Trails to explore the state's Civil War history and visit battlefields and museums.
- **Maryland Wine Trails**: Discover Maryland's emerging wine industry by visiting wineries along the Maryland Wine Trails. Sample local wines and enjoy picturesque vineyard settings.

Maryland invites you to experience its blend of history, culture, and natural beauty. Whether you're touring historical sites, indulging in seafood delicacies, or simply enjoying the coastal views, the Old Line State offers a diverse range of experiences for every traveler. Enjoy your visit to Maryland!

1. Accommodation:
- Look for well-reviewed hotels, inns, or boutique accommodations, especially in historic areas.
- Recommended places: The Ivy Hotel in Baltimore, Annapolis Waterfront Hotel in Annapolis, and Historic Inns of Annapolis.

2. Transportation:
- Utilize public transportation in cities like Baltimore and Washington D.C., where it can be convenient and cost-effective.
- Consider using ride-sharing services or renting a car if you plan to explore rural areas or multiple cities.

3. Food:
- Explore local markets and eateries to enjoy a mix of seafood and diverse cuisine.
- Recommended restaurants: The Blackwall Hitch in Annapolis, Thames Street Oyster House in Baltimore, and Woodberry Kitchen in Baltimore.

4. Attractions:
- Take advantage of free attractions, such as exploring the Inner Harbor in Baltimore, walking along the National Mall in Washington D.C., and visiting historic districts like Annapolis.
- Consider city passes for discounts on multiple attractions, such as the Baltimore Museum of Art or the Maryland Science Center.

5. Outdoor Activities:
- Enjoy the Chesapeake Bay area by exploring parks and waterfronts. Many outdoor activities are budget-friendly.
- Recommended places: Assateague State Park, Great Falls Park, and Sandy Point State Park.

6. Entertainment:
- Attend local events and festivals. Maryland hosts various cultural and music festivals throughout the year.
- Check the schedule for events like the Maryland Renaissance Festival or the Preakness Stakes.

- **Maryland State House Tours (Annapolis):** The Maryland State House offers free guided tours where you can learn about the state's government, history, and architecture. Tours are typically available Monday through Friday.
- **Baltimore Inner Harbor Walking Tours:** While not always guided, the Inner Harbor area of Baltimore offers many attractions and points of interest that you can explore on foot for free. Take a stroll along the waterfront, visit historic ships, and enjoy the views of the city skyline.
- **National Historic Districts:** Many cities and towns in Maryland, such as Annapolis, Baltimore, and Frederick, have designated national historic districts with self-guided

walking tours. Pick up a map from the local visitor center or chamber of commerce and explore the architecture, landmarks, and history of these areas at your own pace.

7. Shopping:
- Explore local shops in historic areas for unique finds and souvenirs.
- Visit outlet malls like Arundel Mills for discounted shopping.

8. Insider Tips:
- **Museum Free Days:** Many museums in Washington D.C. offer free admission on certain days of the week.
- **Water Activities:** Consider budget-friendly water activities such as paddleboarding or kayaking in the Chesapeake Bay.
- **Happy Hours:** Take advantage of happy hour specials at bars and restaurants for discounted drinks and appetizers.

Sample Budget:
- Accommodation (per night): $80 - $150
- Meals (per day): $30 - $50
- Transportation (if needed): $20 - $40
- Attractions and Entertainment: $20 - $40

Final Thoughts:

Maryland, with its mix of history, culture, and outdoor beauty, provides ample opportunities for a luxurious experience on a budget. By exploring local attractions, enjoying diverse cuisine, and taking advantage of free events, you can make the most of your visit without exceeding your budget. Enjoy your budget-friendly luxury trip to Maryland!

Here are the top attractions in Maryland, along with some money-saving tips for visiting each one:

Baltimore: Explore the largest city in Maryland with its historic neighborhoods and cultural attractions.

- Money-Saving Tip: Take advantage of free museums and attractions like the Inner Harbor.

Inner Harbor, Baltimore: Enjoy waterfront views, restaurants, and attractions.

- Money-Saving Tip: Walk along the harbor and explore the free attractions, such as the Maryland Science Center's outdoor exhibits.

Annapolis: Visit the state capital with its historic charm and naval heritage.

- Money-Saving Tip: Take self-guided tours of the United States Naval Academy and the State House for free.

Ocean City: Relax on the sandy beaches and enjoy the boardwalk.

- Money-Saving Tip: Visit during the off-peak season for lower hotel rates and dining discounts.

Assateague Island National Seashore: Discover wild horses and pristine beaches.

- Money-Saving Tip: Bring your own camping gear for budget-friendly beach camping.

National Aquarium, Baltimore: Explore marine life and interactive exhibits.

- Money-Saving Tip: Look for discounted admission on weekdays and online ticket deals.

Antietam National Battlefield: Learn about Civil War history at this historic battlefield.

- Money-Saving Tip: Purchase an America the Beautiful Pass for access to national parks.

Chesapeake Bay: Enjoy outdoor activities and water sports on the bay.

- Money-Saving Tip: Bring your own kayak or paddleboard for budget-friendly fun.

Frederick: Explore a historic town with charming streets and museums.

- Money-Saving Tip: Visit free museums like the National Museum of Civil War Medicine.

Rockville: Experience cultural events and dining in a suburban setting.

- Money-Saving Tip: Attend free outdoor concerts and community events.

C & O Canal National Historical Park: Hike or bike along the scenic canal towpath.

- Money-Saving Tip: Explore the park's trails and enjoy free outdoor activities.

Hagerstown: Discover a city with museums and outdoor attractions.

- Money-Saving Tip: Visit free attractions like the Hagerstown City Park.

Blackwater National Wildlife Refuge: Observe wildlife and enjoy birdwatching.

- Money-Saving Tip: Visit the refuge for free and bring your binoculars.

Fort McHenry National Monument and Historic Shrine, Baltimore: Learn about the War of 1812 and the national anthem.

- Money-Saving Tip: Purchase an annual pass to access multiple national parks.

Maryland Science Center, Baltimore: Explore interactive exhibits and a planetarium.

- Money-Saving Tip: Look for discounts on admission, especially for students and children.

St. Michaels: Experience a charming waterfront town with historic sites.

- Money-Saving Tip: Visit free attractions like the St. Michaels Museum.

Patuxent Research Refuge: Enjoy wildlife and nature trails.

- Money-Saving Tip: Explore the refuge's trails and attend free programs.

B&O Railroad Museum, Baltimore: Learn about the history of railroads.

- Money-Saving Tip: Check for museum discounts and family passes.

Salisbury: Explore a city with cultural attractions and a vibrant downtown.

- Money-Saving Tip: Attend free community events and explore local art galleries.

Deep Creek Lake: Relax by Maryland's largest freshwater lake and enjoy water activities.

- Money-Saving Tip: Rent water sports equipment in advance for cost savings.

Massachusetts

Massachusetts played a pivotal role in the early history of the United States. From the landing of the Pilgrims in Plymouth in 1620 to the revolutionary events in Boston, the state is a living museum of America's colonial past. The academic institutions, including Harvard University, further contribute to the state's intellectual legacy.

Things to Consider:

- **Historical Landmarks:** Explore the historic landmarks of Boston, such as the Freedom Trail, Paul Revere's House, and the Massachusetts State House. These sites offer a glimpse into the state's role in shaping the nation.
- **Cultural Institutions:** Massachusetts is home to world-class museums, theaters, and cultural institutions. Don't miss the Museum of Fine Arts in Boston, the Massachusetts Museum of Contemporary Art (MASS MoCA), and the historic theaters along Boston's Theatre District.
- **Scenic Beauty:** Enjoy the diverse landscapes, from the picturesque Cape Cod beaches to the serene Berkshire Mountains. Massachusetts offers both coastal retreats and opportunities for outdoor adventures.

Local Tips:

- **Boston Neighborhoods:** Explore the distinct neighborhoods of Boston, each with its own character. From the historic charm of Beacon Hill to the vibrant energy of the North End, Boston is a city of neighborhoods waiting to be discovered.
- **Cape Cod Relaxation:** If you're seeking a coastal escape, spend time on Cape Cod. Enjoy the sandy beaches, picturesque lighthouses, and quaint villages that define this iconic New England destination.
- **Fall Foliage:** Experience the breathtaking beauty of fall foliage in Massachusetts. Take a scenic drive through the Berkshires or hike in the state parks to witness the vibrant colors of autumn.

Must-Visit Places:

- **Boston:** Immerse yourself in the rich history and cultural offerings of Boston. Visit the Boston Common, Faneuil Hall, and the Boston Tea Party Ships & Museum.
- **Salem:** Discover the intriguing history of Salem, known for the infamous witch trials. Explore the Salem Witch Museum, historic homes, and waterfront attractions.
- **Cape Cod National Seashore:** Experience the natural beauty of the Cape Cod National Seashore, with its pristine beaches, dunes, and hiking trails.

As you explore Massachusetts, let the blend of history, culture, and natural beauty captivate you. Whether strolling through historic streets or enjoying the coastal landscapes, Massachusetts welcomes you with open arms. Enjoy your time in the Bay State!

1. Accommodation:

- Look for boutique hotels, charming bed and breakfasts, or well-reviewed budget-friendly hotels.

- Recommended places: The Liberty Hotel in Boston, The Porches Inn in North Adams, and The Red Lion Inn in Stockbridge.

2. Transportation:

- Utilize public transportation in cities like Boston, where it's convenient and well-connected.
- Consider walking or biking in areas with historic significance, like the Freedom Trail in Boston.

3. Food:

- Explore local markets, food trucks, and affordable eateries for diverse and authentic cuisine.
- Recommended restaurants: Neptune Oyster in Boston, The Friendly Toast in Cambridge, and Legal Sea Foods.

4. Attractions:

- Take advantage of free attractions, such as walking the Freedom Trail in Boston, exploring Harvard Yard in Cambridge, and visiting historic districts like Salem.
- Consider city passes for discounts on multiple attractions, such as the Boston CityPASS.

5. Outdoor Activities:

- Enjoy the natural beauty of Massachusetts by exploring parks and coastal areas.
- Recommended places: Cape Cod National Seashore, Mount Greylock State Reservation, and the Boston Common.

6. Entertainment:

- Attend local events and festivals. Massachusetts hosts various cultural and art festivals throughout the year.
- Check the schedule for events like the Boston Calling Music Festival or the Boston Film Festival.

- **Massachusetts State House Tours (Boston):** The Massachusetts State House offers free guided tours where you can learn about the state's government, history, and architecture. Tours are typically available Monday through Friday.
- **Freedom Trail (Boston):** While not guided, the Freedom Trail in Boston is a 2.5-mile walking trail that passes by 16 significant historic sites related to the American Revolution. You can explore the trail at your own pace for free, with optional guided tours available for a fee at certain sites.
- **Harvard University Campus Tours (Cambridge):** Harvard University offers free campus tours led by student guides. You can explore the university's historic buildings, landmarks, and academic programs while learning about its history and culture.
- **Boston Public Library Tours (Boston):** The Boston Public Library offers free guided tours of its historic McKim Building, featuring beautiful architecture, artwork, and special collections. Check their website or contact them directly for tour availability.

7. Shopping:

- Explore local shops in historic areas or vibrant neighborhoods for unique finds.
- Visit outlet malls like Wrentham Village Premium Outlets for discounted shopping.

8. Insider Tips:

- **Free Museum Days:** Many museums in Massachusetts offer free admission on specific days or during certain hours.

- **College Towns:** Explore college towns like Cambridge and Amherst for a vibrant atmosphere and affordable dining options.
- **Historical Tours:** Take advantage of free or low-cost historical walking tours in cities like Boston.

Here are the top attractions in Massachusetts, along with some money-saving tips for visiting each one:

Boston: Explore the historic city with its rich history and cultural attractions.

- Money-Saving Tip: Use the Freedom Trail map to explore historic sites on your own for free.

Freedom Trail, Boston: Walk the 2.5-mile trail and visit historic landmarks.

- Money-Saving Tip: Download the free mobile app for a self-guided tour.

Cape Cod: Enjoy beautiful beaches, charming towns, and outdoor activities.

- Money-Saving Tip: Visit public beaches with lower parking fees and explore free nature trails.

Salem: Discover the history of the witch trials and explore maritime heritage.

- Money-Saving Tip: Take advantage of combination tickets for multiple museums.

Plymouth: Step back in time to the Pilgrim era and visit Plymouth Rock.

- Money-Saving Tip: Explore Plimoth Plantation during discounted admission periods.

Harvard University, Cambridge: Explore the historic campus and museums.

- Money-Saving Tip: Enjoy free admission to the Harvard Art Museums on Saturdays from 10 AM to 12 PM.

Fenway Park, Boston: Attend a Red Sox game and experience baseball history.

- Money-Saving Tip: Look for deals on ticket resale websites or visit during weekday games for lower prices.

Cape Cod National Seashore: Discover pristine beaches and scenic landscapes.

- Money-Saving Tip: Purchase an America the Beautiful Pass for access to national parks.

Lexington and Concord: Learn about the American Revolution and historic battles.

- Money-Saving Tip: Visit the Minute Man National Historical Park for free.

Berkshires: Enjoy cultural festivals, museums, and outdoor activities.

- Money-Saving Tip: Attend free outdoor concerts and art events during the summer.

New Bedford: Explore a historic whaling town and visit the New Bedford Whaling Museum.

- Money-Saving Tip: Look for discounted museum admission and family passes.

Museum of Fine Arts, Boston: Admire art collections and exhibitions.

- Money-Saving Tip: Visit on free admission days and enjoy the museum's free guided tours.

Lowell: Discover a city with industrial history and cultural attractions.

- Money-Saving Tip: Explore free attractions like the Lowell National Historical Park.

Mount Greylock State Reservation: Hike to the highest peak in Massachusetts.

- Money-Saving Tip: Enjoy free hiking trails and breathtaking views.

Old Sturbridge Village: Step into the 19th century and experience living history.

- Money-Saving Tip: Check for discounts on village admission and special events.

Plum Island: Relax on a barrier island with beaches and wildlife.

- Money-Saving Tip: Visit the island for free or with a low-cost parking fee.

The Freedom Trail, Boston: Walk the historic trail and explore Boston's past.

- Money-Saving Tip: Download a free self-guided audio tour from the Freedom Trail Foundation.

Saugus Iron Works National Historic Site: Learn about America's first ironworks.

- Money-Saving Tip: Admission to the historic site is free.

Old North Church, Boston: Visit the historic church famous for its role in the American Revolution.

- Money-Saving Tip: Attend free concerts and events at the church.

Cape Cod Rail Trail: Bike along the scenic trail and explore Cape Cod.

Category	Insider Tips
Food	1. Indulge in Maryland's iconic dish, the crab feast, by visiting local seafood markets or crab shacks for freshly caught crabs at reasonable prices.
	2. Explore Baltimore's diverse culinary scene by seeking out hidden gems in neighborhoods like Hampden or Fells Point, where you can find affordable and delicious eats.
	3. Take advantage of happy hour deals at waterfront restaurants along the Chesapeake Bay or Potomac River for discounted seafood and drinks with scenic views.
	4. Visit local farmers' markets like the Baltimore Farmers' Market & Bazaar or the Bethesda Central Farm Market for fresh produce, artisanal foods, and gourmet treats.
Accommodation	1. Stay in charming bed and breakfasts or guesthouses in historic towns like Annapolis or St. Michaels for a cozy and affordable lodging experience.
	2. Consider booking accommodations outside of major tourist areas like Baltimore or Annapolis for lower rates, such as in suburban areas or smaller towns.

	3. Look for budget-friendly options like motels or vacation rentals in beach towns along the Eastern Shore or in rural areas like Western Maryland.
	4. Take advantage of discounts and deals offered by local hotels and inns, especially during the off-peak season or through loyalty programs.
Activities	1. Explore Maryland's scenic outdoor attractions like Assateague Island National Seashore, Great Falls Park, or Patapsco Valley State Park for affordable outdoor adventures.
	2. Visit historical sites and museums with free or low-cost admission, such as the Baltimore Museum of Art, the U.S. Naval Academy Museum, or the Antietam National Battlefield.
	3. Attend local festivals and events celebrating Maryland's culture and heritage, such as the Maryland Seafood Festival, the Maryland Renaissance Festival, or Artscape.
	4. Take advantage of free or low-cost recreational activities like hiking, biking, fishing, or kayaking in Maryland's parks, trails, rivers, and waterways.
Transport	1. Utilize public transportation options in cities like Baltimore or Washington, D.C., including buses, light rail, or the MARC train, to save on transportation costs.
	2. Consider carpooling or ride-sharing services for shared transportation to and from popular destinations or events, helping to reduce fuel and parking expenses.
	3. Explore bike-sharing programs in cities like Baltimore or Annapolis for a convenient and eco-friendly way to get around urban areas and waterfront attractions.
	4. Take advantage of discounted fares or special offers from local transportation providers, such as commuter discounts on trains or buses, for savings on travel expenses.

Montana

Montana is renowned for its pristine landscapes, including Glacier National Park in the northwest and Yellowstone National Park in the southwest. These parks offer opportunities for hiking, camping, wildlife watching, and photography. Additionally, Montana's numerous state parks, forests, and wilderness areas provide a wealth of outdoor activities such as fishing, rafting, skiing, and snowmobiling, depending on the season.

Things to Consider:

- **Vastness**: Montana is the fourth-largest state in the U.S., so be prepared for long drives between destinations. The expansive landscapes make for breathtaking views, but travel times can be longer than expected.
- **Seasonal Weather**: Montana experiences a wide range of weather conditions, with cold winters and warm summers. Be sure to pack accordingly, especially if you plan to visit during the winter months for skiing or snow-related activities.
- **Wildlife**: Montana is home to a diverse range of wildlife, including grizzly bears, wolves, bison, elk, and more. Respect wildlife and follow safety guidelines when exploring the outdoors.

Local Tips:

- **Glacier National Park**: Explore Glacier National Park, often called the "Crown of the Continent." Hike the Going-to-the-Sun Road, take a boat tour on pristine lakes, and marvel at the park's glaciers and rugged terrain.
- **Yellowstone National Park**: Visit the iconic Yellowstone National Park, where you can witness geothermal wonders like Old Faithful, see herds of bison and elk, and explore the Grand Canyon of the Yellowstone.
- **Big Sky**: Discover the mountain town of Big Sky, known for its world-class skiing in the winter and outdoor adventures in the summer. The nearby Big Sky Resort offers a range of activities and stunning views.
- **Missoula**: Explore Missoula, a vibrant city nestled in the Rocky Mountains. Visit the University of Montana campus, stroll along the Clark Fork River, and enjoy the city's arts and cultural scene.
- **Montana's Ghost Towns**: Montana is home to numerous ghost towns that provide a glimpse into the state's mining history. Bannack State Park and Garnet Ghost Town are worth exploring.
- **Fly Fishing**: Montana is famous for its fly fishing opportunities, with numerous pristine rivers and streams. Consider trying your hand at this popular angling activity.
- **National Bison Range**: Witness the beauty of North America's largest land mammal at the National Bison Range near Moiese, Montana. It's a great place for wildlife viewing.

1. Accommodation:

- Explore budget-friendly accommodations like motels, lodges, and cabins, especially in smaller towns.
- Recommended places: The Pollard Hotel in Red Lodge, KwaTaqNuk Resort in Polson, and the Sacajawea Hotel in Three Forks.

2. Transportation:
- Rent a car for flexibility, as Montana's vast landscapes are best explored with your own transportation.
- Plan road trips to scenic destinations, and consider carpooling for longer drives.

3. Food:
- Enjoy local cuisine at affordable diners, cafes, and food trucks. Montana is known for hearty dishes.
- Recommended eateries: The Shack Cafe in Whitefish, The Notorious P.I.G. in Missoula, and Ale Works in Bozeman.

4. Outdoor Activities:
- Take advantage of Montana's stunning natural beauty by exploring its national parks and hiking trails.
- Recommended activities: Glacier National Park, Yellowstone National Park, and hiking in the Bitterroot Mountains.

5. Camping:
- Experience the great outdoors by camping in Montana's beautiful state parks and national forests.
- Campsite fees are often reasonable, and camping allows you to fully immerse yourself in Montana's natural beauty.

6. Hot Springs:
- Relax in one of Montana's natural hot springs, which can be an affordable and rejuvenating experience.
- Recommended hot springs: Quinn's Hot Springs Resort, Fairmont Hot Springs, and Chico Hot Springs.

7. Local Events:
- Attend local events and festivals, which often showcase Montana's cultural richness.
- Check the schedule for events like the Montana Folk Festival or local rodeos.

8. Shopping:
- Explore local markets and shops for unique Montana-made products and souvenirs.
- Consider visiting farmer's markets for fresh, local produce.

9. Insider Tips:
- **National Park Pass:** If visiting multiple national parks, consider purchasing the America the Beautiful Pass for cost savings.
- **Off-Peak Travel:** Prices may be lower during the off-peak season, and you'll encounter fewer crowds.
- **Local Breweries:** Montana has a thriving craft beer scene. Visit local breweries for affordable and unique beer experiences.

Here are the top attractions in Montana, along with some money-saving tips for visiting each one:

Glacier National Park: Explore the stunning landscapes of this national park.

- Money-Saving Tip: Purchase an annual pass or visit during fee-free days for cost savings.

Yellowstone National Park: Discover the geothermal wonders and wildlife of the first national park.

- Money-Saving Tip: Consider camping within the park for budget-friendly lodging.

Missoula: Explore a city known for its cultural scene and outdoor activities.

- Money-Saving Tip: Attend free concerts and outdoor events in Missoula's parks.

Flathead Lake: Enjoy Montana's largest freshwater lake for swimming and boating.

- Money-Saving Tip: Visit state parks around the lake for affordable access.

Little Bighorn Battlefield National Monument: Learn about the history of the Battle of Little Bighorn.

- Money-Saving Tip: Purchase an America the Beautiful Pass for access to national parks.

Bozeman: Experience a city with a vibrant downtown and outdoor adventures.

- Money-Saving Tip: Explore local trails and parks for free outdoor activities.

Bighorn Canyon National Recreation Area: Discover scenic canyons and reservoirs.

- Money-Saving Tip: Enjoy free access to some areas of the recreation area.

Custer-Gallatin National Forest: Hike and camp in the forest's beautiful landscapes.

- Money-Saving Tip: Camping in the forest is a budget-friendly lodging option.

Helena: Visit the state capital with historic sites and cultural attractions.

- Money-Saving Tip: Explore free attractions like the Montana State Capitol building.

Lewis and Clark Caverns State Park: Explore limestone caverns and hiking trails.

- Money-Saving Tip: Check for discounts on cavern tours and consider a state park pass.

Missouri Headwaters State Park: Discover the birthplace of the Missouri River.

- Money-Saving Tip: Visit the park for free and enjoy picnicking and hiking.

Billings: Explore Montana's largest city with cultural events and outdoor activities.

- Money-Saving Tip: Attend free concerts and festivals in Billings' parks.

Big Sky: Enjoy outdoor adventures in a mountain resort town.

- Money-Saving Tip: Hike and explore the area's trails for free activities.

Flathead National Forest: Experience outdoor activities and scenic beauty.

- Money-Saving Tip: Enjoy free access to the forest's recreation areas.

Makoshika State Park: Explore Montana's largest state park with unique rock formations.

- Money-Saving Tip: Visit the park for free and take self-guided hikes.

Garnet Ghost Town: Step back in time and explore a well-preserved ghost town.

- Money-Saving Tip: Admission to Garnet is free, but consider donating to preservation efforts.

Museum of the Rockies, Bozeman: Learn about Montana's history and paleontology.

- Money-Saving Tip: Look for discounts on museum admission and special exhibits.

Glendive: Discover a town with dinosaur fossils and natural beauty.

- Money-Saving Tip: Visit the Makoshika State Park for free outdoor adventures.

Pictograph Cave State Park: Explore caves with Native American rock art.

- Money-Saving Tip: Visit the park for free and enjoy hiking and picnicking.

Havre: Experience a city with historic sites and cultural attractions.

- Money-Saving Tip: Explore free attractions like the Wahkpa Chu'gn Archaeological Site.

Category	Insider Tips
Food	1. Seek out local farmers' markets, such as the Missoula Farmers' Market, for fresh produce and artisanal products at lower prices.
	2. Visit local diners and cafes for hearty meals made with locally sourced ingredients, offering affordable and authentic Montana cuisine.
	3. Head to food trucks or roadside stands for tasty, budget-friendly meals showcasing Montana's culinary delights, like bison burgers or huckleberry treats.
	4. Pack a picnic and enjoy a meal amidst the breathtaking scenery of Montana's national parks or scenic overlooks.
Accommodation	1. Embrace camping in Montana's stunning wilderness, with campgrounds in national forests and state parks offering affordable options with picturesque views.
	2. Consider staying in cozy cabins or lodges in smaller towns like Whitefish or Big Sky for a rustic and budget-friendly lodging experience.
	3. Look for budget motels or family-owned inns in rural areas or along scenic byways for affordable accommodations away from tourist crowds.
	4. Utilize platforms like Airbnb or Vrbo to find unique and affordable lodging options, such as guesthouses or vacation rentals in Montana's charming towns and villages.
Activities	1. Explore hiking trails in Montana's national parks and wilderness areas for stunning views of mountains, lakes, and wildlife, such as Glacier National Park's Highline Trail.

	2. Attend local rodeos or county fairs for authentic Montana entertainment and cultural experiences, often offering affordable admission and family-friendly fun.
	3. Enjoy fishing in Montana's pristine rivers and lakes, with many areas accessible for free or at low cost, providing opportunities for angling enthusiasts of all skill levels.
	4. Take scenic drives along Montana's scenic byways, such as the Beartooth Highway or Going-to-the-Sun Road, for breathtaking vistas of mountains, valleys, and plains.
Transport	1. Rent a car or RV to explore Montana's vast landscapes and remote destinations, with rental options available at airports and major cities like Billings and Bozeman.
	2. Consider carpooling or ridesharing with fellow travelers to share transportation costs and reduce environmental impact when exploring Montana's attractions and scenic drives.
	3. Utilize public transportation options in larger cities like Missoula and Bozeman, such as buses or trolleys, to navigate urban areas and reach nearby attractions and amenities.
	4. Opt for biking or walking in Montana's pedestrian-friendly towns and cities, with many trails and pathways providing opportunities for eco-friendly and budget-friendly transportation.

Nebraska

Nebraska is known for its expansive prairies, fertile farmland, and the Platte River, which serves as a vital stopover point for migratory birds, particularly sandhill cranes. The state offers a mix of outdoor adventures, including hiking, bird-watching, and water sports in its lakes and rivers.

Things to Consider:

- **Omaha and Lincoln**: Nebraska's largest cities, Omaha and Lincoln, are vibrant cultural centers with museums, art galleries, music venues, and a wide range of dining options.
- **Outdoor Activities**: Nebraska's state parks and natural areas provide opportunities for hiking, camping, fishing, and wildlife viewing. The state's diverse landscapes cater to a variety of outdoor interests.
- **Weather**: Nebraska experiences all four seasons, with hot summers and cold winters. Be prepared for varying weather conditions, especially if you plan outdoor activities.

Local Tips:

- **Omaha's Old Market District**: Explore Omaha's historic Old Market District, known for its brick-paved streets, unique shops, restaurants, and art galleries. It's a great place to stroll and soak in the atmosphere.
- **Lincoln's Capitol Building**: Visit the Nebraska State Capitol Building in Lincoln. You can take a guided tour to learn about its architecture and history. Don't forget to view the city from the observation tower.
- **Sandhill Cranes**: If you visit in the spring, witness the spectacular sandhill crane migration along the Platte River. Bird-watching enthusiasts flock to the region for this natural spectacle.
- **Nebraska's Wineries**: Explore Nebraska's wine country, particularly in areas like the Nebraska Wine Trail. Taste local wines and enjoy vineyard tours in a scenic setting.
- **Chimney Rock**: Discover Chimney Rock National Historic Site, a recognizable landmark on the Oregon Trail. It offers a glimpse into the history of westward expansion.
- **Pioneer Trails**: Follow the routes of pioneers and settlers by exploring the Oregon, California, and Mormon Pioneer National Historic Trails, which pass through Nebraska.
- **Wildlife Safari**: Take a wildlife safari in one of Nebraska's wildlife management areas to observe bison, elk, deer, and a variety of bird species.

1. Accommodation:

- Look for budget-friendly hotels, motels, or cozy bed and breakfasts in both urban and rural areas.
- Recommended places: The Magnolia Hotel in Omaha, The Lincoln Marriott Cornhusker Hotel, and The Lied Lodge & Conference Center in Nebraska City.

2. **Transportation:**
   - Consider renting a car to explore Nebraska's attractions at your own pace.
   - Explore public transportation options in cities like Omaha, where it can be convenient and budget-friendly.

3. **Food:**
   - Explore local diners, cafes, and farm-to-table restaurants for affordable and delicious meals.
   - Recommended eateries: The Grey Plume in Omaha, Honest Abe's Burgers & Freedom in Lincoln, and The Chocolate Bar in Grand Island.

4. **Outdoor Activities:**
   - Take advantage of Nebraska's outdoor offerings, including hiking trails, state parks, and scenic overlooks.
   - Recommended activities: Chimney Rock National Historic Site, Smith Falls State Park, and hiking in Indian Cave State Park.

5. **Cultural Attractions:**
   - Explore museums and cultural attractions that showcase Nebraska's history and heritage.
   - Recommended places: The Durham Museum in Omaha, Strategic Air Command & Aerospace Museum in Ashland, and the Nebraska History Museum in Lincoln.

6. **Festivals and Events:**
   - Attend local festivals and events that celebrate Nebraska's culture and community spirit.
   - Check the schedule for events like the Nebraska State Fair in Grand Island or the Berkshire Hathaway Annual Shareholders Meeting in Omaha.

7. **Shopping:**
   - Explore local markets, antique shops, and small boutiques for unique Nebraska-made products.
   - Consider visiting Omaha's Old Market for a blend of shopping, dining, and entertainment.

8. **Insider Tips:**
   - **Free Attractions:** Take advantage of free attractions like the Henry Doorly Zoo in Omaha on certain days or during specific hours.
   - **Explore Small Towns:** Nebraska's small towns often offer unique charm and affordable experiences.
   - **Agri-Tourism:** Explore Nebraska's agricultural scene with visits to local farms or orchards.

Here are the top attractions in Nebraska, along with some money-saving tips for visiting each one:

Omaha: Explore the largest city in Nebraska with its cultural attractions and outdoor activities.

- Money-Saving Tip: Attend free or low-cost events and festivals in Omaha.

Henry Doorly Zoo and Aquarium, Omaha: Visit one of the best zoos in the country.

- Money-Saving Tip: Look for discounted admission rates on certain days or online ticket deals.

Lincoln: Discover the state capital with historic landmarks and cultural events.

- Money-Saving Tip: Explore free attractions like the Nebraska State Capitol building.

Scotts Bluff National Monument: Hike and enjoy panoramic views of the Nebraska plains.

- Money-Saving Tip: Purchase an America the Beautiful Pass for access to national parks.

Chimney Rock National Historic Site: Learn about the Oregon Trail and pioneer history.

- Money-Saving Tip: Admission to the historic site is affordable, and guided tours are available.

Sandhills: Experience the unique Sandhills region with its rolling dunes and grasslands.

- Money-Saving Tip: Explore the Sandhills by taking scenic drives for free.

Niobrara National Scenic River: Enjoy canoeing, tubing, and outdoor adventures.

- Money-Saving Tip: Bring your own equipment for water activities to save on rentals.

Carhenge, Alliance: Visit this quirky replica of Stonehenge made from cars.

- Money-Saving Tip: Admission to Carhenge is free, and it's a fun photo opportunity.

Ponca State Park: Explore nature trails and enjoy wildlife viewing.

- Money-Saving Tip: Visit the park for free or with a low-cost park permit.

Strategic Air Command & Aerospace Museum, Ashland: Learn about aviation and military history.

- Money-Saving Tip: Check for discounts on museum admission and special events.

Agate Fossil Beds National Monument, Harrison: Discover fossils and Native American history.

- Money-Saving Tip: Purchase an America the Beautiful Pass for access to national parks.

Buffalo Bill Ranch State Historical Park, North Platte: Explore the former home of Buffalo Bill.

- Money-Saving Tip: Look for discounts on admission to the historical park.

Platte River: Enjoy birdwatching and outdoor activities along the Platte River.

- Money-Saving Tip: Visit public access areas and nature preserves for free.

Omaha's Old Market: Stroll through historic streets with shops and dining.

- **Money-Saving Tip**: Explore the Old Market's charm on foot and window-shop.

Wildcat Hills State Recreation Area: Hike and enjoy the scenic beauty of the region.

- **Money-Saving Tip**: Visit the recreation area for free and hike its trails.

Stuhr Museum of the Prairie Pioneer, Grand Island: Experience pioneer history and cultural exhibits.

- **Money-Saving Tip**: Look for discounts on museum admission and special programs.

Lake McConaughy: Relax on the sandy beaches and enjoy water sports.

- **Money-Saving Tip**: Consider camping at Lake McConaughy State Recreation Area for affordable lodging.

Scotts Bluff: Hike to the summit and explore the visitor center for historical insights.

- **Money-Saving Tip**: Purchase an America the Beautiful Pass for access to national parks.

Kearney: Visit a city with cultural attractions and events.

- **Money-Saving Tip**: Attend free community events and explore local art galleries.

Category	Insider Tips
Food	1. Visit local farmers' markets in Omaha or Lincoln for fresh produce and locally made goods at affordable prices.
	2. Enjoy Nebraska's famous steak at local steakhouses or diners for a hearty and budget-friendly meal.
	3. Look for "runzas" at local fast-food joints for a taste of Nebraska's iconic comfort food without breaking the bank.
	4. Opt for "hot beef" sandwiches at diners or cafes for a delicious and budget-friendly meal.
Accommodation	1. Consider staying in guesthouses or bed-and-breakfasts for a cozy and affordable lodging experience in smaller towns.
	2. Look for accommodations in college towns like Lincoln or Kearney, where rates may be more budget-friendly.
	3. Utilize discount websites or apps to find deals on hotels and motels in Nebraska's cities and rural areas.
	4. Embrace camping in Nebraska's state parks or recreation areas for a budget-friendly and scenic overnight stay.
Activities	1. Explore the scenic trails and natural beauty of the Niobrara River Valley for outdoor adventures on a budget.
	2. Visit local museums and historical sites like the Strategic Air Command & Aerospace Museum for affordable entertainment.
	3. Attend local fairs, festivals, and county fairs, where you can enjoy live music, food, and entertainment without spending much.
	4. Take advantage of free community events and outdoor concerts held in Nebraska's towns and cities throughout the year.
Transport	1. Consider renting a car for flexibility and convenience in exploring Nebraska's vast and open landscapes.

	2. Utilize ridesharing services or public transportation options in Omaha or Lincoln to save on transportation costs.
	3. Look for scenic drives and road trips in Nebraska, where you can explore the state's natural beauty at your own pace.
	4. Take advantage of bike-sharing programs or rent bicycles to explore urban areas and scenic trails in Nebraska's cities.

Nevada

Nevada's history is closely tied to the mining boom of the mid-19th century. The discovery of silver and gold led to the development of towns such as Virginia City. Today, Nevada is renowned for its modern attractions, including the famous city of Las Vegas.

Things to Consider:

- **Las Vegas Entertainment:** If you're in the mood for excitement and entertainment, Las Vegas is a world-famous destination. Explore the iconic resorts, catch a live show, and try your luck in the casinos along the dazzling Las Vegas Strip.
- **Natural Wonders:** Nevada is home to stunning natural landscapes. Consider exploring the otherworldly beauty of Red Rock Canyon, hiking in the Valley of Fire State Park, or marveling at the vastness of the Great Basin National Park.
- **Outdoor Adventures:** For outdoor enthusiasts, Nevada offers a playground of adventures. From boating on Lake Tahoe to exploring the rugged trails of the Sierra Nevada, the state provides opportunities for both relaxation and thrill-seeking.

Local Tips:

- **Beyond the Strip:** While Las Vegas is famous for its nightlife and entertainment, consider venturing beyond the Strip to discover the local neighborhoods, arts districts, and hidden gems that showcase the city's diverse culture.
- **Historic Sites:** Explore the state's mining history by visiting places like Virginia City. Take a step back in time as you stroll through the well-preserved streets and historic landmarks.
- **Stargazing:** Nevada's clear skies make it an excellent destination for stargazing. Head to remote areas away from city lights to witness a breathtaking night sky filled with stars.

Must-Visit Places:

- **Las Vegas:** Experience the dazzling lights, world-class entertainment, and vibrant nightlife of Las Vegas. Explore the themed resorts, catch a live performance, and enjoy the unique atmosphere of this iconic city.
- **Lake Tahoe:** Discover the stunning beauty of Lake Tahoe, where you can enjoy outdoor activities such as hiking, skiing, and water sports, surrounded by the breathtaking backdrop of the Sierra Nevada mountains.
- **Great Basin National Park:** Venture to the remote beauty of Great Basin National Park, where you can explore ancient bristlecone pine groves, discover limestone caves, and gaze at the star-filled skies.

1. Accommodation:

- Look for hotel deals and consider staying off the Strip in Las Vegas for more budget-friendly options.
- Recommended places: The LINQ Hotel + Experience in Las Vegas, Atlantis Casino Resort Spa in Reno, and The Plaza Hotel & Casino in Downtown Las Vegas.

2. Transportation:
- Explore public transportation options in Las Vegas, like the monorail, or use rideshare services for convenience.
- Renting a car might be cost-effective for exploring destinations outside the major cities.

3. Food:
- Check out affordable dining options, especially during happy hours and off-peak times.
- Recommended restaurants: Lotus of Siam in Las Vegas, Hash House A Go Go in Reno, and Secret Pizza at The Cosmopolitan in Las Vegas.

4. Entertainment:
- Look for discounted show tickets, especially if you book in advance or during non-peak times.
- Take advantage of free attractions like the Fountains of Bellagio in Las Vegas or the street performers on the Strip.

1. **Nevada State Capitol (Carson City):** The Nevada State Capitol offers free guided tours where you can learn about the state's government, history, and architecture. Tours are typically available Monday through Friday.
2. **Las Vegas Strip Walking Tours:** While not guided, you can explore the iconic Las Vegas Strip on foot for free. Take a stroll along the famous boulevard, marvel at the extravagant resorts, and enjoy the vibrant atmosphere of this entertainment capital.
3. **Self-guided Tours of Red Rock Canyon National Conservation Area (Las Vegas):** While there may be a fee for entrance to the scenic drive, Red Rock Canyon offers free self-guided hiking trails and viewpoints where you can explore the stunning desert landscapes and geological formations.
4. **Lake Mead National Recreation Area (Boulder City):** While there may be fees for entrance to certain areas of the recreation area, Lake Mead offers free self-guided scenic drives, picnic areas, and viewpoints where you can enjoy the beauty of the Colorado River and surrounding desert.

5. Outdoor Activities:
- Explore the natural beauty of Nevada by visiting state parks and scenic areas.
- Recommended places: Valley of Fire State Park, Red Rock Canyon National Conservation Area, and Lake Tahoe (part of which is in Nevada).

6. Casino Experience:
- Set a budget for gambling if you plan to try your luck, and take advantage of any player rewards programs.
- Look for affordable table games and budget-friendly slot machines.

7. Shopping:
- Explore outlet malls for discounted shopping, such as Las Vegas North Premium Outlets.
- Downtown Las Vegas offers unique shops and boutiques with affordable options.

8. Insider Tips:

- **Midweek Travel:** Consider traveling during the week for lower hotel rates and fewer crowds.
- **Groupon Deals:** Check Groupon for discounted activities, dining, and shows in Las Vegas and other Nevada cities.
- **Local Events:** Attend local events or festivals, which might offer free or low-cost entertainment.

Top Savings

Las Vegas: Explore the entertainment capital of the world with its iconic hotels, casinos, and shows.

- Money-Saving Tip: Sign up for player's club cards at casinos for potential discounts and offers.

The Las Vegas Strip: Walk along the famous stretch of resorts, restaurants, and attractions.

- Money-Saving Tip: Enjoy the free fountain shows at the Bellagio and explore the themed hotels for free.

Red Rock Canyon National Conservation Area, Las Vegas: Hike, rock climb, and enjoy stunning desert landscapes.

- Money-Saving Tip: Purchase an annual pass for access to the conservation area throughout the year.

Lake Tahoe: Experience the pristine lake and outdoor adventures on the Nevada-California border.

- Money-Saving Tip: Visit during the off-peak season for more affordable lodging rates.

Reno: Discover "The Biggest Little City in the World" with its casinos and cultural events.

- Money-Saving Tip: Check for casino promotions and discounts on dining and entertainment.

Hoover Dam: Tour the historic dam and learn about its engineering marvel.

- Money-Saving Tip: Purchase tour tickets in advance online for discounts and faster entry.

Great Basin National Park: Explore caves, stargaze, and hike in this remote national park.

- Money-Saving Tip: Purchase an America the Beautiful Pass for access to national parks.

Valley of Fire State Park: Witness red rock formations and petroglyphs.

- Money-Saving Tip: Enjoy the park's trails and scenery for the cost of a state park pass.

Lake Mead National Recreation Area: Enjoy boating, fishing, and water sports near Las Vegas.

- Money-Saving Tip: Bring your own water equipment or rent from local vendors for cost savings.

Virginia City: Step back in time to the 1800s with a historic mining town.

- Money-Saving Tip: Explore the town's historic streets and shops without any admission fees.

Carson City: Visit the state capital with its museums and outdoor activities.

- Money-Saving Tip: Attend free events and explore the Nevada State Capitol building.

Elko: Experience cowboy culture and ranching heritage in northeastern Nevada.

- Money-Saving Tip: Attend free rodeo events and explore local art galleries.

National Atomic Testing Museum, Las Vegas: Learn about the history of atomic testing.

- Money-Saving Tip: Look for discounts on museum admission, especially for students and seniors.

Black Rock Desert: Attend Burning Man, an annual cultural event, in this remote desert region.

- Money-Saving Tip: Plan your visit to coincide with Burning Man if interested, but be prepared for camping and ticket expenses.

Ely: Discover a town with historic sites and outdoor adventures.

- Money-Saving Tip: Visit free attractions like the Nevada Northern Railway Museum.

Laughlin: Enjoy gaming and outdoor activities along the Colorado River.

- Money-Saving Tip: Check for casino promotions and discounts on dining.

Mesquite: Experience golfing and outdoor recreation in this desert town.

- Money-Saving Tip: Play golf during twilight hours for lower green fees.

The Mob Museum, Las Vegas: Explore the history of organized crime in America.

- Money-Saving Tip: Look for discounts on museum admission and combo tickets.

Boulder City: Visit the historic town known for its proximity to Hoover Dam.

- Money-Saving Tip: Explore free attractions like the Nevada Southern Railway Museum.

Tonopah: Explore a historic mining town in central Nevada.

- Money-Saving Tip: Visit the Tonopah Historic Mining Park for a nominal admission fee.

Category	Insider Tips
Food	1. Sample affordable eats at local diners or "mom-and-pop" eateries for authentic Nevada cuisine.
	2. Look for casino buffets offering all-you-can-eat meals at reasonable prices, especially during off-peak hours.
	3. Explore Chinatown in Las Vegas for budget-friendly and delicious Asian cuisine options.
	4. Visit food trucks or street vendors for tasty and wallet-friendly snacks while exploring the city.

Accommodation	1. Stay at budget-friendly motels or hostels in Las Vegas or Reno for affordable lodging options.	
	2. Consider booking accommodations away from the Las Vegas Strip for lower rates and quieter stays.	
	3. Look for hotel deals and discounts offered by casino resorts or booking websites for cost-effective stays.	
	4. Utilize loyalty programs or rewards points to save on hotel stays in Nevada.	
Activities	1. Take advantage of free attractions like the iconic Las Vegas Strip or the scenic Red Rock Canyon.	
	2. Visit local museums or art galleries offering discounted admission or free entry days.	
	3. Explore hiking trails in Nevada's national parks or wilderness areas for outdoor adventures.	
	4. Attend free or low-cost live entertainment shows, street performances, or cultural events in Las Vegas.	
Transport	1. Utilize the Las Vegas Monorail or RTC buses for affordable and convenient transportation on the Strip.	
	2. Consider renting a car for exploring Nevada's vast landscapes and attractions at your own pace.	
	3. Look for ride-sharing or carpooling options for shared transportation costs, especially for longer trips.	
	4. Take advantage of shuttle services offered by hotels or casinos for transportation to local attractions.	

New Hampshire

New Hampshire's history is rich with colonial heritage and a significant role in the American Revolution. The state played a crucial part in the early formation of the United States, from hosting revolutionary conventions to being the site of key battles.

Things to Consider:

- **Scenic Beauty:** New Hampshire is renowned for its scenic landscapes. Whether you're exploring the Lakes Region, hiking in the White Mountains, or driving through covered bridges, the state offers a visual feast for nature lovers.
- **Outdoor Recreation:** If you're an outdoor enthusiast, New Hampshire has it all. Enjoy hiking in the Presidential Range, skiing in the winter, or kayaking on the serene lakes during the warmer months.
- **Quaint Towns:** Discover the charm of New Hampshire's small towns. From the historic appeal of Portsmouth to the artsy vibe of Hanover, each town has its own unique character and story to tell.

Local Tips:

- **Fall Foliage:** Experience the breathtaking beauty of fall foliage in New Hampshire. The vibrant colors of autumn make it an ideal time to take scenic drives or hike in the mountains.
- **Outdoor Markets:** Explore local farmers' markets and craft fairs. New Hampshire's communities often host these events, providing a chance to sample local produce, handmade crafts, and engage with the friendly locals.
- **Live Free or Die:** Embrace the state motto, "Live Free or Die," by enjoying the freedom to explore. Whether it's wandering through historic sites or embarking on a spontaneous road trip, New Hampshire encourages a sense of independence.

Must-Visit Places:

- **White Mountains:** Discover the stunning beauty of the White Mountains, home to iconic peaks like Mount Washington. Whether you're hiking, skiing, or simply enjoying the scenic drives, the White Mountains offer a true New England experience.
- **Lake Winnipesaukee:** Explore the largest lake in New Hampshire, Lake Winnipesaukee. Enjoy water activities, cruise on the lake, and savor the tranquility of this beautiful destination.
- **Portsmouth:** Immerse yourself in the history and maritime charm of Portsmouth. Walk along the cobblestone streets, visit historic sites, and enjoy the vibrant arts and culinary scene.

1. Accommodation:

- Explore charming bed and breakfasts, inns, or budget-friendly hotels in towns like North Conway or Portsmouth.
- Recommended places: The Wentworth in Jackson, The Centennial Hotel in Concord, and The Margate Resort in Laconia.

2. Transportation:

- Rent a car to explore New Hampshire's scenic drives and reach attractions in rural areas.
- Consider using public transportation in cities like Manchester and Portsmouth.

3. Outdoor Activities:
- Take advantage of New Hampshire's natural beauty with hiking, kayaking, or exploring the White Mountains.
- Recommended activities: Mount Washington Auto Road, Franconia Notch State Park, and kayaking on Lake Winnipesaukee.

4. Cultural Attractions:
- Explore historic sites, museums, and cultural attractions that showcase New Hampshire's heritage.
- Recommended places: Strawbery Banke Museum in Portsmouth, Canterbury Shaker Village, and the Currier Museum of Art in Manchester.
  - **New Hampshire State House (Concord):** The New Hampshire State House offers free guided tours where you can learn about the state's government, history, and architecture. Tours are typically available Monday through Friday.
  - **White Mountain National Forest (Various Locations):** While there may be fees for certain recreational activities, White Mountain National Forest offers free self-guided hiking trails, scenic drives, and viewpoints where you can explore the natural beauty of the area.
-

5. Scenic Drives:
- Enjoy the beauty of New Hampshire by taking scenic drives like the Kancamagus Highway or the Great North Woods Loop.
- Stop at viewpoints and take in the natural wonders.

6. Local Events:
- Attend local events and festivals that celebrate the changing seasons or New Hampshire's cultural heritage.
- Check the schedule for events like the Portsmouth Maritime Folk Festival or the New Hampshire Highland Games.

7. Shopping:
- Explore local shops, artisan markets, and outlets for unique New Hampshire-made products.
- Visit the Tanger Outlets in Tilton for discounted shopping.

8. Dining:
- Enjoy local cuisine in charming restaurants and cafes. Try New England classics like clam chowder and lobster rolls.
- Recommended restaurants: The Common Man in Plymouth, The Old Salt Restaurant in Hampton, and The Riverwalk Cafe & Music Bar in Nashua.

9. Insider Tips:
- **Free Outdoor Concerts:** Check for free outdoor concerts or live music events happening in town centers or parks.
- **State Parks:** New Hampshire has many beautiful state parks. Consider a state park pass for access to multiple locations.
- **Farm-to-Table Dining:** Explore farm-to-table restaurants for fresh, local ingredients and affordable upscale dining.

Here are the top attractions in New Hampshire, along with some money-saving tips for visiting each one:

White Mountains: Explore the stunning landscapes of the White Mountains region with its hiking trails and outdoor activities.

- Money-Saving Tip: Purchase a White Mountains National Forest Pass for access to recreational areas.

Mount Washington: Visit the highest peak in the Northeast and enjoy breathtaking views.

- Money-Saving Tip: Opt for self-guided exploration or consider the value of guided tours.

Franconia Notch State Park: Discover natural wonders like the Flume Gorge and the Basin.

- Money-Saving Tip: Consider a state park pass for access to multiple parks.

Portsmouth: Explore the historic coastal city with its charming downtown and cultural attractions.

- Money-Saving Tip: Enjoy free events and outdoor concerts in Prescott Park.

Lake Winnipesaukee: Relax by New Hampshire's largest lake and enjoy boating and water sports.

- Money-Saving Tip: Public access beaches and parks offer affordable beach days.

Mount Monadnock: Hike to the summit of this iconic mountain with panoramic views.

- Money-Saving Tip: Purchase a state park pass for parking and hiking.

Kancamagus Highway: Drive along this scenic byway with picturesque views and hiking trails.

- Money-Saving Tip: Explore the highway's natural beauty without entrance fees.

Seacoast Science Center, Rye: Learn about marine life and the coastal environment.

- Money-Saving Tip: Check for discounts on admission and family passes.

Conway: Experience outdoor adventures and explore local shops in this mountain town.

- Money-Saving Tip: Look for deals on outdoor activities and equipment rentals.

Cannon Mountain: Ski or hike at this popular destination in the White Mountains.

- Money-Saving Tip: Consider visiting during non-peak skiing times for lower rates.

Squam Lake: Enjoy the tranquil beauty of this lake known for its clear waters.

- Money-Saving Tip: Visit public access points and enjoy affordable kayaking or fishing.

Diana's Baths, North Conway: Hike to this series of cascading waterfalls in the White Mountains.

- Money-Saving Tip: Enjoy the natural beauty of Diana's Baths with free access.

Strawbery Banke Museum, Portsmouth: Explore historic buildings and learn about early American life.

- Money-Saving Tip: Look for discounts on museum admission and special events.

Presidential Range: Hike and explore the peaks of the Presidential Range in the White Mountains.

- Money-Saving Tip: Consider camping in the White Mountains for budget-friendly lodging.

Canterbury Shaker Village: Step back in time and learn about Shaker history and culture.

- Money-Saving Tip: Check for discounts on village admission and guided tours.

Hampton Beach: Relax on the sandy beach and enjoy seaside entertainment.

- Money-Saving Tip: Visit during the off-peak season for more affordable accommodations.

McAuliffe-Shepard Discovery Center, Concord: Discover space and aviation history.

- Money-Saving Tip: Look for discounts on admission and special programs.

Castle in the Clouds, Moultonborough: Tour a historic mansion with stunning lake views.

- Money-Saving Tip: Purchase tickets online in advance for potential discounts.

Albany: Explore a town near the White Mountains with outdoor activities and natural beauty.

- Money-Saving Tip: Hike and enjoy the White Mountains without additional costs.

Category	Insider Tips
Food	1. Visit local maple syrup farms for free tastings and to purchase maple products directly from producers.
	2. Explore farmers' markets in towns like Concord and Portsmouth for fresh produce and artisanal foods.
	3. Look for seafood shacks along the coast for affordable and delicious seafood, such as lobster rolls.
	4. Visit diners and family-owned restaurants for hearty New England classics like clam chowder and blueberry pie.
Accommodation	1. Camp in New Hampshire's state parks and forests for scenic and affordable camping experiences.
	2. Stay in cozy bed and breakfasts in charming towns like Hanover and North Conway for a true New England experience.
	3. Consider renting cabins or cottages near lakes or mountains for a rustic and budget-friendly getaway.
	4. Look for deals and discounts on accommodations during the shoulder seasons, such as spring and fall.
Activities	1. Hike or drive along the scenic Kancamagus Highway for breathtaking views of the White Mountains.
	2. Explore the charming villages of the Lakes Region, such as Wolfeboro and Meredith, for shopping and dining.
	3. Visit local breweries and wineries for tastings of craft beer and wine, with many offering free or low-cost tours.
	4. Take advantage of free outdoor activities like swimming in lakes, hiking in state parks, and scenic drives.
Transport	1. Rent a car to explore New Hampshire's rural areas and scenic byways, providing flexibility and convenience.
	2. Utilize public transportation options in cities like Manchester and Nashua, such as buses and commuter rail.
	3. Consider biking on the many rail trails and scenic routes throughout the state for a budget-friendly adventure.
	4. Look for carpooling opportunities or ride-sharing services for shared transportation costs, especially for longer distances.

New Jersey

New Jersey has a rich history that spans the colonial era to the industrial age. As one of the original thirteen colonies, the state played a pivotal role in the American Revolution. Today, you can explore historic sites, museums, and neighborhoods that reflect its storied past.

Things to Consider:

- **Beaches and Boardwalks:** New Jersey boasts a beautiful coastline with sandy beaches and iconic boardwalks. From the lively atmosphere of Seaside Heights to the serene beaches of Cape May, the shore offers a variety of experiences.
- **Urban Exploration:** If you're a fan of urban experiences, explore the cities of Newark and Jersey City. Enjoy cultural attractions, diverse cuisine, and the vibrant atmosphere of these bustling urban centers.
- **Parks and Outdoor Activities:** Discover the natural beauty of New Jersey by exploring its state parks and outdoor spaces. The Delaware Water Gap, the Palisades, and the Pine Barrens offer opportunities for hiking, camping, and outdoor adventures.

Local Tips:

- **Diverse Cuisine:** New Jersey is a melting pot of cultures, and its culinary scene reflects this diversity. Indulge in delicious ethnic cuisines, from Italian and Portuguese to Indian and Korean, found in neighborhoods throughout the state.
- **Shopping:** Enjoy tax-free shopping in New Jersey. Explore the malls, outlets, and boutiques for a variety of shopping experiences, including the famous Jersey Gardens Mall.
- **Seasonal Festivals:** Check out seasonal festivals and events happening throughout the state. From the Cherry Blossom Festival in Branch Brook Park to the New Jersey State Fair, there's always something lively and cultural to experience.

Must-Visit Places:

- **Jersey Shore:** Experience the classic American beach culture along the Jersey Shore. Visit iconic boardwalks like those in Wildwood or Point Pleasant, and enjoy the sun, sand, and vibrant coastal atmosphere.
- **Princeton:** Explore the charming town of Princeton, home to the prestigious Princeton University. Walk around the historic campus, visit the university's art museum, and enjoy the quaint surroundings.
- **Liberty State Park:** Enjoy the stunning views of the Manhattan skyline from Liberty State Park in Jersey City. The park also houses the Liberty Science Center and the Central Railroad of New Jersey Terminal.

1. **Accommodation:**

- Look for budget-friendly hotels, inns, or boutique accommodations in cities like Cape May or Princeton.
- Recommended places: Congress Hall in Cape May, Nassau Inn in Princeton, and The Asbury Hotel in Asbury Park.

2. Transportation:

- Utilize public transportation options like NJ Transit for cost-effective travel within the state and to neighboring cities like New York City.
- Consider renting a car for exploring scenic areas like the Delaware Water Gap or the Jersey Shore.

3. Beaches:

- Enjoy the Jersey Shore without breaking the bank. Opt for public beaches that have lower entrance fees or are free.
- Recommended beaches: Wildwood, Cape May, and Seaside Heights.

4. Outdoor Activities:

- Explore state parks and nature reserves for hiking, picnicking, and bird watching.
- Recommended places: High Point State Park, Liberty State Park, and the Palisades Interstate Park.

5. Cultural Attractions:

- Visit museums and cultural attractions that showcase New Jersey's history and arts.
- Recommended places: Grounds For Sculpture in Hamilton, The Newark Museum, and the Thomas Edison National Historical Park in West Orange.

6. Boardwalks:

- Experience the iconic boardwalks along the Jersey Shore. Enjoy affordable treats like saltwater taffy and hot dogs.
- Recommended boardwalks: Atlantic City, Seaside Heights, and Point Pleasant Beach.

7. Dining:

- Explore local diners, seafood shacks, and ethnic eateries for budget-friendly yet delicious meals.
- Recommended restaurants: The Committed Pig in Morristown, Marucas Tomato Pies in Seaside Heights, and Jose Tejas in Iselin.

8. Shopping:

- Visit outlet malls for discounted shopping. The Jersey Gardens Outlet Mall in Elizabeth is a popular choice.
- Explore local markets and downtown areas for unique finds.

9. Insider Tips:

- **Free Events:** Check local event calendars for free concerts, festivals, and community events.
- **Historical Tours:** Join free or low-cost historical walking tours in places like Princeton or Cape May.
- **Weekday Travel:** Consider traveling during the week for potential hotel discounts and fewer crowds.

Here are the top attractions in New Jersey, along with some money-saving tips for visiting each one:

Atlantic City: Explore the famous boardwalk, casinos, and entertainment options.

- Money-Saving Tip: Sign up for casino rewards programs for discounts and promotions.

Jersey Shore: Enjoy the beautiful beaches and vibrant coastal towns along the Jersey Shore.

- Money-Saving Tip: Visit public beaches for lower parking fees and free beach access.

Liberty State Park, Jersey City: Take in views of the Statue of Liberty and Manhattan skyline.

- Money-Saving Tip: Enjoy picnics and outdoor activities in the park for free.

Cape May: Experience a charming Victorian town with historic architecture and beautiful beaches.

- Money-Saving Tip: Explore the town's streets and window-shop without spending.

Six Flags Great Adventure, Jackson: Have fun at the amusement park with rides and entertainment.

- Money-Saving Tip: Look for discounts on tickets online or consider season passes for savings.

Princeton University, Princeton: Explore the historic campus and museums.

- Money-Saving Tip: Enjoy free admission to the Princeton University Art Museum.

Delaware Water Gap National Recreation Area: Hike, swim, and enjoy outdoor activities in this scenic area.

- Money-Saving Tip: Visit for free or with a low-cost park pass for parking.

Ellis Island: Learn about immigration history at this historic site.

- Money-Saving Tip: Purchase a combined ticket for both Ellis Island and the Statue of Liberty to save on admission.

Grounds For Sculpture, Hamilton Township: Discover an art-filled sculpture park and gardens.

- Money-Saving Tip: Check for discounts on admission and special events.

Hoboken: Explore the city with waterfront views of Manhattan and cultural attractions.

- Money-Saving Tip: Attend free outdoor events and festivals in Hoboken.

Newark: Visit the largest city in New Jersey with its museums and cultural institutions.

- Money-Saving Tip: Explore free attractions like the Newark Museum.

The Adventure Aquarium, Camden: Discover marine life and interactive exhibits.

- Money-Saving Tip: Look for online discounts and family passes for the aquarium.

Battleship New Jersey, Camden: Tour the historic battleship on the Delaware River.

- Money-Saving Tip: Check for discounts on admission and guided tours.

New Jersey State Botanical Garden, Ringwood: Enjoy beautiful gardens and natural surroundings.

- Money-Saving Tip: Admission to the botanical garden is free, but donations are appreciated.

Thomas Edison National Historical Park, West Orange: Learn about the inventor's life and work.

- Money-Saving Tip: Check for discounts on guided tours of the Edison laboratory.

Island Beach State Park: Relax on pristine beaches and enjoy outdoor activities.

- Money-Saving Tip: Visit the park for a small entrance fee or consider a season pass.

Monmouth Battlefield State Park: Explore historic battlefields and trails.

- Money-Saving Tip: Visit the park for free or with a low-cost park pass.

New Jersey Pine Barrens: Discover a unique natural area with hiking, wildlife, and scenic beauty.

- Money-Saving Tip: Enjoy the Pine Barrens by hiking and exploring its trails for free.

Morristown: Experience a historic town with museums and cultural attractions.

- Money-Saving Tip: Explore free attractions like the Morristown National Historical Park.

Wildwood: Visit a family-friendly beach town with amusement parks and entertainment.

- Money-Saving Tip: Look for discounted ride tickets and combo deals.

Category	Insider Tips
Food	1. Head to local diners for classic Jersey diner fare like Taylor ham (pork roll) sandwiches and disco fries.
	2. Explore boardwalk eateries along the Jersey Shore for fresh seafood, funnel cakes, and saltwater taffy.
	3. Look for family-owned Italian delis for authentic subs, sandwiches, and freshly made pasta dishes.
	4. Check out local farmers' markets for Jersey-fresh produce, including tomatoes, corn, and blueberries.
Accommodation	1. Consider booking accommodations in smaller towns along the Jersey Shore for more affordable rates.
	2. Look for bed and breakfasts or guesthouses in historic towns like Cape May or Lambertville for a unique stay.
	3. Utilize discount websites or apps to find deals on hotels and accommodations throughout New Jersey.
	4. Check for vacation rental properties in beach towns or rural areas for more budget-friendly options.
Activities	1. Spend a day exploring the boardwalks and beaches of the Jersey Shore, with many beaches offering free access.

	2. Visit state parks like Liberty State Park or Island Beach State Park for outdoor activities like hiking and picnicking.
	3. Attend local festivals and events, such as the Atlantic City Airshow or the New Jersey State Fair, for entertainment.
	4. Take a scenic drive through the picturesque countryside of Hunterdon County or along the Delaware River for stunning views.
Transport	1. Consider using public transportation options like NJ Transit trains or buses for travel within New Jersey and to nearby cities.
	2. Use ride-sharing services or taxis for short-distance travel in urban areas or to access areas not served by public transit.
	3. Look for carpooling opportunities or shared transportation options when traveling longer distances within the state.
	4. Explore biking trails like the Delaware and Raritan Canal Trail or the Sandy Hook Multi-Use Pathway for eco-friendly transportation and sightseeing.

North Dakota

North Dakota boasts diverse landscapes, including the badlands of Theodore Roosevelt National Park, the fertile Red River Valley, and the rugged beauty of the Pembina Gorge. Outdoor enthusiasts will find opportunities for hiking, bird-watching, fishing, and more.

Things to Consider:

- **Theodore Roosevelt National Park**: This national park is a must-visit, known for its striking badlands terrain, scenic drives, and abundant wildlife. The park is divided into three units: North Unit, South Unit, and Elkhorn Ranch Unit.
- **Weather**: North Dakota experiences all four seasons, with cold winters and warm summers. Be prepared for varying weather conditions based on the time of year.
- **Native American Heritage**: North Dakota is home to several Native American tribes, including the Standing Rock Sioux Tribe and the Mandan, Hidatsa, and Arikara Nation. Explore cultural centers and events to learn about their rich heritage.

Local Tips:

- **Fargo**: Visit Fargo, North Dakota's largest city, known for its arts and culture scene, historic downtown district, and vibrant nightlife. The Fargo-Moorhead area offers diverse dining options.
- **Bismarck**: Explore the state capital, Bismarck, with its historical attractions like the North Dakota Heritage Center & State Museum and the State Capitol Building.
- **Medora**: Experience the charming town of Medora, located near Theodore Roosevelt National Park. Attend the Medora Musical, explore the Western-themed attractions, and enjoy stunning views from the Badlands.
- **Fort Union Trading Post**: Discover Fort Union Trading Post National Historic Site, a reconstructed fur trading post that provides insights into the 19th-century fur trade along the Missouri River.
- **Lake Sakakawea**: Enjoy outdoor activities at Lake Sakakawea, North Dakota's largest reservoir. It offers boating, fishing, camping, and scenic viewpoints.
- **Northern Lights**: If you visit during the winter months, keep an eye out for the northern lights (aurora borealis) in the state's dark skies.
- **Pembina Gorge**: Explore the Pembina Gorge State Recreation Area, known for its hiking trails, wildlife viewing, and opportunities for kayaking and tubing.

1. Accommodation:
    - **Budget-Friendly Luxury Hotels:**
    - **The Grand Hotel, Minot:** Offers comfortable and stylish rooms with excellent amenities. Approximate price: $100 per night.
2. Dining:
    - **HoDo Restaurant, Fargo:** Known for its exquisite local cuisine. Average meal cost: $20-$30.
    - **Blarney Stone Pub, Bismarck:** Enjoy Irish fare with a North Dakotan twist. Average meal cost: $15-$25.
3. Attractions:

- **Theodore Roosevelt National Park:** Entry fee of $30 per vehicle, offering stunning landscapes and wildlife.
- **North Dakota Heritage Center & State Museum, Bismarck:** Free entry. Explore North Dakota's rich history and culture.

4. Activities:
   - **Hot Air Balloon Ride:** Experience breathtaking views of the North Dakota landscape. Approximate cost: $200-$250 per person.
   - **Horseback Riding in Medora:** Explore the badlands on horseback. Approximate cost: $40-$60 per hour.

5. Local Experiences:
   - **Fargo's Local Breweries Tour:** Discover local craft beers. Tours usually around $10-$15.
   - **Art Galleries in Grand Forks:** Often free or with a small donation.

6. Transportation:
   - **Car Rental:** Economical option for getting around. Average cost: $30-$50 per day.
   - **Public Transportation:** Affordable, though more limited in rural areas.

7. Shopping:
   - **Prairie Edge, Bismarck:** Offers unique local crafts and souvenirs. Prices vary.

8. Insider Tips:
   - **Seasonal Considerations:** Summer is ideal for outdoor activities, while winter offers beautiful snowy landscapes and potential for snow sports.
   - **Book in Advance:** Especially for accommodation and activities, to get the best deals.

9. Budget Tips:
   - **Eat Like a Local:** Try local diners and food trucks for affordable, authentic meals.
   - **Explore Free Attractions:** Many museums and historical sites offer free or low-cost entry.

Here are the top attractions in North Dakota, along with some money-saving tips for visiting each one:

Theodore Roosevelt National Park: Explore the rugged Badlands landscapes and wildlife.

- Money-Saving Tip: Purchase an America the Beautiful Pass for access to national parks.

Fargo: Discover the largest city in North Dakota with its cultural events and outdoor activities.

- Money-Saving Tip: Attend free concerts and events in Fargo's parks.

Medora: Experience a historic town near Theodore Roosevelt National Park with entertainment and attractions.

- Money-Saving Tip: Check for package deals on lodging and attractions in Medora.

Bismarck: Visit the state capital with museums, historic sites, and recreational areas.

- Money-Saving Tip: Explore free attractions like the North Dakota State Capitol building.

Devils Lake: Enjoy water sports and outdoor adventures on North Dakota's largest natural lake.

- Money-Saving Tip: Visit public access areas and state parks for affordable lakeside activities.

Fort Abraham Lincoln State Park: Explore historic military sites and the On-A-Slant Indian Village.

- Money-Saving Tip: Consider a state park pass for access to multiple parks.

Minot: Discover a city with cultural events, shopping, and outdoor recreation.

- Money-Saving Tip: Attend free community events and explore local parks.

Knife River Indian Villages National Historic Site, Stanton: Learn about Native American history and culture.

- Money-Saving Tip: Admission to the historic site is free.

Lake Sakakawea: Enjoy fishing, boating, and camping on this reservoir along the Missouri River.

- Money-Saving Tip: Bring your own equipment for water activities to save on rentals.

Grand Forks: Experience a city with shopping, dining, and recreational opportunities.

- Money-Saving Tip: Explore local trails and parks for budget-friendly outdoor activities.

Fort Buford State Historic Site, Williston: Learn about the history of Fort Buford and its role in the Indian Wars.

- Money-Saving Tip: Check for discounts on admission and guided tours.

Jamestown: Visit the "Buffalo City" with attractions like the National Buffalo Museum.

- Money-Saving Tip: Look for discounts on museum admission and special events.

Sakakawea Statue, Bismarck: View the iconic statue of Sacagawea, the Lewis and Clark expedition guide.

- Money-Saving Tip: Enjoy the statue and scenic views at no cost.

Sheyenne National Grassland: Explore grasslands and wildlife in southeastern North Dakota.

- Money-Saving Tip: Visit the national grassland for free outdoor experiences.

Maah Daah Hey Trail: Hike, bike, or horseback ride along this scenic trail in the Badlands.

- Money-Saving Tip: Enjoy the trail for free and choose day hikes or rides.

Mandan: Experience cultural festivals, historic sites, and outdoor activities in this city.

- Money-Saving Tip: Attend free community events and explore local parks.

International Peace Garden: Visit this garden on the U.S.-Canada border with floral displays and peace-themed attractions.

- Money-Saving Tip: Admission is free, but there may be a fee for parking.

Rugby: Explore the geographical center of North America and learn about its history.

- Money-Saving Tip: Visit the Geographical Center Monument for a free photo opportunity.

Lake Metigoshe State Park: Enjoy outdoor activities on the lake's shores near the Canadian border.

- Money-Saving Tip: Consider a state park pass for access to multiple parks.

North Dakota Heritage Center & State Museum, Bismarck: Learn about the state's history and culture.

- Money-Saving Tip: Check for discounts on museum admission and special exhibits.

Category	Insider Tips
Food	1. Explore local diners and cafes for hearty Midwestern fare, featuring dishes like hotdish and knoephla soup.
	2. Visit farmers' markets for fresh produce and locally made goods, supporting North Dakota's agricultural community.
	3. Enjoy affordable meals at small-town restaurants and supper clubs, known for generous portions and friendly service.
	4. Look for seasonal events like church suppers and community dinners for homemade meals at reasonable prices.
Accommodation	1. Embrace the outdoors by camping at state parks or recreation areas, offering budget-friendly campsites amidst scenic landscapes.
	2. Stay in cozy bed and breakfasts or guesthouses in charming small towns, providing affordable and personalized lodging options.
	3. Utilize budget motels and roadside inns along major highways for convenient and economical overnight stays.
	4. Consider booking accommodations in advance during the off-peak season for lower rates and fewer crowds.
Activities	1. Explore North Dakota's vast prairies and Badlands by hiking scenic trails in state parks like Theodore Roosevelt National Park.
	2. Visit local museums and cultural centers to learn about North Dakota's Native American heritage and pioneer history.
	3. Attend county fairs, rodeos, and agricultural festivals for authentic Midwestern experiences and family-friendly entertainment.
	4. Take scenic drives along designated routes like the Enchanted Highway or the Sheyenne River Valley Scenic Byway for breathtaking views.
Transport	1. Rent a car for flexibility in exploring North Dakota's expansive landscapes and rural attractions at your own pace.

	2. Utilize local shuttle services or public transportation options in cities like Fargo and Bismarck for affordable and convenient travel.
	3. Consider carpooling with fellow travelers or joining group tours to share transportation costs and explore North Dakota's hidden gems.
	4. Take advantage of bike rental programs or walking tours in urban areas like Grand Forks or Minot for eco-friendly and budget-friendly sightseeing.

Ohio

Once home to ancient cultures like the Adena and Hopewell peoples, Ohio's fertile lands attracted settlers seeking opportunity and freedom. In 1803, it became the 17th state admitted to the Union, earning the nickname "The Buckeye State."

Ohio's strategic location along the Ohio River made it a key player in westward expansion and the Underground Railroad, aiding fugitive slaves seeking freedom in the North.

The state's industrial prowess surged in the 19th century, fueled by innovations like the Wright brothers' first powered flight in Dayton and John D. Rockefeller's Standard Oil Company in Cleveland. Ohio's cities became bustling hubs of manufacturing and commerce, shaping the nation's economy.

Throughout the 20th century, Ohio continued to evolve, contributing to advancements in technology, medicine, and culture. From the birthplace of aviation to the heart of the Rust Belt, Ohio's story reflects the triumphs and challenges of the American experience.

Today, Ohio stands as a testament to the resilience of its people, a blend of innovation and tradition, with vibrant cities, picturesque landscapes, and a spirit of perseverance that defines its identity.

Things to Consider:

- **Cultural Attractions:** Explore the cultural richness of Ohio by visiting museums, theaters, and historical sites. The Rock and Roll Hall of Fame in Cleveland, the Cincinnati Art Museum, and the National Underground Railroad Freedom Center are just a few examples.
- **Outdoor Adventures:** Enjoy the scenic beauty of Ohio's natural landscapes. From the shores of Lake Erie to the Hocking Hills State Park, outdoor enthusiasts can partake in hiking, boating, and other recreational activities.
- **Amish Country:** Experience a more traditional way of life in Ohio's Amish Country. Visit towns like Berlin and Sugarcreek to explore Amish markets, enjoy handmade crafts, and savor delicious homemade treats.

Local Tips:

- **Football Frenzy:** Join in on the football fever in Ohio, a state known for its passionate sports culture. Whether you're cheering for the Ohio State Buckeyes in Columbus or attending a Cleveland Browns game, the energy is contagious.
- **Culinary Delights:** Indulge in Ohio's culinary scene. Try Cincinnati-style chili, a Lake Erie perch sandwich, or enjoy craft beer in the thriving brewery scenes of cities like Cincinnati, Cleveland, and Columbus.
- **Festivals and Events:** Check out Ohio's festivals and events, celebrating everything from arts and culture to agriculture and music. The Ohio State Fair, Oktoberfest Zinzinnati, and the Cleveland International Film Festival are just a few examples.

Must-Visit Places:

- **Cleveland:** Explore the revitalized city of Cleveland, home to the Rock and Roll Hall of Fame, the Cleveland Museum of Art, and the bustling West Side Market.
- **Columbus:** Immerse yourself in the state capital, Columbus, with its vibrant neighborhoods, the Ohio State University campus, and the Scioto Mile riverfront park.
- **Hocking Hills State Park:** Discover the natural wonders of Hocking Hills State Park, featuring stunning rock formations, waterfalls, and scenic trails.

1. **Accommodation:**
    - **Budget-Friendly Luxury Hotels:**
    - **The Cincinnatian Hotel, Cincinnati:** Elegant, historic hotel with modern amenities. Approximate price: $130-$180 per night.
    - **Renaissance Columbus Downtown Hotel, Columbus:** Stylish, upscale accommodation with city views. Approximate price: $150-$200 per night.

2. **Dining:**
    - **Orchids at Palm Court, Cincinnati:** An award-winning fine dining experience. Average meal cost: $30-$50.
    - **The Refectory Restaurant & Bistro, Columbus:** French cuisine in a romantic setting. Average meal cost: $25-$40.

3. **Attractions:**
    - **Cedar Point, Sandusky:** Renowned amusement park with an entry fee of around $50-$70 per person.
    - **Rock & Roll Hall of Fame, Cleveland:** Iconic music museum. Entry fee: $25-$30 per person.

4. **Activities:**
    - **Hot Air Balloon Rides over Amish Country:** Experience breathtaking views. Approximate cost: $200-$250 per person.
    - **Wine Tasting Tours in the Ohio River Valley:** Discover local wineries. Approximate cost: $30-$50 per person.

5. **Local Experiences:**
    - **Short North Arts District, Columbus:** Explore galleries, boutiques, and eateries. Free to stroll, costs vary for purchases.
    - **Cleveland Cultural Gardens:** Beautifully landscaped gardens representing various cultures. Free entry.

6. **Transportation:**
    - **Car Rental:** Convenient for exploring wider areas. Average cost: $35-$55 per day.

- **Public Transit:** Affordable, especially in major cities like Columbus and Cleveland.

7. Shopping:
    - **Easton Town Center, Columbus:** A mix of high-end and budget-friendly stores. Prices vary.
    - **Findlay Market, Cincinnati:** Historic market with local goods and crafts. Prices vary.

8. Insider Tips:
    - **Best Time to Visit:** Late spring to early fall for the best weather.
    - **Advance Bookings:** Recommended for top restaurants and attractions.

9. Budget Tips:
    - **Local Dining:** Discover affordable local cuisines at food trucks and diners.
    - **Free Attractions:** Ohio offers many parks and museums with free or low-cost entry.

Here are the top attractions in Ohio, along with some money-saving tips for visiting each one:

Cedar Point, Sandusky: Enjoy thrilling roller coasters and water rides at this amusement park.

- Money-Saving Tip: Look for discounts on admission tickets and consider visiting on weekdays.

Rock and Roll Hall of Fame, Cleveland: Explore the history of rock music and its legends.

- Money-Saving Tip: Check for discounted admission rates for students, seniors, and military personnel.

Hocking Hills State Park: Discover beautiful hiking trails, waterfalls, and rock formations.

- Money-Saving Tip: Visit state parks during non-peak times to avoid parking fees.

Columbus: Explore the state capital with its museums, parks, and cultural events.

- Money-Saving Tip: Attend free festivals and outdoor concerts in Columbus.

Cincinnati Zoo & Botanical Garden: See a variety of animals and enjoy lush gardens.

- Money-Saving Tip: Look for discounted zoo tickets and family packages.

Amish Country, Holmes County: Experience Amish culture and enjoy homemade food.

- Money-Saving Tip: Visit local Amish markets and shops for affordable handmade products.

Cuyahoga Valley National Park: Hike, bike, and explore scenic landscapes near Cleveland.

- Money-Saving Tip: Purchase an America the Beautiful Pass for access to national parks.

Dayton: Visit the birthplace of aviation with museums and historic sites.

- Money-Saving Tip: Explore free attractions like the National Museum of the U.S. Air Force.

Toledo Zoo: See a wide variety of animals and enjoy family-friendly exhibits.

- Money-Saving Tip: Look for special zoo admission deals and discounts.

Kings Island, Mason: Have fun at this amusement park with rides and entertainment.

- Money-Saving Tip: Buy tickets online in advance for savings and avoid long lines.

Cleveland Museum of Art: Explore a wide range of art collections and special exhibitions.

- Money-Saving Tip: General admission to the museum is free, but some special exhibits may have fees.

Lake Erie Islands: Visit islands like Put-in-Bay and Kelleys Island for outdoor activities and relaxation.

- Money-Saving Tip: Check for discounted ferry tickets and consider weekday visits.

Cleveland Metroparks Zoo: Enjoy wildlife exhibits and educational programs.

- Money-Saving Tip: Look for zoo membership options that offer unlimited visits.

Cedar Bog Nature Preserve, Urbana: Discover a unique ecosystem with boardwalk trails.

- Money-Saving Tip: Visit the nature preserve for a nominal entrance fee.

Cleveland Botanical Garden: Explore beautiful gardens and exhibits in University Circle.

- Money-Saving Tip: Look for discounted admission rates for students and seniors.

Pro Football Hall of Fame, Canton: Learn about the history of American football and its legendary players.

- Money-Saving Tip: Check for discounts on admission, especially for NFL fans.

COSI Columbus: Enjoy interactive science exhibits and educational programs.

- Money-Saving Tip: Look for discounted COSI tickets and family packages.

Great Serpent Mound, Peebles: Visit this ancient effigy mound and learn about Native American history.

- Money-Saving Tip: Admission to the mound is affordable.

Franklin Park Conservatory and Botanical Gardens, Columbus: Experience lush gardens and plant collections.

Category	Insider Tips
Food	1. Explore Ohio's local farmers' markets, such as North Market in Columbus or Findlay Market in Cincinnati, for fresh produce and artisanal products sourced directly from local growers and producers.

	2. Dive into Ohio's culinary scene by trying regional specialties like Cincinnati-style chili or Lake Erie perch sandwiches, which can often be found at family-owned diners or casual eateries across the state.
	3. Take advantage of happy hour specials at Ohio's craft breweries and wineries, where you can sample a variety of locally brewed beers or wines at discounted prices.
	4. Look for food trucks and street food vendors in cities like Cleveland or Columbus, offering a diverse range of affordable and delicious eats, from gourmet tacos to artisanal ice cream.
Accommodation	1. Consider booking accommodations through local bed and breakfasts or guesthouses, where you can often find charming and affordable lodgings with personalized hospitality.
	2. Check out Airbnb or VRBO listings for unique and budget-friendly stays, including cozy cottages in rural areas, historic homes in small towns, or apartments in vibrant urban neighborhoods.
	3. Look for budget-friendly motel chains or independently owned motels along major highways and interstates, offering comfortable accommodations at affordable rates for travelers passing through Ohio.
	4. Explore camping options in Ohio's state parks, where you can pitch a tent or park your RV amidst picturesque natural surroundings, with amenities ranging from basic campsites to full-service campgrounds.
Activities	1. Embark on outdoor adventures in Ohio's state parks and nature reserves, where you can hike scenic trails, go birdwatching, or enjoy picnics in tranquil settings surrounded by lush forests and rolling hills.
	2. Discover Ohio's rich history and cultural heritage by visiting museums and historic sites like the Rock and Roll Hall of Fame in Cleveland, the National Museum of the U.S. Air Force in Dayton, or the Ohio History Center in Columbus.
	3. Attend local festivals and events celebrating Ohio's diverse communities and traditions, such as the Ohio State Fair in Columbus, the Cleveland International Film Festival, or Oktoberfest Zinzinnati in
	4. Take scenic drives along Ohio's countryside roads, exploring charming small towns, scenic overlooks, and roadside attractions like covered bridges, historic landmarks, and quirky roadside diners.
Transport	1. Consider renting a car to explore Ohio's diverse regions and attractions at your own pace, with rental agencies available at major airports, cities, and tourist destinations throughout the state.
	2. Utilize public transportation options in urban areas like Cleveland, Columbus, and Cincinnati, including buses, light rail, and commuter trains, for convenient and affordable travel within city limits.
	3. Look for bike-sharing programs in cities like Columbus or Cleveland, offering a fun and eco-friendly way to explore urban neighborhoods, parks, and scenic waterfront trails at minimal cost.
	4. Plan your travels around Ohio's scenic byways and heritage trails, which showcase the state's natural beauty, cultural landmarks, and historical sites, providing memorable road trip experiences for travelers of

Oklahoma

Oklahoma's history is deeply connected to the forced removal of Native American tribes, known as the Trail of Tears, and the subsequent settlement of various Indigenous nations in the region. The state has a strong cultural identity influenced by Native American heritage, ranching, and the oil industry.

Things to Consider:

- **Native American Culture:** Explore the rich Native American heritage in Oklahoma. Visit tribal museums, such as the Chickasaw Cultural Center or the Cherokee Heritage Center, to learn about the traditions and history of the Indigenous peoples.
- **Scenic Landscapes:** From the rolling plains to the Ouachita Mountains, Oklahoma offers diverse natural landscapes. Enjoy outdoor activities like hiking in the Wichita Mountains Wildlife Refuge or exploring the Talimena Scenic Byway.
- **Live Music and Festivals:** Experience the vibrant music scene in Oklahoma. Attend live performances in cities like Tulsa or Oklahoma City, and check out local festivals celebrating the state's cultural diversity.

Local Tips:

- **Barbecue and Comfort Food:** Indulge in Oklahoma's delicious barbecue and comfort food. Try local favorites like smoked brisket, chicken-fried steak, and the renowned Oklahoma onion burger.
- **Route 66:** Explore the historic Route 66, which cuts through Oklahoma. Visit quirky roadside attractions, vintage diners, and charming towns along this iconic stretch of highway.
- **Art and Museums:** Discover Oklahoma's artistic side by visiting museums and art galleries. The Oklahoma City Museum of Art, the Philbrook Museum of Art in Tulsa, and the National Cowboy & Western Heritage Museum offer diverse cultural experiences.

Must-Visit Places:

- **Oklahoma City:** Explore the state's capital and its attractions, including the Oklahoma City National Memorial, the Bricktown entertainment district, and the Myriad Botanical Gardens.
- **Tulsa:** Experience the vibrant arts scene in Tulsa's Brady Arts District, visit the Gathering Place park, and explore the Philbrook Museum of Art.
- **Chickasaw National Recreation Area:** Enjoy the natural beauty of the Chickasaw National Recreation Area, known for its springs, lakes, and hiking trails.

1. **Accommodation:**
    - **Budget-Friendly Luxury Hotels:**
    - **21c Museum Hotel Oklahoma City:** A boutique hotel with an in-house art museum. Approximate price: $150-$200 per night.
    - **The Mayo Hotel, Tulsa:** Historic hotel with modern amenities and a luxurious feel. Approximate price: $130-$180 per night.

2. **Dining:**
   - **The Paseo Grill, Oklahoma City:** Known for its upscale American cuisine in a romantic setting. Average meal cost: $20-$40.
   - **Juniper Restaurant, Tulsa:** Offers farm-to-table dining with a focus on local ingredients. Average meal cost: $25-$35.
3. **Attractions:**
   - **Oklahoma City National Memorial & Museum:** A poignant and educational experience. Entry fee: $15 per person.
   - **Philbrook Museum of Art, Tulsa:** Stunning art collections in a beautiful villa and gardens. Entry fee: $10-$12 per person.
4. **Activities:**
   - **Hot Air Balloon Rides over the Plains:** See Oklahoma's landscapes from above. Approximate cost: $200-$250 per person.
   - **Horseback Riding in the Wichita Mountains:** Explore scenic trails. Approximate cost: $40-$60 per hour.
5. **Local Experiences:**
   - **Bricktown, Oklahoma City:** Enjoy entertainment, dining, and canal rides. Canal ride cost: around $10-$15.
   - **Tulsa Arts District:** Explore galleries, music venues, and local cafes. Costs vary for purchases.
6. **Transportation:**
   - **Car Rental:** A convenient way to explore the state. Average cost: $30-$50 per day.
   - **Public Transportation:** More available in larger cities; limited in rural areas.
7. **Shopping:**
   - **Plaza District, Oklahoma City:** Boutique shops and local art. Prices vary.
   - **Utica Square, Tulsa:** High-end shopping experience. Prices vary.
8. **Insider Tips:**
   - **Visit During Festivals:** Oklahoma hosts various cultural and music festivals year-round.
   - **Book Accommodations in Advance:** Especially during peak seasons and events.
9. **Budget Tips:**
   - **Dine Locally:** Explore affordable and authentic meals at local eateries.
   - **Free Attractions:** Many museums and parks in Oklahoma offer free admission.

Oklahoma City: Explore the state's capital city with its museums, parks, and cultural events.

- Money-Saving Tip: Attend free concerts, festivals, and outdoor activities in Oklahoma City.

Tulsa: Discover the city with art deco architecture, cultural institutions, and outdoor attractions.

- Money-Saving Tip: Explore free attractions like the Philbrook Museum of Art gardens.

Chickasaw National Recreation Area: Enjoy outdoor activities, hiking trails, and mineral springs.

- Money-Saving Tip: Visit the recreation area for free and explore its natural beauty.

Oklahoma City National Memorial & Museum: Pay tribute to the victims of the Oklahoma City bombing.

- Money-Saving Tip: Check for discounted museum admission rates for students and seniors.

Route 66: Drive along the historic Route 66 with its roadside attractions and nostalgia.

- Money-Saving Tip: Enjoy the scenic drive and visit free attractions along the route.

Wichita Mountains Wildlife Refuge: Explore hiking trails and see bison, elk, and wildlife.

- Money-Saving Tip: Visit the refuge for free outdoor adventures.

National Cowboy & Western Heritage Museum, Oklahoma City: Learn about Western culture and art.

- Money-Saving Tip: Look for discounts on museum admission and special exhibits.

Beavers Bend State Park: Experience outdoor activities, camping, and Broken Bow Lake.

- Money-Saving Tip: Consider a state park pass for access to multiple parks.

Woody Guthrie Center, Tulsa: Discover the life and legacy of the folk singer and songwriter.

- Money-Saving Tip: Check for discounted admission rates and special programs.

Great Salt Plains State Park, Jet: Dig for selenite crystals and enjoy birdwatching.

- Money-Saving Tip: Visit the state park for free crystal digging and outdoor exploration.

Tulsa Botanic Garden: Explore themed gardens and seasonal displays.

- Money-Saving Tip: Look for discounted garden admission rates for children and seniors.

Marland Estate Mansion, Ponca City: Tour the historic mansion and its beautiful gardens.

- Money-Saving Tip: Enjoy affordable guided tours of the mansion.

Oklahoma Aquarium, Jenks: Discover marine life and aquatic exhibits.

- Money-Saving Tip: Check for online discounts and family admission packages.

Alabaster Caverns State Park, Freedom: Explore caves and underground formations.

- Money-Saving Tip: Visit the state park for cave tours with reasonable admission fees.

Science Museum Oklahoma, Oklahoma City: Enjoy hands-on science exhibits and educational programs.

- Money-Saving Tip: Look for discounts on museum admission and family passes.

Will Rogers Memorial Museum, Claremore: Learn about the life and humor of Will Rogers.

- Money-Saving Tip: Check for discounted museum admission rates and special events.

Oklahoma History Center, Oklahoma City: Explore the state's history and cultural heritage.

- Money-Saving Tip: Look for discounts on museum admission and exhibits.

Little Sahara State Park, Waynoka: Experience sand dunes and recreational activities.

- Money-Saving Tip: Visit the state park for a nominal entrance fee and enjoy outdoor adventures.

Cherokee Heritage Center, Tahlequah: Discover Cherokee culture and history.

- Money-Saving Tip: Check for discounts on admission and cultural events.

Blue Whale of Catoosa: Visit the iconic roadside attraction along Route 66.

- Money-Saving Tip: Enjoy the Blue Whale and its pond area for free.

Category	Insider Tips
Food	1. Explore Oklahoma's farmers' markets, such as the Cherry Street Farmers Market in Tulsa or the OSU-OKC Farmers Market, for locally grown produce and artisanal goods.
	2. Indulge in Oklahoma's barbecue culture by visiting local joints like Burn Co. Barbecue in Tulsa or Leo's BBQ in Oklahoma City for mouthwatering ribs, brisket, and pulled pork.
	3. Look for affordable dining options at diners and cafes serving comfort food classics like chicken fried steak, catfish, and Okie-style burgers, often found in small towns and rural areas.
	4. Take advantage of food truck festivals and events across Oklahoma, where you can sample a variety of cuisines from gourmet tacos and artisanal burgers to fusion fare and sweet treats.
Accommodation	1. Consider staying at locally owned bed and breakfasts or guesthouses in charming towns like Guthrie or Medicine Park, where you can enjoy personalized hospitality and unique accommodations.
	2. Explore affordable lodging options on platforms like Airbnb or Vrbo, where you can find cozy cabins, historic cottages, or private rooms in local homes at budget-friendly rates.
	3. Look for budget motels and roadside inns along major highways and interstates, offering basic amenities and convenient stays for travelers passing through Oklahoma.
	4. Embrace outdoor camping in Oklahoma's state parks and recreation areas, where you can pitch a tent or park your RV amidst scenic landscapes, with options ranging from primitive campsites to full-service campgrounds.
Activities	1. Discover Oklahoma's natural wonders by hiking trails in places like the Wichita Mountains Wildlife Refuge, exploring waterfalls at Turner Falls Park, or canoeing on the Illinois River.
	2. Immerse yourself in Oklahoma's cowboy culture and history by visiting attractions like the National Cowboy & Western Heritage Museum in Oklahoma City or the Will Rogers Memorial Museum in Claremore.
	3. Attend local festivals and events celebrating Oklahoma's diverse heritage and traditions, such as the Red Earth Festival in Oklahoma City, the Tulsa State Fair, or the Cherokee National Holiday in Tahlequah.
	4. Take scenic drives along Oklahoma's scenic byways and backroads, exploring small towns, historic landmarks, and natural attractions like the Tallgrass Prairie Preserve or the Great Salt Plains.
Transport	1. Rent a car to explore Oklahoma's vast landscapes and attractions at your own pace, with rental agencies available at major airports, cities, and tourist hubs throughout the state.
	2. Utilize public transportation options in urban areas like Oklahoma City and Tulsa, including buses, trolleys, and bike-sharing programs, for convenient and eco-friendly travel within city limits.
	3. Look for ridesharing services or carpooling opportunities for shared transportation to and from events, attractions, or outdoor adventures across Oklahoma.
	4. Plan road trips along Oklahoma's scenic highways and backroads, taking advantage of fuel-efficient vehicles and budget-friendly travel stops along the way.

Native American Heritage

The Native American heritage in the United States is a rich tapestry woven with diverse cultures, histories, and challenges that have shaped the landscape of the nation. As the original inhabitants of the continent, Native Americans have contributed immeasurably to the cultural mosaic of the USA. In this exploration, we delve into the multifaceted aspects of Native American heritage, from pre-European contact to contemporary challenges, highlighting the resilience and vibrancy of indigenous communities.

Pre-European Contact: A Tapestry of Cultures

1. Diverse Indigenous Nations:

Before the arrival of European settlers, the North American continent was home to a multitude of indigenous nations, each with its unique languages, customs, and traditions. From the Iroquois Confederacy in the Northeast to the Navajo in the Southwest, Native American societies thrived in harmony with the land, developing sophisticated agricultural practices, trade networks, and governance systems.

2. Spiritual Connection to Land:

Central to Native American cultures is a profound spiritual connection to the land. Many tribes regarded the Earth as a living entity, and their spiritual practices were intricately tied to the natural world. Sacred sites, such as the Black Hills for the Lakota Sioux or Mount Shasta for the Modoc, held profound spiritual significance.

3. Oral Traditions:

The preservation of history and cultural values was often achieved through oral traditions. Elders passed down stories, myths, and legends, ensuring the continuity of knowledge from one generation to the next. These narratives not only conveyed historical events but also provided moral lessons and insights into the interconnectedness of all living things.

European Contact: Impact and Adaptation

1. Cultural Exchange and Conflict:

The arrival of European explorers and settlers in the 15th century brought about profound changes. While there were instances of peaceful cultural exchange, interactions more often led to conflicts over land, resources, and differing worldviews. The devastating impact of diseases introduced by Europeans further altered the demographic landscape, causing significant population decline among Native American communities.

2. Forced Relocation and Trail of Tears:

One of the darkest chapters in Native American history is the forced relocation of tribes, particularly the Cherokee, Choctaw, Creek, Chickasaw, and Seminole, known as the Trail of Tears. The Indian Removal Act of 1830 authorized the removal of these nations from their ancestral lands in the Southeast to designated territories west of the Mississippi River, resulting in immense hardship and loss of life.

3. Treaty-Making Era:

Throughout the 19th century, the US government entered into a series of treaties with various Native American tribes. These treaties often involved the ceding of lands in exchange for reserved territories, annuities, and promises of protection. However, the implementation of these agreements was fraught with broken promises, leading to further dispossession and marginalization.

While some of these sites may charge admission fees or offer paid tours, there are also opportunities for free exploration and learning about Native American culture in Oklahoma. Here are a few options:

1. **Chickasaw Cultural Center**: Located in Sulphur, the Chickasaw Cultural Center offers free admission to its campus, which includes exhibits, demonstrations, and cultural performances highlighting Chickasaw history and traditions. Visitors can explore interactive exhibits, watch traditional crafts demonstrations, and enjoy outdoor spaces such as the traditional village and botanical garden.
2. **Red Earth Art Center**: Situated in Oklahoma City, the Red Earth Art Center showcases contemporary and traditional Native American art through rotating exhibits and educational programs. While there may be fees for special events or certain exhibits, general admission to the gallery is often free.
3. **Oklahoma City American Indian Cultural Center and Museum (AICCM)**: Although the AICCM is still under development, it occasionally hosts free events, workshops, and cultural programs that offer opportunities to learn about Native American history, art, and traditions. Keep an eye on their website or social media for upcoming free events.
4. **Tribal Festivals and Events**: Throughout the year, various Native American tribes in Oklahoma host cultural festivals, powwows, and other events that are often open to the public and free to attend. These events typically feature traditional music, dance, food, and arts and crafts, providing a vibrant showcase of Native American culture.
5. **Tribal Historic Sites**: Some tribal nations in Oklahoma maintain historic sites and cultural centers that are open to the public for free or at a nominal cost.

Oregon

Exploring Oregon with a touch of luxury while maintaining a budget is an exciting prospect. Here's a comprehensive guide to help you enjoy Oregon's natural beauty, cultural richness, and urban charm:

1. Accommodation:
- **Budget-Friendly Luxury Hotels:**
- **The Nines, Portland:** A stylish, upscale hotel located in a historic building. Approximate price: $150-$200 per night.
- **Ashland Springs Hotel, Ashland:** Historic charm with modern amenities in a picturesque setting. Approximate price: $120-$170 per night.

2. Dining:
- **Le Pigeon, Portland:** Innovative French cuisine in an intimate setting. Average meal cost: $30-$50.
- **Larks Home Kitchen Cuisine, Ashland:** Farm-to-table fare with a focus on Oregon flavors. Average meal cost: $20-$40.

3. Attractions:
- **Columbia River Gorge National Scenic Area:** Free access to breathtaking landscapes and hikes.
- **Oregon Coast Aquarium, Newport:** A window into marine life. Entry fee: $20-$25 per person.

4. Activities:
- **Wine Tasting in Willamette Valley:** Explore renowned vineyards. Tasting fees: $15-$30 per person.
- **Hot Air Balloon Rides over the Willamette Valley:** Picturesque views of the landscape. Approximate cost: $200-$250 per person.

5. Local Experiences:
- **Portland's Art and Cultural Scene:** Visit galleries, theaters, and music venues. Costs vary.
- **Shakespeare Festival, Ashland:** Renowned theater performances. Ticket prices: $30-$100, depending on the show.

6. Transportation:
- **Car Rental:** Ideal for exploring the diverse regions of Oregon. Average cost: $35-$55 per day.
- **Public Transportation in Portland:** Efficient and budget-friendly.

7. Shopping:
- **Pearl District, Portland:** Upscale boutiques and local artisan shops. Prices vary.
- **Saturday Market, Eugene:** Local crafts, art, and food. Prices vary.

8. Insider Tips:
- **Best Time to Visit:** Late spring through early fall for outdoor activities.
- **Advance Bookings:** Recommended for popular attractions and accommodations.

9. Budget Tips:
- **Eat Like a Local:** Food trucks and local diners offer delicious, affordable options.
- **Enjoy Nature:** Oregon's natural attractions often have minimal to no fees.

Here are the top attractions in Oregon, along with some money-saving tips for visiting each one:

Crater Lake National Park: Explore the stunning Crater Lake, the deepest lake in the United States.

- Money-Saving Tip: Purchase an America the Beautiful Pass for access to national parks.

Portland: Discover Oregon's largest city with its vibrant arts scene, parks, and culinary delights.

- Money-Saving Tip: Enjoy free events, festivals, and outdoor activities in Portland.

Columbia River Gorge: Hike and take in the breathtaking views along the Columbia River.

- Money-Saving Tip: Explore the scenic beauty of the gorge without any entrance fees.

Multnomah Falls: Visit the iconic waterfall in the Columbia River Gorge.

- Money-Saving Tip: Enjoy the falls and nearby hiking trails for free.

Mount Hood: Experience outdoor activities, including skiing and hiking, on Oregon's highest peak.

- Money-Saving Tip: Visit during non-peak seasons for more affordable lodging rates.

Oregon Coast: Enjoy the picturesque coastline with its beaches, cliffs, and charming towns.

- Money-Saving Tip: Explore free public beaches and parks along the coast.

Crater Lake Lodge: Stay at the historic lodge overlooking Crater Lake.

- Money-Saving Tip: Book accommodations well in advance for the best rates.

Powell's City of Books, Portland: Browse the world's largest independent bookstore.

- Money-Saving Tip: Enjoy window-shopping and exploring the store without making a purchase.

Oregon Museum of Science and Industry (OMSI), Portland: Experience interactive science exhibits and educational programs.

- Money-Saving Tip: Look for discounts on museum admission and special exhibitions.

Mount Bachelor: Ski and snowboard in the winter or hike and bike in the summer at this mountain resort.

- Money-Saving Tip: Check for lift ticket discounts and consider renting equipment locally.

Oregon Shakespeare Festival, Ashland: Attend theater performances and cultural events.

- Money-Saving Tip: Look for discounts on show tickets and consider attending matinee performances.

Oregon Zoo, Portland: Visit a variety of animals and enjoy family-friendly exhibits.

- Money-Saving Tip: Check for online discounts and family admission packages.

Deschutes Brewery, Bend: Take a brewery tour and enjoy craft beer tastings.

- Money-Saving Tip: Look for brewery tour discounts and happy hour specials.

Cannon Beach: Relax on the sandy shores and explore Haystack Rock.

- Money-Saving Tip: Visit public access beaches for lower parking fees and free beach access.

Silver Falls State Park: Hike to stunning waterfalls and enjoy outdoor adventures.

- Money-Saving Tip: Consider a state park pass for access to multiple parks.

Oregon Vortex and House of Mystery, Gold Hill: Experience optical illusions and strange phenomena.

- Money-Saving Tip: Visit the vortex for a nominal admission fee.

Tillamook Creamery: Tour the cheese factory and taste delicious dairy products.

- Money-Saving Tip: Enjoy affordable cheese tastings and self-guided tours.

Hood River: Explore a town known for outdoor activities, including windsurfing and kiteboarding.

- Money-Saving Tip: Check for deals on equipment rentals and lessons.

Astoria: Visit the historic coastal town with museums and cultural attractions.

- Money-Saving Tip: Attend free community events and explore historic neighborhoods.

High Desert Museum, Bend: Discover the natural and cultural history of Central Oregon.

- Money-Saving Tip: Look for discounts on museum admission and family passes.

Recap:

Category	Insider Tips
Food	1. Explore Oregon's farmers' markets, such as the Portland Farmers Market or Eugene Saturday Market, for locally sourced produce, artisanal foods, and handcrafted goods.

	2. Indulge in Oregon's vibrant food truck scene, with pods and clusters offering a diverse array of cuisines, from gourmet grilled cheese sandwiches to creative vegan fare and international street food.
	3. Look for affordable dining options at local cafes and diners, serving up Pacific Northwest specialties like fresh seafood, wild-caught salmon, and farm-to-table dishes in cozy settings.
	4. Take advantage of happy hour specials and daily deals at restaurants and bars across Oregon, offering discounted drinks, appetizers, and small plates for budget-conscious diners.
Accommodation	1. Consider staying at rustic lodges, cabins, or yurts in Oregon's state parks and recreation areas, offering affordable accommodations amidst scenic natural settings, with options for camping, hiking, and outdoor recreation.
	2. Explore budget-friendly lodging options on platforms like Airbnb or Vrbo, where you can find unique accommodations like tiny houses, treehouses, or farm stays in rural and urban settings across Oregon.
	3. Look for budget motels and roadside inns along major highways and scenic byways, providing convenient and affordable stays for travelers exploring Oregon's diverse regions and attractions.
	4. Embrace outdoor camping in Oregon's national forests and wilderness areas, where you can pitch a tent or park your RV amidst old-growth forests, mountain lakes, and cascading waterfalls, with options for primitive campsites, dispersed camping, and backcountry adventures.
Activities	1. Discover Oregon's natural wonders by exploring hiking trails in places like the Columbia River Gorge, Oregon Coast, or Cascade Mountains, where you can experience breathtaking vistas, scenic waterfalls, and diverse ecosystems.
	2. Immerse yourself in Oregon's craft beer culture by visiting local breweries, taprooms, and brewpubs, offering tours, tastings, and flights of handcrafted beers, ciders, and spirits brewed with local ingredients and innovative techniques.
	3. Attend local festivals and events celebrating Oregon's diverse communities and cultural traditions, such as the Oregon Shakespeare Festival in Ashland, the Portland Rose Festival, or the Sisters Folk Festival in Central Oregon.
	4. Take scenic drives along Oregon's scenic byways and backroads, exploring charming small towns, historic landmarks, and natural attractions like the Painted Hills, Smith Rock, or the Oregon Dunes, with opportunities for hiking, wildlife viewing, and photography along the way.
Transport	1. Rent a car to explore Oregon's scenic highways and backroads, with rental agencies available at major airports, cities, and tourist destinations throughout the state, providing flexibility and convenience for travelers.
	2. Utilize public transportation options in urban areas like Portland and Eugene, including buses, light rail, and streetcars, for convenient and eco-friendly travel within city limits, with options for day passes, fare discounts, and bike-sharing programs available.
	3. Look for ridesharing services or carpooling opportunities for shared transportation to and from events, attractions, or outdoor adventures across Oregon, providing cost-effective and social travel options for visitors and locals alike.
	4. Plan road trips along Oregon's scenic highways and backroads, taking advantage of fuel-efficient vehicles and budget-friendly travel stops along the way, with opportunities for camping, picnicking, and exploring hidden gems off the beaten path.

Pennsylvania

From the historic streets of Philadelphia to the scenic beauty of the Pocono Mountains, Pennsylvania offers a journey through time and nature.

History and Culture:

- **Philadelphia:** Explore the historic city of Philadelphia, where the Declaration of Independence was signed. Visit Independence Hall, the Liberty Bell, and the iconic Philadelphia Museum of Art with the famous "Rocky Steps."
- **Gettysburg National Military Park:** Step back in time at Gettysburg, the site of a pivotal Civil War battle. Tour the battlefield, visit the museum, and gain insights into this significant period of American history.
- **Pittsburgh:** Discover the vibrant city of Pittsburgh, known for its industrial history and modern revitalization. Explore the Andy Warhol Museum, stroll along the Three Rivers Heritage Trail, and ride the Duquesne Incline for panoramic views.

Nature and Scenic Beauty:

- **Pocono Mountains:** Escape to the picturesque Pocono Mountains for outdoor adventures. Enjoy hiking, skiing, and water activities in this scenic region.
- **Amish Country:** Experience the tranquility of Amish Country in Lancaster County. Explore charming villages, visit farmers' markets, and learn about the Amish way of life.
- **Great Allegheny Passage:** Bike or hike along the Great Allegheny Passage, a scenic trail connecting Pittsburgh to Cumberland, Maryland, offering breathtaking views and outdoor recreation.

Local Tips:

- **Cheesesteaks in Philadelphia:** Indulge in the iconic Philadelphia cheesesteak. Visit famous spots like Pat's King of Steaks or Geno's Steaks for a delicious and authentic experience.
- **Dutch Country Delights:** In Amish Country, savor traditional Pennsylvania Dutch cuisine. Try shoofly pie, scrapple, and handmade pretzels.
- **Fall Foliage:** If your visit aligns with the fall season, witness the spectacular display of fall foliage in Pennsylvania. Explore state parks and scenic drives for the best autumn views.

Must-Visit Places:

- **Hershey:** Visit Hershey, the "Sweetest Place on Earth." Tour the Hershey Chocolate World, visit Hersheypark, and indulge in all things chocolate in this delightful town.
- **Philadelphia Museum of Art:** Channel your inner Rocky Balboa by running up the "Rocky Steps" at the Philadelphia Museum of Art. Enjoy the impressive art collection inside.
- **Rittenhouse Square:** Relax in Rittenhouse Square in Philadelphia, a picturesque park surrounded by shops, cafes, and historic architecture.

1. **Accommodation:**
    - **Budget-Friendly Luxury Hotels:**
    - **The Rittenhouse Hotel, Philadelphia:** A prestigious hotel offering luxury in the heart of the city. Approximate price: $200-$250 per night.
    - **Omni Bedford Springs Resort, Bedford:** Historic resort with spa and golf course. Approximate price: $150-$200 per night.
2. **Dining:**
    - **Vetri Cucina, Philadelphia:** Renowned for its upscale Italian cuisine. Average meal cost: $30-$50.
    - **Le Mont, Pittsburgh:** Fine dining with stunning city views. Average meal cost: $25-$40.
3. **Attractions:**
    - **Philadelphia Museum of Art:** Iconic museum with a rich collection. Entry fee: $20-$25 per person.
    - **Gettysburg National Military Park:** Historical site with free admission; guided tours available at various costs.
4. **Activities:**
    - **Hot Air Balloon Ride over Lancaster County:** Scenic views of Amish country. Approximate cost: $200-$250 per person.
    - **Wine Tasting in the Brandywine Valley:** Explore local vineyards. Tasting fees: $10-$20 per person.
5. **Local Experiences:**
    - **Philadelphia's Historic District:** Explore the Liberty Bell, Independence Hall (free admission), and more.
    - **Pittsburgh's Cultural District:** Theatres, galleries, and live performances. Ticket prices vary.
6. **Transportation:**
    - **Car Rental:** Useful for exploring rural areas and small towns. Average cost: $30-$50 per day.
    - **Public Transit in Cities:** Affordable and convenient in Philadelphia and Pittsburgh.
7. **Shopping:**
    - **King of Prussia Mall, Philadelphia:** A mix of high-end and mainstream retailers. Prices vary.
    - **The Strip District, Pittsburgh:** Local markets and specialty stores. Prices vary.
8. **Insider Tips:**
    - **Best Time to Visit:** Spring and fall for pleasant weather and colorful scenery.
    - **Book in Advance:** Especially for upscale dining and popular attractions.
9. **Budget Tips:**
    - **Local Eats:** Try Pennsylvania's famous cheesesteaks, pretzels, and diners for affordable meals.
    - **Free Attractions:** Many historical sites and museums in Pennsylvania offer free admission.

Philadelphia: Explore the historic city with its museums, historic sites, and cultural events.

- Money-Saving Tip: Visit historic sites like Independence Hall and the Liberty Bell for free.

Pittsburgh: Discover the Steel City with its thriving arts scene, scenic views, and sports events.

- Money-Saving Tip: Attend free concerts, festivals, and outdoor activities in Pittsburgh.

Gettysburg National Military Park: Learn about the Civil War's pivotal battle and its history.

- Money-Saving Tip: Purchase an America the Beautiful Pass for access to national parks.

Hershey: Experience the "Sweetest Place on Earth" with Hersheypark and chocolate-themed attractions.

- Money-Saving Tip: Look for Hersheypark ticket discounts and consider visiting during off-peak times.

Amish Country, Lancaster: Immerse yourself in Amish culture and enjoy homemade food.

- Money-Saving Tip: Visit local Amish markets and shops for affordable handmade products.

Ricketts Glen State Park: Hike to see stunning waterfalls and enjoy outdoor activities.

- Money-Saving Tip: Explore state parks during non-peak times to avoid parking fees.

Frank Lloyd Wright's Fallingwater, Mill Run: Tour the iconic architectural masterpiece.

- Money-Saving Tip: Book your Fallingwater tour tickets online in advance.

Eastern State Penitentiary, Philadelphia: Explore the historic prison and its eerie architecture.

- Money-Saving Tip: Check for discounts on admission and special events.

Presque Isle State Park, Erie: Relax on sandy beaches and enjoy water activities on Lake Erie.

- Money-Saving Tip: Visit the state park for free access to beaches and picnic areas.

Philadelphia Museum of Art: Discover a wide range of art collections and the famous "Rocky Steps."

- Money-Saving Tip: Pay what you wish for museum admission on specific days and hours.

Valley Forge National Historical Park: Learn about the Revolutionary War and history.

- Money-Saving Tip: Explore the park's historical sites and trails for free.

Longwood Gardens, Kennett Square: Enjoy lush gardens and seasonal displays.

- Money-Saving Tip: Look for discounted admission rates for students and seniors.

Lake Erie Wine Country: Explore vineyards and wineries along the Lake Erie shoreline.

- Money-Saving Tip: Enjoy wine tastings and look for special events with discounts.

Phipps Conservatory and Botanical Gardens, Pittsburgh: Experience beautiful gardens and plant collections.

- Money-Saving Tip: Check for discounts on admission rates and special exhibits.

Ride the Rails of Pennsylvania: Take scenic train rides on various historic railways.

- Money-Saving Tip: Look for discounts and package deals for train excursions.

Crayola Experience, Easton: Enjoy colorful and interactive art activities for the whole family.

- Money-Saving Tip: Check for online discounts and family admission packages.

Kennywood Amusement Park, West Mifflin: Have fun at this historic amusement park.

- Money-Saving Tip: Purchase tickets online in advance for potential savings.

Reading Terminal Market, Philadelphia: Sample diverse cuisines and shop for local products.

- Money-Saving Tip: Enjoy food samples and shop for affordable fresh produce.

Bushkill Falls: Hike to the "Niagara of Pennsylvania" and explore the natural beauty.

- Money-Saving Tip: Visit during weekdays or non-peak times for lower admission rates.

Erie Maritime Museum and U.S. Brig Niagara: Learn about naval history and explore a historic ship.

- Money-Saving Tip: Check for discounts on museum admission and ship tours.

Category	Insider Tips
Food	1. Explore Pennsylvania's farmers' markets, such as the Reading Terminal Market in Philadelphia or the Strip District in Pittsburgh, for locally sourced produce, artisanal foods, and ethnic specialties.
	2. Indulge in Pennsylvania's iconic comfort foods like cheesesteaks in Philadelphia, pierogies in Pittsburgh, or Pennsylvania Dutch dishes in Lancaster County, often found at neighborhood delis, diners, and family-owned restaurants.
	3. Look for affordable dining options at local diners and cafes serving up classic American fare, regional favorites, and hearty breakfasts, often found in small towns and rural areas across Pennsylvania.
	4. Take advantage of happy hour specials and weekday deals at bars and taverns across Pennsylvania, offering discounted drinks, appetizers, and pub grub for budget-conscious diners and nightlife enthusiasts.
Accommodation	1. Consider staying at cozy bed and breakfasts or historic inns in Pennsylvania's small towns and countryside, offering personalized hospitality and unique accommodations amidst scenic landscapes and

	2. Explore budget-friendly lodging options on platforms like Airbnb or Vrbo, where you can find affordable stays like guest suites, vacation rentals, or private rooms in local homes in urban and rural areas across
	3. Look for budget motels and roadside inns along major highways and interstates, providing convenient and affordable stays for travelers passing through Pennsylvania's cities and towns.
	4. Embrace outdoor camping in Pennsylvania's state parks and forests, where you can pitch a tent or park your RV amidst nature trails, waterways, and recreational facilities, with options for family-friendly campsites, group camping, and rustic cabins.
Activities	1. Discover Pennsylvania's outdoor attractions by hiking trails in places like Ricketts Glen State Park, exploring waterfalls in the Pocono Mountains, or biking along the Great Allegheny Passage, offering scenic vistas, natural wonders, and recreational opportunities for outdoor
	2. Immerse yourself in Pennsylvania's cultural heritage by visiting historic sites like Independence National Historical Park in Philadelphia, Gettysburg National Military Park, or the Pennsylvania Dutch Country in Lancaster County, where you can explore landmarks, museums, and living history exhibits showcasing the state's rich history and traditions.
	3. Attend local festivals and events celebrating Pennsylvania's diverse communities and cultural traditions, such as the Philadelphia Flower Show, Musikfest in Bethlehem, or the Pennsylvania Renaissance Faire in Lancaster, featuring music, food, crafts, and entertainment for visitors of
	4. Take scenic drives along Pennsylvania's scenic byways and country roads, exploring charming small towns, historic landmarks, and natural attractions like covered bridges, rural landscapes, and scenic overlooks, with opportunities for picnicking, antiquing, and exploring local shops and
Transport	1. Rent a car to explore Pennsylvania's scenic highways and backroads, with rental agencies available at major airports, cities, and tourist destinations throughout the state, providing flexibility and convenience for travelers to explore at their own pace.
	2. Utilize public transportation options in urban areas like Philadelphia and Pittsburgh, including buses, subways, and trolleys, for convenient and eco-friendly travel within city limits, with options for day passes, fare discounts, and bike-sharing programs available for visitors and locals
	3. Look for ridesharing services or carpooling opportunities for shared transportation to and from events, attractions, or outdoor adventures across Pennsylvania, providing cost-effective and social travel options for travelers and residents.
	4. Plan road trips along Pennsylvania's scenic highways and backroads, taking advantage of fuel-efficient vehicles and budget-friendly travel stops along the way, with opportunities for camping, picnicking, and exploring hidden gems off the beaten path.

Rhode Island

Rhode Island, the smallest state with the biggest charm! Tucked away in New England, this pint-sized paradise packs a punch when it comes to history, culture, and coastline. With its rich colonial heritage, stunning beaches, and vibrant arts scene, Rhode Island is a delightful blend of old-world charm and modern-day flair. So grab your clam chowder and get ready to explore the Ocean State's treasures, from Newport's opulent mansions to Providence's quirky neighborhoods. Welcome to Rhode Island, where big adventures come in small packages!

Historic and Coastal Charm:

- **Newport Mansions:** Explore the opulent Newport Mansions, including The Breakers and Marble House, showcasing the Gilded Age's grandeur along the coastline.
- **Providence Waterfront:** Stroll along the Providence Riverwalk, where cobblestone streets, historic architecture, and vibrant cultural events create a charming atmosphere.
- **Historic Landmarks:** Visit historic landmarks such as the Rhode Island State House in Providence and the Roger Williams National Memorial, commemorating the founder of Rhode Island.

Coastal Beauty:

- **Narragansett Bay:** Enjoy the scenic beauty of Narragansett Bay, whether by taking a harbor cruise, exploring coastal parks, or lounging on the beaches.
- **Block Island:** Take a ferry to Block Island, a serene destination with lighthouses, bluffs, and a relaxed island atmosphere.
- **Watch Hill:** Visit Watch Hill, known for its historic carousel, upscale shops, and panoramic views of the Atlantic Ocean.

Local Tips:

- **Seafood Delights:** Indulge in Rhode Island's fresh seafood, particularly its famous clam chowder and clam cakes. Don't miss trying a local favorite—stuffies, which are stuffed quahogs.
- **New England Lighthouses:** Rhode Island is home to several picturesque lighthouses. Visit iconic ones like Beavertail Lighthouse and Castle Hill Lighthouse for stunning coastal views.
- **Waterfire in Providence:** If you're in Providence during the summer or fall, experience WaterFire, an art installation featuring bonfires on the rivers, accompanied by music and events.

Must-Visit Places:

- **The Cliff Walk:** Take a scenic walk along The Cliff Walk in Newport, offering breathtaking views of the Atlantic Ocean and passing by the backyards of the famous Newport Mansions.
- **Brown University:** Explore the Brown University campus in Providence, known for its historic architecture and vibrant student life.
- **Rhode Island Beaches:** Relax on the state's beautiful beaches, such as Misquamicut Beach or Narragansett Town Beach, for sun, sand, and seaside bliss.

1. Accommodation:
   - **Budget-Friendly Luxury Hotels:**
   - **The Chanler at Cliff Walk, Newport:** Elegant hotel with stunning ocean views. Approximate price: $150-$400 per night.
   - **Hotel Providence, Providence:** Upscale boutique hotel in the arts and entertainment district. Approximate price: $150-$200 per night.
2. Dining:
   - **White Horse Tavern, Newport:** America's oldest tavern, offering a high-end dining experience. Average meal cost: $30-$50.
   - **Gracie's, Providence:** Known for its exceptional farm-to-table cuisine. Average meal cost: $25-$40.
3. Attractions:
   - **The Breakers, Newport:** A famous Gilded Age mansion with an entry fee of about $24 per person.
   - **Rhode Island School of Design Museum, Providence:** Offers a diverse art collection. Entry fee: $15-$20 per person.
4. Activities:
   - **Sailing in Narragansett Bay:** Experience the beauty of Rhode Island's coast. Approximate cost: $50-$100 per person.
   - **Wine Tasting at Newport Vineyards:** Enjoy local wines. Tasting fees: $15-$25 per person.
5. Local Experiences:
   - **Cliff Walk, Newport:** A scenic 3.5-mile walk combining natural beauty with architectural history. Free.
   - **WaterFire, Providence:** An award-winning fire sculpture installation on the rivers of downtown Providence (seasonal). Free.
6. Transportation:
   - **Car Rental:** Convenient for exploring the state. Average cost: $40-$60 per day.
   - **Public Transportation:** Available in cities but limited in rural areas.
7. Shopping:
   - **Bowen's Wharf, Newport:** A prime location for shopping and dining, with a range of prices.
   - **Thayer Street, Providence:** Eclectic mix of shops and boutiques. Prices vary.
8. Insider Tips:
   - **Best Time to Visit:** Late spring to early fall for ideal weather.
   - **Advance Bookings:** Recommended for hotels and popular attractions, especially in Newport during the summer.
9. Budget Tips:
   - **Eat Like a Local:** Seafood is a must-try; local clam shacks offer great value.

- **Explore Free Attractions:** Rhode Island offers many beaches, parks, and walking tours with no fee.

This guide blends luxury and affordability, allowing you to enjoy Rhode Island's rich cultural heritage, stunning coastal landscapes, and historical charm. Keep in mind that prices can vary, so it's always a good idea to check current rates and book in advance where possible. Enjoy your Rhode Island adventure!

Here are the top attractions in Rhode Island, along with some money-saving tips for visiting each one:

Providence: Explore the capital city with its historic architecture, culinary scene, and cultural events.

- Money-Saving Tip: Attend free outdoor concerts, festivals, and events in Providence.

Newport: Discover the coastal city known for its historic mansions, beaches, and maritime heritage.

- Money-Saving Tip: Enjoy the Cliff Walk and public beaches for free or at a low cost.

The Breakers, Newport: Tour the opulent Vanderbilt mansion and its grand architecture.

- Money-Saving Tip: Consider purchasing a combination ticket for multiple mansion tours.

Roger Williams Park, Providence: Relax in the expansive park with gardens, a zoo, and a carousel.

- Money-Saving Tip: Explore the park's gardens and outdoor areas for free.

Block Island: Visit the scenic island with beaches, hiking trails, and outdoor activities.

- Money-Saving Tip: Take advantage of day trips and ferry discounts for visitors.

RISD Museum, Providence: Discover art collections and exhibitions at the Rhode Island School of Design.

- Money-Saving Tip: Check for discounts on museum admission, especially for students.

Marble House, Newport: Tour another Vanderbilt mansion with stunning architecture.

- Money-Saving Tip: Consider a combination ticket for multiple mansion tours in Newport.

WaterFire, Providence: Attend the unique art installation with bonfires on the Providence River.

- Money-Saving Tip: Enjoy the event for free and check the schedule for specific dates.

Narragansett Beach: Relax on the sandy shores and enjoy the Atlantic Ocean.

- Money-Saving Tip: Visit public beaches for affordable beach days.

Touro Synagogue, Newport: Explore the historic synagogue, the oldest in the United States.

- Money-Saving Tip: Take advantage of discounted admission for guided tours.

Blackstone River Valley National Historical Park: Learn about the industrial history of the region.

- Money-Saving Tip: Visit the park for free and explore the historical sites.

Providence Children's Museum: Enjoy interactive exhibits and educational programs for kids.

- Money-Saving Tip: Look for discounts on museum admission and family memberships.

Westerly: Experience a coastal town with beaches, parks, and charming downtown areas.

- Money-Saving Tip: Explore local parks and enjoy outdoor activities.

Roger Williams Park Zoo, Providence: See a variety of animals and family-friendly exhibits.

- Money-Saving Tip: Check for online discounts and family admission packages.

Beavertail State Park, Jamestown: Take in panoramic ocean views and explore rocky shores.

- Money-Saving Tip: Visit the state park for a nominal entrance fee.

Fort Adams State Park, Newport: Explore the historic fort and its waterfront location.

- Money-Saving Tip: Enjoy the park's outdoor spaces and views without any fees.

Slater Mill Historic Site, Pawtucket: Learn about the industrial revolution and history.

- Money-Saving Tip: Check for discounts on guided tours and special events.

Sakonnet Vineyard, Little Compton: Visit a local vineyard and enjoy wine tastings.

- Money-Saving Tip: Look for winery tour and tasting package deals.

Ladd Observatory, Providence: Observe the stars and planets during public viewing nights.

- Money-Saving Tip: Attend free public stargazing events at the observatory.

Jamestown: Explore a quaint island town with scenic beauty and outdoor activities.

- Money-Saving Tip: Enjoy the natural beauty of Jamestown without additional costs.

Category	Insider Tips
Food	1. Explore Rhode Island's seafood scene by visiting local seafood shacks and clam shacks for fresh catches like lobster rolls, clam cakes, and chowder, often found along the coast and in beachside towns like

		2. Indulge in Rhode Island's culinary specialties like johnnycakes, stuffies (stuffed quahogs), and coffee milk, which can often be found at local diners, family-owned restaurants, and traditional Rhode Island eateries.
		3. Look for affordable dining options at casual cafes and bistros serving up comfort food classics, seasonal dishes, and farm-to-table fare, often found in historic neighborhoods like Providence's Federal Hill or Newport's Thames Street.
		4. Take advantage of happy hour specials and weekday deals at bars and taverns across Rhode Island, offering discounted drinks, appetizers, and local brews for budget-conscious diners and nightlife enthusiasts.
	Accommodation	1. Consider staying at boutique hotels or historic inns in Rhode Island's charming towns and coastal villages, offering personalized hospitality and unique accommodations amidst scenic landscapes and architectural
		2. Explore budget-friendly lodging options on platforms like Airbnb or Vrbo, where you can find affordable stays like guest suites, vacation rentals, or private rooms in local homes in urban and rural areas across
		3. Look for budget motels and roadside inns along major highways and scenic routes, providing convenient and affordable stays for travelers passing through Rhode Island's cities and towns.
		4. Embrace outdoor camping in Rhode Island's state parks and beaches, where you can pitch a tent or park your RV amidst coastal dunes, woodlands, and waterfront campsites, with options for family-friendly camping, group sites, and rustic cabins.
	Activities	1. Discover Rhode Island's outdoor attractions by exploring hiking trails in places like Arcadia Management Area, biking along the East Bay Bike Path, or kayaking in Narragansett Bay, offering scenic vistas, natural wonders, and recreational opportunities for outdoor enthusiasts.
		2. Immerse yourself in Rhode Island's maritime heritage by visiting historic sites like the Newport Mansions, exploring lighthouses along the coast, or taking harbor cruises and sailing tours, offering insights into the state's seafaring past and coastal culture.
		3. Attend local festivals and events celebrating Rhode Island's diverse communities and cultural traditions, such as the Newport Jazz Festival, the WaterFire Providence, or the South County Hot Air Balloon Festival, featuring music, food, arts, and entertainment for visitors of all ages.
		4. Take scenic drives along Rhode Island's coastal roads and scenic byways, exploring charming small towns, historic landmarks, and natural attractions like wildlife refuges, seaside parks, and coastal cliffs, with opportunities for picnicking, beachcombing, and exploring local shops and galleries along the way.
	Transport	1. Rent a car to explore Rhode Island's scenic coastal drives and historic landmarks, with rental agencies available at major airports, cities, and tourist destinations throughout the state, providing flexibility and convenience for travelers to explore at their own pace.
		2. Utilize public transportation options in urban areas like Providence and Newport, including buses, trolleys, and ferries, for convenient and eco-friendly travel within city limits, with options for day passes, fare discounts, and bike-sharing programs available for visitors and locals
		3. Look for ridesharing services or carpooling opportunities for shared transportation to and from events, attractions, or outdoor adventures across Rhode Island, providing cost-effective and social travel options for travelers and residents.

4. Plan road trips along Rhode Island's scenic coastal routes and rural backroads, taking advantage of fuel-efficient vehicles and budget-friendly travel stops along the way, with opportunities for beach hopping, exploring hidden coves, and indulging in fresh seafood along the

New York state

Every corner tells a story and every skyline paints a picture! From the iconic bustle of New York City to the tranquil beauty of the Adirondack Mountains, this diverse state offers something for everyone. Whether you're exploring the vibrant streets of Manhattan, marveling at the natural wonders of Niagara Falls, or tasting your way through the Finger Lakes wine country, New York State is a playground of possibilities. Soak up the energy of Times Square, wander through historic villages, or escape to the wilderness for a breath of fresh air. Whatever your adventure, get ready to be swept away by the magic of the Empire State!

1. **Accommodation:**
   - Explore budget-friendly hotels, motels, or boutique accommodations. Consider staying in areas outside Manhattan in New York City or in charming towns upstate.
   - Recommended places: Pod 51 Hotel in New York City, The Otesaga Resort Hotel in Cooperstown, and The Sagamore Resort in Bolton Landing.
   - **Camping:** If you enjoy the outdoors, camping can be an extremely affordable option. Look for campgrounds in state parks, national forests, or private campgrounds across New York State. Options range from basic tent sites to RV hookups, with prices varying depending on amenities and location.

2. **Transportation:**
   - Utilize public transportation in cities like New York City, where subways and buses are efficient and cost-effective.
   - Consider walking or biking in areas with pedestrian-friendly infrastructure, especially in cities and towns.

3. **Free Attractions:**
   - Take advantage of free attractions, such as Central Park in New York City, the High Line, and Times Square.
   - Explore state parks with no or minimal entrance fees, like Letchworth State Park or Watkins Glen State Park.

4. **Cultural Experiences:**
   - Visit museums during free hours or on specific days. Many museums offer discounted or free entry on certain times or for students.
   - Recommended places: The Metropolitan Museum of Art in NYC, The Corning Museum of Glass, and The Museum of Modern Art (MoMA).

5. **Outdoor Activities:**

- Explore the natural beauty of New York by hiking in the Adirondacks, exploring the Catskill Mountains, or enjoying the Finger Lakes region.
- Recommended activities: Adirondack Scenic Railroad, Watkins Glen Gorge Trail, and Lake Placid's Mirror Lake.

6. Local Markets:

- Explore local markets for affordable and delicious food. In NYC, consider visiting Chelsea Market or the Union Square Greenmarket.
- Upstate, visit regional farmers' markets for fresh produce and local delicacies.

7. Entertainment:

- Check for discounted Broadway tickets, especially for matinee shows or through online platforms.
- Attend free concerts and events in public spaces, parks, or local community centers.
- **New York State Capitol (Albany):** The New York State Capitol offers free guided tours where you can learn about the state's government, history, and architecture. Tours are typically available Monday through Friday.
- **Central Park (New York City):** While not guided, Central Park offers numerous free self-guided walking tours and activities. You can explore iconic landmarks such as Bethesda Terrace, Bow Bridge, and Strawberry Fields, or participate in free events and performances held throughout the park.
- **Statue of Liberty and Ellis Island (New York City):** While there may be fees for ferry tickets and access to certain areas of the monuments, you can explore the grounds of the Statue of Liberty and Ellis Island for free. Park rangers are available to provide information and answer questions.

8. Dining:

- Explore a variety of dining options, from street food carts to ethnic eateries for budget-friendly yet tasty meals.
- Recommended restaurants: Joe's Pizza in NYC, Dinosaur Bar-B-Que in Syracuse, and Moosewood Restaurant in Ithaca.

9. Insider Tips:

- **City Passes:** Consider city passes for discounts on multiple attractions in New York City.
- **Off-Peak Travel:** Plan visits during the off-peak season for potential hotel discounts and fewer crowds.
- **Student Discounts:** If applicable, inquire about student discounts at attractions, museums, and entertainment venues.

Save on big attractions in NY state.

New York City: Explore the Big Apple with its iconic landmarks, museums, and diverse neighborhoods.

- Money-Saving Tip: Use public transportation, like the subway, for affordable travel within the city.

Niagara Falls: Witness the natural wonder of Niagara Falls and take boat tours for up-close views.

- Money-Saving Tip: Consider visiting during the off-season for lower hotel rates and fewer crowds.

The Adirondacks: Experience the Adirondack Mountains with hiking, camping, and outdoor adventures.

- Money-Saving Tip: Choose state campgrounds for affordable accommodations in the region.

The Catskills: Discover the Catskill Mountains with scenic beauty, hiking trails, and charming towns.

- Money-Saving Tip: Explore free hiking trails and take advantage of low-cost lodging options.

Finger Lakes: Enjoy wine tasting, water sports, and the beauty of the Finger Lakes region.

- Money-Saving Tip: Visit local wineries during happy hours for discounted tastings.

The Hamptons: Experience the upscale coastal communities and beautiful beaches.

- Money-Saving Tip: Visit public beaches for lower parking fees and free access.

Thousand Islands: Explore the scenic islands and take boat tours on the St. Lawrence River.

- Money-Saving Tip: Opt for budget-friendly boat tours and consider camping on some islands.

Lake Placid: Experience the Olympic history, outdoor activities, and serene lakes.

- Money-Saving Tip: Enjoy hiking, swimming, and free outdoor activities in the area.

Saratoga Springs: Attend horse races, visit the springs, and explore the charming downtown.

- Money-Saving Tip: Watch morning horse workouts for free at the Saratoga Race Course.

The Baseball Hall of Fame, Cooperstown: Learn about baseball history and legendary players.

- Money-Saving Tip: Look for discounts on museum admission and special exhibits.

Albany: Discover the state capital with museums, historic sites, and cultural attractions.

- Money-Saving Tip: Explore free attractions like the New York State Capitol building.

The Strong National Museum of Play, Rochester: Enjoy interactive exhibits and family-friendly activities.

- Money-Saving Tip: Check for discounts on museum admission and family memberships.

Letchworth State Park: Explore the "Grand Canyon of the East" with waterfalls and hiking trails.

- Money-Saving Tip: Visit state parks during non-peak times to avoid parking fees.

Storm King Art Center, New Windsor: Discover outdoor sculptures and art installations.

- Money-Saving Tip: Look for discounted admission rates and special events.

Hudson Valley: Experience historic sites, wineries, and the Hudson River Valley's natural beauty.

- Money-Saving Tip: Visit wineries with no tasting fees and enjoy local farmer's markets.

Walkway Over the Hudson, Poughkeepsie: Take a walk or bike ride over the Hudson River.

- Money-Saving Tip: Enjoy the scenic walkway for free and explore nearby parks.

Buffalo: Explore the city with its architectural gems, parks, and cultural institutions.

- Money-Saving Tip: Attend free outdoor concerts and festivals in Buffalo.

Corning Museum of Glass: Witness glassmaking demonstrations and art exhibits.

- Money-Saving Tip: Check for discounts on museum admission and glassmaking classes.

Old Westbury Gardens: Enjoy beautiful gardens and historic architecture on Long Island.

- Money-Saving Tip: Look for discounted admission rates for students and seniors.

Lake George: Relax on the shores of Lake George and enjoy water sports and outdoor activities.

Category	Insider Tips
Food	1. Explore New York's diverse culinary scene by visiting local farmers' markets, food halls, and ethnic neighborhoods like Flushing in Queens or Arthur Avenue in the Bronx for fresh produce, specialty foods, and international cuisines.
	2. Indulge in New York's iconic street foods like hot dogs, pretzels, and pizza slices, which can often be found at food carts, delis, and corner stores in bustling neighborhoods and tourist hotspots across the state.
	3. Look for affordable dining options at local diners, delis, and hole-in-the-wall eateries serving up comfort food classics, regional specialties, and hearty breakfasts, often found in small towns and urban neighborhoods across New York.
	4. Take advantage of happy hour specials and weekday deals at bars, pubs, and breweries across New York, offering discounted drinks, appetizers, and craft beers for budget-conscious diners and nightlife enthusiasts.
Accommodation	1. Consider staying at boutique hotels or historic inns in New York's charming towns and scenic regions, offering personalized hospitality and unique accommodations amidst cultural landmarks, natural landscapes, and architectural gems.
	2. Explore budget-friendly lodging options on platforms like Airbnb or Vrbo, where you can find affordable stays like guest suites, vacation rentals, or private rooms in local homes in urban and rural areas across New York.

		3. Look for budget motels, roadside inns, and bed and breakfasts along major highways and scenic routes, providing convenient and affordable stays for travelers passing through New York's cities and towns.
		4. Embrace outdoor camping in New York's state parks and wilderness areas, where you can pitch a tent or park your RV amidst scenic vistas, hiking trails, and recreational facilities, with options for family-friendly camping, group sites, and rustic cabins.
Activities		1. Discover New York's outdoor attractions by exploring hiking trails in places like the Adirondack Park, biking along the Erie Canalway Trail, or kayaking in the Finger Lakes, offering scenic vistas, natural wonders, and recreational opportunities for outdoor enthusiasts.
		2. Immerse yourself in New York's cultural heritage by visiting historic sites like Ellis Island, exploring museums like the Metropolitan Museum of Art, or attending performances at venues like Carnegie Hall, offering insights into the state's rich history, art, and cultural diversity.
		3. Attend local festivals and events celebrating New York's diverse communities and cultural traditions, such as the New York State Fair, the Rochester Lilac Festival, or the Tribeca Film Festival, featuring music, food, arts, and entertainment for visitors of all ages.
		4. Take scenic drives along New York's scenic byways and country roads, exploring charming small towns, historic landmarks, and natural attractions like waterfalls, wineries, and scenic overlooks, with opportunities for picnicking, antiquing, and exploring local shops and galleries along the way.
Transport		1. Rent a car to explore New York's scenic highways and backroads, with rental agencies available at major airports, cities, and tourist destinations throughout the state, providing flexibility and convenience for travelers to explore at their own pace.
		2. Utilize public transportation options in urban areas like New York City and Buffalo, including buses, subways, and commuter trains, for convenient and eco-friendly travel within city limits, with options for day passes, fare discounts, and bike-sharing programs available for visitors and locals alike.
		3. Look for ridesharing services or carpooling opportunities for shared transportation to and from events, attractions, or outdoor adventures across New York, providing cost-effective and social travel options for travelers and residents.
		4. Plan road trips along New York's scenic routes and heritage trails, taking advantage of fuel-efficient vehicles and budget-friendly travel stops along the way, with opportunities for camping, sightseeing, and indulging in local flavors and experiences across the state.

Washington

Washington is renowned for its diverse geography, which includes the towering peaks of the Cascade Range, the serene waters of Puget Sound, and the rugged coastlines of the Olympic Peninsula. Outdoor enthusiasts will find a wealth of activities, including hiking, skiing, kayaking, and more.

Things to Consider:

- **Seattle**: Seattle, the largest city in Washington, offers a thriving arts and culture scene, world-class museums, iconic landmarks like the Space Needle, and a vibrant culinary landscape.
- **Weather**: Washington experiences a variety of climates, from the rainy and mild coastal areas to the snowy mountain regions. Be prepared for changing weather conditions, especially in the mountains.
- **National Parks**: The state is home to three national parks: Mount Rainier, North Cascades, and Olympic. Each park offers unique natural wonders and outdoor adventures.

Local Tips:

- **Mount Rainier**: Explore Mount Rainier National Park, known for its stunning alpine landscapes, glaciers, and hiking trails. Don't miss the opportunity to witness the wildflower blooms in the summer.
- **Olympic National Park**: Visit Olympic National Park, where you can explore rainforests, rugged coastline, and mountains. The Hoh Rainforest and Hurricane Ridge are popular destinations.
- **San Juan Islands**: Take a ferry to the San Juan Islands, a group of picturesque islands known for whale watching, outdoor activities, and a laid-back island atmosphere.
- **Wineries**: Discover Washington's wine country in regions like Walla Walla and the Yakima Valley. Sample local wines and enjoy the vineyard settings.
- **Leavenworth**: Experience the Bavarian-themed town of Leavenworth, nestled in the Cascade Mountains. It's known for its festivals, shops, and charming atmosphere.
- **Columbia River Gorge**: Explore the Columbia River Gorge, known for its scenic beauty, waterfalls, and outdoor recreational opportunities like hiking and windsurfing.
- **Pike Place Market**: Visit Pike Place Market in Seattle to enjoy fresh seafood, artisanal products, and the famous flying fish at the fish market.
- **Ferries**: Take a ferry ride on Puget Sound to enjoy scenic views of the water and surrounding islands. It's a quintessential Pacific Northwest experience.

Washington State invites you to immerse yourself in its natural wonders, vibrant cities, and a wide range of cultural and outdoor activities. Whether you're seeking adventure in the mountains, relaxation by the water, or cultural exploration, the Evergreen State offers a memorable and diverse experience. Enjoy your visit to Washington!

1. Accommodation:

- Explore budget-friendly hotels, motels, or boutique accommodations. Consider staying in areas like Bellevue or Tacoma for more affordable options.
- Recommended places: Motif Seattle, Hotel Murano in Tacoma, and The Heathman Hotel in Kirkland.

2. Transportation:

- Utilize public transportation in cities like Seattle, where buses and light rail are convenient and cost-effective.
- Consider walking or biking in pedestrian-friendly neighborhoods, especially in Seattle's downtown area.

3. Outdoor Activities:

- Take advantage of Washington's natural wonders. Explore state parks, hike in the Cascade Mountains, or visit the Puget Sound.
- Recommended activities: Hiking in Mount Rainier National Park, exploring Olympic National Park, and visiting Snoqualmie Falls.

4. Cultural Experiences:

- Visit museums during free hours or on specific days. Many museums offer discounted entry or free admission during certain times.
- Recommended places: The Museum of Pop Culture (MoPOP) in Seattle, the Chihuly Garden and Glass, and the Washington State History Museum in Tacoma.
- **Washington State Capitol (Olympia):** The Washington State Capitol offers free guided tours where you can learn about the state's government, history, and architecture. Tours are typically available Monday through Friday.
- **Pike Place Market (Seattle):** While not guided, Pike Place Market offers free self-guided tours where you can explore the market's stalls, shops, and eateries. Experience the sights, sounds, and flavors of this iconic Seattle landmark.
- **Olympic National Park (Port Angeles):** While there may be fees for certain activities and camping, Olympic National Park offers free ranger-led programs, walks, and talks. These programs provide insights into the park's diverse ecosystems, wildlife, and history. Check the park's schedule for upcoming programs.
- **Seattle Public Library Central Branch (Seattle):** The Seattle Public Library Central Branch offers free guided tours of its architectural masterpiece designed by Rem Koolhaas. Learn about the building's innovative design, features, and public art installations.

5. Waterfronts:

- Enjoy Washington's scenic waterfronts. Explore the Seattle waterfront, take a ferry ride, or visit waterfront parks in cities like Tacoma.
- Recommended places: Pike Place Market in Seattle, Tacoma Waterfront, and Alki Beach in West Seattle.

6. Local Markets:

- Explore local markets for fresh produce and unique products. Pike Place Market in Seattle is a must-visit for a vibrant local experience.
- Check out farmers' markets in smaller towns for local flavors.

7. Entertainment:

- Attend free concerts, events, or festivals. Many cities host outdoor concerts or community events during the summer months.
- Explore Seattle's neighborhoods for live music at local venues.

8. Dining:

- Experience a variety of dining options, from food trucks to ethnic eateries, for affordable yet delicious meals.
- Recommended restaurants: Paseo Caribbean Food in Seattle, Duke's Seafood in Tacoma, and Ivar's Acres of Clams on the Seattle waterfront.

9. Insider Tips:

- **City Passes:** Consider city passes for discounts on multiple attractions in Seattle.
- **Happy Hours:** Take advantage of happy hour specials at restaurants and bars for discounted drinks and appetizers.
- **National Park Pass:** If exploring multiple national parks, consider the America the Beautiful Pass for cost savings.

Here are the top attractions in Washington state, along with some money-saving tips for visiting each one:

Seattle: Explore the Emerald City with its iconic Space Needle, museums, and vibrant neighborhoods.

- Money-Saving Tip: Use public transportation, like the Link Light Rail, to get around the city affordably.

Mount Rainier National Park: Discover the stunning landscapes of Mount Rainier, with hiking and scenic drives.

- Money-Saving Tip: Purchase an America the Beautiful Pass for access to national parks.

Olympic National Park: Experience diverse ecosystems, rainforests, and coastal beauty.

- Money-Saving Tip: Visit during the off-season for lower accommodation rates and fewer crowds.

San Juan Islands: Explore the scenic islands with outdoor activities and wildlife viewing.

- Money-Saving Tip: Take advantage of budget-friendly ferry services to reach the islands.

Mount St. Helens: Learn about volcanic history and hike the trails around the famous volcano.

- Money-Saving Tip: Explore visitor centers and trails with free admission.

Leavenworth: Enjoy the Bavarian-themed town with festivals, shops, and outdoor adventures.

- Money-Saving Tip: Attend free events and explore local parks for budget-friendly experiences.

Spokane: Discover the city with its Riverfront Park, outdoor activities, and cultural attractions.

- Money-Saving Tip: Explore free parks and outdoor events in Spokane.

Columbia River Gorge: Hike and admire waterfalls along the Columbia River in this scenic area.

- Money-Saving Tip: Explore the gorge's natural beauty without any entrance fees.

Chihuly Garden and Glass, Seattle: Marvel at the glass artworks and installations by Dale Chihuly.

- Money-Saving Tip: Look for discounted admission rates for students and seniors.

Bainbridge Island: Take a ferry ride to this charming island with parks, beaches, and art galleries.

- Money-Saving Tip: Enjoy the island's natural beauty and public access areas.

Woodinville Wine Country: Experience wine tasting in this wine-producing region near Seattle.

- Money-Saving Tip: Visit wineries with no tasting fees and enjoy happy hour deals.

Tacoma: Explore the city with its museums, parks, and waterfront attractions.

- Money-Saving Tip: Attend free community events and explore local parks.

Mount Baker-Snoqualmie National Forest: Enjoy outdoor activities like hiking and skiing.

- Money-Saving Tip: Explore the forest's trails and recreation areas for free or at a low cost.

Pacific Ocean Beaches: Relax on sandy beaches along the Washington coast.

- Money-Saving Tip: Visit public beaches for affordable beach days and picnics.

North Cascades National Park: Experience rugged mountains and wilderness adventures.

- Money-Saving Tip: Purchase an America the Beautiful Pass for access to the national park.

Fort Worden State Park, Port Townsend: Explore the historic fort and its scenic waterfront location.

- Money-Saving Tip: Enjoy the park's outdoor spaces and views without any fees.

Washington State Capitol, Olympia: Learn about the state's history and government.

- Money-Saving Tip: Take free guided tours of the Capitol building.

Deception Pass State Park: Discover the iconic bridge and stunning views on Whidbey Island.

- Money-Saving Tip: Visit state parks during non-peak times to avoid parking fees.

Maryhill Stonehenge, Goldendale: Visit the replica of Stonehenge and enjoy panoramic views of the Columbia River.

- Money-Saving Tip: Explore the attraction for a nominal entrance fee.

Pike Place Market, Seattle: Shop for fresh produce, artisan crafts, and enjoy street performances.

- Money-Saving Tip: Sample food samples and enjoy the market's lively atmosphere.

Category	Insider Tips
Food	1. Explore Washington's vibrant food scene by visiting local farmers' markets, such as Pike Place Market in Seattle or the Ballard Farmers Market, for fresh produce, artisanal foods, and gourmet treats.
	2. Indulge in Washington's seafood specialties like fresh salmon, oysters, and Dungeness crab, which can often be found at seafood markets, waterfront restaurants, and oyster bars along the Puget Sound and coastal regions.
	3. Look for affordable dining options at casual cafes, bistros, and food trucks serving up Pacific Northwest cuisine, international flavors, and fusion fare, often found in eclectic neighborhoods and culinary hotspots across Washington.
	4. Take advantage of happy hour specials and daily deals at bars, breweries, and wineries across Washington, offering discounted drinks, small plates, and locally crafted beverages for budget-conscious diners and nightlife enthusiasts.
Accommodation	1. Consider staying at cozy bed and breakfasts or waterfront inns in Washington's coastal towns and scenic regions, offering personalized hospitality and unique accommodations amidst natural beauty and coastal charm.
	2. Explore budget-friendly lodging options on platforms like Airbnb or Vrbo, where you can find affordable stays like guesthouses, vacation rentals, or private rooms in local homes in urban and rural areas across Washington.
	3. Look for budget motels, roadside inns, and cabins along major highways and scenic routes, providing convenient and affordable stays for travelers passing through Washington's cities and towns.
	4. Embrace outdoor camping in Washington's state parks and wilderness areas, where you can pitch a tent or park your RV amidst lush forests, mountain vistas, and alpine lakes, with options for family-friendly camping, group sites, and rustic cabins.
Activities	1. Discover Washington's outdoor attractions by exploring hiking trails in places like Olympic National Park, biking along the Burke-Gilman Trail, or kayaking in the San Juan Islands, offering scenic beauty, wildlife encounters, and recreational opportunities for outdoor enthusiasts.
	2. Immerse yourself in Washington's cultural heritage by visiting museums like the Museum of Pop Culture in Seattle, exploring historic sites like Pioneer Square, or attending performances at venues like the Chihuly Garden and Glass, offering insights into the state's art, history, and innovation.
	3. Attend local festivals and events celebrating Washington's diverse communities and cultural traditions, such as the Seattle International Film Festival, the Skagit Valley Tulip Festival, or the Fremont Solstice Parade, featuring music, arts, food, and entertainment for visitors of all ages.
	4. Take scenic drives along Washington's scenic byways and rural roads, exploring charming small towns, natural wonders, and cultural landmarks like Mount Rainier, Leavenworth, or the Columbia River Gorge, with opportunities for picnicking, wine tasting, and exploring local attractions along the way.
Transport	1. Rent a car to explore Washington's scenic highways and backroads, with rental agencies available at major airports, cities, and tourist destinations throughout the state, providing flexibility and convenience for travelers to explore at their own pace.
	2. Utilize public transportation options in urban areas like Seattle and Spokane, including buses, light rail, and ferries, for convenient and eco-friendly travel within city limits, with options for day passes, fare discounts, and bike-sharing programs available for visitors and locals alike.

		3. Look for ridesharing services or carpooling opportunities for shared transportation to and from events, attractions, or outdoor adventures across Washington, providing cost-effective and social travel options for travelers and residents.
		4. Plan road trips along Washington's scenic routes and scenic byways, taking advantage of fuel-efficient vehicles and budget-friendly travel stops along the way, with opportunities for camping, sightseeing, and indulging in local flavors and experiences across the state.

West Virginia

Welcome to the Mountain State, West Virginia! As a first-time visitor, get ready to explore a state known for its stunning landscapes, outdoor adventures, and rich Appalachian heritage. From the scenic beauty of the New River Gorge to the historical charm of small towns, West Virginia offers a unique and welcoming experience.

Outdoor Adventures:

- **New River Gorge:** Discover the majestic New River Gorge, a haven for outdoor enthusiasts. Engage in activities like whitewater rafting, hiking along the rim, and experiencing the iconic New River Gorge Bridge.
- **Seneca Rocks:** Marvel at the impressive Seneca Rocks, a popular destination for rock climbing and hiking. The panoramic views from the summit are worth the climb.
- **Cass Scenic Railroad State Park:** Step back in time at Cass Scenic Railroad State Park, where you can take a scenic train ride through the picturesque landscapes of the Appalachian Mountains.

Historical and Cultural Attractions:

- **Harpers Ferry National Historical Park:** Explore the historic town of Harpers Ferry, known for its role in the Civil War. Visit museums, stroll through the quaint streets, and enjoy the confluence of the Potomac and Shenandoah rivers.
- **Greenbrier Resort:** Experience luxury and history at The Greenbrier, a world-class resort with a storied past. Take a tour of the underground bunker built for Congress during the Cold War.
- **Berkeley Springs:** Relax in Berkeley Springs, a charming town with historic mineral springs. Visit the Berkeley Springs State Park and enjoy the town's arts scene.

Natural Beauty:

- **Blackwater Falls State Park:** Immerse yourself in the beauty of Blackwater Falls State Park. Witness the stunning waterfall, explore hiking trails, and experience the vibrant fall foliage.
- **Dolly Sods Wilderness:** Embark on an adventure in Dolly Sods Wilderness, a unique high-altitude plateau with sweeping vistas, rocky landscapes, and diverse plant life.
- **Cranberry Glades Botanical Area:** Discover the Cranberry Glades Botanical Area, featuring bogs and wetlands with a variety of plant species. Boardwalks make it easy to explore this unique ecosystem.

Local Tips:

- **Scenic Drives:** Enjoy scenic drives through the winding mountain roads. The Highland Scenic Highway and the Coal Heritage Trail offer picturesque views and glimpses of West Virginia's cultural heritage.
- **Appalachian Music:** Immerse yourself in the sounds of Appalachia. Seek out local venues for live performances of bluegrass, folk, and traditional Appalachian music.

- **Farm-to-Table Cuisine:** Experience farm-to-table cuisine in West Virginia. Explore local farmers' markets and restaurants that showcase the region's fresh produce and culinary traditions.

Must-Visit Places:

- **New River Gorge Bridge:** Walk along the catwalk of the New River Gorge Bridge for breathtaking views, especially during the Bridge Day festival when BASE jumpers leap from the bridge.
- **Cheat Lake:** Relax by Cheat Lake near Morgantown, offering boating, fishing, and a tranquil setting.
- **Hawks Nest State Park:** Visit Hawks Nest State Park for its scenic overlook of the New River and enjoy the aerial tramway ride for panoramic views.

1. Accommodation:

- Look for budget-friendly hotels, motels, or cozy cabins in areas close to your points of interest.
- Recommended places: The Greenbrier River Cabins in Hinton, The Historic Blennerhassett Hotel in Parkersburg, and The Smoke Hole Resort in Cabins.

2. Transportation:

- Renting a car is recommended for exploring West Virginia, especially if you plan to visit more remote areas and state parks.
- Take advantage of scenic drives, like the Highland Scenic Highway or the Midland Trail.

3. Outdoor Activities:

- Explore the state's natural beauty by hiking, rafting, or biking in its numerous parks and recreation areas.
- Recommended activities: New River Gorge National Park, Seneca Rocks, and hiking in the Monongahela National Forest.

4. Cultural Experiences:

- Discover West Virginia's rich cultural heritage through local events, folk festivals, and music performances.
- Check for events like the Vandalia Gathering in Charleston or the Mountain State Forest Festival in Elkins.

5. State Parks:

- Visit state parks, many of which offer affordable recreational activities and camping options.
- Recommended parks: Blackwater Falls State Park, Cass Scenic Railroad State Park, and Pipestem Resort State Park.

6. Historic Sites:

- Explore historic towns and sites that showcase West Virginia's unique history.
- Recommended places: Harpers Ferry National Historical Park, Blennerhassett Island Historical State Park, and the Trans-Allegheny Lunatic Asylum in Weston.

7. Local Cuisine:

- Savor local cuisine in charming diners and restaurants, offering hearty Appalachian dishes.
- Try pepperoni rolls, ramps (wild leeks), and apple butter.

- Recommended places: The Custard Stand in Webster Springs, Hillbilly Hot Dogs in Lesage, and DiCarlo's Pizza in Wheeling.

8. **Festivals:**
   - Attend local festivals celebrating music, art, and heritage.
   - Check for events like the West Virginia State Folk Festival in Glenville or the Appalachian String Band Music Festival in Clifftop.

9. **Insider Tips:**
   - **Scenic Train Rides:** Consider taking scenic train rides like the Cass Scenic Railroad or the Durbin & Greenbrier Valley Railroad.
   - **State Forests:** Explore lesser-known state forests for quiet hiking and camping experiences.
   - **Local Crafts:** Purchase handmade crafts and souvenirs from local artisans.

Here are the top attractions in West Virginia, along with some money-saving tips for visiting each one:

New River Gorge National Park and Preserve: Explore the scenic beauty of the New River Gorge, with hiking, rafting, and rock climbing.

- Money-Saving Tip: Purchase an America the Beautiful Pass for access to national parks.

Harpers Ferry National Historical Park: Learn about Civil War history and hike along the confluence of the Potomac and Shenandoah rivers.

- Money-Saving Tip: Check for discounts on park entrance fees and ranger-led programs.

Seneca Rocks: Experience rock climbing and hiking in the Monongahela National Forest.

- Money-Saving Tip: Enjoy the natural beauty of Seneca Rocks for free.

Cass Scenic Railroad State Park: Ride the historic steam-driven locomotives and explore the mountain scenery.

- Money-Saving Tip: Check for discounts on train tickets and consider package deals.

Charleston: Explore the state capital with its museums, historic sites, and cultural events.

- Money-Saving Tip: Attend free concerts, festivals, and outdoor activities in Charleston.

Greenbrier Resort, White Sulphur Springs: Visit the historic resort with its luxurious amenities and golf courses.

- Money-Saving Tip: Consider visiting during off-peak times for lower accommodation rates.

Blackwater Falls State Park: See the stunning waterfall and enjoy outdoor activities in the park.

- Money-Saving Tip: Visit state parks during non-peak times to avoid parking fees.

Babcock State Park: Discover the iconic Glade Creek Grist Mill and hiking trails.

- Money-Saving Tip: Enjoy the state park's scenic beauty and outdoor adventures.

The Greenbrier River Trail: Hike, bike, or horseback ride along this scenic rail trail.

- Money-Saving Tip: Explore the trail's beauty and outdoor activities for free.

Wheeling: Explore the city with its historic architecture, festivals, and cultural attractions.

- Money-Saving Tip: Attend free community events and explore local parks.

West Virginia State Museum, Charleston: Learn about the state's history and cultural heritage.

- Money-Saving Tip: Check for discounts on museum admission and special exhibitions.

Cheat Lake: Relax on the shores of Cheat Lake and enjoy water sports and outdoor activities.

- Money-Saving Tip: Visit public access points and parks for affordable lakeside experiences.

Stonewall Resort State Park, Roanoke: Enjoy the scenic lake, golfing, and outdoor recreation.

- Money-Saving Tip: Look for lodging and activity packages for potential savings.

Beckley Exhibition Coal Mine: Experience an underground coal mine tour and learn about coal mining history.

- Money-Saving Tip: Check for discounted admission rates and guided tours.

Trans-Allegheny Lunatic Asylum, Weston: Tour the historic asylum and its intriguing architecture.

- Money-Saving Tip: Look for discounts on guided tours and special events.

New River Train Excursions: Ride vintage passenger cars through the New River Gorge.

- Money-Saving Tip: Check for discounts on train excursions and consider family packages.

Hiking and Outdoor Adventures: West Virginia offers numerous hiking trails, state parks, and outdoor adventures.

- Money-Saving Tip: Enjoy free hiking trails and outdoor activities in the state's natural areas.

Davis and Thomas: Visit the charming towns in Tucker County known for outdoor recreation and small-town charm.

- Money-Saving Tip: Explore local parks and enjoy affordable dining options.

Berkeley Springs: Experience the historic town with natural springs, spas, and art galleries.

- Money-Saving Tip: Visit the springs in the state park for free relaxation.

Food	1. Explore West Virginia's farm-to-table dining scene by visiting local farmers' markets, such as the Capitol Market in Charleston or the Bridgeport Farmers Market, for fresh produce, artisanal foods, and
	2. Indulge in West Virginia's Appalachian cuisine by trying regional specialties like pepperoni rolls, ramps, and biscuits with gravy, which can often be found at local diners, family-owned restaurants, and country
	3. Look for affordable dining options at roadside BBQ joints, mom-and-pop eateries, and country buffets serving up hearty comfort foods, homestyle dishes, and Southern favorites, often found in small towns and rural communities throughout West Virginia.
	4. Take advantage of happy hour specials and daily deals at bars, pubs, and breweries across West Virginia, offering discounted drinks, appetizers, and craft beers for budget-conscious diners and nightlife
Accommodation	1. Consider staying at cozy bed and breakfasts or rustic lodges in West Virginia's scenic regions and mountain towns, offering personalized hospitality and unique accommodations amidst natural beauty and
	2. Explore budget-friendly lodging options on platforms like Airbnb or Vrbo, where you can find affordable stays like cabins, cottages, or vacation rentals in rural and remote areas across West Virginia.
	3. Look for budget motels, roadside inns, and campgrounds along major highways and scenic routes, providing convenient and affordable stays for travelers passing through West Virginia's cities and towns.
	4. Embrace outdoor camping in West Virginia's state parks and national forests, where you can pitch a tent or park your RV amidst mountain vistas, forested trails, and scenic rivers, with options for family-friendly camping, group sites, and primitive campsites.
Activities	1. Discover West Virginia's outdoor attractions by exploring hiking trails in places like the New River Gorge, biking along the Greenbrier River Trail, or whitewater rafting on the Gauley River, offering adrenaline-pumping adventures and natural wonders for outdoor enthusiasts.
	2. Immerse yourself in West Virginia's cultural heritage by visiting historic sites like Harpers Ferry, exploring museums like the Huntington Museum of Art, or attending festivals like the Mountain State Forest Festival, offering insights into the state's history, art, and Appalachian traditions.
	3. Attend local festivals and events celebrating West Virginia's diverse communities and cultural traditions, such as the Mothman Festival in Point Pleasant, the West Virginia Pumpkin Festival, or the Ramps and Rail Festival in Elkins, featuring music, crafts, food, and entertainment for
	4. Take scenic drives along West Virginia's scenic byways and country roads, exploring charming small towns, historic landmarks, and natural attractions like Blackwater Falls, Seneca Rocks, or the Cass Scenic Railroad, with opportunities for picnicking, wildlife viewing, and exploring local heritage sites along the way.
Transport	1. Rent a car to explore West Virginia's scenic highways and backroads, with rental agencies available at major airports, cities, and tourist destinations throughout the state, providing flexibility and convenience for travelers to explore at their own pace.
	2. Utilize public transportation options in urban areas like Charleston and Morgantown, including buses, trolleys, and shuttles, for convenient and eco-friendly travel within city limits, with options for day passes, fare discounts, and bike-sharing programs available for visitors and locals

	3. Look for ridesharing services or carpooling opportunities for shared transportation to and from events, attractions, or outdoor adventures across West Virginia, providing cost-effective and social travel options for travelers and residents.
	4. Plan road trips along West Virginia's scenic routes and heritage trails, taking advantage of fuel-efficient vehicles and budget-friendly travel stops along the way, with opportunities for camping, sightseeing, and indulging in local flavors and experiences across the Mountain State.

Wisconsin

The Badger State, a place where natural beauty, outdoor adventures, and a rich cultural heritage come together to create a diverse and welcoming destination in the Midwest region of the United States. Wisconsin offers a mix of charming cities, picturesque lakes, and rural landscapes. Whether you're exploring the vibrant city of Milwaukee, enjoying the serenity of the Northwoods, or savoring the state's famous cheese and beer, Wisconsin has something to offer every traveler. Here's an introduction to Wisconsin, along with some key things to consider and local tips for your visit:

Wisconsin is known for its beautiful landscapes, including the Great Lakes, rolling farmland, and the Northwoods. Outdoor enthusiasts can indulge in activities such as hiking, biking, fishing, and boating, depending on the season.

Things to Consider:

- **Milwaukee**: Milwaukee is Wisconsin's largest city and offers a vibrant arts and culture scene, historic neighborhoods, and a waterfront along Lake Michigan.
- **Seasonal Weather**: Wisconsin experiences four distinct seasons. Summers are warm and humid, while winters can be cold with snowfall. Plan your activities and clothing accordingly.
- **Cheese and Beer**: Wisconsin is famous for its cheese and craft beer. Be sure to sample local varieties and visit cheese factories and breweries.

Local Tips:

- **Door County**: Explore Door County, a picturesque peninsula known for its scenic beauty, charming villages, and waterfront activities. Visit state parks, lighthouses, and enjoy cherry picking in season.
- **Wisconsin Dells**: Experience the natural beauty and family-friendly attractions in Wisconsin Dells, known for its unique rock formations and water parks.
- **Madison**: Visit the state capital, Madison, home to the University of Wisconsin-Madison. Enjoy the farmer's market at Capitol Square and explore the city's vibrant neighborhoods.
- **Green Bay**: Catch a Green Bay Packers football game at Lambeau Field, an iconic sporting venue, or visit the Green Bay Packers Hall of Fame.
- **Northwoods**: Escape to the Northwoods region, which offers a peaceful retreat with lakes, forests, and outdoor recreational opportunities such as fishing and boating.
- **Harley-Davidson Museum**: Motorcycle enthusiasts should not miss the Harley-Davidson Museum in Milwaukee, which showcases the history and culture of this iconic American brand.
- **Frank Lloyd Wright Sites**: Explore architectural gems designed by Frank Lloyd Wright, including Taliesin in Spring Green and the SC Johnson campus in Racine.
- **Beer Gardens**: Enjoy a classic beer garden experience in Milwaukee's Estabrook Park or one of the many other beer gardens throughout the state.

Accommodation:

- **Boutique Hotels:** Look for boutique hotels or charming bed and breakfasts in cities like Madison, Milwaukee, and Door County. These often offer a more personalized and luxurious experience at reasonable prices.
- **Vacation Rentals:** Consider renting a vacation home or cabin near one of Wisconsin's scenic lakes or in the countryside. Websites like Airbnb and Vrbo have numerous options that can provide a sense of seclusion and luxury.

Dining:

- **Farm-to-Table Restaurants:** Wisconsin is known for its fresh produce and dairy. Enjoy upscale farm-to-table dining experiences that showcase local ingredients without breaking the bank.
- **Supper Clubs:** Visit one of Wisconsin's iconic supper clubs for a taste of classic Midwest cuisine in a cozy, nostalgic atmosphere. It's a unique and affordable way to dine luxuriously.

Activities:

- **State Parks:** Explore Wisconsin's natural beauty by visiting state parks like Devil's Lake, Peninsula State Park, or Governor Dodge State Park. Enjoy hiking, picnicking, and swimming amidst stunning landscapes.
- **Museums and Art Galleries:** Many museums and art galleries in Wisconsin offer free or low-cost admission on specific days or during certain hours. Check their websites for details.
- **Brewery and Winery Tours:** Wisconsin is famous for its craft breweries and wineries. Take advantage of free or affordable tours and tastings to sample locally-made beverages.

Entertainment:

- **Live Music:** Check out local event listings for free outdoor concerts or affordable live music performances at bars and small venues. Madison and Milwaukee have vibrant music scenes.
- **Theater and Performing Arts:** Keep an eye out for discounted tickets to theatrical productions, concerts, and dance performances, especially in college towns like Madison.

Wisconsin State Capitol (Madison): The Wisconsin State Capitol offers free guided tours where you can learn about the state's government, history, and architecture. Tours are typically available Monday through Friday.

Self-guided Tours of Historic Neighborhoods: Many cities and towns in Wisconsin, such as Milwaukee, Madison, and La Crosse, have historic neighborhoods with self-guided walking tours. Pick up a map from the local visitor center or historical society and explore the architecture, landmarks, and history of these areas at your own pace.

University of Wisconsin-Madison Campus Tours (Madison): The University of Wisconsin-Madison offers free campus tours led by student guides. You can explore the university's historic buildings, landmarks, and academic programs while learning about its history and culture.

Relaxation:

- **Spas:** Look for day spas or wellness centers that offer budget-friendly spa packages, massages, and relaxation treatments.

- **Hot Springs:** Consider a trip to hot springs like the one in the Wisconsin Dells area for a natural and rejuvenating soak.

Shopping:

- **Outlet Malls:** Visit outlet malls like Johnson Creek Premium Outlets or Pleasant Prairie Premium Outlets for luxury brand shopping at discounted prices.

Transportation:

- **Public Transportation:** Use public transportation in cities like Madison and Milwaukee to save on parking and gas expenses. It's an eco-friendly and budget-friendly option.

Special Events:

- **Festivals:** Plan your trip around one of Wisconsin's many festivals, such as the EAA AirVenture in Oshkosh or Summerfest in Milwaukee, which offer a mix of entertainment, food, and culture.

Additional Tips:

- **Travel Off-Peak:** Consider visiting Wisconsin during the shoulder seasons (spring or fall) when accommodation prices are lower, and attractions are less crowded.
- **Discount Passes:** Check if there are any discount passes or city cards that offer savings on multiple attractions and activities.
- **Local Coupons:** Look for local coupons and discounts in brochures, at visitor centers, or online to maximize savings on dining and activities.

Here are the top attractions in Wisconsin, along with some money-saving tips for visiting each one:

Milwaukee: Explore Wisconsin's largest city with its museums, breweries, and lakefront activities.

- Money-Saving Tip: Attend free events and festivals along Milwaukee's lakefront.

Madison: Visit the state capital with its historic landmarks, gardens, and vibrant downtown.

- Money-Saving Tip: Explore free attractions like the Wisconsin State Capitol building.

Wisconsin Dells: Experience water parks, outdoor adventures, and the unique rock formations.

- Money-Saving Tip: Look for package deals and discounted water park admissions.

Green Bay: Discover the city with its football heritage, museums, and family-friendly attractions.

- Money-Saving Tip: Check for discounts on museum admission and stadium tours.

Door County: Enjoy the picturesque peninsula with its scenic beauty, parks, and charming villages.

- Money-Saving Tip: Explore free public beaches and parks along Lake Michigan.

Devil's Lake State Park: Hike, swim, and rock climb in one of Wisconsin's most popular state parks.

- Money-Saving Tip: Visit during non-peak times to avoid parking fees.

EAA AirVenture, Oshkosh: Attend the annual aviation event with airshows and aircraft displays.

- Money-Saving Tip: Look for early-bird ticket discounts and consider camping on-site.

Frank Lloyd Wright Trail: Explore the architectural legacy of Frank Lloyd Wright.

- Money-Saving Tip: Visit exterior views of the buildings for free, or choose guided tours selectively.

Lake Geneva: Relax by the lake, take boat tours, and explore the town's shops and restaurants.

- Money-Saving Tip: Enjoy free public access to the lake and lakeside paths.

Taliesin, Spring Green: Tour the former home and studio of architect Frank Lloyd Wright.

- Money-Saving Tip: Check for discounts on tour packages and student rates.

Wisconsin State Fair, West Allis: Experience the annual fair with entertainment, food, and exhibits.

- Money-Saving Tip: Look for advance ticket deals and special admission days.

Cave of the Mounds, Blue Mounds: Explore the underground cave system with stunning formations.

- Money-Saving Tip: Check for discounted cave tour rates and package deals.

Old World Wisconsin, Eagle: Step back in time and experience life in historic Wisconsin.

- Money-Saving Tip: Look for discounts on admission and special events.

Ice Age National Scenic Trail: Hike along this trail that highlights Wisconsin's glacial history.

- Money-Saving Tip: Enjoy the trail for free and explore different segments.

Harley-Davidson Museum, Milwaukee: Discover the history of the iconic motorcycle company.

- Money-Saving Tip: Check for discounts on museum admission and special exhibits.

Cedarburg: Visit the charming town with historic buildings, art galleries, and unique shops.

- Money-Saving Tip: Explore the town's historic district and enjoy affordable dining options.

Bayfield: Experience the gateway to the Apostle Islands with outdoor activities and Lake Superior views.

- Money-Saving Tip: Explore free public access areas along the lake.

Manitowoc: Discover the maritime history of the city with museums and lakefront attractions.

- Money-Saving Tip: Attend free community events and explore local parks.

Kettle Moraine State Forest: Hike, camp, and enjoy outdoor adventures in this state forest.

- Money-Saving Tip: Visit the forest for free or at a low cost and enjoy its natural beauty.

La Crosse: Explore the city along the Mississippi River with its parks, festivals, and river activities.

- Money-Saving Tip: Attend free concerts and events along the riverfront.

Category	Insider Tips
Food	1. Explore Wisconsin's dairy heritage by visiting local cheese factories, such as Carr Valley Cheese or Widmer's Cheese Cellars, for cheese tastings, factory tours, and artisanal cheeses made with local milk.
	2. Indulge in Wisconsin's supper club tradition by dining at classic supper clubs like The HobNob in Racine or Ishnala Supper Club in Wisconsin Dells, where you can enjoy cocktails, relish trays, and hearty comfort foods in a nostalgic setting.
	3. Look for affordable dining options at casual taverns, breweries, and fish fries serving up Wisconsin favorites like bratwurst, beer-battered fish, and Friday night fish fries, often found in small towns and rural communities across the state.
	4. Take advantage of food festivals and events celebrating Wisconsin's culinary heritage, such as the Wisconsin State Fair, the Brat Fest in Madison, or the Cheese Curd Festival in Ellsworth, featuring music, food, and fun for visitors of all ages.
Accommodation	1. Consider staying at cozy bed and breakfasts or historic inns in Wisconsin's charming towns and scenic regions, offering personalized hospitality and unique accommodations amidst natural beauty and
	2. Explore budget-friendly lodging options on platforms like Airbnb or Vrbo, where you can find affordable stays like cabins, cottages, or vacation rentals in lakeside towns and rural areas across Wisconsin.
	3. Look for budget motels, roadside inns, and campgrounds along major highways and scenic routes, providing convenient and affordable stays for travelers passing through Wisconsin's cities and towns.
	4. Embrace outdoor camping in Wisconsin's state parks and forests, where you can pitch a tent or park your RV amidst scenic landscapes, hiking trails, and recreational facilities, with options for family-friendly camping, group sites, and rustic cabins.
Activities	1. Discover Wisconsin's outdoor attractions by exploring hiking trails in places like Devil's Lake State Park, biking along the Elroy-Sparta Trail, or kayaking on the Door County Peninsula, offering scenic beauty and outdoor adventures for nature lovers.

		2. Immerse yourself in Wisconsin's cultural heritage by visiting historic sites like Old World Wisconsin, exploring museums like the Milwaukee Art Museum, or attending festivals like Summerfest in Milwaukee, offering insights into the state's history, art, and diverse communities.
		3. Attend local festivals and events celebrating Wisconsin's traditions and industries, such as the EAA AirVenture in Oshkosh, the Cranberry Festival in Warrens, or Oktoberfest in La Crosse, featuring music, food, crafts, and entertainment for visitors of all ages.
		4. Take scenic drives along Wisconsin's scenic byways and rural roads, exploring charming small towns, historic landmarks, and natural attractions like waterfalls, orchards, and dairy farms, with opportunities for picnicking, wine tasting, and exploring local shops and attractions along
	Transport	1. Rent a car to explore Wisconsin's scenic highways and backroads, with rental agencies available at major airports, cities, and tourist destinations throughout the state, providing flexibility and convenience for travelers to explore at their own pace.
		2. Utilize public transportation options in urban areas like Milwaukee and Madison, including buses, trolleys, and commuter trains, for convenient and eco-friendly travel within city limits, with options for day passes, fare discounts, and bike-sharing programs available for visitors and locals
		3. Look for ridesharing services or carpooling opportunities for shared transportation to and from events, attractions, or outdoor adventures across Wisconsin, providing cost-effective and social travel options for travelers and residents.
		4. Plan road trips along Wisconsin's scenic routes and heritage trails, taking advantage of fuel-efficient vehicles and budget-friendly travel stops along the way, with opportunities for camping, sightseeing, and indulging in local flavors and experiences across the Badger State.

Wyoming

The Cowboy State, Wyoming! Get ready to experience the vastness of the American West, where expansive landscapes, rugged mountains, and abundant wildlife await. From the iconic Yellowstone National Park to the historic charm of Jackson Hole, Wyoming offers a true taste of frontier spirit and natural wonders.

Yellowstone National Park:

- **Old Faithful:** Witness the awe-inspiring eruptions of Old Faithful, one of Yellowstone's most famous geysers. The park is home to a vast array of geothermal features, including hot springs and geysers.
- **Grand Canyon of the Yellowstone:** Marvel at the stunning Grand Canyon of the Yellowstone, with its thundering waterfalls and colorful canyon walls.
- **Wildlife Viewing:** Experience unparalleled wildlife viewing opportunities. Keep an eye out for bison, elk, bears, and the elusive wolves that inhabit the park.

Grand Teton National Park:

- **Grand Teton Range:** Explore the majestic Grand Teton Range, characterized by rugged peaks and pristine alpine lakes. Take in the breathtaking scenery along the Teton Crest Trail or the Jenny Lake Loop.
- **Jackson Hole:** Discover the charming town of Jackson Hole, known for its rustic charm, art galleries, and outdoor activities. Stroll through the iconic town square with its elk antler arches.
- **Snake River:** Enjoy a scenic float trip or go whitewater rafting on the Snake River, offering stunning views of the Teton Range and chances to spot wildlife along the riverbanks.

Cultural and Historical Sites:

- **Buffalo Bill Center of the West:** Immerse yourself in the history of the American West at the Buffalo Bill Center of the West in Cody. Explore exhibits on Native American cultures, Western art, and the life of Buffalo Bill Cody.
- **Fossil Butte National Monument:** Journey to Fossil Butte National Monument, where you can see well-preserved fossils from the Eocene epoch, providing a glimpse into ancient Wyoming.
- **Oregon Trail Ruts:** Visit the Oregon Trail Ruts near Guernsey State Park, where pioneers left their mark on the landscape as they journeyed westward.

Local Tips:

- **Dark Sky Reserves:** Experience the brilliance of Wyoming's night skies. Visit designated Dark Sky Reserves, such as Grand Teton National Park or Devils Tower National Monument, for exceptional stargazing.
- **Western Cuisine:** Indulge in hearty Western cuisine. Try bison steaks, elk burgers, and other local delicacies that reflect Wyoming's ranching heritage.
- **Rodeos:** Attend a rodeo for an authentic taste of cowboy culture. Many towns host rodeos during the summer, featuring bull riding, barrel racing, and other rodeo events.

Must-Visit Places:

- **Devils Tower National Monument:** Stand in awe of Devils Tower, a unique geological formation that rises dramatically from the surrounding landscape.
- **Hot Springs State Park:** Relax in the healing waters of Hot Springs State Park in Thermopolis, known for its natural hot springs.
- **Medicine Bow National Forest:** Explore the scenic beauty of Medicine Bow National Forest, offering hiking trails, alpine lakes, and panoramic vistas.

Accommodation:

- **National Park Lodges:** Stay in lodges within national parks like Yellowstone or Grand Teton. While some may seem pricey, they often offer affordable rooms, and you'll have easy access to the parks' natural wonders.
- **Camping and Glamping:** Enjoy the great outdoors by camping in scenic areas. Many campgrounds are budget-friendly, or you can opt for glamping experiences that offer comfort and luxury in nature.

Dining:

- **Local Eateries:** Wyoming has charming local restaurants and diners where you can savor hearty meals without the high price tags. Try regional specialties like bison or elk burgers.
- **Pack a Picnic:** Purchase local produce and artisanal goods from farmers' markets and create your own gourmet picnic to enjoy in the picturesque outdoors.

Activities:

- **National Parks:** Wyoming is home to iconic national parks like Yellowstone and Grand Teton. The cost of entry is well worth the incredible natural beauty and wildlife viewing opportunities.
- **Hiking and Wildlife Viewing:** Explore hiking trails in the parks and national forests. Keep an eye out for free ranger-led programs and guided wildlife tours.
- **Hot Springs:** Relax in natural hot springs like those in Thermopolis, which offer a soothing and budget-friendly way to unwind.

Entertainment:

- **Wyoming State Capitol (Cheyenne):** The Wyoming State Capitol offers free guided tours where you can learn about the state's government, history, and architecture. Tours are typically available Monday through Friday.
- **Yellowstone National Park (Various Locations):** While there may be fees for certain activities and camping, Yellowstone National Park offers free ranger-led programs, walks, and talks. These programs provide insights into the park's geology, wildlife, and history. Check the park's schedule for upcoming programs.
- **Grand Teton National Park (Moose):** Similar to Yellowstone, Grand Teton National Park offers free ranger-led programs, walks, and talks. These programs focus on the park's natural and cultural resources, including wildlife, geology, and human history.
- **Stargazing:** Wyoming's vast, dark skies make it an ideal destination for stargazing. Many areas offer free astronomy programs and events.
- **Local Music and Art:** Check out local music events, art galleries, and cultural festivals for affordable entertainment options.

Relaxation:

- **Spas and Wellness Centers:** Consider visiting a spa or wellness center for budget-friendly treatments, massages, and relaxation therapies.

Shopping:

- **Local Boutiques:** Support local artisans and boutiques in towns like Jackson Hole, Cody, or Laramie, where you can find unique, handcrafted items.
- **Antique Stores:** Explore antique shops for hidden gems and vintage treasures.

Transportation:

- **Carpooling:** If traveling with a group, consider carpooling to share gas and transportation costs.

Special Events:

- **Rodeos:** Attend local rodeos, which are an integral part of Wyoming's culture. Tickets are often affordable, and the experience is unforgettable.
- **Festivals:** Look for seasonal festivals, such as Cheyenne Frontier Days, which offer a mix of rodeo, concerts, and cultural events.

Additional Tips:

- **Off-Peak Travel:** Visit Wyoming in the shoulder seasons (spring or fall) to avoid crowds and take advantage of lower accommodation rates.
- **National Park Pass:** If you plan to visit multiple national parks in the U.S., consider purchasing an America the Beautiful Pass, which grants access to numerous federal lands, including Wyoming's national parks.
- **Local Discounts:** Check for local discounts and coupons at visitor centers, hotels, and online resources to save on dining and activities.

Here are the top attractions in Wyoming, along with some money-saving tips for visiting each one:

Yellowstone National Park: Explore the first national park with its geothermal wonders, wildlife, and hiking trails.

- Money-Saving Tip: Purchase an America the Beautiful Pass for access to national parks.

Grand Teton National Park: Discover the rugged beauty of the Teton Range with hiking, wildlife viewing, and scenic drives.

- Money-Saving Tip: Visit during the off-season for lower accommodation rates and fewer crowds.

Jackson Hole: Experience the outdoor paradise with skiing, hiking, and charming downtown shops.

- Money-Saving Tip: Look for package deals on ski passes and consider off-peak travel.

Devils Tower National Monument: Witness the iconic natural monument and its unique geological features.

- Money-Saving Tip: Enjoy the monument's surroundings and visitor center for free.

Cody: Explore the town known for its Western heritage, museums, and outdoor activities.

- Money-Saving Tip: Attend free events and rodeos in Cody during the summer.

Bighorn Mountains: Enjoy outdoor adventures, camping, and scenic beauty in this mountain range.

- Money-Saving Tip: Choose free or low-cost campgrounds in the Bighorn National Forest.

Cheyenne: Visit the state capital with its historic sites, museums, and rodeo events.

- Money-Saving Tip: Explore free attractions like the Wyoming State Capitol building.

Hot Springs State Park, Thermopolis: Relax in natural hot springs and explore the park's attractions.

- Money-Saving Tip: Visit the park's hot springs for a nominal fee.

Flaming Gorge National Recreation Area: Experience water sports, fishing, and outdoor activities.

- Money-Saving Tip: Enjoy free access to some recreation areas and hiking trails.

Wind River Range: Hike and backpack in this remote mountain range known for its pristine wilderness.

- Money-Saving Tip: Choose free or low-cost backcountry camping sites.

Buffalo Bill Center of the West, Cody: Discover five museums in one complex dedicated to Western history.

- Money-Saving Tip: Check for discounts on admission and special exhibitions.

Fossil Butte National Monument: Explore the fossil-rich butte and its paleontological treasures.

- Money-Saving Tip: Enjoy the monument's visitor center and hiking trails for free.

Wyoming Dinosaur Center, Thermopolis: Learn about dinosaurs and fossils with interactive exhibits.

- Money-Saving Tip: Look for discounts on museum admission and family passes.

Medicine Bow National Forest: Hike, camp, and enjoy outdoor activities in this forested area.

- Money-Saving Tip: Visit the forest's trailheads and picnic areas for free.

National Historic Trails Interpretive Center, Casper: Learn about the historic trails that passed through Wyoming.

- Money-Saving Tip: Check for discounts on admission and special programs.

Yellowstone River: Raft, fish, or enjoy scenic drives along the river's picturesque landscapes.

- Money-Saving Tip: Look for deals on guided rafting trips and fishing excursions.

Sinks Canyon State Park, Lander: Witness a natural phenomenon where the river disappears into a cave.

- Money-Saving Tip: Explore the park's hiking trails and geological features for free.

Vedauwoo Recreation Area: Rock climb, hike, and picnic in this unique granite formation area.

- Money-Saving Tip: Enjoy outdoor activities and rock formations without any entrance fees.

Shoshone National Forest: Experience outdoor adventures and camping in the nation's first national forest.

- Money-Saving Tip: Choose free or low-cost campgrounds in the forest.

Category	Insider Tips
Food	1. Explore Wyoming's cowboy cuisine by dining at local steakhouses and ranches, such as the Historic Irma Hotel in Cody or the Snake River Grill in Jackson Hole, for hearty cuts of beef, bison, and game meats.
	2. Indulge in Wyoming's Western fare by trying regional specialties like bison burgers, trout, and elk chili, which can often be found at local diners, roadside
	3. Look for affordable dining options at casual eateries, breweries, and cafes serving up comfort foods, homestyle dishes, and cowboy breakfasts, often found in small towns and rural communities throughout Wyoming.
	4. Take advantage of food festivals and events celebrating Wyoming's culinary heritage, such as the Wyoming Brewers Festival in Cheyenne, the Jackson Hole Food & Wine Festival, or the Chuckwagon Cookoff in Lander, featuring
Accommodation	1. Consider staying at guest ranches or dude ranches in Wyoming's scenic regions and mountain valleys, offering immersive Western experiences, horseback riding, and cozy accommodations amidst natural beauty and cowboy
	2. Explore budget-friendly lodging options on platforms like Airbnb or Vrbo, where you can find affordable stays like cabins, cottages, or vacation rentals in
	3. Look for budget motels, roadside inns, and campgrounds along major highways and scenic routes, providing convenient and affordable stays for
	4. Embrace outdoor camping in Wyoming's national parks and wilderness areas, where you can pitch a tent or park your RV amidst mountain vistas, alpine meadows, and star-filled skies, with options for family-friendly camping,
Activities	1. Discover Wyoming's outdoor attractions by exploring hiking trails in places like Grand Teton National Park, biking along the Snake River Canyon, or fishing in Yellowstone Lake, offering scenic beauty and outdoor adventures for nature
	2. Immerse yourself in Wyoming's cowboy culture by visiting historic sites like the Buffalo Bill Center of the West in Cody, attending rodeos like Cheyenne Frontier Days, or taking trail rides in places like the Big Horn Mountains, offering
	3. Attend local festivals and events celebrating Wyoming's wildlife and natural wonders, such as the Jackson Hole Elk Fest, the Cody Stampede Rodeo, or the Wind River Wild Horse Sanctuary Open House, featuring music, arts, and

		4. Take scenic drives along Wyoming's scenic byways and backroads, exploring charming small towns, historic landmarks, and natural attractions like Devils Tower, Hot Springs State Park, or the Wind River Range, with opportunities for picnicking, wildlife viewing, and exploring local shops and attractions along the
Transport		1. Rent a car to explore Wyoming's scenic highways and backroads, with rental agencies available at major airports, cities, and tourist destinations throughout the state, providing flexibility and convenience for travelers to explore at their
		2. Utilize public transportation options in urban areas like Cheyenne and Jackson, including buses, shuttles, and trolleys, for convenient and eco-friendly travel within city limits, with options for day passes, fare discounts, and bike-
		3. Look for ridesharing services or carpooling opportunities for shared transportation to and from events, attractions, or outdoor adventures across Wyoming, providing cost-effective and social travel options for travelers and
		4. Plan road trips along Wyoming's scenic routes and heritage trails, taking advantage of fuel-efficient vehicles and budget-friendly travel stops along the way, with opportunities for camping, sightseeing, and indulging in local flavors

Solutions to Common Problems

Now we have completed the granular assessment of how to save in the USA, let's look at how things can go wrong...

Common Complaints	Solutions
1. High Healthcare Costs	1. **Purchase Travel Insurance:** Cover medical
2. Complex Visa Processes	2. **Plan Early:** Start visa applications well in advance.
3. Transportation Challenges	3. **Use Ride-Sharing Apps:** Easier than public
4. Language Barriers	4. **Use Translation Apps:** Facilitates communication.
5. Tipping Culture Uncertainty	5. **Research Tipping Norms:** Be aware of local
6. Limited Public Restrooms	6. **Plan Rest Stops:** Utilize facilities when available.
7. Mobile Data Costs for Travelers	7. **Get Local SIM Card:** Affordable data while in the
8. Crowded Tourist Attractions	8. **Visit Off-Peak Times:** Less crowded during
9. Lack of Public Transportation in Rural Areas	9. **Rent a Car:** Explore remote areas with flexibility.

1. **High Costs**: Complaint: Many tourists find that traveling in the USA can be expensive, from accommodation and dining to transportation and attractions.
2. Solution:
    - Take advantage of free attractions and activities: Many museums, parks, and cultural sites offer free admission or donation-based entry.
    - Use public transportation: Opt for public transportation or ride-sharing services instead of taxis or rental cars to save on transportation costs.
    - Look for discounts: Use discount websites, coupon books, and travel passes to save money on attractions, dining, and transportation.
3. **Long Wait Times**: Complaint: Tourists may experience long wait times at popular attractions, restaurants, and transportation hubs.
4. Solution:
    - Purchase tickets in advance: Book tickets for attractions, tours, and transportation services online to skip the line and secure your spot.
    - Avoid peak hours: Plan your visits to popular attractions during off-peak hours or on weekdays to avoid crowds and long wait times.
    - Use express passes: Some attractions offer express or fast-track passes for an additional fee, allowing you to bypass long lines and queues.
5. **Language Barriers**: Complaint: Non-English speaking tourists may encounter language barriers when communicating with locals or navigating in unfamiliar areas.
6. Solution:
    - Use translation apps: Download translation apps or carry a pocket dictionary to help with basic communication in English.
    - Seek assistance: Don't hesitate to ask for help or clarification from hotel staff, tour guides, or fellow travelers if you encounter language barriers.
    - Learn basic phrases: Familiarize yourself with essential phrases and greetings in English to facilitate communication in everyday situations.

7. **Cultural Differences**: Complaint: Tourists may experience culture shock or misunderstandings due to differences in customs, etiquette, or social norms.
8. Solution:
    - Research cultural norms: Before traveling to the USA, learn about American customs, etiquette, and social expectations to avoid unintentional misunderstandings.
    - Be open-minded: Approach cultural differences with an open mind and willingness to learn, respecting local customs and traditions.
    - Ask questions: If you're unsure about appropriate behavior in a particular situation, don't hesitate to ask locals or tour guides for guidance.
9. **Safety Concerns**: Complaint: Tourists may feel unsafe or concerned about crime, particularly in urban areas or tourist hotspots.
10. Solution:
    - Stay informed: Research safety tips and travel advisories for the specific destinations you plan to visit in the USA.
    - Use common sense: Exercise caution and be vigilant of your surroundings, especially in crowded or unfamiliar areas.
    - Secure belongings: Keep your belongings secure and be mindful of pickpockets or theft in crowded tourist areas.
    - Trust your instincts: If you feel uncomfortable or unsafe in a situation, trust your instincts and remove yourself from the situation if possible.

Freebies to be cautious of...

While there are many legitimate freebies and promotional offers available in the USA, it's essential to be cautious of certain situations that may come with hidden costs or obligations. Here are some freebies to be careful of:

1. **Time Share Presentations**: Companies offering free gifts or vacations in exchange for attending a timeshare presentation often employ high-pressure sales tactics to persuade attendees to purchase a timeshare or vacation club membership. Be wary of offers that require attendance at a presentation and thoroughly research the company before committing to anything.
2. **Free Trials with Automatic Renewal**: Some companies offer free trials of products or services but require credit card information upfront and automatically enroll participants in a subscription or membership program if they don't cancel before the trial period ends. Read the terms and conditions carefully and set a reminder to cancel if you're not interested in continuing the service.
3. **"Free" Vacation Packages**: Beware of offers for free vacation packages that require payment for taxes, fees, or additional services. These offers may come with hidden costs or require attendees to sit through sales presentations for timeshares or vacation clubs.
4. **"Free" Seminars or Workshops**: Some seminars or workshops advertised as free may be sales pitches for expensive educational programs, investment opportunities, or financial products. Attendees may feel pressured to make a purchase or investment after attending the seminar.
5. **"Free" Prize Offers**: Offers for free prizes, such as gift cards, vacations, or electronics, may require participants to provide personal information or pay shipping

and handling fees. These offers may be a guise to collect personal data for marketing purposes or may come with hidden costs.
6. **Door-to-Door Sales**: Be cautious of freebies offered by door-to-door salespeople, particularly if they pressure you to make a purchase or sign a contract on the spot. Research the company and its products/services before making any decisions.

Avoid Unexpected Costs

Unexpected Costs	How to Minimize
Currency Exchange Fees	Use credit cards with no foreign transaction fees or withdraw cash from ATMs with low or no fees.
Sales Tax	Research and budget for sales tax rates in different states and cities. Look for tax-free shopping days or exemptions for certain items.
Tipping	Familiarize yourself with tipping customs and percentages. Use apps or calculators to help calculate tips accurately.
Healthcare Expenses	Purchase travel insurance that covers medical emergencies. Use in-network healthcare providers and pharmacies if needed.
Transportation Costs	Use public transportation, rideshare services, or walk whenever possible. Look for discount passes or pre-book transportation options.
Roaming Charges	Purchase a local SIM card or use international roaming plans from your mobile carrier. Utilize Wi-Fi networks for communication whenever available.
Parking Fees	Research parking options in advance and look for free or discounted parking areas. Consider using public transportation or rideshare services to avoid parking costs.
Attractions and Tours	Look for discounted tickets, online deals, or combination passes for attractions. Consider free or low-cost activities such as hiking, museums with suggested donations, or exploring nature parks.

Getting Out

The airspace over the United States is one of the busiest and most heavily trafficked airspaces in the world but flying is not the only option to leave:

1. Buses:

Depending on your location and destination, overland travel options such as buses or trains may be more affordable than flying, especially for shorter distances or neighboring countries. Bus fares vary widely depending on the distance and the operator. On average, short-distance trips (within the same state or neighboring states) may start at around $10 to $30, while longer trips across multiple states could range from $50 to $150 or more.

How to Score Discounts:

- Book Early: Like airlines, bus companies often offer cheaper fares for those who book in advance.
- Use Discount Websites: Websites like Wanderu, Busbud, and Megabus offer discounted fares and promotions for various bus companies.
- Student and Senior Discounts: Many bus companies offer discounted fares for students and seniors. Make sure to inquire about these discounts when booking.
- Loyalty Programs: Some bus companies have loyalty programs that offer perks and discounts for frequent travelers.
- Travel Off-Peak: Traveling during non-peak hours or on weekdays can sometimes result in lower fares.
- Bundle Tickets: Some bus companies offer discounts for purchasing round-trip or multi-leg tickets.

2. Trains:

rain fares vary depending on the route, class of service, and time of booking. Short-distance trips (e.g., regional routes) may start at around $20 to $50, while long-distance trips (e.g., cross-country journeys) could range from $100 to $500 or more.

How to Score Discounts:

- Book in Advance: Train tickets are often cheaper when booked in advance, especially for long-distance routes.
- Rail Passes: Consider purchasing rail passes like Amtrak's USA Rail Pass or regional passes for specific areas to save money on multiple journeys.
- Discounts for Groups: Amtrak offers group discounts for parties of 20 or more traveling together.

- Senior, Student, and Military Discounts: Amtrak offers discounts for seniors, students, and members of the military. Make sure to check eligibility and inquire about these discounts when booking.
- Special Promotions: Keep an eye out for special promotions and deals offered by Amtrak, such as limited-time discounts and companion fares.
- Check Regional Rail Providers: In addition to Amtrak, some regions have their own commuter and regional rail services that may offer discounted fares.

3. Ferries:

erry fares vary depending on the route, distance, type of ferry (e.g., passenger-only or vehicle ferry), and time of year. Short ferry rides (e.g., between neighboring islands or across a river) may start at around $10 to $20, while longer ferry journeys (e.g., between mainland USA and Alaska) could range from $50 to several hundred dollars.

How to Score Discounts:

- Book Online: Many ferry companies offer discounts for booking tickets online in advance.
- Multi-Trip Passes: Some ferry operators offer multi-trip passes or commuter passes for frequent travelers.
- Special Discounts: Ferry companies may offer discounts for seniors, students, military personnel, and residents of certain areas. Check eligibility requirements and inquire about available discounts.
- Travel Off-Peak: Fares may be cheaper during non-peak hours or outside of the tourist season.
- Group Discounts: Some ferry companies offer discounts for groups traveling together. Inquire about group rates when booking.

4. Planes:

Look for budget airlines that offer discounted fares for international flights. Airlines like Spirit, Frontier, or Southwest Airlines often provide competitive prices, especially if you book well in advance or are flexible with your travel dates.

How to Score Discounts:

- Book Early: Airfares are often cheaper when booked well in advance, especially for popular routes and peak travel periods.
- Use Flight Comparison Websites: Compare prices across multiple airlines and booking platforms to find the best deals.
- Sign Up for Alerts: Subscribe to fare alerts from airlines and travel websites to be notified of price drops and special promotions.
- Be Flexible with Dates and Destinations: Being flexible with your travel dates and destinations can help you find cheaper fares. Consider flying midweek or during off-peak seasons.

- Look for Budget Airlines: Budget airlines like Southwest Airlines, Spirit Airlines, and Frontier Airlines often offer lower fares, especially for domestic flights within the USA.
- Use Travel Rewards and Miles: If you have frequent flyer miles or credit card rewards points, consider using them to offset the cost of your flights.
- Take Advantage of Sales and Promotions: Keep an eye out for airline sales, promotional codes, and special offers, which can sometimes result in significant savings.
- Consider Connecting Flights: Opting for connecting flights instead of direct flights can sometimes be cheaper, especially for long-haul journeys.
- Bundle Flights and Accommodation: Some travel websites offer discounts for booking flights and accommodation together as part of a package deal.

Cheapest airport lounges

Is there anything superior to an airport lounge as a pre-travel experience? Finding the cheapest airport lounges in the USA can vary depending on the airport and the lounge network. However, here are some options along with starting prices, benefits, and potential passes or credit cards to maximize savings:

1. **Priority Pass Lounges**: Priority Pass is a popular lounge network that offers access to various lounges worldwide, including many in the USA. The cost of a Priority Pass membership varies depending on the level:
    - **Starting Price**: The Standard membership starts at around $99 per year, with additional fees per lounge visit.
    - **Benefits**: Access to a network of over 1,300 airport lounges worldwide, regardless of the airline or class of travel. Lounges typically offer amenities such as comfortable seating, complimentary snacks and beverages, Wi-Fi, and sometimes showers and business facilities.
    - **Maximizing Savings**: Some premium credit cards offer Priority Pass memberships as a complimentary benefit. For example, the Chase Sapphire Reserve, The Platinum Card from American Express, and the Hilton Honors American Express Aspire Card all come with Priority Pass Select memberships included.
2. **Airport-Specific Lounges**: Some airports in the USA have their own independent lounges or lounges operated by airlines. These lounges may offer more affordable access options:
    - **Starting Price**: Prices can vary widely, but some lounges offer day passes starting around $25 to $50 per person.
    - **Benefits**: Lounge amenities typically include comfortable seating, complimentary snacks and beverages (alcoholic and non-alcoholic), Wi-Fi, and sometimes showers and business facilities.
    - **Maximizing Savings**: Some credit cards offer lounge access benefits that can be used at specific lounges or networks. For example, the United Club Card offers access to United Club lounges, while the Delta SkyMiles Reserve American Express Card offers access to Delta Sky Club lounges.
3. **Credit Card Lounge Access**: Several premium credit cards offer complimentary lounge access as a benefit, either through specific lounge networks or their own proprietary programs:
    - **Starting Price**: Annual fees for these cards can range from $450 to $695 or more, depending on the card.
    - **Benefits**: Complimentary access to select airport lounges worldwide, along with other travel benefits such as travel credits, elite status, and airport security program memberships.
    - **Maximizing Savings**: Look for credit cards that offer lounge access as part of a broader suite of travel benefits that align with your travel habits and preferences. Compare the annual fee against the value of the benefits to ensure you're getting the most out of the card.

Here are some highly regarded airport lounges in the USA known for their exceptional services and amenities:

1. **The Centurion Lounge (Various Locations)**: Operated by American Express, The Centurion Lounge is known for its upscale amenities and services. Locations in major airports like Dallas/Fort Worth (DFW), Miami (MIA), and Las Vegas (LAS) offer premium food and beverage options, including signature cocktails crafted by renowned mixologists, as well as amenities like shower suites, relaxation areas, and high-speed Wi-Fi.
2. **Delta Sky Club (Various Locations)**: Delta Air Lines operates its network of Sky Club lounges in airports across the USA. Sky Clubs typically offer comfortable seating, complimentary snacks and beverages (including alcoholic options), Wi-Fi, and sometimes additional amenities like showers and business centers. Locations in airports like Atlanta (ATL), New York-JFK, and Los Angeles (LAX) are particularly popular.
3. **United Polaris Lounge (Chicago O'Hare International Airport)**: United Airlines' Polaris Lounge at Chicago O'Hare (ORD) is renowned for its luxurious amenities and services, specifically designed for international premium travelers. The lounge features private dining areas with a la carte menus curated by celebrity chefs, relaxation spaces with daybeds and showers, and premium bar offerings.
4. **American Airlines Flagship Lounge (Various Locations)**: American Airlines' Flagship Lounges are available in select airports, including New York-JFK, Los Angeles (LAX), and Miami (MIA). These lounges offer a premium experience with enhanced food and beverage options, including chef-inspired menus and premium wine selections. Some locations also feature shower suites and dedicated dining areas.
5. **Alaska Lounge (Various Locations)**: Alaska Airlines operates its network of Alaska Lounges in airports like Seattle-Tacoma (SEA), Portland (PDX), and Los Angeles (LAX). These lounges offer a relaxed atmosphere with complimentary snacks and beverages, including local craft beer and wine selections. Some locations also feature amenities like shower facilities and business centers.

Checklist of top 20 things not to miss

- ☑ Visit the Grand Canyon in Arizona
- ☑ Explore New York City's Times Square
- ☑ Take a road trip along the Pacific Coast Highway in California
- ☑ Experience the magic of Disney World in Florida
- ☑ Walk the Freedom Trail in Boston, Massachusetts
- ☑ See the Statue of Liberty in New York Harbor
- ☑ Visit the Smithsonian museums in Washington, D.C.
- ☑ Take a helicopter tour of the Las Vegas Strip in Nevada
- ☑ Explore the French Quarter in New Orleans, Louisiana
- ☑ Go hiking in Yellowstone National Park, Wyoming
- ☑ Attend a Broadway show in New York City
- ☑ Visit the White House in Washington, D.C.
- ☑ Explore the historic neighborhoods of San Francisco, California
- ☑ See the Northern Lights in Alaska
- ☑ Go wine tasting in Napa Valley, California
- ☑ Visit the Kennedy Space Center in Florida
- ☑ Take a cruise to the Hawaiian Islands
- ☑ Explore the art galleries of Santa Fe, New Mexico
- ☑ Attend a live music concert in Nashville, Tennessee
- ☑ Experience the natural beauty of the Great Smoky Mountains in Tennessee and North Carolina

Recap chart showing how to have a $10,000 trip to for $1,000

Expense Category	Normal Cost	Hack	Recommendations to Save
Accommodation	$3,000	$300	Use blindbooking, last minute reservations and mix in Camping in numerous national parks and campsites across the country offering affordable or even free camping grounds. Additionally, consider alternative lodging options like hostels, guesthouses, or budget motels, especially if you're traveling in a group and can split the cost.
Transportation	$1,000	$100	2. Utilize relocation services for free transport, budget airlines, buses, uber / lyft coupons, and ride-sharing services instead of taxis or rental cars. Look for discounted tickets and travel passes.
Food and Dining	$2,000	$200	3. Opt for budget-friendly dining options such as street food, food trucks, and local markets. Cook your meals occasionally to save money on dining out.
Attractions and Tours	$2,000	$100	4. Take advantage of free attractions, museums, and parks. Look for discounts on attraction tickets, tours, and activities through online booking websites or tourist passes like America the beautiful. **By purchasing the pass for $80, you would save $1,495 on entrance fees alone.**
Miscellaneous		$300	5. Set aside a contingency fund for unexpected expenses. Limit impulse purchases like starbucks and prioritize spending on experiences that matter most to you.
Total Estimated Cost		$10,000	$10,000
Total Estimated Savings		$9,000	$9,000

Experiencing a luxurious $10,000 trip to the USA on a budget of $1,000 is not only possible but also an adventure filled with thrills and unforgettable experiences.

1. **Accommodations**:
    - **Day Passes to Five-Star Hotels**: Instead of booking traditional overnight stays, take advantage of day passes offered by luxury hotels. Many five-star hotels offer day passes to their pools, spas, and amenities for a fraction of the cost of a room. Treat yourself to a day of relaxation and luxury without breaking the bank.

- **Camping**: Embrace the great outdoors by camping in national parks or campgrounds. Camping fees are significantly cheaper than hotel rooms and offer the chance to immerse yourself in nature's beauty. Bring your own tent or rent camping gear for an affordable outdoor experience.

2. **Exploring National Parks**:
   - **National Park Pass**: Invest in an America the Beautiful National Parks Pass, which grants access to over 2,000 federal recreation sites, including national parks, forests, and monuments. Use the pass to explore iconic destinations like Yellowstone, Yosemite, and the Grand Canyon for free or at a discounted rate.

3. **Transportation**:
   - **Relocation Cars and RVs**: Take advantage of relocation deals offered by car rental companies and RV providers. These deals allow you to rent vehicles for a nominal fee (sometimes even for free) in exchange for relocating them to a different location. Enjoy the flexibility of road tripping across the country while saving on transportation costs.

4. **Visiting Landmarks**:
   - **Statue of Liberty**: Utilize your National Park Pass to access the Statue of Liberty and Ellis Island for free. Take a ferry ride to Liberty Island and marvel at Lady Liberty up close, then explore the Ellis Island National Museum of Immigration to learn about the millions of immigrants who passed through its halls.

5. **Dining**:
   - **Too Good To Go**: Download the Too Good To Go app to discover surplus meals from local restaurants at discounted prices. Enjoy gourmet meals at a fraction of the cost while reducing food waste. This eco-friendly dining option allows you to sample diverse cuisines without overspending.

By following these recommendations and prioritizing budget-friendly options, you can enjoy a $10,000 trip to the USA for just $1,000. With careful planning and resourcefulness, you can make the most of your travel budget and create unforgettable experiences without breaking the bank.

1. **Museum Free Days**: Many museums across the USA offer free admission on certain days of the week or month. Research the museum's website or contact them directly to find out about their free days and plan your visit accordingly.
2. **City Passes and Tourist Discounts**: Look for city passes or tourist discount cards that offer discounted or free admission to multiple attractions. These passes often include popular sights and can save you a significant amount of money compared to paying for each attraction individually. here are 63 designated national parks in the United States. Entrance fees to national parks typically range from $20 to $35 per vehicle for a seven-day pass, depending on the park. However, some parks have higher fees for specific activities or special permits. Assuming an average entrance fee of $25 per park, visiting all 63 national parks without the America the Beautiful Pass would cost $1,575. **By purchasing the pass for $80, you would save $1,495 on entrance fees alone.**
3. **Library Passes**: Many public libraries offer passes or discounts to local attractions that cardholders can check out for free or at a reduced cost. Check with local library to see if they offer any such programs and take advantage of them to save on

admission fees. In many cases, foreigners can get a library card in the USA, although specific policies can vary depending on the library system
4. **Outdoor Viewing Areas**: For attractions such as iconic landmarks or city skylines, consider visiting nearby outdoor viewing areas or public parks where you can enjoy similar views for free. This is a great option for attractions like the Statue of Liberty, where you can take a free ride on the Staten Island Ferry for views of the statue and the New York City skyline.
5. **Local Tours and Walking Routes**: Instead of paying for guided tours or hop-on-hop-off buses, explore attractions on your own using self-guided walking tours, audio guides, or online resources. Many cities have free or low-cost walking routes that take you past major landmarks and attractions.

Understand

Understanding the history of the United States is crucial for making sense of its present-day context. Here are some key historical events that have shaped the nation:

Picture this: It's 1776, and the Declaration of Independence is signed, sealing the deal on the thirteen American colonies' break from British rule. Fast forward to the American Revolution from 1775 to 1783, where fiery battles paved the way for the birth of the United States.

Now, hold onto your tri-cornered hats because things are about to get monumental! In 1787, delegates gathered for the Constitutional Convention, ready to tackle the shortcomings of the Articles of Confederation. Their brainpower birthed none other than the U.S. Constitution, a document still revered today.

Zooming ahead to 1803, President Thomas Jefferson pulls off a real estate deal for the ages—the Louisiana Purchase. Imagine doubling the size of the country in one swoop! It's like a historical Black Friday sale.

But wait, there's drama brewing in the mid-19th century! The Civil War erupts from 1861 to 1865, pitting the Northern states against the Southern states in a clash over slavery and states' rights. Enter President Abraham Lincoln, stage left, with his game-changing Emancipation Proclamation in 1863, setting the stage for freedom's triumph.

Now, cue the Reconstruction Era from 1865 to 1877, where the nation rolls up its sleeves to rebuild after the war's devastation. It's a time of hope, healing, and the arduous journey toward racial equality.

Fast forward again to the late 19th century, and America is in full swing—literally! The Industrial Revolution kicks into high gear, transforming the nation with technological marvels and bustling cities. It's like the Gilded Age, where wealth and excess reign supreme.

But don't get too comfortable in your top hat and tails because here comes the Progressive Era in the early 20th century. Think Theodore Roosevelt, Woodrow Wilson, and a wave of reforms aimed at tackling social injustices and curbing corruption.

Then, bam! World War I erupts from 1914 to 1918, thrusting the United States onto the global stage as a major player. The Roaring Twenties follow—a decade of jazz, flappers, and economic boom times. But the party comes crashing down with the Great Depression in 1929, plunging the nation into darkness.

Fear not, for President Franklin D. Roosevelt rides to the rescue with his New Deal programs, offering a glimmer of hope amidst the economic despair. World War II soon follows, from 1939 to 1945, with the United States emerging as a beacon of freedom and democracy.

But the fight for justice rages on, with the Civil Rights Movement shaking the nation to its core in the 1950s and 1960s. It's a time of marches, protests, and monumental legislative victories like the Civil Rights Act of 1964 and the Voting Rights Act of 1965.

Yet, even in the midst of progress, turmoil brews on the international stage. The Vietnam War from 1955 to 1975 divides the nation like never before, while the Cold War simmers with tension between the United States and the Soviet Union.

And let's not forget the race to the stars! The Space Race from 1957 to 1975 sees America and the Soviet Union duking it out for cosmic supremacy, culminating in Neil Armstrong's iconic moonwalk.

The 1990s saw the end of the Cold War and the collapse of the Soviet Union, leading to a period of relative global stability. The United States emerged as the world's sole superpower, but domestically, issues such as the Gulf War, the rise of the internet, and debates over healthcare reform dominated the agenda.

The turn of the millennium brought both prosperity and adversity. The dot-com bubble burst in the early 2000s, leading to an economic recession. The September 11, 2001 terrorist attacks fundamentally changed the country's approach to national security and led to military interventions in Afghanistan and Iraq. The presidency of Barack Obama from 2009 to 2017 marked a historic moment with his election as the first African American president. His tenure was defined by efforts to address the Great Recession, healthcare reform with the Affordable Care Act, and attempts to tackle climate change.

In recent years, the United States has grappled with increasing political polarization, social unrest, and challenges to democratic norms. The election of Donald Trump in 2016 brought a populist and unconventional style of leadership, marked by controversial policies on immigration, trade, and foreign relations. The COVID-19 pandemic, which began in 2020, further exposed societal divisions and economic vulnerabilities, leading to unprecedented government interventions to mitigate the crisis.

Throughout these years, technological advancements, cultural shifts, and demographic changes have shaped American society. From the rise of Silicon Valley and the digital revolution to movements for civil rights, LGBTQ+ rights, and environmental activism, the United States continues to evolve as a complex and dynamic nation facing both opportunities and challenges in the 21st century.

Phew! What a rollercoaster ride through history! From the birth of a nation to the triumph of civil rights, America's story is a testament to resilience, courage, and the enduring quest for a more perfect union but there's also tiny tales which haven't been much told. Here are just a few:

1. **The Great Molasses Flood**: In 1919, a massive storage tank holding over 2 million gallons of molasses burst in Boston's North End, unleashing a 25-foot wave of molasses that swept through the streets at speeds of up to 35 miles per hour. The disaster, known as the Great Molasses Flood, resulted in 21 deaths and 150 injuries, as well as significant property damage. It remains one of the most unusual and deadly industrial accidents in American history.

2. **The U.S. Camel Corps**: In the mid-19th century, the U.S. Army experimented with using camels as pack animals in the arid regions of the American Southwest. The U.S. Camel Corps, established in 1856, imported camels from the Middle East and employed them in various military expeditions and surveys. While the experiment ultimately proved unsuccessful due to logistical challenges and the outbreak of the Civil War, it left behind a quirky footnote in American military history.
3. **The Great Emu War**: In 1932, the Australian government faced a unique problem: a population explosion of emus in Western Australia was wreaking havoc on crops and farmland. In response, the government deployed military personnel armed with machine guns to cull the emu population, leading to a series of bizarre and comical encounters known as the "Great Emu War." Despite their efforts, the soldiers struggled to effectively control the emu population, and the "war" ended in defeat for the human forces.
4. **The Greenbrier Bunker**: Deep beneath the luxury Greenbrier resort in West Virginia lies a secret underground bunker built during the Cold War era to house members of the U.S. Congress in the event of a nuclear attack. The bunker, which remained classified until its existence was revealed in 1992, was equipped with living quarters, medical facilities, a cafeteria, and communication systems designed to sustain up to 1,100 people for over 60 days. Today, the bunker serves as a museum and tourist attraction, offering visitors a glimpse into the country's Cold War history.
5. **The Battle of Athens**: In 1946, a group of returning World War II veterans in Athens, Tennessee, staged an armed rebellion against a corrupt local government accused of voter fraud and election rigging. Known as the Battle of Athens, the conflict culminated in a shootout between the veterans and law enforcement officers, resulting in casualties on both sides. Ultimately, the veterans emerged victorious, and the incident led to reforms in the electoral system and increased transparency in local government.

Values

The American national psyche is a complex and multifaceted construct shaped by a multitude of historical, cultural, social, and economic factors. At its core, the American psyche reflects a deeply ingrained sense of individualism, optimism, and resilience, often characterized by the belief in the American Dream—the idea that through hard work, determination, and opportunity, anyone can achieve success and prosperity.

Americans have long celebrated the virtues of independence, autonomy, and personal freedom. This ethos is reflected in various aspects of American life, from the emphasis on entrepreneurship and innovation to the strong tradition of civil liberties and individual rights enshrined in the Constitution.

Alongside individualism, optimism plays a central role in shaping the American psyche. Despite facing numerous challenges and setbacks throughout its history, the United States has maintained a steadfast belief in progress, growth, and the possibility of a better future. This optimism is deeply rooted in the country's founding principles and is perpetuated through cultural narratives, such as the idea of American exceptionalism—the belief that the United States occupies a unique and privileged place in the world.

However, the American psyche is not devoid of contradictions or complexities. While optimism and individualism are celebrated, they can also foster a culture of hyper-competitiveness, materialism, and inequality. The relentless pursuit of success and upward mobility can lead to a sense of alienation, anxiety, and isolation, particularly among those who feel marginalized or left behind by the American Dream.

Moreover, the American psyche is also deeply influenced by its history of immigration and diversity. As a nation of immigrants, the United States has always been characterized by its rich tapestry of cultures, languages, and identities. This diversity has both enriched the American experience and contributed to tensions and conflicts over issues of race, ethnicity, and national identity.

In recent years, the American psyche has been further shaped by political polarization, economic uncertainty, and social upheaval. The rise of populist movements, the erosion of trust in institutions, and the growing divide between urban and rural communities have all contributed to a sense of disillusionment and fragmentation within American society.

Despite these challenges, the American psyche remains resilient and adaptable. Throughout its history, the United States has faced numerous crises and upheavals, from economic depressions and world wars to civil rights struggles and terrorist attacks. In each instance, Americans have demonstrated a remarkable capacity to come together, overcome adversity, and forge a path forward.

Understanding how the "average" American thinks can be challenging given the diversity of perspectives, backgrounds, and experiences across the country. However, there are some common traits and cultural nuances that can provide insights into American thinking:

1. **Individualism**: Americans often value individualism and independence, placing importance on personal freedom, self-reliance, and autonomy. This mindset can manifest in attitudes towards entrepreneurship, personal responsibility, and the pursuit of individual goals and aspirations.
2. **Optimism**: There is a pervasive sense of optimism and can-do attitude among many Americans, characterized by a belief in the possibility of success, progress, and improvement. This optimism often fuels resilience in the face of challenges and a willingness to embrace change and innovation.
3. **Pragmatism**: Americans tend to be pragmatic and results-oriented, prioritizing practical solutions and efficiency in problem-solving. This pragmatic mindset can be seen in various aspects of American life, from business and technology to politics and everyday decision-making.
4. **Diversity and Inclusion**: The United States is a melting pot of cultures, ethnicities, and backgrounds, and many Americans value diversity and inclusion as core principles of society. Embracing multiculturalism, celebrating differences, and promoting equality and social justice are important values for many Americans.
5. **Patriotism**: Patriotism and national pride are strong sentiments for many Americans, with a deep attachment to symbols of American identity such as the flag, the national anthem, and historical figures like the Founding Fathers. This patriotism can manifest in expressions of loyalty to the country and a sense of pride in American achievements and values.

The secret to saving HUGE amounts of money when travelling to USA is...

Your mindset. Money is an emotional topic, if you associate words like cheapskate, Miser (and its £9.50 to go into Charles Dickens London house, oh the Irony) with being thrifty when traveling you are likely to say 'F-it' and spend your money needlessly because you associate pain with saving money. You pay now for an immediate reward. Our brains are prehistoric; they focus on surviving day to day. Travel companies and hotels know this and put trillions into making you believe you will be happier when you spend on their products or services. Our poor brains are up against outdated programming and an onslaught of advertisements bombarding us with the message: spending money on travel equals PLEASURE. To correct this carefully lodged propaganda in your frontal cortex, you need to imagine your future self.

Saving money does not make you a cheapskate. It makes you smart. How do people get rich? They invest their money. They don't go out and earn it; they let their money earn more money. So every time you want to spend money, imagine this: while you travel, your money is working for you, not you for money. While you sleep, the money, you've invested is going up and up. That's a pleasure a pricey entrance fee can't give you. Thinking about putting your money to work for you tricks your brain into believing you are not withholding pleasure from yourself, you are saving your money to invest so you can go to even more amazing places. You are thus turning thrifty travel into a pleasure fueled sport.

When you've got money invested - If you want to splash your cash on a first-class airplane seat - you can. I can't tell you how to invest your money, only that you should. Saving $20 on taxis doesn't seem like much, but over time you could save upwards of $15,000 a year, which is a deposit for a house which you can rent on Airbnb to finance more travel. Your brain making money looks like your brain on cocaine, so tell yourself saving money is making money.

Scientists have proved that imagining your future self is the easiest way to associate pleasure with saving money. You can download FaceApp — which will give you a picture of what you will look like older and grayer, or you can take a deep breath just before spending money and ask yourself if you will regret the purchase later.

The easiest ways to waste money traveling are:

Getting a taxi. The solution to this is to always download the google map before you go. Many taxi drivers will drive you around for 15 minutes when the place you were trying to get to is a 5-minute walk... remember while not getting an overpriced taxi to tell yourself, 'I am saving money to free myself for more travel.'
Spending money on overpriced food when hungry. The solution: carry snacks. A banana and an apple will cost you, in most places, less than a dollar.

Spending on entrance fees to top-rated attractions. If you really want to do it, spend the money happily. If you're conflicted, sleep on it. I don't regret spending $200 on a sky dive over the Great Barrier Reef; I regret going to the top of the shard on a cloudy day in USA for $60. Only you can know, but make sure it's your decision and not the marketing directors at said top-rated attraction.

Telling yourself 'you only have the chance to see/eat/experience it now'. While this might be true, make sure YOU WANT to spend the money. Money spent is money you can't invest, and often you can have the same experience for much less.

You can experience luxurious travel on a small budget, which will trick your brain into thinking you're already a high-roller, which will mean you'll be more likely to act like one and invest your money. Stay in five-star hotels for $5 by booking on the day of your stay on booking.com to enjoy last-minute deals. You can go to fancy restaurants using daily deal sites. Ask your airline about last-minute upgrades to first-class or business. I paid $100 extra on a $179 ticket to Cuba from Germany to be bumped to Business Class. When you ask, it will surprise you what you can get both at hotels and airlines.

Travel, as the saying goes, is the only thing you spend money on that makes you richer. You can easily waste money, making it difficult to enjoy that metaphysical wealth. The biggest money saving secret is to turn bargain hunting into a pleasurable activity, not an annoyance. Budgeting consciously can be fun, don't feel disappointed because you don't spend the $60 to go into an attraction. Feel good because soon that $60 will soon earn money for you. Meaning, you'll have the time and money to enjoy more metaphysical wealth while your bank balance increases.

So there it is. You can save a small fortune by being strategic with your trip planning. We've arranged everything in the guide to offer the best bang for your buck. Which means we took the view that if it's not an excellent investment for your money, we wouldn't include it. Why would a guide called 'Super Cheap' include lots of overpriced attractions? That said, if you think we've missed something or have unanswered questions, ping me an email: philgtang@gmail.com I'm on central Europe time and usually reply within 8 hours of getting your mail. We like to think of our guide books as evolving organisms helping our readers travel better cheaper. We use reader questions via email to update this book year round so you'll be helping other readers and yourself.

Don't put your dreams off!

Time is a currency you never get back and travel is its greatest return on investment. Plus, now you know you can visit USA for a fraction of the price most would have you believe.

Thank you for reading

Dear **Lovely Reader**,

If you have found this book useful, please consider writing a quick review on Amazon.

One person from every 1000 readers leaves a review on Amazon. It would mean more than you could ever know if you were one of our 1 in 1000 people to take the time to write a brief review.

Thank you so much for reading again and for spending your time and investing your trips future in Super Cheap Insider Guides.

One last note, please don't listen to anyone who says 'Oh no, you can't visit USA on a budget'. Unlike you, they didn't have this book. You can do ANYWHERE on a budget with the right insider advice and planning. Sure, learning to travel to USA on a budget that doesn't compromise on anything or drastically compromise on safety or comfort levels is a skill, but this guide has done the detective work for you. Now it is time for you to put the advice into action.

Phil and the Super Cheap Insider Guides Team

P.S If you need any more super cheap tips we'd love to hear from you e-mail me at philgtang@gmail.com, we have a lot of contacts in every region, so if there's a specific bargain you're hunting we can help you find it.

Your Next Book is Free

DISCOVER YOUR NEXT VACATION

☑ LUXURY ON A BUDGET APPROACH
☑ CHOOSE FROM 107 DESTINATIONS
☑ EACH BOOK PACKED WITH REAL-TIME LOCAL TIPS

Our American city guides are packed with THOUSANDS MORE TIPS for American cities.

GET A FREE BOOK: Simply leave an honest review and send a screenshot and proof of purchase to philgtang@gmail.com with the name of the book you'd like to have for free.

COUNTRY GUIDES

Super Cheap AUSTRALIA
Super Cheap AUSTRIA
Super Cheap CANADA
Super Cheap DENMARK
Super Cheap FIJI
Super Cheap FINLAND
Super Cheap FRANCE
Super Cheap GREAT BRITAIN
Super Cheap GERMANY
Super Cheap ICELAND
Super Cheap ITALY
Super Cheap IRELAND
Super Cheap JAPAN
Super Cheap MALDIVES
Super Cheap MEXICO
Super Cheap NETHERLANDS
Super Cheap NEW ZEALAND
Super Cheap NORWAY
Super Cheap SOUTH KOREA
Super Cheap SPAIN
Super Cheap SWITZERLAND
Super Cheap UAE
Super Cheap UNITED STATES

CITIES / TOWNS

Super Cheap ADELAIDE
Super Cheap ALASKA
Super Cheap AUSTIN
Super Cheap BANFF
Super Cheap BANGKOK
Super Cheap BARCELONA

Super Cheap BELFAST
Super Cheap BERMUDA
Super Cheap BORA BORA
Super Cheap BRITISH VIRGIN ISLANDS
Super Cheap BUDAPEST
Super Cheap Great Barrier Reef
Super Cheap CAMBRIDGE
Super Cheap CANCUN
Super Cheap CHIANG MAI
Super Cheap CHICAGO
Super Cheap Copenhagen
Super Cheap DOHA
Super Cheap DUBAI
Super Cheap DUBLIN
Super Cheap EDINBURGH
Super Cheap GALWAY
Super Cheap Guadeloupe
Super Cheap HELSINKI
Super Cheap LIMA
Super Cheap LISBON
Super Cheap MALAGA
Super Cheap Martinique
Super Cheap Machu Pichu
Super Cheap MIAMI
Super Cheap Milan
Super Cheap Montpellier
Super Cheap NASHVILLE
Super Cheap NAPA
Super Cheap NEW ORLEANS
Super Cheap NEW YORK
Super Cheap PARIS
Super Cheap PRAGUE
Super Cheap St. Vincent and the Grenadines
Super Cheap SEYCHELLES
Super Cheap SINGAPORE
Super Cheap ST LUCIA
Super Cheap TORONTO
Super Cheap Turks and Caicos
Super Cheap VANCOUVER
Super Cheap VENICE
Super Cheap VIENNA
Super Cheap YOSEMITE
Super Cheap ZURICH
Super Cheap ZANZIBAR

Bonus Travel Hacks

I've included these bonus travel hacks to help you plan and enjoy your trip to USA cheaply, joyfully, and smoothly. Perhaps they will even inspire you to start or renew a passion for long-term travel.

Common pitfalls when it comes to allocating money to your desires while traveling

Beware of Malleable mental accounting

Let's say you budgeted spending only $30 per day in USA but then you say well if I was at home I'd be spending $30 on food as an everyday purchase so you add another $30 to your budget. Don't fall into that trap as the likelihood is you still have expenses at home even if its just the cost of keeping your freezer going.

Beware of impulse purchases in USA

Restaurants that you haven't researched and just idle into can sometimes turn out to be great, but more often, they turn out to suck, especially if they are near tourist attractions. Make yourself a travel itinerary including where you'll eat breakfast and lunch. Dinner is always more expensive, so the meal best to enjoy at home or as a takeaway. This book is full of incredible cheap eats. All you have to do is plan to go to them.

Social media and FOMO (Fear of Missing Out)

'The pull of seeing acquaintances spend money on travel can often be a more powerful motivator to spend more while traveling than seeing an advertisement.' Beware of what you allow to influence you and go back to the question, what's the best money I can spend today?

Now-or-never sales strategies

One reason tourists are targeted by salespeople is the success of the now-or-never strategy. If you don't spend the money now… your never get the opportunity again. Rarely is this true.

Instead of spending your money on something you might not actually desire, take five minutes. Ask yourself, do I really want this? And return to the answer in five minutes. Your body will either say an absolute yes with a warm, excited feeling or a no with a weak, obscure feeling.

Unexpected costs

> "Holding on to anger is like grasping a hot coal with the intent of throwing it at someone else; you only hurt yourself." The Buddha.

One downside to traveling is unexpected costs. When these spring up from airlines, accommodation providers, tours and on and on, they feel like a punch in the gut. During the pandemic my earnings fell to 20% of what they are normally. No one was traveling, no one was buying travel guides. My accountant out of nowhere significantly raised his fee for the year despite the fact there was a lot less money to count. I was so angry I consulted a lawyer who told me you will spend more taking him to court than you will paying his bill. I had to get myself into a good feeling place before I paid his bill, so I googled how to feel good paying someone who has scammed you.

The answer: Write down that you will receive 10 times the amount you are paying from an unexpected source. I did that. Four months later, the accountant wrote to me. He had applied for a COVID subsidy for me and I would receive… you guessed it almost exactly 10 times his fee.

Make of that what you want. I don't wish to get embroiled in a conversation about what many term 'woo-woo', but the result of my writing that I would receive 10 times the amount made me feel much, much better when paying him. And ultimately, that was a gift in itself. So next time some airline or train operator or hotel/ Airbnb sticks you with an unexpected fee, immediately write that you will receive 10 times the amount you are paying from an unexpected source. Rise your vibe and skip the added price of feeling angry.

Hack your allocations for your USA Trip

"The best trick for saving is to eliminate the decision to save." Perry Wright of Duke University.

Put the money you plan to spend in USA on a pre-paid card in the local currency. This cuts out two problems - not knowing how much you've spent and totally avoiding expensive currency conversion fees.

You could even create separate spaces. This much for transportation, this for tours/entertainment, accommodation and food. We are reluctant to spend money that is pre-assigned to categories or uses.

Write that you want to enjoy a $3,000 trip for $500 to your USA trip. Countless research shows when you put goals in writing, you have a higher chance of following through.

Spend all the money you want to on buying experiences in USA

"Experiences are like good relatives that stay for a while and then leave. Objects are like relatives who move in and stay past their welcome." Daniel Gilbert, psychologist from Harvard University.

Economic and psychological research shows we are happier buying brief experiences on vacation rather than buying stuff to wear so give yourself freedom to spend on experiences knowing that the value you get back is many many times over.

Make saving money a game

There's one day a year where all the thrift shops where me and my family live sell everything there for a $1. My wife and I hold a contest where we take $5 and buy an entire outfit for each other. Whoever's outfit is liked more wins. We also look online to see whose outfit would have cost more to buy new. This year, my wife even snagged me an Armani coat for $1. I liked the coat when she showed it to me, but when I found out it was $500 new; I liked it and wore it a lot more.

Quadruple your money

Every-time you want to spend money, imagine it quadrupled. So the $10 you want to spend is actually $40. Now imagine that what you want to buy is four times the price. Do you still want it? If yes, go enjoy. If not, you've just saved yourself money, know you can choose to invest it in a way that quadruples or allocate it to something you really want to give you a greater return.

Understand what having unlimited amounts of money to spend in USA actually looks like

Let's look at what it would be like to have unlimited amounts of money to spend on your trip to USA.

Isolation

You take a private jet to your private USA hotel. There you are lavished with the best food, drink, and entertainment. Spending vast amounts of money on vacation equals being isolated.

If you're on your honeymoon and you want to be alone with your Amore, this is wonderful, but it can be equally wonderful to make new friends. Know this a study 'carried out by Brigham Young University, Utah found that while obesity increased risk of death by 30%, loneliness increased it by half.'

Comfort

Money can buy you late check outs of five-star hotels and priority boarding on airlines, all of which add up to comfort. But as this book has shown you, saving money in USA doesn't minimize comfort, that's just a lie travel agencies littered with glossy brochures want you to believe.

You can do late-check outs for free with the right credit cards and priority boarding can be purchased with a lot of airlines from $4. If you want to go big with first-class or business, flights offset your own travel costs by renting your own home or you can upgrade at the airport often for a fraction of what you would have paid booking a business flight online.

MORE TIPS TO FIND CHEAP FLIGHTS

"The use of travelling is to regulate imagination by reality, and instead of thinking how things may be, to see them as they are." Samuel Jackson

If you're working full-time, you can save yourself a lot of money by requesting your time off from work starting in the middle of the week. Tuesdays and Wednesdays are the cheapest days to fly. You can save thousands just by adjusting your time off.

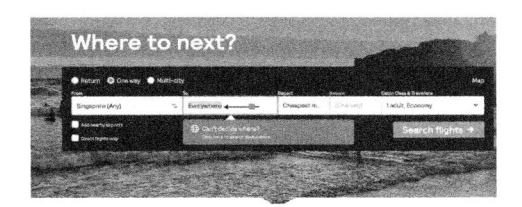

The simplest secret to booking cheap flights is open parameters. Let's say you want to fly from Chicago to Paris. You enter the USA in from and select USA under to. You may find flights from New York City to Paris for $70. Then you just need to find a cheap flight to NYC. Make sure you calculate full costs, including if you need airport accommodation and of course getting to and from airports, **but in nearly every instance open parameters will save you at least half the cost of the flight.**

 If you're not sure about where you want to go, use open parameters to show you the cheapest destinations from your city. Start with skyscanner.net they include the low-cost airlines that others like Kayak leave out. Google Flights can also show you cheap destinations. To see these leave the WHERE TO section blank. Open parameters can also show you the cheapest dates to fly. If you're flexible, you can save up to 80% of the flight cost. Always check the weather at your destination before you book. Sometimes a $400 flight will be $20, because it's monsoon season. But hey, if you like the rain, why not?

ALWAYS USE A PRIVATE BROWSER TO BOOK FLIGHTS

Skyscanner and other sites track your IP address and put prices up and down based on what they determine your strength of conviction to buy. e.g. if you've booked one-way and are looking for the return, these sites will jack the prices up by in most cases 50%. Incognito browsing pays.

Use a VPN such as Hola to book your flight from your destination

Install Hola, change your destination to the country you are flying to. The location from which a ticket is booked can affect the price significantly as algorithms consider local buying power.

Choose the right time to buy your ticket.

Choose the right time to buy your ticket, as purchasing tickets on a Sunday has been proven to be cheaper. If you can only book during the week, try to do it on a Tuesday.

Mistake fares

Email alerts from individual carriers are where you can find the best 'mistake fares". This is where a computer error has resulted in an airline offering the wrong fare. In my experience, it's best to sign up to individual carriers email lists, but if you ARE lazy Secret Flying puts together a daily roster of mistake fares. Visit https://www.secretflying.com/errorfare/ to see if there're any errors that can benefit you.

Fly late for cheaper prices

Red-eye flights, the ones that leave later in the day, are typically cheaper and less crowded, so aim to book that flight if possible. You will also get through the airport much quicker at the end of the day. Just make sure there's ground transport available for when you land. You don't want to save $50 on the airfare and spend it on a taxi to your accommodation.

Use this APP for same day flights

If your plans are flexible, use 'Get The Flight Out' (http://www.gtfoflights.com/) a fare tracker Hopper that shows you same-day deeply discounted flights. This is best for long-haul flights with major carriers. You can often find a British Airways round-trip from JFK Airport to Heathrow for $300. If you booked this in advance, you'd pay at least double.

Take an empty water bottle with you

Airport prices on food and drinks are sky high. It disgusts me to see some airports charging $10 for a bottle of water. ALWAYS take an empty water bottle with you. It's relatively unknown, but most airports have drinking water fountains past the security check. Just type in your airport name to wateratairports.com to locate the fountain. Then once you've passed security (because they don't allow you to take 100ml or more of liquids) you can freely refill your bottle with water.

Round-the-World (RTW) Tickets

It is always cheaper to book your flights using a DIY approach. First, you may decide you want to stay longer in one country, and a RTW will charge you a hefty fee for changing your flight. Secondly, it all depends on where and when you travel and as we have discussed, there are many ways to ensure you pay way less than $1,500 for a year of flights. If you're travelling long-haul, the best strategy is to buy a return ticket, say New York, to Bangkok and then take cheap flights or transport around Asia and even to Australia and beyond.

Cut your costs to and from airports

Don't you hate it when getting to and from the airport is more expensive than your flight! And this is true in so many cities, especially European ones. For some reason, Google often shows the most expensive options. Use Omio to compare the cheapest transport options and save on airport transfer costs.

Car sharing instead of taxis

Check if USA has car sharing at the airport. Often they'll be tons of cars parked at the airport that are half the price of taking a taxi into the city. In most instances, you register your driving licence on an app and scan the code on the car to get going.

Checking Bags

Sometimes you need to check bags. If you do, put an AirTag inside. That way, you'll be about to see when you land where your bag is. This saves you the nail biting wait at baggage claim. And if worse comes to worst, and you see your bag is actually in another city, you can calmly stroll over to customer services and show them where your bag is.

Is it cheaper and more convenient to send your bags ahead?

Before you check your bags, check if it's cheaper to send them ahead of you with sendmybag.com obviously if you're staying in an Airbnb, you'll need to ask the hosts permission or you can time them to arrive the day after you. Hotels are normally very amenable.

What Credit Card Gives The Best Air Miles?

You can slash the cost of flights just for spending on a piece of plastic.

LET'S TALK ABOUT DEBT

Before we go into the best cards for each country, let's first talk about debt. The US system offers the best and biggest rewards. Why? Because they rely on the fact that many people living in the US will not pay their cards in full and the card will earn the bank significant interest payments. Other countries have a very different attitude towards money, debt, and saving than Americans. Thus in Germany and Austria the offerings aren't as favourable as the UK, USA and Australia, where debt culture is more widely embraced. The takeaway here is this: **Only spend on one of these cards when you have set-up an automatic total monthly balance repayment. Don't let banks profit from your lizard brain!**

The best air-mile credit cards for those living in the UK

Amex Preferred Rewards Gold comes out top for those living in the UK for 2024.

Here are the benefits:

- 20,000-point bonus on £3,000 spend in first three months. These can be used towards flights with British Airways, Virgin Atlantic, Emirates and Etihad, and often other rewards, such as hotel stays and car hire.
- 1 point per £1 spent
- 1 point = 1 airline point
- Two free visits a year to airport lounges
- No fee in year one, then £140/yr

The downside:

- Fail to repay fully and it's 59.9% rep APR interest, incl fee

You'll need to cancel before the £140/yr fee kicks in year two if you want to avoid it.

The best air-mile credit cards for those living in Canada

Aeroplan is the superior rewards program in Canada. The card has a high earn rate for Aeroplan Points, generating 1.5 points per $1 spent on eligible purchases. Look at the specifics of the eligible purchases https://www.aircanada.com/ca/en/aco/home/aeroplan/earn.html. If you're not spending on these things AMEX's Membership Rewards program offers you the best returns in Canada.

The best air-mile credit cards for those living in Germany

If you have a German bank account, you can apply for a Lufthansa credit card.

Earn 50,000 award miles if you spend $3,000 in purchases and paying the annual fee, both within the first 90 days.

Earn 2 award miles per $1 spent on ticket purchases directly from Miles & More integrated airline partners.

Earn 1 award mile per $1 spent on all other purchases.

The downsides

the €89 annual fee

Limited to fly with Lufthansa and its partners but you can capitalise on perks like the companion pass and airport lounge vouchers.

You need excellent credit to get this card.

The best air-mile credit cards for those living in Austria

"In Austria, Miles & More offers you a special credit card. You get miles for each purchase with the credit card. The Miles & More program calculates miles earned based on the distance flown and booking class. For European flights, the booking class is a flat rate. For intercontinental flights, mileage is calculated by multiplying the booking class by the distance flown." They offer a calculator so you can see how many points you could earn: https://www.miles-and-more.com/at/en/earn/airlines/mileage-calculator.html

The best air-mile credit cards for those living in USA:

"The American Express card is the best known and oldest to earn miles, thanks to its membership Rewards program. When making payments with this card, points are added, which can then be exchanged for miles from airlines such as Iberia, Air Europa, Emirates or Alitalia." More information is available here: https://www.americanexpress.com/es-es/

The best air-mile credit cards for those living in Australia

ANZ Rewards Black comes out top for 2024.

180,000 bonus ANZ Reward Points (can get an $800 gift card) and $0 annual fee for the first year with the ANZ Rewards Black
Points Per Spend: 1 Velocity point on purchases of up to $5,000 per statement period and 0.5 Velocity points thereafter.
Annual Fee: $0 in the first year, then $375 after.
Ns no set minimum income required, however, there is a minimum credit limit of $15,000 on this card.

Here are some ways you can hack points onto this card: https://www.pointhacks.com.au/credit-cards/anz-rewards-black-guide/

The best air-mile credit card solution for those living in the USA with a POOR credit score

The downside to Airline Mile cards is that they require good or excellent credit scores, meaning 690 or higher.

If you have bad credit and want to use credit card air lines you will need to rebuild your credit poor. The Credit One Bank® Platinum Visa® for Rebuilding Credit is a good credit card for people with bad credit who don't want to place a deposit on a secured card. The Credit One Platinum Visa offers a $300 credit limit, rewards, and the potential for credit-limit increases, which in time will help rebuild your score.

PLEASE don't sign-up for any of these cards if you can't trust yourself to repay it in full monthly. This will only lead to stress for you.

Frequent Flyer Memberships

"Points" and "miles" are often used interchangeably, but they're usually two very different things. Maximise and diversify your rewards by utilising both.

A frequent-flyer program (FFP) is a loyalty program offered by an airline. They are designed to encourage airline customers to fly more to accumulate points (also called miles, kilometres, or segments) which can be redeemed for air travel or other rewards.

You can sign up with any FFP program for free. There are three major airline alliances in the world: Oneworld, SkyTeam and Star Alliance. I am with One World https://www.oneworld.com/members because the points can be accrued and used for most flights.

The best return on your points is to use them for international business or first class flights with lie-flat seats. You would need 3 times more miles compared to an economy flight, but if you paid cash, you'd pay 5 - 10 times more than the cost of the economy flight, so it really pays to use your points only for upgrades. The worst value for your miles is to buy an economy seat or worse, a gift from the airlines gift-shop.

Sign up for a family/household account to pool miles together. If you share a common address, you can claim the miles with most airlines. You can use AwardWallet to keep track of your miles. Remember that they only last for 2 years, so use them before they expire.

How to spend money

Bank ATM fees vary from $2.50 per transaction to as high as $5 or more, depending on the ATM and the country. You can completely skip those fees by paying with card and using a card which can hold multiple currencies.

Budget travel hacking begins with a strategy to spend without fees. Your individual strategy depends on the country you legally reside in as to what cards are available. Happily there are some fin-tech solutions which can save you thousands on those pesky ATM withdrawal fees and are widely available globally. Here are a selection of cards you can pre-charge with currency for USA:

N26

N26 is a 12-year-old digital bank. I have been using them for over 6 years. The key advantage is fee-free card transactions abroad. They have a very elegant app, where you can check your timeline for all transactions listed in real time or manage your in-app security anywhere. The card you receive is a Mastercard so you can use it everywhere. If you lose the card, you don't have to call anyone, just open the app and swipe 'lock card'. It puts your purchases into a graph automatically so you can see what you spend on. You can open an account from abroad entirely online, all you need is your passport and a camera
n26.com

Revolut

Revolut is a multi-currency account that allows you to hold and exchange 29 currencies and spend fee-free abroad. It's a UK based neobank, but accepts customers from all over the world.

Wise debit card

If you're going to be in one place for a long time, the Wise debit card is like having your travel money on a card – it lets you spend money at the real exchange rate.

Monzo

Monzo is good if your UK based. They offer a fee-free UK account. Fee-free international money transfers and fee-free spending abroad.

The downside

The cards above are debit cards, meaning you need to have money in those accounts to spend it. This comes with one big downside: safety. Credit card issuers' have "zero liability" meaning you're not liable for unauthorised charges. All the cards listed above do provide cover for unauthorised charges but times vary greatly in how quickly you'd get your money back if it were stolen.

The best option is to check in your country to see which credit cards are the best for travelling and set up monthly payments to repay the whole amount so you don't pay unnecessary interest. In the USA, Schwab regularly ranks at the top for travel credit cards. Credit cards are always the safer option when abroad simply because you get your money back faster if its stolen and if you're renting cars, most will give you free insurance when you book the car rental using the card, saving you money.

Always withdraw money; never exchange.

Money exchanges, whether they be on the streets or in the airports will NEVER give you a good exchange rate. Do not bring bundles of cash. Instead, withdraw local currency from the ATM as needed and try to use only free ATMs. Many in airports charge you a fee to withdraw cash. Look for bigger ATMs attached to banks to avoid this.

Recap

- Take cash from local, non-charging ATMs for the best rates.
- Never change at airport exchange desks unless you absolutely have to, then just change just enough to be able get to a bank ATM.
- Bring a spare credit card for emergencies.
- Split cash in various places on your person (pockets, shoes) and in your luggage. It's never sensible to keep your cash or cards all in one place.
- In higher risk areas, use a money belt under your clothes or put $50 in your shoe or bra.

Revolut
Revolut is a multi-currency account that allows you to hold and exchange 29 currencies and spend fee-free abroad. It's a UK based neobank, but accepts customers from all over the world.

Wise debit card
If you're going to be in one place for a long time the Wise debit card is like having your travel money on a card – it lets you spend money at the real exchange rate.

Monzo
Monzo is good if your UK based. They offer a fee-free UK account. Fee-free international money transfers and fee-free spending abroad.

The downside

The cards above are debit cards, meaning you need to have money in those accounts to spend it. This comes with one big downside: safety. Credit card issuers' have "zero liability" meaning you're not liable for unauthorised charges. All of the cards listed above do provide cover for unauthorised charges but times vary greatly in how quickly you'd get your money back if it were stolen.

The best option is to check in your country to see which credit cards are the best for travelling and set up monthly payments to repay the whole amount so you don't pay unnecessary interest. In the USA, Schwab[4] regularly ranks at the top for travel credit cards. Credit cards are always the safer option when abroad simply because you get your money back faster if its stolen and if you're renting cars, most will give you free insurance when you book the car rental using the card, saving you money.

Always withdraw money; never exchange.

Money exchanges whether they be on the streets or in the airports will NEVER give you a good exchange rate. Do not bring bundles of cash. Instead withdraw local currency from the ATM as needed and try to use only free ATM's. Many in airports charge you a fee to withdraw cash. Look for bigger ATM's attached to banks to avoid this.

Recap

- Take cash from local, non-charging ATMs for the best rates.
- Never change at airport exchange desks unless you absolutely have to, then just change just enough to be able get to a bank ATM.
- Bring a spare credit card for emergencies.
- Split cash in various places on your person (pockets, shoes) and in your luggage. Its never sensible to keep your cash or cards all in one place.
- In higher risk areas, use a money belt under your clothes or put $50 in your shoe or bra.

---

[4] Charles Schwab High Yield Checking accounts refund every single ATM fee worldwide, require no minimum balance and have no monthly fee.

How NOT to be ripped off

> "One of the great things about travel is that you find out how many good, kind people there are."
> — Edith Wharton

The quote above may seem ill placed in a chapter entitled how not to be ripped off, but I included it to remind you that the vast majority of people do not want to rip you off. In fact, scammers are normally limited to three situations:

1. Around heavily visited attractions - these places are targeted purposively due to sheer footfall. Many criminals believe ripping people off is simply a numbers game.
2. In cities or countries with low-salaries or communist ideologies. If they can't make money in the country, they seek to scam foreigners. If you have travelled to India, Morocco or Cuba you will have observed this phenomenon.
3. When you are stuck and the person helping you know you have limited options.

Scammers know that most people will avoid confrontation. Don't feel bad about utterly ignoring someone and saying no. Here are six strategies to avoid being ripped off:

1. **Never ever agree to pay as much as you want. Always decide on a price before.**

Whoever you're dealing with is trained to tell you, they are uninterested in money. This is a trap. If you let people do this they will ask for MUCH MORE money at the end, and because you have used there service, you will feel obliged to pay. This is a conman's trick and nothing more.

2. Pack light

You can move faster and easier. If you take heavy luggage, you will end up taking taxis which are comparatively very costly over time.

3. NEVER use the airport taxi service. Plan to use public transport before you reach the airport.

4. Don't buy a sim card from the airport. Buy from the local supermarkets it will cost 50% less.

5. Eat at local restaurants serving regional food

Food defines culture. Exploring all delights available to the palate doesn't need to cost enormous sums.

6. **Ask the locals what something should cost,** and try not to pay over that.

7. **If you find yourself with limited options.** e.g. your taxi dumps you on the side of the road because you refuse to pay more (common in India and parts of South America) don't act desperate and negotiate as if you have other options or you will be extorted.

8. Don't blindly rely on social media[5]

Let's say you post in a Facebook group that you want tips for travelling to The Maldives. A lot of the comments you will receive come from guides, hosts and restaurants doing their own promotion. It's estimated that 50% or more of Facebook's current monthly active users are fake. And what's worse, a recent study found Social media platforms leave 95% of reported fake accounts up. These accounts are the digital versions of the men who hang around the Grand Palace in Bangkok telling tourists its closed, to divert you to shops where they will receive a commission for bringing you.

It can also be the case that genuine comments come from people who have totally different interests, beliefs and yes, budgets to yours. Make your experience your own and don't believe every comment you read.

Bottom line: use caution when accepting recommendations on social media and always fact-check with your own research.

Small tweaks on the road add up to big differences in your bank balance

Take advantage of other hotel amenities

If you fancy a swim but you're nowhere near the ocean, try the nearest hotel with a pool. As long as you buy a drink, the hotel staff will probably grant you access.

Fill up your mini bar for free.

Fill up your mini bar for free by storing things from the breakfast bar or grocery shop in your mini bar to give you a greater selection of drinks and food without the hefty price tag.

Save yourself some ironing

Use the steam from the shower to get rid of wrinkles in clothing. If something is creased, leave it trapped with the steam in the bathroom overnight for even better results.

See somewhere else for free

Opt for long stopovers, allowing you to experience another city without spending much money.

Wear your heaviest clothes

On the plane to save weight in your pack, allowing you to bring more with you. Big coats can then be used as pillows to make your flight more comfortable.

Don't get lost while you're away.

Find where you want to go using Google Maps, then type 'OK Maps' into the search bar to store this information for offline viewing.

---

[5] https://arstechnica.com/tech-policy/2019/12/social-media-platforms-leave-95-of-reported-fake-accounts-up-study-finds/

Use car renting services

Share Now or Car2Go allow you to hire a car for 2 hours for $25 in a lot of European countries.

Share Rides

Use sites like blablacar.com to find others who are driving in your direction. It can be 80% cheaper than normal transport. Just check the drivers reviews.

Use free gym passes

Get a free gym day pass by googling the name of a local gym and free day pass.

When asked by people providing you a service where you are from..

If there's no price list for the service you are asking for, when asked where you are from, Say you are from a lesser-known poorer country. I normally say Macedonia, and if they don't know where it is, add it's a poor country. If you say UK, USA, the majority of Europe bar the well-known poorer countries taxi drivers, tour operators etc will match the price to what they think you pay at home.

Set-up a New Uber/ other car hailing app account for discounts

By googling you can find offers with $50 free for new users in most cities for Uber/ Lyft/ Bolt and alike. Just set up a new gmail.com email account to take advantage.

Where and How to Make Friends

"People don't take trips, trips take people." – John Steinbeck

Become popular at the airport

Want to become popular at the airport? Pack a power bar with multiple outlets and just see how many friends you can make. It's amazing how many people forget their chargers, or who packed them in the luggage that they checked in.

Stay in Hostels

First of all, Hostels don't have to be shared dorms, and they cater to a much wider demographic than is assumed. Hostels are a better environment for meeting people than hotels, and more importantly, they tended to open up excursion opportunities that further opened up that opportunity.

Or take up a hobby

If hostels are a definite no-no for you; find an interest. Take up a hobby where you will meet people. I've dived for years and the nature of diving is you're always paired up with a dive buddy. I met a lot of interesting people that way.

Small tweaks on the road add up to big differences in your bank balance

Take advantage of other hotel's amenities

If you fancy a swim but you're nowhere near the ocean, try the nearest hotel with a pool. As long as you buy a drink, the hotel staff will likely grant you access.

Fill up your mini bar for free.

Fill up your mini bar for free by storing things from the breakfast bar or grocery shop in your mini bar to give you a greater selection of drinks and food without the hefty price tag.

Save yourself some ironing

Use the steam from the shower to get rid of wrinkles in clothing. If something is creased, leave it trapped with the steam in the bathroom overnight for even better results.

See somewhere else for free

Opt for long stopovers, allowing you to experience another city without spending much money.

Wear your heaviest clothes

on the plane to save weight in your pack, allowing you to bring more with you. Big coats can then be used as pillows to make your flight more comfortable.

Don't get lost while you're away.

Find where you want to go using Google Maps, then type 'OK Maps' into the search bar to store this information for offline viewing.

Use car renting services

Share Now or Car2Go allow you to hire a car for 2 hours for $25 in a lot of Europe.

Share Rides

Use sites like blablacar.com to find others who are driving in your direction. It can be 80% cheaper than normal transport. Just check the drivers reviews.

Use free gym passes

Get a free gym day pass by googling the name of a local gym and free day pass.

When asked by people providing you a service where you are from..

If there's no price list for the service you are asking for, when asked where you are from, Say you are from a lesser-known poorer country. I normally say Macedonia, and if they don't know where it is, add it's a poor country. If you say UK, USA, the majority of Europe bar the well-known poorer countries taxi drivers, tour operators etc will match the price to what they think you pay at home.

Set-up a New Uber/ other car hailing app account for discounts

By googling you can find offers with $50 free for new users in most cities for Uber/ Lyft/ Bolt and alike. Just set up a new gmail.com email account to take advantage.

Where and How to Make Friends

"People don't take trips, trips take people." – John Steinbeck

Become popular at the airport

Want to become popular at the airport? Pack a power bar with multiple outlets and just see how many friends you can make. It's amazing how many people forget their chargers, or who packed them in the luggage that they checked in.

Stay in Hostels

First of all, Hostels don't have to be shared dorms, and they cater to a much wider demographic than is assumed. Hostels are a better environment for meeting people than hotels, and more importantly they tended to open up excursion opportunities that further opened up that opportunity.

Or take up a hobby

If hostels are a definite no-no for you; find an interest. Take up a hobby where you will meet people. I've dived for years and the nature of diving is you're always paired up with a dive buddy. I met a lot of interesting people that way.

When unpleasantries come your way...

We all have our good and bad days travelling, and on a bad day you can feel like just taking a flight home. Here are some ways to overcome common travel problems:

Anxiety when flying

It has been over 40 years since a plane has been brought down by turbulence. Repeat that number to yourself: 40 years! Planes are built to withstand lighting strikes, extreme storms and ultimately can adjust course to get out of their way. Landing and take-off are when the most accidents happen, but you have statistically three times the chance of winning a huge jackpot lottery, then you do of dying in a plane crash.

If you feel afraid on the flight, focus on your breathing saying the word 'smooth' over and over until the flight is smooth. Always check the airline safety record on airlinerating.com I was surprised to learn Ryanair and Easyjet as much less safe than Wizz Air according to those ratings because they sell similarly priced flights. If there is extreme turbulence, I feel much better knowing I'm in a 7 star safety plane.

Wanting to sleep instead of seeing new places

This is a common problem. Just relax, there's little point doing fun things when you feel tired. Factor in jet-lag to your travel plans. When you're rested and alert you'll enjoy your new temporary home much more. Many people hate the first week of a long-trip because of jet-lag and often blame this on their first destination, but its rarely true. Ask travellers who 'hate' a particular place and you will see that very often they either had jet-lag or an unpleasant journey there.

Going over budget

Come back from a trip to a monster credit card bill? Hopefully, this guide has prevented you from returning to an unwanted bill. Of course, there are costs that can creep up and this is a reminder about how to prevent them making their way on to your credit card bill:

- To and from the airport. Solution: leave adequate time and take the cheapest method - book before.

- Baggage. Solution: take hand luggage and post things you might need to yourself.

- Eating out. Solution: go to cheap eats places and suggest those to friends.

- Parking. Solution: use apps to find free parking

- Tipping. Solution Leave a modest tip and tell the server you will write them a nice review.

- Souvenirs. Solution: fridge magnets only.

- Giving to the poor. (This one still gets me, but if you're giving away $10 a day - it adds up) Solution: volunteer your time instead and recognise that in tourist destinations many beggars are run by organised crime gangs.

Price v Comfort

I love traveling. I don't love struggling. I like decent accommodation, being able to eat properly and see places and enjoy. I am never in the mood for low-cost airlines or crappy transfers, so here's what I do to save money.

- Avoid organised tours unless you are going to a place where safety is a real issue. They are expensive and constrain your wanderlust to typical things. I only recommend them in Algeria, Iran and Papua New Guinea - where language and gender views pose serious problems all cured by a reputable tour organiser.
- Eat what the locals do.
- Cook in your Airbnb/ hostel where restaurants are expensive.
- Shop at local markets.
- Spend time choosing your flight, and check the operator on arilineratings.com
- Mix up hostels and Airbnbs. Hostels for meeting people, Airbnb for relaxing and feeling 'at home'.

Not knowing where free toilets are

Use Toilet Finder - https://play.google.com/store/apps/details?id=com.bto.toilet&hl=en

Your Airbnb is awful

Airbnb customer service is notoriously bad. Help yourself out. Try to sort things out with the host, but if you can't, take photos of everything e.g bed, bathroom, mess, doors, contact them within 24 hours. Tell them you had to leave and pay for new accommodation. Ask politely for a full refund including booking fees. With photographic evidence and your new accommodation receipt, they can't refuse.

The airline loses your bag

Go to the Luggage desk before leaving the airport and report the bag missing. Hopefully you've headed the advice to put an AirTag in your checked bag and you can show them where to find your bag. Most airlines will give you an overnight bag, ask where you're staying and return the bag to you within three days. It's extremely rare for Airlines to lose your bag due to technological innovation, but if that happens you should submit an insurance claim after the three days is up, including receipts for everything you had to buy in the interim.

Your travel companion lets you down

Whether it's a breakup or a friend cancelling, it sucks and can ramp up costs. The easiest solution to finding a new travel companion is to go to a well-reviewed hostel and find someone you want to travel with. You should spend at least three days getting to know this person before you suggest travelling together. Finding someone in person is always better than finding someone online, because you can get a better idea of whether you will have a smooth journey together. Travel can make or break friendships.

Culture shock

I had one of the strongest culture shocks while spending 6 months in Japan. It was overwhelming how much I had to prepare when I went outside of the door (googling words and sentences what to use, where to go, which station and train line to use, what is this food called in Japanese and how does its look etc.). I was so tired constantly but in the end I just let go and went with my extremely bad Japanese. If you feel culture shocked its because your brain is referencing your surroundings to what you know. Stop comparing, have Google translate downloaded and relax.

Your Car rental insurance is crazy expensive

I always use carrentals.com and book with a credit card. Most credit cards will give you free insurance for the car, so you don't need to pay the extra. Some unsavoury companies will bump the price up when you arrive. Ask to speak to a manager. If this doesn't resolve, it google "consumer ombudsman for NAME OF COUNTRY." and seek an immediate full refund on the balance difference you paid. It is illegal in most countries to alter the price of a rental car when the person arrives to pickup a pre-arranged car.

A note on Car Rental Insurance

Always always always rent a car with a credit card that has rental vehicle coverage built into the card and is automatically applied when you rent a car. Then there's no need to buy additional rental insurance (check with your card on the coverage they protect some exclude collision coverage). Do yourself a favour when you step up to the desk to rent the car tell the agent you're already covered and won't be buying anything today. They work on commission and you'll save time and your patience avoiding the upselling.

You're sick

First off ALWAYS, purchase travel insurance. Including emergency transport up to $500k even to back home, which is usually less than $10 additional. I use https://www.comparethemarket.com/travel-insurance/ to find the best days. If I am sick I normally check into a hotel with room service and ride it out.

Make a Medication Travel Kit

Take travel sized medications with you:

- Antidiarrheal medication (for example, bismuth subsalicylate, loperamide)
- Medicine for pain or fever (such as acetaminophen, aspirin, or ibuprofen)
- Throat Lozenges

Save yourself from most travel related hassles

- Do not make jokes with immigration and customs staff. A misunderstanding can lead to HUGE fines.

- Book the most direct flight you can find nonstop if possible.

- Carry a US$50 bill for emergency cash. I have entered a country and all ATM and credit card systems were down. US$ can be exchanged nearly anywhere in the world and is useful in extreme situations, but where possible don't exchange, as you will lose money.

- Check, and recheck, required visas and such BEFORE the day of your trip. Some countries, for instance, require a ticket out of the country in order to enter. Others, like the US and Australia, require electronic authorisation in advance.

- Airport security is asinine and inconsistent around the world. Keep this in mind when connecting flights. Always leave at least 2 hours for international connections or international to domestic. In Stansted for example, they force you to buy one of their plastic bags, and remove your liquids from your own plastic bag…. just to make money from you. And this adds to the time it will take to get through security, so lines are long.

- Wiki travel is perfect to use for a lay of the land.

- Expensive luggage rarely lasts longer than cheap luggage, in my experience. Fancy leather bags are toast with air travel.

Food

- When it comes to food, eat in local restaurants, not tourist-geared joints. Any place with the menu in three or more languages is going to be overpriced.

- Take a spork - a knife, spoon and fork all in one.

Water Bottle

Take a water bottle with a filter. We love these ones from Water to Go.

Empty it before airport security and separate the bottle and filter as some airport people will try and claim it has liquids…

Bug Sprays

If you're heading somewhere tropical spray your clothes with Permethrin before you travel. It lasts 40 washes and saves space in your bag. A 'Bite Away' zapper can be used after the bite to totally erase it. It cuts down on the itching and erases the bite from your skin.

Order free mini's

Don't buy those expensive travel sized toiletries, order travel sized freebies online. This gives you the opportunity to try brands you've never used before, and who knows, you might even find your new favourite soap.

Take a waterproof bag

If you're travelling alone you can swim without worrying about your phone, wallet and passport laying on the beach.

You can also use it as a source of entertainment on those ultra budget flights.

Make a private entertainment centre anywhere

Always take an eye-mask, earplugs, a scarf and a kindle reader - so you can sleep and entertain yourself anywhere!

The best Travel Gadgets

The door alarm

If you're nervous and staying in private rooms or airbnbs take a door alarm. For those times when you just don't feel safe, it can help you fall asleep. You can get tiny ones for less than $10 from Amazon: https://www.Amazon.com/Travel-door-alarm/s?k=Travel+door+alarm

Smart Blanket

Amazon sells a 6 in 1 heating blanket that is very useful for cold plane or bus trips. Its great if you have poor circulation as it becomes a detachable Foot Warmer: Amazon http://amzn.to/2hTYIOP I paid $49.00.

The coat that becomes a tent

https://www.adiff.com/products/tent-jacket. This is great if you're going to be doing a lot of camping.

Clever Tank Top with Secret Pockets

Keep your valuables safe in this top. Perfect for all climates.

on Amazon for $39.90

Optical Camera Lens for Smartphones and Tablets

Leave your bulky camera at home. Turn your device into a high-performance camera. Buy on Amazon for $9.95

Travel-sized Wireless Router with USB Media Storage

Convert any wired network to a wireless network. Buy on Amazon for $17.99

Buy a Scrubba Bag to wash your clothes on the go

Or a cheaper imitable. You can wash your clothes on the go.

Hacks for Families

Rent an Airbnb apartment so you can cook

Apartments are much better for families, as you have all the amenities you'd have at home. They are normally cheaper per person too. We are the first travel guide publisher to include Airbnb's in our recommendations if you think any of these need updating you can email me at philgtang@gmail.com

Shop at local markets

Eat seasonal products and local products. Get closer to the local market and observe the prices and the offer. What you can find more easily, will be the cheapest.

Take Free Tours

Download free podcast tours of the destination you are visiting. The podcast will tell you where to start, where to go, and what to look for. Often you can find multiple podcast tours of the same place. Listen to all of them if you like, each one will tell you a little something new.

Pack Extra Ear Phones

If you go on a museum tour, they often have audio guides. Instead of having to rent one for each person, take some extra earphones. Most audio tour devices have a place to plug in a second set.

Buy Souvenirs Ahead of Time

If you are buying souvenirs somewhere touristy, you are paying a premium price. By ordering the same exact products online, you can save a lot of money.

Use Cheap Transportation

Do as the locals do, including weekly passes.

Carry Reusable Water Bottles

Spending money on water and other beverages can quickly add up. Instead of paying for drinks, take some refillable water bottles.

Combine Attractions

Many major cities offer ticket bundles where one price gets you into 5 or 6 popular attractions. You will need to plan ahead of time to decide what things you plan to do on vacation and see if they are selling these activities together.

Pack Snacks

Granola bars, apples, baby carrots, bananas, cheese crackers, juice boxes, pretzels, fruit snacks, apple sauce, grapes, and veggie chips.

Stick to Carry-On Bags

Do not pay to check a large bag. Even a small child can pull a carry-on.

Visit free art galleries and museums

Just google the name + free days.

Eat Street Food

There's a lot of unnecessary fear around this. You can watch the food prepared. Go for the stands that have a steady queue.

Travel Gadgets for Families

Dropcam

Are what-if scenarios playing out in your head? Then you need Dropcam.

'Dropcam HD Internet Wi-Fi Video Monitoring Cameras help you watch what you love from anywhere. In less than a minute, you'll have it setup and securely streaming video to you over your home Wi-Fi. Watch what you love while away with Dropcam HD.'

Approximate Price: $139

Kelty-Child-Carrier

Voted as one of the best hiking essentials if you're traveling with kids and can carry a child up to 18kg.

Jetkids Bedbox

No more giving up your own personal space on the plane with this suitcase that becomes a bed.

How I got hooked on luxury on a budget travelling

'We're on holiday' is what my dad used to say to justify getting us in so much debt we lost our home and all our things when I was 11. We moved from the suburban bliss of Hemel Hempstead to a run down council estate in inner-city London, near my dad's new job as a refuge collector, a fancy word for dustbin man. I lost all my school friends while watching my dad go through a nervous breakdown.

My dad loved walking up a hotel lobby desk without a care in the world. So much so, that he booked overpriced holidays on credit cards. A lot of holidays. As it turned out, we couldn't afford any of them. In the end, my dad had no choice but to declare bankruptcy. When my mum realised, he'd racked up so much debt our family unit dissolved. A neat and perhaps as painless a summary of events that lead me to my life's passion: budget travel that doesn't compromise on fun, safety or comfort.

I started travelling full-time at the age of 18. I wrote the first Super Cheap Insider guide for friends visiting Norway - which I did for a month on less than $250. When sales reached 10,000 I decided to form the Super Cheap Insider Guides company. As I know from first-hand experience debt can be a noose around our necks, and saying 'oh come on, we're on vacation' isn't a get out of jail free card. In fact, its the reverse of what travel is supposed to bring you - freedom.

Before I embarked upon writing Super Cheap Insider guides, many, many people told me that my dream was impossible. Travelling on a budget could never be comfortable. I hope this guide has proved to you what I have known for a long-time: budget travel can feel luxurious when you know and use the insider hacks.

And apologies if I depressed you with my tale of woe. My dad is now happily remarried and works as a chef in USA at a fancy hotel - the kind he used to take us to!

A final word...

There's a simple system you can use to think about budget travel. In life, we can choose two of the following: cheap, fast, or quality. So if you want it Cheap and fast you will get a lower quality service. Fast-food is the perfect example. The system holds true for purchasing anything while travelling. I always choose cheap and quality, except at times where I am really limited on time. Normally, you can make small tweaks to make this work for you. Ultimately, you must make choices about what's most important to you and heed your heart's desires.

'Your heart is the most powerful muscle in your body. Do what it says.' Jen Sincero

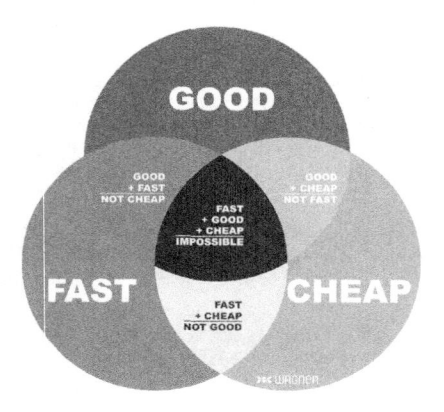

If you've found this book useful, please select some stars, it would mean genuinely make my day to see I've helped you.

Copyright

Published in Great Britain in 2024 by Super Cheap Insider Guides LTD.

Copyright © 2024 Super Cheap Insider Guides LTD.

The right of Phil G A Tang to be identified as the Author of the Work has been asserted in accordance with the Copyright, Designs and Patents Act 1988.

All rights reserved.

No part of this publication may be reproduced, stored in a retrieval system, or transmitted, in any form or by any means without the prior written permission of the publisher, nor be otherwise circulated in any form of binding or cover other than that in which it is published and without a similar condition being imposed on the subsequent purchaser.

All rights reserved. No part of this publication may be reproduced, distributed, or transmitted in any form or by any means, including photocopying, recording, or other electronic or mechanical methods, without the prior written permission of the publisher, except in the case of brief quotations embodied in critical reviews and certain other noncommercial uses permitted by copyright law.

Printed in Great Britain
by Amazon